T0281511

Lecture Notes in Computer Science   14408

Founding Editors

Gerhard Goos
Juris Hartmanis

The series Lecture Notes in Computer Science (LNCS), including its subseries Lecture Notes in Artificial Intelligence (LNAI) and Lecture Notes in Bioinformatics (LNBI), has established itself as a medium for the publication of new developments in computer science and information technology research, teaching, and education.

LNCS enjoys close cooperation with the computer science R & D community, the series counts many renowned academics among its volume editors and paper authors, and collaborates with prestigious societies. Its mission is to serve this international community by providing an invaluable service, mainly focused on the publication of conference and workshop proceedings and postproceedings. LNCS commenced publication in 1973.

Huimin Lu · Michael Blumenstein ·
Sung-Bae Cho · Cheng-Lin Liu · Yasushi Yagi ·
Tohru Kamiya
Editors

Pattern Recognition

7th Asian Conference, ACPR 2023
Kitakyushu, Japan, November 5–8, 2023
Proceedings, Part III

Springer

Editors
Huimin Lu
Kyushu Institute of Technology
Kitakyushu, Fukuoka, Japan

Michael Blumenstein
The University of Sydney
Sydney, NSW, Australia

Sung-Bae Cho 🆔
Yonsei University
Seoul, Korea (Republic of)

Cheng-Lin Liu
Chinese Academy of Sciences
Beijing, China

Yasushi Yagi
Osaka University
Osaka, Ibaraki, Japan

Tohru Kamiya
Kyushu Institute of Technology
Kitakyushu, Japan

ISSN 0302-9743   ISSN 1611-3349 (electronic)
Lecture Notes in Computer Science
ISBN 978-3-031-47664-8   ISBN 978-3-031-47665-5 (eBook)
https://doi.org/10.1007/978-3-031-47665-5

This Springer imprint is published by the registered company Springer Nature Switzerland AG
The registered company address is: Gewerbestrasse 11, 6330 Cham, Switzerland

Paper in this product is recyclable.

Preface for ACPR 2023 Proceedings

Pattern recognition stands at the core of artificial intelligence and has been evolving significantly in recent years. These proceedings include high-quality original research papers presented at the 7th Asian Conference on Pattern Recognition (ACPR 2023), which was successfully held in Kitakyushu, Japan from November 5th to November 8th, 2023. The conference welcomed participants from all over the world to meet physically in beautiful Kitakyushu to exchange ideas, as we did in our past ACPR series of conferences. The conference was operated in a hybrid format allowing for both on-site and virtual participation. With all your participation and contributions, we believe ACPR 2023 was a special and memorable conference in history!

ACPR 2023 was the 7th conference of its series since it was launched in 2011 in Beijing, followed by ACPR 2013 in Okinawa, Japan, ACPR 2015 in Kuala Lumpur, Malaysia, ACPR 2017 in Nanjing, China, ACPR 2019 in Auckland, New Zealand, and ACPR 2021 in Jeju Island, South Korea. As we know, ACPR was initiated to promote pattern recognition theory, technologies and applications in the Asia-Pacific region. Over the years, it has actually welcomed authors from all over the world.

ACPR 2023 focused on four important areas of pattern recognition: pattern recognition and machine learning, computer vision and robot vision, signal processing, and media processing and interaction, covering various technical aspects.

ACPR 2023 received 164 submissions from 21 countries. The program chairs invited 141 program committee members and additional reviewers. Each paper was single blindly reviewed by at least two reviewers, and most papers received three reviews each. Finally, 93 papers were accepted for presentation in the program, resulting in an acceptance rate of 56.7%.

The technical program of ACPR was scheduled over four days (5–8 November 2023), including two workshops, four keynote speeches, and nine oral sessions.

The keynote speeches were presented by internationally renowned researchers. Tatsuya Harada, from University of Tokyo, Japan, gave a speech titled "Learning to reconstruct deformable 3D objects". Longin Jan Latecki, from Temple University, USA, gave a speech titled "Image retrieval by training different query views to retrieve the same database images". Jingyi Yu, Shanghai Tech University, China, gave a speech titled "Bridging recognition and reconstruction: Generative techniques on digital human, animal, and beyond". Mark Nixon, from University of Southampton, UK, gave a speech titled "Gait Biometrics – from then to now and the deep revolution".

Organizing a large event is a challenging task, requiring intensive teamwork. We would like to thank all members of the organizing committee for their hard work, with guidance from the steering committee. The program chairs, publication chairs, publicity chairs, workshop chairs, tutorial chairs, exhibition/demo chairs, sponsorship chairs, finance chairs, local organizing chairs, and webmaster all led their respective committees and worked together closely to make ACPR 2023 successful. Our special thanks go to the many reviewers, whom we cannot name one by one, for constructive comments to improve the papers. We thank all the authors who submitted their papers, which is the most important part of a scientific conference. Finally, we would like to acknowledge the student volunteers from our local organizers.

We hope this proceedings could be a valuable resource for the researchers and practitioners in the field of pattern recognition.

November 2023

Cheng-Lin Liu
Yasushi Yagi
Tohru Kamiya
Michael Blumenstein
Huimin Lu
Wankou Yang
Sung-Bae Cho

Organization

Steering Committee

Seong-Whan Lee	Korea University, South Korea
Cheng-Lin Liu	Chinese Academy of Sciences, China
Umapada Pal	Indian Statistical Institute, India
Tieniu Tan	Nanjing University, China
Yasushi Yagi	Osaka University, Japan

General Chairs

Cheng-Lin Liu	Chinese Academy of Sciences, China
Yasushi Yagi	Osaka University, Japan
Tohru Kamiya	Kyushu Institute of Technology, Japan

Program Chairs

Michael Blumenstein	University of Sydney, Australia
Huimin Lu	Kyushu Institute of Technology, Japan
Wankou Yang	Southeast University, China
Sung-Bae Cho	Yonsei University, South Korea

Publication Chairs

Yujie Li	Kyushu Institute of Technology, Japan
Xizhao Wang	Shenzhen University, China
Manu Malek	Stevens Institute of Technology, USA

Publicity Chairs

Jihua Zhu	Xi'an Jiaotong University, China
Limei Peng	Kyungpook National University, South Korea
Shinya Takahashi	Fukuoka University, Japan

Workshop Chairs

JooKooi Tan   Kyushu Institute of Technology, Japan
Weihua Ou   Guizhou Normal University, China
Jinjia Zhou   Hosei University, Japan

Tutorial Chairs

Shenglin Mu   Ehime University, Japan
Xing Xu   University of Electronic Science and Technology
                         of China, China
Tohlu Matsushima   Kyushu Institute of Technology, Japan

Exhibition/Demo Chairs

Zongyuan Ge   Monash University, Australia
Yuya Nishida   Kyushu Institute of Technology, Japan
Wendy Flores-Fuentes   Universidad Autónoma de Baja California,
                         Mexico

Sponsorship Chairs

Rushi Lan   Guilin University of Electronic Technology, China
Keiichiro Yonezawa   Kyushu Institute of Technology, Japan
Jože Guna   University of Ljubljana, Slovenia

Finance Chairs

Quan Zhou   Nanjing University of Posts and
                         Telecommunications, China
Ainul Akmar Mokhtar   Universiti Teknologi Petronas, Malaysia
Shota Nakashima   Yamaguchi University, Japan

Local Organizing Chairs

Nobuo Sakai   Kyushu Institute of Technology, Japan
Naoyuki Tsuruta   Fukuoka University, Japan
Xiaoqing Wen   Kyushu Institute of Technology, Japan

Webmaster

Jintong Cai   Southeast University, China

Program Committee Members

Alireza Alaei
Noriko Takemura
Yuchao Zheng
Michael Cree
Jingyi Wang
Cairong Zhao
Minh Nguyen
Huimin Lu
Jinshi Cui
Renlong Hang
Takayoshi Yamashita
Hirotake Yamazoe
Weiqi Yan
Weihua Ou
Umapada Pal
Wankou Yang
Shuo Yang
Koichi Ito
Qiguang Miao
Yirui Wu
Jaesik Choi
Nobuo Sakai
Songcan Chen
Sukalpa Chanda
Xin Jin
Masayuki Tanaka
Fumihiko Sakaue
Jaehwa Park
Hiroaki Kawashima
Hiroshi Tanaka
Wendy Flores-Fuentes
Yasushi Makihara
Jože Guna
Yanwu Xu
Guangwei Gao
Rushi Lan
Kazuhiro Hotta

Shinya Takahashi
Xing Xu
Weifeng Liu
Kaushik Roy
Quan Zhou
Daisuke Miyazaki
Byoungchul Ko
Sung-Bae Cho
Yoshito Mekada
Kar-Ann Toh
Martin Stommel
Tohru Kamiya
Xiaoqing Wen
Xiaoyi Jiang
Jihua Zhu
Michael Blumenstein
Andrew Tzer-Yeu Chen
Shohei Nobuhara
Yoshihiko Mochizuki
Yasutomo Kawanishi
Jinjia Zhou
Yusuyuki Sugaya
Ikuhisa Mitsugami
Yubao Sun
Dong-Gyu Lee
Yuzuko Utsumi
Saumik Bhattacharya
Masaaki Iiyama
Shang-Hong Lai
Shivakumara Palaiahnakote
Limei Peng
Jookooi Tan
Shenglin Mu
Zongyuan Ge
Ainul Mokhtar
Shota Nakashima
Naoyuki Tsuruta

Chunyan Ma
Sung-Ho Bae
Gong Cheng
Sungjoon Choi
Andreas Dengel
Junyu Dong
Bo Du
Jianjiang Feng
Fei Gao
Hitoshi Habe
Tsubasa Hirakawa
Maiya Hori
Yoshihisa Ijiri
Kohei Inoue
Yumi Iwashita
Taeeui Kam
Kunio Kashino
Sangpil Kim
Jinkyu Kim
Hui Kong
Seong-Whan Lee
Namhoon Lee
Xuelong Li
Zhu Li
Zechao Li
Junxia Li
Jia Li
Qingshan Liu
Feng Lu
Jiayi Ma
Brendan Mccane
Tetsuro Morimoto

Hajime Nagahara
Masashi Nishiyama
Naoko Nitta
Kazunori Okada
Srikanta Pal
Partha Pratim Roy
Hong-Bin Shen
Atsushi Shimada
Xiangbo Shu
Heung-Il Suk
Jun Sun
Minhyuk Sung
Tomokazu Takahashi
Kenichiro Tanaka
Ngo Thanh Trung
Christian Wallraven
Qi Wang
Xiushen Wei
Yihong Wu
Haiyuan Wu
Guiyu Xia
Guisong Xia
Yong Xu
Junchi Yan
Keiji Yanai
Xucheng Yin
Xianghua Ying
Kaihua Zhang
Shanshan Zhang
Hao Zhang
Jiang Yu Zheng
Wangmeng Zuo

Contents – Part III

Anisotropic Operator Based on Adaptable Metric-Convolution Stage-Depth Filtering Applied to Depth Completion

Vanel Lazcano[1]($\boxtimes$) iD, Iván Ramírez[2], and Felipe Calderero[3]

[1] Facultad de Ciencia, Ingeniería y Tecnología, Núcleo de Matemática, Física y Estadística, Universidad Mayor, Manuel Montt 318, Providencia, Chile
vanel.lazcano@umayor.cl
[2] Facultad de Ciencia, Ingeniería y Tecnología, Escuela de Ingeniería, Universidad Mayor, Manuel Montt 318, Providencia, Chile
ivan.ramirez@umayor.cl
[3] VP @ Ladorian - Digital School Madrid, Madrid, Spain

Abstract. Nowadays, depth maps are a crucial source of information for many applications based on artificial vision. Applications such as video games, 3D cinema, or unmanned autonomous vehicle control strongly depend on data extracted from depth maps. Depth maps can be estimated by algorithms or acquired by sensors (such as Kinect sensor, Time-of-Flight camera, or LiDAR sensor). Acquired depth data frequently contains holes or data with low confidence levels. An interpolation model is necessary to solve the problem of lack of data or complete these holes in depth maps. We constructed a manifold given the image domain and a metric whose parameters are learned from the data. The primary approach is to provide the parameterized metric enough flexibility to estimate the manifold's shape correctly. Additionally, the proposal embedded depth estimation in a pipeline considering convolution stages and the anisotropic metric. We estimated the parameters' proposal using the PSO algorithm. We assessed our proposal using the publicly available KITTI Depth Completion Suite dataset. Obtained results show that this proposal outperforms our previous implementation and other contemporary models. Additionally, we performed an ablation study of the model showing that the critical component of the model is the first convolution stage, meaning this stage that enforces the edges of the color image is a crucial component of the model.

Keywords: Depth maps · Infinity Laplacian · Depth Completion · Depth Filtering

1 Introduction

Nowadays, depth maps are essential information for many applications, such as 3D cinema, video games, or unmanned autonomous vehicles. The depth map is a

H. Lu et al. (Eds.): ACPR 2023, LNCS 14408, pp. 1–14, 2023.
https://doi.org/10.1007/978-3-031-47665-5_1

picture of a scene where every element of the picture contains the distance from each object in the scene concerning a fixed point (a sensor). A Depth map can be acquired by an algorithm (stereo algorithm) or sensor (Kinect, Time-Of-Flight Camera, or LiDAR). The information given by the sensor presents points with low confidence levels and regions of the depth map with a need for more information. The high-performance standards of the applications make the completion of depth maps in areas without data necessary. This paper proposes a model to interpolate depth data based on the infinity Laplacian. We solve numerically the degenerated second-order partial differential equation associated with the infinity Laplacian. Given the domain $\Omega \subset \mathbb{R}^2$ and a metric $d_{\mathbf{x},\mathbf{y}}$ we constructed a manifold $\mathcal{M} = (\Omega, d_{\mathbf{xy}})$, in which the available data is embedded. We solve the second-order degenerated partial differential equation in the manifold.

The contribution of this paper is:

i) The addition of a filter that eliminates outliers in the available depth data.
ii) The use of an anisotropic metric.
iii) Ablation study.

In Sect. 2 we present a literature review of similar works to the one we propose. In Sect. 3, we propose a model to complete sparse depth maps. Section 5 presents the implementation of the Particle Swarm Optimization algorithm to estimate the parameters of the proposal. In Sects. 6 and 7, we present our performed experiments and the used dataset, and finally, we give our conclusions in Sect. 8.

2   Related Works

The objective of the depth completion is to interpolate sparse depth maps in order to generate dense depth maps. Some depth interpolation models use only the available depth data. In contrast, others use additional information (a scene color reference image) to perform the depth completion guided by the color image [10, 15, 20, 24]. The idea behind guided methods is to guide the completion process by taking into account regional characteristics of the image, such as edges or smoothness.

Nowadays, many proposals use CNN (Convolutional Neural Networks) to interpolate sparse depth maps [4, 6, 8, 15, 18, 25]. In work presented in [18], a depth completion process is performed considering CNN without the reference color image. Authors simultaneously interpolate the sparse depth information and reconstruct a scene gray-level image. Authors evaluated their model in a publicly available dataset and found that it outperforms contemporaneous models that use data extracted from that color reference image [25].

In [6], the authors represented the image using Depth Coefficients, avoiding inter-object mixing. In [4], a model is presented to classify depth information using a normalized convolutional neural network (NCNN) network-based input trust.

The work in [16] uses spatial dispersion networks. These networks, which are affinities-based models, are used to finish depth maps, but this model needs help with under-representing fixed affinities and over-smoothing. In general, estimates of independent affinity matrices are over-parameterized using conventional approaches. The authors provided a successful model that uses a dynamic attention-based technique to discover the affinity between neighboring pixels. Diffusion suppression, attention maps, and a non-linear propagation model are all used in the model. The model avoids over-smoothing the final solution and produces better results with fewer iterations than traditional spatial propagation networks.

On the other hand, methods that do not use neural networks are presented in [7,14,23]. The work of Lazcano et al. [14] presents an experimental assessment of a practical implementation of the infinity Laplacian used to interpolate depth maps. Authors compared the performance of their proposal using different metrics ($\mathcal{L}^1$, $\mathcal{L}^2$, and $\mathcal{L}^{\frac{1}{2}}$) and different color spaces (RGB, XYZ, CIE-Lab, and CMY). The authors applied their proposal to depth and optical flow completion. The model called PDC [23] presents a non-deep learning model (or classical model). The authors remove misaligned points from the depth data by filtering it. The reference color image is then divided into superpixels. The authors constructed a convex hull as a set of the most inline points used to define a superpixel. This superpixel is used to fit the local depth data if a plane is inadequate locally. The filtered and residual data are then interpolated using a pinhole camera model. According to their KITTI Depth Completion Suite findings, obtained results using the proposal outperform models based on more traditional concepts, such as variational models or morphological operations. A piecewise depth map completion model is stated in the work of Krauss et al. [7]. The model divides color images into superpixels based on regions with similar depth values. They suppose these superpixels correspond to pixels from the same objects and were acquired using a cost map. The results are comparable to those of state-of-the-art algorithms. In their analysis of the KITTI dataset, the authors show the effects of each processing stage and overall performance.

The authors in [1] applied the AMLE or infinity Laplacian to elevation models or optical flow completion in [14,21]. The authors of [13] applied the bAMLE to complete depth data but did not experiment with various metrics or color spaces. Furthermore, surfaces embedded in $\mathbb{R}^3$ given a few iso-level curves were completed using the Infinity Laplacian operator [2]. Finally, new databases have been constructed, and protocols are defined to systematically assess the performance of depth completion methods such as KITTI [25] or NYU_V2. Recently the work in [5] shows applications of the infinity Laplacian in segmentation, completion of color images, and clustering.

3   Proposed Model

We used a pipeline presented in [12] to complete depth maps. We can follow two paths in Fig. 1. The first is the green path, and the second is the red-dotted path. We use a binary parameter, "reversible", to select which path we follow. If the parameter is 0, we follow the green path, and if the parameter is 1, we follow the red-dotted path. First, we explain the green path. The pipeline starts with a color reference image of the scene. To enforce the color reference images' features, we processed the image with a battery of Gabor Filters and max pool the output of the filters (namely stage SC1), and to eliminate outliers, we used a pre-filter applied to the acquired depth map. Then, the infinity Laplacian interpolates the available depth data. Finally, the output of the infinity Laplacian is filtered by a battery of convolutional filters, and the output is max pooled (SC2).

In Fig. 1, we show the pipeline we will explain in detail in this section.

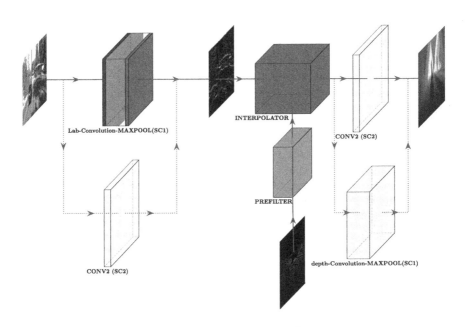

Fig. 1. Pipeline used to complete depth maps.

3.1 Interpolation Model

To interpolate the data, we use the infinity Laplacian. Let us consider $u : \Omega \subset \mathbb{R}^2 \to \mathbb{R}$ the map to interpolate. We solve the infinity Laplacian to interpolate the available data,

$$\Delta_{\infty,g} u = 0 \in \Omega, \tag{1}$$

with the boundary condition $u\big|_{\partial \mathcal{O}} = \theta$, and $\mathcal{O}$ is where the available data is located and θ is the available depth data. Given the domain Ω and the metric

g, we constructed a manifold $\mathcal{M} = (\Omega, g)$ where the infinity Laplacian should be solved. To solve the infinity Laplacian in the manifold, we solve,

$$\Delta_{\infty,g} u = D^2_{\mathcal{M}} u \left(\frac{\nabla u}{|\nabla u|}, \frac{\nabla u}{|\nabla u|} \right) = 0, \tag{2}$$

which is a degenerated second-order partial differential equation.

3.2 Depth Map Filtering

Pre-filtering of the data eliminates some outliers of the acquired depth data. The pre-filtering is a morphological operation that depends on the depth values of a pixel $\mathbf{x}$ and its neighborhood. Figure 2 shows the considered neighborhood and the central point,

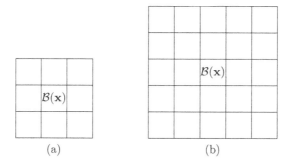

(a)   (b)

Fig. 2. Neighborhood $\mathcal{B}(\mathbf{x})$ is considered to implement the depth filtering. The neighbor is of the size P around the x point. (a) The neighborhood of size $P = 1$. (b) neighborhood of size $P = 2$

Figure 2 shows the neighborhood around every point $\mathbf{x}$ of the acquired depth map. The acquired data has the following codification:

$$\text{depth}(\mathbf{x}) = \begin{cases} \text{depth}(\mathbf{x}) = -1 & \text{no data} \\ \text{depth}(\mathbf{x}) \neq -1 & \text{available data} \end{cases} \tag{3}$$

The main idea is that we start with a point, called the central point $\mathbf{x}$. We check if this point is valid, meaning that it is not an outlier ($\text{depth}(\mathbf{x}) \neq -1$). If it is valid, we look at all the points around it ($\mathbf{y} \in \mathcal{B}(\mathbf{x})$). If all of these points $\mathbf{y}$ are also valid and their depth is less than the depth of the central point, then we know that the central point is an outlier. In this case, we eliminate the point by setting its $\text{depth}(\mathbf{x})$ to -1.

Practically, we implemented this filtering addition to the depth value of the surrounding points of $\mathbf{x}$ and compared it with a threshold (θ_f) times $\text{depth}(\mathbf{x})$, i.e.:

$$\text{if } \left(\sum_{\mathbf{y} \in \mathcal{B}(\mathbf{x}), \, \mathbf{y} \neq \mathbf{x}} [\theta_f \text{depth}(\mathbf{y}) > \text{depth}(\mathbf{x})] \right) > 1, \ \text{depth}(\mathbf{x}) = -1. \qquad (4)$$

We estimated the θ_f in the training stage.

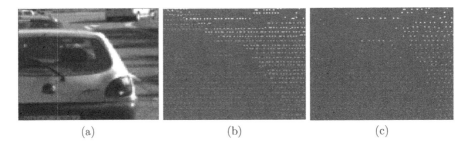

(a)   (b)   (c)

Fig. 3. Examples of depth filtering. (a) Reference color image. (b) Acquired depth data. (c) Filtered depth data.

In Fig. 3, we show an example of the depth data Pre-filtering. Figure 3 (a) shows a cropped color reference image. In (b), we show its corresponding depth map acquired by a laser. In (c), we show the output of our filter. We observe in (b) that most of the data (in yellow color) on the car's surface present larger depth values than the surrounding available data, meaning that all those yellow points are outliers. Our filter eliminates these outliers, as we show in (c). The resulting depth map contains less available data, but the new data has less outliers that finally improves the performance of our model.

The Fig. 3 (a) shows a cropped color reference image of a car. The second image (b) shows the corresponding depth map of the car, which was acquired by a LiDAR. The third image (c) shows the output of a proposed Filter that was applied to the depth map (b).

In the second Fig. 3 (b), we can see that the data on the car's surface (in yellow color) has larger depth values than the surrounding data. This means that these yellow points are outliers (depth data that are significantly different from the surrounding data). The filter in the third image (c) eliminates these outliers. In other words, the filter helps to remove inaccurate data from the depth map, which makes the depth map more accurate and reliable.

4 Practical Model Implementation

As presented in [19], infinity Laplacian can be computed as the average value between the positive eikonal operator and the negative infinity operator,

$$\frac{\|\nabla u(\mathbf{x})\|_{\xi}^{+} + \|\nabla u(\mathbf{x})\|_{\xi}^{-}}{2} = 0. \qquad (5)$$

The positive eikonal operator is a non-local gradient defined as:

$$\|\nabla u(\mathbf{x})\|_\xi^+ = \frac{u(\mathbf{y}) - u(\mathbf{x})}{d_{\mathbf{xy}}}, \tag{6}$$

where $\mathbf{y}$ is a position in a neighborhood $\mathcal{N}(\mathbf{x})$ around $\mathbf{x}$, that maximizes the ratio in Eq. 6, and $d_{\mathbf{xy}}$ is the distance between $\mathbf{x}$ and $\mathbf{y}$. The negative eikonal operator is a non-local gradient defined as:

$$\|\nabla u(\mathbf{x})\|_\xi^- = \frac{u(\mathbf{z}) - u(\mathbf{x})}{d_{\mathbf{xz}}}, \tag{7}$$

where $\mathbf{z}$ is a position in a neighborhood $\mathcal{N}(\mathbf{x})$ that maximizes the ratio in Eq. 7.

4.1 Numerical Model for the Infinity Laplacian

Given the above definitions, the numerical model for the infinity Laplacian as in [13]: Let $\mathbf{y}, \mathbf{z}$ be the location that maximizes the positive eikonal and minimizes the negative eikonal operator, respectively. Taking into account these definitions is possible to state the infinity Laplacian,

$$\frac{1}{2}\left(\left(\frac{u(\mathbf{y}) - u(\mathbf{x})}{d_{\mathbf{xy}}}\right) + \left(\frac{u(\mathbf{z}) - u(\mathbf{x})}{d_{\mathbf{xz}}}\right)\right) = 0. \tag{8}$$

The solution of Eq. (8) is given by:

$$u(\mathbf{x}) = \frac{d_{\mathbf{xz}}u(\mathbf{y}) + d_{\mathbf{xy}}u(\mathbf{z})}{d_{\mathbf{xz}} + d_{\mathbf{xy}}}. \tag{9}$$

The iterated version of the infinity Laplacian is given by,

$$u^{k+1}(\mathbf{x}) = \frac{d_{\mathbf{xz}}u^k(\mathbf{y}) + d_{\mathbf{xy}}u^k(\mathbf{z})}{d_{\mathbf{xz}} + d_{\mathbf{xy}}} \quad k = 1, 2, 3, ... \tag{10}$$

4.2 Considered Metric

As we see in the section above, the eikonal operator depends on the distance between two points in the manifold. To estimate the distance, we use a metric composed of one spatial term and a photometric term. We considered a metric different from $\mathcal{L}^2$; the considered metric gives more flexibility to the manifold's shape estimation. We state the assumed metric:

$$d_{\mathbf{xy}} = (\kappa_x\|\mathbf{x} - \mathbf{y}\|^p + \kappa_y\|I(\mathbf{x}) - I(\mathbf{y})\|^s)^q \tag{11}$$

where κ_x, κ_c, p, q, and r are parameters of the model that have to be empirically estimated.

In this paper, we considered an adaptable metric. This metric has a balance term, balancing between the space and photometric terms. The expression for this metric is given by:

$$d_{\mathbf{xy}} = (\kappa_x\gamma(\mathbf{x})\|\mathbf{x} - \mathbf{y}\|^p + \kappa_c(1 - \gamma(\mathbf{x}))\|I(\mathbf{x}) - I(\mathbf{y})\|^s)^q \tag{12}$$

where $\gamma(\mathbf{x})$ is given by,

$$\gamma(\mathbf{x}) = \frac{1}{1 + e^{\beta_\gamma(\|\mathbf{x}-\mathbf{y}\| - \tau_\gamma \|I(\mathbf{x})-I(\mathbf{y})\|)}} \tag{13}$$

where β_γ and τ_γ are parameters of the balance term that must be empirically estimated. This balance term is defined as $\gamma : \Omega \subset \mathbb{R}^2 \rightarrow [0,1]$. The main idea behind the balance term [9] is that if the spatial term is larger than the photometric term ($\gamma(\mathbf{x}) \approx 0$), the distance will be measured using mainly $\|I(\mathbf{x}) - I(\mathbf{y})\|$. On the other hand, if the photometric term is larger than the spatial term ($\gamma(\mathbf{x}) \approx 1$), the distance will be computed mainly using the spatial term. If $\gamma(x) = 0.5$, we recover the distance stated in Eq. 11. In Fig. 4 we show and example of computation of balance term $\gamma(x)$ in a color reference image, In Fig. 4 in (a), we present a color reference image. In (b), we show the balance term color coded. In Yellow we present values of $\gamma(\mathbf{x}) > 0.5$ and in orange $0\gamma(\mathbf{x}) < 0.5$. Comparing the color image (a) and $\gamma(\mathbf{x})$ in (b), we observe that larger values of γ are located in regions where shadows are present, and mainly the spatial term is used to compute distances. Both terms are used in other regions, such as the sky or on the road.

(a)   (b)

Fig. 4. Example of balance term $\gamma(\mathbf{x})$ computer for an urban color reference image. (a) color reference image. (b) color-coded balance map $\gamma(\mathbf{x})$ larger gamma values are color-coded with yellow and orange representing $\gamma = 0.46$.

5   Training the Model

We have estimated the parameter of our model using the KITTI dataset [17]. We used five color reference images, their corresponding depth, and their ground truth. We estimated the best parameters that minimize the MSE (mean square error) and MAE (mean absolute error) error, defined by:

$$MSE(\mu_j) = \sqrt{\frac{1}{NP} \sum_{i=1}^{NP} (out(\mu_j, i) - gt(i))^2}, \tag{14}$$

and,

$$MAE(\mu_j) = \frac{1}{NP} \sum_{i=1}^{NP} |out(\mu_j, i) - gt(i)|, \tag{15}$$

where gt is the provided ground truth, out is the completed depth map, μ_j is used as the parameter to obtain $out(\mu_j)$, and NP is the number of points where we compared the estimated depth with the ground truth. We minimized fitness,

$$J(\mu_j) = MSE(\mu_j) + MAE(\mu_j) \tag{16}$$

Fig. 5. The training set is used to estimate the model's parameters. The training set is extracted from the KITTI depth completion suite. (a), (b) and (c) color reference images. (e), (f), and (g) corresponding depth map.

We use the Particle Swarm Optimization (PSO) algorithm to minimize the fitness. We created 40 random μ_i individuals, and then according to the dynamic of velocity and acceleration for each individual, we evolved them for 30 iterations. In each iteration, we selected the individual that presented the best performance. In 5 we show the training set extracted from the KITTI dataset.

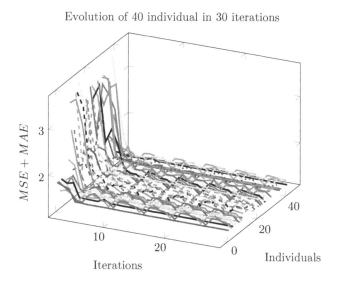

Fig. 6. Performance evolution of 40 individuals in 30 iterations.

In Fig. 6, we show the evolution of the 40 individuals of the training set. We present the $MSE + MAE$ of each individual. The final performance reached by the proposal was fitness=1.3122 $(MSE + MAE)$.

6 Dataset and Experiments

6.1 Dataset

We use the KITTI depth completion suite [17] to train our model and to evaluate the model. The KITTI dataset contains 1000 color images, its depth map, and its corresponding ground truth. We showed above an example of the KITTI dataset in Fig. 5.

6.2 Experiments

We used three images to train our models and 997 images to test our model. We evaluate our model and compare our obtained performance with many models already presented in the literature. We also performed an ablation test to determine the most critical component of our model.

7 Results

We trained our models on 997 images from the KITTI dataset. We then evaluated the performance of our models on the entire dataset, using two metrics: the mean squared error (MSE) and the mean absolute error (MAE). The results of our evaluation are shown in Table 1. As we show Table 1, our model performs better than our previous version of the model and other models that were developed around the same time [11] or [23]. However, some more complex models use neural networks to learn morphological operations [3] that perform even better than our model.

Table 1. Obtained results by our model and comparison with other models.

Model	MSE	MAE	$MAE + MSE$
Our proposal	1.1252	0.3045	1.4297
CANDAR [11]	1.1397	0.3132	1.4529
PDC [23]	1.2866	0.2932	1.5798
Deep Fusion Networks [22]	1.2067	0.4299	1.6366
Morpho Networks [3]	1.0455	0.3105	1.3560

Table 2. Results of the ablation test in our proposal.

Stage	MSE	MAE	$MSE + MAE$
Prefiltering	1.1260	0.3124	1.4384
1st Convolutional Stage	1.6700	0.2956	1.9656
2nd Convolutional Stage	1.1256	0.3055	1.4311
Complete proposal	1.1252	0.3045	1.4297

7.1   Ablation Test

We conducted a series of experiments to see how each stage of our proposal contributes to its overall performance. We removed each stage individually and measured the impact on the performance. The results of these experiments are shown in Table 2. The table shows that the convolutional stage is the most crucial stage, followed by the interpolator and the prefiltering of the depth. The postfiltering stage has the most negligible impact on the performance. In Table 2, the most critical part of our model is the convolutional stage SC1. This convolutional stage selects features that enforce edges of the color reference image, improving the model's performance. In Fig. 7, we show examples of the completed depth map in images extracted from the KITTI dataset. In Fig. 7 (a), we show the reference color image, where we observe a person riding a bike. In (b), we offer the sparse depth map; the amount of available data is 4.51% of the size of the image. In (c), we show the ground truth acquired by LiDAR. Finally, in (d), we offer our completed depth map. We observed that we recovered much information about the scene: the person riding the bike, a traffic sign, a parked bike on the street, and a small car. We compare the ground truth depth map in Fig. 7 (c) with the completed depth map in Fig. 7 (d). The ground truth depth map is the actual depth map of the scene, and the completed depth map is the depth map we generated using the available data. As a qualitative evaluation, we look at the regions where the available data is located. These regions have a similar color code in both the ground truth depth map and the completed depth map.

(a)   (b)

(c)   (d)

Fig. 7. Examples of completed depth maps. (a) reference color image. (b) Available sparse depth map. (c) ground truth. (d) Completed depth map.

This fact means that the completed depth map is a good representation of the actual depth map in these regions.

(a)   (b)

(c)   (d)

Fig. 8. Examples of completed depth maps where our proposal fails. (a) reference color image. (b) Available sparse depth map. (c) ground truth. (d) Completed depth map.

In Fig. 8 we present an example where our proposal fails. Figure 8 shows that our model fails due to transparent objects like car windows. We observe in (d) that the edges of the window present errors in the completion.

8   Conclusions

We have proposed a model to complete sparse depth based on the infinity Laplacian embedded in a convolutional pipeline. The convolutional pipeline considers two convolutional stages and the infinity Laplacian to complete depth maps. As a prefiltering stage, we implemented a morphological operator to eliminate outliers of the available depth data. We embedded the depth data in a manifold given a metric in the image domain. We proposed a variable metric that uses a balance mechanism that depends on spatial tern and the photometric term. The inclusion of these two components improves the performance of our model, outperforming our previous version of it. The proposal also outperforms contemporaneous depth completion models and performs similarly to more complex neural network models. In the performed ablation test, we discovered that the most critical stage is the first convolutional stage that enforces edges of the reference color image, which helps in the correct diffusion of the available data. In future work, we will use more contemporaneous interpolation models.

References

1. Almansa, A., Cao, F., Gousseau, Y., Rougé, B.: Interpolation of digital elevation models using Amle and related methods. IEEE Trans. Geosci. Rem. Sens. **40**(2), 314–325 (2002)

2. Caselles, V., Igual, L., Sander, O.: An axiomatic approach to scalar data interpolation on surfaces. Numer. Math. **102**(3), 383–411 (2006)
3. Dimitrievski, M.D., Veelaert, P., Philips, W.: Learning morphological operators for depth completion. In: Advanced Concepts for Intelligent Vision Systems Conference. IEEE (2018)
4. Eldesokey, A., Felsberg, M., Holmquist, K., Persson, M.: Uncertainty-aware CNNs for depth completion: uncertainty from beginning to end. In: Proceedings of the IEEE/CVF Conference on Computer Vision and Pattern Recognition (CVPR). IEEE, June 2020
5. Ennaji, H., Quéau, Y., Elmoataz, A.: Tug of war games and PDES on graphs with applications in image and high dimensional data processing. Sci. Rep. **13**(1), 2045–2322 (2023)
6. Imran, S., Long, Y., Liu, X., Morris, D.: Depth coefficients for depth completion. In: Proceedings of the IEEE Conference on Computer Vision and Pattern Recognition, pp. 12438–12447. IEEE (2019)
7. Krauss, B., Schroeder, G., Gustke, M., Hussein, A.: Deterministic guided lidar depth map completion, pp. 824–831. IEEE Intelligent Vehicles Symposium (IV), IEEE (2021). https://doi.org/10.1109/IV48863.2021.9575867
8. Lai, W.S., Huang, J.B., Ahuja, N., Yang, M.H.: Fast and accurate image super-resolution with deep Laplacian pyramid network. Trans. Pattern Anal. Mach. Intell. **41**(11), 2599–2613 (2019)
9. Lazcano, V.: Some problems in depth enhanced video processing, Ph.D. thesis. Universitat Pompeu Fabra, Barcelona, Spain (2016). http://hdl.handle.net/10803/373917
10. Lazcano, V., Arias, P., Facciolo, G., Caselles, V.: A gradient based neighborhood filter for disparity interpolation. In: 2012 19th IEEE International Conference on Image Processing, pp. 873–876. IEEE (2012). https://doi.org/10.1109/ICIP.2012.6466999
11. Lazcano, V., Calderero, F.: Hybrid model convolutional stage-positive definite metric operator-infinity Laplacian applied to depth completion, pp. 174–179. 2022 Tenth International Symposium on Computing and Networking Workshops (CANDARW), IEEE (2022). https://doi.org/10.1109/CANDARW57323.2022.00085
12. Lazcano, V., Calderero, F.: Hybrid pipeline infinity Laplacian plus convolutional stage applied to depth completion. In: Smys, S., Tavares, J.M.R.S., Balas, V.E. (eds.) Computational Vision and Bio-Inspired Computing. AISC, vol. 1420, pp. 119–134. Springer, Singapore (2022). https://doi.org/10.1007/978-981-16-9573-5_8
13. Lazcano, V., Calderero, F., Ballester, C.: Depth image completion using anisotropic operators. In: Abraham, A., et al. (eds.) SoCPaR 2020. AISC, vol. 1383, pp. 593–604. Springer, Cham (2021). https://doi.org/10.1007/978-3-030-73689-7_57
14. Lazcano, V., Calderero, F., Ballester, C.: Comparing different metrics on an anisotropic depth completion model. Int. J. Hybrid Intell. Syst. **1**, 87–99 (2021)
15. Li, Y., J.B. Huang, Ahuja, N., Yang, M.H.: Joint image filtering with depth convolutional networks. Trans. Pattern Anal. Mach. Intell. **41**(8), 1909–1923 (2019). https://doi.org/10.1109/TPAMI.2018.2890623
16. Lin, Y., Cheng, T., Zhong, Q., Zhou, W., Yang, H.: Dynamic spatial propagation network for depth completion. In: AAAI 2022 Conference on Artificial Intelligence, AAAI (2022)
17. Liu, L., Liao, Y., Wang, Y., Geiger, A., Liu, Y.: Learning steering kernels for guided depth completion. IEEE Trans. Image Process. **30**, 2850–2861 (2021)

18. Lu, K., Barnes, N., Anwar, S., Zheng, L.: From depth what can you see? Depth completion via auxiliary image reconstruction. In: Proceedings of the IEEE/CVF Conference on Computer Vision and Pattern Recognition (CVPR). IEEE, June 2020

19. Manfredi, J., Oberman, A., Svirodov, A.: Nonlinear elliptic partial differential equations and p-harmonic functions on graphs. Differ. Integ. Eq. **28**(12), 79–102 (2012)

20. Park, J., Kim, H., Yu-Wing, T., Brown, M., Kweon, I.: High quality depth map upsampling for 3d-TOF cameras. In: 2011 International Conference on Computer Vision, pp. 1623–1630. IEEE (2011). https://doi.org/10.1109/ICCV.2011.6126423

21. Raad, L., Oliver, M., Ballester, C., Haro, G., Meinhardt, E.: On anisotropic optical flow inpainting algorithms. IPOL. Image Process. On Line **10**, 78–104 (2020)

22. Shivakumar, S., Nguyen, T., Miller, I., Chen, S., Kumar, V., Taylor, C.: DfuseNet: deep fusion of RGB and sparse depth information for image guided dense depth completion. In: 2019 IEEE Intelligent Transportation Systems Conference (ITSC), pp. 13–20. IEEE (2019). https://doi.org/10.1109/ITSC.2019.8917294

23. Teutscher, D., Mangat, P., Wassermueller, O.: PDC: piecewise depth completion utilizing Superpixels. In: IEEE International Intelligent Transportation Systems Conference (ITSC), pp. 2752–2758. IEEE, Indianapolis, USA (2021)

24. Tomasi, C., Manduchi, R.: Bilateral filter for gray and color images. In: Sixth International Conference on Computer Vision (IEEE Press), pp. 839–846. IEEE (1998)

25. Uhrig, J., Schneider, N., Schneider, L., Franke, U., Brox, T., Geiger, A.: Sparsity invariant CNNs. In: International Conference on 3D Vision (3DV), pp. 11–20 (2017)

Stable Character Recognition Strategy Using Ventilation Manipulation in ERP-Based Brain-Computer Interface

Dogeun Park[1] , Young-Gi Ju[1] , and Dong-Ok Won[1,2]($\boxtimes$)

[1] Dept. of Artificial Intelligence Congervence, Hallym University, Chuncheon, Republic of Korea
{B22008,D20504,dongok.won}@hallym.ac.kr
[2] College of Medicine, Hallym University, Chuncheon, Republic of Korea

Abstract. Brain-computer interface (BCI) technology is a system that uses brain signals to assist in controlling devices in the outside world. Among the many methods of implementing BCI, one of the most representative method is event-related potential (ERP)-based BCI. However, ERP-based speller averages data through multiple trials to enhance performance and require continuous visual attention from subjects simultaneously. In particular, long-term experimental sessions can cause visual and cognitive fatigue in users. As a result, the performance of the ERP-based BCI could be degraded. Sighing is a natural phenomenon and one of the methods to stabilize physiological mechanisms in a short period of time. This experiment assumed that a proposed two-minute ventilation pattern using cyclic sighing could change the user's physiological attention state. The second assumption is that the proposed method may improve character recognition accuracy. To ascertain the feasibility of the proposed method, a total of five subjects participated in the experiment, and each participant was requested to experience two sessions. The counter-balancing method was implemented to prevent the carry-over effect of the experiment. These results indicate that the proposed short-term ventilation pattern performed better than the general ventilation pattern in terms of character recognition in the ERP-based BCI speller task and led our assumptions in a positive direction. In light of this, we suggest that the proposed method utilizing cyclic sighing could be used for long-term BCI protocols with respect to stability and robustness.

Keywords: Brain-computer interface · Event-related potential · Character recognition · Ventilation manipulation · Cyclic sighing · Attention

1 Introduction

Many people around the world are restricted in body movement and communication due to fatal cranial nerve diseases, cerebrovascular diseases, and amyotrophic lateral sclerosis (ALS). Brain-computer interface (BCI) system uses

H. Lu et al. (Eds.): ACPR 2023, LNCS 14408, pp. 15–25, 2023.
https://doi.org/10.1007/978-3-031-47665-5_2

brain signals to assist in controlling devices in the outside world [1–3]. Among the methods for implementing BCI systems, the most widely used application are mu-rhythm, steady state visually evoked potential (SSVEP), and event-related potential (ERP) (e.g. [2,4–6]).

P300 is one of the most studied and symbolic component of ERPs and it is widely used in BCI research [7]. The representative paradigm was developed by Farwell and Donchin and consists of the 6 × 6 matrix row-column paradigm (RCP) [6]. Moreover, single character paradigm (SCP) [8], checkerboard paradigm (CBP) [9], random set presentation (RSP) [10] and famous faces [11] have been proposed to improve the performance in ERP-based BCI speller paradigm.

The biggest advantage of ERP-based BCI is a representative endogenous attention-based task that does not require intensive user training. In addition, signal averaging through multiple trials allows subjects to achieve very high performance speller accuracy and can be calibrated in a short time. However, this paradigm has a noticeable disadvantage. The ERP-based speller task presents a repetitive stimulus of about 10 sequences per a character to improve brain signal classification performance. Since this requires continuous visual attention from the user, a high level of cognitive and visual fatigue is inevitable [3,7,8]. Collecting multiple trials to improve performance over a long period is contrary to the original purpose in terms of performance enhancement because it can be burdensome for users and could degrade character recognition rates due to fatigue.

One study to improve this problem showed a significant performance improvement in the P300-based BCI paradigm with a 6-minute meditative mindfulness induction (MMI) [12]. Mindfulness meditation is widely used for the purpose of improving awareness of the current state and involves breathing. However, mindfulness-based meditation goes through a extended period of training process to be effective, which is not an acute effect in general [13,14]. Moreover, one study provides evidence that practicing attention to internal body sense, one of the main features of meditation, is not associated with enhanced cardiac interoceptive awareness [15]. Humans spontaneously sigh a few times per hour, and rodents sigh dozens of times per hour [16]. Sighing is an evolutionary behavior among mammals that gradually decreases to 20 times per hour within a year of birth [17]. Additionally, the frequency of sighing is sensitive to cognitive, emotional, and behavioral demands. In healthy individuals, stressful situations induce more frequent sighing compared to emotionally neutral conditions [18]. Likewise, sighing is a very natural phenomenon and also a very important respiratory pattern simultaneously. During normal breathing, sighs improve gas exchange and inflate collapsed alveoli [16]. This ventilation pattern is a natural phenomenon to reduces physiological arousal and makes the condition stable. In a comparative study of four different breathing patterns, including mindfulness meditation and cyclic sighing, showed cyclic sighing was more effective in relieving sympathetic nerves than mindfulness meditation. In addition, the phys-

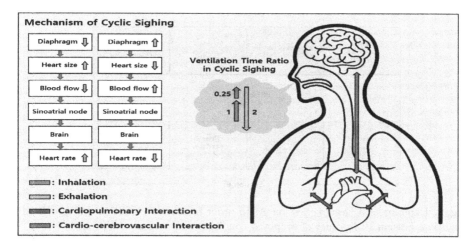

Fig. 1. The components of cyclic sighing(two inhalations and one exhalation) and physiological mechanisms.

iological and psychological effects of cyclic sighing seem not only acute, but also to persist over time [14, 19, 20].

Based on the findings of these previous researches, we first assumed that a short-term respiratory pattern using cyclic sighing can change physiological attention state. The second assumption that we reckoned was that the proposed ventilation method could enhance character recognition performance. Furthermore, sighing for more than five minutes can cause the subject to become excessively stable and drowsy. Therefore, this study investigated the change in character recognition performance according to cyclic sighing for two minutes in the ongoing experimental paradigm in P300-based BCI systems. To test the feasibility of the proposed method, we organized two experimental sessions and two different conditions. A total of five subjects participated in this preliminary study. All data were analyzed using multi-channel electroencephalogram (EEG) equipment and regularized linear discriminant analysis with shrinkage [21].

2 Methods

2.1 Experimental Paradigm

a. Visual Stimuli Setting
In this experiment, the event-related potential (ERP)-based 6 × 6 matrix row-column paradigm (RCP) [6] was set up using MATLAB (MathWorks, Natick, MA, USA) with psychtoolbox (http://psychtoolbox.org), and the stimulus-time interval (STI) was set to 80 ms and the inter-stimulus interval (ISI) was set to 135 ms, respectively.

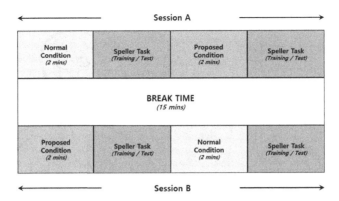

Fig. 2. Experimental Design (Session A: In order of normal condition and proposed condition, Session B: In order of proposed condition and normal condition).

b. Ventilation Pattern

To verify our hypothesis, we investigated the effect of cyclic sighing on the ERP-based speller paradigm, as shown in Fig. 1. Cyclic sighing consists of two inhalations using the nasal cavity, one inhalation using the oral cavity, and participants were asked to exhale about two times longer than the inhalation. Firstly, each participant was requested to take double inhalations, and maximum inhalation was requested on the first breath. The second inhalation was performed to maximize the amount of oxygen by maximizing the alveoli [14]. However, long-term cyclic sighing could reduce physiological arousal, and this may cause drowsiness. Therefore, we applied a two-minute ventilation pattern using cyclic sighing for the proposed condition.

c. Experimental Design

As shown in Fig. 2., the experiment consists of Session A and Session B. Each subject participated in both sessions. In session A, it was carried out in the order of normal condition and proposed condition. After an average of 15 min of rest, it was carried out in the opposite order to minimize the carry-over effect in session B. The data set was divided into a training set and a test set, and the training set consisted of twenty characters (HALLYMUNIVERSITYAIML) and the test set consisted of twenty-two characters (BRAINCOMPUTERINTERFACE). In each session under normal conditions, each subject was not requested to do anything to induce normal breathing for two minutes. On the other hand, in the proposed condition, each subject was asked to do cyclic sighing for two minutes.

2.2   Data Acquisition

Five subjects participated in the experimental paradigm. All subjects have not experienced cardiovascular, cerebrovascular disease and respiratory system issues. Participants conducted an experiment in an experimental environment

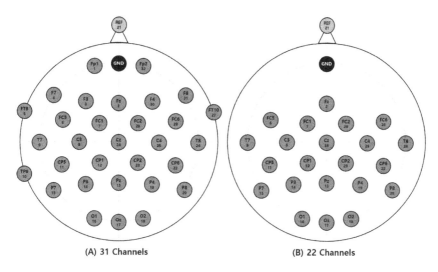

(A) 31 Channels   (B) 22 Channels

Fig. 3. 31 channels of EEG data were collected and 22 channels of EEG data were selected in this experiment.

with a distance from the monitor of about 1.2 m and a temperature of about 24 °C. In the experiment, actiCHamp (Brain Products, Germany) was used as an amplifier. As shown in Fig. 3. (A), 31 channels of data were obtained at 1000 Hz through the international 10–20 system. This study was approved by the Institutional Review Board of Hallym University [HIRD-2022-056].

2.3   Data Analysis

a. Preprocessing
We used MATLAB with the BBCI toolbox (http://bbci.de/toolbox) for data analysis. All electroencephalogram (EEG) data was down-sampled at 100 Hz for analysis. In this study, we selected only 22 electrode channels (Fz, FC5, FC1, FC2, FC6, T7, C3, Cz, C4, T8, CP5, CP1, CP2, CP6, P7, P3, Pz, P4, P8, O1, Oz, O2) in Fig. 3. (B). and band-pass filtered at 0.1–30 Hz with a Chebyshev filter for off-line analysis. Additionally, we applied the common average reference (CAR) to remove artifacts.

b. Epoching and Classification
After EEG data are signal pre-processed, we used Python for the rest of the processing. All training set and test set data were segmented from -200 to 1000 ms and the pre-stimulus interval from -200 to 0 ms for baseline correction. We applied regularized linear discriminant analysis with shrinkage [21] for training and test data to proceed with offline analysis.

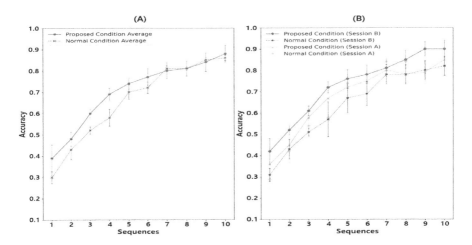

Fig. 4. Comparison of character recognition accuracy by condition((A): Mean comparison between two conditions, (B): Mean comparison between two conditions by sessions).

3   Results

3.1   Average Character Recognition Accuracy Across All Subjects

As shown in Fig. 4., shows the character recognition accuracy over sequences for five subjects. In particular, (A) in Fig. 4., compares the Proposed Condition Average and the Normal Condition Average for all sessions. It shows an improvement in performance for all sequences except sequences 7–9. (B) in Fig. 4 shows the condition average for all subjects by session. In this figure, the proposed condition in session A outperforms the normal condition in session A on sequences 1–4 while the proposed condition underperforms on sequences 5–10. On the other hand, the proposed condition in session B outperforms the normal condition in session B in all sequences.

3.2   Individual Subject Character Recognition and ERPs Patterns

For further analysis, we examined the character recognition rates for individual subjects. Figure 5 shows the comparison of individual subject performance in session A, and Fig. 6 shows the comparison of individual subject performance in session B. In Fig. 5, the individual subjects' performance in the proposed condition does not show a large difference from the normal condition overall. However, it is important to note that the overall performance is dominated by sequences 1–6. In addition, in Fig. 6., all subjects except subject2 and subject4 showed higher character recognition accuracy in all sequences than in the normal condition. In particular, session 6 shows a rapid increase overall in accuracy for sequences with fewer trials. To further examine the ERPs analysis, we compared the P300 patterns of the first condition of Session A (the normal condition) and the first condition of Session B (the proposed condition) for Subject5. Figure 7. (A) shows the first condition of Session A, and Fig. 7. (B) shows the first condition of Session B. In terms of amplitude and latency, the P300 pattern (B) is larger than (A) in Fig. 7 and most subjects showed similar patterns. This suggests that our proposed breathing pattern could change the ERPs pattern.

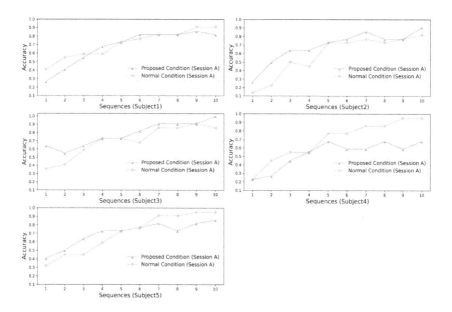

Fig. 5. Comparison of Proposed and Normal Condition by subject in Session A.

4   Discussion and Conclusion

In this study, we investigated the effects of a 2-min ventilation pattern using cyclic sighing on ERPs pattern and character recognition performance using ERP-based BCI speller task. The results in Fig. 4 show positive results for our hypothesis. In Fig. 5 and Fig. 6, the analysis for individual subject suggests that the proposed condition is generally better than the normal condition. However, the difference in performance between the proposed and normal conditions in Session A was not outstanding. This may be due to decreased attention caused by eye and cognitive fatigue [7,8]. Nevertheless, the similar level of performance between the two conditions indicates that the proposed method is robust and stable in the experimental environment. In addition, as shown in B of Fig. 4, the proposed condition in both sessions rapidly improves performance on a small number of sequences (1–4).

Furthermore, we analyzed the ERP patterns to identify physiological changes. As shown in Fig. 7, subject5's ERP in the proposed condition was larger than

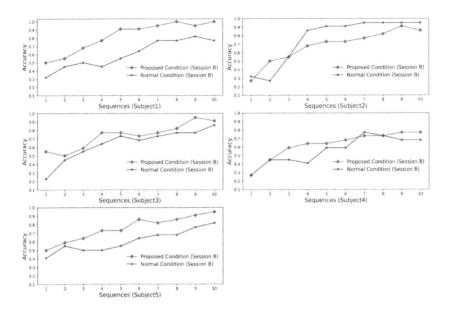

Fig. 6. Comparison of Proposed and Normal Condition by subject in Session B.

the normal condition in terms of amplitude and latency. Since the amplitude and latency of ERPs are used as features in the classifier, we believe this has a positive impact on classification performance.

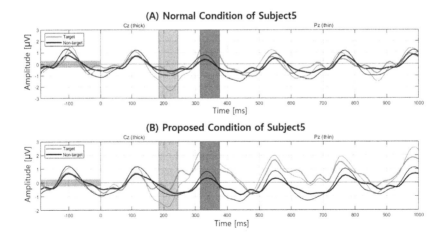

Fig. 7. ERPs Pattern in the Cz and Pz regions of Subject5 ((A): First Condition in Session A, (B): First Condition in Session B).

Interestingly, although session B was implemented after session A, the proposed condition in session B performed better than both the normal condition and the proposed condition in session A, and meaningfully better for the entire sequence from sequence 1 to 10. In addition, subject4 was vulnerable to eye fatigue due to dry eye syndrome after the first task in session A. Figure 8 shows a further analysis excluding subject4, which showed stable high character recognition performance in the proposed condition.

One of the biggest challenges in the BCI field is BCI illiteracy [22]. Although researchers in various fields are making efforts to solve it, it remains a difficult problem. While subject selection is a crucial aspect of BCI research, our proposed method shows promise in achieving higher character recognition performance independent of subject selection. Although our work requires additional subjects and statistical measurement, our results are very encouraging for future research on improving BCI-based character recognition performance.

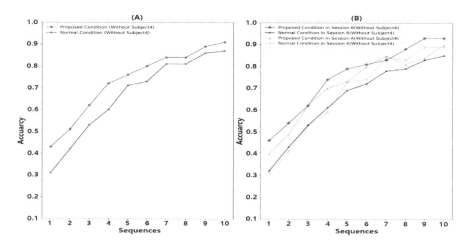

Fig. 8. Comparison of character recognition accuracy by condition((A): Mean comparison excluding subject4 between two conditions, (B): Mean comparison excluding subject4 between two conditions by sessions).

Acknowledgements. This work was supported by Institute of Information & Communications Technology Planning & Evaluation (IITP) grant funded by the Korea government (the Ministry of Science and ICT (MSIT)) (No. 2017-0-00451, Development of BCI based Brain and Cognitive Computing Technology for Recognizing User's Intentions using Deep Learning) and partly supported by the National Research Foundation of Korea (NRF) grant funded by the Korea government (MSIT) (No. 2022R1A5A8019303) and Basic Science Research Program through the National Research Foundation of Korea(NRF) funded by the Ministry of Education(RS-2023-00250246).

References

1. Won, D.-O., Hwang, H.-J., Kim, D.-M., Müller, K.-R., Lee, S.-W.: Motion-based rapid serial visual presentation for gaze-independent brain-computer interfaces. IEEE Trans. Neural Syst. Rehabil. Eng. **26**(2), 334–343 (2018)
2. Hwang, H.-J., Kwon, K., Im, C.-H.: Neurofeedback-based motor imagery training for brain-computer interface (BCI). J. Neurosci. Methods **179**(1), 150–156 (2009)
3. Wolpaw, J.R., Birbaumer, N., McFarland, D.J., Pfurtscheller, G., Vaughan, T.M.: Brain-computer interfaces for communication and control. Clin. Neurophysiol. **113**(6), 767–791 (2002)
4. Blankertz, B., Dornhege, G., Krauledat, M., Müller, K.-R., Curio, G.: The non-invasive Berlin Brain-Computer Interface: Fast acquisition of effective performance in untrained subjects. Neuroimage **37**(2), 539–550 (2007)
5. Müller-Putz, G.R., Scherer, R., Brauneis, C., Pfurtscheller, G.: Steady-state visual evoked potential (SSVEP)-based communication: impact of harmonic frequency components. J. Neural Eng. **2**(4), 123 (2005)
6. Farwell, L.A., Donchin, E.: Talking off the top of your head: toward a mental prosthesis utilizing event-related brain potentials. Electroencephalogr. Clin. Neurophysiol. **70**(6), 510–523 (1988)
7. Abiri, R., Borhani, S., Sellers, E.W., Jiang, Y., Zhao, X.: A comprehensive review of EEG-based brain-computer interface paradigms. J. Neural Eng. **16**(1), 011001 (2019)
8. Fazel-Rezai, R., Allison, B., Guger, C., Sellers, E., Kleih, S., Kübler, A.: P300 brain computer interface: current challenges and emerging trends. Front. Neuroeng. **5**, 1–11 (2012)
9. Townsend, G., et al.: A novel p300-based brain-computer interface stimulus presentation paradigm: moving beyond rows and columns. Clin. Neurophysiol. **121**(7), 1109–1120 (2010)
10. Yeom, S.-K., Fazli, S., Müller, K.-R., Lee, S.-W.: An efficient ERP-based brain-computer interface using random set presentation and face familiarity. PLoS ONE **9**(11), e111157 (2014)
11. Kaufmann, T., Schulz, S.M., Grünzinger, C., Kübler, A.: Flashing characters with famous faces improves ERP-based brain-computer interface performance. J. Neural Eng. **8**(5), 056016 (2011)
12. Lakey, C.E., Berry, D.R., Sellers, E.W.: Manipulating attention via mindfulness induction improves P300-based brain-computer interface performance. J. Neural Eng. **8**(2), 025019 (2011)
13. Wielgosz, J., Schuyler, B.S., Lutz, A., Davidson, R.J.: Long-term mindfulness training is associated with reliable differences in resting respiration rate. Sci. Rep. **6**(1), 27533 (2016)
14. Balban, M.Y., et al.: Brief structured respiration practices enhance mood and reduce physiological arousal. Cell Rep. Med. **4**(1), 100895 (2023)
15. Khalsa, S.S., Rudrauf, D., Hassanpour, M.S., Davidson, R.J., Tranel, D.: The practice of meditation is not associated with improved interoceptive awareness of the heartbeat. Psychophysiology **57**(2), e13479 (2019)
16. Li, P., et al.: The peptidergic control circuit for sighing. Nature **530**(7590), 293–297 (2016)
17. Li, P., Yackle, K.: Sighing. Curr. Biol. **27**(3), R88–R89 (2017)
18. Guyon, A.J., et al.: Respiratory variability, sighing, anxiety, and breathing symptoms in low- and high-anxious music students before and after performing. Front. Psychol. **11**, 303 (2020)

19. Severs, L., Vlemincx, E., Ramirez, J.-M.: The psychophysiology of the sigh: I: the sigh from the physiological perspective. Biol. Psychol. **170**, 108313 (2022)
20. Vlemincx, E., Severs, L., Ramirez, J.-M.: The psychophysiology of the sigh: II: the sigh from the psychological perspective. Biol. Psychol. **6**, 108386 (2022)
21. Blankertz, B., Lemm, S., Treder, M., Haufe, S., Müller, K.-R.: Single-trial analysis and classification of ERP components - a tutorial. Neuroimage **56**(2), 814–825 (2011)
22. Lee, M.-H., et al.: EEG dataset and OpenBMI toolbox for three BCI paradigms: an investigation into BCI illiteracy. GigaScience **8**(5), 01 (2019)

Exploring CycleGAN for Bias Reduction in Gender Classification: Generative Modelling for Diversifying Data Augmentation

Dimitri Hooftman[1(✉)], S. Sahand Mohammadi Ziabari[1] (iD), and Joop Snijder[2]

[1] Faculty of Science, Mathematics and Computer Science, University of Amsterdam, 1098 XH Amsterdam, The Netherlands
Dimitri.hooftman@student.uva.nl, s.s.mohammadiziabari@uva.nl
[2] Info Support, 3905 TG Veenendaal, The Netherlands
joop.snijder@infosupport.com

Abstract. Deep learning algorithms have become more prevalent in real world applications. With these developments, bias is observed in the predictions made by these algorithms. One of the reasons for this is the algorithm's capture of bias existing in the data set being used. This paper investigates the influence of using generative adversarial networks (GANs) as a gender-to-gender data pre-processing step on the bias and accuracy measured for a VGG-16 gender classification model. A cyclic generative adversarial network (CycleGAN) is trained on the Adience data set to perform the gender-to-gender data augmentation. This architecture allows for an unpaired domain mapping and results in two generators that double the training images generating a male for every female and vice versa. The VGG-16 gender classification model uses training data to produce an accuracy that indicates its performance. In addition, the model's fairness is calculated using demographic parity and equalized odds to indicate its bias. The evaluation of the results provided by the proposed methodology in this paper shows that the accuracy decreases when Cycle-GAN pre-processing is applied. In addition, the bias also decreases, especially when measured on an imbalanced data set. However, the decrease in bias needs to be more significant to change our evaluation of the model from unfair to fair, showing the proposed methodology to be effective but insufficient to remove bias from the data set.

Keywords: Generative modelling · Generative adversarial networks · CycleGAN · Data augmentation · Bias · Gender classification

1 Introduction

The predictive power of deep learning algorithms has led them to be widely used in real-world applications [6]. A prominent example of a widely used machine-learning technique is the supervised learning method, which can, for instance, provide a gender classifier of images by learning a mapping between an input image and a corresponding predicted class [12]. An unintended lack of diversity in the input is a problem observed in using images as data to train these algorithms [16]. For instance, this unintended lack of diversity could be introduced by a selection bias in the compilation process of a data set [21]. Using these data sets could introduce "over-fitting" in the downstream training process and lead to sub-optimal behavior in the real world where complexity and diversity are common. Examples of this sub-optimal behavior are observed for different types of training data, like images and word embeddings, induced by the learned bias existing in the training data [2, 23]. For instance, a model trained on a biased training data set shows that the activity of cooking is over 33 percent more likely to involve females than males [25].

What has been studied is using methods like over-sampling and prevailing data augmentation methods like rotations, flips, and rescales to increase diversity in data sets used for downstream tasks [23]. In addition, GANs have been used as a data augmentation method to improve generalizability in Computerized Tomography (CT) segmentation tasks [18]. However, the impact of using cyclic GANs to increase data set diversity to reduce bias on downstream tasks needs to be explored more. This thesis project aims to quantify this approach's impact on reducing bias in the downstream task of gender classification. In addition to reducing bias, maintaining or increasing the performance of a model trained in a downstream task is also of interest. Numerous studies have shown that including pre-processing steps using adversarial networks has increased performance when using deep neural networks downstream [17]. Using a GAN is described as one of the most promising modeling techniques for using data augmentation [24].

This paper hypothesizes that augmenting the training data into different domains will reduce bias and retain potential model performance on a downstream task. The reduced bias is hypothesized to be caused by the balance in training examples of different domains, for example, males and females. This hypothesis will be tested using a balanced and an unbalanced training data set to perform measurements. The retained performance is hypothesized to be caused by an increased amount of training data. A downside of the proposed data augmentation could be decreased performance on downstream tasks. To make this transparent, the predictive performance of downstream tasks is also evaluated. As data augmentation is a pre-processing technique used to increase downstream performance, the diversification of the data set should ideally not decrease downstream performance. The difference in performance will be tested using baseline measurements.

Obtaining this quantified knowledge could benefit both research areas mentioned before. For bias reduction, it could open up a new avenue of research into complex methods like configurable data augmentation using a GAN to generate a diverse data set based on a less-diverse data set. For the pre-processing field, this research will verify that using a GAN as a data augmentation method increases the performance on downstream tasks [19]. To make the mentioned knowledge objectives more concrete, the following research question is proposed: *How does pre-processing using GANs as a gender-to-gender data augmentation step influence the accuracy and bias of a VGG-16 Convolutional Neural Network performing a gender classification task?* To answer the research question, it is essential to gather measurements of the impact of the data augmentation method on the performance and bias of the downstream task of gender classification. These measurements are gathered using a well-known VGG-16 model architecture adjusted to perform binary classification. On top of this, it is important to create a data augmentation method that can perform the gender-to-gender generation.

This paper is organized as follows: Sect. 2 covers the literature review and related work. Section 3 explains the methodology that has been used. The results of this paper will be presented in Sect. 5, following the evaluation in Sect. 4. Finally, the paper will be concluded in Sect. 6.

2   Related Work

The research gap described in the previous section indicates a goal of mitigating bias without reducing downstream performance. To quantitatively assess the bias reduction, the research questions mention both VGG-16 gender classification models and the image to image translating CycleGAN model. These areas of research will be explored in this Section.

2.1   Gender Classification

Deep neural networks have demonstrated excellent performance in recognizing the gender of human faces [14]. Eidinger et al. used a standard linear SVM trained on the Local Binary Pattern (LBP) and Four-Patch LBP features (FPLBP) extracted from the Adience data set. They showed a 77 percent accuracy when training on the near-frontal faces [5]. They, however, added that their tests leave room for future work as a drop in performance is observed when using the Adience data set as a benchmark. As the Adience data set is made available, it will be considered for this paper. Hassner et al. report a 79.3 percent accuracy when using the same features but adjusting the Adience data set by a Frontalization process. This process detects facial features and rotates them to create a frontal face [9]. This accuracy is improved upon by Levi and Hassner using a deep-convolutional neural network for gender classification [15]. They used a network architecture comprising three convolutional layers and two fully-connected layers with a small number of neurons. They used all rotations of the original images in the Adience data set to show the performance of the network architecture instead of the improved performance by preprocessing. This approach has been shown to have an 86.8 percent accuracy. Dehgan et al. improved on this by using a larger amount of data to train on though it is unclear how this data set was aggregated [3]. In addition, it is unclear how the images' labels were provided. They stated that a team of human annotators was used through a semi-supervised procedure. For pre-processing the images, they used techniques that perform horizontal flips and random crop augmentation. They applied a specific but undisclosed deep network architecture for gender classification on the Adience benchmark and obtain an accuracy of 91 percent. Lapuschkin et al. considered the influence of model initialization with weights pre-trained on a real-world data set. Their results were reported using a VGG-16 model, pre-trained on the well-known ImageNet and IMDB-WIKI data sets. In addition, it was fine-tuned on the Adience data set using both face alignment techniques simultaneously [14]. They stated that three major factors contribute to performance improvements on the gender classification task. (1) Changes in architecture. (2) Prior knowledge via pre-training. (3) Optional data set preparation via alignment pre-processing. The VGG-16 model consists of 13 convolutional layers of small kernel size followed by two fully connected layers. Using the VGG-16 model, an accuracy of 92.6 percent is attained using a weight initialization based on ImageNet. Improved results on the gender classification task have also been published. These, however, use the improved ResNet model architecture to increase accuracy [13]. As the difference in performance and bias is to be measured based on pre-processing techniques, the model architecture is kept constant in both measurements, and this is why performance and bias using models that differ from VGG-16 on the Adience data set are not considered further in this paper.

2.2 CycleGAN

Image-to-image translation using a cycle-consistent adversarial network was introduced by Zhu et al. [26]. This method makes it possible to perform unpaired image translation without paired training data, as obtaining this data can be difficult and expensive [26]. They applied this method to various applications, including collection style transfer, object transfiguration, season transfer, and photo enhancement [26]. The cycle-consistent adversarial network is an architecture built from two GANs. These networks are optimized using a loss function that first includes an adversarial loss allowing it to learn the domain mapping. Second, it includes a cycle consistency loss that ensures the source and generated results are related. This additional loss optimizes the generators to produce a translation instead of a random output in the target domain. Almahairi et al. build on this idea by introducing an augmented CycleGAN, which can perform many-to-many mapping [1]. They captured variations in the generated domain by learning stochastic mapping by inferring information about the source which is not captured in the generated result. Qualitative results show the effectiveness of the many-to-many mapping approach in generating multiple females for a given male and vice versa, indicating the viability of successfully generating male-to-female and female-to-male images [1]. Using a CycleGAN architecture as a data augmentation method for pre-processing images has already been shown adequately for the task of CT segmentation [18]. They use the GANs to render a non-contrast version of training images based on the original contrast CT image. They observed that segmentation performance significantly improved when additional synthetic images were used for training. Hammami et al. use a CycleGAN as an unsupervised method that generates images of different modalities in a similar domain. These images are used to train a downstream model that can perform multi-organ detection, which has been shown to improve the intended task significantly [8].

2.3 Bias Reduction

Mehrabi et al. describe that, like people, algorithms are vulnerable to biases that render their decisions "unfair" [16]. Fairness is defined as the "absence of prejudice or favoritism towards an individual or group based on their inherent or acquired characteristics [16]. Research has been carried out into the reduction of bias in data sets. Wu et al. described that recent studies found substantial disparities in the accuracy rate of classifying gender of dark-skin females [23]. In their research, Wu et al. described the usage of preprocessing to balance the skin-type composition of a data set. Using the

ImageDataGenerator, familiar data augmentation techniques like horizontal flips and re-scaling can be performed. By using the *ImageDataGenerator*, they increased the percentage of dark-skin males from 1.3 percent to 15.21 percent and dark skin females from 2.5 percent to 16.03 percent. An example is given about facial recognition software in digital cameras, which over-predict Asians as blinking. These biased predictions are said to stem from the hidden or neglected biases in data or algorithms [16].

3 Methodology

The methodology provided in this section is followed to answer the research question stated in Sect. 1. Figure 1 shows a broad overview of the applied methodology. Both the CycleGAN pipeline and the gender classification pipeline use the Adience benchmark data set as their input. It is used to both train and evaluate the CycleGAN and VGG-16 CNN architecture.

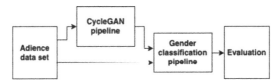

Fig. 1. Overview of methodology.

To further detail these parts of the methodology, this Section will first describe the data set being used. After this, the CycleGAN pipeline will be explained. Next, the gender classification pipeline will be shown to incorporate this data set and the CycleGAN pipeline results. Finally, the evaluation will be elaborated so it is clear what is measured.

3.1 Adience Data Set

The data set used in this classification pipeline is the Adience data set published in 2014 [5]. This data set contains photos of faces with binary gender labels and has been used in similar classification pipelines [5, 14]. The data set contains faces of different angles, with different light settings, and of different sharpness. A fundamental design principle of this data set is that it is as accurate as possible to challenging real-world conditions. As such, it presents all the variations in appearance, noise, pose, lighting, and more that can be expected of images taken without careful preparation or posing [5]. The images are collected using a face detector described by Viola and Jones [22] based on images collected from Flickr albums. All images were manually labeled for gender using both the image themselves and any available contextual information [5]. From the Adience data set, 19.370 images have been used. These images come from 2284 unique individuals. The coarse and landmark images provided by the data set have been used; this brings the total up to 38.740. Of these, 16.240 images have a male gender label. The other 22.500 have a female gender label. For further usage in downstream tasks, the data set is split into a training/validation and test set based on the task for which the model is trained.

The coarse and landmark images were used as Lapuschkin et al. stated that all models benefit the most from combining the coarse-aligned and the landmark-aligned data sets for training [14]. Finally, the data in the Adience data set is divided into five folds. These folds have been created to evenly distribute the individuals into subsets to prevent over-fitting on a fold, as multiple images of the same unique individual are in the Adience data set.

3.2 CycleGAN Pipeline

The GAN gender-to-gender data augmentation method uses the CycleGAN architecture described in [26] trained on the Adience data set. This architecture uses a GAN to learn two mappings. The first mapping is a generator function G that takes an image in domain X and generates an image that is indistinguishable from domain Y. This is done by optimizing the generator and the discriminator D_y, which learns to label images in domain Y as real or fake based on the generated images from generator G and images from domain Y. The image resulting from equation G: X -> Y is then used as input for the second mapping, which is a generator function F that takes the image in domain Y and generates an image that is indistinguishable from domain X. This is again through optimizing a generator F and discriminator D_x, essentially learning the inverse of G shown as equation F: Y -> X. The result of this CycleGAN architecture thus results in two generators and two discriminators. Figure 2 shows the architecture of CycleGAN.

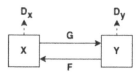

Fig. 2. CycleGAN architecture as shown by [26]. The cyclic nature between generator X and Y, which translates between domain X and Y.

For this specific application, generator G will be able to generate a female image based on the image of a male. Furthermore, generator F will be able to generate a male image based on the image of a female. The discriminator D_y will determine whether the female image generated by generator G is real or fake. Moreover, the discriminator.

D_x will determine whether the male image generated by generator F is real or fake. Both these generators and discriminators will be trained simultaneously as described in common GAN architectures.

Generator. The generator model used for this CycleGAN architecture is similar to a residual neural network. The downsampling before the Residual Blocks is done through a layer of 2D Convolution. An Instance Normalization layer and a ReLu Activation layer follow this. After the residual blocks, the upsampling is done through a layer of 2D Transposed Convolution. This convolutional layer is followed again by an Instance Normalization and ReLu Activation layer. The Residual Blocks use a familiar layer configuration starting with Reflection Padding, followed by a 2D Convolution, Instance Normalization, and a ReLu Activation layer. These layers are repeated twice, but instead of a second Activation layer, the input to the Residual Block is added to the result provided by the Residual Block. The complete overview is shown in Table 1 (a).

Discriminator. The discriminator model used for this Cycle-GAN architecture uses a layer configuration shown in Table 1 (b). The down-sampling is again done through a layer of 2D Convolution with a vertical and horizontal stride of 2. An Instance Normalization layer, Leaky ReLu Activation and 2D Convolution layer follow this. Both the architecture of the generator and the architecture of the discriminator could potentially be improved upon by investigating optimizations to the layers described in Table 1 (a, b). This optimization would, however, introduce the need to compare generated results past the current qualitative approach. The objective of this paper is not to find an improved CycleGAN architecture. The CycleGAN is used to generate domain translations, so the impact of using these in the training data set can be examined. For this reason, an improved CycleGAN architecture is not considered further.

Table 1. (a) Layers of generator in CycleGAN architecture. (b) Layers of discriminator in CycleGAN architecture.

(a)

Layer (type)	Output Shape	Parameter #
Input Layer	[224, 224, 3]	0
2D reflection padding	[230, 230, 3]	0
2D Convolution	[224, 224, 64]	9.408
Instance normalization	[224, 224, 64]	128
ReLu activation	[224, 224, 64]	0
ResNet Block (9x)	[56, 56, 256]	12.400.640
2D transpose convolution	[112, 112, 12]	294.912
Instance normalization	[112, 112, 12]	256
ReLu activation	[112, 112, 12]	0
2D transpose convolution	[224, 224, 64]	73.728
Instance normalization	[224, 224, 64]	128
ReLu activation	[224, 224, 64]	0
2D reflection padding	[230, 230, 64]	0
2D Convolution	[224, 224, 3]	9.411
Tanh Activation	[224, 224, 3]	0

(b)

Layer (type)	Output Shape	Parameter #
Input Layer	[224, 224, 3]	0
2D Convolution	[112, 112, 64]	3.316
Leaky ReLu activation	[112, 112, 64]	0
2D Convolution	[56, 56, 128]	131.072
Instance normalization	[56, 56, 128]	256
Leaky ReLu activation	[56, 56, 128]	0
2D Convolution	[28, 28, 256]	524.288
Instance normalization	[28, 28, 256]	512
Leaky ReLu activation	[28, 28, 256]	0
2D Convolution	[28, 28, 512]	2.097.162
Instance normalization	[28, 28, 512]	1024
Leaky ReLu activation	[28, 28, 512]	0
2D convolution	[28, 28, 1]	8.193

Loss function. The total loss of this CycleGAN architecture is shown in Fig. 2 comprises the loss function for both the aforementioned GANs using domain X and Y as input; these networks adopt the architecture described by [11]. Only optimizing this loss function still has the potential to create realistic but unrelated images. This behavior happens because the loss of the discriminators optimizes how well the generated images fits in the other domain, but this does not say anything about how related the image is to the original. This behavior requires a third component to the loss function penalizing a difference between the input x and the output of $F(G(x))$ and vice versa. Calculating the loss of the generator is done by calculating the mean square error between the continuous evaluation of the discriminator and a vector of the same shape containing an evaluation for which all of the generated images are classified as being real, essentially evaluating how real the discriminator perceived the generated image to be and converging towards a real prediction for every input. Calculating the discriminator's loss is also done by first calculating the mean square error of evaluating a real image and a vector of the same shape containing an evaluation for which all of the real images are classified as being real. Secondly, the mean square error is calculated for evaluating a fake image and a vector of the same shape containing an evaluation for which all of the fake images are classified as being fake. This loss function evaluates how well the discriminator can identify the fake image as fake and how well the discriminator can identify the real image as real, converging towards all correct predictions.

$$L(G, F, D_x, D_y) = L_{GAN}(G, D_y, X, Y) + L_{GAN}(F, D_x, Y, X) \\ + \lambda L_{CYC}(G, F) + \lambda L_{CYC}(F, G) + L_{IDEN}(G, F) \qquad (1)$$

Finally, the cycle loss is calculated using the mean square error between the real image and the corresponding generated image in the same domain, converging toward related images. Using this loss function, the two generators and two discriminators in the CycleGAN architecture are trained by performing a forward pass and propagating the calculated gradient back through the trainable variables. The optimization is done through an Adam optimizer, and the model is initialized using a random normal distribution, based on the implementation described by [26]. 90% of the images are used as training data for male and female domains. The remaining 10% will remain available for quantitative inspection. The model is trained on the training data for 150 epochs. After training this architecture using the three-part loss function shown in Eq. 1 for optimization, it can be used at inference time to generate a translated image for a corresponding source image.

Pre-processing. Before training the CycleGAN architecture, the input images go through a preprocessing stage. The default implementation of the CycleGAN architecture provided by Zhu et al. performs both a random crop and random flip, followed by normalizing the images. In the default implementation, the random crop uses a resize based on the nearest neighbor resize method. The resize method was changed to the bi-linear because the nearest neighbor resize method would overemphasize the black corners in the coarse images, resulting in an increasingly dark image generated by the CycleGAN generators.

Learning rate. After 100 epochs of training, the learning rate of both discriminators was adjusted from 2e-4 to 5e-4. This adjustment is made because the discriminators seemed to underperform in classifying images as fake in a specific domain. The tolerant discriminator led to generators that would not consistently provide a mapping from gender to gender but instead learned to map to the same gender as this obtains the highest cycle consistency. The trained generators, however, do not lead to the intended gender mapping, which is why the discriminators' learning rate was increased while optimizing the GANs.

3.3 Gender Classification Pipeline

To investigate the impact of the pre-processing using the CycleGAN model, a gender classification pipeline is created for four configurations. The first serves as a benchmark with pre-processing as it was done in [14]. The second compares the benchmark with the CycleGAN pre-processing in the training stage. The last two serve as a comparison when there is an imbalance in the training data; this essentially means the same two configurations are run for a different data set. The gender classification of facial images is done using a VGG-16 Convolutional Neural Network (CNN) architecture described by Simonyan and Zisserman [20]. The VGG-16 model is initialized using the ImageNet pre-trained weights. Because the model has to perform binary classification of males and females, the fully connected top layers of the VGG-16 model are removed, and the remaining weights are frozen so they will not change while training the model. To this base of the VGG-16 model, additional layers are added to provide the single result in the final layer. To train the VGG-16 model, a train and test split is done for the Adience data set. This split is done for all folds, so the unique individuals are distributed evenly. The training data is pre-processed by performing a random crop, a random flip, and normalization. A potential data augmenting step replaced the pre-processing stage depending on the pipeline's configuration. The generators from the CycleGAN are used to randomly provide a translated image, for which the label is changed accordingly. Multiple epochs are performed while training the model. This pre-processing approach provides the original and the translated version of the source image to the model for training. The training data is split into folds and used for training models validated on a holdout fold. Performing training iterations for all holdout folds will result in learning curves indicating at what epoch the training should stop to prevent over-fitting. The training of the VGG-16 CNN is done using the objective function of increased performance on the gender classification task using well-known optimization methods described in [7]. After determining the optimal number of epochs obtained through k-fold cross-validation, the final VGG-16 model is trained on all training folds and used to evaluate the test data.

4 Evaluation

The test data is classified after training the VGG-16 model for different pre-processing configurations using the training and validation data. These classifications are evaluated to compare the performance and the bias after using the different pre-processing techniques. To measure the performance difference, the model performance is measured by its accuracy calculated as the fraction of correct decisions. The predictions on the test set are also used to evaluate the bias of the models resulting from different pre-processing configurations. Evaluating the bias is done by calculating the demographic parity and the equal odds. The demographic parity measures the balance of the positive (and negative) predictions by evaluating the predictive equality and equality of opportunity between groups [4]. The equal odds measures the balance of classification errors like false positive and false negatives rates between groups [4]. To summarize the meth-odology provided in this Section, Fig. 3 shows a graphical overview of the data sets, models, decisions, and actions taken to provide the results used to answer the research questions provided in Sect. 1.

5 Results

This section tries to investigate the impact of using a CycleGAN architecture as a data-augmenting pre-processing method. First, the training of the CycleGAN and its resulting generators will be discussed. After this, the different configurations of the gender classification pipeline will be evaluated so the bias and performance can be reported.

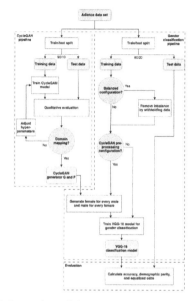

Fig. 3. Detailed overview of data sets, models, decisions, and actions.

5.1 CycleGAN

To demonstrate the CycleGAN's effectiveness, several domain translations are shown in Fig. 4. None of the loss functions of the networks seems to converge towards zero, indicating that the networks keep learning on each new epoch. Because of this equilibrium in generator and discriminator loss, the generators are expected to keep improving, generating fake domain mappings. In addition, both the male-to-female and female-to-male GANs seem to learn at a similar pace.

An observation made by empirically inspecting the results of the CycleGAN generators is that images of infants do not translate as noticeably as images of other age categories. This behavior is shown in Fig. 5b. This result is notable as infants are not underrepresented in the data, as shown in Fig. 5a; the number of labels below ten years old is almost the largest group in the Adience data set. The creators of the Adience data set report that ages between zero and two are the second largest group in the data set, behind ages between 25 and 32 [5].

Fig. 4. Source and corresponding generated image provided by the CycleGAN generators.

Under-representation in the data is thus not an obvious explanation. An alternative explanation of this result could be that images in both the male and female domains are similar for this age range. Thus, the generators do not learn as strong a mapping between the domains because the discriminators do not judge them fake as often.

5.2 Gender Classification

This Section will show the evaluation of the balanced and imbalanced data configuration. Only the prevailing pre-processing techniques described in Sect. 3 are used for this configuration. The training data was split into a train and validation set to determine around what epoch to stop the training process and use the model. The average validation accuracy is shown in Fig. 6, which increases meaningfully until around epoch 60. The average is calculated from the accuracy measured for each fold. These individual results are shown in the background of Fig. 6.

Common pre-processing. To evaluate the baseline for both the balanced and unbalanced data set configuration, the models are trained up until epoch 55 for the former configuration and epoch 63 for the latter configuration. As the first configuration is for a balanced data set, and the second configuration is for an unbalanced data set that is not highly unbalanced, the accuracy is measured as the fraction of correct decisions. These accuracy results are provided in Table 2 for both configurations. Both results are similar to the reference paper mentioned in Sect. 3. However, it is important to recognize that this benchmark was reported for an unbalanced data set. The demographic parity difference and equalized odds difference are also provided in Table 2. Both for the balanced data and unbalanced data set, values above 0.8 are observed, which is quite far from 0. This indicates that demographic parity and equalized odds have not been achieved.

Based on the information in Fig. 6, the decision is made to train the final VGG-16 gender classification models for around 60 epochs. This allows it to reach the expected accuracy without potentially over-fitting the test data. The results of this training process and the accuracy as measured on the test data are shown in Fig. 7. As the model seems

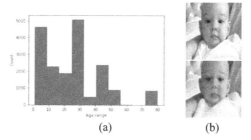

(a)   (b)

Fig. 5. (a) shows an overview of the age labels provided in the Adience data set. (b) shows an example of a female source image for an infant on the top row, below the corresponding generated male image. Upon quantitative inspection, it does not seem that the generator applies gender-altering mapping.

stagnated with little fluctuations around epoch 60 but does not show specific over-fitting just before or after 60 epochs, the model with the highest accuracy between epoch 55 and epoch 65 is chosen. Results for this are shown in Fig. 7. To evaluate fairness, demographic parity is used to measure the probability of a particular prediction depending on sensitive group membership, as reported in Table 2. The results are reported as the difference between the largest and the lowest group-level selection rate across all values of the sensitive feature. The demographic parity difference of 0 means all groups have the same selection rate. In addition, an equalized odds difference of 0 means that all groups have the same true positive, true negative, false positive, and false negative rate.

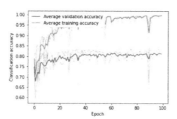

Fig. 6. Accuracy of VGG-16 model at gender classification on validation set. The background of this plot shows the validation and training accuracy per fold.

CycleGAN pre-processing. To compare the balanced and unbalanced data set configuration with CycleGAN pre-processing applied, the models are trained until epoch 60 for the balanced configuration and epoch 58 for the unbalanced configuration. The accuracy is again reported as the fraction of correct decisions in Table 2. Compared to the benchmark, the VGG-16 gender classification models do not seem to have improved performance when trained on data augmented with a gender-to-gender transformation. Instead, a decrease in performance is observed. The demographic parity and equalized odds differences are again calculated and provided in Table 2.

A decrease is observed for the demographic parity difference, especially for the unbalanced data set configuration. For the equalized odds difference, no decrease can

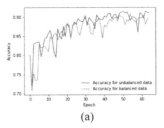
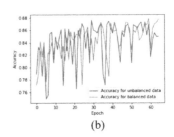

(a)   (b)

Fig. 7. Showcase of the intricacies of the VGG-16 gender classification model's training process on the test dataset. (a) shows the model's accuracy for the balanced and unbalanced training data set configuration. (b) shows the model's accuracy for which both the balanced and unbalanced training images were augmented using a CycleGAN. Here the accuracy in the initial phase of the training seems to be higher.

be observed for the balanced data set, but a decrease can be observed for the imbalanced data set. This indicates that the preprocessing using a gender-to-gender transformation does seem to positively impact the demographic parity and the equalized odds, mainly when the data is imbalanced. It is, however, important to recognize that the demographic parity difference and equalized odds difference remain far from zero. This indicates that demographic parity and equalized odds have again not been achieved.

Table 2. The result of different configurations of the gender classification pipeline with the amount of training data used, the pre-processing configuration, accuracy, demographic parity, and equalized odds.

Male #	Female #	CycleGAN	Accuracy	Parity	Odds
13.024	13.024	No	0.911	0.815	0.890
13.024	17.966	No	0.915	0.828	0.905
13.024	13.024	Yes	0.877	0.758	0.892
13.024	17.966	Yes	0.873	0.738	0.844

6   Conclusion

This paper examines the impact of using generative adversarial networks (GANs) as a gender-to-gender data pre-processing step on bias and accuracy in a VGG-16 gender classification model. A cyclic generative adversarial network (CycleGAN) is trained on the Adience dataset to augment the data by transforming images from one gender to another. The VGG-16 model's accuracy and fairness are evaluated using demographic parity and equalized odds. The results show that while the bias decreases, the decrease is not significant enough to eliminate bias entirely, indicating that the proposed methodology is effective but insufficient for bias removal.

References

1. Almahairi, A., Rajeswar, S., Sordoni, A., Bachman, P., Aaron C.: Augmented CycleGAN: learning many-to-many mappings from unpaired data. CoRR arXiv:1802.10151 (2018)
2. Bolukbasi, T., Chang, KW., Zou, JY., Saligrama, V., Kalai, AT.: Man is to computer programmer as woman is to homemaker? debiasing word embeddings. In: Lee D., Sugiyama M., Luxburg U., Guyon I., Garnett R. (eds.) Advances in Neural Information Processing Systems, vol. 29. Curran Associates, Inc (2016)
3. Dehghan, A., Ortiz, EG., Shu, G., Masood. SZ.: DAGER: deep age, gender and emotion recognition using convolutional neural network. CoRR arXiv:1702.04280 (2017)
4. Dignum V.: Responsible Artificial Intelligence: How to Develop and Use AI in a Responsible Way. Springer International Publishing, Cham (2020) https://doi.org/10.1007/978-3-030-303 71-6
5. Eidinger, E., Enbar, R., Hassner, T.: Age and gender estimation of unfiltered faces. IEEE Trans. Inf. Forensics Secur. **9**(12), 2170–2179 (2014)
6. Gong, Z. Zhong, P., Hu, W.: Diversity in Machine Learning. CoRR arXiv:1807.01477 (2018)
7. Goodfellow, I., Bengio, Y., Courville, A.: Deep Learning. MIT Press. http://www.deeplearn ingbook.org (2016)
8. Hammami, M., Friboulet, D., Kechichian, R.: CycleGAN based data augmentation for multi-organ detection in ct images via yolo. In: 2020 IEEE International Conference on Image Processing (ICIP). 390–393 (2020)
9. Hassner, T., Harel, S., Paz, E., Enbar, R.:. Effective face frontalization in unconstrained images. CoRR arXiv:/1411.7964 (2014)
10. He, K., Zhang, X., Ren, S., Sun, J.: Deep residual learning for image recognition. CoRR arXiv:/1512.03385 (2015)
11. Johnson, J., Alahi, A., Fei-Fei, L.: Perceptual losses for real-time style transfer and super-resolution. CoRR arXiv:1603.08155 (2016)
12. Jordan, M.I., Mitchell, T.M.: Machine learning: trends, perspectives, and prospects. Sci. **349**(6245), 255–260 (2015)
13. Kho, JB.: Multi-expert gender classification on age group by integrating deep neural networks. CoRR arXiv:1809.01990 (2018)
14. Lapuschkin, S., Binder, A., Muller, KR., Samek. W.: Understanding and comparing deep neural networks for age and gender classification. In: Proceedings of the IEEE International Conference on Computer Vision (ICCV) Workshops (2017)
15. Levi, G., Hassner, T.: Age and gender classification using convolutional neural networks. In: 2015 IEEE Conference on Computer Vision and Pattern Recognition Workshops (CVPRW) (2015), 34–42 (2015)
16. Mehrabi, N., Morstatter, F., Saxena, N., Lerman, K., Galstyan, A.: A survey on bias and fairness in machine learning arXiv:1908.09635v3 (2022)
17. Massimo Salvi, U., Acharya, R., Molinari, F., Meiburger, K.M.: The impact of pre- and post-image processing techniques on deep learning frameworks: A comprehensive review for digital pathology image analysis. Comput. Biol. Med. **128**(2021), 104129 (2021)
18. Sandfort, V., Yan, K., Pickhardt, P., Summers, R.: Data augmentation using generative adversarial networks (CycleGAN) to improve generalizability in CT segmentation tasks. Sci. Rep. 9 (2019)
19. Shorten, C., Khoshgoftaar, T.: A survey on Image Data Augmentation for Deep Learning. J. Big Data **6**, 60 (2019). https://doi.org/10.1186/s40537-019-0197-0
20. Simonyan, K., Zisserman, A.: Very deep convolutional networks for large-scale image recognition. In International Conference on Learning Representations (2015)
21. Torralba, A., Efros, AA.: Unbiased look at dataset bias, 1521–1528 (2011)

22. Viola, P., Jones, M.: Robust real-time face detection. In: Proceedings Eighth IEEE International Conference on Computer Vision (2001)
23. Wu, W., Protopapas, P., Yang, Z. Michalatos, P.: Gender classification and bias mitigation in facial images. CoRR arXiv2007.06141 (2020)
24. Yang, S., Xiao, W., Zhang, M., Guo, S., Zhao, J., Shen, F.: Image data augmentation for deep learning: a survey, arXiv:2204.08610 (2022)
25. Zhao, J., Wang, T., Yatskar, M., Ordonez, V., Chang KW.: Men also like shopping: reducing gender bias amplification using corpus-level constraints. In: Proceedings of the 2017 Conference on Empirical Methods in Natural Language Processing. Association for Computational Linguistics, Copenhagen, Denmark, 2979–2989 (2017)
26. Zhu, JY., Park, T., Isola, P., Efros, AA.: Unpaired image-to-image translation using cycle-consistent adversarial networks. CoRR arXiv:1703.10593 (2017)

Knee Osteoarthritis Diagnostic System Based on 3D Multi-task Convolutional Neural Network: Data from the Osteoarthritis Initiative

Khin Wee Lai[1]([✉]) [iD], Pauline Shan Qing Yeoh[1] [iD], Siew Li Goh[2] [iD],
Khairunnisa Hasikin[1] [iD], and Xiang Wu[3] [iD]

[1] Department of Biomedical Engineering, University Malaya, Kuala Lumpur, Malaysia
{lai.khinwee,khairunnisa}@um.edu.my
[2] Sports Medicine Department, University Malaya, Kuala Lumpur, Malaysia
gsiewli@um.edu.my
[3] School of Medical Information and Engineering, Xuzhou Medical University, Xuzhou, China
wuxiang@xzhmu.edu.cn

Abstract. Since knee osteoarthritis is a 3D complexity, one of the most effective tools to diagnose this disease is through Magnetic Resonance Imaging (MRI). Due to the 3D nature of the MRI scans, different 3D deep learning models related to osteoarthritis diagnosis have been proposed, but they are mostly single-task models. This study aims to offer a computationally efficient approach that involves 3D medical data by leveraging multi-task learning, transfer learning and depthwise separable convolutions. We proposed a 3D multi-task model for knee osteoarthritis diagnosis that takes 3D MRI as input and provides segmentation masks and OA severity as the outputs. We validated our proposed model with transfer learning and compared the results with single-task models. The model's performance was measured by different metrics, such as balanced accuracy, Dice Similarity Score and F1 score based on the tasks. The balanced accuracy of the model achieved 0.745 and 0.920 for 3-class classification and 5-class segmentation tasks, respectively. The proposed multi-task model showed better performance in classification tasks compared to classification single-task models. The proposed model offers as a computationally efficient approach to encourage the use of 3D medical data in healthcare applications.

Keywords: Convolutional Neural Networks · Deep Learning · Knee Osteoarthritis · Multi-Task Learning · Transfer Learning

1 Introduction

Knee Osteoarthritis (OA) is a prevalent degenerative joint condition among the elderly that negatively impacts one's mobility and quality of life [1]. In the current clinical practice, OA diagnosis primarily relies on radiographic confirmation, however, it is not capable to provide clear visualization of the early structural changes of OA, which makes Magnetic Resonance Imaging (MRI) the better imaging tool for OA diagnosis [2].

H. Lu et al. (Eds.): ACPR 2023, LNCS 14408, pp. 41–51, 2023.
https://doi.org/10.1007/978-3-031-47665-5_4

Current clinical practice relies on manual inspection of the medical images which are tedious and prone to interrater variability, especially when dealing with large number of patients. Deep learning, particularly convolutional neural networks (CNN) emerged as a powerful artificial intelligence technique to establish fully automated computer aided diagnosis that can automatically process complex medical data, overcoming the need for manual procedures [3].

In the field of diagnosis of OA disease, most deep learning models are designed to perform a single-task separately, mainly focused on two categories of tasks: segmentation and classification [4]. Most of the existing studies utilize 2D CNNs in either of the tasks [5, 6]. However, acknowledging that OA in the knee affects the whole knee joint [7], one major limitation of 2D CNNs is that it cannot take the whole 3D MRI volume into account. Recent studies have proposed implementation of 3D CNN [8] because 3D CNNs can fully utilize the spatial information of volumetric medical image data to extract more distinguishable representations, either on segmentation [9, 10] or classification [11–13] tasks on MRI images respectively. Multi-task learning has been successfully applied in deep learning applications to optimize multiple tasks simultaneously within a single neural network. The superior performance of multi-task models over single-task models is well studied in recent studies [14, 15]. To effectively utilize the volumetric information of MRI that is in 3D by nature, we propose a 3D multi-task model for knee OA diagnosis that combines segmentation and classification tasks simultaneously, which was not previously explored in the existing literature.

Theoretically, 3D CNNs are computationally expensive in terms of data size, model parameter and memory required as well as the computational resources required. In this work, we aim to offer a computationally efficient approach. We reduce the size and complexity of the model by implementing depthwise separable convolutions in the proposed model. Besides, we also incorporate transfer learning to enhance model performance. Moreover, by implementing multi-task model, the parameters are shared in some lower layers, allowing the model to be more parameter-efficient. Not only it can reduce the amount of computation as compared to training different tasks independently, multi-task training and transfer learning of the model can optimize the use of limited available medical dataset. All these aforementioned implementations might lead to improved efficiency of the 3D model with reduced overall computational cost required to comprehensively analyze and process 3D medical data using 3D CNN.

Our motivation is to develop a computationally efficient 3D model for knee OA diagnosis by incorporating three different techniques which are depthwise separable convolutions, transfer learning and multi-task learning. The contribution of this work are as follows:

- Development of a single stage end-to-end multi-task deep learning model for segmenting and classifying OA stages from knee MRI volumes. To the best of our knowledge, this is one of the first works that utilizes 3D multi-task neural network to perform two different tasks simultaneously in healthcare application, specifically in knee OA detection.
- Validation of the proposed multi-task model against the single-task segmentation and classification models.

– Investigation of performance on the integration of transfer learning in the deep learning models, specifically in the proposed multi-task model.

2 Methodology

2.1 Data Acquisition and Pre-processing

400 3D sagittal Double Echo Steady State (DESS) knee MRI scans were obtained from Osteoarthritis Initiative (OAI) public dataset where the respective ground truth segmentation masks were obtained from Zuse Institute Berlin (ZIB) [10]. All volumes were resized to $160 \times 160 \times 160$ due to graphical processing unit restrictions. The segmentation mask provided consists of background (BG), femoral bone (FB), femoral cartilage (FC), tibial bone (TB) and tibial cartilage (TC) and are assigned with class labels ranging from 0 to 4. A common OA grading scale, Kellgren-Lawrence (KL) grading were used to classify the MRI volumes into No OA, Early OA, and Severe OA classes. KL grade 0 was considered as "No OA", KL grades of 1 and 2 were categorised into "Early OA" and KL grades 3 and 4 were categorised as "Severe OA". The data were split into train, validation, and test sets, with a ratio of 7:2:1. The description of the dataset used in this study is presented in Table 1.

Table 1. Description of dataset used.

KL-Grade Score	Number of MRI volumes	3-Class Classification	Number of MRI volumes
0	87	No OA	87
1	48	Early OA	143
2	95		
3	108	OA	170
4	62		

2.2 Multi-task Neural Network Architecture

Figure 1 displays the proposed multi-task model architecture. The proposed multi-task model integrates classification and segmentation tasks in a single stage end-to-end network that adopts the encoder-decoder architecture based on U-Net. To integrate transfer learning in our model, we take 3D ResNet-18 [16] as the encoder of the model. The choice of using the 3D ResNet-18's feature extractor as the encoder is motivated by its superior ability in knee osteoarthritis diagnosis based on prior work [13]. The multi-task model has a shared encoder for two different tasks, where the classification branch is extended from the bottleneck with the classifier. To overcome the expensive computational cost of 3D CNN, where it involves large input data that requires a lot of computational power and memory, the segmentation branch is implemented using a decoder that is make up of 3D depthwise separable convolutional blocks [17]. Each depthwise separable convolutional block consist of double of two sets of convolutions, where the first set is $3 \times 3 \times 3$ depthwise convolution, followed by a $1 \times 1 \times 1$ pointwise convolution. After each pointwise convolution, there is a batch normalization layer and ReLU activation function layer. The classifier block includes an average pooling layer, three fully connected layer (with layer outputs of 128, 32 and 3 respectively), and a SoftMax layer. A ReLU activation function layer and dropout layer with rate of 0.5 is added after each of the first two fully connected layers.

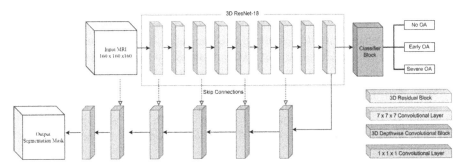

Fig. 1. Architecture of Proposed Multi-task Model.

2.3   Transfer Learning

Transfer learning has emerged as a promising tool in medical imaging applications by allowing the transfer of knowledge learned from larger non-medical dataset to the target medical applications. To investigate the potential of transfer learning in interpreting MRI volumes by integrating this technique into our proposed multi-task model, we implemented the proposed multi-task model in two different approaches: (i) training the network from scratch and (ii) using ImageNet [18] pretrained weights from the Torchvision package in PyTorch library [19] as initial weights. Since only the feature extractor part of the 3D ResNet-18 is utilized in this work, only the feature extractor layers are retained, and the final classification layers are discarded. Hence, only pre-trained weights of the retained layers are transferred and fine-tuned. Given that the available pretrained weights are in 2D and the models implemented in this work requires 3D weights, the 2D weights are replicated along the third dimension to match the dimensions required by the 3D model.

2.4   Training Specification

All models in this work are implemented using PyTorch on workstation equipped with Xeon W-2225 Central Processing Unit Intel and Graphics Processing Unit (GPU) NVIDIA RTX A6000 with Random Access Memory (RAM) of 32.0 GB. The training of the models utilized the ADAM optimizer with a learning rate of 1e-4 and batch size of 2. The models were allowed to train to a maximum epoch of 100 with an early stop where the training will stop when the model does not improve for 10 consecutive epochs. For the loss function, we computed and combined different loss functions for different tasks to a multi-task loss function such that it can optimize two tasks simultaneously. The Cross Entropy Loss and Dice Loss are implemented in this study for classification and segmentation tasks, respectively. The segmentation loss and the classification loss employed can be expressed as the equations below.

$$Segmentation\,Loss(p, q) = 1 - \frac{2\sum_{i=1}^{N} p_i q_i}{\sum_{i=1}^{N} p_i^2 + \sum_{i=1}^{N} q_i^2} \tag{1}$$

$$Classification\,Loss(p, q) = -\sum_{i=1}^{N} p_i \log(q_i) \tag{2}$$

where p is the ground truth value, q is the predicted probability for ith class and N is total number of classes. The multi-task loss function used in this work is formulated as below:

$$Multitask\,loss = \lambda(Segmentation\,Loss) + (1 - \lambda)Classification\,Loss \tag{3}$$

where λ is the weight of the segmentation task in the loss function. The λ provides a trade-off between the segmentation and classification tasks. Multiple experiments were conducted to find the optimal λ for the model, with search range from 0.1 to 0.9 with a step of 0.2, and λ was finally set to 0.7.

2.5 Evaluation

In this work, we evaluated the performance of the model through different metrics for the two different tasks. For segmentation performance, it is evaluated through the following metrics: Balanced Accuracy (BA) (defined as the average of recall), Dice Similarity Coefficient (DSC) and Jaccard Similarity Coefficient (JSC). For the classification task, the metrics used are: Balanced Accuracy, F1- score and Area Under the Curve of Receiver Operating Characteristic (AUC). To evaluate the multi-class segmentation and classification performance quantitatively, the average of the metric scores were computed to indicate the overall performance of the models for respective tasks.

3 Results and Discussion

Table 2 summarizes the performance of the proposed multi-task model and single-task models, with and without transfer learning. The segmentation baseline model is obtained by extracting the whole encoder-decoder network without the classifier whereas the classification baseline model is obtained by extracting the encoder path and the classifier only.

The proposed multi-task model reported superior performance than classification baseline model in terms of classification performance, while simultaneously perform segmentation task. When all the models are trained from scratch, the findings revealed that multi-task model (BA: 0.716) achieved 117% or 2 × improvement in terms of balanced accuracy compared to the classification baseline model (BA: 0.330). The proposed

Table 2. Comparison of Segmentation and Classification Performance between Proposed Multi-task Model and Single-task Models.

Model	Classification			Segmentation		
	Balanced Accuracy	F1 score	AUC	Balanced Accuracy	DSC	JSC
Segmentation Model (S)				0.939	0.931	0.879
Segmentation Model (TL)				0.939	0.930	0.877
Proposed Model (S)	0.716	0.710	0.825	0.928	0.924	0.866
Proposed Model (TL)	0.745	0.753	0.926	0.920	0.923	0.865
Classification Model (S)	0.330	0.283	0.530			
Classification Model (TL)	0.727	0.723	0.767			

Note: S = Trained from Scratch, TL = Trained with Transfer Learning

multi-task model displayed a small decrease of 1% and 2% in segmentation performance compared to segmentation baseline models when the models are trained from scratch and with transfer learning, respectively. According to the results obtained, the segmentation performance of all the models is generally excellent, achieving at least 0.920 for DSC and balanced accuracy. In summary, it is observed that multi-task models demonstrated improved classification performance but had minimal impact on the segmentation performance. Table 3 presents the classification performance by class respectively for the proposed model trained from scratch and transfer learning.

Table 3. Classification Performance per Class of the Proposed Multi-task Model

	Trained from Scratch			Trained with Transfer Learning		
	No OA	Early OA	Severe OA	No OA	Early OA	Severe OA
Recall	0.800	0.563	0.786	0.700	0.750	0.786
F1 score	0.800	0.621	0.710	0.737	0.706	0.815
AUC	0.830	0.740	0.904	0.930	0.891	0.956

The effectiveness of transfer learning is demonstrated in the proposed multi-task model, where it achieved classification balanced accuracy of 0.745, surpassed proposed model that trained from scratch (BA: 0.716) with improvement in classification performance by 4%, and 2% above the classification baseline model with transfer learning (BA: 0.727). With transfer learning, the classification performance of the proposed model increases by 4% with a slight drop of 1% of segmentation performance in terms of balanced accuracy. According to Table 3, transfer learning improves the ability to identify Early OA knees by 33% (Recall: 0.750), with a higher discriminatory ability of 0.891 AUC score. The ability to detect Severe OA knees increases as well with transfer learning, with enhancement of the F1score and AUC metrics by 15% and 6% respectively. However, there are no obvious differences in segmentation performance between with and without transfer learning, as presented in Table 2.

Besides, transfer learning's ability to enhance classification performance is also demonstrated with a quicker convergence time. When the proposed model is trained from scratch, it takes 24 h 40 min to complete 78 training epochs, however, with transfer learning, the model converges quicker within 42 training epochs, taking 13 h 15 min. Generally, training deep learning models requires plenty of training data, which is challenging and computationally expensive, especially in the medical applications. In this work, we leveraged the potential of transfer learning and multi-task learning to address this issue. The multi-task model allows more efficient use of available data which is helpful in our case because the volume of knee MRI data in our dataset is limited. By sharing the same feature extractor or encoder, the multi-task model is able to extract more significant features related to OA severity to improve classification performance while training with limited datasets.

We further compare our proposed model with several commonly used models in both segmentation and classification tasks. The results are presented in Table 4. When the proposed model is trained from scratch, it outperformed the other 3 classification models, 3D DenseNet-121 [20], 3D ResNeXt-50 [21], and 3D VGG-16 [22], in terms of balanced accuracy and F1-score. This demonstrates the effectiveness of multi-task learning technique. The superiority of transfer learning is demonstrated in Proposed Model (TL), which achieved the best classification scores compared to the other models. This indicates that our proposed model leverages the information from segmentation tasks to improve the classification performance. However, in terms of segmentation performance, the proposed model did not surpass the performance of 3D U-Net [23] and 3D V-Net [24].

Based on our results, integrating transfer learning, and early stopping in our proposed multi-task model achieve better classification results while preventing overfitting. Our proposed multi-task model with transfer learning achieved AUC of 0.926 and DSC of 0.923 for classification and segmentation tasks, respectively. Using the computational setup as described in the 'Methodology' section, the proposed multi-task model has about 34.986 million parameters and requires 139.946 MB memory, taking 3.13 s for inference to provide segmentation mask and classification output from a knee MRI volume. Furthermore, a multi-task model can complete two tasks in half of the total time of two single-task models. Besides, to address the complexity issue of 3D CNN, depthwise separable convolutions is utilized to lower the computational cost by minimizing the amount of parameters and computations while able to fully utilize the 3D volume information from the volumetric medical images. These findings demonstrate a promising research direction for developing efficient 3D deep learning models in medical imaging applications to handle complex 3D data, particularly in real world conditions where computation resources may be limited. With this 3D multitask model, new opportunities

Table 4. Performance Comparison of Segmentation and Classification Performance with existing models

Model	Classification			Segmentation		
	Balanced Accuracy	F1 score	AUC	Balanced Accuracy	DSC	JSC
Proposed Model (S)	0.716	0.710	0.825	0.928	0.924	0.866
Proposed Model (TL)	0.745	0.753	0.926	0.920	0.923	0.865
3D DenseNet-121	0.705	0.707	0.866			
3D ResNeXt-50	0.591	0.577	0.735			
3D VGG-16	0.310	0.300	0.596			
3D U-Net				0.934	0.936	0.887
3D V-Net				0.949	0.921	0.863

Note: S = Trained from Scratch, TL = Trained with Transfer Learning

on advancing the diagnosis of life-threatening disease can be further explored, such as on automated heart condition detection while simultaneously providing heart segmentations from tagged MRI scans that is crucial for comprehensive assessment of the heart [25].

In this paper, a single stage end-to-end 3D multi-task approach that carries out two tasks simultaneously is proposed. The proposed multi-task model is an ongoing effort to develop an early knee osteoarthritis system and there is a need for further research to optimize the model's performance in detecting early incidence of the disease. It is important to note that early detection of OA is crucial for effective clinical interventions to halt the disease progression and mitigate disability in later stages [26]. Moreover, previous studies either utilizes segmentation output to perform or refine classification prediction or to improve a target segmentation task on specific region of interest by utilizing the information extracted from the segmentation output. To further enhance our model's performance on early OA detection, we can extend the model by leveraging the segmentation mask as an output and input simultaneously. Since the encoder of the proposed model adopts 3D ResNet-18, the encoder can be easily exchanged to other CNN models to improve the model or to be adapted to other applications. Future work should also investigate the model's generalization ability and clinical relevance by testing on different independent clinical datasets. Lastly, future works can involve comparisons considering aspects of computational efficiency such as model parameters and floating-point operations per second, enabling a comprehensive assessment of the practical applicability of different models by comparing their computational efficiency.

4   Conclusion

In this study, we proposed a 3D fully convolutional neural network that effectively integrates multi-task learning and transfer learning techniques for knee OA diagnosis. Although the model's segmentation performance does not show any significant improvement, we leveraged the benefits of both techniques in the classification tasks, achieving overall AUC of 0.926 and boosted the AUC score of Early OA detection to 0.891. While the results are promising, future works can explore on further enhancing the model's performance across all aspects as well as improving its generalizability. These findings not only bring new research directions on efficient computations of 3D CNN for healthcare applications involving 3D medical data, but it also potentiating the diagnosis of OA in the early stage using 3D MRI. Overall, the proposed multi-task model offers as a computationally efficient approach applicable to various domains where limited training data and computational resources are available.

Acknowledgements. The research was funded by The Unveiling & Leading Project of Xuzhou Medical University under Grant No. JBGS202204 and The National Key Research and Development Program of China under Grant No. 2020YFC2006600. Data used in the preparation of this paper was obtained from Osteoarthritis Initiative (OAI), whereas the annotated dataset was obtained from Zuse Institute Berlin (OAI-ZIB).

References

1. Faisal, A., Ng, S.-C., Goh, S.-L., Lai, K.W.: Knee cartilage segmentation and thickness computation from ultrasound images. Med. Biol. Eng. Comput. **56**, 657–669 (2018). https://doi.org/10.1007/s11517-017-1710-2
2. Yong, C.W., Lai, K.W., Murphy, B.P., Hum, Y.C.: Comparative study of encoder-decoder-based convolutional neural networks in cartilage delineation from knee magnetic resonance images. Curr. Med. Imaging **17**, 981–987 (2021). https://doi.org/10.2174/1573405616666620 1214122409
3. Anis, S., et al.: An overview of deep learning approaches in chest radiograph. IEEE Access **8**, 182347–182354 (2020). https://doi.org/10.1109/ACCESS.2020.3028390
4. Yeoh, P.S.Q., et al.: Emergence of deep learning in knee osteoarthritis diagnosis. Comput. Intell. Neurosci. **2021** (2021). https://doi.org/10.1155/2021/4931437
5. Prasoon, A., Petersen, K., Igel, C., Lauze, F., Dam, E., Nielsen, M.: Deep feature learning for knee cartilage segmentation using a triplanar convolutional neural network. In: Sakuma, I., Barillot, C., Navab, N. (eds.) Medical Image Computing and Computer-Assisted Intervention–MICCAI 2013, LNCS, vol. 8150, pp. 246–253. Springer, Heidelberg (2013). https://doi.org/10.1007/978-3-642-40763-5_31
6. Pedoia, V., Lee, J., Norman, B., Link, T.M., Majumdar, S.: Diagnosing osteoarthritis from T2 maps using deep learning: an analysis of the entire osteoarthritis Initiative baseline cohort. Osteoarthritis Cartilage **27**, 1002–1010 (2019). https://doi.org/10.1016/j.joca.2019.02.800
7. Teoh, Y.X., et al.: Discovering knee osteoarthritis imaging features for diagnosis and prognosis: review of manual imaging grading and machine learning approaches. J. Healthc. Eng. **2022** (2022). https://doi.org/10.1155/2022/4138666
8. Zhou, Z., Zhao, G., Kijowski, R., Liu, F.: Deep convolutional neural network for segmentation of knee joint anatomy. Magn. Reson. Med. **80**, 2759–2770 (2018). https://doi.org/10.1002/mrm.27229

9. Tack, A., Zachow, S.: Accurate automated volumetry of cartilage of the knee using convolutional neural networks: data from the osteoarthritis initiative. In: 2019 IEEE 16th International Symposium on Biomedical Imaging (ISBI 2019), pp. 40–43. IEEE, New York (2019). https://doi.org/10.1109/ISBI.2019.8759201

10. Ambellan, F., Tack, A., Ehlke, M., Zachow, S.: Automated segmentation of knee bone and cartilage combining statistical shape knowledge and convolutional neural networks: data from the Osteoarthritis Initiative. Med. Image Anal. **52**, 109–118 (2019). https://doi.org/10.1016/j.media.2018.11.009

11. Tolpadi, A.A., Lee, J.J., Pedoia, V., Majumdar, S.: Deep learning predicts total knee replacement from magnetic resonance images. Sci. Rep. **10**, 1–12 (2020). https://doi.org/10.1038/s41598-020-63395-9

12. Martinez, A.M., et al.: Discovering knee osteoarthritis bone shape features using deep learning. Osteoarthritis Cartilage **27**, S386–S387 (2019). https://doi.org/10.1016/j.joca.2019.02.386

13. Yeoh, P.S.Q., Lai, K.W., Goh, S.L., Hasikin, K., Wu, X., Li, P.: Transfer learning assisted 3D deep learning models for knee osteoarthritis detection: data from the osteoarthritis initiative. Front. Bioeng. Biotechnol. **11** (2023). https://doi.org/10.3389/fbioe.2023.1164655

14. Amyar, A., Modzelewski, R., Li, H., Ruan, S.: Multi-task deep learning based CT imaging analysis for COVID-19 pneumonia: classification and segmentation. Comput. Biol. Med. **126**, 104037 (2020). https://doi.org/10.1016/j.compbiomed.2020.104037

15. Liu, M., et al.: A multi-model deep convolutional neural network for automatic hippocampus segmentation and classification in Alzheimer's disease. Neuroimage **208**, 116459 (2020). https://doi.org/10.1016/j.neuroimage.2019.116459

16. He, K., Zhang, X., Ren, S., Sun, J.: Deep residual learning for image recognition. In: 2016 IEEE Conference on Computer Vision and Pattern Recognition (CVPR), pp. 770–778. IEEE, New York (2016). https://doi.org/10.1109/CVPR.2016.90

17. Sifre, L.: Rigid-motion scattering for image classification. Ecole Polytechniq. (2014)

18. Deng, J., Dong, W., Socher, R., Li, L.-J., Li, K., Fei-Fei, L.: Imagenet: a large-scale hierarchical image database. In: 2009 IEEE Conference on Computer Vision and Pattern Recognition, pp. 248–255. IEEE, New York (2009). https://doi.org/10.1109/CVPR.2009.5206848

19. Paszke, A., et al.: Pytorch: an imperative style, high-performance deep learning library. In: Advances in Neural Information Processing Systems 32 (NIPS 2019), pp. 8024–8035. NIPS, California (2019)

20. Huang, G., Liu, Z., Van Der Maaten, L., Weinberger, K.Q.: Densely connected convolutional networks. In: 30th IEEE Conference on Computer Vision and Pattern Recognition, pp. 2261–2269. IEEE, New York (2017). https://doi.org/10.1109/CVPR.2017.243

21. Xie, S., Girshick, R., Dollár, P., Tu, Z., He, K.: Aggregated residual transformations for deep neural networks. In: 30th IEEE Conference on Computer Vision and Pattern Recognition (CVPR), pp. 5987–5995. IEEE, New York (2017). https://doi.org/10.1109/CVPR.2017.634

22. Simonyan, K., Zisserman, A.: Very deep convolutional networks for large-scale image recognition. arXiv preprint arXiv:1409.1556 (2014). https://doi.org/10.48550/arXiv.1409.1556

23. Çiçek, Ö., Abdulkadir, A., Lienkamp, S.S., Brox, T., Ronneberger, O.: 3D U-Net: learning dense volumetric segmentation from sparse annotation. In: Ourselin, S., Joskowicz, L., Sabuncu, M., Unal, G., Wells, W. (eds.) Medical Image Computing and Computer-Assisted Intervention–MICCAI 2016, LNCS, vol. 9901, pp. 424–432. Springer, Cham (2016). https://doi.org/10.1007/978-3-319-46723-8_49

24. Milletari, F., Navab, N., Ahmadi, S.-A.: V-net: fully convolutional neural networks for volumetric medical image segmentation. In: 2016 Fourth IEEE International Conference on 3D Vision (3DV), pp. 565–571. IEEE, New York (2016). https://doi.org/10.1109/3DV.2016.79

25. Jahanzad, Z., et al.: Regional assessment of LV wall in infarcted heart using tagged MRI and cardiac modelling. Phys. Med. Biol. **60**, 4015 (2015). https://doi.org/10.1088/0031-9155/60/10/4015

26. Yong, C.W., et al.: Knee osteoarthritis severity classification with ordinal regression module. Multim. Tools Appl. **81**, 41497–41509 (2021). https://doi.org/10.1007/s11042-021-10557-0

Multi-step Air Quality Index Forecasting Based on Parallel Multi-input Transformers

Jie Xie[1,2(✉)], Jun Li[1], Mingying Zhu[3,4,5], and Qiong Wang[1]

[1] School of Computer and Electronic Information and School of Artificial Intelligence, Nanjing Normal University, Nanjing 210046, People's Republic of China
`xiej8734@gmail.com`
[2] Key Laboratory of Modern Acoustics, MOE, Nanjing University, Nanjing, China
[3] School of Economics, Nanjing University, 22 Hankou Road, Nanjing 210093, Jiangsu, China
[4] Johns Hopkins University, Hopkins, USA
[5] Nanjing Center for Chinese and American Studies, Nanjing University, 162 Shanghai Road, Nanjing, Jiangsu, China

Abstract. Air quality index (AQI) forecasting is a hot research topic that has been widely explored by the whole society. To better understand environmental quality, numerous methods have been proposed for investigating air pollutant data. Previous studies have used deep learning-based methods for AQI forecasting, but few studies investigate parallel multi-input deep models for multi-step hourly AQI forecasting. In this study, a novel parallel multi-input transformer architecture is proposed for multi-step hourly AQI forecasting. To model the air quality data, the transformer is selected and compared with four bidirectional-long-short term memory-based models. Moreover, parallel variable embedding is used to boost forecasting performance. Experimental results using air quality data collected in Shanghai show that our proposed method achieves superior performance against various competing methods.

Keywords: AQI forecasting · Multi-input Transformer · Multi-step forecasting

1 Introduction

With the continuous development of the industrial economy and urbanization, air pollution has become a serious problem that harms residents' physical and mental health [22]. Therefore, it is becoming evermore important to prevent and manage air pollution problems. As a standard of measuring air pollution levels, Air Quality Index (AQI) can be derived from the concentrations of $PM_{2.5}$, PM_{10}, O_3, NO_2, SO_2, CO [12]. To help combat the air pollution problem, accurate AQI prediction is regarded as an achievable way which offers a reliable reference for citizen's outdoor activities and government policies [9].

H. Lu et al. (Eds.): ACPR 2023, LNCS 14408, pp. 52–63, 2023.
https://doi.org/10.1007/978-3-031-47665-5_5

For current AQI forecasting methods, they can be grouped into three categories: classical regression-based algorithms, machine learning regression-based algorithms, and deep learning algorithms [11,24]. For classical regression-based algorithms, two widely used methods are multiple linear regression [4] and autoregressive integrated moving average [8]. For machine learning regression-based algorithms, support vector regression [21], decision trees [5], random forest [6,15], and K-nearest neighbors regression [15] are four machine learning algorithms that have been used for AQI prediction. As one of the fastest-growing topics, deep learning has shown amazing performance in various pattern recognition tasks. For AQI forecasting, different deep learning architectures have been proposed: convolutional neural networks (CNN), recurrent neural networks (RNN), long-short term memory neural networks (LSTM), gated recurrent unit (GRU), encoder-decoder neural networks, transformer. Although most recent studies have investigated deep learning algorithms for AQI forecasting, few works applied multiple variables parallelly for multi-step AQI forecasting which might limit its performance.

In this study, we propose a parallel multi-input transformer neural network to forecast AQI. Specifically, different single-variable-based models are first evaluated to select the candidate for multi-variable-based models. Then, a correlation-based variable selection method is used to optimize variables to construct transformer-based models. Finally, a novel parallel multi-input transformer architecture is constructed for predicting AQI.

This paper is organized as follows. Section 2 describes the related work. In Sect. 3, data preprocessing, variable selection, and multi-input transformer architecture are described. Section 4 provides the datasets and experimental details. Section 5 analyzes the results. Finally, the conclusion and future work are given in Sect. 5.4.

2   Related Work

AQI forecasting has attracted much attention in recent years. Wu et al. [16] proposed a hybrid AQI forecasting model to enhance forecasting accuracy including Variational mode decomposition (VMD), sample entropy (SE), and an LSTM neural network. Xu et al. [18] developed a novel hybrid model for multi-step daily AQI forecasting, where VMD and the least absolute shrinkage and selector operation (LASSO) were used for preprocessing and reshaping the input data. Then, a stacked auto-encoder (SAE) was proposed to reduce dimension and extract features. Finally, the deep echo state network was used for forecasting. Zhan et al. [19] developed a dynamic decomposition framework by adding the time window based on empirical mode decomposition, ensemble empirical mode decomposition, and complementary ensemble empirical mode decomposition with adaptive noise (CEEMDAN). Moreover, a decomposition-ensemble broad learning system was proposed for air quality index forecasting based on a broad learning system. Zhao et al. [22] developed a novel statistical learning framework integrating the spatial autocorrelation variables, feature selection, and support vector regression

(SVR) for AQI prediction in which correlation analysis and time series analysis were used to extract the spatial-temporal features. Wu et al. [17] developed a new ensemble learning model for AQI forecasting, where CEEMDAN was introduced to decompose the nonlinear and nonstationary AQI history data series. Then, fuzzy entropy (FE) was selected as the feature indicator to recombine the sub-series with similar trends to avoid the problem of over-decomposition and reduce the computing time. Finally, an ensemble LSTM neural network was established to forecast each reconstructed sub-series.

Su et al. [13] proposed a new ST (spatio-temporal) correlation hybrid prediction model named ST-EXMG (ELM-XGBoost-MLP (multilayer perceptron)-GAT (graph attention networks))-AE-XGBoost for AQI forecasting.

Most aforementioned studies used data decomposition, feature selection, and deep learning models to build an AQI forecasting system. As for the deep learning models, LSTM variants are the most frequency used method. Recently, transformer variants have often been used for time series forecasting due to their success in pattern recognition tasks including Reformer [7], Informer [23], Autoformer [2]. For AQI forecasting, Feng et al. [2] proposed a novel encoder-decoder model named Enhanced Autoformer to improve the AQI prediction. However, few studies explored multi-input parallel deep learning models for AQI forecasting.

3 Proposed Method

In this study, we develop a novel parallel multi-input transformer for AQI forecasting which can be divided into three steps: preprocessing, variable selection, and multi-input transformer. The conceptual framework of the proposed method is shown in Fig. 1.

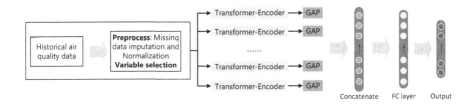

Fig. 1. The structure of proposed parallel multi-input transformer. Here, the input to the model consists of multiple variables based on the variable selection result. Here, GAP denotes global average pooling, and FC denotes fully connected.

3.1 Data Preprocessing

Using data collected by monitoring stations might suffer from data loss in a specific period because of machine failure, regular inspection and maintenance, unstable transmission, and other uncontrollable factors. However, the loss of data will directly affect the performance of subsequent data analysis. Therefore, it is important to fill in the missing value to ensure the model performance [10]. Previous studies have proposed several methods for filling missing values: (1) a fixed value of 0 or 9999, (2) a mean value of the previous and next value of current data, (3) interpolation, (4) k-nearest neighbor, etc. In this study, we empirically use the mean value of the previous and next values to fill in the missing data. Next, we apply Mix-Max normalization to the dataset as follows:

$$x_j = \frac{x_j - min(x_j)}{max(x_j) - min(x_j)} \tag{1}$$

Here, $max(\cdot)$ and $min(\cdot)$ denotes the maximal and minimal value of x_j.

3.2 Variable Selection

Since we aim to create a parallel multi-input transformer model for AQI forecasting, it is important to select suitable variables as the input. Here, we use the Spearman Correlation Coefficient to create multiple types of variables as the input, which has been used in previous studies [14,20]. Figure 2 shows the correlation coefficients between seven air quality variables. Based on the grading standards of ρ shown in Table 1, we can observe that different variables have a different correlation degree with AQI. For instance, PM_{10} and SO_2 are very strongly correlated with AQI. However, the correlation between AQI and O_3 is very weak. It should be noted that the ρ value in Fig. 2 is the mean value over nine sites. For some sites, O_3 is negatively correlated with AQI. Therefore, in this study, we will construct two types of combinations of variables including (1) all seven variables, and (2) those variables that are positively correlated with AQI.

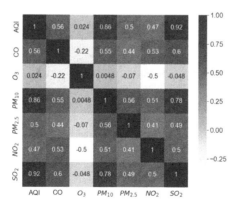

Fig. 2. Mean Spearman Correlation Coefficient (ρ) between seven air quality variables over nine sites.

Table 1. Grading table of Spearman Correlation Coefficient (ρ).

Grading Standards	Correlation Degree
$\rho = 0$	no correlation
$0 < \rho \leq 0.19$	very weak
$0.20 \leq \rho \leq 0.39$	weak
$0.40 \leq \rho \leq 0.59$	moderate
$0.60 \leq \rho \leq 0.79$	strong
$0.80 \leq \rho < 1.00$	very strong
$\rho = 1.00$	monotonic correlation

3.3 Parallel Multi-input Transformer

Transformer is entirely built upon attention mechanisms, which makes it possible to access any part of a sequence regardless of its distance to the target [1]. Initially, the transformer is proposed for machine translation but is rapidly applied in other research areas for its great success. The standard transformer is organized in an encoder-decoder manner, where identical encoder modules are stacked at the bottom of stacked decoder modules.

In this study, we use a transformer encoder to encode the input air quality data into the hidden information matrix. For each encoder, it is composed of Layer Normalization, a multi-head attention layer, and a position-wise feedforward layer. A pictorial representation of this transformer architecture is shown in Fig. 3. Here, the use of position embedding is investigated in our parallel multi-input transformer architecture.

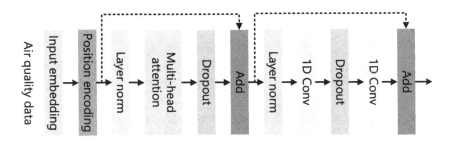

Fig. 3. The architecture of transformer encoder.

Multi-head Attention. Given the input x, it is used as the input for the multi-head attention mechanism. For the multi-head attention mechanism, it is a transformation of Q, K, and V by h different linear conversions for projection, and finally, the different results of attention are sutured together. The concept can be expressed as follows:

$$MultiHead(Q, K, V) = Concat(head_1, head_2, ..., head_h)W^o \qquad (2)$$

$$head_i = Attention(QW_i^Q, KW_i^K, VW_i^V) \qquad (3)$$

where W_i^Q, W_i^K, $W_i^V \in \mathbb{R}^{d_{model} \times d_k}$, and $W^o \in \mathbb{R}^{d_{model} \times hd_v}$.

Parallel Transformer. Similar to [3], parallel series embedding can adequately capture both temporal and variable-wise dependencies and boost the performance of transformer-based models. In this study, we apply a transformer model to each variable in parallel, which is then processed by 1D global average pooling (GAP). Then, the outputs of each GAP are concatenated and processed by a multi-layer perceptron to achieve the final forecasting result.

4   Experimental Details

4.1   Datasets

For AQI forecasting, the air quality data from nine air quality monitoring stations in Shanghai City, China, were obtained from *The Chinese Ministry of Environmental Protection*. Figure 4 shows the location map of Shanghai. The experimental data were collected from 2014-05-13 to 2020-12-31 at an hourly rate, which consists of AQI, CO, O_3, NO_2, SO_2, PM_{10}, and $PM_{2.5}$.

Fig. 4. Distribution of air quality monitoring stations in Shanghai City. Here, there are nine monitoring stations across seven districts.

4.2   Experimental Settings

The parameters of parallel multi-input transformer are experimentally found to achieve the best performance by considering both RMSE and efficiency. For multi-head attention, the head size is 256, the number of heads is 4, and the dropout is 0.25. For the feed-forward part, the filter sizes of the first and second Conv1D are set to 4 and the input embedding size is set to 24, the dropout is 0.25. The transformer encoder is repeated 4 times. For the multi-layer perceptron head, the dense size and dropout are 64 and 0.4. For training parameters, we use the Adam algorithm to optimize the network with a learning rate of 0.0001, batch size is 64, and epoch size is 200.

5   Results and Discussion

In this section, we first discuss the performance of our model during the training and inference period. We train and validate the model using the data collected from 2014-05-12 to 2019-12-31. The rest data is used for testing.

5.1   Evaluation Metrics

To verify the accuracy of the proposed method in predicting AQI, two commonly used performance metrics are used to evaluate the results of the model: root mean square error (RMSE) and R^2.

$$RMSE = \sqrt{\frac{1}{n}\sum_{i=1}^{n}(|y_i' - y_i|)} \tag{4}$$

$$R^2 = 1 - \frac{\sum_{i=1}^{n}(y_i - \hat{y}_i)^2}{\sum_{i=1}^{n}(y_i' - \hat{y}_i)^2} \tag{5}$$

where y_i' and y_i represent the actual and predicted value of AQI, respectively, n is the number of data points contained in the test set, and i is the compilation of test data, $\hat{y}_i$ the average value of n observed samples. For RMSE, a lower value indicates better performance. However, a higher value of R^2 indicates better performance.

5.2   Performance of Single-Input Multi-step Model

The AQI forecasting performance of the proposed method is compared with biLSTM, stack-biLSTM, CNN-biLSTM-v1, and CNN-biLSTM-v2. Tables 2, 3 and 4 show 3-step, 6-step, and 9-step forecasting results using five different architectures, where AQI is used as the model input. From the tables, we can observe that the transformer-based model can achieve the best performance in terms of both RMSE and R^2. For various monitoring stations, the performance is very different. The performance of 1148A is the worst, while the result of 1142A is the best in terms of RMSE and R^2. Considering different steps in multi-step ahead AQI forecasting, it is natural that the forecasting performance deteriorates due to the increasing prediction horizons. Among four biLSTM-based models, stack-biLSTM achieves the best performance where the averaged RMSE and R^2 for 3-step, 6-step, and 9-step forecasting are 7.5101 and 0.8288, 9.7164 and 0.7127, 11.1694 and 0.6198, respectively. Therefore, both transformer and stack-biLSTM will be selected as the basic block for the subsequent multi-input multi-step analysis.

Table 2. Comparison of **3-step** forecasting results using different models in terms of RMSE ↓ and R^2 ↑, where AQI is used as the input.

Metric	Method	1142A	1143A	1144A	1145A	1146A	1147A	1148A	1149A	1150A	Mean
RMSE	biLSTM	5.7927	9.4096	6.8628	7.5125	7.4767	8.1573	9.6585	6.1925	6.7555	7.5353
	stack-biLSTM	5.7672	9.3872	6.8365	7.4620	7.3632	8.1951	9.6254	6.1985	6.7560	7.5101
	CNN-biLSTM-v1	5.8343	9.5170	7.0031	7.6536	7.4941	8.2194	9.5698	6.3006	6.8592	7.6057
	CNN-biLSTM-v2	5.8685	9.4614	6.9991	7.6445	7.5151	8.1831	9.5682	6.3065	6.8385	7.5983
	Transformer	5.7431	9.3192	6.8678	7.4989	7.3724	8.0932	9.5359	6.1846	6.7551	**7.4856**
R^2	biLSTM	0.8325	0.8158	0.8432	0.8311	0.8304	0.8170	0.8018	0.8467	0.8305	0.8277
	stack-biLSTM	0.8340	0.8166	0.8444	0.8334	0.8355	0.8153	0.8032	0.8464	0.8305	0.8288
	CNN-biLSTM-v1	0.8301	0.8115	0.8367	0.8247	0.8296	0.8142	0.8054	0.8413	0.8252	0.8243
	CNN-biLSTM-v2	0.8281	0.8137	0.8369	0.8252	0.8286	0.8158	0.8055	0.8410	0.8263	0.8246
	Transformer	0.8354	0.8193	0.8430	0.8318	0.8351	0.8198	0.8068	0.8471	0.8305	**0.8299**

Table 3. Comparison of **6-step** forecasting results using different models in terms of RMSE ↓ and R^2 ↑, where AQI is used as the input.

Metric	Method	1142A	1143A	1144A	1145A	1146A	1147A	1148A	1149A	1150A	Mean
RMSE	biLSTM	7.5781	11.9582	8.9781	9.9010	9.6351	10.4189	12.0198	8.1957	8.7114	9.7107
	stack-biLSTM	7.6263	12.0462	8.9841	9.8806	9.5206	10.3877	12.0723	8.2235	8.7065	9.7164
	CNN-biLSTM-v1	7.6616	12.0460	9.0787	10.0153	9.6847	10.4811	12.0302	8.2741	8.7893	9.7845
	CNN-biLSTM-v2	7.7354	12.0107	9.0553	9.9808	9.7050	10.5326	11.9847	8.2335	8.8093	9.7830
	Transformer	7.4880	11.7925	8.8869	9.6849	9.5138	10.2649	11.9166	8.0954	8.6357	**9.5865**
R^2	biLSTM	0.7134	0.7025	0.7317	0.7068	0.7183	0.7015	0.6931	0.7315	0.7182	0.7130
	stack-biLSTM	0.7098	0.6981	0.7313	0.7080	0.7250	0.7032	0.6904	0.7297	0.7185	0.7127
	CNN-biLSTM-v1	0.7071	0.6981	0.7256	0.7000	0.7154	0.6979	0.6926	0.7263	0.7131	0.7085
	CNN-biLSTM-v2	0.7014	0.6999	0.7271	0.7020	0.7142	0.6949	0.6949	0.7290	0.7118	0.7084
	Transformer	0.7202	0.7107	0.7371	0.7195	0.7254	0.7102	0.6984	0.7380	0.7230	**0.7203**

5.3 Performance of Multi-input Multi-step Model

Figures 5 and 6 show the forecasting results using all seven variables and optimized variables as the input in parallel. Here, optimized variables are selected based on the ρ value, where those variables are positively correlated with AQI. Compared to a single-input multi-step model, the multi-input multi-step model can achieve better forecasting performance, which verifies the effectiveness of having more variables to construct the model. Multi-input transformer with positively correlated variables as the input can achieve an RMSE of 6.488, 8.7978,

Table 4. Comparison of **9-step** forecasting results using different models in terms of RMSE ↓ and R^2 ↑, where AQI is used as the input.

Metric	Method	1142A	1143A	1144A	1145A	1146A	1147A	1148A	1149A	1150A	Mean
RMSE	biLSTM	8.7977	13.8244	10.4122	11.4434	11.1173	11.8833	13.7453	9.5555	10.0543	11.2037
	stack-biLSTM	8.8092	13.7301	10.4684	11.4518	11.0394	11.8265	13.6538	9.5392	10.0064	11.1694
	CNN-biLSTM-v1	8.8565	13.7776	10.5275	11.5903	11.2051	11.9440	13.7415	9.6398	10.1596	11.2713
	CNN-biLSTM-v2	8.8445	13.8409	10.5102	11.5557	11.1326	11.9175	13.7085	9.5565	10.1010	11.2408
	Transformer	8.6346	13.5435	10.2555	11.1797	10.9084	11.7506	13.5681	9.3674	9.9604	**11.0187**
R^2	biLSTM	0.6139	0.6025	0.6392	0.6084	0.6251	0.6117	0.5988	0.6351	0.6246	0.6177
	stack-biLSTM	0.6128	0.6079	0.6353	0.6078	0.6303	0.6154	0.6041	0.6363	0.6282	0.6198
	CNN-biLSTM-v1	0.6087	0.6052	0.6312	0.5983	0.6191	0.6077	0.5990	0.6286	0.6167	0.6127
	CNN-biLSTM-v2	0.6097	0.6016	0.6324	0.6007	0.6241	0.6095	0.6009	0.6350	0.6211	0.6150
	Transformer	0.6280	0.6185	0.6500	0.6263	0.6390	0.6203	0.6090	0.6493	0.6316	**0.6302**

and 10.4585 for 3-step, 6-step, and 9-step AQI forecasting, respectively, which are the best in the four models. However, the best performance for 3-step and 6-step is obtained using position encoding, and the best performance for 9-step AQI forecasting is obtained without position encoding.

Similar to the single-input model, the forecasting performance deteriorates due to the increasing prediction horizons. For short-horizon (3-step) forecasting, the proposed model has an R^2 of 0.8715, meaning that the proposed model fits the AQI series well. Furthermore, experimental results demonstrate that our proposed model can forecast future AQI grades accurately. Therefore, the public can schedule their outdoor activities and take some protection measures against air pollution in advance according to the predicted AQI grade.

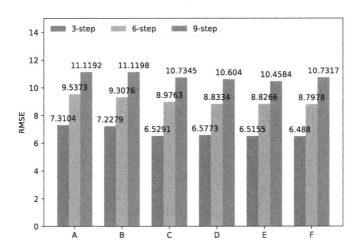

Fig. 5. Comparison of **multi-step** forecasting results using multi-input stack-biLSTM and multi-input transformer in terms of **RMSE** ↓. Here, A: multi-stack-biLSTM with all variables, B: multi-stack-biLSTM with optimized variables, C: multi-transformer with all variables, D: multi-transformer with optimized variables, E: multi-transformer with all variables using position encoding, F: multi-transformer with optimized variables using position encoding.

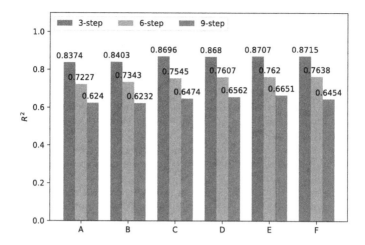

Fig. 6. Comparison of **multi-step** forecasting results using multi-input stack-biLSTM and multi-input transformer in terms of R^2 ↓. Here, A: multi-stack-biLSTM with all variables, B: multi-stack-biLSTM with optimized variables, C: multi-transformer with all variables, D: multi-transformer with optimized variables, E: multi-transformer with all variables using position encoding, F: multi-transformer with optimized variables using position encoding.

5.4   Conclusion

We propose a novel parallel multi-input transformer architecture for AQI forecasting, which is essential for public health protection and air pollution reduction. In the proposed model, five single-input deep learning models are first employed to forecast AQI, where the best-performing architecture is selected for constructing multi-input models. Then, multiple variables are optimized based on the Spearman Correlation Coefficients. Finally, the final experimental results demonstrate the effectiveness of multi-input architectures and variable optimization. Moreover, the performance of the proposed method is superior to those of all compared models. Future work aims to investigate data decomposition and data from nearby stations for improving performance.

Acknowledgements. This work is Supported by the Fundamental Research Funds for the Central Universities (grants No. 020414380195). This work is supported by National Natural Science Foundation of China (Grant No: 32371556, 61902154 and 72004092).

References

1. Cai, L., Janowicz, K., Mai, G., Yan, B., Zhu, R.: Traffic transformer: capturing the continuity and periodicity of time series for traffic forecasting. Trans. GIS **24**(3), 736–755 (2020)

2. Feng, H., Zhang, X.: A novel encoder-decoder model based on autoformer for air quality index prediction. PLOS ONE **18**(4), e0284293 (2023)
3. Feng, X., Lyu, Z.: How features benefit: parallel series embedding for multivariate time series forecasting with transformer. In: 2022 IEEE 34th International Conference on Tools with Artificial Intelligence (ICTAI), pp. 967–975. IEEE (2022)
4. Ganesh, S.S., Modali, S.H., Palreddy, S.R., Arulmozhivarman, P.: Forecasting air quality index using regression models: a case study on Delhi and Houston. In: 2017 International Conference on Trends in Electronics and Informatics (ICEI), pp. 248–254. IEEE (2017)
5. Jamal, A., Nodehi, R.N.: Predicting air quality index based on meteorological data: a comparison of regression analysis, artificial neural networks and decision tree. J. Air Pollut. Health **2**(1), 27–38 (2017)
6. Ketu, S.: Spatial air quality index and air pollutant concentration prediction using linear regression based recursive feature elimination with random forest regression (RFERF): a case study in India. Nat. Hazards **114**(2), 2109–2138 (2022)
7. Kitaev, N., Kaiser, Ł., Levskaya, A.: Reformer: the efficient transformer. arXiv preprint arXiv:2001.04451 (2020)
8. Kumar, A., Goyal, P.: Forecasting of daily air quality index in Delhi. Sci. Total Environ. **409**(24), 5517–5523 (2011)
9. Liu, C.C., Lin, T.C., Yuan, K.Y., Chiueh, P.T.: Spatio-temporal prediction and factor identification of urban air quality using support vector machine. Urban Clim. **41**, 101055 (2022)
10. Ma, J., Cheng, J.C.: Estimation of the building energy use intensity in the urban scale by integrating GIS and big data technology. Appl. Energy **183**, 182–192 (2016)
11. Méndez, M., Merayo, M.G., Núñez, M.: Machine learning algorithms to forecast air quality: a survey. Artif. Intell. Rev. **56**, 10031–10066 (2023). https://doi.org/10.1007/s10462-023-10424-4
12. Nigam, S., Rao, B., Kumar, N., Mhaisalkar, V.: Air quality index-a comparative study for assessing the status of air quality. Res. J. Eng. Technol. **6**(2), 267–274 (2015)
13. Su, M., Liu, H., Yu, C., Duan, Z.: A novel AQI forecasting method based on fusing temporal correlation forecasting with spatial correlation forecasting. Atmos. Pollut. Res. **14**(4), 101717 (2023)
14. Sun, W., Li, Z.: Hourly PM2.5 concentration forecasting based on feature extraction and stacking-driven ensemble model for the winter of the Beijing-Tianjin-Hebei area. Atmos. Pollut. Res. **11**(6), 110–121 (2020)
15. Tella, A., Balogun, A.L., Adebisi, N., Abdullah, S.: Spatial assessment of PM10 hotspots using Random Forest, K-nearest neighbour and Naïve Bayes. Atmos. Pollut. Res. **12**(10), 101202 (2021)
16. Wu, Q., Lin, H.: Daily urban air quality index forecasting based on variational mode decomposition, sample entropy and LSTM neural network. Sustain. Urban Areas **50**, 101657 (2019)
17. Wu, Z., Zhao, W., Lv, Y.: An ensemble LSTM-based AQI forecasting model with decomposition-reconstruction technique via CEEMDAN and fuzzy entropy. Air Qual. Atmos. Health **15**(12), 2299–2311 (2022)
18. Xu, Y., Liu, H., Duan, Z.: A novel hybrid model for multi-step daily AQI forecasting driven by air pollution big data. Air Qual. Atmos. Health **13**, 197–207 (2020)
19. Zhan, C., Jiang, W., Lin, F., Zhang, S., Li, B.: A decomposition-ensemble broad learning system for AQI forecasting. Neural Comput. Appl. **34**(21), 18461–18472 (2022)

20. Zhang, L., et al.: Trend analysis and forecast of PM2.5 in Fuzhou, China using the
    Arima model. Ecol. Indic. **95**, 702–710 (2018)
21. Zhao, X., Wu, Z., Qiu, J., Wei, Y.: A novel hybrid algorithm with static and
    dynamic models for air quality index forecasting. Nonlinear Dyn. **111**, 1–13 (2023)
22. Zhao, Z., Wu, J., Cai, F., Zhang, S., Wang, Y.G.: A statistical learning frame-
    work for spatial-temporal feature selection and application to air quality index
    forecasting. Ecol. Ind. **144**, 109416 (2022)
23. Zhou, H., et al.: Informer: beyond efficient transformer for long sequence time-series
    forecasting. In: Proceedings of the AAAI Conference on Artificial Intelligence, vol.
    35, pp. 11106–11115 (2021)
24. Zhu, M., Xie, J.: Investigation of nearby monitoring station for hourly PM2.5
    forecasting using parallel multi-input 1D-CNN-biLSTM. Exp. Syst. Appl. **211**,
    118707 (2023)

One-shot Video-based Person Re-identification based on SAM Attention and Reciprocal Nearest Neighbors Metric

Ji Zhang, Yuchang Yin, and Hongyuan Wang$^{(\boxtimes)}$

Changzhou University, Changzhou Jiangsu 213164, China
hywang@cczu.edu.cn

Abstract. Pedestrian re-identification (Re-ID) is used to solves the recognition and retrieval of pedestrians across cameras. To solve the difficulties of label annotation in Re-ID, a one-shot video-based Re-ID method is applied. For the problem of large number of neural network parameters and weak feature extraction ability of the model, the SAM attention module is embedded. The module is plug-and-play without any additional parameters, while it can capture the hidden information in samples and improve the discriminative of model. To address the problem of low accuracy of label estimation, a reciprocal nearest neighbours metric is designed. The metric is capable of constructing closer nearest-neighbour relationships between samples, combining the Mahalanobis distance and Jaccard distance to significantly improve the accuracy of label estimation and model performance. The effectiveness of our method in this paper is extensively experimented on two video-based Re-ID datasets, MARS and DukeMTMC-VideoReID.

Keywords: Video-based Person Re-identification · One-shot Learning · Semi-supervised Learning

1 Introduction

Pedestrian re-identification (Re-ID) is a technique for detecting the presence of a specific pedestrian in a network of multiple cameras [1–5]. It plays an important role in intelligent video surveillance systems and has a wide range of applications in the field of public safety. With the developments of smart cities, a large number of cameras have been installed in cities and huge amount of video data is generated all the time. How to process video data efficiently is an important problem encountered by security personnel nowadays. Re-ID plays an important role in this regard, which reduce the consumption of manpower and economy effectively.

Most of the existing video-based pedestrian Re-ID methods use supervised based methods [6–10], which are extremely dependent on data annotation. But it is laborious and time-consuming for large-scale data annotations. Compared with supervised based methods, massive data annotations are not necessary for semi-supervised based methods. But these methods do not fully utilize the hidden information of unlabeled data, which

H. Lu et al. (Eds.): ACPR 2023, LNCS 14408, pp. 64–78, 2023.
https://doi.org/10.1007/978-3-031-47665-5_6

cause the performances of them are not as good as desired. One-shot Re-ID methods adopt a different training philosophy, which use only one labeled video clip for each identity in the training set, and the rest are unlabeled data. The current mainstream approach uses an incremental learning strategy to first assign pseudo-labels to the unlabeled data, then select some reliable pseudo-labeled data to merge with the original training set, and finally use the merged new data set to train the model again. Obviously, assignment of labels plays an important role in these methods, because it determines the assignment of pseudo-labels directly, and the correct assignment of pseudo-labels has a great impact on the next training. In other words, a correct pseudo-label sample has a positive effect on the training, while a wrong one provides wrong supervision information and prevents the model from learning the hidden information of the sample.

In this paper, a novel one-shot video-based pedestrian Re-ID method is designed based on SAM attention module and reciprocal nearest neighbor metric. The whole process can be briefly divided into three steps: (1) Initialize the model using labeled data. (2) Assign pseudo-labels for unlabeled data and select some reliable pseudo-labels to be combined with labeled data as a new training set. (3) Train the model again using the new training set. Due to the few number of initial labeled samples, the trained model is not discriminative enough. To address the problem of few number of labeled samples and low discriminative ability at the begining of training, we embed SAM attention module [11] in our network. In label estimation, in order to improve the accuracy of pseudo-label assignment, we design a reciprocal nearest neighbor metric, with k-reciprocal encoding [12], Mahalanobis metric and Jaccard metric for nearest neighbor samples, which is more robust and tighter and improves the accuracy of pseudo-label assignment. The main contributions of this paper are as follow:

(1) The SAM attention module is embedded in our network, which is flexible and effective to enhance the model discrimination without increasing the training burden.
(2) A reciprocal nearest neighbor metric is designed for pseudo-label estimation, which can effectively improve the accuracy of pseudo-label prediction.
(3) Our method in this paper focuses on the video-based pedestrian Re-ID problem under one-shot, and achieves competitive performance on two large-scale video pedestrian datasets, MARS and DukeMTMC-VideoReID.

2 Related Works

In recent years, video-based pedestrian Re-ID with deep learning has developed rapidly and achieved impressive results on major datasets [13–17]. Compared with image-based pedestrian Re-ID, video-based pedestrian Re-ID contains more pedestrian identity information and is accompanied by more noise and challenges. How to obtain sequence-level discriminant features is the core of supervised video-based pedestrian Re-ID. To address this problem, based on the spatio-temporal information of videos, many researchers extract more effective pedestrian features by integrating attention mechanisms. Li et al. propose a spatio-temporal attention module that discovers discriminative parts from pedestrian images and extract valid information without being affected by problems such as occlusion [13]; Hou et al. combine the attention mechanism with adversarial generative networks to design a spatio-temporal completion network, which recover the occluded parts of pedestrian through the network, instead of discarding them, to effectively deal with the occlusion problem [14]; Li et al. draw on the work in image pedestrian Re-ID to explore multi-scale temporal cues in video sequences [15]; Liu et al. introduce a non-local attention module and reduce the computational complexity of extracting spatio-temporal features [16]; Eom et al. propose a spatio-temporal memory network, where spatial memory stores the features of the extracted spatial interference terms and temporal memory stores the attention used to optimize temporal patterns, this network improves the performance of attention mechanisms in the field of video-based pedestrian Re-ID [17].

Semi-supervised video-based Re-ID has been less studied, and most of the work focuses on semi-supervised video-based Re-ID under one-shot [18–24]. Zhu et al. use a semi-supervised dictionary learning approach to study the cross-view problem in video-based Re-ID by converting videos under different cameras into coding coefficients in the feature space to reduce the variation and differences between different cameras [18]; Liu et al. propose a metric boosting algorithm that iterates between model upgrading and label estimation, mainly for the problems of difficult sample mining and label propagation, and achieves good results on three datasets [19]. Wu et al. improve the framework of iterative training by drawing on the experience in [19], they also optimize the sampling strategy and the algorithm for pseudo-label assignment [20]. Similar to this iterative training approach, Ye et al. design a framework for dynamic graph matching to improve the label estimation process by continuously changing the graph structure, and also design a joint matching strategy to fully extract video information and reduce false matches [21]. Although all of the above methods are semi-supervised methods, the training and data selection strategies are different from each other. In particular, the traditional principle of nearest neighbor assignment is still used in label estimation, and pseudo-label estimation errors often occur. The method in this paper focuses on the problem of one-shot video-based Re-ID, using SAM attention as well as reciprocal nearest neighbor metric, which can effectively utilize unlabeled samples and improve the accuracy of pseudo-label prediction.

3 Method

3.1 Main Framework

Figure 1 shows the overall framework of our method proposed in this paper. The whole process consists of model initialization, label assignment, dynamic selection and model update. Firstly, the model is initialized using labeled samples. In previous works, ResNet-50 is the common choice. For the dual consideration of feature extraction and computation consumption of our model, the SAM attention module is embedded in ResNet-50. In label assignment, the reciprocal nearest neighbor metric is used, which is better in reflecting the relationships of samples and improving the accuracy of label estimation effectively, compared with the Euclidean metric. After each selection of pseudo-labeled data, the labeled data are merged with the selected pseudo-labeled data as the training set for the next training. The whole process is continuously iterated, and eventually all unlabeled data are selected.

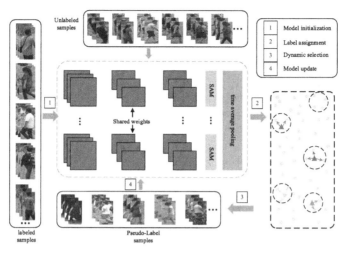

Fig. 1. The main framework

3.2 SAM Attention Module

In one-shot Re-ID, the labeled samples are unique for each identity. These samples are used to train the model firstly, then estimate labels for unlabeled ones with the model. However, due to the small amount of these labeled samples, researchers usually do not use more complex network structures. On the one hand, a complex network structure will trigger a huge amount of computation; on the other hand, a complex network structure does not necessarily enhance the feature extraction ability and discriminative ability of the model, but it may even fall into overfitting. To address the above problems, the SAM attention module is added into the ResNet-50 network, which is a plug-and-play module that does not require much adjustment of the network structure.

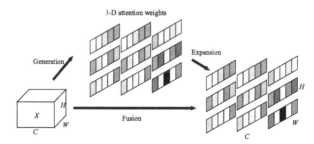

Fig. 2. 3-D attention weights

Existing attention models usually extract features from channels or image spaces only, which limit the flexibility of attention weights for network learning. In addition, the structures of these attention models are usually very complex, which bring enormous amount of computation. In contrast, the SAM module is simple and effective in that it considers both spatial dimensions and channel dimensions and it is able to obtain 3-dimensional attention weights directly from the current neurons, as shown in Fig. 2, where $X \in \mathbf{R}^{C \times H \times W}$ is the input feature map, and C is the channel number of X. The SAM energy function is shown in Eq. (1), which is derived in [11] detailly:

$$e_t^* = \frac{4\left(\hat{\sigma}^2 + \lambda\right)}{\left(t - \hat{\mu}\right)^2 + 2\hat{\sigma} + 2\lambda} \tag{1}$$

$$\hat{\mu} = \frac{1}{M} \sum_{i=1}^{M} x_i \tag{2}$$

$$\hat{\sigma}^2 = \frac{1}{M} \sum_{i=1}^{M} \left(x_i - \hat{\mu}\right)^2 \tag{3}$$

In Eq. (1), t is an objective neuron in one of the channels of input feature X, and x_i denotes other neurons in this channel, and i is the index of spatial dimensions. $M = H \times W$ denotes the number of neurons in the spatial dimension, and λ is a hyper-parameters. $\hat{\mu}$ and $\hat{\sigma}^2$ denote the mean and variance of all neurons in the channel, as shown in Eq. (2) and Eq. (3), respectively. The above formula indicates that, the smaller e_t^*, the larger t. That is, t is more pronounced than other neurons, and the network can thus learn more features.

Integrate the attention weights of each dimension with input features, and the final feature representation is shown in Eq. (4):

$$\tilde{X} = sigmoid\left(\frac{1}{E}\right) \odot X \tag{4}$$

where, $\tilde{X}$ denotes the output feature, and E groups all e_t^* across channel and spatial dimensions. Sigmoid is added to restrict too large value in E.

SAM attention module is very flexible and modular, which is combined with the ResNet-50 network in this paper, and in order to adapt to the classification task of pedestrian Re-ID, a temporal average pooling layer is added at the end of the network to extract sequence-level features.

From Fig. 3, it can be seen that SAM attention module can be inserted into each layer, from Layer1 to Layer4. In order to extract sequence-level features, a time average pooling layer is added after Layer4 and SAM modules. With these SAM modules, many valuable clues can be captured, and the discriminative ability of the model can be enhanced, but the computational cost has not increased significantly, due to its lightweight structure.

3.3 Reciprocal Nearest Neighbor Metric

Label estimation is currently the main challenge in semi-supervised Re-ID. How to assign correct pseudo-labels for unlabeled sample plays a crucial role in model training. The nearest neighbor method with Euclidean distance metric is commonly used to assign pseudo-labels. Equation (5) represents the Euclidean distance $d(v_i, v_j)$ between labeled sample v_i and unlabeled sample v_j:

$$d\left(v_i, v_j\right) = \|v_i - v_j\| \tag{5}$$

According to Formula (5), unlabeled data is assigned the label of the labeled data which is closest to it. However, in the process of label allocation, it is inevitable that unlabeled data is mislabeled (assigned error pseudo-label), especially when the discriminant power of the model is not strong enough. With the nearest neighbor method, when the number of mislabeled samples is large, it can greatly weaken the performance of the model. To address this problem, k-reciprocal encoding is used in our model for label estimation. In the field of pedestrian Re-ID, k-reciprocal encoding is initially used for re-ranking.

In this paper, reciprocal encoding is applied as the distance metric for one-shot label estimation of unlabeled samples. Assuming u_i is an unlabeled data, $G = \{g_i | i = 1, 2, ..., N\}$ denotes N labeled data, and the k-nearest neighbor of u_i is defined as $N(u_i, k)$ as shown in Eq. (6):

$$N(u_i, k) = \{g_1^0, g_2^0, ..., g_k^0\}, |N(u_i, k)| = k \tag{6}$$

where, |.| denotes the number of candidates in the set. Based on the k-nearest neighbor of u_i, the k-reciprocal nearest neighbor of u_i is denoted as $R(u_i, k)$:

$$R(u_i, k) = \{g_i | (g_i \in N(u_i, k)) \bigwedge (u_i \in N(g_i, k)) \tag{7}$$

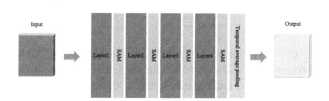

Fig. 3. Network structure diagram with SAM module

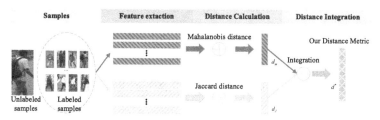

Fig. 4. Reciprocal nearest neighbour metric

As shown in Eq. (7), an unlabeled sample and a labeled sample are called k-reciprocal nearest neighbors, when they are k-nearest neighbors of each other. Compared with k-nearest neighbors, k-reciprocal nearest neighbors reflect the relationships of samples better. At the procedure of label assignment, when an unlabeled sample and a labeled sample are k-reciprocal nearest neighbors, it can be considered that the likelihood of them belonging to the same category is very high. Based on this assumption, a reciprocal nearest neighbor metric is proposed for label estimation in this paper, as shown in Fig. 4.

It can be seen from Fig. 4 that the reciprocal nearest neighbor metric consists of three components:

(1) extract the features x_{u_i} and x_{g_i} of unlabeled data u_i and labeled data g_i, respectively,
(2) calculate the Mahalanobis distance $d_M(u_i, g_i)$ and Jaccard distance $d_J(u_i, g_i)$, as shown in Eq. (8) and Eq. (9),

$$d_M(u_i, g_i) = \sqrt{(u_i - g_i)^T \sum{}^{-1} (u_i - g_i)} \qquad (8)$$

$$d_J(u_i, g_i) = 1 - \frac{|R(u_i, k) \cap R(g_i, k)|}{|R(u_i, k) \cup R(g_i, k)|} \qquad (9)$$

In Eq. (8), $\sum$ is covariance matrix of u_i and g_i, the superscripts T and -1 denote matrix transpose and inverse. In Eq. (9), $R(\cdot, k)$ denotes the k-nearest neighbor of $\cdot$, and | and || and |·| denotes the number of samples in $\cdot$. If sample u_i and g_i belong to the same category, there are many same samples in $R(u_i, k)$ and $R(g_i, k)$. This means that, the more the number of same samples in $R(u_i, k)$ and $R(g_i, k)$, the more similar of u_i and g_i, and the closer $d_J(u_i, g_i)$ tends to zero.

(1) Our reciprocal nearest neighbor metric $d^*(u_i, g_i)$ is defined with Mahalanobis distance $d_M(u_i, g_i)$ and Jaccard distance $d_J(u_i, g_i)$ as follow,

$$d^*(u_i, g_i) = (1 - \lambda)d_M(u_i, g_i) + \lambda d_J(u_i, g_i) \qquad (10)$$

where, $\lambda(0 < \lambda < 1)$ is balance factor. With this metric, we can mine the information of reciprocal nearest neighbors between unlabeled and labeled data, and the accuracy of pseudo-label estimation and the robustness of the model can be improved.

4   Experiments and Results

4.1   Datasets and Evaluation Indicators

In our experiments, two mainstream large-scale datasets of video pedestrian Re-ID, MARS [25] and DukeMTMC-VideoReID [20], are used. In MARS, there are 20,478 video clips captured by 6 cameras, in which 17,503 are valid clips and the rest 3,248 are interference clips. The total number of pedestrians present in MARS is 1,261, and 625 in the training set and 636 in the test set. In DukeMTMC-VideoReID, there are 1,812 pedestrians and 4,832 video clips, wherein 702 pedestrians and 2196 clips in the training set, and 702 pedestrians and 2636 clips in the test set, in additional 408 interference pedestrians, which is the subset of DukeMTMC [26]. To demonstrate the performance of our model, two indicators, Cumulative Matching Characteristic (CMC) and Mean Average Precision (mAP), are used as evaluation indicators.

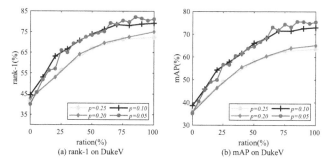

Fig. 5. Comparison of results for different p of the DukeMTMC-VideoReID

4.2 Experimental settings

In this paper, GPU 2080ti is used and the experimental settings are the same as [20]. The stochastic gradient descent (SGD) optimization method with momentum of 0.5 and weight attenuation of 0.0005 is adopted. The overall learning rate is initialized to 0.1 and decays to 0.01 in the 15 epochs. The loss function is Cross Entropy Loss.

4.3 Experimental Results and Comparison

Parameter Selection Experiments

In this section, we analyze the parameter $p(0 < p < 1)$, which control the number of pseudo-label samples selected each time. Figure 5 shows the results with $p = 0.05$, $p = 0.10$, $p = 0.20$, $p = 0.25$ on the DukeMTMC-VideoReID dataset, respectively.

As shown in Fig. 5, it can be seen that, the smaller p selected, the better performance achieved. This is because fewer reliable pseudo-label samples are selected when p is small. Although there may be mislabeled samples contained in those selected pseudo-label samples, the number is too small to impact the performance of our model. But we also find that, p is not necessarily as small as possible. Because the fewer samples selected each time, the higher consumption in model training. In order to achieve a balance between speed and accuracy, we set $p = 0.05$ and $p = 0.10$ in the following experiments.

In addition to parameter p, k and λ can also affect the result of reciprocal nearest neighbor metric (RNM). Table 1 and Table 2 show the RNM results for different k values and different λ values on the DukeMTMC-VideoReID dataset, respectively.

As shown in Table 1, we set $p = 0.10$, $\lambda = 0.3$ and select $k = 5, 10, 15, 20$ for comparison In our experiments. Our RNM model achieves the best score in rank-1, rank-5, rank-20 and mAP, when $k = 10$. In the following experiments, we set $k = 10$.

As shown in Table 2, we set $p = 0.10$, $k = 10$ and select $\lambda=0.3, 0.5$ for comparison In our experiments. Our RNM model achieves the best score in rank-1, rank-5, rank-20 and mAP, when $\lambda = 0.3$. In the following experiments, we set $\lambda = 0.3$.

Effectiveness Experiments of SAM Attention Module

In this section, effectiveness of SAM attention module embedded in our model is compared with EGU [20] and PL [27] on DukeMTMC-VideoReID and MARS datasets.

Table 1. Comparison of RNM (%) for different k on DukeMTMC-VideoReID

k	rank-1	rank-5	rank-20	mAP
20	71.70	85.30	92.30	63.60
15	78.50	91.60	95.70	72.30
10	**79.20**	**92.20**	**95.40**	**73.00**
5	77.10	89.00	94.60	69.40

Table 2. Comparison of RNM (%) for different λ on DukeMTMC-VideoReID

λ	rank-1	rank-5	rank-20	mAP
0.30	**79.20**	**92.20**	**95.40**	**73.00**
0.50	75.40	88.00	93.90	67.50

As shown in Table 3, with SAM($p = 0.10$), rank-1 and mAP of our model achieves 75.6% and 67.6%, respectively, on DukeMTMC-VideoReID dataset, which exceeds the performance of EUG ($p = 0.05$) and PL ($p = 0.05$). Compared to EUG ($p = 0.10$), rank-1 and mAP of our model exceed 4.81% and 5.84%, respectively. Compared to PL ($p = 0.10$), rank-1 and mAP of our model exceed 4.6% and 5.7%, respectively. Similar results can also be obtained, when compared SAM ($p = 0.10$) with EUG ($p = 0.05$) and PL ($p = 0.05$).

As shown in Table 4, with SAM ($p = 0.10$), rank-1 and mAP of our model achieves 60.7% and 41.5%, respectively, on MARS dataset, which exceeds the performance of EUG ($p = 0.10$) and PL ($p = 0.10$), lower than the performance of EUG ($p = 0.05$) and PL ($p = 0.05$). Similarly,with SAM ($p = 0.05$), rank-1 and mAP of our model achieves 63.7% and 43.9%, respectively, which exceed the performance of EUG ($p = 0.05$) and PL ($p = 0.05$).

Table 3. Comparison(%) of SAM with EUG and PL on DukeMTMC-VideoReID

Methods	rank-1	rank-5	rank-20	mAP
EUG [20] ($p = 0.10$)	70.79	83.61	89.60	61.76
EUG [20] ($p = 0.05$)	72.79	84.18	91.45	63.23
PL [27] ($p = 0.10$)	71.00	83.80	90.30	61.90
PL [27] ($p = 0.05$)	72.90	84.30	91.40	63.30
SAM ($p = 0.10$)	**75.60**	**87.60**	**92.00**	**67.60**
SAM ($p = 0.05$)	**77.60**	**89.60**	**94.40**	**69.20**

Table 4. Comparison(%) of SAM with other methods on MARS

Methods	rank-1	rank-5	rank-20	mAP
EUG [20] ($p = 0.10$)	57.62	69.64	78.08	34.68
EUG [20] ($p = 0.05$)	62.67	74.94	82.57	42.45
PL [27] ($p = 0.10$)	57.90	70.30	79.30	34.90
PL [27] ($p = 0.05$)	62.80	75.20	83.80	42.60
SAM ($p = 0.10$)	**60.70**	**74.00**	**81.90**	**41.50**
SAM ($p = 0.05$)	**63.70**	**76.00**	**82.30**	**43.90**

With above experiments, it can be seen that, because of the flexible and lightweight characteristics of the SAM attention module, our model can effectively captures hidden information in video data and extracts more discriminative features, without increasing network parameters and without modifying the overall structure significantly, because of the flexible and lightweight characteristics of the SAM attention module.

Effectiveness Experiments of Reciprocal Nearest Neighbor Metric

In this section, effectiveness of RNM (reciprocal nearest neighbor metric) used in our model is compared with EGU [20] and PL [27] on DukeMTMC-VideoReID and MARS datasets.

As shown in Table 5, with RNM ($p = 0.10$), rank-1 and mAP of our model achieves 79.2% and 73.0%, respectively, on DukeMTMC-VideoReID dataset, which exceeds the performance of EUG ($p = 0.05$) and PL ($p = 0.05$). Compared to EUG ($p = 0.10$), rank-1 and mAP of our model exceed 8.41% and 11.24%, respectively. Compared to PL ($p = 0.10$), rank-1 and mAP of our model exceed 8.2% and 11.1%, respectively. Similar results can also be obtained, when compared RNM ($p = 0.10$) with EUG ($p = 0.05$) and PL ($p = 0.05$).

As shown in Table 6, with RNM ($p = 0.10$), rank-1 and mAP of our model exceed the performance of EUG ($p = 0.05$) and PL ($p = 0.05$) on MARS dataset. Compared to EUG ($p = 0.10$), rank-1 and mAP of our model exceed 7.18% and 8.52%, respectively. Compared to PL ($p = 0.10$), rank-1 and mAP of our model exceed 6.9% and 8.3%, respectively. Similar results can also be obtained, when compared RNM ($p = 0.05$) with EUG ($p = 0.05$) and PL ($p = 0.05$).

In RNM, it is assumed that, two samples that are k-nearest to each other are highly likely to belong to the same category. Experiments have shown that, compared to the commonly used Euclidean distance, RNM makes labeled data and pseudo-labeled data to connect much more closer to each other, which can improve the accuracy of pseudo-label estimation.

Ablation Experiments

In ablation experiments, in order to demonstrate the effectiveness of SAM and RNM, we use EUG as baseline and the framework used in our model is the same as that in EUG.

Table 5. Comparison(%) of RNM with other methods on DukeMTMC-VideoReID

Methods	rank-1	rank-5	rank-20	mAP
EUG [20] ($p = 0.10$)	70.79	83.61	89.60	61.76
EUG [20] ($p = 0.05$)	72.79	84.18	91.45	63.23
PL [27] ($p = 0.10$)	71.00	83.80	90.30	61.90
PL [27] ($p = 0.05$)	72.90	84.30	91.40	63.30
RNM ($p = 0.10$)	**79.20**	**92.20**	**95.40**	**73.00**
RNM($p = 0.05$)	**81.20**	**92.70**	**95.60**	**75.40**

Table 6. Comparison (%) of RNM with other methods on MARS

Methods	rank-1	rank-5	rank-20	mAP
EUG [20] ($p = 0.10$)	57.62	69.64	78.08	34.68
EUG [20] ($p = 0.05$)	62.67	74.94	82.57	42.45
PL [27] ($p = 0.10$)	57.90	70.30	79.30	4.90
PL [27] ($p = 0.05$)	62.80	75.20	83.80	42.60
RNM ($p = 0.10$)	**64.80**	**79.50**	**86.90**	**43.20**
RNM ($p = 0.05$)	**66.30**	**80.40**	**87.50**	**44.80**

As shown in Table 7, when $p = 0.10$, rank-1 of SAM, RNM and SAM + RNM are 75.6%, 79.2% and 80.5%, and mAP of them are 67.6%, 73% and 74.4%, respectively. All of the scores exceed the scores with EUG. Similar results can be obtained, when compared SAM, RNM and SAM + RNM with EUG. It can be seen that, performance improvements are achieved on DukeMTMC-VideoReID dataset, whether using SAM, RNM or SAM + RNM, which demonstrates the effectiveness of our method.

As shown in Table 8, when $p = 0.10$ and 0.05, SAM, RNM and SAM + RNM are better than EUG, which demonstrates the effectiveness of our method.

Generally speaking, both SAM and RNM outperform EUG on both datasets, which demonstrates the effectiveness of SAM and RNM. Specifically, when using both SAM and RNM simultaneously, the performance of our model achieves an better performance than using SAM or RNM alone. With above experiments, we can see that, compared SAM with RNM, the latter contributes more to the network. This is because RNM acts on the process of label estimation directly, and significantly improves the accuracy of pseudo-label assignment, which reduces the proportion of erroneous samples in the model and helps to generate a robust model. SAM, on the other hand, focuses on extracting hidden features from video data and relies on models with strong discriminative power to play its role.

Table 7. Ablation Experiments on DukeMTMC-VideoReID

Methods	rank-1	rank-5	rank-20	mAP
EUG [20] ($p = 0.10$)	70.79	83.61	89.60	61.76
SAM ($p = 0.10$)	75.60	87.60	92.00	67.60
RNM ($p = 0.10$)	79.20	92.20	95.40	73.00
SAM + RNM ($p = 0.10$)	**80.50**	**92.70**	**96.20**	**74.40**
EUG [20] ($p = 0.05$)	72.79	84.18	91.45	63.23
SAM ($p = 0.05$)	77.60	89.60	94.40	69.20
RNM ($p = 0.05$)	81.20	92.70	95.60	75.40
SAM + RNM ($p = 0.05$)	**82.20**	**92.50**	**96.40**	**75.60**

Table 8. Ablation Experiments on MARS

Methods	rank-1	rank-5	rank-20	mAP
EUG [20] ($p = 0.10$)	57.62	69.64	78.08	34.68
SAM ($p = 0.10$)	60.70	74.00	81.90	41.50
RNM ($p = 0.10$)	64.80	79.50	86.90	43.20
SAM + RNM ($p = 0.10$)	**66.80**	**80.90**	**87.70**	**45.80**
EUG [20] ($p = 0.05$)	62.67	74.94	82.57	42.45
SAM ($p = 0.05$)	63.70	76.00	82.30	43.90
RNM ($p = 0.05$)	66.30	80.40	87.50	44.80
SAM + RNM ($p = 0.05$)	**67.60**	**81.20**	**88.70**	**47.90**

Comparison with Other Advanced Methods

In order to demonstrate the superiority of our method, a large number of experiments are conducted on two commonly used large datasets in this section to compare it with the current advanced one-shot video-based pedestrian Re-ID methods, including Stepwise [19], EUG [20], DGM + IDE [21], SCLU [22], LGF [23], PL [27], and BUC [28]. Among them, Baseline (one shot) [20] indicates that only the initial labeled samples are used for training, without any progressive learning methods, and Supervised [20] indicates that all labeled samples are used for training the baseline. From Table 9, it can be seen that the method SAM + RNM proposed in this paper achieves significant performance improvement compared to the Baseline (one shot) and unsupervised method BUC (only use single labeled samples for training), and also surpasses traditional semi-supervised methods such as DGM + IDE and Stepwise. Compared with some one-shot methods, including EUG, SCLU, and PL, the performance of our SAM + RNM method exceeds all above methods, which demonstrate the effectiveness of the proposed method.

In summary, the method proposed in this paper has achieved excellent performance on DukeMTMC-VideoReID and MARS datasets, which indicates that our model, with

Table 9. Comparison with Some Advance Methods on Large-Scale Datasets

Methods	MARS				DukeMTMC-VideoReID			
	rank-1	rank-5	rank-20	mAP	rank-1	rank-5	rank-20	mAP
Baseline(one-shot) [20]	36.20	50.20	61.90	15.50	39.60	56.80	67.00	33.30
Supervised [20]	80.8	92.1	96.1	63.7	83.6	94.6	97.6	78.3
Stepwise [19]	41.20	55.60	66.80	19.70	56.30	70.40	79.20	46.80
EUG($p = 0.10$) [20]	57.62	69.64	78.08	34.68	70.79	83.61	89.60	61.76
EUG($p = 0.05$) [20]	62.67	74.94	82.57	42.45	72.79	84.18	91.45	63.23
DGM + IDE [21]	36.80	54.00	68.50	16.90	42.40	57.90	69.30	33.60
SCLU($p = 0.10$) [22]	61.97	76.52	84.34	41.47	72.79	84.19	91.03	62.99
SCLU($p = 0.05$) [22]	63.74	78.44	85.51	42.74	72.79	85.04	90.31	63.15
LGF [23]	58.80	69.00	78.50	36.20	86.30	96.00	98.60	82.70
PL($p = 0.10$) [27]	57.90	70.30	79.30	34.90	71.00	83.80	90.30	61.90
PL($p = 0.05$) [27]	62.80	75.20	83.80	42.60	72.90	84.30	91.40	63.30
BUC [28]	55.10	68.30	-	29.40	74.80	86.80	-	66.70
SAM + RNM($p = 0.10$)	**66.80**	**80.90**	**87.70**	**45.80**	**80.50**	**92.70**	**96.20**	**74.40**
SAM + RNM($p = 0.05$)	**67.60**	**81.20**	**88.70**	**47.90**	**82.20**	**92.50**	**96.40**	**75.60**

SAM and RNM, can effectively improve the performance of feature extraction, reduce the mislabel in pseudo-label assignment, and enhance the robustness and discrimination.

5 Conclusion

In this paper, we focus on the problem of one-shot video-based pedestrian Re ID. To address the issue of insufficient labeled data under this one-shot settings, SAM attention module is embedded in the network to improve the ability of feature extraction and the discriminative power. In order to further improve the accuracy of label prediction, we design RNM, which can assign pseudo-labels for unlabeled samples more accurately. The excellent performance on two large-scale datasets proves that, the effectiveness of our method. But it should be noted that, although our method proposed in this paper achieves competitive performance, there are still issues with incorrect label assignment and long training time in the later stage, which require further exploration.

References

1. Liu, J., Zha, Z.J., Wu, W., et al.: Spatial-temporal correlation and topology learning for person re-identification in videos. In: Proceedings of the IEEE/CVF Conference on Computer Vision and Pattern Recognition. Piscataway: IEEE, pp. 4370–4379 (2021)

2. Zhang, Y.P., Wang, H.Y., Zhang, J., et al.: One-shot Video-based Person Re-identification Based on Neighborhood Center Iteration Strategy. J. Softw. **32**(12), 4025–4035 (2021)

3. Dai, C.C., Wang, H.Y., Ni, T.G., et al.: Person Re-Identification Based on Deep Convolutional Generative Adversarial Network and Expanded Neighbor Reranking. Comput. Res. Dev. **56**(8), 1632–1641 (2019)

4. Ni, T., Gu, X., Wang, H., et al.: Discriminative deep transfer metric learning for cross-scenario person re-identification. J. Electron. Imaging **27**(4), 043026 (2018)

5. Wang, H., Ding, Z., Zhang, J., et al.: Person reidentification by semisupervised dictionary rectification learning with retraining module. J. Electron. Imaging **27**(4), 043043 (2018)

6. Sun, X., Zheng, L.: Dissecting person re-identification from the viewpoint of viewpoint. In: Proceedings of the IEEE/CVF Conference on Computer Vision and Pattern Recognition. Piscataway: IEEE, pp. 608–617 (2019)

7. Zhang, Z., Lan, C., Zeng, W., et al.: Densely semantically aligned person re-identification. In: Proceedings of the IEEE/CVF Conference on Computer Vision and Pattern Recognition. Piscataway: IEEE, pp. 667–676 (2019)

8. Zheng, L., Yang, Y., Hauptmann, A.G.: Person re-identification: past, present and future[EB/OL]. (2016–10–10)[2022–06–11]. https://arxiv.org/pdf/1610.02984.pdf

9. Ye, M., Shen, J., Lin, G., et al.: Deep learning for person re-identification: a survey and outlook. In: IEEE Transactions on Pattern Analysis and Machine Intelligence: 1–1 (2021)

10. Navaneet, K.L., Todi, V., Babu, R.V., et al.: All for one: Frame-wise rank loss for improving video-based person re-identification. In: ICASSP 2019–2019 IEEE International Conference on Acoustics, Speech and Signal Processing (ICASSP). Piscataway: IEEE, pp. 2472–2476 (2019)

11. Yang, L., Zhang, R.Y., Li, L., et al.: Simam: A simple, parameter-free attention module for convolutional neural networks. In:International Conference on Machine Learning. New York: ICML, pp. 11863–11874 (2021)

12. Zhong, Z., Zheng, L., Cao, D., et al.: Re-ranking person re-identification with k-reciprocal encoding. In: Proceedings of the IEEE Conference on Computer Vision and Pattern Recognition. Piscataway: IEEE, pp. 1318–1327 (2017)

13. Li, S., Bak, S., Carr, P., et al.: Diversity regularized spatiotemporal attention for video-based person re-identification. In: Proceedings of the IEEE Conference on Computer Vision and Pattern Recognition. Piscataway, NJ: IEEE, pp. 369–378 (2018)

14. Hou, R., Ma, B., Chang, H., et al.: Vrstc: Occlusion-free video person re-identification. In: Proceedings of the IEEE/CVF Conference on Computer Vision and Pattern Recognition. Piscataway: IEEE, pp. 7183–7192 (2019)

15. Li, J., Wang, J., Tian, Q., et al.: Global-local temporal representations for video person re-identification. In: Proceedings of the IEEE/CVF International Conference on Computer Vision. Piscataway: IEEE, pp. 3958–3967 (2019)

16. Liu, C.T., Wu, C.W., Wang, Y.C.F., et al.: Spatially and temporally efficient non-local attention network for video-based person re-identification[EB/OL]. (2019–08–05)[2022–06–11]. https:// arxiv.org/ pdf/1908.01683. pdf

17. Eom, C., Lee, G., Lee, J., et al.: Video-based Person Re-identification with Spatial and Temporal Memory Networks. In: Proceedings of the IEEE/CVF International Conference on Computer Vision. Piscataway: IEEE, pp. 12036–12045 (2021)

18. Zhu, X., Jing, X.Y., Yang, L., et al.: Semi-supervised cross-view projection-based dictionary learning for video-based person re-identification[J]. IEEE Trans. Circuits Syst. Video Technol. **28**(10), 2599–2611 (2017)

19. Liu, Z., Wang, D., Lu, H.: Stepwise metric promotion for unsupervised video person re-identification. In: Proceedings of the IEEE International Conference on Computer Vision. Piscataway: IEEE, pp. 2429–2438 (2017)

20. Wu, Y., Lin, Y., Dong, X., et al.: Exploit the unknown gradually: one-shot video-based person re-identification by stepwise learning. In: Proceedings of the IEEE Conference on Computer Vision and Pattern Recognition. Piscataway: IEEE, pp. 5177–5186 (2018)

21. Ye, M., Li, J., Ma, A.J., et al.: Dynamic graph co-matching for unsupervised video-based person re-identification. IEEE Trans. Image Process. **28**(6), 2976–2990 (2019)

22. Yin, J., Li, B., Wan, F., et al.: A new data selection strategy for one-shot video-based person re-identification. In: 2019 IEEE International Conference on Image Processing (ICIP). Piscataway: IEEE, pp. 1227–1231 (2019)

23. Zhao, C., Zhang, Z., Yan, J., et al.: Local-global feature for video-based one-shot person re-identification. In: ICASSP 2020–2020 IEEE International Conference on Acoustics, Speech and Signal Processing (ICASSP). Piscataway: IEEE, pp. 3662–3666 (2020)

24. Liu, M., Qu, L., Nie, L., et al.: Iterative local-global collaboration learning towards one-shot video person re-identification. IEEE Trans. Image Process. **29**, 9360–9372 (2020)

25. Zheng, L., Shen, L., Tian L, et al. Scalable person re-identification: a benchmark. In: Proceedings of the IEEE international conference on computer vision. Piscataway: IEEE, pp. 1116–1124 (2015)

26. Ristani, E., Solera, F., Zou, R., et al.: Performance measures and a data set for multi-target, multi-camera tracking. In: European conference on computer vision, pp. 17–35. Springer, Berlin (2016)

27. Wu, Y., Lin, Y., Dong, X., et al.: Progressive learning for person re-identification with one example. IEEE Trans. Image Process. **28**(6), 2872–2881 (2019)

28. Lin, Y., Dong, X., Zheng, L., et al.: A bottom-up clustering approach to unsupervised person re-identification. In: Proceedings of the AAAI Conference on Artificial Intelligence. Menlo Park, CA: AAAI, 33(01), pp. 8738–8745 (2019)

Three-Dimensional Object Detection Network Based on Coordinate Attention and Overlapping Region Penalty Mechanisms

Wenxin Li[1], Shiyu Zhu[2], Hongzhi Liu[3], Pinzheng Zhang[3], and Xiaoqin Zhang[1]([✉])

[1] School of Information and Electronic Engineering (Sussex Artificial Intelligence Institute), Zhejiang Gongshang University, Hangzhou 310018, China
zhxq@zjgsu.edu.cn
[2] National Key Laboratory of Transient of Physics, Nanjing University of Science and Technology, Nanjing 210094, China
[3] School of Computer Science and Engineering, Southeast University, Nanjing 210096, China

Abstract. Three-dimensional target detection is a key technology in the fields of autonomous driving and robot control for applications such as self-driving cars and unmanned aircraft systems. In order to achieve high detection accuracy, this paper proposes a 3D target detection network with a coordinate attention training mechanism that generates voting feature points for better detection ability and an overlap region penalty mechanism that reduces false detection. In comparative experiments on public large-scale 3D datasets including the Scannet dataset and SUN-RGB-D dataset, the proposed method obtained an average detection accuracy mAP of 60.1% and 58.0% with an intersection ratio of 0.25, which demonstrates its superior effectiveness over the current main algorithms such as F-PointNet, VoxelNet and MV3D. The improved method is expected to achieve higher accuracy for 3D object detection relying only on point cloud information.

Keywords: Three-dimensional object detection · Point cloud · Hough voting · Coordinate attention training · Overlap region,VoteNet

1 Introduction

1.1 Research Background

With the development of computers and information technology in recent years, driverless vehicles, drones, virtual reality and other technologies are gradually affecting our daily lives. Google has launched Waymo, a driverless car, Baidu has launched Apollo, a driverless car driving platform, and DJI and other companies have launched drone products that enable autonomous navigation. All of the above products invariably require the use of target detection technology to achieve environment awareness. However, two-dimensional target detection methods cannot cope with complex environments, and the accuracy and stability of existing three-dimensional target detection methods still cannot support the safe and stable operation of self-driving cars and drones, etc. Therefore, it is of significance to carry out research on three-dimensional target detection algorithms.

© The Author(s), under exclusive license to Springer Nature Switzerland AG 2023
H. Lu et al. (Eds.): ACPR 2023, LNCS 14408, pp. 79–92, 2023.
https://doi.org/10.1007/978-3-031-47665-5_7

1.2 Related Research

With the successful application of deep learning techniques to tasks such as object recognition and the semantic segmentation of 2D images, and the undertaking of projects in fields such as face recognition [1] and scene segmentation [2], point cloud target detection methods based on deep learning have gradually become a hot research topic. The existing deep learning-based 3D point cloud target detection algorithms can be divided into three categories: point-based algorithms, voxel-based algorithms, and image and point cloud fusion-based algorithms.

Point-based algorithms involve the direct processing of the original point cloud data, and these algorithms preserve the original point cloud information to the maximum extent. Point-based algorithms have the characteristics of high accuracy but large computation, and are often used in scenes with a small scene space and more point cloud data. Shi S et al. [3] proposed the PointRCNN target detection algorithm. The first step of this algorithm, through the backbone network PointNet++ [4], is to semantically segment the original point cloud data, segment the target points and generate bounding boxes on these points, and the second step is to transfer the generated bounding boxes to a unified standard coordinate system by means of coordinate transformation based on many bounding boxes generated in the first step, and then remove the redundant bounding boxes by non-maximal value suppression. This algorithm has a shortage of large computational volume. Qi C R et al. [5] proposed the VoteNet target detection algorithm, which uses PointNet++ as the backbone network, extracts feature points as seed points, votes to derive the centroid of the target and generates candidate regions with reference to the idea of Hough voting, and finally generates the bounding box. The concept of voting in this algorithm fits the disorder of point clouds, but the accuracy is poor in the case of fewer point clouds.

The idea of voxel-based algorithms is to convert the disordered point cloud data into a tightly ordered voxel block, after which the point cloud can be learned using a convolutional structure. The voxel-based method has the characteristics of less computation and higher detection speed, but is lower in detection accuracy. Zhou Y [6] et al. proposed a voxel-based 3D target detection algorithm, VoxelNet, which proposes a voxel feature encoding module, which voxelizes the original point cloud and then uses the farthest point sampling within a single voxel block for feature extraction, after which a three-dimensional CNN is used to extract features for the entire voxel space. Yan Y et al. [7] proposed the SECOND target detection network in response to the fact that the presence of many empty voxel blocks in the voxelized space can cause a waste of computational resources, and this algorithm uses sparse convolution. Lang A H et al. [8] proposed a voxelization method, which only voxelizes the X and Y axes of the 3D space and the segmented space is shaped like a column, and then uses 2D convolution for sampling and learning, which has the advantages of small computation and fast detection speed, but the detection accuracy is relatively low. Shi S et al. [9] proposed the PV-RCNN target detection algorithm, which combines the advantages of voxel-based and point-based methods; the network first voxelizes the 3D space and then learns the features by fusing sparse convolution with key point sampling, after which the candidate regions are extracted by the RPN network, and then the features of key points are obtained using farthest point sampling and point set abstraction.

The idea of the target detection method based on image and point cloud fusion is to fuse the advantages of image and point cloud for target detection. Chen X et al. [10] proposed the MV3D detection method fusing three feature maps: point cloud front view, point cloud bird's eye view and RGB images, which are extracted using three network branches, respectively, and finally fused and fitted to a bounding box. Qi C R et al. [11] proposed the Frustum-PointNet target detection algorithm, which extracts candidate regions from RGB images, projects the candidate regions into the aligned 3D space to form the cone of the view point cloud candidate regions, and obtains the final target borders through 3D feature extraction and bounding box estimation. This method based on image and point cloud fusion requires aligned image and point cloud data, and the network structure is mostly complex.

1.3 Proposed Method

The above target detection algorithm has achieved certain results, but still cannot meet the needs of practical applications. Therefore, this paper retains the advantages of the voting mechanism to fit the disorderly nature of point clouds on the basis of the VoteNet detection algorithm, and improves its disadvantage of poor performance in the case of sparse point cloud data.

This paper introduces a voting feature point generation module to mine the feature information of points to generate voting feature points to improve the accuracy of voting, and proposes an overlapping region penalty mechanism to reduce the number of cases of false detection. The proposed network structure is described in the following sections from backbone network, voting feature point generation, target center prediction, overlapping region penalty mechanism and loss function. In the experimental part, the dataset and parameter setting are explained, and the ablation experiment is carried out to compare and analyze the results.

2 Network Structure

The network structure proposed in this paper is shown in Fig. 1. It can be divided into three parts: the first part is the backbone network module, the second part is the voting feature point generation module, and the third part is the target center prediction module.

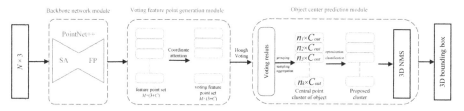

Fig. 1. Overall network structure.

The network takes $N \times 3$ raw point cloud data as input, where N represents the number of points as N and 3 indicates the dimensions of the data. The three-dimensional coordinates (X, Y, Z) of the point cloud are inputted into the backbone network to sample and learn the features of the points, extract the features of C channels from them, and output the $M \times (3 + C)$ feature set of M points. The feature set of these points generates new voting feature points with dimensions $M \times (3 + C)$ through the coordinate attention [12] mechanism. The voting feature points are voted by the Hough Voting module of the deep neural network, which independently generates ballots from each seed through the multilayer perception mechanism (MLP), expressing the centers of the objects in terms of coordinates. These voted centroids are then subjected to the operation of sampling group aggregation to generate K clusters of points representing the center of the target object, and the C_{out} is the channel numbers of the central point cluster. Then, the point cloud data in each of the previous groups are transformed by coordinates separately, reduced to the coordinate axis with its center as the origin, and then the proposed cluster of the object is derived by a PointNet-like operation. Finally, the low scoring and duplicate objects are filtered by means of Non-Maximum Suppression (NMS) in 3D to obtain the final K' 3D bounding box of the target detection results.

2.1   Backbone Network Module

The backbone network module uses a PointNet++ network structure to learn the features of points and outputs a set of M feature points. The backbone network contains four point set abstraction (SA) layers and two feature up-sampling (FP) layers. The backbone network module consists of four point SA layers as the encoding part, and the SA layers transform the point cloud features using MLP and randomly sample the original point cloud with n points sampled at the farthest point. Each SA layer is composed of $(n, r, [c_1, ..., c_k])$ set parameters, where n is the number of sampling points, r is the radius of the sampling area, and $[c_1, ..., c_k]$ is the number of MLP channels. The decoding part of the backbone network consists of two FP layers. The FP layer upsamples the point cloud by inserting the features of the input points into the output points, and the features of each output point are the weighted average of the features of its three nearest input points, after which the features are connected by MLP.

2.2   Voting Feature Point Generation Module

After the features of the points are generated by the backbone network, the voting feature points are then generated by the voting feature point generation module. This module mainly consists of a coordinate attention mechanism, where the input is the features of the points generated by the backbone network and the output is the voting feature points for the subsequent voting operation, where the attention mechanism is added to help the model to assign a different weight to each of the channels and further aid in feature extraction by assigning different weights. This module can improve the shortcomings of the original VoteNet in the case of low point cloud data and can improve the performance of the network.

The structure of the coordinate attention mechanism is shown in Fig. 2. The first layer of this attention mechanism consists of two average pooling modules to encode each channel along the horizontal coordinate and the vertical coordinate, respectively, so that the location information and global features of the points could be captured. And then

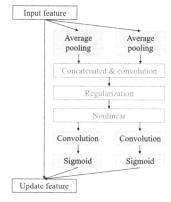

Fig. 2. Coordinate attention mechanism network structure.

the location information and global features are stitched together and passed through a convolutional layer, followed by regularization and a nonlinear layer. The nonlinear layer is the h-swish activation function, and after the features are split and passed through the convolutional layer and the Sigmoid activation function, respectively, the features are finally updated by multiplying the original input feature by the two weights, and the voting feature points are output, and the voting feature points are shown as red dots in Fig. 3.

Fig. 3. Voting feature points.

2.3 Target Center Prediction Module

In the target center prediction module, voting is performed based on the voting feature points, and then the voting target center points are sampled, grouped, and clustered to obtain a set of points as the target center point cluster, and the clustering method is based on the spatial similarity of uniform sampling and grouping, in which K subsets of the voting set are selected using the farthest point sampling method. Then, the neighboring points are aggregated by the K nearest neighbor algorithm to form the target center point cluster. As shown in Fig. 4, the green points are the points obtained by voting, and the red points are the target centroid clusters obtained after sampling, grouping and aggregation. Then, we generate the candidate regions and generate the bounding boxes through the optimization classification, and finally, we obtain the final target 3D bounding boxes through the 3D NMS.

Fig. 4. Target center cluster obtained by voting.

2.4   Overlapping Region Penalty Mechanism

In the prediction information generated for a sample scene, the predicted borders produce overlapping results in different objects. The overlap between some objects can be considered reasonable due to the characteristics of their appearance. However, the overlap between objects of the same type is largely absent in the dataset and in reality. Therefore, to address this property and the common phenomenon of overlapping prediction borders in the prediction results, this paper proposes a penalty mechanism for overlapping regions.

The volume calculation of the overlapping region is based on the determination and calculation of the estimated coordinates of the given borders between similar objects. As shown in Fig. 5a, objects that obtain the same classification prediction in the same scene are sampled to obtain the two vertexes on the diagonal of the body in its predicted border and the geometric center of the border. The two objects *P1* and *P2* in red and blue color in Fig. 5a are the prediction boxes of two samples in the same classification. *Px_Max* and *Px_Min* are the two points on the diagonal of the box body with the largest and smallest 3D coordinate values, and *Px_Cen* is the center of the box. The two vertexes on the diagonal of the body contain both the position and dimensional information of the whole rectangular prediction frame. According to the relative positions of the computed geometric centers *P1_Cen* and *P2_Cen* in Fig. 5b, whether two predicted bounding boxes overlap can be judged by the 3D size of the bounding box. If overlapped, in Fig. 5c and Fig. 5d, the two vertexes in the body diagonals of the overlapping region box in green color can be selected from the two original predicted bounding boxes. Which *Op_Max* and *Op_Min* used to be the vertexes of the predicted largest and smallest 3D coordinate values and also the reference points for calculating the overlapping area of the two original predicted bounding boxes.

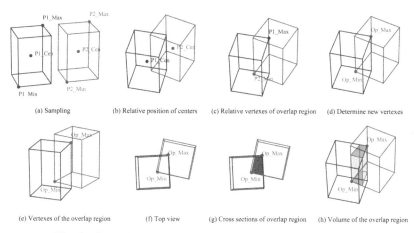

Fig. 5. Illustration of penalty mechanism for overlapping regions.

Based on obtaining the body diagonal vertexes $Op\_Max(x_1, y_1, z_1)$ and $Op\_Min(x_2, y_2, z_2)$ of the borders of the overlapping region in Fig. 5e, the area of the overlapping cross section in the top view of Fig. 5f can be calculated as A_{cs} which represents the green area in Fig. 5g. Because the boundary box in the dataset only has yaw angle but no pitch and roll angle data, the predicted overlap region should be the upright quadrilateral or cuboid. The volume of the overlapping region of similar objects in the scene in Fig. 5h is accumulated for the loss of the overlapping region penalty term in formula 1.

$$L_{overlap} = \sum |A_{cs} \times (z_1 - z_2)| \tag{1}$$

2.5 Loss Function

The loss function of the network is weighted by five components, which include voting loss, target loss, 3D edge loss, semantic classification loss, and overlapping region loss.

$$L = L_{vote} + \lambda_1 L_{obj-cls} + \lambda_2 L_{box} + \lambda_3 L_{sem-cls} + \lambda_4 L_{overlap} \tag{2}$$

The voting loss L_{vote} calculates the error between the voted feature points and the true value, by calculating the distance between the voting feature points that need to be voted and the true target centroid. The target loss $L_{obj-cls}$ is calculated as the error between the centroid of the target derived from voting and the true value, and is a cross-entropy loss function with the value of parameter λ_1 set to 0.5.

$$L_{box} = L_{center-reg} + 0.1 L_{angle-cls} + L_{angle-reg} + 0.1 L_{size-cls} + L_{size-reg} \tag{3}$$

The calculation method of border loss L_{box} is shown in formula 3. $L_{center-reg}$ is the residual between the observed and true values of the border center point. $L_{angle-cls}$ and $L_{angle-reg}$ are the angular error of the border. $L_{size-cls}$ and $L_{size-reg}$ are the position error of the eight corners of the border box cumulatively. The residual of the border center point is derived by calculating the Euclidean distance between the observed and true values, and the position error of the border box is derived by calculating the distance between each corner of the predicted border box and each corner of the true border box, and the value of parameter λ_2 is set to 1. The semantic classification loss $L_{sem-cls}$ is calculated by cross-entropy between the predicted classification information and the true value, and the value of parameter λ_3 is set to 0.1. The overlap region loss $L_{overlap}$ reduces the probability of border offset by calculating the size of the overlap region between the predicted border and the true border, and the value of parameter λ_4 is set to 0.1.

3   Experiment

This section introduces the experimental dataset, training parameter settings, evaluation metrics, experimental data, ablation experiments and visualization results analysis. The point cloud target detection method proposed in this paper is compared with other methods, and the impact of the voting feature point generation module and the overlapping region penalty mechanism proposed in this paper on the algorithm is demonstrated through ablation experiments. Finally, the performance of the algorithm proposed in this paper is analyzed concretely through visualization results.

3.1   Dataset

In this paper, we used the publicly available dataset ScanNet dataset [13] with the SUN-RGBD [14] dataset for experiments.

ScanNet. A point cloud dataset of indoor scenes reconstructed using RGB-D video, and the dataset contains 1513 frames of point cloud data. The indoor scenes of the ScanNet dataset are large in space, and the number of targets in a scene is large. In the experiments, the dataset is processed in the same way as VoteNet, with 1201 frames of the ScanNet dataset as the training set and 312 frames of the dataset as the test set.

SUN RGB-D. A single-view 3D scene dataset. The dataset contains more than 10000 RGB-D depth images, and the depth maps are converted into point cloud data before formal training. In the experiment, the train set contains 5282 samples and the test set contains 5050 samples.

3.2   Training Parameter Setting

The hardware configuration was: Ubuntu 16.04 operating system, the GPU model was Tesla V100, the GPU acceleration tool was CUDA 10.2, and the deep learning framework was Pytorch1.7. The training parameters were set as follows: the optimizer was Adam, the batch size was 4, the training epoch was 200, the initial learning rate was 0.001, and the learning rate decayed to 0.1 times the original after the number of training epochs reached 80, 120, and 160, the regularization decay ratio was 0.5, and the regularization decay was 0.5 every 20 training epochs.

3.3 Evaluation Metrics

Compared with semantic classification and recognition, evaluating the accuracy of 3D border prediction is more challenging as it requires calculating the overlap between the predicted result and the actual label, which is affected by different poses and sizes. To be able to accurately evaluate the accuracy of object detection, the evaluation metrics used in this paper were the average precision (AP) of the borders of each classified target object, and the mean average precision (mAP) of all classified targets. Firstly, the intersection over union (IoU) ratio between the predicted edge and the actual edge is calculated, and the accuracy of the predicted edge is judged according to the size of the intersection over union ratio. In order to accurately reflect the performance of the proposed algorithm, the evaluation indexes chosen in this paper are consistent with those of VoteNet, and the accuracy thresholds of 0.25 and 0.5 are calculated, respectively.

3.4 Experimental Data

Table 1 shows the detection accuracy performance of the proposed algorithm based on the publicly available dataset ScanNet and compares it with other representative and well-performing algorithms. Both the DSS (deep sliding shapes) [15] and 3D-SIS [16] algorithms fuse the features of RGB images and point clouds. DSS is a fusion of RGB image feature information with point cloud features in the output part, and 3D-SIS uses CNN to extract the features of the image and map the image features to the voxels in 3D. F-PointNet [11] is a two-stage detection network that uses a two-dimensional target detection algorithm to obtain a two-dimensional bounding box on the image, and then projects it into a three-dimensional point cloud to finally obtain a three-dimensional bounding box using a three-dimensional target detection network. MRCNN2D-3D [15, 16] uses Mask-RCNN [17] as an image instance segmentation network, projects the instance segmentation results into 3D space, and fuses them with the 3D instance segmentation results to obtain the target object borders. GSPN [18] uses parsing synthesis method to generate candidate regions and compared to the traditional methods of generating candidate regions, GSPN has superior performance.

Table 1. Performance of different methods on ScanNet dataset.

Method	mAP@0.25	mAP@0.5
DSS	15.2	6.8
MRCNN2D-3D	17.3	10.5
F-PointNet	19.8	10.8
GSPN	30.6	17.7
3D-SIS	40.2	22.5
VoteNet	58.6	33.5
Ours	**60.1**	**36.4**

Table 2a. Performance on various types of targets in the ScanNet dataset mAP@0.25.

	cab	bed	chair	sofa	tabl	door	wind	bkshf	curt	pic
Votenet	36.3	87.9	**88.7**	89.6	58.8	47.3	38.1	44.6	47.2	**7.8**
Ours	**38.3**	**89.5**	87.5	**90.5**	**58.8**	**48.1**	**42.4**	**49.6**	**49.1**	6.7

Table 2b. Performance on various types of targets in the ScanNet dataset mAP@0.25.

	cntr	desk	fridg	showr	toil	sink	bath	ofurn	mAP
Votenet	56.1	71.7	45.4	57.1	94.9	**54.7**	**92.1**	37.2	58.7
Ours	**57.9**	**72.3**	**48.7**	**62.1**	**96.4**	49.5	91.2	**43.3**	**60.1**

Table 3a. Performance on various types of targets in the ScanNet dataset mAP@0.5.

	cab	bed	chair	sofa	tabl	door	wind	bkshf	curt	pic
Votenet	8.1	76.1	67.2	68.8	42.4	15.3	6.4	28.0	11.6	**1.2**
Ours	**9.6**	**80.6**	**77.5**	**72.2**	**46.4**	**16.7**	**12.3**	**32.8**	**12.0**	0.8

Table 3b. Performance on various types of targets in the ScanNet dataset mAP@0.5.

	cntr	desk	fridg	showr	toil	sink	bath	ofurn	mAP
Votenet	9.5	**37.5**	27.8	10.0	**86.5**	16.8	78.9	11.7	33.5
Ours	**18.2**	36.8	**30.5**	**16.2**	73.8	**25.3**	**82.7**	**18.6**	**36.4**

The average accuracy based on the ScanNet dataset is shown in the table above. The first column is the name of the algorithm compared, the second column is the average accuracy when the IoU ratio is set to 0.25, and the third column is the average accuracy when the IoU is set to 0.5. From the data, we can see that the proposed method performs best when the intersection ratio is set to 0.25 and 0.5. Compared with VoteNet, the average accuracy is improved by 1.5% when the intersection ratio is set to 0.25 and 2.9% when the intersection ratio is set to 0.5, which indicates that the proposed algorithm is more accurate than VoteNet on average.

The proposed method outperforms other methods in terms of average accuracy, and the paper also focuses on the performance regarding various targets in the ScanNet dataset. The data in Table 2a and 2b are the accuracies when the intersection ratio is set to 0.25, and the data in Table 3a and 3b are the accuracies when the intersection ratio is set to 0.5. The proposed method maintains or improves the high accuracy of the VoteNet for categories such as bed, chair, sofa, and bathtub. This is attributed to the coordinate attention and overlapping region penalty mechanisms that mainly enhance these categories. However, categories with low accuracy, such as cabinet and picture, still perform poorly due to their far location in the scene, sparse point cloud data, and indistinct features. From the four tables, it is easy to see that the detection accuracy of proposed method is higher than that of VoteNet on most of the targets.

Table 4. Accuracy performance on SUN-RGBD dataset mAP@0.25.

	bathtub	bed	bkshf	chair	desk	dresser	nstnd	sofa	table	toilet	mAP
Votenet	74.4	83.0	28.8	**75.3**	22.0	**29.8**	**62.2**	64.0	47.3	90.1	57.7
Ours	**75.5**	**83.2**	**29.3**	74.8	**22.7**	27.4	62.0	**66.5**	**48.0**	**90.5**	**58.0**

Table 4 shows the detection accuracy of the proposed algorithm based on the SUN-RGBD dataset, as shown in Table 4; the proposed algorithm has 0.3% higher average accuracy compared with VoteNet, and the detection accuracy is higher for target objects including bathtubs, beds, bookcases, desks, sofas, tables and toilets, with the detection accuracy of sofas being improved by 2.5%. However, the detection accuracy for chairs, cupboards and bedside tables is slightly lower than that of VoteNet.

Combining the two datasets, the recognition accuracy of some categories of objects decreases or remains at a low level. The reason may be that the network improvement proposed in this paper, is before the 3D Hough voting. In the stage of generating voting feature points, if the point cloud data of the target is missing due to light, occlusion and other factors, the local point cloud data will be missing, which will cause the generated voting feature points to shift, and eventually lead to inaccurate voting and prediction results.

3.5 Ablation Experiment

In order to test the effects of the proposed voting feature point generation module and the overlapping region penalty mechanism on the network, ablation experiments are performed on the ScanNet dataset in this paper.

Table 5. Ablation experiment data.

Voting Feature Point Generation Module	Overlapping Region Penalty Mechanism	mAP@0.25	mAP@0.5
×	×	58.6	33.5
√	×	59.7	35.4
×	√	58.6	36.0
√	√	**60.1**	**36.4**

The ablation experimental data are shown in Table 5. The voting feature point generation module improves the model performance when the intersection ratio is set to 0.25, and the overlap region penalty mechanism improves the model performance when the intersection ratio is 0.5. The proposed method in this paper uses both of them, and the network performance achieves further improvement.

3.6 Visualization Results Analysis

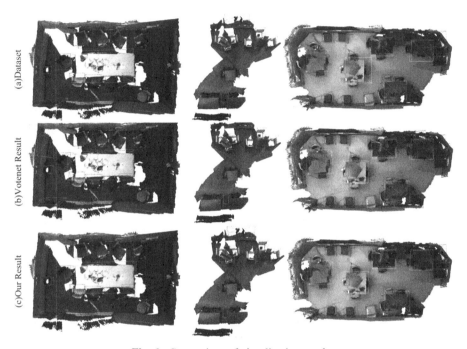

Fig. 6. Comparison of visualization results.

In order to more intuitively show the performance of the network model proposed in this paper for semantic classification, center prediction, and edge prediction of objects in scenes, the same scenes are visualized in this paper in terms of dataset labels, VoteNet model prediction results, and model prediction results in this paper. As shown in Fig. 6, the first row is the standard bounding box on the dataset, the second row is the visualization of the detection results of VoteNet, and the third row is the visualization of the detection results of the algorithm proposed in this paper. The three rows are three different scenes. In the first row of scenes, VoteNet has false detection in both the upper and lower right of the scene; in the second row of scenes, VoteNet fails to detect the target in the left side of the scene; and in the third row of scenes, the algorithm proposed in this paper and VoteNet both have false detection in the more complicated case in the lower right. Overall, the performance of the network model in this paper is relatively good in classifying and predicting the size of sofas, tables, chairs, garbage bins, doors and other objects, and the overlapping of the prediction frames of similar adjacent objects has been reduced, which proves that the voting feature point generation module and the overlapping region penalty mechanism play a certain role, providing a certain improvement in its performance compared with that of VoteNet. However, in the case of tightly arranged targets and the detection of small targets, there are cases of false detections and omissions in this paper, and there is still room for improvement.

4 Conclusion

This paper proposes a voting feature point generation module to mine the feature information of points to generate voting feature points to improve the accuracy of voting, and an overlap region penalty mechanism to reduce the number of cases of false detection. After comparison experiments and ablation experiments, the proposed method showed good performance on both the ScanNet dataset and SUN RGB-D dataset. The experimental data on ScanNet and SUN RGB-D dataset show that the proposed method achieves better performance than VoteNet. However, in some complex cases, there are cases of false detection and missed detection, and there is still room for improvement. The proposed method is an improvement on the famous method, i.e. VoteNet, and improves the accuracy. In the future, this improvement can be considered and applied in some more advanced algorithms and higher performance backbone network, add the comparison experiments with other methods to provide reference for the improvement of the method.

Acknowledgments. The research was supported by the Zhejiang Provincial Natural Science Foundation of China (Grant No. LQ21A040007), and Scientific Research Fund of Zhejiang Provincial Education Department (Grant No. Y201941856).

References

1. Ss, A., Svavp, B.: Techniques and challenges of face recognition: a critical review. Procedia Comput. Sci. **143**, 536–543 (2018)
2. Yu, H., Yang, Z., Tan, L., et al.: Methods and datasets on semantic segmentation: a review. Neurocomputing **304**, 82–103 (2018)
3. Shi, S., Wang, X., Li, H.: Pointrcnn: 3d object proposal generation and detection from point cloud. In: Proceedings of the IEEE/CVF Conference on Computer Vision and Pattern Recognition, pp. 770–779 (2019)
4. Qi, C.R., Yi, L., Su, H., et al.: Pointnet++: deep hierarchical feature learning on point sets in a metric space. In: Advances in Neural Information Processing Systems, 30 (2017)
5. Qi, C.R., Litany, O., He, K., et al.: Deep hough voting for 3d object detection in point clouds. In: Proceedings of the IEEE/CVF International Conference on Computer Vision, pp. 9277–9286 (2019)
6. Zhou, Y., Tuzel, O.: Voxelnet: end-to-end learning for point cloud based 3d object detection. In: Proceedings of the IEEE Conference on Computer Vision and Pattern Recognition, pp. 4490–4499 (2018)
7. Yan, Y., Mao, Y., Li, B.: Second: sparsely embedded convolutional detection. Sensors **18**(10), 3337 (2018)
8. Lang, A.H., Vora, S., Caesar, H., et al.: Pointpillars: fast encoders for object detection from point clouds. In: Proceedings of the IEEE/CVF Conference on Computer Vision and Pattern Recognition, pp. 12697–12705 (2019)

9. Shi, S., Guo, C., Jiang, L., et al.: Pv-rcnn: point-voxel feature set abstraction for 3d object detection. In: Proceedings of the IEEE/CVF Conference on Computer Vision and Pattern Recognition, pp. 10529–10538 (2020)

10. Chen, X., Ma, H., Wan, J., et al.: Multi-view 3d object detection network for autonomous driving. In: Proceedings of the IEEE conference on Computer Vision and Pattern Recognition, pp. 1907–1915 (2017)

11. Qi, C.R., Liu, W., Wu, C., et al.: Frustum pointnets for 3d object detection from rgb-d data. In: Proceedings of the IEEE Conference on Computer Vision and Pattern Recognition, pp. 918–927 (2018)

12. Hou, Q., Zhou, D., Feng, J.: Coordinate attention for efficient mobile network design. In: Proceedings of the IEEE/CVF Conference on Computer Vision and Pattern Recognition, pp. 13713–13722 (2021)

13. Dai, A., Chang, A.X., Savva, M., et al.: Scannet: Richly-annotated 3d reconstructions of indoor scenes. In: Proceedings of the IEEE Conference on Computer Vision and Pattern Recognition, pp. 5828–5839 (2017)

14. Song, S., Lichtenberg, S.P., Xiao, J.: Sun rgb-d: A rgb-d scene understanding benchmark suite. In: Proceedings of the IEEE Conference on Computer Vision and Pattern Recognition, pp. 567–576 (2015)

15. Song, S., Xiao, J.: Deep sliding shapes for amodal 3d object detection in rgb-d images. In: Proceedings of the IEEE Conference on Computer Vision and Pattern Recognition, pp. 808–816 (2016)

16. Hou, J., Dai, A., Nießner, M.: 3d-sis: 3d semantic instance segmentation of rgb-d scans. In: Proceedings of the IEEE/CVF Conference on Computer Vision and Pattern Recognition, pp. 4421–4430 (2019)

17. He, K., Gkioxari, G., Dollár, P., et al.: Mask r-cnn. In: Proceedings of the IEEE International Conference on Computer Vision, pp. 2961–2969 (2017)

18. Yi, L., Zhao, W., Wang, H., et al.: Gspn: generative shape proposal network for 3d instance segmentation in point cloud. In: Proceedings of the IEEE/CVF Conference on Computer Vision and Pattern Recognition, pp. 3947–3956

Discriminative Region Enhancing and Suppression Network for Fine-Grained Visual Categorization

Guanhua Wu📶, Cheng Pang$^{(\boxtimes)}$📶, Rushi Lan📶, Yilin Zhang, and Pingping Zhou

Guilin University of Electronic Technology, Guilin 541004, China
pangcheng3@guet.edu.cn

Abstract. Attention mechanisms are intensively devoted to local feature abstraction for fine-grained visual categorization. A limitation of attention-based methods is that they focus on salient region mining and feature extraction, while ignoring the ability to incorporate discriminative and complementary features from other parts of the image. In order to address this issue, we introduce a novel network known as the Discriminative Region Enhancing and Suppression Network (DRESNet). This network efficiently extracts a wide range of diverse and complementary features, thereby enhancing the final representation. Specifically, a plug-and-play salient region diffusion (SRD) module is proposed to explicitly enhances the salient features extracted by any backbone network. The SRD module can adaptively adjust the weights of regions and redirect attention to other non-discriminative regions to generate different complementary features. The proposed discriminative region enhancing and suppression network is free from bounding boxes or part annotations and can be trained end-to-end. Our proposed method demonstrates competitive performance on three fine-grained classification benchmark datasets, as supported by extensive experimental results. Additionally, it is compatible with widely used frameworks currently in use.

Keywords: Fine-grained Visual Categorization · Attention mechanism · Region enhancing and suppression

1 Introduction

Fine-grained visual categorization (FGVC) has garnered growing research interest [2–4] in recent years, driven by its promising applications in diverse real-world scenarios such as intelligent retail [24], intelligent transportation [11], and conservation [1]. FGVC aims to recognizing images belonging to multiple sub-categories within the same category, e.g., different species of birds [23], models of cars [13] and aircrafts [18]. As different subcategory objects share a similar physical structure (i.e., all kinds of birds have a head, wings, and a tail), and could be only be distinguished by subtle local regions, as shown in Fig. 1. Due to

Fig. 1. Samples belonging to the same sub-category share a similar physical structure (i.e., all kinds of birds have a head, wings, and a tail) and appearance, making it infeasible to visually distinguish between them.

low inter-class variances, it further increases the difficulty of fine-grained image classification.

To extract discriminative features for classification, a key process is to focus on the feature representations of different parts of the object. Some previous works [14,25,29,31] rely mainly on predefined bounding boxes and part annotations to locate the distinguishable regions, and then extract part-specific features for fine-grained classification. However, these hand-craft annotations are not optimal for FGVC, the collection of which can be very costly. In recent years, weakly supervised learning using labels in image-level has become the mainstream method for FGVC. Some recent methods [7,22,26,33] attempt to locate the distinguishable regions and learn effective feature representations using attention mechanisms, channel clustering, and other techniques, without requiring bounding box/part annotations. Although these methods are effective, there are still potential limitations: 1) attention-based networks tend to focus on globally salient features while ignore other local discriminative features which potentially carry complementary information for the salient ones; 2) part-based sampling methods are easily affected by the number and size of the sampled parts. These pre-defined parameters greatly limit the effectiveness and flexibility of the model. Therefore, how to effectively extract diverse salient features and how to integrate reasonably these features into the final representation are worthy of discussion for the fine-grained classification task.

In this paper, we propose a discriminative region enhancing and suppression network (DRESNet) to address the above limitations by generating a set of integral fine-grained features including the globally salient features and their complementary features. More specifically, DRESNet does not focus on how to capture accurate distinguishable parts, but enhances and suppresses the salient parts in the feature map in an adaptive way and then forces the following network to mine other discriminative regions containing potentially complementary features. Some observations show that the most salient region of an image is tend to be noticed by the attention models in the first time, then the feature abstraction of this region is enhanced while that of other regions is suppressed. As a result, visual cues from suppressed features may be absent in the learned features. However, a set of integral features consisting of both globally salient features and other local features are crucial for FGVC tasks [6,9].

The proposed DRESNet consists of a feature extraction backbone network and a salient region diffusion (SRD) module. By inserting salient region diffusion module into various stages of the backbone network, it efficiently extracts various potential features. SRD module enhances and suppresses features to obtain part-specific representations. Note that, in the suppression operation, SRD module does not require additional complex hyperparameters to suppress salient regions information. Instead, it effectively expands the discriminative region through a learnable way (suppress excessive feature expression of salient regions while encourage feature expression from adjacent non-salient regions). We demonstrate hat the feature learning of the backbone networks could be substantially improved in this way.

Our contributions are summarized as follows: (1) We propose a salient region diffusion (SRD) module, which enhances the prominent features of the network. Additionally, through an adaptive learning-based suppression process, SRD can compel the network to learn more complementary features. (2) Our proposed region enhancing and suppression network (DRESNet) achieves competitive results on three benchmark fine-grained classification datasets.

2   Related Work

Fine-grained visual categorization (FGVC) aims to identify visually similar subcategories within the same basic category, e.g., different species of birds [23], models of cars [13] and aircraft [18]. Currently, research on weakly supervised fine-grained visual categorization methods mainly focuses on three aspects: fine-grained feature learning, discriminative region localization, and visual attention mechanisms.

2.1   Fine-Grained Feature Learning

In order to more accurately describe the subtle differences between fine-grained categories, Lin et al. [15] proposed a bilinear model consisting of two feature extractors. This model adopts a translation-invariant approach to extract features from different parts of the image and fuse them, thereby enhancing the ability to learn fine-grained features. However, the use of bilinear features generated by the outer product results in extremely high dimensions, which increases the computational complexity. To address this issue, Gao et al. [8] attempted to approximate the second-order statistics of the original bilinear pooling operation by applying Tensor Sketch to reduce the dimensionality of bilinear features. Kong et al. [12] used a low-rank approximation for the covariance matrix and further learned low-rank bilinear classifiers, which significantly reduced the computation time and effective number of parameters. In addition, Yu et al. [27] proposed a cross-layer bilinear pooling method to integrate multiple cross-layer bilinear features and capture part relationships in the features from inter layers.

2.2 Discriminative Region Localization

Localization-based methods capture discriminative semantic parts of fine-grained objects and then construct intermediate representations corresponding to these parts for final classification. Fu et al. [7] proposed a recurrent attention convolutional neural network, which recursively learns discriminative regions region-based feature representation at multiple scales in a mutually reinforced way. Yang et al. [26] utilized self-supervision attention mechanism to effectively locate regions in images that contain more semantic features. In [34], a part proposal network generates multiple local attention maps and s part rectification network learns rich part-specific features. Zhang et al. [28] proposed a multi-scale learning network, which predicts the position of objects and local regions information through the attention object location module and attention part proposal module.

2.3 Visual Attention Mechanisms

In fine-grained image classification tasks, introducing visual attention mechanisms helps to capture subtle inter-class differences in the image. Ding et al. [6] proposed a selective sparse sampling learning method that learns a set of sparse attention for obtaining discriminative and complementary regions. Similar to [6], TASN [33] regards the regions with high responses in the attention map as informative parts, and proposes a trilinear attention sampling network to learn fine-grained feature representations. Through attention-based samplers, TASN can re-sample the focused regions in the image to emphasize fine-grained details. Sun et al. [22] proposed a one-squeeze multi-excitation module to extract features from multiple attention regions and proposed a multi-attention multi-class constraint to enhance the correlation of attention features. Zhang et al. [30] introduced a progressively enhancing strategy by highlighting important regions through class activation maps.

3   Method

In visual attention models, we observe that the learning of features in salient regions may hinder its further feature abstraction in non-salient regions. As

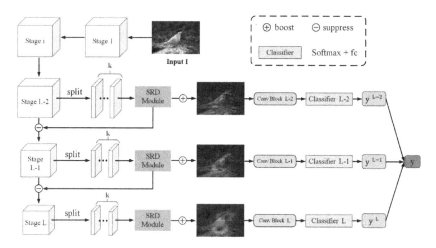

Fig. 2. Overview of the discriminative region enhancing and suppression network (DRESNet). Any backbone networks can be used coupled with the proposed salient region diffusion (SRD) module, for further mining complementary features for FGVC. The Conv Block consists of two convolutional layers followed by a max-pooling layer. $\oplus$ represents boosting feature and $\ominus$ represents suppressing feature.

a result, the complementary information and discriminative cues being beneficial to FGVC are eliminated. To tackle this issue, we present discriminative region enhancing and suppression network (DRESNet) that mine diverse potential useful features that be masked by the other salient features stage-by-stage, and each stage integrates different feature embedding for the last discriminative fine-grained representation. In addition, it can be easily implemented on various convolutional neural networks, such as VGG [21] and ResNet [10]. The DRESNet network structure, illustrated in Fig. 2.

3.1 Salient Region Diffusion Module

The method base on attention model tends to highlight the most distinct feature regions. However, such mechanism hurts the further exploration of the rich information from other regions in an image. Thus, we propose a simple yet effective salient region diffusion (SRD) module to encourage the diffusion of the attention from salient regions to more other regions, obtaining discriminative and complementary features.

As illustrated in Fig. 3, suppose $X \in R^{C \times W \times H}$ is the feature map of an image extracted from backbone network, where C, W, and H indicate the number of channels, width, and height of the feature map, respectively. In the enhancing step, SRD module simply splits X evenly into k vertical groups along the width dimension. This clearly indicates that the feature map will be composed of these k multiple local features, where each group is represented as $X_i \in R^{C \times (W/k) \times H}, i = [1, 2, ..., k]$. Then, the importance of each group is cal-

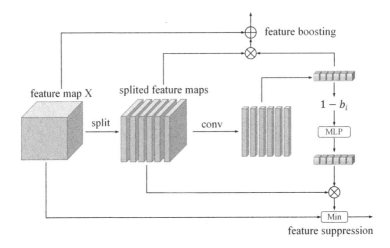

Fig. 3. The proposed Salient Region Diffusion (SRD) module diffuses the visual attention from salient region to more other region in an image, obtaining discriminative and complementary features. The SRD module explicitly divides the feature map into multiple groups along the width dimension, facilitating the extraction of corresponding enhancement and suppression factors.

culated using a convolutional layer (Conv) followed by a Rectified Linear Unit (ReLU) operation.

$$e_i = ReLU(Conv(X_i)) \tag{1}$$

where $e_i = [e_1, e_2, ..., e_k] \in R^{(1 \times (W/k) \times H)}$ denotes the spatial attention score of the i-th group of feature in X. $Conv$ is a 1×1 kernel sized convolutional layer, where the output channel is set to 1. This configuration enables us to study the importance of the corresponding area. ReLU is applied to remove negative activation values. Afterwards, we apply the global average pooling (GAP) operation to e_i, followed by the application of the softmax function to map the resulting values to the range $[0, 1]$ for normalization:

$$b_i = \frac{exp(GAP(e_i))}{\sum_{j=1}^{k} exp(e_j)} \tag{2}$$

$B = [b_1, b_2, ..., b_k] \in R$ represents the importance of the region. For input feature map X, we obtain enhanced feature F_e by enhancing its most salient part.

$$F_e = X + B \otimes X \tag{3}$$

where $\otimes$ denotes element-wise multiplication. F_e represents the enhanced features obtained through the enhanced steps of the SRD module in different network output stages.

$$F_p = Conv\_Block(F_e) \tag{4}$$

Here $Conv\_Block$ represents the combination of two convolution layers and a global average pooling. The F_p is then fed into the classifier for prediction, obtaining the class probability of the input image.

SRD module suppresses the most salient features to extract complementary attention features. More specifically, in the suppression operation, we do not set a fixed hyperparameter as the upper bound of x and regard it as a starting point to be suppressed. We believe that the larger the value in the enhancement factor b_i, the more important the corresponding group feature is, and the greater the degree of suppression of this feature. Using the learning ability of the fully connected layer, SRD module adaptively suppresses discriminative regions. Formally, the output of the learnable suppression factor is:

$$s_i = \sigma(MLP(1 - b_i)) \tag{5}$$

$S = [s_1, s_2, ..., s_k]$ represents the suppression factor of group i features. The SRD module can improve the learning ability of the network with the help of the non-linear mapping and powerful fitting ability of multilayer perceptron (MLP). σ is the sigmoid function that can normalizes the suppression factor. Since the parameters in MLP are trained with the classification target, the learnable SRD module can adaptively suppress the discriminative region without greatly impairing its extraction ability.

Finally, we obtain the suppressed feature X_s by calculating the minimum value between the original feature X and $S \otimes X$. The suppressed feature X_s is then passed to the following network to obtain other salient features.

$$X_s = Min(X, S \otimes X) \tag{6}$$

Min denotes the application of element-wise minimum operation on X and $S \otimes X$ to suppress the discriminative region.

3.2 Loss Function

Our framework is illustrated in Fig. 2. Based on single branch DRESNet, we can extract multiple complementary discriminative features from multiple stages of the network. In this paper, we use ResNet50 as a feature extractor, which has S stages (i.e., $L = 5$). With the increase of the number of layers, the features extracted by ResNet50 can more abstract and represent higher level semantic information. In DRESNet, our goal is to optimize the feature representation in the s-th stage. To this end, the SRD module is inserted into the last three stages of ResNet50. The part-specific representation F_p corresponding to different stagescan be obtained from Eq. (4). During the training phase, the classification loss for the last three stages (i.e., $i = L - 2, L - 1, L$) of DRESNet can be formulated as follows:

$$L_i = -y^T \log(y_i), y_i = classifier_i(F_i) \tag{7}$$

where y is the ground-truth label corresponding to the input image. $y_i \in R^C$ represents the predicted probability of the i-th stage, where C is the number of classes. Therefore, The overall optimization objective of DRESNet during the training phase is:

$$L_{total} = \sum_{i=1}^{T} L_i \qquad (8)$$

Where $T = 3$ represents the number of salient features enhanced by the SRD module in the last three stages of the network. During inference, we calculate the sum of prediction scores for all enhanced part-specific features to obtain the final prediction result.

4   Experiments

4.1   Dataset and Implementation Details

We conducted experiments on three benchmarked datasets for fine-grained classification, including CUB-200-2011 [23], Stanford Cars [13], and FGVC-Aircraft [18]. Table 1 provides detailed statistical data on the number of categories and the standard train-test split. In this paper, we evaluate categorization performance using Top-1 accuracy as the metric.

Table 1. The statistics information of the three widely used Fine-Grained Visual Categorization datasets.

Dataset	Category	Train	Test
CUB-200-2011 [23]	200	5994	5974
FGVC-Aircraft [18]	100	6667	3333
Stanford Cars [13]	196	8144	8041

For all experiments, we utilized pre-trained VGG16 [21] and ResNet50 [10] models on ImageNet [5] as backbone networks for feature extraction from input images. Then, SRD module is inserted into the last three output feature of ResNet50's $res3\_4$, $res4\_6$ and $res5\_3$ (VGG16's $relu3\_3$, $relu4\_3$ and $relu5\_3$). To ensure fair comparison, we maintained the same resolution as other methods. During the training phase, the input image was resized to a fixed size of 550×550 and subsequently randomly cropped to 448×448, accompanied by random horizontal flipping. During the testing stage, the input image was resized to 550×550 and cropped from the center to 448×448. According to the standards in the literature, we set up stochastic gradient descent (SGD) optimizer with a momentum of 0.9 and weight decay of $1e^{-5}$ to optimize the training process. The model trained for 200 epochs, with the learning rate of the backbone initialized at 0.0002 and the other newly added layers set to 0.002. During training, the learning rate was adjusted using the cosine annealing strategy [16]. The batch size is 16. Our model was implemented in Pytorch and trained end-to-end on a single GTX 2080Ti GPU, without any bounding box or part annotation.

4.2   Experimental Results

We compared the proposed DRESNet with state-of-the-art methods on three popular benchmarked fine-grained datasets: CUB-200-2011 [23], Stanford Cars [13], and FGVC Aircraft [18]. The results are shown in Table 2, with the top and second-best values highlighted in **bold** and underline, respectively. Our method achieved significant performance improvements on these three datasets compared to existing techniques.

Table 2. Comparison results on CUB-200-2011, FGVC-Aircraft and Stanford Cars datasets. (The top-1 accuracy is reported in %)

Method	Backbone	CUB-200-2011	Stanford Cars	FGVC-Aircraft
BCNN [15]	VGG16	84.1	91.3	84.1
CBP [8]	VGG16	84.1	91.3	84.1
LRBP [12]	VGG16	84.2	90.9	87.3
HBP [27]	VGG16	**87.1**	**93.7**	90.3
RA-CNN [7]	VGG16	85.3	92.5	88.1
MA-CNN [32]	VGG16	86.5	92.8	89.9
Ours	VGG16	87.0	93.6	**91.6**
Cross-X [17]	ResNet50	87.7	94.6	92.6
S3N [6]	ResNet50	88.5	94.5	**93.0**
CIN [9]	ResNet50	87.5	94.1	92.6
MAMC [22]	ResNet50	86.2	92.8	-
NTS [26]	ResNet50	87.5	93.9	91.4
TASN [33]	ResNet50	87.9	93.8	-
MOMN [19]	ResNet50	88.3	93.2	90.3
API [35]	ResNet50	87.7	**94.8**	**93.0**
MGE-CNN [30]	ResNet50	88.5	93.9	-
Ours	ResNet50	**89.3**	94.5	92.7

Results on CUB200-2011 [23]: CUB-200-2011 [23] is the most challenging benchmark in fine-grained image classification tasks, and our models based on VGG16 and ResNet50 have achieved state-of-the-art performance on this dataset. Compared with fine-grained feature learning methods BCNN [15], CBP [8], and LRBP [12], our method outperforms them by 5.2%, 5.3%, and 5.1%, respectively. MA-CNN [32], TASN [33], and S3N [6] capture subtle inter-class differences in images by introducing visual attention mechanisms. Due to the introduction of feature enhancement and suppression, our proposed method achieves superior accuracy compared to them to varying degrees.

Results on Stanford Cars [13]: This dataset contains more images than CUB-200-2011, but the car images present less structure variations than the

bird images. The proposed methods consistently wins MOMN [19], MGE-CNN
[30], CIN [9], and TASN [33] to varying degrees. Cross-X [17] performs robust
multi-scale feature learning by using relationships between different images and
between different network layers. The accuracy of Cross-X [17] is 0.1% higher
than our proposed method. Unlike other methods that use a single image, API
[35] learns to recognize each image in a pair by adaptively considering feature
priorities and pairs them for comparison step by step. It's accuracy is 0.3% higher
than our proposed method.

Results on FGVC-Aircraft [18]: Our method achieved competitive performance on the FGVC-Aircraft dataset [18]. Compared to RA-CNN [7] and MA-
CNN [32], our method outperforms them by 4.6% and 2.8% respectively. Based
on ResNet50, our model's performance is 0.1%, 1.3%, and 2.4% higher than CIN
[9], NTS [26], and MOMN [19] respectively. S3N [6] uses sparse attention and
selective sampling to capture diverse and discriminative details of parts without
losing contextual information. In this dataset, the top-1 accuracy of S3N [6] is
slightly higher than our method.

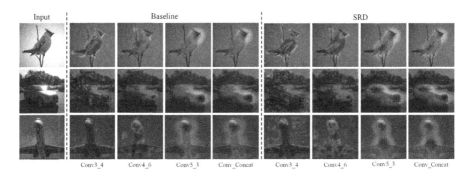

Fig. 4. Visualizations of activation maps in different layers. Feature maps obtained
with the proposed SRD have learnt more discriminative body parts of the target. These
parts need not to be the most salient features but help to distinguish the confusing
sub-categories.

4.3   Visualization Analysis

To better understand the enhancing and suppressing effects of the SRD module on features, we visualized activation maps of ResNet50 [10] with and without the SRD module on three benchmark datasets for fine-grained classification
tasks, and the results are shown in Fig. 4. The activation maps were obtained
by averaging activation values over the channel dimension of the given feature map. Based on ResNet50, we applied the Grad-CAM [20] algorithm to
visualize the $Conv3\_4$, $Conv4\_6$, $Conv5\_3$, and $Conv\_concat$ feature maps
of ResNet50 [10] on the three validation sets. We concatenate the $Conv3\_4$,

*Conv*4_6, *Conv*5_3 feature map attention pooled by different middle feature maps to get a refined *Conv_concat* feature map. By comparing the heatmaps of the baseline and DRESNet on *Conv*3 and *Conv_concat*, we can demonstrate that the SRD module plays a crucial role in enhancing the baseline and extracting additional complementary features. Taking the bird in Fig. 4 as an example, in the absence of SRD configuration, the baseline network only focuses on the salient head region while disregarding equally significant wing segments. The visualization experiments demonstrate the capability of SRDs for mining multiple different discriminative object parts.

5 Conclusion

In this paper, we propose a new discriminative region enhancing and suppression network for weakly supervised fine-grained image classification, focusing on how to extract the most salient features and complementary attention features. Specifically, we introduce a salient region diffusion (SRD) module, which can be considered as a significant dropout scheme, enabling the network to adaptively mine potentially important information at different levels of importance. Visualization of the feature maps demonstrates that the SRD mines multiple complementary discriminative object parts in different network levels. Our proposed network demonstrates impressive performance on the three most difficult FGVC datasets, outperforming the majority of attention-based methods due to our redesigned attention mechanism. Furthermore, it exhibits exceptional efficacy in handling non-rigid targets featuring multiple body joints.

Acknowledgement. This work is partially supported by the Guangxi Science and Technology Project (2021GXNSFBA220035, AD20159034), the Open Funds from Guilin University of Electronic Technology, Guangxi Key Laboratory of Image and Graphic Intelligent Processing (GIIP2208) and the National Natural Science Foundation of China (61962014).

References

1. Aggrawal, P., Anand, S.: Computer vision applications in wildlife conservation (2020)
2. Angelova, A., Zhu, S.: Efficient object detection and segmentation for fine-grained recognition. In: Proceedings of the IEEE Conference on Computer Vision and Pattern Recognition, pp. 811–818 (2013)
3. Branson, S., Beijbom, O., Belongie, S.: Efficient large-scale structured learning. In: Proceedings of the IEEE Conference on Computer Vision and Pattern Recognition, pp. 1806–1813 (2013)
4. Branson, S., Van Horn, G., Belongie, S., Perona, P.: Bird species categorization using pose normalized deep convolutional nets. arXiv preprint arXiv:1406.2952 (2014)
5. Deng, J., Dong, W., Socher, R., Li, L.J., Li, K., Fei-Fei, L.: ImageNet: a large-scale hierarchical image database. In: 2009 IEEE Conference on Computer Vision and Pattern Recognition, pp. 248–255. IEEE (2009)

6. Ding, Y., Zhou, Y., Zhu, Y., Ye, Q., Jiao, J.: Selective sparse sampling for fine-grained image recognition. In: Proceedings of the IEEE/CVF International Conference on Computer Vision, pp. 6599–6608 (2019)

7. Fu, J., Zheng, H., Mei, T.: Look closer to see better: recurrent attention convolutional neural network for fine-grained image recognition. In: Proceedings of the IEEE Conference on Computer Vision and Pattern Recognition, pp. 4438–4446 (2017)

8. Gao, Y., Beijbom, O., Zhang, N., Darrell, T.: Compact bilinear pooling. In: Proceedings of the IEEE Conference on Computer Vision and Pattern Recognition, pp. 317–326 (2016)

9. Gao, Y., Han, X., Wang, X., Huang, W., Scott, M.: Channel interaction networks for fine-grained image categorization. In: Proceedings of the AAAI Conference on Artificial Intelligence, vol. 34, pp. 10818–10825 (2020)

10. He, K., Zhang, X., Ren, S., Sun, J.: Deep residual learning for image recognition. In: Proceedings of the IEEE Conference on Computer Vision and Pattern Recognition, pp. 770–778 (2016)

11. Khan, S.D., Ullah, H.: A survey of advances in vision-based vehicle re-identification. Comput. Vis. Image Underst. **182**, 50–63 (2019)

12. Kong, S., Fowlkes, C.: Low-rank bilinear pooling for fine-grained classification. In: Proceedings of the IEEE Conference on Computer Vision and Pattern Recognition, pp. 365–374 (2017)

13. Krause, J., Stark, M., Deng, J., Fei-Fei, L.: 3D object representations for fine-grained categorization. In: Proceedings of the IEEE International Conference on Computer Vision Workshops, pp. 554–561 (2013)

14. Lin, D., Shen, X., Lu, C., Jia, J.: Deep LAC: deep localization, alignment and classification for fine-grained recognition. In: Proceedings of the IEEE Conference on Computer Vision and Pattern Recognition, pp. 1666–1674 (2015)

15. Lin, T.Y., RoyChowdhury, A., Maji, S.: Bilinear CNN models for fine-grained visual recognition. In: Proceedings of the IEEE International Conference on Computer Vision, pp. 1449–1457 (2015)

16. Loshchilov, I., Hutter, F.: SGDR: stochastic gradient descent with warm restarts. arXiv preprint arXiv:1608.03983 (2016)

17. Luo, W., et al.: Cross-X learning for fine-grained visual categorization. In: Proceedings of the IEEE/CVF International Conference on Computer Vision, pp. 8242–8251 (2019)

18. Maji, S., Rahtu, E., Kannala, J., Blaschko, M., Vedaldi, A.: Fine-grained visual classification of aircraft. arXiv preprint arXiv:1306.5151 (2013)

19. Min, S., Yao, H., Xie, H., Zha, Z.J., Zhang, Y.: Multi-objective matrix normalization for fine-grained visual recognition. IEEE Trans. Image Process. **29**, 4996–5009 (2020)

20. Selvaraju, R.R., Cogswell, M., Das, A., Vedantam, R., Parikh, D., Batra, D.: Grad-CAM: visual explanations from deep networks via gradient-based localization. In: Proceedings of the IEEE International Conference on Computer Vision, pp. 618–626 (2017)

21. Simonyan, K., Zisserman, A.: Very deep convolutional networks for large-scale image recognition. arXiv preprint arXiv:1409.1556 (2014)

22. Sun, M., Yuan, Y., Zhou, F., Ding, E.: Multi-attention multi-class constraint for fine-grained image recognition. In: Ferrari, V., Hebert, M., Sminchisescu, C., Weiss, Y. (eds.) ECCV 2018. LNCS, vol. 11220, pp. 834–850. Springer, Cham (2018). https://doi.org/10.1007/978-3-030-01270-0_49

23. Wah, C., Branson, S., Welinder, P., Perona, P., Belongie, S.: The Caltech-UCSD Birds-200-2011 dataset (2011)
24. Wei, X.S., Cui, Q., Yang, L., Wang, P., Liu, L.: RPC: a large-scale retail product checkout dataset. arXiv preprint arXiv:1901.07249 (2019)
25. Wei, X.S., Xie, C.W., Wu, J., Shen, C.: Mask-CNN: localizing parts and selecting descriptors for fine-grained bird species categorization. Pattern Recogn. **76**, 704–714 (2018)
26. Yang, Z., Luo, T., Wang, D., Hu, Z., Gao, J., Wang, L.: Learning to navigate for fine-grained classification. In: Ferrari, V., Hebert, M., Sminchisescu, C., Weiss, Y. (eds.) Computer Vision – ECCV 2018. LNCS, vol. 11218, pp. 438–454. Springer, Cham (2018). https://doi.org/10.1007/978-3-030-01264-9_26
27. Yu, C., Zhao, X., Zheng, Q., Zhang, P., You, X.: Hierarchical bilinear pooling for fine-grained visual recognition. In: Ferrari, V., Hebert, M., Sminchisescu, C., Weiss, Y. (eds.) ECCV 2018. LNCS, vol. 11220, pp. 595–610. Springer, Cham (2018). https://doi.org/10.1007/978-3-030-01270-0_35
28. Zhang, F., Li, M., Zhai, G., Liu, Y.: Multi-branch and multi-scale attention learning for fine-grained visual categorization. In: Lokoč, J., et al. (eds.) MMM 2021. LNCS, vol. 12572, pp. 136–147. Springer, Cham (2021). https://doi.org/10.1007/978-3-030-67832-6_12
29. Zhang, H., et al.: SPDA-CNN: unifying semantic part detection and abstraction for fine-grained recognition. In: Proceedings of the IEEE Conference on Computer Vision and Pattern Recognition, pp. 1143–1152 (2016)
30. Zhang, L., Huang, S., Liu, W., Tao, D.: Learning a mixture of granularity-specific experts for fine-grained categorization. In: Proceedings of the IEEE/CVF International Conference on Computer Vision, pp. 8331–8340 (2019)
31. Zhang, N., Donahue, J., Girshick, R., Darrell, T.: Part-based R-CNNs for fine-grained category detection. In: Fleet, D., Pajdla, T., Schiele, B., Tuytelaars, T. (eds.) ECCV 2014. LNCS, vol. 8689, pp. 834–849. Springer, Cham (2014). https://doi.org/10.1007/978-3-319-10590-1_54
32. Zheng, H., Fu, J., Mei, T., Luo, J.: Learning multi-attention convolutional neural network for fine-grained image recognition. In: Proceedings of the IEEE International Conference on Computer Vision, pp. 5209–5217 (2017)
33. Zheng, H., Fu, J., Zha, Z.J., Luo, J.: Looking for the devil in the details: learning trilinear attention sampling network for fine-grained image recognition. In: Proceedings of the IEEE/CVF Conference on Computer Vision and Pattern Recognition, pp. 5012–5021 (2019)
34. Zheng, H., Fu, J., Zha, Z.J., Luo, J., Mei, T.: Learning rich part hierarchies with progressive attention networks for fine-grained image recognition. IEEE Trans. Image Process. **29**, 476–488 (2019)
35. Zhuang, P., Wang, Y., Qiao, Y.: Learning attentive pairwise interaction for fine-grained classification. In: Proceedings of the AAAI Conference on Artificial Intelligence, vol. 34, pp. 13130–13137 (2020)

Edge Based Architecture for Total Energy Regression Models for Computational Materials Science

Kangmo Yeo[1] , Sukmin Jeong[2(✉)] , and Soo-Hyung Kim[1(✉)]

[1] Department of Artificial Intelligence Convergence, Chonnam National University, Gwangju 61186, Republic of Korea
shkim@jnu.ac.kr
[2] Department of Physics and Research Institute of Physics and Chemistry, Jeonbuk National University, Jeonju 54896, Republic of Korea
jsm@jbnu.ac.kr

Abstract. It is widely acknowledged that artificial intelligence (AI) technology has been extensively applied and has achieved remarkable advancements in various fields. The field of computational materials science has also embraced AI techniques in diverse ways. Today, computational materials science plays a crucial role in the development of cutting-edge materials, including pharmaceuticals, catalysts, semiconductors, and batteries. One significant task in this field is the regression of the total energy of atomic structures that form various materials. In this study, we propose a modified model architecture aimed at improving the performance of existing total energy regression models. Traditional total energy regression models calculate the total energy by summing the energies of individual nodes represented in the atomic structure graph. However, our approach suggests a modified architecture that not only predicts the energy for nodes but also incorporates energy prediction for edges in the graph. This novel architecture achieved a 3.9% reduction in energy error compared to the base model. Moreover, its simplicity provides the advantage of general applicability to other total energy regression models.

Keywords: Computational materials science · Atomic structure

1 Introduction

Artificial intelligence (AI) has already demonstrated its powerful performance and efficiency through numerous examples. In the field of natural science, AI is rapidly improving efficiency, comparable to the fourth wave. One area where AI algorithms have been introduced and are making a significant impact is computational materials science [1–5]. This field, which primarily simulates the properties and phenomena of materials, is gaining attention across various industries, including semiconductors, batteries, light-emitting devices, chemistry, new drug development, catalysts, and solar cells [6–14].

© The Author(s), under exclusive license to Springer Nature Switzerland AG 2023
H. Lu et al. (Eds.): ACPR 2023, LNCS 14408, pp. 106–112, 2023.
https://doi.org/10.1007/978-3-031-47665-5_9

Density Functional Theory (DFT) [15,16], proposed in the 1970s, boasts surprisingly high accuracy and has become a major method in the field of computational science. However, DFT methods require large computational resources at the cost of high accuracy [10,17,18]. Recently, AI technology has been rapidly introduced to solve these problems and has achieved considerable results. However, it still lacks accuracy compared to the DFT method [19].

A fundamental and central task in computational materials science is to calculate the total energy for a given atomic structure. A total energy regression AI model called machine learning potential is based on calculating the total energy by predicting and summing the contributions of each target atom to the total energy [20–24]. This method has a similar structure to the empirical potential, which is a traditional method of calculating total energy.

We propose a new architecture that considers both atoms and bonds. This approach is more physically intuitive as the total energy of a material consists of both the energy of the atoms themselves and the energy of chemical bonds. This architecture is more natural and similar to DFT calculations. If the architecture of the AI model is similar to how DFT calculations work, then it can be expected that the AI model will learn more easily. This effect is especially effective in non-metallic materials with clear chemical bonds rather than metallic materials with ambiguous bonds. Any AI model that interprets atomic structure as a graph and calculates total energy can benefit from this approach and improve its performance.

2   Background and Base Model

Machine Learning Potential. In 2007, Behler and Parrinello first proposed an AI architecture for regressing total energy based on atomic positions [20]. Density functional theory-based first-principles calculations are one of the most widely used methodologies in computational materials science and can calculate various properties for materials. Total energy is one of the most basic and essential physical quantities in property calculations. Total energy is a kind of function that takes atomic structure as a variable, meaning the type and arrangement of atoms that make up an arbitrary material. For example, an atomic structure containing N atoms is expressed as an atomic number $\mathbf{Z} = \{Z_1, Z_2, Z_3, ..., Z_N\}$ and each atom's position $\mathbf{R} = \{\mathbf{r}_1, \mathbf{r}_2, \mathbf{r}_3, ..., \mathbf{r}_N\}$ where $\mathbf{r}_i$ is a Cartesian coordinate $\mathbf{r}_i = \{x_i, y_i, z_i\}$. The traditional computational chemical methodology of empirical potential was adopted. According to this methodology, total energy E_{total} is

$$E_{total} = \sum_i E_i \tag{1}$$

where E_i is the contribution of the i_{th} atom to total energy. The architecture of machine learning potential is shown in Fig. 1. Almost all machine learning potentials published so far have a structure like this. In Fig. 1, G_i^{φ} is an input vector of size φ transformed by symmetric function.

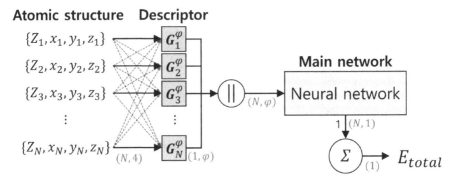

Fig. 1. Basic architecture of a machine learning potential [20]. The gray and pink boxes represent the descriptor and main network, respectively. All black and dotted arrows indicate the flow of data. The round circle represents an operation that calculates the sum of input values. The data shape at each step is indicated by blue numbers. (Color figure online)

Base Model. The model proposed in this study is based on GemNet-OC [25] and uses a similar architecture. GemNet-OC is a graph neural network (GNN) that represents an atomic system as a graph G = (V, E), where the set of graph nodes, V, represents each atom and the set of edges, E, is defined as all pairs of atoms within a certain cutoff distance. The first model, similar to state-of-the-art GNNs, was proposed in 1997 but only gained popularity after several works demonstrated its potential for a wide range of graph-related tasks [26]. GemNet-OC evolves the two-level message passing scheme proposed in MXMNet into an interaction layer and utilizes both edge and node embeddings. GemNet-OC is a model based on Geometric Message Passing Neural Networks (GemNet) [27], which uses a similar architecture and improves the accuracy of forces experienced by atoms.

3   Datasets

We used the Open Catalyst 2022 (OC22) dataset for model training [19]. The OC22 dataset is designed to enable the development of generalizable machine learning (ML) models for catalysts, particularly for oxygen and hydrogen evolution reactions and oxide electrocatalysis. The dataset consists of oxide surface structures combined with constituent elements and oxide surface structures with adsorbed molecules, as well as defects such as atomic substitution and vacancies. By providing a diverse and representative training dataset, OC22 aims to support the development of generalized models that can accurately predict catalytic reactions on oxide surfaces. Models generated from this dataset are expected to accelerate the discovery and design of new catalysts for a wide range of applications.

The primary task of OC20 is to regress the total energy obtained through first-principles calculations based on DFT from the atomic structure. The dataset is divided into training/validation/test sets and each set includes both material surface structures and surface structures with adsorbed molecules. The dataset includes 19,142 material surface structures and 43,189 surface structures with adsorbed molecules, with a total of 9,854,504 data points. Diversity in surface structure and adsorption structure was prioritized when constructing the dataset to ensure that a generalized model can be built.

4   Edge Based Architecture of GemNet-OC

GemNet-OC is a graph neural network (GNN) that represents atomic systems as graphs, with its architecture being improved to map the energy of the edge embedding using GemNet as a base model. In this architecture, nodes and edges are embedded respectively, with the edge embedding being used to regress the force received by atoms. An architecture similar to the empirical potential for the total energy was proposed, as shown in Eq. (1) and Fig. 1.

However, the total energy can also be described in terms of heat statistics. Specifically, it can be expressed as

$$E_{total} = \Omega + \sum_i \mu_i \qquad (2)$$

where Ω is the formation energy representing chemical interaction between atoms and μ_i is the energy of one atom in terms of thermostatistics. The formation energy Ω can be further expressed as $\Omega = \sum_m e_m$, which is the sum of the binding energies e_m of atomic pairs. The binding energies e_m of atomic pairs are mapped to the values from the edges of the atomic structure graph by the main network.

This structure has several advantages. Firstly, μ_i is more consistent about the placement of atoms than E_i, making the model easier to train. Secondly, the total energy naturally regresses by the formation energy calculated as the sum of the binding energies. To reflect these formulas, the architecture was modified to map energy to edges as well. The modified architecture can be seen in Fig. 2.

5   Results

Due to limited computational resources, only 200,000 training data points (1/40 of the total OC22 dataset) were used for training over 9 epochs. However, since the same dataset was used for all models being compared and 200,000 is still a large number of data points, it is still meaningful to test the performance of the models. The training and validation errors were reduced equally for all models, indicating that there was no underfitting or overfitting (Fig. 3). The inset of Fig. 3-b shows that the validation error of GemNet-EB (shown in red) is about 3.9% smaller than that of the base model GemNet-OC (shown in green).

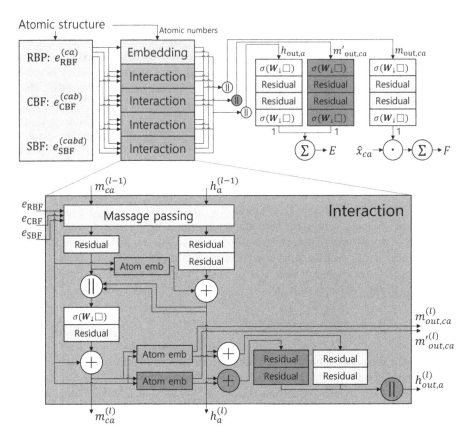

Fig. 2. Main network of the GemNet-EB architecture. Changes are highlighted in orange. □ denotes the layer's input, ‖ concatenation, σ a non-linearity. The massage passing block and Embedding block have same architecture with the GemNet-OC [25]. (Color figure online)

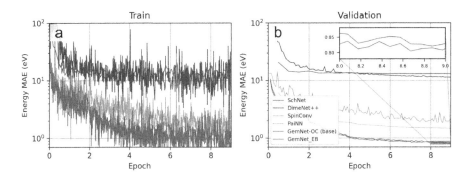

Fig. 3. Energy mean absolute error (MAE) of train (a) and validation (b) respectively. The x-axis represents the epoch and the y-axis represents the MAE on a log scale. The inset in (b) is a zoom-in of the red box zone at the bottom right. (Color figure online)

6   Conclusion

We proposed a new and improved architecture for regressing the total energy from atomic structures. Our newly proposed GemNet-EB model achieved a 3.9% lower validation error than the base model. Of course, other experiments are possible, but further studies are needed because it is difficult to test more than this due to the limitation of computer resources. However, this study is still significant because we applied the new concept of the total energy prediction model, as shown in Eq. (2), and achieved a low validation error rate with this method. There is a significant difference in errors between the other models and the GemNet base model, indicating that the edge embedding of the GemNet-OC model also plays an important role in total energy regression. By directly mapping bond energy using edge embedding, we were able to improve the accuracy of the model. While edge embedding is indirectly reflected in node embedding through the interaction block, we were able to improve performance by directly connecting it to total energy regression.

However, considering that the accuracy of DFT calculations used for surface structure and surface adsorption energy studies is less than 0.01 eV, there is still room for improvement. Since our new method is not limited to any specific model or architecture and can be applied to any GNN-based model for atomic structures, our proposed new architecture can serve as a foundation for advancing machine learning potential.

Acknowledgement. This research was supported by Basic Science Research Program through the National Research Foundation of Korea (NRF) funded by the Ministry of Education (NRF-2021R1I1A3A04036408) and also supported by Institute of Information & communications Technology Planning & Evaluation (IITP) grant funded by the Korea government (MSIT) (No. 2021-0-02068, Artificial Intelligence Innovation Hub).

References

1. Butler, K.: Machine learning for molecular and materials science. Nature **559**, 547–555 (2018)
2. Schmidt, J.: Recent advances and applications of machine learning in solid-state materials science. npj Comput. Mater. **5**, 83 (2019)
3. Wei, J.: Machine learning in materials science. InfoMat **1**, 338–358 (2019)
4. Morgan, D.: Opportunities and challenges for machine learning in materials science. Ann. Rev. **50**, 71–103 (2020)
5. Fiedler, L.: Deep dive into machine learning density functional theory for materials science and chemistry. Phys. Rev. Mater. **6**, 040301 (2022)
6. Ladha, D.: A review on density functional theory-based study on two-dimensional materials used in batteries. Mater. Today. Chem. **11**, 94–111 (2019)
7. Adekoya, D.: DFT-guided design and fabrication of carbon-nitride-based materials for energy storage devices: a review. Nanomicro Lett. **13**, 13 (2021)
8. Liang, Q.: Transition metal compounds family for Li-S batteries: the DFT-guide for suppressing polysulfides shuttle. Adv. Funct. Mater. **33**, 2300825 (2023)

9. Neugebauer, J.: Density functional theory in materials science. WIREs Comput. Mol. Sci. **3**, 438–448 (2013)
10. Mattsson, A.: Designing meaningful density functional theory calculations in materials science-a primer. Model. Simul. Mat. Sci. Eng. **13**, R1 (2005)
11. Tandon, H.: A brief review on importance of DFT in drug design. Res. Med. Eng. Sci. **7**, 791–795 (2019)
12. Sade, V.: Current trends in computer aided drug design and a highlight of drugs discovered via computational techniques: a review. Eur. J. Med. Chem. **224**, 113705 (2021)
13. Weijing, D.: The application of DFT in catalysis and adsorption reaction system. Energy Procedia **152**, 997–1002 (2018)
14. Liao, X.: Density functional theory for electrocatalysis. Energy Environ. Mater. **5**, 157–185 (2021)
15. Hohenberg, P.: Inhomogeneous electron gas. Phys. Rev. **136**, B864 (1964)
16. Kohn, W.: Self-consistent equations including exchange and correlation effects. Phys. Rev. **140**, A1133 (1965)
17. Zhang, L.: Deep potential molecular dynamics: a scalable model with the accuracy of quantum mechanics. Phys. Rev. Lett. **120**, 143001 (2018)
18. Chandrasekaran, A.: Solving the electronic structure problem with machine learning. npj Comput. Mater. **5**, 22 (2019)
19. Tran, R.: The Open Catalyst 2022 (OC22) dataset and challenges for oxide electrocatalysts. ACS Catal. **13**(5), 3066–3084 (2023)
20. Behler, J.: Generalied neural-network representation of high-dimensional potential-energy surface. Phys. Rev. Lett. **98**, 146401 (2007)
21. Bartók, A.: Gaussian approximation potentials: the accuracy of quantum mechanics, without the electrons. Phys. Rev. Lett. **104**, 136403 (2010)
22. Artith, N.: An implementation of artificial neural-network potentials for atomistic materials simulations: performance for TiO_2. Comput. Mater. Sci. **114**, 135–150 (2016)
23. Schütt, K.: SchNet - a deep learning architecture for molecules and materials. J. Chem. Phys. **148**, 24 (2018)
24. Lee, K.: SIMPLE-NN: an efficient package for training and executing neural-network interatomic potentials. Comput. Phys. Comm. **242**, 95–103 (2019)
25. Gasteiger, J.: GemNet-OC: developing graph neural networks for large and diverse molecular simulation datasets. arXiv preprint arXiv:2204.02782 (2022)
26. Zelinsky, N.: A neural device for searching direct correlations between structures and properties of chemical compounds. J. Chem. Inf. Comput. Sci. **37**, 715–721 (1997)
27. Gasteiger, J., Becker, F., Günnemann, S.: GemNet: universal directional graph neural networks for molecules. In: 35th Conference on Neural Information Processing Systems, vol. 34, pp. 6790–6802 (2021)

Multiscale Transformer-Based for Multimodal Affective States Estimation from Physiological Signals

Ngoc Tu Vu, Van Thong Huynh, Hyung-Jeong Yang, and Soo-Hyung Kim[✉]

Department of AI Convergence, Chonnam National University,
Gwangju, South Korea
{tu369,vthuynh,hjyang,shkim}@jnu.ac.kr

Abstract. In recent times, the estimation of affective states from physiological data has garnered considerable attention within the research community owing to its wide-ranging applicability in daily life scenarios. The advancement of wearable technology has facilitated the collection of physiological signals, thereby highlighting the necessity for a resilient system capable of effectively discerning and interpreting user states. This work introduces an innovative methodology aimed at addressing the Valence-Arousal estimation, through the utilization of physiological signals. Our proposed model presents an efficient multi-scale transformer-based architecture for fusing signals from multiple modern sensors to tackle Emotion Recognition task. Our approach involves applying a multi-modal technique combined with scaling data to establish the relationship between internal body signals and human emotions. Additionally, we utilize Transformer and Gaussian transformation techniques to improve signal encoding effectiveness and overall performance. Our proposed model demonstrates compelling performance on the CASE dataset, achieving an impressive Root Mean Squared Error (RMSE) of 1.45.

Keywords: Affective states analysis · Physiological signals · Multimodal · Mental health

1 Introduction

Recognizing emotions is a fundamental aspect of human communication, and the ability to accurately detect emotional states has significant impacts on a range of applications, from healthcare to human-computer interaction. Emotions are often reflected in physiological signals [26], facial [8], and speech [24]. Recently, the use of physiological signals for affective computing has gained considerable attention due to its potential to provide objective measures of emotional states in real time [21].

Recently, there has been a growing interest in developing machine learning algorithms for affective computing using physiological signals [2,4,5,22,28].

H. Lu et al. (Eds.): ACPR 2023, LNCS 14408, pp. 113–122, 2023.
https://doi.org/10.1007/978-3-031-47665-5_10

These algorithms can be used to classify emotional states, predict changes in emotional states over time, or identify the specific features of physiological signals that are most informative for detecting emotional states. There has also been interested in developing wearable sensors that can capture physiological signals in real-world settings, such as in the workplace or in social situations [20].

The use of end-to-end deep learning architectures for physiological signals has the potential to simplify the development and deployment of an emotion recognition system [21]. By eliminating the need for preprocessing steps, these architectures can reduce the complexity and time required for system development, as well as improve the scalability and accuracy of the system. In addition, end-to-end architectures can enable the development of systems that can process multiple physiological signals simultaneously, such as heart rate, respiration, and electrodermal activity, providing more comprehensive and accurate measures of emotional states.

Despite the potential benefits of end-to-end deep learning architectures for affective computing, there are still challenges that need to be addressed. One challenge is to develop architectures that can handle noisy and non-stationary physiological signals, which can be affected by movement artifacts, signal drift, and other sources of noise. Another challenge is to ensure that the learned features are interpretable and meaningful, which can help improve the transparency and explainability of the system.

In this paper, we propose an end-to-end multi-scale architecture for continuous emotion regression with physiological signals. We evaluate the performance of the proposed architecture using CASE dataset [25], which contains data collected from experiments carried out in a laboratory setting.

2 Related Works

2.1 Continuous Emotion Recognition from Multimodal Physiological Signal

The utilization of physiological signals has been widely acknowledged as one of the most reliable data forms for affective science and affective computing. Although individuals are capable of manipulating their physical signals such as facial expressions or speech, consciously controlling their internal state is a daunting task. Therefore, analysis of signals from the human body represents a reliable and robust approach to fully recognizing and comprehending an individual's emotional state [1, 26]. This reliability factor is especially crucial in medical applications, such as mental health treatment or mental illness diagnosis.

Recognizing affect from physiological data remains a significant challenge, not only during the data acquisition process but also in terms of emotion assessment. Laboratory-based research dominates the field of affective science due to the control it affords over experimental variables. Researchers can carefully select and prepare emotional stimuli, and employ various sensor devices to trace and record a subject's emotional state with minimal unexpected event, interference [21]. However, most of these studies rely on discrete indirect methods, such as quizzes, surveys, or discrete emotion categories for emotion assessment, which overlook the time-varying nature of human emotional experience. Sharma et al. [25] introduced Joystick-based emotion reporting interface (JERI) to overcome a limitation in emotion assessment. JERI enables the simultaneous annotation of valence and arousal, allowing for moment-to-moment emotion assessment. The Continuously Annotated Signals of Emotion (CASE) dataset, acquired using JERI, provides additional information for researchers to identify the timing of emotional triggers.

In addition, it is claimed that a single physiological signal is relatively difficult to precisely reflect human emotional changes. Therefore, recently, there has been much research focusing on detecting human emotion through multimodal physiological signals. There are many types of physiological signal used in these studies. While some studies record heart-related signals such as electrocardiographic (ECG) [7,17,18], blood volume pulse (BVP) [15,33], others use electrical activity of the brain (Electroencephalogram/EEG) [13,14] or muscle electrical reaction (Electromyogram/EMG) [19,23]. Furthermore, some even employ skin temperature (SKT) [19], skin sweat glands (EDA) [13,23], the depth and rate of breathing (respiratory/RSP) [23].

2.2 Transformer-Based Method for in Multimodal Emotion Recognition from Physiological Signal

Similar to other emotion recognition problems that involve physical signals, affective computing in physiological data has witnessed extensive adoption of machine learning techniques, particularly deep learning methodologies. Dominguez et al. [4] employed various conventional machine learning techniques, including Gaussian naive Bayes, k-Nearest Neighbors, and support vector machines, for valence-arousal estimation. However, these approaches are heavily dependent on the quality of handcrafted feature selection and feature extraction processes. To overcome this challenge, other studies [5,22,28] proposed the use of Deep Learning techniques for an end-to-end approach, where the model learns to extract features automatically without the need for pre-designed feature descriptors.

With the advancement of deep learning, various state-of-the-art techniques have been used to analyze physiological signals. Santamaria et al. [22] used convolutional neural networks (CNN) with 1D convolution layers for emotion detection, while Harper et al. [5] combined CNNs with frequently used recurring neural networks (RNN) for emotion recognition from ECG signals. Since their introduction in 2016, Transformers [27] have emerged as preferred models in the field of deep learning. Their robust performance in natural language processing, a type of data that shares some characteristics similar to time-series data, has demonstrated the potential of Transformers when applied to time-series signals. As a result, recent research in the time series domain has utilized Transformers as the core module in their model architecture [9,10,30]. For physiological signals, some studies have proposed using Transformers and their variants to detect emotions [28,29,31,32]. In the works of Vazquez et al. [28,29], they focused on applying pre-trained Transformers for multimodal signal processing. However, this is still a very basic application of Transformer modules. Wu et al. [31] and Yang et al. [32] proposed using more advanced techniques of Transformer-based models, which are self-supervised and Convolution-augmented transformers for single- and multimodal signal processing. Although these studies have demonstrated the effectiveness of transformers for physiological signals, they often feed the model with fixed original size signals, which may lead to the loss of global feature information. To address this issue, we propose a new multi-scale transformer-based architecture for multimodal emotional recognition.

3   Proposed Approach

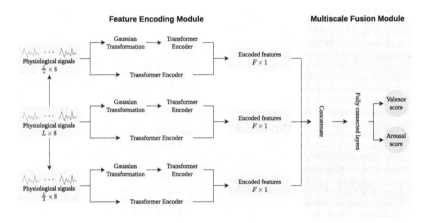

Fig. 1. An overview of our proposed architecture.

3.1   Problem Definition

The emotion recognition in multimodal physiological signal problem takes as input 8 physiological signals, namely ECG, BVP, EMG_CORU, EMG_TRAP, EMG_ZYGO, GRS, RSP and SKT, extracted from human subjects during emotion-inducing stimuli. This is denoted as the 8 sequence with L length. In the affective computing field, the objective of the emotion recognition problem varies depending on the indicated emotional models. In the scope of this study, following the use of the SAM (Self-Assessment Manikin) [3] model of the CASE dataset, the problem objective is the estimated Valence-Arousal (V-A) value. The V-A score consists of two continuous floating-point numbers ranging from 0.5 to 9.5. A value of 0.5 denotes the most negative valence or the lowest arousal, 5 indicates the neutral valence or arousal, and 9.5 indicates the most positive valence or the highest arousal.

3.2 Methodology

We constructed a new multiscale architecture for the estimation of valence arousal from 8 physiological signals. Our architecture consists of two core modules: Feature encoding module and multiscale fusion module. The process involves feeding raw physiological data into a feature encoding module, designed to extract vital information across varying global and local scales. Subsequently, the multi-scale features are fused and utilized for the estimation of Valence-Arousal scores. The overall architecture is shown in Fig. 1.

Feature Encoding. To enable the feature encoding module to extract global features for the estimator and eliminate noise and interference information from the input, we employ 1-Dimensional average pooling to scale the 8 input signals into three different lengths: L, $L/2$, and $L/4$. This process helps to improve the model's ability to extract useful information and eliminate unwanted noise and interference.

Then, we simultaneously apply two types of feature encoders, which are the Gaussian transform [16] and the transformer encoder [27]. The transformer encoder block is used as multi-headed self-attention as its core mechanism. Given an input sequential signal $S \in R^{L \times C}$, where L represents the length of the signal sequence and $C = 8$ is the number of channels (signal modalities), we apply a positional encoding and embedding layer to convert the raw input into a sequence of tokens. Subsequently, the tokens are fed into transformer layers consisting of multi-headed self-attention (MSA) [27], layer normalization (LN), and multilayer perceptron (MLP) blocks. Each element is formalized in the following equations:

$$y^i = MSA(LN(x^i)) + x^i \tag{1}$$

$$x^{l+i} = MLP(LN(y^i)) + y^i \tag{2}$$

Here, i represents the index of the token, and x^i denotes the generated feature's token. It is worth noting that since the multi-headed self-attention mechanism allows multiple sequences to be processed in parallel, all 8 signal channels are fed into the Transformer Encoder at once.

The Gaussian transform [16] is traditionally employed to kernelize linear models by nonlinearly transforming input features via a single layer and subsequently training a linear model on top of the transformed features. However, in the context of deep learning architectures, random features can also be leveraged, given their ability to perform dimensionality reduction or approximate certain functions via random projections. As a non-parametric technique, this transformation maps input data to a more compressed representation that excludes noise information while still enabling computationally efficient processing. Such a technique may serve as a valuable supplement to Transformer Encoder architectures, compensating for any missing information.

Multi-scale Fusion. From the features extracted from the feature encoder module on different scales, we fuse them using the concatenation operation. The concatenated features are then fed through a series of fully connected layers (FCN) for the estimation of the 2 valence and arousal scores. The Rectified Linear Unit (ReLU) activation function is chosen for its ability to introduce non-linearity into the model, thus contributing to the accuracy of the score estimation. The effectiveness of this approach lies in its ability to efficiently estimate the desired scores while maintaining a simple and straightforward architecture.

4   Experimental and Results

4.1   Dataset

CASE dataset [25] contains data from several physiological sensors and continuous annotations of emotion. These data were acquired from 30 subjects while they watched several video-stimuli and simultaneously reported their emotional experience using JERI. The devices used include sensors for electrocardiography (ECG), blood volume pulse (BVP), galvanic skin response (GSR), respiration (RSP), skin temperature (SKT) and electromyography (EMG). These sensors return 8 types of physiological signals: ECG, BVP, EMG_CORU, EMG_TRAP, EMG_ZYGO, GRS, RSP and SKT. Emotional stimuli consisted of 11 videos, ranging in duration from 120 to 197 s. The annotation and physiological data were collected at a sampling rate of 20 Hz and 1000 Hz, respectively. The initial range of valence arousal scores was established at $[-26225, 26225]$.

We evaluate our approach with four different scenarios:

– Across-time scenario: Each sample represents a single person watching a single video, and the training and test sets are divided based on time. Specifically, the earlier parts of the video are used for training, while the later parts are reserved for testing.
– Across-subject scenario: Participants are randomly assigned to groups, and all samples from a given group belong to either the train or test set depending on the fold.
– Across-elicitor scenario: Each subject has two samples (videos) per quadrant in the arousal-valence space. For each fold, both samples related to a given quadrant are excluded, resulting in four folds, with one quadrant excluded in each fold.
– Across-version scenario: Each subject has two samples per quadrant in the arousal-valence space. In this scenario, one sample is used to train the model, and the other sample is used for testing, resulting in two folds.

4.2   Experiments Setup

Our networks were implemented using the TensorFlow framework. We trained our models using the AdamW optimizer [12] with a learning rate of 0.001 and the Cosine annealing warm restarts scheduler [11] over 10 epochs. The MSE loss function was used to optimize the network, and the evaluation stage is done with RMSE. The sequence length was set to 2048. We utilized 4 transformer layers for the transformer encoder, with each Attention module containing 4 heads. The hidden dimension of the transformer was set to 1024. All training and testing processes were conducted on a GTX 3090 GPU.

Table 1. RMSE on the test data with different scenarios.

Approach	Scenario	Arousal	Valence
Hinduja et al. [6]	Across-time	1.82	1.76
	Across-subject	1.33	1.31
	Across-elicitor	1.03	1.10
	Across-version	0.99	1.07
	Avg	1.292	1.31
Ours - without transformer on original signals	Across-time	1.550	1.612
	Across-subject	1.478	1.592
	Across-elicitor	1.600	1.653
	Across-version	1.595	1.548
	Avg	1.556	1.601
• Ours	Across-time	1.503	1.639
	Across-subject	1.336	1.345
	Across-elicitor	1.509	1.514
	Across-version	1.369	1.352
	Avg	1.430	1.463

4.3 Results

Table 1 presents the results of our model in the test set in terms of the evaluation at different scenarios. Overall, the final RMSE score for the valence and arousal estimation task that we gain is 1.447. Our model showcases promising performance in comparison to the approach presented by Hinduja et al. [6]. It achieves a slightly lower score of 0.077 in Arousal and 0.153 in Valence score.

In detail, our model achieved the best performance in the across-subject scenario, with an arousal score of 1.336 and a valence score of 1.345. These results suggest that our model can effectively generalize to new subjects and accurately capture the emotion change after fully viewing the entire video-viewing process. Meanwhile, the relatively low performance in the across-elicitor scenario, with scores of 1.509 and 1.514 in arousal and valence, respectively, suggests that our model did not perform well in inferring emotional states that were not seen during training, given the specific emotional states learned previously. In the context of the across-time scenario, our results demonstrate a significantly improved performance compared to that of Hinduja et al. [6]. Specifically, our model achieves noteworthy enhancements in both Arousal and Valence scores, with a margin of 0.317 in Arousal and 0.121 in Valence. This substantial improvement opens up promising avenues for our future research.

5   Conclusion

This paper proposes a new multiscale architecture for multimodal emotional recognition from physiological signals. Our approach involves encoding the signal with the transformer encoder at multiple scales to capture both global and local features and obtain more informative representations. Our method achieved decent results on the CASE dataset.

Acknowledgments. This work was supported by the National Research Foundation of Korea (NRF) grant funded by the Korea government (MSIT) (RS-2023-00219107). This work was also supported by Institute of Information & communications Technology Planning & Evaluation (IITP) grant funded by the Artificial Intelligence Convergence Innovation Human Resources Development (IITP-2023-RS-2023-00256629) grant funded by the Korea government (MSIT).

References

1. Ahmad, Z., Khan, N.: A survey on physiological signal-based emotion recognition. Bioengineering **9**(11), 688 (2022)
2. Algarni, M., Saeed, F., Al-Hadhrami, T., Ghabban, F., Al-Sarem, M.: Deep learning-based approach for emotion recognition using electroencephalography (EEG) signals using bi-directional long short-term memory (Bi-LSTM). Sensors **22**(8), 2976 (2022)
3. Bradley, M.M., Lang, P.J.: Measuring emotion: the self-assessment manikin and the semantic differential. J. Behav. Ther. Exp. Psychiatry **25**(1), 49–59 (1994)
4. Domínguez-Jiménez, J.A., Campo-Landines, K.C., Martínez-Santos, J.C., Delahoz, E.J., Contreras-Ortiz, S.H.: A machine learning model for emotion recognition from physiological signals. Biomed. Sig. Process. Control **55**, 101646 (2020)
5. Harper, R., Southern, J.: A Bayesian deep learning framework for end-to-end prediction of emotion from heartbeat. IEEE Trans. Affect. Comput. **13**(2), 985–991 (2020)
6. Hinduja, S., Bilalpur, M., Jivnani, L., Canavan, S.: Multimodal temporal modeling of emotion using physiological signals (2023)
7. Hu, L., Yang, J., Chen, M., Qian, Y., Rodrigues, J.J.: SCAI-SVSC: smart clothing for effective interaction with a sustainable vital sign collection. Fut. Gener. Comput. Syst. **86**, 329–338 (2018)
8. Li, S., Deng, W.: Deep facial expression recognition: a survey. IEEE Trans. Affect. Comput. **13**(3), 1195–1215 (2020)
9. Li, S., et al.: Enhancing the locality and breaking the memory bottleneck of transformer on time series forecasting. In: Advances in Neural Information Processing Systems, vol. 32 (2019)

10. Li, Y., Peng, X., Zhang, J., Li, Z., Wen, M.: DCT-GAN: dilated convolutional transformer-based GAN for time series anomaly detection. IEEE Trans. Knowl. Data Eng. **35**, 3632–3644 (2021)

11. Loshchilov, I., Hutter, F.: SGDR: stochastic gradient descent with warm restarts. arXiv preprint arXiv:1608.03983 (2016)

12. Loshchilov, I., Hutter, F.: Decoupled weight decay regularization. arXiv preprint arXiv:1711.05101 (2017)

13. Martens, T., Niemann, M., Dick, U.: Sensor measures of affective leaning. Front. Psychol. **11**, 379 (2020)

14. Nakisa, B., Rastgoo, M.N., Rakotonirainy, A., Maire, F., Chandran, V.: Long short term memory hyperparameter optimization for a neural network based emotion recognition framework. IEEE Access **6**, 49325–49338 (2018)

15. Ragot, M., Martin, N., Em, S., Pallamin, N., Diverrez, J.-M.: Emotion recognition using physiological signals: laboratory vs. wearable sensors. In: Ahram, T., Falcão, C. (eds.) AHFE 2017. AISC, vol. 608, pp. 15–22. Springer, Cham (2018). https://doi.org/10.1007/978-3-319-60639-2_2

16. Rahimi, A., Recht, B.: Random features for large-scale kernel machines. In: Advances in Neural Information Processing Systems, vol. 20 (2007)

17. Rattanyu, K., Mizukawa, M.: Emotion recognition using biological signal in intelligent space. In: Jacko, J.A. (ed.) HCI 2011. LNCS, vol. 6763, pp. 586–592. Springer, Heidelberg (2011). https://doi.org/10.1007/978-3-642-21616-9_66

18. Rattanyu, K., Ohkura, M., Mizukawa, M.: Emotion monitoring from physiological signals for service robots in the living space. In: ICCAS 2010, pp. 580–583. IEEE (2010)

19. Romeo, L., Cavallo, A., Pepa, L., Bianchi-Berthouze, N., Pontil, M.: Multiple instance learning for emotion recognition using physiological signals. IEEE Trans. Affect. Comput. **13**(1), 389–407 (2019)

20. Saganowski, S., Behnke, M., Komoszyńska, J., Kunc, D., Perz, B., Kazienko, P.: A system for collecting emotionally annotated physiological signals in daily life using wearables. In: 2021 9th International Conference on Affective Computing and Intelligent Interaction Workshops and Demos (ACIIW), pp. 1–3. IEEE (2021)

21. Saganowski, S., Perz, B., Polak, A., Kazienko, P.: Emotion recognition for everyday life using physiological signals from wearables: a systematic literature review. IEEE Trans. Affect. Comput. **14**, 1876–1897 (2022)

22. Santamaria-Granados, L., Munoz-Organero, M., Ramirez-Gonzalez, G., Abdulhay, E., Arunkumar, N.: Using deep convolutional neural network for emotion detection on a physiological signals dataset (amigos). IEEE Access **7**, 57–67 (2018)

23. Schmidt, P., Dürichen, R., Reiss, A., Van Laerhoven, K., Plötz, T.: Multi-target affect detection in the wild: an exploratory study. In: Proceedings of the 2019 ACM International Symposium on Wearable Computers, pp. 211–219 (2019)

24. Schuller, B.W.: Speech emotion recognition: two decades in a nutshell, benchmarks, and ongoing trends. Commun. ACM **61**(5), 90–99 (2018)

25. Sharma, K., Castellini, C., van den Broek, E.L., Albu-Schaeffer, A., Schwenker, F.: A dataset of continuous affect annotations and physiological signals for emotion analysis. Sci. Data **6**(1), 196 (2019)

26. Shu, L., et al.: A review of emotion recognition using physiological signals. Sensors **18**(7), 2074 (2018)

27. Vaswani, A., et al.: Attention is all you need. In: Advances in Neural Information Processing Systems, vol. 30 (2017)

28. Vazquez-Rodriguez, J., Lefebvre, G., Cumin, J., Crowley, J.L.: Emotion recognition with pre-trained transformers using multimodal signals. In: 2022 10th International Conference on Affective Computing and Intelligent Interaction (ACII), pp. 1–8. IEEE (2022)

29. Vazquez-Rodriguez, J., Lefebvre, G., Cumin, J., Crowley, J.L.: Transformer-based self-supervised learning for emotion recognition. In: 2022 26th International Conference on Pattern Recognition (ICPR), pp. 2605–2612. IEEE (2022)

30. Wu, N., Green, B., Ben, X., O'Banion, S.: Deep transformer models for time series forecasting: The influenza prevalence case. arXiv preprint arXiv:2001.08317 (2020)

31. Wu, Y., Daoudi, M., Amad, A.: Transformer-based self-supervised multimodal representation learning for wearable emotion recognition. IEEE Trans. Affect. Comput. (2023)

32. Yang, K., et al.: Mobile emotion recognition via multiple physiological signals using convolution-augmented transformer. In: Proceedings of the 2022 International Conference on Multimedia Retrieval, pp. 562–570 (2022)

33. Zhao, B., Wang, Z., Yu, Z., Guo, B.: EmotionSense: emotion recognition based on wearable wristband. In: 2018 IEEE SmartWorld, Ubiquitous Intelligence & Computing, Advanced & Trusted Computing, Scalable Computing & Communications, Cloud & Big Data Computing, Internet of People and Smart City Innovation (SmartWorld/SCALCOM/UIC/ATC/CBDCom/IOP/SCI), pp. 346–355. IEEE (2018)

Frequency Mixup Manipulation Based Unsupervised Domain Adaptation for Brain Disease Identification

Yooseung Shin[1], Junyeong Maeng[1], Kwanseok Oh[1], and Heung-Il Suk[1,2(✉)]

[1] Department of Artificial Intelligence, Korea University, Seoul, Republic of Korea
{usxxng,mjy8086,ksohh,hisuk}@korea.ac.kr
[2] Department of Brain and Cognitive Engineering, Korea University, Seoul, Republic of Korea

Abstract. Unsupervised Domain Adaptation (UDA), which transfers the learned knowledge from a labeled source domain to an unlabeled target domain, has been widely utilized in various medical image analysis approaches. Recent advances in UDA have shown that manipulating the frequency domain between source and target distributions can significantly alleviate the domain shift problem. However, a potential drawback of these methods is the loss of semantic information in the low-frequency spectrum, which can make it difficult to consider semantic information across the entire frequency spectrum. To deal with this problem, we propose a frequency mixup manipulation that utilizes the overall semantic information of the frequency spectrum in brain disease identification. In the first step, we perform self-adversarial disentangling based on frequency manipulation to pretrain the model for intensity-invariant feature extraction. Then, we effectively align the distributions of both the source and target domains by using mixed-frequency domains. In the extensive experiments on ADNI and AIBL datasets, our proposed method achieved outstanding performance over other UDA-based approaches in medical image classification. Code is available at: https://github.com/ku-milab/FMM.

Keywords: Unsupervised domain adaptation · Frequency manipulation · Medical image reconstruction · sMRI

1 Introduction

Accurate diagnosis of brain diseases is critical, as it allows for early intervention and treatment and helps advance neuroscience studies. Recently, machine learning-based approaches [9,26] have made significant strides in identifying brain diseases such as Alzheimer's disease. Those existing methods assume that various medical images are based on homogeneous data distribution and utilize an identical model among different domain datasets. In other words, a model trained on a source domain is directly applied to the target domain without adjusting the domain difference [5]. However, in real-world applications, the presence of inter-domain heterogeneity can challenge the validity of this assumption. Differences in data distribution between domains can arise from variations in scanner protocols, demographic information of cohorts within sites, etc. This distribution discrepancy between training and test data, also known as domain shift [2], can reduce the performance of models across different domains.

To alleviate the domain shift, Unsupervised Domain Adaptation (UDA), which transfers well-trained knowledge from sufficiently labeled source data to unlabeled target data [19], has been widely exploited. Recently, various UDA methodologies [3,6,16] for effective domain transfer have been proposed. Deep-CORAL [16] minimizes domain shift by aligning the second-order statistics of source and target distributions without requiring any target labels. DANN [3] is a widely used adversarial learning-based domain adaptation method in modern medical imaging tasks. AD^2A [6] proposed an attention-guided deep domain adaptation strategy to identify brain disease in multi-site MRI. However, since these methods utilize the pixel-level distributional characteristics of samples in the spatial domain, they are sensitive to noise or variations in input data and limited in their ability to adapt to significant changes in input data distribution, which are commonly encountered in real-world scenarios. More recently, the outstanding performance of UDA has been achieved through research [15,21,22,24] by aligning the frequency domain between source and target distributions, which effectively relieves the domain shift problem. Those frequency-based methods propose a simple image translation strategy by replacing the low-frequency spectrum between the source and target domains. They achieve remarkable performance by transforming images through (Fast) Fourier Transform (FFT) and inverse FFT (iFFT) [14] for frequency manipulation and simply training on the transformed images. However, they have a limitation in that the optimum portion of the low-frequency has to be selected manually for optimal performance. In addition, since the semantic information of the original image may be lost in the process of replacing the low-frequency spectrum, the overfitting problem can occur with a fixed high-frequency spectrum [18].

To address the limitations mentioned above, we propose a novel adversarial training network based on self-adversarial disentanglement and frequency mixup strategy by exploiting the full scale of the frequency spectrum. In medical imaging, the amplitude refers to the intensity or brightness of a pixel in an image. The phase, on the other hand, represents the local orientation or direction of the intensity changes in the image. In intra-domain adaptation process, we get the intensity-shifted source domain by integrating the amplitude and phase from the intensity-transformed and the original source domain, respectively. Our proposed model learns to extract intensity-invariant representation based on a self-adversarial training approach [27] by leveraging the intensity-shifted and original source domain. The self-adversarial disentangling method can effectively pre-train models that are robust to intensity variations (*i.e.*, domain shift problem). Based on the pretrained model using the source domain only, in the inter-domain adaptation process, we reconstruct a novel amplitude-mixed target domain by mixing the amplitudes from the source and target domains, respectively, utilizing the mixup technique [25]. Unlike low-frequency domain replacement methods, mixing all-frequency domains can include low-level statistics from the target domain while effectively preserving low-level statistics of the source domain. Through domain transfer using the amplitude-mixed target domain, we solved the domain shift problem and demonstrated it in the brain disease classification task.

The main contributions of this work are as follows: (1) We propose a novel image translation-based adversarial training network by frequency mixup manipulation to exploit the semantic information of the source and target domains without loss of information in the frequency domain. (2) We show the generalizability of our proposed method in the pretraining step through self-adversarial disentangling by utilizing the frequency manipulation of the intensity-shifted source domain. (3) Our proposed method outperforms the existing methods for UDA robustly.

2   Related Work

2.1   Frequency-Based UDA

Unsupervised domain adaptation (UDA) has been explored to transfer knowledge from a sufficiently labeled (source) domain to an unlabeled unseen (target) domain. Recent studies [22,24] reveal that a simple alignment of the frequency domain between the source and target distributions can remarkably improve the performance of UDA. On the one hand, Yang *et al.* [22] proposes Fourier domain adaptation (FDA) by replacing the source frequency with the target frequency at the low-level to resolve the discrepancy between the source and target distributions. To be specific, the frequency replacement results in a reconstructed source image in the target style, which presents a reduced disparity between different domains. They suggest that a simple Fourier transform operation can achieve state-of-the-art performance on domain adaptation benchmarks without requiring individual training for domain alignment. On the other hand, Zakazov *et al.* [24] proposes a very light and transparent approach to perform test-time domain adaptation. The idea is to substitute the target low-level frequency space components that are deemed to reflect the style of an image.

As such, most frequency-based methodologies reconstruct images by replacing low-level frequencies through Fourier transform operations in each domain. This demonstrates improved UDA performance through a simple alignment of low-level statistics between source and target distribution. However, these methods encounter limitations in accurately discerning between low and high-frequency regions, which subsequently imposes a challenge in manually pinpointing the optimal region for enhancing performance. To alleviate these problem, we introduce a frequency mixup strategy by exploiting the full scale of the frequency spectrum.

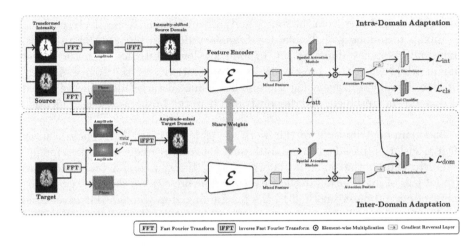

Fig. 1. Overall framework of our proposed method that consists of intra-domain adaptation and inter-domain adaptation processes.

2.2 Adversarial Training for Domain-Invariant Features

Adversarial training [1,3,7,17] is a practical approach for learning domain-invariant features by leveraging adversarial learning to minimize the domain discrepancy between different datasets. The basic idea of adversarial training is to train models that generate realistic data samples and distinguish between actual and generated samples at the same time. In the context of domain-invariant feature representation, by using a discriminator that attempts to distinguish between source and target domain features, the feature encoder is encouraged to learn domain-invariant representations that are not discriminative with respect to domain labels. This minimizes the domain discrepancy, leading to more robust and transferable features. In recent studies, Levi et al. [11] learns a feature representation that is both robust and domain invariant. By using a variant of DANN on the source domain and its corresponding target domain, the proposed method learns a feature representation constrained not to discriminate between the source and target examples and can achieve a more robust representation. Yang et al. [23] proposes a novel dual-module network architecture to promote learning domain invariant features. Furthermore, they improved performance by using a discrepancy loss to find the discrepancy of the prediction results and the feature distribution between the two modules.

3   Proposed Method

Let $\mathbf{X}_s \in \mathbb{R}^{h \times w \times d \times 1}$ denotes three-dimensional structural magnetic resonance imaging (sMRI), and $\mathbf{Y}_s$ refers to the category label in the source domain, i.e., $\mathcal{D}_s = \{(\mathbf{X}_s, \mathbf{Y}_s)\}$. In contrast, there is no category label in the target domain, i.e., $\mathcal{D}_t = \{(\mathbf{X}_t)\}$. The goal of our proposed method is to train a classification model on $\mathcal{D}_s$ and $\mathcal{D}_t$ that can perform well on unseen target domains. As shown in Fig. 1, we describe the crucial components of our proposed framework, which comprises intra-domain adaptation for pretaining using the frequency manipulation, attention-based feature encoder, and inter-domain adaptation for domain transfer.

3.1 Intra-domain Adaptation

In the first step of an intra-domain adaptation process, we use random noise transformation in the source domain to create an intensity-transformed source domain $\mathbf{X}_{is}$. Then we can get an identity-shifted source domain, which maintains the semantic characteristics of the source domain while containing the information of different intensity distributions. For this purpose, we utilize FFT algorithm [14] in mixing the information of the intensity-transformed and the original source domain. The amplitude of the intensity-transformed source domain and the phase of the original source domain is combined through iFFT process to synthesize the intensity-shifted source domain. In detail, let $\mathbf{A}, \mathbf{P}$ be the amplitude and phase components of the FFT F of an image. And then they fed to iFFT to generate the reconstructed intensity-shifted source domain $\mathcal{D}_{IS}$ as follows:

$$\mathcal{D}_{IS} = F^{-1}(\mathbf{A}(F(\mathbf{X}_{is})) \times \mathbf{P}(F(\mathbf{X}_{s}))). \tag{1}$$

We adopted a label classifier $\mathcal{C}_L$ for identifying the label of the given images and an intensity discriminator $\mathcal{C}_I$ which plays a role in making the encoder $\mathcal{E}$ to be robust in intensity differences. The cross-entropy loss $\mathcal{L}_{ce}$ for minimizing $\mathcal{C}_L$ and maximizing $\mathcal{C}_I$ with gradient reversal layer [3] is as follows:

$$\mathcal{L}_{cls} = \mathcal{L}_{ce}(\mathcal{C}_L(\mathbf{X}_s, \mathbf{Y}_s)), \mathcal{L}_{int} = \mathcal{L}_{ce}(\mathcal{C}_I(\mathbf{X}, \mathbf{Y}_i)). \tag{2}$$

3.2 Attention-Based Feature Encoder

We design a 3D convolutional neural network to extract features of brain MRIs from source and target domains. The feature encoder $\mathcal{E}$ includes 10 convolutional layers comprised of $3 \times 3 \times 3$ kernels, followed by batch normalization and ReLU in each convolution layer. Subsequently, the downsampling operation is conducted to the even-numbered convolution layers for hierarchical feature extraction. Previous studies [12,13,20] have demonstrated that brain disorders are highly associated with specific regions in the brain. Based on this proposition, we designed an attention module to automatically identify brain regions closely related to brain diseases in brain MRIs. As shown in Fig. 1, the mixed feature generated by the last layer of the feature encoder is used as an input of the proposed attention module. In the spatial attention module, the outputs of average pooling and max pooling from the mixed feature are concatenated. Then, they pass through a convolution layer to generate spatial attention maps $\mathbf{AM}$. Finally, the sigmoid function δ is used to calculate the attentive score of $\mathbf{AM}$. Mathematically, the spatial attention map $\mathbf{SA}$ is defined as:

$$\mathbf{SA} = \delta(Conv^{3 \times 3 \times 3}([\mathbf{AM}_{max}, \mathbf{AM}_{avg}])). \tag{3}$$

To make our model robust to domain differences, we need to maintain attentional consistency between $\mathbf{SA}_s$ and $\mathbf{SA}_t$, which represents attention maps for the source domain and target domain, respectively. We design an attention consistency loss to transfer semantic information from the source domain to the target domain. Attention consistency loss, which calculates the mean square difference between $\mathbf{SA}_s$ and $\mathbf{SA}_t$ is defined as follows:

$$\mathcal{L}_{\text{att}} = \frac{1}{N \times H \times W \times D} \sum_{i=1}^{N} \|\mathbf{SA}_s - \mathbf{SA}_t\|. \tag{4}$$

3.3 Inter-domain Adaptation

In inter-domain adaptation process, we extract the frequencies of the source and target domain, respectively, using FFT operation. Inspired by the mixup technique [25], we devise a novel image translation strategy by linearly interpolating between the amplitude spectrum of two domains. The equation of the frequency amplitude mixup **FAM** is defined as:

$$\mathbf{FAM} = (1 - \lambda)\mathbf{A}(F(\mathbf{X}_t)) + \lambda\mathbf{A}(F(\mathbf{X}_s)), \tag{5}$$

where $\lambda \sim U(0,1)$ refers to a random value within a fixed range.

The mixed amplitude spectrum is combined with the phase of the target image and fed to iFFT, generating the reconstructed amplitude-mixed target domain $\mathcal{D}_{\text{MT}}$ as follows:

$$\mathcal{D}_{\text{MT}} = F^{-1}(\mathbf{FAM} \times \mathbf{P}(F(\mathbf{X}_t))). \tag{6}$$

To reduce the domain gap between the source and target domain, domain classifier $\mathcal{C}_{\text{D}}$ is designed to distinguish MRI features from different domains, same as the intra-domain adaptation step.

$$\mathcal{L}_{\text{dom}} = \mathcal{L}_{ce}(\mathcal{C}_{\text{D}}(\mathbf{X}, \mathbf{Y}_{\text{d}})). \tag{7}$$

3.4 Objective Function

Our objective function was performed with the goal of minimization even though the negative loss for maximization was included for the domain classification loss. Since our domain classifier already includes a gradient reversal layer in the module, backpropagation is performed by multiplying a negative constant to maximize the loss function. As a result, we jointly minimize the label classification loss $\mathcal{L}_{\text{cls}}$, the attention consistency loss $\mathcal{L}_{\text{att}}$, and maximize the domain classification loss $\mathcal{L}_{\text{dom}}$. The overall objective function of our proposed method is defined as follows:

$$\mathcal{L}_{\text{total}} = \mathcal{L}_{\text{cls}} + \mathcal{L}_{\text{att}} - \mathcal{L}_{\text{dom}}. \tag{8}$$

4   Experiments

4.1   Dataset

ADNI Dataset. We used the Alzheimer's Disease Neuroimaging Initiative (ADNI) dataset, which is a public dataset utilized for brain disease-related research [8]. This dataset consists of ADNI-1, ADNI-2, and ADNI-3, which refer to the different site domains. We excluded data from ADNI-1 and ADNI-2, which also belong to ADNI-3, for the sake of independent evaluation. After pruning, ADNI-1 contains 431 subjects with T1-weighted sMRIs, and ADNI-2, ADNI-3 contain 360, 398 subjects, respectively.

AIBL Dataset. To demonstrate the effectiveness of domain adaptation in other domains, we additionally used the Australian Imaging Biomarkers and Lifestyle Study of Ageing (AIBL) dataset, which seeks to discover which biomarkers, cognitive characteristics, and health and lifestyle factors determine the development of Alzheimer's disease. AIBL contains 577 subjects with T1-weighted sMRIs. We conducted the experiment by dividing the training and test data at a ratio of 8:2 for all subjects in each domain.

4.2   Implementation

In the intra-domain adaptation process, we pretrained the model for 50 epochs to adapt the feature encoder $\mathcal{E}$ from the source to the target domain. Subsequently, the trained feature encoder was fine-tuned for 100 epochs in the inter-domain adaptation process. The best model selection was performed underlying the AUC score via simple hold-out validation. As implementation details in both steps (*i.e.*, intra-/inter-domain adaptation process), Adam [10] is exploited as the optimizer with an initial learning rate of 1e−4, and the batch size is set to 4.

4.3   Experiments and Analysis

In the experiments, we compared our proposed network with state-of-the-art UDA methods [4,6,16], which have been widely used in modern medical imaging tasks. We utilized the structure of our backbone feature encoder for experimenting with DANN and Deep-CORAL. To demonstrate the validity of our proposed method in various metrics, we utilized four metrics for performance evaluation in the experiment, *i.e.*, accuracy (ACC), sensitivity (SEN), specificity (SPE), and AUC curve (AUC), which evaluate the classification performance. We conducted an experiment, as shown in Table 1, based on a scenario for domain adaptation from the source domain to the target domain. We can see that the overall performance of our proposed method is better than that of the other UDA approaches. This demonstrates that 1) Fourier frequency manipulation-based self-adversarial disentanglement in intra-domain adaptation and 2) frequency mixup-based domain transfer in inter-domain adaptation in our proposed

Table 1. Performance of our proposed method and baseline methods in AD identification (*i.e.*, AD vs. CN classification) in different domain transfer settings.

Source → Target	Method	ACC	SEN	SPE	AUC
ADNI-1 → ADNI-2	DANN [4]	84.77	75.00	92.50	83.75
	Deep-CORAL [16]	84.72	75.00	92.50	83.75
	AD^2A [6]	86.11	75.00	95.00	85.00
	Ours	**90.28**	**81.25**	**97.50**	**89.37**
ADNI-1 → ADNI-3	DANN [4]	88.75	84.62	**89.55**	87.08
	Deep-CORAL [16]	85.00	76.92	86.57	81.74
	AD^2A [6]	88.75	92.31	88.06	90.18
	Ours	**90.00**	**100.0**	88.06	**94.03**
ADNI-2 → ADNI-1	DANN [4]	77.01	69.23	**83.33**	76.28
	Deep-CORAL [16]	74.71	64.10	83.33	73.72
	AD^2A [6]	78.16	**92.31**	66.67	79.49
	Ours	**81.61**	89.74	75.00	**82.37**
ADNI-2 → ADNI-3	DANN [4]	81.25	84.62	80.59	82.61
	Deep-CORAL [16]	83.75	69.23	**86.57**	77.90
	AD^2A [6]	83.75	100.0	80.60	90.30
	Ours	**86.25**	**100.0**	83.58	**91.79**
ADNI-1 → AIBL	DANN [4]	74.14	69.56	75.27	72.42
	Deep-CORAL [16]	87.07	65.22	88.17	80.46
	AD^2A [6]	85.34	73.91	88.17	81.04
	Ours	**89.65**	**78.26**	**92.47**	**85.37**
ADNI-2 → AIBL	DANN [4]	67.24	**91.30**	61.29	76.30
	Deep-CORAL [16]	71.55	52.17	76.34	64.26
	AD^2A [6]	71.55	82.61	68.82	75.71
	Ours	**83.62**	86.96	**82.79**	**84.88**

Table 2. Performance of our proposed method and ablating Fourier frequency manipulation (FFM) in intra-domain adaptation.

Source → Target	Method	ACC	SEN	SPE	AUC
ADNI-1 → ADNI-2	w/o FFM	87.50	71.87	**100.0**	85.93
	Ours	**90.28**	**81.25**	97.50	**89.37**
ADNI-1 → ADNI-3	w/o FFM	80.00	92.31	77.62	84.96
	Ours	**90.00**	**100.0**	**88.06**	**94.03**
ADNI-2 → ADNI-1	w/o FFM	77.01	76.92	**77.08**	77.00
	Ours	**81.61**	**89.74**	75.00	**82.37**
ADNI-2 → ADNI-3	w/o FFM	85.00	100.0	82.09	91.04
	Ours	**86.25**	100.0	**83.58**	**91.79**
ADNI-1 → AIBL	w/o FFM	85.34	73.91	88.17	81.04
	Ours	**89.65**	**78.26**	**92.47**	**85.37**
ADNI-2 → AIBL	w/o FFM	81.90	69.56	**84.95**	77.25
	Ours	**83.62**	**86.96**	82.79	**84.88**

method can effectively align domain distributions. We also visualized the domain distribution adapted by our proposed method and the original domain distribution in Fig. 2 to verify the effectiveness of our proposed model in distribution alignment.

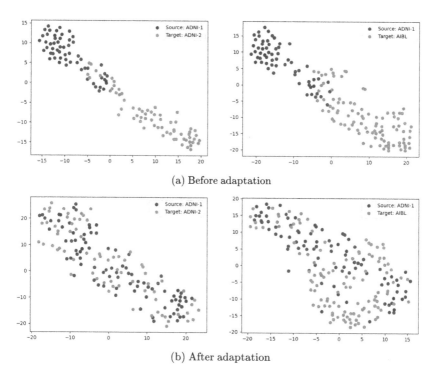

(a) Before adaptation

(b) After adaptation

Fig. 2. Visualization of (a) the original distribution and (b) the distribution after adaptation of the proposed our method for each domain (*i.e.*, ADNI-1, ADNI-2, AIBL).

Table 3. Performance of our proposed method and ablating attention consistency loss (AC).

Source → Target	Method	ACC	SEN	SPE	AUC
ADNI-1 → ADNI-2	w/o AC	87.50	81.25	92.50	86.87
	Ours	**90.28**	**81.25**	**97.50**	**89.37**
ADNI-1 → ADNI-3	w/o AC	85.00	92.31	83.58	87.94
	Ours	**90.00**	**100.0**	**88.06**	**94.03**
ADNI-2 → ADNI-1	w/o AC	77.01	76.92	**77.08**	77.00
	Ours	**81.61**	**89.74**	75.00	**82.37**
ADNI-2 → ADNI-3	w/o AC	82.50	100.0	79.10	89.55
	Ours	**86.25**	**100.0**	**83.58**	**91.79**
ADNI-1 → AIBL	w/o AC	88.79	69.56	**93.55**	81.56
	Ours	**89.65**	**78.26**	92.47	**85.37**
ADNI-2 → AIBL	w/o AC	77.59	82.61	76.34	79.48
	Ours	**83.62**	**86.96**	**82.79**	**84.88**

Table 4. Performance of our proposed method and adopting two image translation strategies in inter-domain adaptation.

Source → Target	Method	ACC	SEN	SPE	AUC
ADNI-1 → ADNI-2	Fda [22]	80.55	**87.50**	75.00	81.25
	Mixup [25]	88.89	84.37	92.50	88.44
	Ours	**90.28**	81.25	**97.50**	**89.37**
ADNI-1 → ADNI-3	Fda [22]	88.75	92.31	88.06	90.18
	Mixup [25]	87.50	92.31	86.57	89.44
	Ours	**90.00**	**100.0**	88.06	**94.03**
ADNI-2 → ADNI-1	Fda [22]	78.17	66.67	**87.50**	77.08
	Mixup [25]	75.86	61.54	87.50	74.52
	Ours	**81.61**	**89.74**	75.00	**82.37**
ADNI-2 → ADNI-3	Fda [22]	80.00	100.0	76.12	88.06
	Mixup [25]	83.75	100.0	80.60	90.30
	Ours	**86.25**	**100.0**	**83.58**	**91.79**
ADNI-1 → AIBL	Fda [22]	81.90	78.26	82.79	80.53
	Mixup [25]	85.34	73.91	88.17	81.04
	Ours	**89.65**	**78.26**	**92.47**	**85.37**
ADNI-2 → AIBL	Fda [22]	80.17	78.26	80.64	79.45
	Mixup [25]	74.14	82.61	72.04	77.32
	Ours	**83.62**	**86.96**	**82.79**	**84.88**

4.4 Ablation Analysis

In order to assess the efficacy of self-adversarial disentanglement using Fourier frequency manipulation, we conducted an ablation experiment with and without using Fourier frequency manipulation in the intra-domain adaptation process. As seen in Table 2, utilizing Fourier frequency manipulation for the intensity-shifted source domain results in better performance within overall evaluation metrics. This reveals that manipulating frequencies of the source domain using the Fourier transform operation can make the model robust to the intensity differences.

Our proposed combination with the attention consistency loss empowers the domain invariant semantic representations, thus enhancing diagnosis performance on unseen target domains. Besides the attention consistency loss, our attention module helps highlight discriminative regions across different domains, while others can only focus on a single domain. To verify these attention mechanisms, we conducted an ablation experiment with and without computing attention consistency loss in the inter-domain adaptation process. From Table 3, we can derive that attention consistency loss is useful in boosting learning performance.

We also compared with the previous low-frequency replacing method (*i.e.*, Fda [22]) and the vanilla mixup method [25] to demonstrate the effectiveness of the proposed frequency mixup strategy, as shown in Table 4. Using the Fda method, which replaces low-frequency, occurs overfitting in the high-frequency region due to loss of low-frequency information [18] and showed poor results in the overall evaluation metrics. The results of adopting the vanilla mixup technique are slightly better than those using Fda but worse than our proposed method. Through this ablation study, we demonstrated the effectiveness of our mixup technique at the frequency semantic-level rather than other mixing strategies.

5   Conclusion

In this paper, we proposed a frequency mixup manipulation-based unsupervised domain adaptation model to alleviate domain shifts in brain disease identification. The proposed model comprises two main steps: intra-domain adaptation and inter-domain adaptation. In the intra-domain adaptation step, a pre-training process is conducted to enhance the intensity-invariant feature extraction capability of the model. This is achieved by using self-adversarial disentangling with frequency manipulation-based intensity-shifted domains. In the inter-domain adaptation step, a domain transfer process is performed, where the reconstructed image through frequency mixup is used to train a model that is robust to domain adaptation. Our experimental results demonstrate that the proposed method outperforms state-of-the-art UDA methods in terms of accuracy and effectiveness.

Acknowledgements. This work was supported by National Research Foundation of Korea (NRF) grant funded by the Korea government (MSIT) No. 2022R1A2C2006865 (Development of deep learning techniques for data-driven medical knowledge graph generation and interpretable multi-modal electronic health records analysis) and No. 2019-0-00079 (Department of Artificial Intelligence (Korea University)).

References

1. Bai, T., Luo, J., Zhao, J., Wen, B., Wang, Q.: Recent advances in adversarial training for adversarial robustness. arXiv preprint arXiv:2102.01356 (2021)
2. Ben-David, S., Blitzer, J., Crammer, K., Pereira, F.: Analysis of representations for domain adaptation. In: Advances in Neural Information Processing Systems, vol. 19 (2006)
3. Ganin, Y., Lempitsky, V.: Unsupervised domain adaptation by backpropagation. In: International Conference on Machine Learning, pp. 1180–1189. PMLR (2015)
4. Ganin, Y., et al.: Domain-adversarial training of neural networks. J. Mach. Learn. Res. **17**(1), 2096–2030 (2016)
5. Guan, H., Liu, M.: Domain adaptation for medical image analysis: a survey. IEEE Trans. Biomed. Eng. **69**(3), 1173–1185 (2021)

6. Guan, H., Liu, Y., Yang, E., Yap, P.T., Shen, D., Liu, M.: Multi-site MRI harmonization via attention-guided deep domain adaptation for brain disorder identification. Med. Image Anal. **71**, 102076 (2021)
7. Hoffman, J., et al.: CyCADA: cycle-consistent adversarial domain adaptation. In: International Conference on Machine Learning, pp. 1989–1998. PMLR (2018)
8. Jack, C.R., Jr., et al.: The Alzheimer's disease neuroimaging initiative (ADNI): MRI methods. J. Magn. Reson. Imaging Official J. Int. Soc. Magn. Reson. Med. **27**(4), 685–691 (2008)
9. Khan, P., et al.: Machine learning and deep learning approaches for brain disease diagnosis: principles and recent advances. IEEE Access **9**, 37622–37655 (2021)
10. Kingma, D.P., Ba, J.: Adam: a method for stochastic optimization. arXiv preprint arXiv:1412.6980 (2014)
11. Levi, M., Attias, I., Kontorovich, A.: Domain invariant adversarial learning. arXiv preprint arXiv:2104.00322 (2021)
12. Lian, C., Liu, M., Zhang, J., Shen, D.: Hierarchical fully convolutional network for joint atrophy localization and Alzheimer's disease diagnosis using structural MRI. IEEE Trans. Pattern Anal. Mach. Intell. **42**(4), 880–893 (2018)
13. Mu, Y., Gage, F.H.: Adult hippocampal neurogenesis and its role in Alzheimer's disease. Mol. Neurodegener. **6**(1), 1–9 (2011)
14. Nussbaumer, H.J.: The fast Fourier transform. In: Fast Fourier Transform and Convolution Algorithms. Springer Series in Information Sciences, vol. 2. Springer, Heidelberg (1982). https://doi.org/10.1007/978-3-642-81897-4_4
15. Sharifzadeh, M., Tehrani, A.K., Benali, H., Rivaz, H.: Ultrasound domain adaptation using frequency domain analysis. In: 2021 IEEE International Ultrasonics Symposium, pp. 1–4. IEEE (2021)
16. Sun, B., Feng, J., Saenko, K.: Correlation alignment for unsupervised domain adaptation. In: Csurka, G. (ed.) Domain Adaptation in Computer Vision Applications. ACVPR, pp. 153–171. Springer, Cham (2017). https://doi.org/10.1007/978-3-319-58347-1_8
17. Tzeng, E., Hoffman, J., Saenko, K., Darrell, T.: Adversarial discriminative domain adaptation. In: Proceedings of the IEEE Conference on Computer Vision and Pattern Recognition, pp. 7167–7176 (2017)
18. Wang, H., Wu, X., Huang, Z., Xing, E.P.: High-frequency component helps explain the generalization of convolutional neural networks. In: Proceedings of the IEEE/CVF Conference on Computer Vision and Pattern Recognition, pp. 8684–8694 (2020)
19. Wilson, G., Cook, D.J.: A survey of unsupervised deep domain adaptation. ACM Trans. Intell. Syst. Technol. **11**(5), 1–46 (2020)
20. Woo, S., Park, J., Lee, J.-Y., Kweon, I.S.: CBAM: convolutional block attention module. In: Ferrari, V., Hebert, M., Sminchisescu, C., Weiss, Y. (eds.) ECCV 2018. LNCS, vol. 11211, pp. 3–19. Springer, Cham (2018). https://doi.org/10.1007/978-3-030-01234-2_1
21. Yang, C., Guo, X., Chen, Z., Yuan, Y.: Source free domain adaptation for medical image segmentation with Fourier style mining. Med. Image Anal. **79**, 102457 (2022)
22. Yang, Y., Soatto, S.: FDA: Fourier domain adaptation for semantic segmentation. In: Proceedings of the IEEE/CVF Conference on Computer Vision and Pattern Recognition, pp. 4085–4095 (2020)
23. Yang, Y., Zhang, T., Li, G., Kim, T., Wang, G.: An unsupervised domain adaptation model based on dual-module adversarial training. Neurocomputing **475**, 102–111 (2022)

24. Zakazov, I., Shaposhnikov, V., Bespalov, I., Dylov, D.V.: Feather-light Fourier domain adaptation in magnetic resonance imaging. In: Kamnitsas, K., et al. (eds.) Domain Adaptation and Representation Transfer, DART 2022. LNCS, vol. 13542, pp. 88–97. Springer, Cham (2022). https://doi.org/10.1007/978-3-031-16852-9_9
25. Zhang, H., Cisse, M., Dauphin, Y.N., Lopez-Paz, D.: mixup: beyond empirical risk minimization. arXiv preprint arXiv:1710.09412 (2017)
26. Zhang, L., Wang, M., Liu, M., Zhang, D.: A survey on deep learning for neuroimaging-based brain disorder analysis. Front. Neurosci. **14**, 779 (2020)
27. Zhou, Q., Gu, Q., Pang, J., Lu, X., Ma, L.: Self-adversarial disentangling for specific domain adaptation. arXiv preprint arXiv:2108.03553 (2021)

SSC-l_0: Sparse Subspace Clustering with the l_0 Inequality Constraint

Yangbo Wang[1,2], Jie Zhou[1,2,3]($\boxtimes$), Qingshui Lin[4], Jianglin Lu[5], and Can Gao[2,3]

[1] National Engineering Laboratory for Big Data System Computing Technology, Shenzhen University, Shenzhen 518060, China
2070276074@email.szu.edu.cn, jie_jpu@163.com
[2] College of Computer Science and Software Engineering, Shenzhen University, Shenzhen 518060, China
[3] SZU Branch, Shenzhen Institute of Artificial Intelligence and Robotics for Society, Shenzhen 518060, China
[4] Basic Teaching Department, Liaoning Technical University, Huludao 125105, China
[5] College of Engineering, Northeastern University, Boston, MA 02115, USA
lu.jiang@northeastern.edu

Abstract. Self-expression learning methods often obtain a coefficient matrix to measure the similarity between pairs of samples. However, directly using all points to represent a fixed sample in a class under the self-expression framework may not be ideal, as points from other classes participate in the representing process. To alleviate this issue, this study attempts to achieve representation learning between points only coming from the same class. In practice, it is easier for data points from the same class to represent each other than that from different classes. So, when reconstructing a point, if the number of non-zero elements in the coefficient vector is limited, a model is more likely to select data points from the class where the reconstructed point lies to complete the reconstruction work. Based on this idea, we propose Sparse Subspace Clustering with the l_0 inequality constraint (SSC-l_0). In SSC-l_0, the l_0 inequality constraint determines the maximum number of non-zero elements in the coefficient vector, which helps SSC-l_0 to conduct representation learning among the points in the same class. After introducing the simplex constraint to ensure the translation invariance of the model, an optimization method concerning l_0 inequality constraint is formed to solve the proposed SSC-l_0, and its convergence is theoretically analyzed. Extensive experiments on well-known datasets demonstrate the superiority of SSC-l_0 compared to several state-of-the-art methods.

Keywords: Sparse subspace clustering · l_0 inequality constraint · simplex constraint · self-expression learning · graph learning

---

This work was supported by the National Natural Science Foundation of China (No. 62076164), Shenzhen Science and Technology Program (No. JCYJ20210324094601005), and Guangdong Basic and Applied Basic Research Foundation (No. 2021A1515011861).

H. Lu et al. (Eds.): ACPR 2023, LNCS 14408, pp. 136–149, 2023.
https://doi.org/10.1007/978-3-031-47665-5_12

1   Introduction

As an important branch of the field of pattern recognition, clustering has been extensively developed in the past few decades. Commonly used clustering methods include prototype-based clustering [1], matrix factorization-based clustering [2], and graph-based clustering [3], etc. Among them, graph-based clustering has attracted much attention because it can exploit the geometrical structure information of the data [4,5].

As a typical graph-based clustering method, Spectral Clustering (SC) [6] often achieves superior clustering performance when handling datasets with high dimensions. In the spectral clustering method, a low-dimensional representation of data is first constructed by utilizing the predetermined similarity matrix. Subsequently, SC yields the discrete clustering result by calling the spectral rotation method [7] or using k-Means methods [8] based on the relaxed spectral solutions. So, the similarity matrix plays a critical role in spectral clustering. Similarity matrix construction methods often include two types, point-pairwise distance-based methods and self-expression learning methods-based. The typical point-pairwise distance-based methods include the Gaussian kernel method, adaptive neighbors [9,10], typicality-aware adaptive graph [11], and so on. These methods construct sparse similarity matrices by learning sample neighborhood structure information.

The self-expression learning methods, including the Sparse Subspace Clustering (SSC) [12], Low-Rank Representation (LRR) [13], Block-Diagonal Representation (BDR) [14], and their extensions [15,16], have been reported and achieved desired performance. Among them, SSC [12] aims to group data drawn from a union of multiple linear subspaces. When the subspaces from which data are drawn are independent, SSC can obtain desired performance by learning a sparse affinity matrix. LRR [13] minimizes the rank of the coefficient matrix to recover the row space of the data. BDR [14] proposes a novel regularizer for directly pursuing a coefficient matrix with the block diagonal property. Iteratively Reweighted Least Squares (IRLS) [15] solves a joint low-rank and sparse minimization problem. Least Squares Regression (LSR) [16] minimizes the F-norm of the coefficient matrix to achieve that the correlated samples have similar coefficient vectors. Simplex Sparse Representation (SSR) [17] introduces the simplex constraint to ensure the translation invariance of the model.

The above self-expression learning-based methods seek sparse or low-rank representation coefficient matrices to measure the similarity between pairs of samples. However, in these methods, the way that directly uses all sample points to represent a fixed sample may not be ideal since points from other classes also participate in the representing process. Therefore, the generated similarity matrix is not reliable and affects the performance of downstream tasks.

To alleviate this issue, we propose Sparse Subspace Clustering with the l_0 inequality constraint (SSC-l_0). SSC-l_0 aims to achieve a representation learning mechanism in which only the points coming from the same class are expected to be used for representing each sample in this class.

The main contributions of this work are listed as follows:

1. A new self-expression learning method, named Sparse Subspace Clustering with the l_0 inequality constraint (SSC-l_0), is proposed. In SSC-l_0, the l_0 inequality constraint constrains the number of non-zero elements in the coefficient vector, which helps SSC-l_0 to conduct representation learning among the points in the same class.
2. By introducing the simplex constraint to ensure the translation invariance of the model, an optimization method concerning l_0 inequality constraint is presented to solve the proposed SSC-l_0, and its convergence is theoretically analyzed. Since the l_0 inequality constraint problem is difficult to be solved, the proposed optimization method has the potential to be widely used sparse learning models.
3. Extensive experiments on benchmark datasets demonstrate the superiority of SSC-l_0.

The rest of this paper is organized as follows. In Sect. 2, we introduce some notations and the related methods. In Sect. 3, we elaborate on the proposed SSC-l_0 and its corresponding optimization algorithm. Experimental results are reported in Sect. 4. Finally, Sect. 5 concludes the paper.

2   Related Works

2.1   Notations

In this study, the bold uppercase letters and lowercase italic letters are used to stand for the matrices and scalars, respectively, such as $\mathbf{X} = [\mathbf{x}_1; \mathbf{x}_2; \cdots ; \mathbf{x}_n] \in \mathbb{R}^{n \times d}$ represents a data matrix, where d and n denote the dimensions and the number of samples, respectively. The bold lowercase letters stand for vectors, such as $\mathbf{x}_i \in \mathbb{R}^{1 \times d}$ is a sample point. $Tr(\mathbf{A})$ and $\mathbf{A}^T$ stand for the trace and the transpose of matrix $\mathbf{A}$, respectively. $\mathbf{A} \geq \mathbf{0}$ means that each element $a_{ij} \geq 0$ in $\mathbf{A}$.

2.2   Sparse Subspace Clustering

Let $\left\{ \mathbf{x}_j \in \mathbb{R}^{1 \times d} \right\}_{j=1}^{n}$ be a set of data points drawn from a union of c independent linear subspaces $\{ \mathcal{S}_i \}_{i=1}^{c}$. Let n_i is the number of data points drawn from the subspace $\mathcal{S}_i$, d_i is dimension of $\mathcal{S}_i$, and $\mathbf{Y}_i$ a data matrix corresponding to subspace $\mathcal{S}_i$. If $n_i \geq d_i$, the points that are drawn from the subspace $\mathcal{S}_i$ is *self-expressive* [12]. This means that if $\mathbf{x}$ is a new data point in $\mathcal{S}_i$, then it can be represented as a linear combination of d_i points in the same subspace. Denoting $\mathbf{z}_i \in \mathbb{R}^{1 \times n_i}$ is a fragment of the coefficient vector, and it corresponds to the data matrix $\mathbf{Y}_i$. If we let $\mathbf{X}$ be a data matrix with proper permutation, i.e., $\mathbf{X} = [\mathbf{Y}_1, \mathbf{Y}_1, \cdots , \mathbf{Y}_c]$, for any data point $\mathbf{x}$, there exists a vector $\mathbf{s} = [\mathbf{z}_1, \mathbf{z}_2, \cdots , \mathbf{z}_c] \in \mathbb{R}^{1 \times n}$ such that $\mathbf{x} = \mathbf{s}\mathbf{X}$, where $\mathbf{z}_i \neq \mathbf{0}$ and $\mathbf{z}_j = \mathbf{0}$ for all $j \neq i$ ($\mathbf{z}_i \in \mathbb{R}^{1 \times n_i}$ is the fragment corresponding to points in the same subspace as $\mathbf{x}$). And such a $\mathbf{s}$ can be sought by solving the following problem:

$$\min_{\mathbf{s}} ||\mathbf{s}||_0, \quad \text{s.t.} \quad \mathbf{x} = \mathbf{s}\mathbf{X}, \tag{1}$$

where $||\mathbf{s}||_0$ represents the number of non-zero elements in row vector $\mathbf{s}$. This can be proved by the following Theorem 1.

Theorem 1. *Denoting $\mathbf{s}^*$ is the optimal solution to the problem* (1). *Let $\mathbf{X}$ be a data matrix with proper permutation and $\mathbf{x} \in \mathcal{S}_i$, then $\mathbf{s}^* = [\mathbf{z}_1, \mathbf{z}_2, \cdots, \mathbf{z}_c] \in \mathbb{R}^{1 \times n}$, where $\mathbf{z}_i \neq \mathbf{0}$ and $\mathbf{z}_j = \mathbf{0}$ for all $j \neq i$.*

Proof. Let $\mathbf{s}^* = \mathbf{s}_\uparrow^* + \mathbf{s}_\downarrow^*$, where $\mathbf{s}_\uparrow^* = [0, 0, \cdots, \mathbf{z}_i, \cdots 0] \in \mathbb{R}^{1 \times n}$ and $\mathbf{s}_\downarrow^* = [\mathbf{z}_1, \mathbf{z}_2, \cdots, \mathbf{z}_{i-1}, \mathbf{0}, \mathbf{z}_{i+1}, \cdots, \mathbf{z}_c] \in \mathbb{R}^{1 \times n}$. It has Theorem 1 holds when we show that $\mathbf{s}_\downarrow^* = \mathbf{0}$.

Let $\mathbf{s}_\downarrow^* \neq \mathbf{0}$, since $\mathbf{s}^* = \mathbf{s}_\uparrow^* + \mathbf{s}_\downarrow^*$, it has $\mathbf{x} = \mathbf{s}^* \mathbf{X} = (\mathbf{s}_\uparrow^* + \mathbf{s}_\downarrow^*)\mathbf{X}$. According to the independence assumption [12], it has $\mathbf{x} \in \mathcal{S}_i$, $\mathbf{s}_\uparrow^* \mathbf{X} \in \mathcal{S}_i$, and $\mathbf{s}_\downarrow^* \mathbf{X} \notin \mathcal{S}_i$. Thus, we have $\mathbf{s}_\downarrow^* \mathbf{X} = \mathbf{0}$. This implies that

$$\mathbf{x} = \mathbf{s}^* \mathbf{X} = \mathbf{s}_\uparrow^* \mathbf{X} \tag{2}$$

which means that $\mathbf{s}_\uparrow^*$ is also a solution of Eq. (1). And we have $||\mathbf{s}_\uparrow^*||_0 < ||\mathbf{s}_\uparrow^* + \mathbf{s}_\downarrow^*||_0 = ||\mathbf{s}^*||_0$, which conflicts with $\mathbf{s}^*$ being the optimal solution to Eq. (1). So we have $\mathbf{s}_\downarrow^* = \mathbf{0}$. The Theorem 1 holds. ∎

The matrix format of Eq. (1) is as follows:

$$\min_{\mathbf{S}} \sum_{i=1}^{n} ||\mathbf{s}_i||_0, \quad \text{s.t.} \quad \mathbf{X} = \mathbf{S}\mathbf{X}, \tag{3}$$

where $\mathbf{S} = [\mathbf{s}_1; \mathbf{s}_2; \cdots; \mathbf{s}_n] \in \mathbb{R}^{n \times n}$ is a coefficient matrix, and $\mathbf{s}_i \in \mathbb{R}^{1 \times n}$ is a coefficient vector corresponding to the point $\mathbf{x}_i$.

Theorem 1 demonstrates that when the subspaces are independent, any sample $\mathbf{x}_i$ can be represented by the samples coming from the same class. And $s_{ij} = 0$ if samples $\mathbf{x}_j$ and $\mathbf{x}_i$ come from different classes.

According to Theorem 1, when $\mathbf{X}$ is properly permuted and subspaces are independent, the coefficient matrix $\mathbf{S}$ has a block diagonal structure, which can be used to improve clustering performance.

3   Sparse Subspace Clustering with the l_0 Inequality Constraint

3.1   Motivation of SSC-l_0

Most self-expression learning methods seek a sparse or low-rank representation coefficient matrix and minimize the difference between the original samples and their reconstructed estimations. The objective functions of SSC, LRR, and their extensions [14–16] can be generalized as follows:

$$\min_{\mathbf{S}} ||\mathbf{X} - \mathbf{S}\mathbf{X}||_F^2 + \gamma \mathcal{R}(\mathbf{S}), \tag{4}$$

where $\mathbf{S}$ is a reconstruction coefficient matrix, $||\mathbf{X} - \mathbf{SX}||_F^2$ indicates the self-expression reconstruction loss. $\mathcal{R}(\mathbf{S})$ is a regularization term, which guarantees that $\mathbf{S}$ is sparse or low-rank, or has a strict block diagonal structure, etc.

Numerous studies have shown that self-expression learning methods achieve impressive performance in clustering tasks [13]. However, in Eq. (4), directly using all points to represent a fixed sample in a class may degrade the quality of the learned similarity matrix, as points from other classes also participate in the representing process. To alleviate this issue, we attempt to achieve representation learning between points of the same class. However, this work is not easy because the ground truth labels are not provided beforehand. According to Theorem 1, the permuted coefficient matrix has a block diagonal structure when the subspaces from which the data are drawn are independent. Thus, such block diagonal structures can be used to guide the similarity measurements among samples. However, real data often do not qualify the subspace independence assumption [18].

In practice, it is easier for data points from the same class to represent each other than that from different classes. Thus, when reconstructing a point, if the number of non-zero elements in the coefficient vector is limited, a model is more likely to select data points from the class where the reconstructed point lies to complete the reconstruction process. This means that introducing the l_0 inequality constraint may improve the performance of the self-expression learning model.

3.2 Objective Function of SSC-l_0

According to the discussion in Sect. 3.1, introducing the l_0 inequality constraint may improve the performance of the self-expression learning model. The proposed objective function is as follows:

$$\min_{\mathbf{S}} \ ||\mathbf{X} - \mathbf{SX}||_F^2 + \gamma ||\mathbf{S}||_F^2,$$
$$\text{s.t. } \mathbf{S} \geq 0, \mathbf{S1}^T = \mathbf{1}^T, ||\mathbf{s}_i||_0 < k \ (i = 1, 2, \cdots, n), \tag{5}$$

where $\mathbf{S} = [\mathbf{s}_1; \mathbf{s}_2; \cdots ; \mathbf{s}_n] \in \mathbb{R}^{n \times n}$ is a reconstruction coefficient matrix, γ is a non-negative balance parameter, and k is a constant. The constraint $||\mathbf{s}_i||_0 \leq k$ means that the max number of non-zero elements in the coefficient vector $\mathbf{s}_i$ is k.

By introducing the l_0 inequality constraint $||\mathbf{s}_i||_0 \leq k$, in the first term of Eq. (5), each sample is represented as a linear combination of the samples that are more likely from the class that the represented sample belongs to. Since the coefficient matrix is non-negative, the elements in the coefficient matrix can reflect the similarity between the sample pairs. The l_2 norm $||\mathbf{s}_i||_2^2$ can be utilized to avoid overfitting on $\mathbf{s}_i$. The constraint $\mathbf{s}_i \mathbf{1}^T = 1$ can be used to ensure the translation invariance [17].

3.3   Optimization of SSC-l_0

First, because of the difficulty of solving model Eq. (5), we turn to optimize the following model:

$$\min_{S,M} \ ||X - MX||_F^2 + \alpha||M - S||_F^2 + \gamma||S||_F^2,$$
$$\text{s.t.} \ \ S \geq 0, S1^T = 1^T, ||s_i||_0 \leq k \ (i = 1, 2, \cdots, n), \tag{6}$$

where α is a non-negative parameter. Problem (6) can be transformed into the problem (5) when α is large enough. And the problem (6) can be minimized using the following iterative algorithm:

Updating M. When S is fixed, problem (6) becomes:

$$\min_{M} \ ||X - MX||_F^2 + \alpha||M - S||_F^2. \tag{7}$$

Setting the derivative of Eq. (7) with respect to M to zero, it has:

$$M = \left(XX^T + \alpha S\right)\left(XX^T + \alpha I\right)^{-1}. \tag{8}$$

Updating S. When M is fixed, problem (6) becomes:

$$\min_{S} \ \alpha||M - S||_F^2 + \gamma||S||_F^2,$$
$$\text{s.t.} \ \ S \geq 0, S1^T = 1^T, ||s_i||_0 \leq k \ (i = 1, 2, \cdots, n). \tag{9}$$

Since problem (9) is independent of each s_i, problem (9) can be converted into subproblems:

$$\min_{s_i} \ \alpha||m_i - s_i||_2^2 + \gamma||s_i||_2^2,$$
$$\text{s.t.} \ \ s_i \geq 0, s_i 1^T = 1, ||s_i||_0 \leq k,$$
$$\Leftrightarrow \min_{s_i} \ \mathcal{O}(s_i) = ||s_i - u_i||_2^2, \tag{10}$$
$$\text{s.t.} \ \ s_i \geq 0, s_i 1^T = 1, ||s_i||_0 \leq k,$$

where $u_i = \frac{\alpha}{\alpha+\gamma} m_i$.

Obviously, Eq. (10) seems to be an NP-hard problem. Some methods sparsify the vector s_i obtained from all samples [19]. However, the convergence of this solving method cannot be guaranteed theoretically. Here, we attempt to identify an equivalent problem to Eq. (10) that is readily solvable.

Denoting $\check{\Gamma}$ is a set that includes the indices corresponding to the first k largest elements in u_i. Then, the optimal solution to the following problem (11) is also an optimal solution to the problem (10). To prove this, we propose further the following definitions, lemmas, and theorems.

$$\min_{s_i \geq 0, s_i 1^T = 1, s_{ij} = 0 \ if j \notin \check{\Gamma}(i)} \left\{ \mathcal{O}_1 = \sum_{j \in \check{\Gamma}(i)} (s_{ij} - u_{ij})^2 \right\}. \tag{11}$$

Definition 1. *Let* $\mathbf{s}_i$ *satisfy the constraints of Eq.* (10). *If there is at least one non-zero element* s_{ij} ($s_{ij} > 0$) *in* $\mathbf{s}_i$ *that satisfies* $j \notin \check{\Gamma}(i)$, *then* $\mathbf{s}_i$ *is called a* ζ *solution of Eq.* (10).

Definition 2. $\Pi\left(\mathbf{s}_i, \check{\Gamma}(i)\right) = \sum_{j=1}^{n} \mathcal{A}(s_{ij}, j)$, *where* $\mathcal{A}(s_{ij}, j) = 1$ *if* $s_{ij} > 0$ *and* $j \in \check{\Gamma}(i)$; *otherwise* $\mathcal{A}(s_{ij}, j) = 0$.

Lemma 1. *For any* ζ *solution* $\ddot{\mathbf{s}}_i$ *of Eq.* (10), *there exists another solution* $\widetilde{\mathbf{s}}_i$ *of Eq.* (10) *that satisfies* $\Pi\left(\widetilde{\mathbf{s}}_i, \check{\Gamma}(i)\right) = \Pi\left(\ddot{\mathbf{s}}_i, \check{\Gamma}(i)\right) + 1$ *such that* $\mathcal{O}\left(\widetilde{\mathbf{s}}_i\right) \leq \mathcal{O}\left(\ddot{\mathbf{s}}_i\right)$.

Proof. Let $\tau \notin \check{\Gamma}(i)$ and $\epsilon \in \check{\Gamma}(i)$ be indices that satisfy $\ddot{\mathbf{s}}_i = [\cdots, \ddot{s}_{i\tau}, \cdots, \ddot{s}_{i\epsilon}, \cdots]$ and $\widetilde{\mathbf{s}}_i = [\cdots, \widetilde{s}_{i\tau}, \cdots, \widetilde{s}_{i\epsilon}, \cdots]$, where $u_{i\tau} \leq u_{i\epsilon}$, $\ddot{s}_{i\epsilon} = 0$, $\widetilde{s}_{i\tau} = 0$, $\ddot{s}_{i\tau} = \widetilde{s}_{i\epsilon} > 0$, and $\ddot{s}_{ij} = \widetilde{s}_{ij}$ for any $j \neq \tau$ and $j \neq \epsilon$.

Thus, one has:

$$\left(\ddot{s}_{i\tau} - u_{i\tau}\right)^2 + \left(\ddot{s}_{i\epsilon} - u_{i\epsilon}\right)^2 \geq \left(\widetilde{s}_{i\tau} - u_{i\tau}\right)^2 + \left(\widetilde{s}_{i\epsilon} - u_{i\epsilon}\right)^2, \tag{12}$$

which means $\mathcal{O}\left(\widetilde{\mathbf{s}}_i\right) \leq \mathcal{O}\left(\ddot{\mathbf{s}}_i\right)$. Thus, Lemma 1 holds. ∎

Lemma 2. *For any* ζ *solution* $\ddot{\mathbf{s}}_i$ *of Eq.* (10), *there exists another non-*ζ *solution* $\widetilde{\mathbf{s}}_i$ *of Eq.* (10) *such that* $\mathcal{O}\left(\widetilde{\mathbf{s}}_i\right) \leq \mathcal{O}\left(\ddot{\mathbf{s}}_i\right)$.

Proof. Lemma 2 holds when Lemma 1 holds. ∎

Lemma 3. *Let* $\mathbf{s}_i^*$ *be the optimal solution of Eq.* (10), *there exists a non-*ζ *solution* $\ddot{\mathbf{s}}_i^*$ *that satisfy* $\mathcal{O}\left(\ddot{\mathbf{s}}_i^*\right) = \mathcal{O}\left(\mathbf{s}_i^*\right)$.

Proof. Obviously, Lemma 3 holds when Lemma 2 holds. ∎

Lemma 3 demonstrates that if $\mathbf{s}_i^*$ is an optimal solution of Eq. (10) and it is a ζ solution, then there exists a non-ζ solution $\ddot{\mathbf{s}}_i^*$ which is also an optimal solution to the problem (10).

Theorem 2. *Let* $\bar{\mathbf{s}}_i^*$ *be the optimal solution to the problem* (11), *then* $\bar{\mathbf{s}}_i^*$ *is also an optimal solution to the problem* (10).

Proof. Let $\mathbf{s}_i^*$ be the optimal solution of Eq. (10), according to Lemma 3, there exists a non-ζ solution $\ddot{\mathbf{s}}_i^*$ that satisfy $\mathcal{O}\left(\ddot{\mathbf{s}}_i^*\right) = \mathcal{O}\left(\mathbf{s}_i^*\right)$. And it has:

$$\mathcal{O}\left(\ddot{\mathbf{s}}_i^*\right) = \check{\sigma} + \mathcal{O}_1\left(\ddot{\mathbf{s}}_i^*\right), \tag{13}$$

where $\check{\sigma} = \sum_{j=1, j \notin \check{\Gamma}(i)}^{n} \left(0 - u_{ij}\right)^2$, and $\ddot{\mathbf{s}}_i^* \geq \mathbf{0}$, $\ddot{\mathbf{s}}_i^* \mathbf{1}^T = 1$, $\|\ddot{\mathbf{s}}_i^*\|_0 \leq k$. Considering $\check{\Gamma}(i)$ is fixed, $\check{\sigma}$ is a constant. And we have $\mathcal{O}\left(\bar{\mathbf{s}}_i^*\right) = \check{\sigma} + \mathcal{O}_1\left(\bar{\mathbf{s}}_i^*\right)$. Since $\bar{\mathbf{s}}_i^*$ is the optimal solution to the problem (11), we have $\mathcal{O}_1\left(\bar{\mathbf{s}}_i^*\right) \leq \mathcal{O}_1\left(\ddot{\mathbf{s}}_i^*\right)$. So, $\mathcal{O}\left(\bar{\mathbf{s}}_i^*\right) \leq \mathcal{O}\left(\ddot{\mathbf{s}}_i^*\right) = \mathcal{O}\left(\mathbf{s}_i^*\right)$. Thus, Theorem 2 holds. ∎

The problem (11) can be transformed into a vector format. We can solve it easily by utilizing the KKT conditions and the Newton method [17].

Algorithm 1 Sparse Subspace Clustering with the l_0 inequality constraint (SSC-l_0)

Input: Data matrix $\mathbf{X} \in \mathbf{R}^{n \times d}$
Parameter: α, γ, and k.
Output: $\mathbf{S} \in \mathbf{R}^{n \times n}$.

1: Initialize $\mathbf{S}$.
2: Initialize $\mathbf{M}$ with formula (8).
3: **while** Iterations $t \leq T$ and not converge **do**
4:     Update $\check{I}(i)$ for any i;
5:     Update $\mathbf{S}$ by solving the problem (11);
6:     Update $\mathbf{M}$ with formula (8).
7: **end while**
8: **return S**.

The algorithm of SSC-l_0 is summarized in Algorithm 1. Assume that Algorithm 1 iterates at most T times. The time cost of updating $\mathbf{M}$ is $O(T(dn^2 + n^3))$, where n is the number of samples and d is the number of features. The time cost of solving the problem (11) is $O(T(n\ k\ log\ k))$ [20], where k is the maximum number of non-zero elements in the coefficient vector. Given that $k \ll n$, the overall time complexity of SSC-l_0 is $O(n^3)$.

After a non-negative coefficient matrix $\mathbf{S}$ is learned, spectral clustering can be executed based on the produced $\mathbf{S}$.

In Algorithm 1, the optimal solutions for $\mathbf{M}$ and $\mathbf{S}$ can be obtained by solving problems (8) and (11). Then,

$$J_{SSC-l_0}\left(\mathbf{M}^{(t)}, \mathbf{S}^{(t)}\right) \leq J_{SSC-l_0}\left(\mathbf{M}^{(t-1)}, \mathbf{S}^{(t)}\right) \leq J_{SSC-l_0}\left(\mathbf{M}^{(t-1)}, \mathbf{S}^{(t-1)}\right), \tag{14}$$

where $t-1$ and t represent the $(t-1)$th and tth iteration, respectively. Inequality Eq. (14) indicates that the objective function values of SSC-l_0 decrease monotonically, i.e., SSC-l_0 is convergent.

4   Experiments

In this study, all experiments are conducted on a personal computer with i5-9500 CPU @3.00 GHz and 8 GB RAM. The codes are implemented in MATLAB R2021a 64 bit.

4.1   Datasets and Comparison Methods

Ten image datasets are utilized for experiments, including five face image datasets (Yale, Jaffe [21], ORL1024 [22], PIE [23] and FERET [24]), and four handwritten digit image datasets (Binary[1], Semeion[2], Digit[3], and Minist[4]), and one palm image dataset (Palm) [9]. The details of these datasets are shown in Table 1.

Table 1. The Benchmark Datasets.

Datasets	Samples	Size	Clusters	Datasets	Samples	Size	Clusters
Yale	165	32 * 32	15	Binary	1404	20 * 16	36
Jaffe	213	26 * 26	10	Semeion	1593	16 * 16	10
ORL1024	400	32 * 32	40	Digit	1797	8 * 8	10
FERET	1400	40 * 40	200	Minist	4000	28 * 28	10
PIE	1632	32 * 32	68	Palm	2000	16 * 16	100

Seven clustering methods are selected for comparison, including Least Squares Regression (LSR1) [16], Sparse Subspace Clustering (SSC) [12], Low-Rank Representation (LRR) [13], Iteratively Reweighted Least Squares (IRLS) [15], Block-Diagonal Representation (BDR) [14], Clustering with Typicality-aware Adaptive Graph (CTAG) [11], and the Simplex Sparse Representation (SSR) [17]. Please see Sect. 1 for more details on these methods.

SSC-l_0 and seven other methods vary parameters in the range of $\{10^{-3}, 10^{-2}, 10^{-1}, 10^0, 10^1, 10^2, 10^3\}$. Spectral clustering is applied to coefficient matrices, followed by post-processing with k-means. To reduce sensitivity to initialization, k-means is repeated 50 times, and the reported result is the average of the 20 trials with the lowest loss.

4.2   Clustering Analysis

Clustering Performance. Table 2 shows the ACC values obtained by the different methods on the selected benchmark datasets. In Table 2, the best results are exhibited in bold and the second-best results are marked in brackets. The average results of each method over all selected datasets are listed as the last row in Table 2. From Table 2, we have the following observations:

1. LRR and IRLS rank second and third, respectively, in terms of average ACC values among the eight methods. This can be attributed to their ability to restore the row space of the data by learning a coefficient matrix with a low-rank structure. This characteristic aids in enhancing their robustness and improving their clustering ability.
2. SSR exhibits the lowest average ACC value, which can be attributed to the absence of an effective regularization term.

[1] https://cs.nyu.edu/~roweis/data/.
[2] https://archive.ics.uci.edu/ml/index.php.
[3] http://www.escience.cn/people/fpnie/index.html.
[4] http://www.cad.zju.edu.cn/home/dengcai/Data/MLData.html.

Table 2. ACC Values of the SSC-l_0 and the Selected Methods on Benchmark Datasets. (%)

Datasets	LSR1	SSC	LLR	IRLS	BDR	SSR	CTAG	SSC-l_0
Yale	49.33	46.79	(50.61)	47.06	48.55	48.09	49.67	**54.97**
Jaffe	96.74	94.37	95.02	93.57	**100.00**	95.96	(97.18)	**100.00**
ORL	64.71	63.35	(65.53)	65.13	59.66	57.20	62.94	**70.64**
FERET	32.75	38.30	33.54	34.19	(38.62)	34.83	29.60	**39.50**
PIE	70.64	48.92	**71.24**	69.61	56.87	50.89	31.95	(70.94)
Binary	36.05	25.77	35.68	35.08	6.12	5.46	(43.54)	**45.17**
Semeion	57.29	56.57	58.26	(58.46)	57.61	57.74	54.11	**60.18**
Digit	47.74	**70.60**	64.15	59.55	58.13	60.52	61.62	(69.79)
Minist	37.49	(39.41)	37.04	38.30	37.58	31.01	38.34	**44.10**
Palm	80.32	67.35	(82.03)	80.41	66.98	66.08	82.01	**91.13**
Avg.	57.31	55.14	(59.31)	58.14	53.01	50.78	55.10	**64.64**

3. SSC-l_0 achieves the best ACC values across all selected datasets except PIE and Digit. The reason is that SSC-l_0 tends to represent each sample as a linear combination of the samples from the same class under the l_0 inequality constraint. However, the other seven methods lack this ability. In general, data points coming from the same class are easier to represent each other. When reconstructing a point, if the number of non-zero elements in the coefficient vector is limited, it is more likely to select data points from the same class to complete the corresponding reconstruction work. Therefore, the l_0 inequality constraint can improve the performance of the SSC-l_0.

Visualization of the Similarity Matrix. Figure 1 visualizes the coefficient matrix obtained by SSC-l_0 on datasets including Jaffe, PIE, and Palm. In Fig. 1, the coefficient matrix exhibits a block-diagonal structure, indicating that similar samples in SSC-l_0 tend to belong to the same class. This characteristic enhances the clustering performance of SSC-l_0. The reason for showing the block-diagonal structure is that if the number of non-zero elements in the coefficient vector is limited, when reconstructing a point, it is more likely to select a point of the class to which the reconstruction point belongs.

Parameter Sensitivity. SSC-l_0 has three parameters: α, γ, and k. Figure 2 illustrates the impact of these parameters on SSC-l_0 performance across different datasets. The results indicate that SSC-l_0 is sensitive to the values of α, γ, and k. To obtain optimal performance, a grid search method is recommended for parameter selection in SSC-l_0.

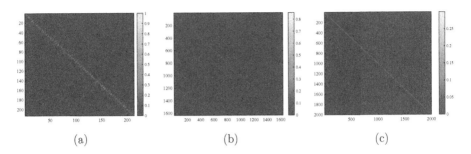

Fig. 1. The coefficient matrix obtained by SSC-l_0 on the different datasets. (a) Jaffe. (b) PIE. (c) Palm.

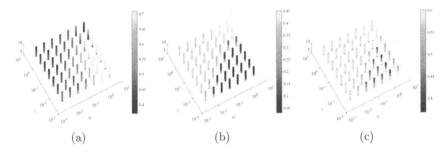

Fig. 2. ACC values of SSC-l_0 on different datasets when varying parameters α, γ, and k. (a) PIE. (b) Binary. (c) Semeion. The color in the figure reflects the ACC values.

Convergence Analysis. Figure 3 shows the convergence curves of SSC-l_0 on datasets Yale, ORL1024, and FERET. From Fig. 3, the objective function values of SSC-l_0 decrease monotonically and SSC-l_0 converges after 100 iterations.

4.3   Robustness Analysis

To compare the robustness of the eight methods, the following experiments are designed:

1. In the ORL2116 dataset, 20% of the samples are randomly selected and added salt and pepper noise. The noisy densities are 0.1, 0.2, 0.3, 0.4, and 0.5. Figure 4(a) illustrates the original ORL2116 dataset and noisy ORL2116 datasets. Figure 5(a) presents the performances of eight methods on these noisy datasets.
2. In the ORL1024 dataset, 20% of the samples are randomly selected and added random noisy blocks. The sizes of the noisy blocks were 5×5, 10×10, 15×15, 20×20, and 25×25 pixels. Figure 4(b) displays the original ORL1024 dataset and the corresponding noisy ORL1024 datasets. The performances of different methods on these noisy datasets are presented in Fig. 5(b).
3. In the Jaffe dataset, 20% of the samples are randomly selected and added random noisy blocks. The sizes of the noisy blocks were $4 * 4$, $8 * 8$, $12 * 12$,

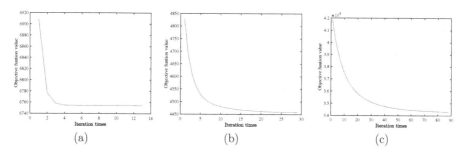

(a)   (b)   (c)

Fig. 3. Convergence curves of SSC-l_0 on different datasets. (a) Yale.(b) ORL1024. (c) FERET.

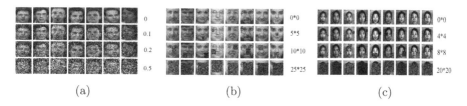

(a)   (b)   (c)

Fig. 4. Original dataset and noisy datasets. (a) ORL2116. (b) ORL1024. (c) Jaffe.

16 * 16 and 20 * 20 pixels. Figure 4(c) displays the original Jaafe dataset and the corresponding noisy Jaffe datasets. The performances of different methods on these noisy datasets are presented in Fig. 5(c).

Form Fig. 5, although the performance of the eight methods degrades as increasing the noise levels, SSC-l_0 achieve almost the best results no matter which noise levels are involved, which demonstrates further that SSC-l_0 has high robustness. The reason is as follows. Clean points have better representation ability compared to noisy points. When the number of non-zero elements in the coefficient vector is limited, clean points are more likely to be used for reconstruction. Thus, constraining the number of non-zero elements can improve model robustness. SSC and SSR use l_1 regularization and l_1 equation constraint to induce sparsity in the coefficient matrix, but they do not directly constrain the number of non-zero elements in the coefficient vector. In contrast, SSC-l_0 can precisely control the number of non-zero elements, leading to better performance.

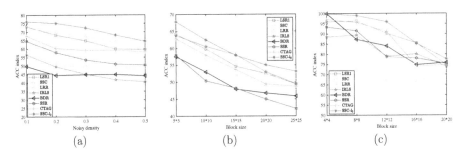

Fig. 5. Performance of different clustering methods on the noisy datasets with different noise levels. (a) Noisy ORL2116 datasets with different noise densities. (b) Noisy ORL1024 datasets with different sizes noisy blocks. (c) Noisy Jaffe datasets with different sizes noisy blocks.

5   Conclusions

Considering data points coming from the same class are easier to represent each other and when the number of non-zero elements in the coefficient vector is limited, a model is more likely to select data points from the same class to complete corresponding reconstruction work, we propose Sparse Subspace Clustering with the l_0 inequality constraint (SSC-l_0) to conduct representation learning among the points in the same class. By introducing the simplex constraint, an optimization method concerning l_0 inequality constraint is proposed, and its convergence is also theoretically analyzed. Since the l_0 inequality constraint problem is difficult to be solved, the proposed optimization method can be widely used in lots of sparse learning models. Extensive experiments demonstrate the superiority of SSC-l_0. Establishing a one-step clustering method based on SSC-l_0 may further improve the performance of the proposed clustering model, which is our next work.

References

1. Zhou, J., Pedrycz, W., Wan, J., et al.: Low-rank linear embedding for robust clustering. IEEE Trans. Knowl. Data Eng. **35**(5), 5060–5075 (2022)
2. Li, X., Chen, M., Wang, Q.: Discrimination-aware projected matrix factorization. IEEE Trans. Knowl. Data Eng. **32**, 809–814 (2019)
3. Lu, J., Wang, H., Zhou, J., et al.: Low-rank adaptive graph embedding for unsupervised feature extraction. Pattern Recogn. **113**, 107758 (2021)
4. Wang, Y., Gao, C., Zhou, J.: Geometrical structure preservation joint with self-expression maintenance for adaptive graph learning. Neurocomputing **501**, 436–450 (2022)
5. Lu, J., Lai, Z., Wang, H., et al.: Generalized embedding regression: a framework for supervised feature extraction. IEEE Trans. Neural Netw. Learn. Syst. **33**, 185–199 (2022)

6. Ng, A., Jordan, M., Weiss, Y.: On spectral clustering: analysis and an algorithm. In: Advances in Neural Information Processing Systems, Vancouver, pp. 849–856. MIT (2002)

7. Stella, X., Shi, J.: Multiclass spectral clustering. In: Proceedings of the 9th IEEE International Conference on Computer Vision, Nice, pp. 313–319. IEEE Computer Society (2003)

8. MacQueen, J.: Some methods for classification and analysis of multivariate observations. In: Proceedings of the Fifth Berkeley Symposium on Mathematical Statistics and Probability, pp. 281–297 (1967)

9. Nie, F., Wang, X., Huang, H.: Clustering and projected clustering with adaptive neighbors. In: Proceedings of the 20th ACM SIGKDD International Conference on Knowledge Discovery and Data Mining, New York, pp. 977–986. ACM (2014)

10. Lu, J., Lin, J., Lai, Z., et al.: Target redirected regression with dynamic neighborhood structure. Inf. Sci. **544**, 564–584 (2021)

11. Zhou, J., Gao, C., Wang, X., et al.: Typicality-aware adaptive similarity matrix for unsupervised learning. IEEE Trans. Neural Netw. Learn. Syst. (2023). https://doi.org/10.1109/TNNLS.2023.3243914

12. Elhamifar, E., Vidal, R.: Sparse subspace clustering: algorithm, theory, and applications. IEEE Trans. Pattern Anal. Mach. Intell. **35**, 2765–2781 (2013)

13. Liu, G., Lin, Z., Yan, S., et al.: Robust recovery of subspace structures by low-rank representation. IEEE Trans. Pattern Anal. Mach. Intell. **35**, 171–184 (2013)

14. Lu, C., Feng, J., Lin, Z., et al.: Subspace clustering by block diagonal representation. IEEE Trans. Pattern Anal. Mach. Intell. **41**, 487–501 (2019)

15. Lu, C., Lin, Z., Yan, S.: Smoothed low rank and sparse matrix recovery by iteratively reweighted least squares minimization. IEEE Trans. Image Process. **24**, 646–654 (2015)

16. Lu, C.-Y., Min, H., Zhao, Z.-Q., Zhu, L., Huang, D.-S., Yan, S.: Robust and efficient subspace segmentation via least squares regression. In: Fitzgibbon, A., Lazebnik, S., Perona, P., Sato, Y., Schmid, C. (eds.) ECCV 2012. LNCS, vol. 7578, pp. 347–360. Springer, Heidelberg (2012). https://doi.org/10.1007/978-3-642-33786-4_26

17. Huang, J., Nie, F., Huang, H.: A new simplex sparse learning model to measure data similarity for clustering. In: Proceedings of the 24th International Conference on Artificial Intelligence, Buenos Aires, pp. 3569–3575. AAAI (2015)

18. Maggu, J., Majumdar, A., Chouzenoux, E.: Transformed subspace clustering. IEEE Trans. Knowl. Data Eng. **33**, 1796–1801 (2020)

19. Zelnik-Manor, L., Perona, P.: Self-tuning spectral clustering, in: Advances in Neural Information Processing Systems, Montreal, pp. 1601–1608 (2004)

20. Condat, L.: Fast projection onto the simplex and the l-1 ball. Math. Program. **158**, 575–585 (2016)

21. Lyons, M., Budynek, J., Akamatsu, S.: Automatic classification of single facial images. IEEE Trans. Pattern Anal. Mach. Intell. **21**, 1357–1362 (1999)

22. Samaria, F., Harter, A.: Parameterisation of a stochastic model for human face identification. In: Proceedings of 1994 IEEE Workshop on Applications of Computer Vision, Sarasota, pp. 138–142. IEEE (1994)

23. Sim, T., Baker, S., Bsat, M.: The CMU Pose, illumination and expression database of human faces. Carnegie Mellon University Technical Report CMU-RI-TR-OI-02 (2001)

24. Phillips, P., Moon, H., Rizvi, S., et al.: The FERET evaluation methodology for face-recognition algorithms. IEEE Trans. Pattern Anal. Mach. Intell. **22**, 1090–1104 (2000)

Pixel-Wise Detection of Road Obstacles on Drivable Areas by Introducing Maximized Entropy to Synboost Framework

Carlos David Ardon Munoz$^{(\boxtimes)}$ iD, Masashi Nishiyama iD, and Yoshio Iwai iD

Tottori University, 101 Minami 4-chome, Koyama-cho, Tottori 680-8550, Japan
m22j4003x@edu.tottori-u.ac.jp, {nishiyama,iwai}@tottori-u.ac.jp
https://www.tottori-u.ac.jp/

Abstract. Semantic segmentation plays a crucial role in understanding the surroundings of a vehicle in the context of autonomous driving. Nevertheless, segmentation networks are typically trained on a closed-set of inliers, leading to misclassification of anomalies as in-distribution objects. This is especially dangerous for obstacles on roads, such as stones, that usually are small and blend well with the background. Numerous frameworks have been proposed to detect out-of-distribution objects in driving scenes. Some of these frameworks use softmax cross-entropy measurements as an attention mechanism for a dissimilarity network to find anomalies. However, a significant limitation arises from the segmentation network's tendency toward overconfidence in its predictions, resulting in low cross-entropy in regions where anomalies are present. This suggests that normal cross-entropy is a low-quality prior for anomaly detection. Therefore, for the task of detecting stones on roads, we propose utilizing a fined-tuned segmentation network with a changed target, from semantic segmentation to maximize the cross-entropy in anomalous areas. With this, we feed the dissimilarity network with a better prior image. Furthermore, due to the lack of datasets with enough samples of stones for pixel-wise detection, we synthetically added stones on images of driving scenes to create a dataset for fine-tuning and training. The results of our comparative experiments showed that our model attains the highest average precision while having the lowest false positive rate at 95% true positive rate when evaluating on a real-stone image dataset.

Keywords: Anomaly classification · Semantic segmentation · Computer vision

1 Introduction

Understanding surroundings through images is an important task in applications such as autonomous vehicles and robots, where it is vital to identify abnormal objects that may be a danger to vehicles and must be avoided. For this study,

H. Lu et al. (Eds.): ACPR 2023, LNCS 14408, pp. 150–161, 2023.
https://doi.org/10.1007/978-3-031-47665-5_13

we focus on a subclass of anomalies, stones. Because those are a type of obstacle commonly found on roads and dangerous to vehicles. Additionally, keeping roads clear of obstacles, such as stones, is a continuous task done by local governments and municipalities. Who regularly conduct car patrols with experts to manually identify obstacles so they can take appropriate corrective action. However, by requiring the intervention of experts, the efficiency of detection is limited since the frequency of patrols is normally low. This increases the time that obstacles are dangerous to vehicles, raising the probability of accidents and damage. Thereby, developing a support system for detecting this type of obstacle can help to overcome these problems by allowing automatic detection during patrolling.

Given the critical need of efficient anomaly detection systems, many techniques have been applied to perform anomaly detection from a single monocular RGB image. For example, uncertainty measurements in semantic segmentation, such as softmax entropy and the difference between the two largest softmax values (softmax distance), have been used to statistically detect areas of low segmentation reliability and classify them as anomalies [1]. Additionally, generating a photo-realistic image (image re-synthesis) from a semantic segmentation map and comparing it with the original image can be used to detect anomalies. As the segmentation network will not be able to understand anomalies, they will not appear in the reconstruction [2]. Thus, the areas with significant differences between the two images are classified as anomalies. Finally, the framework Synboost [3] complements the results of both techniques by using a dissimilarity network to find differences between the input and synthesized images with softmax entropy and softmax distance as attention mechanisms. However, when anomalies blend well with its surroundings or only span a few pixels in the image, which is the case for most stones on the road, the softmax cross-entropy is low and does not contribute much with the framework's prediction ability.

Therefore, in Sect. 2, we propose a method to overcome the limitations of Synboost [3] and improve detection accuracy of anomalies in a constrained setting, namely, small anomalies laying on the drivable area (Fig. 1). We call these kinds of anomalies, road obstacles. In Sect. 3, we describe the process of training the dissimilarity network of Synboost using a dataset with synthetically added obstacles to compensate for the lack of anomalies examples in usual datasets. Furthermore, we introduce to our framework a neural network that strives to maximize cross-entropy in regions where there are anomalies [4]. With this, we increase the cross-entropy even for small anomalies that previously were unnoticeable on softmax entropy and softmax distance images, in consequence, they produce a better contribution to the final prediction, acting as attention mechanisms. Finally, in Sect. 4, we present our conclusions, highlighting how our framework enhances the pixel-wise detection accuracy for stones and significantly reduces false positives compared to previous methods.

Fig. 1. Drivable area. The region-of-interest are roads and sidewalks, which are highlighted in white in this image. We employed semantic segmentation inference to identify the contours of this area. Any anomaly completely enclosure within the drivable area is a road obstacle for this research.

2   Proposed Framework

2.1   Related Methods

We built our framework on top of Synboost [3]. This framework combines two techniques for anomaly detection. The first one is using uncertainty measurements, softmax entropy and softmax distance. The second one is image re-synthesis, that compares the original input with a generated image to find differences between both. We expect that anomalous regions in the original image look different in the generated one. The outputs of uncertainty measurements and image re-synthesis are used as inputs for a dissimilarity network that carries out a binary classification for each pixel with classes for anomaly and non-anomaly. This framework achieves state-of-the-art performance for anomaly detection with minimal computational cost for training since it is designed to use pre-trained models and only requires training for the dissimilarity network.

We chose this model to build upon our framework because it addresses different scenarios when dealing with semantic segmentation anomalies [3]. The first scenario occurs when an anomaly is misclassified as any of the inlier classes, resulting in low entropy due to overconfidence but a significantly different re-synthesized image if the object is large. The second scenario involves over-segmentation of the anomaly, with different sections assigned to different classes, leading usually to higher entropy. The final scenario occurs when the anomaly goes undetected and is classified as part of its surroundings. In this case, the anomalous area appears different in the re-synthesized image, particularly if it is sufficiently large. However, Synboost still has a low accuracy for detecting objects that blend with the background (low entropy) and only encompass a few

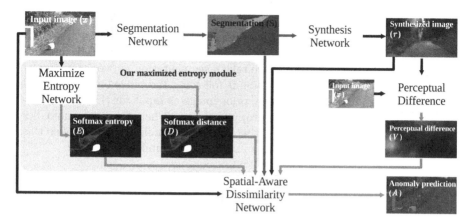

Fig. 2. Outline of our framework architecture. In Synboost [3], softmax entropy and softmax difference images are taken from the semantic segmentation network. In our framework, we introduced to the Synboost framework a Maximized entropy network [4] fine-tuned using the loss function showed in Eq. (2). Thus, this module specializes in creating prior images to feed into the Spatial-Aware Dissimilarity Network that produces the anomaly prediction (highlighted with white contours for better visualization).

pixels in the images (similar synthesized image), which is the case for most road obstacles, including stones, as both approaches fail to detect the anomaly.

2.2 Our Framework Architecture

Figure 2 shows an outline of the proposed framework. We use a pre-trained segmentation network with a WideResNet38 backbone, which is trained on Cityscapes dataset [5] according to [6]. For the synthesis network, we take a pre-trained model from the CC-FPSE framework [7], which is a conditional generative adversarial network. In the case of the perceptual difference V, we simply take a pre-trained VGG19 on ImageNet dataset as a feature extractor to find differences between the original and generated images, following the same procedure as Synboost [3]:

$$V(x,r) = \sum_{i=1}^{N} \frac{1}{M_i} \left\| F^{(i)}(x) - F^{(i)}(r) \right\|_1,\qquad(1)$$

where $F^{(i)}$ is the i-th layer with M_i elements in the VGG network with N layers. This equation computes the perceptual difference as the sum of the absolute differences between the feature representations of the original image x and the generated image r across all layers of the VGG network. Therefore, it captures the perceptual variations and discrepancies between the two images in feature space.

Furthermore, because neural networks tend to be overconfident in their predictions, the cross-entropy can be low even in regions where an anomaly exists. In consequence, the uncertainty measures may not contribute much to the final prediction. To deal with this problem, we take a segmentation network pre-trained on the Cityscapes dataset and fine-tune it following the procedure of [4]. With this, we aim to create a better-quality prior image as input for the dissimilarity network that maximizes the cross-entropy on regions where there are anomalies, while minimizing it on regions where there are no anomalies. To accomplish this, during fine-tuning, we modify the loss function to minimize the target:

$$L = (1 - \lambda)\mathbb{E}_{(x,y)\sim\mathcal{D}_{in}}[\ell_{in}(f(x), y(x)] \\ + \lambda\mathbb{E}_{(x')\sim\mathcal{D}_{out}}[\ell_{out}(f(x'))], \tag{2}$$

where

$$\ell_{in}(f(x), y(x)) = -\sum_{j\in C} \mathbb{1}_{j=y(x)} \log(f_j(x)), \tag{3}$$

$$\ell_{out}(f(x')) = -\sum_{j\in C} \frac{1}{q} \log(f_j(x')), \tag{4}$$

where, $(x, y) \sim \mathcal{D}_{in}$ stands for an in-distribution example, while $(x') \sim \mathcal{D}_{out}$ is an out-of-distribution example. $f(x)$ indicates the softmax probabilities for a predicted class and $y(x)$ the corresponding ground truth. λ is a value in the range of $[0, 1]$ that controls the weight between the two single objectives. $\mathbb{1}_{j=y(x)}$ is an indicator function that yields 1 when $j = y(x)$ and zero otherwise. C is the set of q classes. The minimization of the single objective for the out-of-distribution part is equivalent to maximizing entropy in anomalous regions as stated in [4].

We can interpret this new objective as follows: for in-distribution pixels, minimizing Eq. (3), which represents the standard cross-entropy loss function when using one-hot encoding, is equivalent to maximizing the softmax value for the true class. On the other hand, for out-of-distribution pixels, Eq. (4) yields the lowest loss value when the predictions in the softmax layer are uniformly distributed across all classes. Consequently, for outlier pixels, we encourage the one-hot encoding vector to have the same value in every class. This is the reason why the logarithm in Eq. (4) is divided by the number of classes q. Such a vector will yield a high value when evaluated with Shannon entropy, hence the term "Maximized entropy". Shannon entropy, also known as relative entropy, is defined as follows:

$$E(f(x)) = -\sum_{j\in C} f_j(x) \log(f_j(x)), \tag{5}$$

where $f(x)$ indicates the softmax probabilities predicted by the segmentation model. We use this equation to obtain the entropy image E in Fig. 2.

In Table 1, we present an overview of the models used in our framework. The segmentation, synthesis, and perceptual difference networks are pre-trained models that can be seamlessly integrated into the framework. Regarding the Maximized entropy network, it starts as a segmentation network pre-trained on Cityscapes that we subsequently fine-tune on our composite training set using

Table 1. Model and datasets overview.

Model	Training set	Training details
Segmentation	Cityscapes	Pre-trained
Synthesis	Cityscapes	Pre-trained
Perceptual difference	ImageNet	Pre-trained
Maximized entropy	Our composite dataset	Fine-tuned
Dissimilarity	Our composite dataset	Trained

Eq. (2) as loss function. Lastly, the Dissimilarity network is trained from random initialization, employing our composite training set.

2.3 Ensemble

Because the prior images used as inputs to the dissimilarity network are also anomaly predictions, it is feasible to combine them with the dissimilarity network output generated in the last step of Fig. 2. To accomplish this, we use a weighted sum to generate a more robust prediction (A_e). We refer to this procedure as ensemble, and it can be applied to both Synboost and our model using the following equation in a pixel-wise manner:

$$A_e = w_1 A + w_2 E + w_3 D + w_4 V, \tag{6}$$

where A, E, D, and V represent the output from the dissimilarity network, softmax entropy, softmax distance, and perceptual difference images, respectively. To find the values for the weights w_1, w_2, w_3, and w_4 to combine these images for ensemble, we applied a grid search restricted to values that satisfy $w_1 + w_2 + w_3 + w_4 = 1$.

This means that prior images can be used in two ways: first, as inputs for the dissimilarity network where they serve as attention mechanisms, and second, as part of an ensemble together with the dissimilarity network output.

3 Experiments

3.1 Dataset

For the training set, we started from the same methodology used in Synboost training. Consequently, we took Cityscapes training set (2975 images) using the objects labeled as void class as samples for anomalies and inferred semantic segmentation for image S in Fig. 2. To train the dissimilarity network to find differences between the original and synthesized images, we added a copy of each image and randomly swapped labels for known objects in the ground truth semantic segmentation map before image synthesis. These objects look quite different in the synthesized image and are also used as anomalies samples. For

156   C. D. Ardon Munoz et al.

Fig. 3. Stones included as road obstacles.

this part of the dataset, we used the modified ground truth segmentation for image S in Fig. 2.

On top of that, we synthetically added one stone on a random position of the drivable area per image. The stone dataset (Fig. 3) consists of images of four stones (83, 87, 120 and 70 images per stone, respectively) taken from different orientations and illumination conditions (left only, right only, and both). We used stones 1 and 2 for training, while stones 3 and 4 were used only for evaluation. In addition, we used six images from different spots in our University's campus as backgrounds to synthetically add stones. Applying image augmentation techniques (horizontal flip, cropping, and adjusting brightness) we added 192 images to the training set. Finally, to conduct experiments with real-stone images, we placed stones, and we took 153 images from seven spots in our University's campus. In sum, the training set contains 6142 images when only using composite images and 6295 images when including real-stone images, as shown in Table 2. Lastly, in Fig. 4 we show some examples of composite images.

For evaluation, we built a 147 real-stone images dataset. We placed stones 3 and 4 and took photos in six spots in the University's campus that were not used for training. With this, all evaluations for experiments are run using places and stones unseen during training. Additionally, using a real-obstacle dataset for evaluation prevents our experiments from yielding unrealistic results caused by the use of synthetic data during training. For instance, a model might unrealistically excel at identifying merely pasted objects rather than genuine obstacles [8].

Table 2. Composition of training set.

Type	Source	Number of images
Composite	Cityscapes	5950
Composite	Our background set	192
Total composite images		**6142**
Real	Our real-stone set	153
Total composite + real-stone images	**6295**	

Fig. 4. Composite images. Examples of composite image used for training. In the top row there are examples of backgrounds from Cityscapes. While in the bottom row, there are examples of our backgrounds. The stones synthetically added are highlighted by a solid line rectangle.

3.2 Experimental Conditions

The region-of-interest (ROI) for evaluation of anomaly detection in our experiments comprises all pixels that belong to road or sideways. As well as regions assigned to other classes enclosed within the road or sidewalk. While the road obstacles that we want to detect are objects on the drivable area that do not belong to any known classes from the Cityscapes dataset [5]. We used average precision (AP) as the primary metric, as well as false positive rate at 95% true positive rate (FPR95), that are fitted for highly imbalance classification problems, such as anomaly detection.

For the first experiment, we used our dataset with only composites images to train Synboost's and our model's dissimilarity network, as well as fine-tuning a segmentation network to maximize entropy on anomalous areas. For the second experiment, we added 192 images with real-stone images into the training set, which improved performance for all models despite the small sample size.

Table 3. Hyperparameters used for training and fine-tuning.

	Dissimilarity network training	Maximized entropy network fine-tuning
Hyperparameter	Value	Value
Learning rate	0.0001	0.00001
Betas (Adam)	0.5, 0.999	0.9, 0.999
Epochs	30	20
Batch size	8	8

Table 4. Best weights for Eq. (6) for our model according to a grid search.

Model	Training set	w_1	w_2	w_3	w_4
Synboost	Composite images only	1	0	0	0
	Composite + real-stone images	1	0	0	0
Ours	Composite images only	0.85	0.15	0	0
	Composite + real-stone images	0.55	0.45	0	0

We trained the dissimilarity networks for 30 epochs five times per model from random initializations. In the case of entropy maximization, we fine-tuned the segmentation network for 20 epochs with $\lambda = 0.9$ in Eq. (2). In both cases, we selected the epoch with the lowest lost value on the evaluation set as the best epoch. In Table 3, we show the hyperparameters used for training and fine-tuning.

The experiments were conducted on a computer running Ubuntu 20.04.4 LTS, with Python 3.6.9, PyTorch 1.10.1, CUDA 11.4, and a NVIDIA GeForce RTX 3090 GPU with 24 GB of RAM.

3.3   Results

The outcome of a grid search for the best ensemble weights for Synboost and our model when using Eq. (6) are shown in Table 4. In the case of Synboost, we obtained that $w_1 = 1$ for both training sets, which means that it only uses the dissimilarity network output. In other words, Synboost does not benefit from ensemble. On the other hand, for our model we obtained that the dissimilarity output (w_1) is combined with softmax entropy (w_2) to create the final prediction. However, w_3 and w_4 are zero for both training sets which means that softmax distance and perceptual difference are not used for ensemble with our model.

Consequently, using the ensemble weights during testing, the results of the best networks when evaluating on real-stone images are shown in Table 5, where Synboost achieved its best performance without ensemble while our model did it using ensemble. All models improve when a small set of real-stone images are added to the training set.

Table 5. Performance comparison between best networks.

Method	Composite images only		Composite + real-stone images	
	AP ↑	FPR95 ↓	AP ↑	FPR95 ↓
Synboost [3]	64.2	7.07	67.0	4.92
Maximized entropy [4]	76.8	2.02	85.5	0.30
Ours	**86.6**	**0.29**	**91.0**	**0.13**

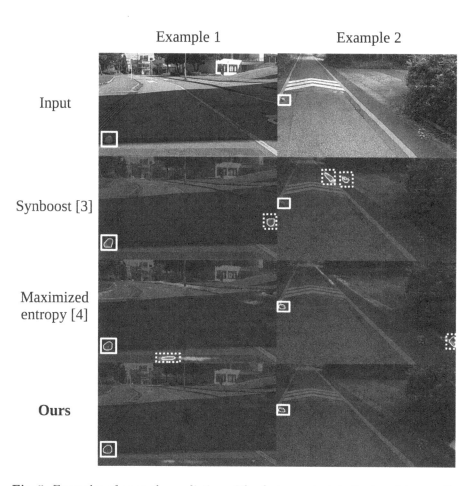

Fig. 5. Examples of anomaly predictions. The first row depicts the input image, the ground-truth anomaly is highlighted by a solid line rectangle for visualization purposes only. For the inferences, false positives are highlighted by a dotted line rectangle. The model's anomaly prediction is indicated by a contour line. In the case of Synboost (second row), it detected the obstacle for the first example but failed to detect it for the second. In both cases, it produced false positives. For Maximized entropy (third row), it spotted correctly the obstacles in both cases, however, it also yielded false positives. In contrast, our model (fourth row) successfully recognized the obstacles in both cases without false positives.

Our experiments demonstrated that our model outperforms previous models in terms of achieving the highest average precision (AP) while simultaneously having the lowest false positive rate at 95% true positive rate (FPR95) when evaluated on a real-stone dataset. In Fig. 5, we present examples of pixel-wise anomaly prediction, where each image contains a single road obstacle. The contour lines indicate the pixels classified as anomalies by each model. Ground-truth anomalies are highlighted with solid line rectangles, while false positives are marked with dotted line rectangles.

4   Conclusions

In this paper, we presented a framework to detect small anomalies laying on roads, such as stones. We demonstrated that using maximized entropy, as an attention mechanism for a dissimilarity network, improves the average precision and false positive rate at 95% true positive rate in pixel-wise anomaly detection. Furthermore, the difference between the results from the two experiments, due to the inclusion of the small sample of real-stone images in the training set, indicates that there is still room for improvement in the composite dataset creation.

Regarding the use of ensemble, the values found from grid-search confirms that standard softmax entropy do not contribute much to the final anomaly prediction of road obstacles, as we found that the highest AP values for Syn-boost were achieved without taken into consideration any of the prior images for ensemble. While our model with maximized entropy uses softmax entropy images along with the dissimilarity network output in ensemble to create the final anomaly prediction. In other words, while normal softmax entropy serves as an attention mechanism for the dissimilarity network, it doesn't improve the final result when using ensemble. On the other hand, maximized entropy is beneficial in both scenarios.

In future work, we intend to conduct experiments using a composite dataset with additional types of road obstacles aside from stones to create a more general anomaly detection system. For this purpose, we plan to create a composite dataset using objects not present in the in-distribution label set of Cityscapes, treating them as obstacles. We also aim to develop a framework with local image synthesis, constraint to the drivable area to avoid synthesizing whole images and thus, reducing the computational of inferences.

References

1. Rottmann, M., et al.: Prediction error meta classification in semantic segmentation: detection via aggregated dispersion measures of Softmax probabilities. In: 2020 International Joint Conference on Neural Networks (IJCNN), Glasgow, UK, pp. 1–9 (2020)
2. Lis, K., Nakka, K.K., Fua, P., Salzmann, M.: Detecting the unexpected via image resynthesis. In: 2019 IEEE/CVF International Conference on Computer Vision (ICCV), Seoul, South Korea, pp. 2152–2161 (2019)

3. Di Biase, G., Blum, H., Siegwart, R., Cadena, C.: Pixel-wise anomaly detection in complex driving scenes. In: 2021 IEEE/CVF Conference on Computer Vision and Pattern Recognition (CVPR), Nashville, TN, USA, pp. 16913–16922 (2021)
4. Chan, R., Rottmann, M., Gottschalk, H.: Entropy maximization and meta classification for out-of- distribution detection in semantic segmentation. In: 2021 IEEE/CVF International Conference on Computer Vision (ICCV), Montreal, QC, Canada, pp. 5108–5117 (2021)
5. Cordts, M. et al.: The cityscapes dataset for semantic urban scene understanding. In: Proceedings of the IEEE Conference on Computer Vision and Pattern Recognition (CVPR), Las Vegas, NV, USA, pp. 3213–3223 (2016)
6. Zhu, Y. et al.: Improving semantic segmentation via video propagation and label relaxation. In: 2019 IEEE/ CVF Conference on Computer Vision and Pattern Recognition (CVPR), Long Beach, CA, USA, pp. 8848–8857 (2019)
7. Liu, X., Yin, G., Shao, J., Wang, X.: Learning to predict layout-to-image conditional convolutions for semantic image synthesis. In: Advances in Neural Information Processing Systems, Red Hook, NY, USA (2019)
8. Bogdoll, D., Uhlemeyer, S., Kowol, K., Zollner, M.: Perception datasets for anomaly detection in autonomous driving: a survey. In: 2023 IEEE Intelligent Vehicles Symposium (IV), Anchorage, AK, USA, pp. 1–8 (2023)

Gender Classification from Gait Energy and Posture Images Using Multi-stage Network

Tak-Man Leung and Kwok-Leung Chan[✉]

Department of Electrical Engineering, City University of Hong Kong, Hong Kong, China
takmleung2-c@my.cityu.edu.hk, itklchan@cityu.edu.hk

Abstract. Gait-based gender classification from an image sequence captured at a distance from human subjects can provide valuation information for video surveillance. One common approach is to adopt machine learning for the prediction of the gender class. Algorithms perform gender classification based on spatio-temporal feature, e.g., Gait Energy Image (GEI), extracted from the video. Although GEI can concisely characterize the movements over a gait cycle, it has some limitations. For instance, GEI lacks photometric information and does not exhibit a clear posture of the subject. To improve gender classification, we think that more features must be utilized. In this paper, we propose a gender classification framework that exploits not only the GEI, but also the characteristic poses of the walking cycle. The proposed framework is a multi-stream and multi-stage network that is capable of gradually learning the gait features from multiple modality inputs acquired in multiple views. The extracted features are fused and input to the classifier which is trained with ensemble learning. We evaluate and compare the performance of our proposed model with a variety of gait-based gender classification methods on two benchmark datasets. Through thorough experimentations, we demonstrate that our proposed model achieves higher gender classification accuracy than the methods that utilize only either GEI, or posture image.

Keywords: gait classification · gait energy image · walking cycle · ensemble learning

1 Introduction

Humans can recognize gender class at ease. To replicate this capability in machine is a challenging problem. Automatic gender classification is a useful function in many systems, e.g., surveillance, micromarketing. Information on gender of visitors in the crowd flow is of great commercial value for better shop arrangement and allocation, better promotion management and human flow arrangement. Automatic gender recognition also plays an important role in human-machine interaction and security control.

Gait is useful visual information. Image of walking human may be captured with camera set at a long distance from the subject. Still, human gait, showing posture and walking style, is visible in the image. Therefore, gait-based gender recognition from image is a feasible approach. Many research [1] adopt the gait-based approach, e.g.,

H. Lu et al. (Eds.): ACPR 2023, LNCS 14408, pp. 162–173, 2023.
https://doi.org/10.1007/978-3-031-47665-5_14

activity recognition, tracking, person identification, gender classification, etc. Gait can be recognized based on structural information such as stride parameters. Liao et al. [2] proposed a gait recognition method based on 3D human pose estimated from images with a convolutional neural network (CNN). This type of method usually demands an initialization phase, such as model construction, and the optimization of a large number of free parameters. Alternatively, methods can purely rely on appearance features extracted from image. This type of method has the advantage of lower computational cost. For instance, in each image the gait silhouette is segmented. Feature is then computed from the silhouette sequence, e.g., Gait Energy Image (GEI) [3]. GEI, computed as an average silhouette image, characterizes the movements of the subject over a gait cycle. However, the classification accuracy may be low on image sequences acquired at some viewing angles due to the highly similar GEIs of both gender classes. The average silhouette does not display the distinctive posture of the subject clearly. We therefore propose a multi-stage gender classification framework with the inputs of GEI and poses extracted from the walking cycle. We design the training process to allow the feature extractor network gradually learns from a variety of inputs. The multiple features are fed to the classifier network which is trained by ensemble learning. We train our proposed model on two benchmark gait datasets. Through thorough experimentations, we demonstrate that our proposed model outperforms other gender classification methods. The contributions of our work are as follows:

- GEI provides concise representation of movement that can be used for gender classi-fication. However, GEI lacks photometric information and does not clearly dis-play the body shape. We observe that postures, such as stance and swing images of the walking cycle, exhibit unique features that can provide complementary information for gender classification. In order to improve the gender classification accuracy, we exploit multiple modality inputs of GEI and postures.
- We propose a multi-stream network for feature extraction from the multiple modality inputs. The extracted features are fused and fed to the classifier. We design the training process to allow the feature extractor network gradually learns from a variety of inputs. The proposed multi-stage framework, through ensemble learning, predicts the gender class irrespective of other factors such as viewing angle and walking status.
- We adopt data augmentation to address the class imbalance problem of the gait dataset. Investigation is performed on two benchmark datasets. Comparison analysis is car-ried out with recently proposed methods based on deterministic and deep learning approaches. We demonstrate that our proposed model outperforms these reference methods that only utilize either GEI, or posture image.

The rest of this paper is organized as follows. The related research on gender classi-fication is reviewed in Sect. 2. We focus on the gait-based gender recognition techniques and the datasets created for gender classification research. Our proposed gender classifi-cation framework is described in Sect. 3. Experimentations are performed on two publicly available gait datasets. Quantitative measures are adopted for performance evaluation. In Sect. 4, we compare the performance of our proposed model with a variety of gender classification methods. Section 5 presents the ablation study performed on our proposed gender classification model. Finally, we draw the conclusion in Sect. 6.

2 Related Work

Gait-based gender classification methods, depending on the way to extract visual information from the images, can be grouped into two categories - deterministic algorithm, deep learning-based model.

Deterministic algorithm performs gender classification via computation of hand-crafted features, followed by gender prediction from the feature vector. Yu et al. [4] utilized GEI as the appearance-based gait feature. In [5], the textural feature, local binary pattern (LBP), is computed from GEI and then input to the classifier. Hu and Wang [6] proposed Gait Principal Component Image to represent the movement of body in one gait period. The features are then input to the K nearest neighbor classifier. Support vector machine (SVM) is a popular choice of classifier in many recently proposed methods, e.g., [5], due to its robustness. Saini and Singh [7] proposed a gender recognition system using SVM and multi-linear discriminant analysis as classifier. Do et al. [8] proposed a view-dependent gender classification system. The viewing angle (i.e., the walking direction) is first estimated. The gender of the human captured in arbitrary view is predicted with multiple view dependent SVM classifiers.

Deep learning brings forth rapid advancement in computer vision. In contrast to deterministic algorithms, deep learning is machine learning based on learning data representations. With the development of CNN [9] and the use of graphics processing units, significant advancement has been reported. CNN model is trained to learn feature extraction with the use of training dataset. In many research, it is found that features extracted by deep learning-based algorithms can vastly outperform hand-crafted features computed by deterministic algorithms. Gait-based gender classification also benefits from the adoption of CNN model.

Shiraga et al. [10] developed a gait recognition method from GEI with the use of CNN. Zhang et al. [11], proposed a complex gait recognition framework which contains two parallel Siamese networks. While similar/dissimilar GEIs are used to train the two networks. Only one Siamese network is used for testing. The gait feature extracted by the network is fed to the classifier. These two methods [10, 11] are used for human identification. Takemura et al. [12] have studied and compared some CNN gait recognition models. Sakata et al. [13] first proposed a network for classifying gender, age group, and age from GEI. It contains one convolutional block and three parallel fully connected layers. They further proposed a larger network to address the same classification problem. It contains 13 structurally identical convolutional blocks organized in three layers. Xu et al. [14] proposed a CNN framework for real-time gender classification. From a single image, the human silhouette is segmented by graph-cut. Based on the single silhouette, a gait cycle is synthesized by the phase-aware reconstructor [15]. The gait cycle is then input to GaitSet [16] for gait recognition. In training, two images from two viewing angles are selected. The two synthesized gait cycles are fed into two GaitSet networks for model learning. In the testing phase, only one image frame is used as input and one GaitSet is utilized as feature extractor. The method has the advantage of quick response since recognition is performed per image instead of waiting for the acquisition of the whole gait cycle. GEI, containing a mixture of static and dynamic gait features from the original image sequence, provides distinctive features for gait recognition. Features extracted from synthesized gait cycle will be less precise. Moreover, the complex framework with two networks demands high computational load in training.

Besides using the single input of GEI, some research utilizes additional input information and adopts multi-stream framework for gender classification. Bei et al. [17] proposed a two-stream CNN to combine GEI and optical flow information. A single GEI image lacks temporal information of the walking cycle. To address this limitation, they proposed a new average silhouette subGEI, which is computed from fewer image frames than the complete gait cycle. Temporal information, characterized by the optical flow map, is then computed from two adjacent subGEIs. Russel and Selvaraj [18] proposed a unified model with the input of GEI to six parallel CNNs. The parallel network contains varying number of convolution layers. Each GEI is transformed into a multi-scale representation for the network to learn the discriminative gait features. In summary, deep learning models can achieve higher gender classification accuracy than deterministic algorithms. However, they demand the optimization of a number of hyperparameters and the computation of a large number of system parameters. Moreover, they also heavily rely on loss functions.

In order to facilitate the development of data driven gait recognition model, various gait datasets have been created. Accurate CNN model demands training on large dataset. For instance, gait databases should contain videos capturing a large number of human subjects. Each subject should be instructed to walk in different directions, and/or recorded by multiple cameras set in a wide range of viewpoints. Sakata et al. [13] trained their frameworks on a single-view gait dataset OU-ISIR LP [19, 20]. OU-ISIR LP is a large dataset containing 32,753 females and 31,093 males with a wide range of ages. The videos were captured by a single camera. Moreover, the dataset provides the pre-computed GEIs. Xu et al. [14] trained their model on a multi-view gait dataset OU-ISIR MVLP [12, 21]. OU-ISIR MVLP contains videos captured by 14 cameras set in different view angles. The dataset also provides a total of 267,386 pre-computed GEIs. Zhang and Wang [22] created a small gait dataset IRIP Gait Database. It only contains 32 male subjects and 28 female subjects. The Soton database [23] is a relatively old dataset. It contains 400 subjects with unique multi-modal data (e.g., multi-view gait records, face images). CASIA [24] is also a gait database with multi-view images. The CASIA B gait dataset consists of videos captured from 124 subjects, each with 11 viewing angles and 3 walking conditions. Another large-scale dataset GREW [25] was created for research on gait recognition in the wild. It provides silhouette sequences, GEIs, and optical flow maps, computed from videos captured from 26,345 subjects.

3 Gender Classification Framework

GEI, which is computed from the silhouette images over a gait cycle, concisely represents the movement of the subject. Figure 1 (a) and (b) show the GEIs of a male and a female respectively. To observe the difference between the two GEIs, we perform image subtraction and enhance the difference of GEIs with gamma correction for better visualization as shown in Fig. 1 (c). The brighter pixels in the subtraction result correspond to larger difference between the two GEIs. Gender recognition based on GEI learns from the difference of male and female GEIs in gender prediction. Besides the exploitation of movement information, we propose a framework that also learns the difference of male and female postures. Figure 1 (d) and (e) show the images of a male and a female at the same posture of the walking cycle respectively. The subtraction result, as shown in Fig. 1 (f), illustrates the difference of the postures. It is clear that the difference of postures can provide complementary information to that from the difference of GEIs. Gender recognition model can learn other features from posture images and benefit gender classification. In order to improve the gender recognition accuracy, we therefore propose a multi-stream multi-stage gender classification framework with the inputs of GEI, and the stance and swing images extracted from the walking cycle.

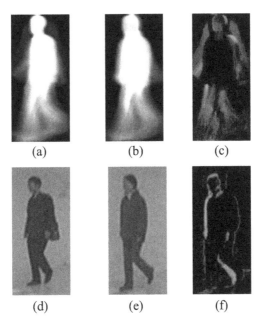

(a)   (b)   (c)

(d)   (e)   (f)

Fig. 1. Difference of male and female GEIs and posture images: (a) male GEI; (b) female GEI; (c) difference between male and female GEIs; (d) male posture image; (e) female posture image; (f) difference between male and female posture images. The difference images are enhanced by gamma correction with the same factor of 0.5 for better visualization.

Figure 2 shows the proposed gender classification framework. Stage 1 contains three parallel streams of CNN, which are trained to extract gait features from the input images. The first input is the GEI image computed from the silhouette sequence. The second and the third inputs are the stance and swing images extracted from the walking cycle. The feature vectors extracted by the CNNs are concatenated. Ensemble learning is adopted to train the Stage 2 CNN for gender prediction. Based on the proposed framework, we design the gender classification model.

We design a CNN for gait feature extraction from the input of GEI. As shown in Fig. 3, the GEI CNN model consists of convolutional layers, max-pooling layers, and batch normalization layers. If we use the single-stage network for gender classification, a densely-connected layer and an output layer are added. For the multi-stage gender classification model, the feature vector is fused with the other feature vectors and fed into the Stage 2 CNN.

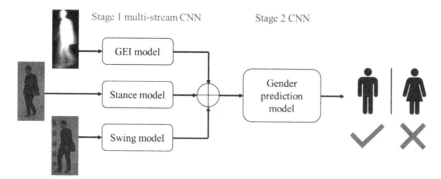

Fig. 2. Proposed gender classification framework.

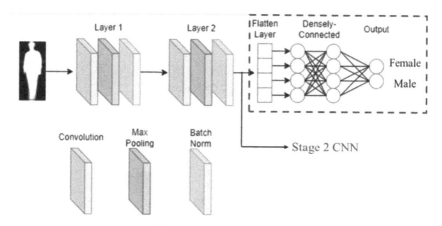

Fig. 3. GEI CNN model.

The gait of human walking is periodic. Within one walking cycle, one foot stays on the ground (stance phase) for about 60% of the cycle, and then lifts off the ground (swing phase) for about 40% of the cycle. Besides GEI, some state-of-the-art methods exploit pose information for gait recognition. Kwon et al. [26] proposed the joint swing energy which is computed from the skeletons found in three coordinate planes. Zhao et al. [27] utilized a pre-trained convolutional network to generate the pose heatmap from RGB images. We propose the gender classification framework which also extracts posture related features from image sequence. The images of the stance and swing phases of the right leg are extracted from the video and fed into the respective CNN models as shown in Fig. 2. The Stance CNN and Swing CNN models have the same structure as the GEI CNN model (see Fig. 3).

The feature vectors (each has the dimension of $1 \times 1{,}024$) extracted by the three CNN models as mentioned previously, are fused to form a wide feature vector of $1 \times 3{,}072$. It is then reshaped to 128×24 and input to Stage 2 CNN. Ensemble learning is adopted to train the CNN for the final gender prediction output. Figure 4 shows the Stage 2 CNN model. There are two convolutional blocks, each containing a convolutional layer, a max-pooling layer, and a batch normalization layer.

There is an imbalance problem in gait dataset. For instance, the CASIA B gait dataset [24] contains 10,187 male GEIs and 3,405 female GEIs. To address this problem, we adopt data augmentation to increase the number of female GEIs to the same as the male counterpart. First, a new female GEI is generated by blending of two original female GEIs as shown in Fig. 5. A total of 45,559 new female GEIs are generated, from which 6,782 are randomly selected as the augmented female data. We also sample more stance and swing images from videos of female subjects.

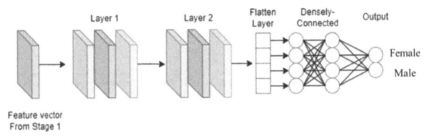

Fig. 4. Stage 2 CNN model.

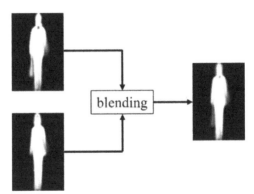

Fig. 5. Generation of augmented female GEI.

The GEI CNN model, Stance CNN model, and Swing CNN model are trained independently. Inputs from two different angles are combined to form one set of samples. As for the CASIA B dataset, a total of 55 sets are generated. We adopt 5-fold cross-validation as the training method and categorical cross entropy CE as the loss function

$$CE(x) = -\sum_{i=1}^{C} y_i \log(f(x_i)) \tag{1}$$

where y_i is the ground truth label for gender class i, x_i is the score for gender class i, f is the activation function sigmoid, C is the number of gender classes. Each set of samples is divided into 80% training set and 20% testing set. From the training set, 20% of the samples are reserved for validation. The model is trained on each set 10 times. The total number of training epochs is 2750. The extracted features are fused and fed to the Stage 2 CNN classifier. The whole framework is further trained through ensemble learning with the dataset divided into 80% training set and 20% validation set.

4 Experiments and Results

We train our proposed model on a computer with Intel i5 CPU, Nvidia GeForce RTX 3060 GPU, 32 GB RAM, and 1 TB disk memory. We evaluate and compare the performance of our proposed framework with state-of-the-art gait-based gender classification methods on two benchmark datasets CASIA B [24] and OU-ISIR MVLP [12, 21]. The reference methods include texture-based algorithm, posture-based algorithm, and deep-learning based model. El-Alfy et al. [5] proposed a texture-based gender recognition algorithm based on fuzzy local binary pattern (FLBP*) features extracted from GEI. SVM is adopted for the prediction of the gender of the walking subject. Experimental results on CASIA B dataset demonstrate that FLBP* outperforms four other LBP-based methods. Isaac et al. [28] proposed a posture-based gender classification method. Instead of demanding a complete gait cycle, they proposed a method that extracts features from each frame of the image sequence. Gender classification, called pose-based voting (PBV), is achieved based on the most probable predictions. Experimentations were performed on CASIA B dataset with two feature extraction techniques: elliptic Fourier descriptors (PBV-EFD), consolidate vector of row-column summation (PBV-RCS). Linear discriminant analysis is adopted for gender classification. The two models achieve high gender classification accuracy, even surpassing the CNN + SVM method. Russel and Selvaraj [18] proposed a complex gender classification framework containing six parallel CNNs with the input of GEI. The parallel networks contain varying number of convolution layers. Besides evaluating the performance of gender classification from multiple networks, they also investigate the performance of individual networks. For comparison, we select a single network model CNN C_customized which has similar complexity as our proposed model.

To evaluate the gender classification accuracy, we calculate the Recall (Re), Precision (Pr), and total accuracy (Acc)

$$Recall = \frac{TP}{TP + FN} \tag{2}$$

$$Precision = \frac{TP}{TP + FP} \tag{3}$$

$$Acc = \frac{TP + TN}{TP + FP + TN + FN} \tag{4}$$

where TP is True Positive, TN is True Negative, FP is False Positive, and FN is False Negative.

Table 1. Comparison of our proposed model with other methods on CASIA B dataset.

Method	Re	Pr	Acc
FLBP* [5]	0.964	0.965	0.964
PBV-EFD [28]	-	-	0.953
PBV-RCS [28]	-	-	0.979
CNN C_customized [18]	0.929	0.995	0.960
Our proposed model	0.983	0.979	0.981

Table 1 compares the performance of our proposed model and four state-of-the-art methods as mentioned above on CASIA B dataset in terms of Re, Pr, and Acc. The best result is highlighted in red. The second best result is highlighted in blue. FLBP* extracts feature from GEI. PBV extracts features from posture. Our proposed model outperforms these two methods with features from both GEI and posture images. CNN C_customized also extracts feature from GEI. Although it achieves the highest Pr, Acc is relatively low due to low value of Re. Our proposed model achieves uniformly high values in Re, Pr, and Acc. As compared with the four recently proposed methods covering deterministic algorithms and CNN model, our proposed achieves the best score in Re and Acc, and the second best score in Pr.

Table 2. Comparison of our proposed model with other methods on OU-ISIR MVLP dataset.

Method	Acc
GEINet [10]	0.939
GaitSet [16]	0.927
Xu [14]	0.943
Our proposed model	0.943

GEINet [10] is an eight-layered network with the input of GEI to two triplets (convolution, pooling, normalization) and two fully connected layers. GaitSct [16] is a flexible multi-stream CNN framework with the input of gait silhouette sequence. Xu et al. [14] proposed a CNN framework. The model contains two GaitSet networks for two reconstructed gait silhouette sequences during training, while only one GaitSet network is used for testing. These deep learning based methods exploit inputs of GEI, single original gait sequence, and multi-view synthesized gait sequences. Table 2 compares the performance of our proposed model and three methods as mentioned above on OU-ISIR MVLP dataset in terms of Acc. Our proposed model outperforms both GEINet and GaitSet. GaitSet, with the input of a large number of gait silhouettes in parallel, is a complex network. Our proposed model, which is a relatively simpler network with the inputs of GEI and posture images, can perform as good as Xu et al. [14] complex framework with two GaitSet networks.

5 Ablation Study

We evaluate and compare Stage 1 GEI CNN and our proposed model (Stage 1 + Stage 2). Tables 3 and 4 show the performance of all models on CASIA B dataset and OU-ISIR-MVLP dataset respectively.

Table 3. Performance evaluation of Stage 1 GEI CNN and Stage 1 + Stage 2 CNN on CASIA B dataset.

Model	Female Recall	Female Precision	Male Recall	Male Precision	Acc
Stage 1 (only GEI CNN)	0.870	0.881	0.879	0.869	0.875
Stage 1 + Stage 2	0.992	0.964	0.973	0.994	0.981

Table 4. Performance evaluation of Stage 1 GEI CNN and Stage 1 + Stage 2 CNN on OU-ISIR MVLP dataset.

Model	Female Recall	Female Precision	Male Recall	Male Precision	Acc
Stage 1 (only GEI CNN)	0.844	0.778	0.789	0.852	0.815
Stage 1 + Stage 2	0.942	0.947	0.945	0.940	0.943

Our proposed model achieves higher Re, Pr, and Acc than the GEI CNN on both datasets. It demonstrates that the proposed framework, that exploits features from both GEI and postures, achieves higher gender classification accuracy than the model that only utilizes GEI. Table 5 compares the inference time per one set of inputs (GEI, stance image, swing image) and the number of parameters of Stage 1 CNN and our proposed model. Stage 1, a multi-stream CNN, contains most parameters of the framework. That guarantees the feature extractor has sufficient analytical power to extract useful features from the multiple modality inputs.

Table 5. Inference time per single set of GEI/Stance/Swing images and number of parameters of our proposed model.

Model	Inference time (sec)	Number of parameters
Stage 1	0.029	52 M
Stage 1 + Stage 2	0.327	53 M

6 Conclusion

We propose a multi-stream gender classification framework with heterogeneous inputs of GEI, stance image, and swing image. We adopt ensemble learning to train our proposed model. Experiments are performed to evaluate and compare the performance of our proposed model with other gait-based gender classification methods on benchmark datasets. We demonstrate that our proposed model with features extracted from multiple modality inputs achieves higher gender classification accuracy than a variety of recently proposed methods that only utilize a single type of visual input such as GEI or posture image.

References

1. Harris, E.J., Khoo, I.-H., Demircan, E.: A survey of human gait-based artificial intelligence applications. Front. Robot. AI **8**, Article 749274 (2022)
2. Liao, R., Yu, S., An, W., Huang, Y.: A model-based gait recognition method with body pose and human prior knowledge. Pattern Recogn.Recogn. **98**, 107069 (2020)
3. Han, J., Bhanu, B.: Individual recognition using gait energy image. IEEE Trans. Pattern Anal. Mach. Intell.Intell. **28**(2), 316–322 (2006)
4. Yu, S., Tan, T., Huang, K., Jia, K., Wu, X.: A study on gait-based gender classification. IEEE Trans. Image Process. **18**(8), 1905–1910 (2009)
5. El-Alfy, E.-S.M., Binsaadoon, A.G.: Automated gait-based gender identification using fuzzy local binary patterns with tuned parameters. J. Ambient. Intell. Humaniz. Comput.Intell. Humaniz. Comput. **10**, 2495–2504 (2019)
6. Hu, M., Wang, Y.: A new approach for gender classification based on gait analysis. In: Proceedings of International Conference on Image and Graphics, pp. 869–874 (2009)
7. Saini, A., Singh, H.: Enhanced human identity and gender recognition from gait sequences using SVM and MDA. Int. J. Comput. Appl. **119**(2) (2015)
8. Do, T.D., Nguyen, V.H., Kim, H.: Real-time and robust multiple-view gender classification using gait features in video surveillance. Pattern Anal. Appl. **23**, 399–413 (2020)
9. Krizhevsky, A., Sutskever, I., Hinton, G.E.: ImageNet classification with deep convolutional neural networks. In: Proceedings of the 25th International Conference on Neural Information Processing Systems, vol. 1, pp. 1097–1105 (2012)
10. Shiraga, K., Makihara, Y., Muramatsu, D., Echigo, T., Yagi, Y.: Geinet: view-invariant gait recognition using a convolutional neural network. In: Proceedings of International Conference on Biometrics, pp. 1–8 (2016)
11. Zhang, C., Liu, W., Ma, H., Fu, H.: Siamese neural network based gait recognition for human identification. In: Proceedings of IEEE International Conference on Acoustics, Speech and Signal Processing, pp. 2832–2836 (2016)
12. Takemura, N., Makihara, Y., Muramatsu, D., Echigo, T., Yagi, Y.: Multi-view large population gait dataset and its performance evaluation for cross-view gait recognition. IPSJ Trans. Comput. Vision Appl. **10**(4), 1–14 (2018)
13. Sakata, A., Takemura, N., Yagi, Y.: Gait-based age estimation using multi-stage convolutional neural network. IPSJ Trans. Comput. Vision Appl. **11**(4), 1–10 (2019)
14. Xu, C., et al.: Real-time gait-based age estimation and gender classification from a single image. In: Proceedings of the IEEE/CVF Conference on Applications of Computer Vision, pp. 3460–3470 (2021)

15. Xu, C., Makihara, Y., Li, X., Yagi, Y., Lu, J.: Gait recognition from a single image using a phase-aware gait cycle reconstruction network. In: Vedaldi, A., Bischof, H., Brox, T., Frahm, J.-M. (eds.) ECCV 2020. LNCS, vol. 12364, pp. 386–403. Springer, Cham (2020). https://doi.org/10.1007/978-3-030-58529-7_23

16. Chao, H., He, Y., Zhang, J., Feng, J.: GaitSet: regarding gait as a set for cross-view gait recognition. In: Proceedings of the AAAI Conference on Artificial Intelligence, vol. 33, no. 1, pp. 8126–8133 (2019)

17. Bei, S., Deng, J., Zhen, Z., Shaojing, S.: Gender recognition via fused silhouette features based on visual sensors. IEEE Sens. J. 19(20), 9496–9503 (2019)

18. Russel, N.S., Selvaraj, A.: Gender discrimination, age group classification and carried object recognition from gait energy image using fusion of parallel convolutional neural network. IET Image Proc. **15**, 239–251 (2021)

19. Xu, C., Makihara, Y., Ogi, G., Li, X., Yagi, Y., Lu, J.: The OU-ISIR gait database comprising the large population dataset with age and performance evaluation of age estimation. IPSJ Trans. Comput. Vision Appl. **9**(24), 1–14 (2017)

20. OU-ISIR Gait Database, Large Population Dataset with Age. http://www.am.sanken.osaka-u.ac.jp/BiometricDB/GaitLPAge.html

21. The OU-ISIR Gait Database, Multi-view Large Population Dataset. http://www.am.sanken.osaka-u.ac.jp/BiometricDB/GaitMVLP.html

22. Zhang, D., Wang, Y.: Gender recognition based on fusion of face and gait information. In: Proceeding of International Conference on Machine Learning and Cybernetics, pp. 62–67 (2008)

23. Samangooei, S., Bustard, J.D., Seely, R.D., Nixon, M.S., Carter, J.N.: Acquisition and analysis of a dataset comprising gait, ear, and semantic data. In: Multibiometrics for Human Identification. Cambridge University Press, Chapter 12 (2011)

24. CASIA Gait Database. http://www.sinobiometrics.com

25. Zhu, Z., et al.: Gait recognition in the wild: a benchmark. In: Proceedings of IEEE International Conference on Computer Vision, pp. 14789–14799 (2021)

26. Kwon, B., Lee, S.: Joint swing energy for skeleton-based gender classification. IEEE Access **9**, 28334–28348 (2021)

27. Zhao, L., Guo, L., Zhang, R., Xie, X., Ye, X.: MmGaitSet: multimodal based gait recognition for countering carrying and clothing changes. Appl. Intell.Intell. **52**, 2023–2036 (2022)

28. Isaac, E.R.H.P., Elias, S., Rajagopalan, S., Easwarakumar, K.S.: Multiview gait-based gender classification through pose-based voting. Pattern Recogn. Lett.Recogn. Lett. **126**, 41–50 (2019)

Oil Temperature Prediction Method Based on Deep Learning and Digital Twins

Zengxu Bian[1], Zhibo Wan[1(⊠)], Feiyu Li[1], Dejun Liu[2], and Zhihan Lyu[3(⊠)]

[1] Qingdao University, Qingdao, China
wzbdata@163.com
[2] China Academy of Railway Sciences, Beijing, China
[3] Uppsala University, Uppsala, Sweden
lvzhihan@gmail.com

Abstract. Oil temperature is an important indicator of transformer health. Oil temperature prediction is widely used in transformer state detection, fault diagnosis and other fields. However, there are many factors affecting the transformer oil temperature, such as season, weather, load, holidays and so on. In order to dig out the relationship between oil temperature and various influencing factors and make more accurate prediction tasks, this paper proposes a multi-step prediction model of long-term sequence oil temperature based on particle swarm optimization (PSO) and Pyraformer and combines it with digital twin system. Pyraformer can capture a wide range of time dependence, and we use PSO to optimize its hyper-parameters to improve the prediction accuracy. At the same time, the digital twin system can provide more data support and real-time feedback for the prediction model, and further improve the accuracy and reliability of the model. At the same time, the digital twin system can also react to management activities such as prediction and detection. Experiments on two datasets with different time unit steps show that PSO-Pyraformer has the highest prediction accuracy in the long-term multi-step prediction task of multivariate to univariate.

Keywords: Oil temperature prediction · Pyraformer · PSO · Digital twins system · Parameter optimization

1 Introduction

As one of the indispensable components in the power system, the transformer undertakes important tasks such as power transmission and distribution [1]. Especially, the transformer oil temperature is an important index to evaluate the state of the transformer, which usually needs to be monitored and predicted in real time [2]. The traditional prediction method based on physical model needs to consider a large number of physical factors, and is easily affected by model deviation and uncertainty. With the development of intelligent technology, the use of multi-source data to establish prediction models has become a hot research field [3].

The current traditional hyperparameter optimization method selects the optimal combination by traversing the given hyperparameter combination. However, for long-term

© The Author(s), under exclusive license to Springer Nature Switzerland AG 2023
H. Lu et al. (Eds.): ACPR 2023, LNCS 14408, pp. 174–184, 2023.
https://doi.org/10.1007/978-3-031-47665-5_15

series forecasting problems, the hyperparameter space is often very large, and the grid search method is inefficient. For example, Bayesian optimization methods estimate the performance of different hyperparameter combinations by building a model, and choose the combination with the highest performance. This method can find the optimal solution within a limited number of trials, but for long-term series forecasting problems, time factors and dynamic changes of the model need to be considered.

Liu et al. (2022) proposed a low-complexity pyramidal attention for long-range time series modeling and forecasting named Pyraformer [4]. Pyraformer can achieve higher prediction accuracy with less time and memory consumption in single-step and long-term multi-step prediction tasks [5]. However, this algorithm also has some challenges, such as choosing an appropriate hierarchical structure and model parameters, as well as computational and memory overhead when processing long sequences, etc. Therefore, proper tuning and parameter selection are required in the application.

Therefore, this paper discusses the feasibility and advantages of using PSO-Pyraformer model to predict transformer oil temperature from multivariate to univariate, and proposes a method combined with digital twin system. The digital twin system can provide real-time feed back and more comprehensive data support for the model, making the prediction model more accurate.

The main contributions of this study are as follows:

(1) It can better capture many factors related to oil temperature: the change of oil temperature is affected by many factors, such as ambient temperature, turbine load, running time and so on [6]. Using multivariate to predict single variables can more fully consider the relationship between these factors, thereby improving the prediction accuracy.
(2) Give full play to the advantages of PSO algorithm and Pyraformer model: PSO algorithm has global search ability, can adjust each parameter adaptively, optimize the prediction model, and combine with Pyraformer model to further improve the generalization and accuracy of the model.
(3) A digital twin system for transformer oil temperature prediction is constructed. A variety of indicators and oil temperature prediction results will be displayed in the system, providing reliable data support for transformer supervision and prediction system. Deep learning and digital twin technology are integrated to provide decision-making for transformer management. At the same time, it is convenient for managers to carry out real-time monitoring and management.

The rest of the paper: Part 2: establishment of prediction model; Part 3: the establishment of digital twin system; Part 4: experiment part; Part 5: summary and outlook for the future.

2 Research Methods and Model Establishment

2.1 PSO

The particle swarm algorithm simulates the group behaviour of natural groups such as birds and fish to find the optimal solution to multivariate nonlinear problems [7]. The basic idea is to find the global optimal solution by constantly testing the search space.

In this algorithm, the ith particle has a position $\vec{x}_i(t)$ and velocity $\vec{vx}_i(t)$ at time t. The update formula of particle velocity and position is:

$$v\_i(t+1) = \rho * v\_i(t) + \alpha * rand\_1 * (pbest\_i - x\_i(t)) + \beta * rand\_2 * (gbest - x\_i(t)) \tag{1}$$

$$x\_i(t+1) = x\_i(t) + v\_i(t+1) \tag{2}$$

Here, ρ is the inertia weight control parameter, α and β are acceleration factors, rand_1 and rand_2 are random numbers ranging from 0 to 1.

Use the PSO algorithm to adjust the parameters of the Pyraformer model to minimize the value of the objective function. The PSO algorithm optimizes parameters by simulating the behavior of a flock of birds, and finds the optimal solution through continuous iteration. By fusing the PSO and Pyraformer models, the optimization ability of the PSO algorithm can be combined with the prediction ability of the Pyraformer model, thereby improving the accuracy and reliability of predicting oil temperature.

2.2 Pyraformer

Compared to the general attention mechanism model, The core part of Pyraformer is the introduction of pyramid attention module(PAM) [8]. Different from the traditional attention mechanism. The specific form is as follows:

$$\begin{cases} X_l^{(s)} = A_l^{(s)} \cup C_l^{(s)} \cup P_l^{(s)} & (3) \\ A_l^{(s)} = \left\{ x_j^{(s)} : |j - l| \leq \frac{a-1}{2}, 1 \leq j \leq \frac{L}{c^{s-1}} \right\} & (4) \\ C_l^{(s)} = \left\{ x_j^{(s-1)} : (l-1)c < j \leq lc \right\} if\ s \geq 2\ else\ \emptyset & (5) \\ P_l^{(s)} = \left\{ x_j^{(s+1)} : j = \lceil l/c \rceil \right\} if\ s \leq S - 1\ else\ \emptyset & (6) \end{cases}$$

In the above formula. $X_1^{(s)}$ adjacent nodes of each node on three different scales: includes $A_1^{(s)}$, $C_1^{(s)}$, $P_1^{(s)}$. It simplifies the attention at the node $x_1^{(s)}$ to:

$$y_i = \sum_{l \in X_l^{(s)}} \frac{exp(q_i k_l^T / \sqrt{d_K}) v_l}{\sum_{l \in X_l^{(s)}} exp(q_i k_l^T / \sqrt{d_K})} \tag{7}$$

In the formula, $X_1^{(s)}$ represents a set of neighboring nodes at three scales. By introducing multi-scale information capture and long-distance dependence modeling, the pyramid attention mechanism can provide more comprehensive and diversified context information [9], enhance model performance and generalization ability [10], and effectively improve prediction accuracy.

The advantage of the Pyraformer algorithm is that it can efficiently process long-term series data and can capture dependencies at different scales. It has achieved good performance in some time series forecasting tasks.

2.3   Proposed PSO-Pyraformer Prediction Model

The advantages of the PSO algorithm and the Pyraformer model are comprehensively utilized. (1) The PSO algorithm can search for the optimal solution globally, and the Pyraformer model can accurately predict the oil temperature. (2) The PSO algorithm can improve the prediction accuracy of the Pyraformer model by iteratively optimizing parameters. (3) The fusion of the two algorithms can complement each other's advantages, thereby improving the accuracy and stability of the prediction results. (4) The PSO algorithm can avoid falling into a local optimal solution, thereby increasing the robustness and generalization ability of the model (Fig. 1).

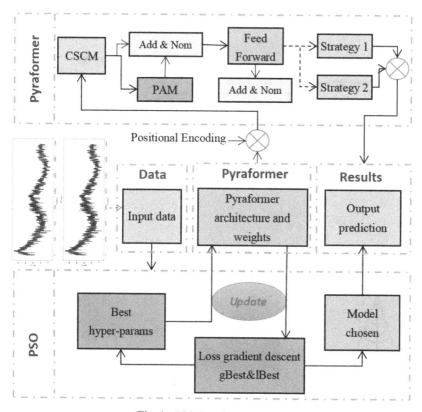

Fig. 1. PSO-Pyraformer model.

In the above framework, the PSO algorithm and the Pyraformer model interact through input data. Here, our goal is to use the PSO algorithm to update the hyper-parameters in Pyraformer to improve the accuracy of model prediction. Specifically, the scheme follows the following steps:

Step 1: The input data is passed to Pyraformer for processing data features and making predictions.

Step 2: PSO algorithm calculates individual fitness according to the current particle position (hyper-parameter) to find the best weight combination.

Step 3: The PSO algorithm updates the particle velocity and position according to the global optimal and local optimal solutions.

Step 4: The updated hyper-parameters are passed to the Pyraformer model, and steps 1–3 are repeated until the stopping condition is reached.

Step 5: The optimal weight used by the entire system is sent back to the model for prediction.

3 Digital Twins System

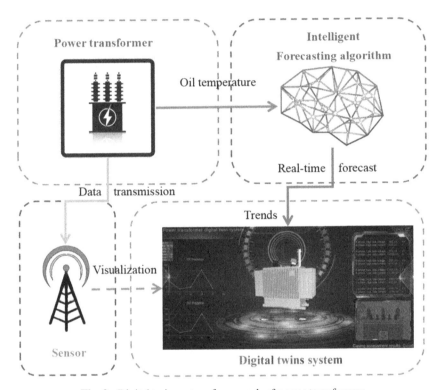

Fig. 2. Digital twin system framework of power transformer.

The following are the steps to establish a transformer digital twin system [11] (Fig. 2):

Step 1: Sensor data collection: Collect the historical data of the transformer, including transformer temperature, humidity, load and other information. In this study, TCP/IP protocol simulation is constructed locally [12].

Step 2: Physical model establishment: A mathematical model is constructed to describe the thermodynamic behavior of the transformer, and various factors affecting the temperature of the transformer are considered.

Step 3: Data-driven model training: historical data is used to train the data-driven model [13]. The data-driven model we used is the PSO-Pyraformer proposed in this study.

Step 4: Prediction application: The real-time environmental parameters are input into the digital twin system [14], and the trained model is used to predict the oil temperature.

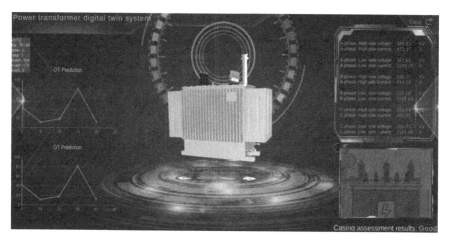

Fig. 3. Interface of the Digital Twin System.

As shown in Fig. 3, it is the view of the power transformer digital twin system. These include oil temperature prediction function, key indicator display, etc. The advantages of the transformer oil temperature prediction digital twin system are as follows:

(1) Real-time monitoring: The digital twin system can obtain the environmental parameters of the transformer in real time and make real-time prediction. This helps to detect potential problems and anomalies in time, and take necessary measures in advance to prevent equipment failure and downtime [15].

(2) Prediction accuracy: By combining mathematical models and historical data for training, the digital twin system can provide relatively accurate oil temperature prediction. It can consider the combined effects of multiple factors, such as load change, ambient temperature, humidity, etc., thereby increasing the accuracy of prediction [16].

(3) Cost savings: By predicting transformer oil temperature, the digital twin system can help optimize equipment maintenance plans and resource allocation. It can guide maintenance personnel to carry out the necessary maintenance or repair when needed, reduce unnecessary maintenance costs and downtime, and reduce operating costs [17].

(4) Risk management: The digital twin system can help identify potential equipment problems in advance and reduce the risk of sudden failures [18]. By providing accurate oil temperature prediction, it can help operators to formulate corresponding preventive measures to reduce the impact of equipment failure on production and operation [19, 20].

4   Analytical Study

4.1   Experimental Data

Since the primary forecasting model in this study comes from the long-term series forecasting model Informer proposed in the article published by (zhou et al., 2021) [21].

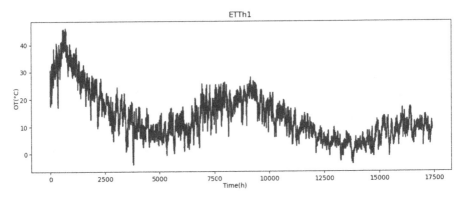

Fig. 4.   Data curve of data set ETTh1.

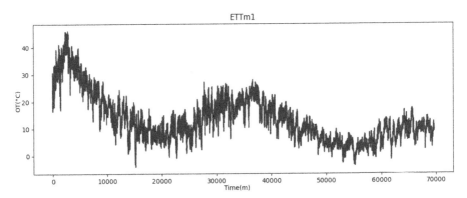

Fig. 5.   Data curve of data set ETTm1.

The experimental data comes from the oil temperature data sets mentioned in this paper: ETTh1 and ETTm1. The experimental data comes from two site transformers from 2016/07 to 2018/07. Among them, ETTh1 is in units of hours, and one piece of oil temperature data is collected every hour. ETTm1 collects one piece of data every 15 min [22]. Figures 4 and 5 is an overall view of two datasets showing evident seasonal trends.

4.2   Evaluation Indicators

We choose the most commonly used three evaluation indicators, MSE (Mean Square Error), RMSE (Root Mean Square Error) and MAE (Mean Absolute Error), to evaluate the performance of the prediction model [23]. The smaller these errors are, the better the performance of the method [24].

$$MAE = \left(\sum_{i=1}^{n} \left| \widehat{Y}_i - Y_i \right| \right) / n \tag{8}$$

$$MSE = \left(\sum_{i=1}^{n} \left(\widehat{Y}_i - Y_i \right)^2 \right) / n \tag{9}$$

$$MAE = \left(\sum_{i=1}^{n} \left| \widehat{Y}_i - Y_i \right| \right) / n \tag{10}$$

n is the number of samples. Prediction: $\widehat{Y} = \{\hat{y}_1, \hat{y}_2, \cdots, \hat{y}_n\}$, True: $Y = \{y_1, y_2, \cdots, y_n\}$, MAE, MSE, RMSE $\in [0, +\infty)$.

4.3 Experimental Results

We evaluated the long-term prediction performance of PSO-Pyraformer on ETTh1 and ETTm1. It is worth noting that these two data sets contain six power load variables and oil temperature, which is a multi-variable to univariate time series prediction problem [25].

We compared it with four common models with better prediction results, including LSTM, Informer, LongTrans and Pyraformer. These algorithms are more representative in the field of long-term sequence prediction. The comparison results can not only prove the prediction advantages of the proposed compared to other algorithms. At the same time, it can be explained that the PSO improves the prediction accuracy of the Pyraformer.

As shown in Table 1, the proposed method outperforms other benchmarks.

4.4 Evaluation of Experimental Results

In order to better demonstrate the superiority of the proposed method, this paper uses three percentage indicators $P_{MSE}(\%)$, $P_{RMSE}(\%)$, $P_{MAE}(\%)$, corresponding to MSE, RMSE, and MAE. This evaluation indicator reflects the proposed algorithm's superiority over other models.

$$P_{MSE}\% = \left| \frac{MSE_{BM} - MSE_{PM}}{MSE_{BM}} \right| \times 100\% \tag{11}$$

$$P_{RMSE}\% = \left| \frac{RMSE_{BM} - RMSE_{PM}}{RMSE_{BM}} \right| \times 100\% \tag{12}$$

$$P_{MAE}\% = \left| \frac{MAE_{BM} - MAE_{PM}}{MAE_{BM}} \right| \times 100\% \tag{13}$$

where: MSE_{BM}, $RMSE_{BM}$, MAE_{BM} is the value of the evaluation index of the benchmark method, MSE_{PM}, $RMSE_{PM}$, MAE_{PM} is the value of the evaluation index of the proposed method. As shown in the Table 2, compared with LSTM, when $l \in \{168, 336, 720\}$, the MSE of Pyraformer on ETTh1 is reduced by 36.96%, 37.42% and 54.54%. Compared with the best model Pyraformer, MSE also decreased by 5.44%, 5.71% and 12.81%.

Table 1. Comparison test (The multi-step prediction results on the two datasets are compared, where ETTh1 is three steps, and the predicted input lengths I are 168,336, and 720, respectively. The three prediction steps on ETTm1 are 96,288 and 672, respectively. The input length o = l.The best results are highlighted in bold.).

Data		Evaluation	Prediction Methods				
Metrics			LSTM	Informer	LongTrans	Pyraformer	Proposed
ETTh1	168	MSE	1.212	1.075	0.983	0.808	**0.764**
		RMSE	1.100	1.036	0.991	0.898	**0.874**
		MAE	0.867	0.801	0.766	0.683	**0.667**
	336	MSE	1.424	1.329	1.100	0.945	**0.891**
		RMSE	1.193	1.152	1.073	0.972	**0.943**
		MAE	0.995	0.911	0.869	0.766	**0.735**
	720	MSE	1.960	1.384	1.411	1.022	**0.891**
		RMSE	1.400	1.176	1.084	1.010	**0.943**
		MAE	1.322	0.950	0.991	0.806	**0.755**
ETTm1	96	MSE	1.339	0.556	0.554	0.480	**0.476**
		RMSE	1.157	0.745	0.744	0.692	**0.689**
		MAE	0.913	0.537	0.499	0.486	**0.478**
	288	MSE	1.740	0.841	0.786	0.754	**0.691**
		RMSE	1.319	0.917	0.886	0.868	**0.831**
		MAE	1.124	0.705	0.676	0.659	**0.615**
	672	MSE	2.736	0.921	1.169	0.857	**0.751**
		RMSE	1.654	0.959	1.081	0.925	**0.866**
		MAE	1.555	0.753	0.868	0.707	**0.647**

Table 2. The proposed method optimizes the percentage Compared with other models.

Data		Metrics	Proposed vs LSTM	Proposed vs Informer	Proposed vs. LongTrans	Proposed vs Pyraformer
ETTh1	168	P_{MSE} (%)	36.96%	28.93%	22.27%	5.44%
		P_{RMSE} (%)	20.54%	15.63%	11.80%	2.67%
		P_{MAE} (%)	23.06%	16.72%	12.92%	2.34%
	336	P_{MSE} (%)	37.42%	32.95%	19.00%	5.71%
		P_{RMSE} (%)	20.95%	18.14%	12.11%	2.98%
		P_{MAE} (%)	26.13%	19.31%	15.42%	4.04%
	720	P_{MSE} (%)	54.54%	35.62%	36.85%	12.81%
		P_{RMSE} (%)	32.64%	19.81%	13.00%	6.63%

(continued)

Table 2. (*continued*)

Data		Metrics	Proposed vs LSTM	Proposed vs Informer	Proposed vs. LongTrans	Proposed vs Pyraformer
ETTm1	96	P_{MAE} (%)	42.88%	20.52%	23.81%	6.32%
		P_{MSE} (%)	64.45%	14.38%	14.07%	0.83%
		P_{RMSE} (%)	40.44%	7.51%	7.39%	0.43%
	288	P_{MAE} (%)	47.64%	10.98%	4.20%	1.64%
		P_{MSE} (%)	60.28%	17.83%	12.08%	8.35%
		P_{RMSE} (%)	36.99%	9.37%	6.20%	4.26%
	672	P_{MAE} (%)	45.28%	12.76%	9.02%	6.67%
		P_{MSE} (%)	72.55%	18.45%	35.75%	12.36%
		P_{RMSE} (%)	47.64%	9.69%	19.88%	6.37%
		P_{MAE} (%)	58.39%	14.07%	25.46%	8.48%

5   Conclusion

In the study of Pyraformer, the author concludes by mentioning in the future work, they would like to explore how to adapt to learn the hyper-parameters. Based on this, this study proposes a PSO-Pyraformer hyper-parameter optimization prediction model. The prediction model is applied to the digital twin model of power transformer. In this way, to improve the accuracy of long time series multi-step multi-variable to single variable prediction and contribute to the intelligent management of the transformer. In the future, we hope to combine with the previous research, further study the oil temperature prediction of single variable to single variable with shorter step size, and deeply combine with the digital twin system to enrich the application.

References

1. Thiviyanathan, V.A., Ker, P.J., Leong, Y.S., et al.: Power transformer insulation system: a review on the reactions, fault detection, challenges and future prospects. Alexandria Eng. J. (2022)
2. Abbasi, A.R.: Fault detection and diagnosis in power transformers: a comprehensive review and classification of publications and methods. Electr. Power Syst. Res. **209**, 107990 (2022)
3. Li, K., Ye, H., Li, W., et al.: Transformer fault identification method based on multi-source data. In: 18th International Conference on AC and DC Power Transmission (ACDC 2022). IET 2022, pp. 791–795 (2022)
4. Liu, S., Yu, H., Liao, C., et al.: Pyraformer: low-complexity pyramidal attention for long-range time series modeling and forecasting. In: International Conference on Learning Representations (2021)
5. Zeng, A., Chen, M., Zhang, L., et al.: Are transformers effective for time series forecasting?. arXiv preprint arXiv:2205.13504 (2022)

6. Cilliyuz, Y., Bicen, Y., Aras, F., et al.: Measurements and performance evaluations of natural ester and mineral oil-immersed identical transformers. Int. J. Electr. Power Energy Syst. **125**, 106517 (2021)
7. Marini, F., Walczak, B.: Particle swarm optimization (PSO). A tutorial. Chemometr. Intell. Lab. Syst. **149**, 153–165 (2015)
8. Li, H., Xiong, P., An, J., et al.: Pyramid attention network for semantic segmentation. arXiv preprint arXiv:1805.10180 (2018)
9. Wang, J., Xu, G., Yan, F., et al.: Defect transformer: an efficient hybrid transformer architecture for surface defect detection. Measurement **211**, 112614 (2023)
10. Feng, C., Su, M., Xu, L., et al.: A novel generalization ability-enhanced approach for corrosion fatigue life prediction of marine welded structures. Int. J. Fatigue **166**, 107222 (2023)
11. Moutis, P., Alizadeh-Mousavi, O.: Digital twin of distribution power transformer for real-time monitoring of medium voltage from low voltage measurements. IEEE Trans. Power Deliv. **36**(4), 1952–1963 (2020)
12. Hassan, M., Jain, R.: High Performance TCP/IP Networking. Prentice Hall, Upper Saddle River (2003)
13. Jin, Y., Yan, D., Zhang, X., et al.: A data-driven model predictive control for lighting system based on historical occupancy in an office building: methodology development. In: Building Simulation, vol. 14, pp. 219–235. Tsinghua University Press (2021)
14. Nasirahmadi, A., Hensel, O.: Toward the next generation of digitalization in agriculture based on digital twin paradigm. Sensors **22**(2), 498 (2022)
15. Sleiti, A.K., Kapat, J.S., Vesely, L.: Digital twin in energy industry: proposed robust digital twin for power plant and other complex capital-intensive large engineering systems. Energy Rep. **8**, 3704–3726 (2022)
16. Lin, J., Ma, J., Zhu, J., et al.: Short-term load forecasting based on LSTM networks considering attention mechanism. Int. J. Electr. Power Energy Syst. **137**, 107818 (2022)
17. Zhong, D., Xia, Z., Zhu, Y., et al.: Overview of predictive maintenance based on digital twin technology. Heliyon (2023)
18. Aivaliotis, P., Georgoulias, K., Chryssolouris, G.: The use of digital twin for predictive maintenance in manufacturing. Int. J. Comput. Integr. Manuf. **32**(11), 1067–1080 (2019)
19. Naqvi, S.M.R., Ghufran, M., Meraghni, S., et al.: Human knowledge centered maintenance decision support in digital twin environment. J. Manuf. Syst. **65**, 528–537 (2022)
20. Dhiman, H.S., Deb, D., Muyeen, S.M., et al.: Wind turbine gearbox anomaly detection based on adaptive threshold and twin support vector machines. IEEE Trans. Energy Convers. **36**(4), 3462–3469 (2021)
21. Zhou, H., Zhang, S., Peng, J., et al.: Informer: beyond efficient transformer for long sequence time-series forecasting. In: Proceedings of the AAAI Conference on Artificial Intelligence, vol. 35, no. 12, pp. 11106–11115 (2021)
22. Nie, Y., Nguyen, N.H., Sinthong, P., et al.: A time series is worth 64 words: long-term forecasting with transformers. arXiv preprint arXiv:2211.14730 (2022)
23. Willmott, C.J., Matsuura, K.: Advantages of the mean absolute error (MAE) over the root mean square error (RMSE) in assessing average model performance. Climate Res. **30**(1), 79–82 (2005)
24. Chicco, D., Warrens, M.J., Jurman, G.: The coefficient of determination R-squared is more informative than SMAPE, MAE, MAPE, MSE and RMSE in regression analysis evaluation. PeerJ Comput. Sci. **7**, e623 (2021)
25. Lim, B., Arık, S.Ö., Loeff, N., et al.: Temporal fusion transformers for interpretable multi-horizon time series forecasting. Int. J. Forecast. **37**(4), 1748–1764 (2021)

Feature Channel Adaptive Enhancement for Fine-Grained Visual Classification

Dingzhou Xie⬤, Cheng Pang$^{(\boxtimes)}$⬤, Guanhua Wu⬤, and Rushi Lan⬤

Guilin University of Electronic Technology, Guilin 541004, China
pangcheng3@guet.edu.cn

Abstract. Fine-grained classification poses greater challenges compared to basic-level image classification due to the visually similar sub-species. To distinguish between confusing species, we introduce a novel framework based on feature channel adaptive enhancement and attention erasure. On one hand, a lightweight module employing both channel attention and spatial attention is designed, adaptively enhancing the feature expression of important areas and obtaining more discriminative feature vectors. On the other hand, we incorporate attention erasure methods that compel the network to concentrate on less prominent areas, thereby enhancing the network's robustness. Our method can be seamlessly integrated into various backbone networks. Finally, an evaluation of our approach is conducted across diverse public datasets, accompanied by a comprehensive comparative analysis against state-of-the-art methodologies. The experimental findings substantiate the efficacy and viability of our method in real-world scenarios, exemplifying noteworthy breakthroughs in intricate fine-grained classification endeavors.

Keywords: Fine-grained Visual Classification · Feature Channel Enhancement · Attention Erasure

1 Introduction

Fine-grained visual classification represents a substantial and intricate challenge within the realm of computer vision. Unlike traditional object classification tasks, fine-grained classification requires precise differentiation among objects with similar appearances but belonging to different subcategories. This task holds practical value in various domains such as animal recognition [20], plant classification [28], and car vehicle recognition [22]. However, As shown in Fig. 1, fine-grained classification presents a delicate balance between similarity and difference. Objects with similar appearances exhibit subtle local differences that often encompass crucial features determining their categories. Conventional classification methods struggle to capture these minute differences, resulting in poor performance. To overcome this challenge, extensive research has introduced innovative methods and techniques for fine-grained classification. Examples include local feature extraction [12,13,30], key part localization [6,24,36,37,40], metric learning [5,7,32,43], and attention-based mechanisms [19,26,41]. These approaches aim to extract discriminative features from local or

H. Lu et al. (Eds.): ACPR 2023, LNCS 14408, pp. 185–198, 2023.
https://doi.org/10.1007/978-3-031-47665-5_16

key details, thereby enhancing classification performance by learning subtle differences between categories. Despite the progress made in this area, fine-grained classification still faces several challenges. On one hand, accurate classifiers often require large amounts of fine-grained data and annotations [2, 16, 23, 38] due to the nuanced differences among categories. This limits the scope and scalability of fine-grained classification methods. On the other hand, traditional fine-grained classification methods are often sensitive to image changes and noise, resulting in a decline in classification performance in complex scenes. Therefore, this paper proposes a comprehensive method named "Channel Feature Adaptive Enhancement". Our approach will focus on the extraction of local details and the learning of discriminative features, while exploring how to reduce intra-class variability and improve classifier robustness. At the outset, the extraction of features from both shallow and deep layers is facilitated through the utilization of a convolutional neural network (CNN). Our designed feature enhancement mechanism learns to emphasize key detail features, thereby improving classification performance. Additionally, an attention mechanism is introduced to highlight regions with significant fine-grained differences. This combination of feature augmentation and attention enables us to capture subtle differences more accurately and achieves significant performance gains in fine-grained classification tasks. Secondly, to address confusion among objects with similar appearances, we employ attention erasure. This technique erases highly discriminative areas, reducing intra-class differences, weakening features with high similarity to other categories, and encouraging the network to learn from previously unattended areas. This approach enhances classification accuracy and robustness, effectively reducing the risk of misclassification. In summary, the following constitute the principal contributions of this work:

1. We propose a feature enhancement module that accurately enhances discriminative regions in images.
2. We improve the channel attention mechanism by doubling the value of channels greater than the mean value calculated from the feature map after global average pooling. This assigns higher scores to important channels.
3. We introduce an informative mining module that masks a strong feature and facilitates the learning of complementary features.

2   Related Work

In the realm of fine-grained visual classification tasks, researchers have introduced various methods to enhance, suppress, and diversify features, aiming to improve classification performance. We describe several commonly employed techniques:

2.1   Local Feature Enhancement

Local feature enhancement methods aim to extract crucial local information from objects to enhance classification performance. For instance, Spatial Transformer

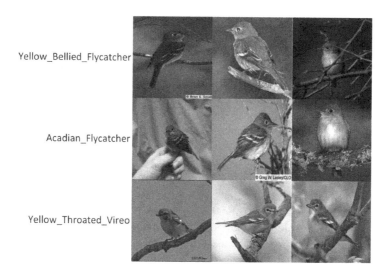

Fig. 1. In FGVC images, the same subclass exhibits significant appearance variations, whereas different categories demonstrate subtle appearance disparities.

Networks (STN) [18] uses spatial transformer modules to adaptively learn local regions of interest of images to improve the representation ability of key local features. In addition, Part-based Convolutional Neural Networks (PCNN) [29] divides the image into different parts, and classifies each part independently, and then combines the classification results of each part.

2.2 Global Feature Enhancement

Global feature augmentation methods concentrate on capturing the overall feature representation of the entire object. For example, Multi-scale CNNs [35] employ convolution kernels of varying scales to extract feature representations at different levels. Additionally, Spatial Pyramid Pooling (SPP) [9] divides the image into multiple spatial levels and performs pooling operations on the features within each level, allowing the capture of global information at different scales.

2.3 Attention Mechanism

The attention mechanism plays a pivotal role in fine-grained classification by automatically learning to focus on key regions or features. For instance, Squeeze-and-Excitation Networks (SENet) [11] employ a gating mechanism to adaptively adjust the importance of feature channels, thereby enhancing key features that contribute to classification. Moreover, the attention mechanism can generate region-specific attention heatmaps, offering interpretable explanations.

2.4 Feature Suppression

Feature suppression methods aim to reduce noise or irrelevant information that may interfere with classification tasks. For instance, DropBlock [8] randomly drops features in specific regions during training to minimize the impact of redundant information on classification. Additionally, Feature Dropout [31]enhances the model's learning by randomly discarding feature channels during training, promoting the exploration of other relevant features.

2.5 Feature Diversification

Feature diversification methods aim to generate multiple features with different transformations to enhance the robustness of classification models. For example, Cutout [3] randomly occludes a portion of the image, forcing the model to learn more resilient feature representations. Furthermore, the utilization of data augmentation techniques, including rotation, scaling, and translation, can facilitate the generation of a diverse array of features.

By comprehensively employing these methods, the performance of fine-grained visual classification tasks can be further enhanced, resulting in increased accuracy and reliability in classification results. However, several challenges, such as class imbalance, occlusion, and pose variation, remain unresolved and merit further exploration and resolution in future research.

3 Method

In this section, a comprehensive depiction of the proposed method is presented, where in Fig. 2 offers an illustrative overview of the framework. Our model consists of two lightweight modules: (1) Feature Channel Adaptive Augmentation module (FCAE), which focuses on learning multiple discriminative part-specific representations with maximum diversity. (2) Information Sufficient Mining Module (ISMM), which randomly erases highly discriminative components to guide the network in learning complementary information.

3.1 Feature Channel Adaptive Enhancement Module

The implementation of the FE method is shown in Fig. 3. The feature map $X_i \in R^{C \times W \times H}$, derived from the final three layers of the backbone network, with C, W, H, and i denoting the channel count, width, height, and layer index, respectively. Drawing inspiration from [30], we adopt a simple approach of taking the maximum value of each pixel along the channel dimension, resulting in $A_i \in R^{1 \times W \times H}$:

$$A_i = \max\left(X_i\right) \in \mathrm{R}^{1 \times \mathrm{W} \times \mathrm{H}} \tag{1}$$

Subsequently, we calculate a score for each pixel. Multiplying A_i by a hyperparameter λ and adding it to X_i, we obtain a new feature map F_i:

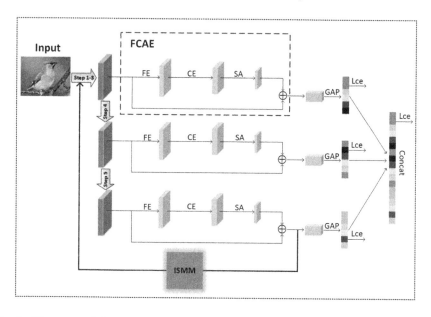

Fig. 2. The general framework of our model is composed of two major modules: (1) The Feature Channel Adaptive Augmentation module (2) The Information Sufficient Mining Module. (FCAE is comprised of three sub-methods, with the intricate process of ISMM illustrated in Fig. 4.)

$$F_i = ((softmax(A_i)) * X_i * \lambda + X_i) \tag{2}$$

At this stage, we aim to enhance globally relevant information. To emphasize discriminative local regions, we employ an attention mechanism inspired by [34]. The feature map F_i undergoes channel attention enhancement (CE), which determines the importance of each channel. We perform global average pooling on all channels and calculate the mean value across all channels.

$$mean = GAP\left(CA\left(F_i\right)\right) \tag{3}$$

If a specific channel's value exceeds the mean, it is doubled; otherwise, it remains unchanged. Upon the application of a sigmoid activation function, the resulting values are subjected to multiplication with F_i:

$$F_i = \begin{cases} 2 * F_i, & if F_i > mean \\ F_i, & otherwise \end{cases} \tag{4}$$

Subsequently, the spatial attention (SA) mechanism is employed to capture relationships between different positions in the feature map, assigning varying weights to each position.

$$F_i = (SA\left(F_i\right)) + F_i \tag{5}$$

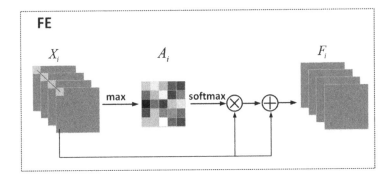

Fig. 3. The feature map X_i, generated by the backbone network, undergoes a process where the maximum value is extracted from the channel dimension to derive A_i. Subsequently, the score of each pixel value is computed and added to X_i, resulting in the feature map F_i after global feature enhancement.

3.2 Information Sufficient Mining Module

The implementation of the ISMM method is shown in Fig. 4. In order to further mine information and utilize attention resources, we take the last layer feature map of the backbone through the FCAE attention map as the attention activation map to extract the key information in the feature map. To fuse the features, we utilize a 1×1 convolution. Subsequently, the attention weight for each group of feature map channels is calculated, we employ global average pooling to select the top k sheets (where k is equal to the batch size). Randomly choosing one image, we apply bilinear interpolation [21] to upsample it to the original image's size. Subsequently, the introduction of a random threshold enables the classification of pixel values, whereby values below the threshold are identified as 0 and those surpassing the threshold as 1. Ultimately, an element-wise multiplication is executed between the acquired mask and the original image, resulting in the creation of the erased image. By employing attention erasure, we can filter out important stimuli that have already been learned and focus on less significant stimuli that may not have been well-learned. By adopting this approach, the efficiency of information processing is effectively heightened, while concurrently optimizing the allocation and utilization of attention resources.

3.3 Network Design

Various convolutional neural network structures can readily incorporate our method. ResNet [10] serves as an example, with its feature extraction process comprising five stages, where the spatial size of the feature map is halved after each stage. Given the abundance of semantic information within the deep feature maps, we opt to insert the Feature Channel Adaptive Enhancement module (FCAE) at the conclusion of the third, fourth, and fifth stages. Our method is very flexible and can adapt to classification tasks of different granularities by

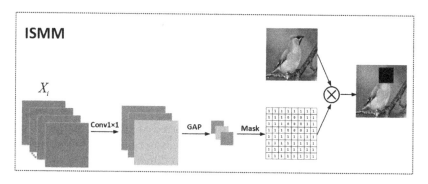

Fig. 4. The attention map is reduced in dimensionality through conv1×1, followed by global average pooling along the channel dimension. A mask is then randomly selected and multiplied with the original image.

directly adjusting the number of FCAEs, and can be customized according to the needs of specific tasks.

4 Experiments

In this section, the performance of the proposed method is evaluated across three fine-grained classification datasets: Caltech UCSD-Birds (CUB) [20], Stanford Cars (CAR) [22], and FGVC-Aircraft (AIR) [27], with detailed information provided in Table 1. The implementation details of our method are extensively discussed in Sect. 4.1, while Sect. 4.2 presents a comparative analysis of our method's accuracy performance against state-of-the-art approaches, showcasing its competitive advantage. Sections 4.3 and 4.4 encompass comprehensive ablation experiments and visualization analyses, aiming to highlight the distinctive features and efficacy of our method. By presenting both experimental results and visualizations, a comprehensive understanding of the robustness and efficiency of our method is provided. Through meticulous evaluations and extensive analyses, the superior performance of our method in fine-grained classification tasks is conclusively demonstrated.

Table 1. The statistics information of the three widely used Fine-Grained Visual Categorization datasets.

Dataset	Catagory	Train	Test
CUB-200-2011 [20]	200	5994	5974
FGVC-Aircraft [27]	100	6667	3333
Stanford Cars [22]	196	8144	8041

4.1   Implementation Details

All experiments were conducted using PyTorch [17], with a version higher than 1.12, on an NVIDIA A100 GPU. The performance evaluation of our method employed the widely adopted ResNet50 as the backbone network, which had been pretrained on the ImageNet dataset. The incorporation of the FCAE module was performed at the conclusion of phases 3, 4, and 5 in our methodology, while the integration of the ISMM module occurred at the termination of phase five. During the training process, the input images were resized to dimensions of 550×550 and subsequently randomly cropped to dimensions of 448×448 to augment the training set. Furthermore, random horizontal flipping was implemented as an auxiliary augmentation technique. For testing purposes, the input images were resized to 550×550 and cropped from the center to dimensions of 448×448. In our approach, a hyperparameter $\lambda=0.5$ was set. To optimize the model, we utilized the stochastic gradient descent (SGD) optimizer with a momentum of 0.9. The model underwent training for 300 epochs, employing a weight decay of 0.00001 and a batch size of 16. The learning rate of the backbone layer was set to 0.002, while the learning rate of the new layer was set to 0.02. We adjusted the learning rate using a cosine annealing scheduler [25].

4.2   Compared with State-of-the-Art Methods

Table 2 showcases a comparative analysis between our method and recent fine-grained classification approaches across the CUB 2002011, Stanford Cars, and FGVC-Aircraft datasets. DeepLAC [23] and Part-RCNN [38] are both component positioning-based methods. DeepLAC [23] initially employs a convolutional neural network to extract image features, followed by the introduction of a local localization module to identify important regions within object images. Part-RCNN [38] first generates candidate object areas in the image using the candidate frame generation algorithm. Subsequently, for each candidate box, the object is decomposed into parts, and features are extracted for each part. Among the attention-based methods, RA-CNN [6], MA-CNN [40], API-Net [43], PCA [39], AC-Net [19], and AKEN [14] are noteworthy. RA-CNN [6] incorporates a circular attention mechanism, allowing the network to dynamically focus attention on the intricate details crucial for fine-grained classification. MA-CNN [40] integrates multiple attention modules, each responsible for producing an attention map for a distinct region of the image, directing the network's focus toward regions with higher discriminative properties. API-Net [43] introduces a pairing interaction mechanism, where selected feature regions undergo pairwise interactions with each other. PCA [39] leverages a co-attention mechanism to learn the association and importance between different regions in an image. The co-attention network consists of a local feature extraction module and a progressive attention module. AC-Net [19] employs an attention mechanism to select and weigh key regions in feature representations. By incorporating a convolutional binary neural tree structure, the model sequentially performs feature selection and learning, progressively focusing on meaningful areas from a global to local perspective. AKEN [14] integrates attention mechanisms and kernel encoding to extract and encode fine-grained features. Attention mechanisms select and weigh important features, aiding in distinguishing between different fine-grained categories. Kernel encoding captures specific feature information by encoding selected features. Guided Zoom [1] and S3N [4] fall under the category of local area amplification methods. Guided Zoom [1] utilizes the interplay of local area amplification and model feedback to acquire insights into model decision-making and confidence. This information serves as guidance for improved decision-making. S3N [4] employs an adaptive sparse sampling strategy to selectively sample local regions within the image. HOI [33] proposes a high-level interaction method, where the high-level interaction module leverages associations between different features in the image to enhance and integrate features. Specific weights and combinations are learned to reinforce and highlight features relevant to fine-grained classification tasks. SPS [15] randomly selects a subset of training samples and exchanges them with other samples, generating new sample pairs. CIN [7] introduces a channel interaction module that facilitates interaction and information transfer between channels. This module utilizes convolution operations and attention mechanisms to enable information exchange and joint feature learning across channels. LIO [42] utilizes unlabeled data for self-supervised learning. By designing self-supervised tasks, the model learns structural information about objects. Each of the above methods possesses its unique advantages and characteristics. However, our proposed method exhibits superior performance across the three datasets, which can be attributed to the exceptional components we have introduced.

Table 2. Comparison results on CUB-200-2011, FGVC-Aircraft and Stanford Cars datasets. "-" means no data

]Method	Backbone	CUB-200-2011	FGVC-Aircraft	Stanford Cars
DeepLAC [23]	VGG	80.3	–	–
Part-RCNN [38]	VGG	81.6	–	–
RA-CNN [6]	VGG	85.3	88.1	92.5
MA-CNN [40]	VGG	86.5	89.9	92.8
SPS [15]	ResNet50	87.3	92.3	94.4
API-Net [43]	ResNet50	87.7	93.0	94.8
HOI [33]	ResNet50	89.5	92.8	**95.3**
PCA [39]	ResNet50	88.3	92.4	94.3
AC-Net [19]	ResNet50	88.1	92.4	94.6
Guided Zoom [1]	ResNet50	87.7	90.7	93.0
CIN [7]	ResNet50	87.5	92.6	94.1
LIO [42]	ResNet50	88.0	92.7	94.5
S3N [4]	ResNet50	88.5	92.8	94.7
FBSD [30]	ResNet50	89.3	92.7	94.4
AKEN [14]	ResNet50	86.2	93.3	92.6
Ours	ResNet50	**89.6**	**93.3**	95.1

4.3 Ablation Experiment

A series of ablation experiments were conducted to evaluate the effectiveness of each module for fine-grained classification. Initially, we conducted classification experiments using a baseline model that solely comprised the backbone network. Subsequently, we gradually introduced the two modules we designed and integrated them with the backbone network individually. Finally, we compared the performance of using a single module versus using both modules simultaneously. The experimental results are presented in Table 3. When employing only the backbone network, the classification accuracy achieved a benchmark level. Upon introducing the FCAE module, the accuracy improved by 2.7% on the bird dataset1.8% on the airplane dataset, and 4.4% on the Stanford car dataset. The introduction of the ISMM module resulted in respective accuracy improvements of 3%, 1.3%, and 4.8% on the three datasets. Remarkably, the best classification results were obtained when both modules were introduced simultaneously, resulting in an improvement of 4.1%, 3%, and 5.3% compared to the baseline. Utilizing the combination of both modules yielded the highest accuracy, significantly outperforming the usage of a single module.

Table 3. Ablation Study on Three Benchmark Datasets

Method	CUB-200-2011	FGVC-Aircraft	Stanford Cars
Resnet50	85.5	90.3	89.8
Resnet50 + FCAE	88.2	92.1	94.2
Resnet50+ISMM	88.5	91.6	94.6
Resnet50+FCAE+ISMM	89.6	93.3	95.1

4.4 Visualization

To visually showcase the effectiveness of our proposed method, the utilization of GradCAM is employed. As depicted in Table 4, when compared to the baseline, a tendency of the baseline to learn global features is observed. In scenarios where the target and background exhibit similarity, the baseline is prone to capturing background noise. Conversely, our method progressively captures global information during the initial stages, which encompasses the assimilation of learned background noise. However, as the network delves deeper into subsequent stages, the learned features become more localized, resulting in precise and targeted focus on the target. The method exhibits remarkable consistency in addressing different categories, emphasizing its robustness and reliability in making classification decisions. This consistency highlights the network's sensitivity to capturing fine-grained features (Fig. 5).

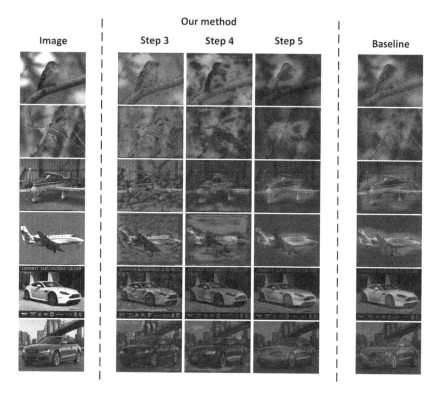

Fig. 5. Compared with the baseline, our method can better learn the discriminative local area, and can accurately distinguish the target and the background when the target is similar to the background.

5 Conclusion

In this study, we propose an approach for fine-grained classification tasks, aiming to improve classification performance by learning feature channel adaptive enhancement and information sufficient mining. First, the feature channel adaptive augmentation module aims to learn different discriminative part representations. Then use the information sufficient mining module to filter the learned important stimuli and focus on the less important stimuli. Our proposed method based on feature channel adaptive augmentation has achieved remarkable progress in meeting the challenges of fine-grained classification tasks. By enhancing useful global information, mining key information, and utilizing attention resources, our method is able to improve classification performance and adapt to different task demands.

Acknowledgements. This work is partially supported by the Guangxi Science and Technology Project (2021GXNSFBA220035, AD20159034), the Open Funds from Guilin University of Electronic Technology, Guangxi Key Laboratory of Image and

Graphic Intelligent Processing (GIIP2208) and the National Natural Science Foundation of China (61962014).

References

1. Bargal, S.A., et al.: Guided zoom: zooming into network evidence to refine fine-grained model decisions. IEEE Trans. Pattern Anal. Mach. Intell. **43**(11), 4196–4202 (2021)
2. Branson, S., Van Horn, G., Belongie, S., Perona, P.: Bird species categorization using pose normalized deep convolutional nets. arXiv preprint arXiv:1406.2952 (2014)
3. DeVries, T., Taylor, G.W.: Improved regularization of convolutional neural networks with cutout. arXiv preprint arXiv:1708.04552 (2017)
4. Ding, Y., Zhou, Y., Zhu, Y., Ye, Q., Jiao, J.: Selective sparse sampling for fine-grained image recognition. In: Proceedings of the IEEE/CVF International Conference on Computer Vision, pp. 6599–6608 (2019)
5. Dubey, A., Gupta, O., Guo, P., Raskar, R., Farrell, R., Naik, N.: Pairwise confusion for fine-grained visual classification. In: Proceedings of the European Conference on Computer Vision (ECCV), pp. 70–86 (2018)
6. Fu, J., Zheng, H., Mei, T.: Look closer to see better: recurrent attention convolutional neural network for fine-grained image recognition. In: Proceedings of the IEEE Conference on Computer Vision and Pattern Recognition, pp. 4438–4446 (2017)
7. Gao, Y., Han, X., Wang, X., Huang, W., Scott, M.: Channel interaction networks for fine-grained image categorization. In: Proceedings of the AAAI Conference on Artificial Intelligence, vol. 34, pp. 10818–10825 (2020)
8. Ghiasi, G., Lin, T.Y., Le, Q.V.: Dropblock: a regularization method for convolutional networks. Adv. Neural Inf. Process. Syst. **31** (2018)
9. He, K., Zhang, X., Ren, S., Sun, J.: Spatial pyramid pooling in deep convolutional networks for visual recognition. IEEE Trans. Pattern Anal. Mach. Intell. **37**(9), 1904–1916 (2015)
10. He, K., Zhang, X., Ren, S., Sun, J.: Deep residual learning for image recognition. In: Proceedings of the IEEE Conference on Computer Vision and Pattern Recognition, pp. 770–778 (2016)
11. Hu, J., Shen, L., Sun, G.: Squeeze-and-excitation networks. In: Proceedings of the IEEE Conference on Computer Vision and Pattern Recognition, pp. 7132–7141 (2018)
12. Hu, T., Qi, H., Huang, Q., Lu, Y.: See better before looking closer: weakly supervised data augmentation network for fine-grained visual classification. arXiv preprint arXiv:1901.09891 (2019)
13. Hu, T., Xu, J., Huang, C., Qi, H., Huang, Q., Lu, Y.: Weakly supervised bilinear attention network for fine-grained visual classification. arXiv preprint arXiv:1808.02152 (2018)
14. Hu, Y., Yang, Y., Zhang, J., Cao, X., Zhen, X.: Attentional kernel encoding networks for fine-grained visual categorization. IEEE Trans. Circuits Syst. Video Technol. **31**(1), 301–314 (2020)
15. Huang, S., Wang, X., Tao, D.: Stochastic partial swap: enhanced model generalization and interpretability for fine-grained recognition. In: Proceedings of the IEEE/CVF International Conference on Computer Vision, pp. 620–629 (2021)

16. Huang, S., Xu, Z., Tao, D., Zhang, Y.: Part-stacked CNN for fine-grained visual categorization. In: Proceedings of the IEEE Conference on Computer Vision and Pattern Recognition, pp. 1173–1182 (2016)
17. Imambi, S., Prakash, K.B., Kanagachidambaresan, G.: Pytorch. Programming with TensorFlow: Solution for Edge Computing Applications, pp. 87–104 (2021)
18. Jaderberg, M., et al.: Spatial transformer networks. Adv. Neural Inf. Process. Syst. **28** (2015)
19. Ji, R., et al.: Attention convolutional binary neural tree for fine-grained visual categorization. In: Proceedings of the IEEE/CVF Conference on Computer Vision and Pattern Recognition, pp. 10468–10477 (2020)
20. Khosla, A., Jayadevaprakash, N., Yao, B., Li, F.F.: Novel dataset for fine-grained image categorization: stanford dogs. In: Proceedings of the CVPR Workshop on Fine-Grained Visual Categorization (FGVC), vol. 2. Citeseer (2011)
21. Kirkland, E.J., Kirkland, E.J.: Bilinear interpolation. In: Advanced Computing in Electron Microscopy, pp. 261–263 (2010)
22. Krause, J., Stark, M., Deng, J., Fei-Fei, L.: 3d object representations for fine-grained categorization. In: Proceedings of the IEEE International Conference on Computer Vision Workshops, pp. 554–561 (2013)
23. Lin, D., Shen, X., Lu, C., Jia, J.: Deep lac: deep localization, alignment and classification for fine-grained recognition. In: Proceedings of the IEEE Conference on Computer Vision and Pattern Recognition, pp. 1666–1674 (2015)
24. Liu, C., Xie, H., Zha, Z.J., Ma, L., Yu, L., Zhang, Y.: Filtration and distillation: enhancing region attention for fine-grained visual categorization. In: Proceedings of the AAAI Conference on Artificial Intelligence, vol. 34, pp. 11555–11562 (2020)
25. Loshchilov, I., Hutter, F.: Sgdr: stochastic gradient descent with warm restarts. arXiv preprint arXiv:1608.03983 (2016)
26. Luo, W., et al.: Cross-x learning for fine-grained visual categorization. In: Proceedings of the IEEE/CVF International Conference on Computer Vision, pp. 8242–8251 (2019)
27. Maji, S., Rahtu, E., Kannala, J., Blaschko, M., Vedaldi, A.: Fine-grained visual classification of aircraft. arXiv preprint arXiv:1306.5151 (2013)
28. Nilsback, M.E., Zisserman, A.: Automated flower classification over a large number of classes. In: 2008 Sixth Indian Conference on Computer Vision, Graphics & Image Processing, pp. 722–729. IEEE (2008)
29. Ouyang, W., et al.: Deepid-net: object detection with deformable part based convolutional neural networks. IEEE Trans. Pattern Anal. Mach. Intell. **39**(7), 1320–1334 (2016)
30. Song, J., Yang, R.: Feature boosting, suppression, and diversification for fine-grained visual classification. In: 2021 International Joint Conference on Neural Networks (IJCNN), pp. 1–8. IEEE (2021)
31. Srivastava, N., Hinton, G., Krizhevsky, A., Sutskever, I., Salakhutdinov, R.: Dropout: a simple way to prevent neural networks from overfitting. J. Mach. Learn. Res. **15**(1), 1929–1958 (2014)
32. Sun, M., Yuan, Y., Zhou, F., Ding, E.: Multi-attention multi-class constraint for fine-grained image recognition. In: Proceedings of the European Conference on Computer Vision (ECCV), pp. 805–821 (2018)
33. Wang, J., Li, N., Luo, Z., Zhong, Z., Li, S.: High-order-interaction for weakly supervised fine-grained visual categorization. Neurocomputing **464**, 27–36 (2021)
34. Woo, S., Park, J., Lee, J.Y., Kweon, I.S.: Cbam: convolutional block attention module. In: Proceedings of the European Conference on Computer Vision (ECCV), pp. 3–19 (2018)

35. Yang, S., Ramanan, D.: Multi-scale recognition with dag-CNNs. In: Proceedings of the IEEE International Conference on Computer Vision, pp. 1215–1223 (2015)

36. Yang, Z., Luo, T., Wang, D., Hu, Z., Gao, J., Wang, L.: Learning to navigate for fine-grained classification. In: Proceedings of the European Conference on Computer Vision (ECCV), pp. 420–435 (2018)

37. Zhang, L., Huang, S., Liu, W., Tao, D.: Learning a mixture of granularity-specific experts for fine-grained categorization. In: Proceedings of the IEEE/CVF International Conference on Computer Vision, pp. 8331–8340 (2019)

38. Zhang, N., Donahue, J., Girshick, R., Darrell, T.: Part-based R-CNNs for fine-grained category detection. In: Fleet, D., Pajdla, T., Schiele, B., Tuytelaars, T. (eds.) ECCV 2014. LNCS, vol. 8689, pp. 834–849. Springer, Cham (2014). https://doi.org/10.1007/978-3-319-10590-1_54

39. Zhang, T., Chang, D., Ma, Z., Guo, J.: Progressive co-attention network for fine-grained visual classification. In: 2021 International Conference on Visual Communications and Image Processing (VCIP), pp. 1–5. IEEE (2021)

40. Zheng, H., Fu, J., Mei, T., Luo, J.: Learning multi-attention convolutional neural network for fine-grained image recognition. In: Proceedings of the IEEE International Conference on Computer Vision, pp. 5209–5217 (2017)

41. Zheng, H., Fu, J., Zha, Z.J., Luo, J.: Looking for the devil in the details: learning trilinear attention sampling network for fine-grained image recognition. In: Proceedings of the IEEE/CVF Conference on Computer Vision and Pattern Recognition, pp. 5012–5021 (2019)

42. Zhou, M., Bai, Y., Zhang, W., Zhao, T., Mei, T.: Look-into-object: self-supervised structure modeling for object recognition. In: Proceedings of the IEEE/CVF Conference on Computer Vision and Pattern Recognition, pp. 11774–11783 (2020)

43. Zhuang, P., Wang, Y., Qiao, Y.: Learning attentive pairwise interaction for fine-grained classification. In: Proceedings of the AAAI Conference on Artificial Intelligence, vol. 34, pp. 13130–13137 (2020)

Visualizing CNN: An Experimental Comparative Study

Xinyi Xu[✉], Shi Tu, Yunfan Xue, and Lin Chai

School of Automation, Southeast University, Nanjing 210096, China
xuxinyi@seu.edu.cn

Abstract. To intuitively and accurately understand the decision mechanism of Convolutional Neural Networks(CNN), CNN visualization, as an essential part of explainable deep learning, has gradually become a hot topic in artificial intelligence. There have been many achievements in CNN visualization research, such as Gradients, Deconvolution, Class Activation Maps(CAM), etc. But there has been no systematic comparative study on CNN visualization algorithms. The choice of visualization algorithm is critical for accurately explaining the decision process of CNNs. Therefore, an experimental evaluation research on representative CNN visualization algorithms is conducted in this paper for ResNet50 and VGG16 on Caltech101, ImageNet, and VOC2007. The visualization performance is assessed in four aspects: causality, anti-disturbance capability, usability, and computational complexity, and suggestions for selecting CNN visualization algorithms are proposed based on the experimental results.

Keywords: Explainable deep learning · CNN visualization · Performance metrics · Experimental study

1 Introduction

In recent years, the popularity of artificial intelligence has remained high and has achieved significant achievements in various fields, such as urban security, automatic driving, and intelligent healthcare [1,2]. Image recognition based on deep convolutional neural networks, as the most basic application of artificial intelligence in machine vision, surpasses traditional machine learning methods and provides a robust feature extraction backbone network for downstream tasks such as object detection and segmentation. In image recognition tasks, numerous models with strong generalization abilities and fast computation speed have been developed. The most representative networks are AlexNet, VGG, ResNet, DenseNet, and DarkNet.

To improve performance and tackle more complex scenarios, CNNs often have stacking depths of dozens of layers, resulting in highly non-linear and complex models. This leads to difficulties in understanding the decision-making process

H. Lu et al. (Eds.): ACPR 2023, LNCS 14408, pp. 199–212, 2023.
https://doi.org/10.1007/978-3-031-47665-5_17

and working mechanisms of CNNs, which poses increasing security risks. Therefore, explainable deep learning has gradually become popular in recent years.

The most intuitive and effective method for uncovering the secrets of CNN is visualization, which can present CNN's decisions in the form of saliency maps, such as Local Interpretable Model-agnostic Explanations(LIME), Randomized Input Sampling for Explanation(RISE), CAM, GradCAM, etc. The saliency maps demonstrate the importance of each pixel in the input image.

As a visualization algorithm proposed for explaining the trustworthiness of CNN's decisions, its reliability must also be evaluated. From an experimental perspective, it can be divided into two categories for evaluation: human-oriented evaluations and machine-oriented metrics. Human-oriented evaluations are subjective judgments, such as designing questionnaires and gathering professional test group members for testing. However, this method will consume much workforce, and the interviewees significantly affect the reliability, making it difficult to standardize and conduct large-scale experiments. On the other hand, machine-oriented metrics evaluate the visualization algorithm by formulating specific rules and providing a quantitative or qualitative criterion. Although this evaluation method is easy to conduct, different approaches have their focuses and cannot fully cover all the properties that visualization algorithms should possess.

There has been considerable researches on algorithms for visualizing CNNs. Still, there is a lack of systematic comparative studies and no clear guidelines for selecting visualization algorithms. Thus, in this study, we selected two representative CNNs, ResNet50 [3] and VGG16 [4], and conducted experiments on 3 mainstream datasets: Caltech101, ImageNet, and VOC2007. We evaluated the performance of various visualization algorithms in terms of causality, anti-disturbance capability, usability, and computational complexity. We compared the performances of different visualization algorithms and provided suggestions on selecting a suitable visualization algorithm.

The main contributions of this paper are as follows:

- We thoroughly summarize seven representative algorithms of CNN visualization;
- We trained the ResNet50 and VGG16 on three datasets: Caltech101, ImageNet, and VOC2007. Then, explanations are made on ResNet50 and VGG16 by using visualization algorithms to be evaluated;
- Evaluate and compare the performance of different visualization algorithms in terms of causality, anti-disturbance capability, usability, and computational complexity;
- Based on the comparative experimental results of visualization algorithms, suggestions are proposed for selecting CNN visualization algorithms.

2   Related Works

There have been some comparative studies on the visualization algorithms of CNN for image recognition.

Yang [5] designed a unified evaluation framework to assess the reliability of visualization algorithms from three aspects: generalizability, fidelity, and persuasibility. Yang [6] copied objects in MSCOCO into MiniPlaces to construct the Benchmarking Attribution Methods(BAM) evaluation dataset and proposed three complementary metrics, Model Contrast Score(MCS), Input Dependence Rate(IDR), and Input Independence Rate(IIR). Brunke [7] conducted a comparative study on visual methods for input perturbations, investigating the impact of neutral baseline images on saliency map generation and performance evaluation. Poppi [8] introduced the concept of Coherency. They used it with Complexity and Average Drop to form the Average DCC(ADCC) assessment metric to perform a comparative study of existing CAM-like algorithms. Samuel [9] designed three human subject experiments to evaluate mainstream visualization algorithms based on predictability, reliability, and consistency. Li [10] designed an annotation tool and constructed a rich hierarchy of evaluation datasets through fine manual annotation. They evaluated visualization algorithms based on accuracy, persuasibility, and class discrimination. Brocki [11] compared perturbation-based visualization algorithms and analyzed and estimated the artifacts caused by perturbations, aiming to eliminate the impact of artifacts on perturbation-based visualization algorithms. Wang [12] argued that the existing evaluation metrics lack rationality and fail to accurately reflect the quality of effective visualizations. In response to this problem, they proposed the faithfulness and plausibility criteria to evaluate visualization algorithms better.

Although Kadir [13] summarized the existing evaluation methods for visualization algorithms and proposed two categories, their work lacks a systematic comparative experimental study. Li [14] proposed a new metric, Intersection between the salient area and the ground truth mask over the Salient Region(IoSR), combining five existing quantitative metrics to evaluate the quality of saliency maps, which is most relevant to our work. Although their work compared multiple metrics, there are no inductive suggestions provided for researchers when selecting visualization algorithms.

Therefore, this article mainly provides selection guidance from causality, anti-disturbance capability, usability, and computational complexity through comparative experimental research on visualization algorithms.

3   Visualization Algorithms

Visualization is the most intuitive and effective means of understanding the decision-making process of CNN. Visualization algorithms can be roughly divided into three categories: (1) perturbation-based methods, which perturb the input and observe the changes of the output; (2) backpropagation-based methods, which propagate gradients, activations, or feature maps back to the input layer and highlight key regions; (3) model-based methods, which construct CNNs that are instinctly explainable. Numerous innovative results have been achieved in each category, and in this section, we will introduce the most commonly used visualization algorithms as candidates for comparative experiments. The visualization results is shown in Fig. 1.

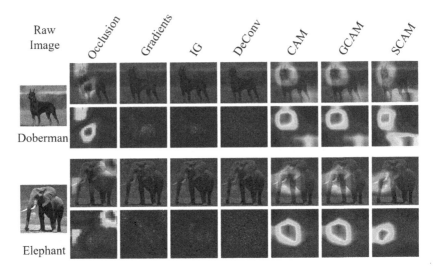

Fig. 1. The visualization results of Occlusion, Gradients, Integrated Gradients, Deconvolution, Class Activation Map, GradCAM and ScoreCAM.

Note: In the following description, the input image is denoted as $I \in \mathbb{R}^{h \times w \times chn}$, h, w, chn representing the height, width, and channels, respectively. The CNN to be explained is denoted as $f : \mathbb{R}^{h \times w \times chn} \rightarrow \mathbb{R}^{N}$, N representing classes. c means the class to be observed during the decision process of CNN.

3.1 Occlusion

A fixed-size occluding block is used to cover the image, and the saliency values of each pixel are obtained by using a sliding window based on the change in CNN's prediction [15].

$$\text{Sal}_{\text{Occlusion}}\left(I; f, r, \phi\right)^c = \sum_{p \in P} \frac{f^c\left(I\right) - f^c\left(\phi\left(I; p\right)\right)}{r^2} \mathbb{I}\left(p\right) \qquad (1)$$

r means the size of the window, P is the set of images with sliding masked areas, ϕ is the method of occlusion, $\mathbb{I}\left(p\right)$ is the indicator function with 1 inside the masked area while 0 outside.

3.2 Gradients

Propagate the gradients of a specific output to the input layer, using them as sensitivity maps to explain the importance of each input pixel [16].

$$\text{Sal}_{\text{Gradients}}\left(I; f\right)^c = \left.\frac{\partial f^c\left(\hat{I}\right)}{\partial \hat{I}}\right|_{\hat{I}=I} \qquad (2)$$

3.3   Integrated Gradients

Directly using the gradients can be greatly influenced by noise. Therefore, it is crucial to consider a smooth transformation from the baseline input to the original input when calculating the gradients. By accumulating the changes in gradients during this transformation process, noise can be avoided [17].

$$\text{Sal}_{\text{IG}}\left(I; f, I_{\text{base}}\right)^c = \left(I - I_{\text{base}}\right) \times \int_{\alpha=0}^{1} \left.\frac{\partial f^c \left(I_{\text{base}} + \alpha \times \left(\hat{I} - I_{\text{base}}\right)\right)}{\partial \hat{I}}\right|_{\hat{I}=I} d_\alpha \tag{3}$$

I_{base} is the predefined baseline image.

3.4   Deconvolution

In forward propagation, the location of the maxpooling is recorded as "switches" [18]. During the backpropagation, the deconvolution result is obtained using the matrix's transpose when encountering a convolutional layer. When facing a maxpooling layer, the position of the maximum value recorded by "switches" is used to fill in the up-sampling result, and the others are filled with 0.

$$\text{Sal}_{\text{Deconvolution}}\left(I; f\right)^c = \text{unpool}\left(\text{ReLU}\left(K_l^T \times A_{l-1}\right), S_l\right) \tag{4}$$

A is the activation of specific layers, S is the recorded location Switches, l is the current layer, K is the convolutional kernel.

3.5   Class Activation Maps

By utilizing information such as activation, gradient, and feature maps during the forward propagation process of the network, saliency maps are obtained by combining these features and mapping back to the input layer. CAM [19] requires the last layer of the CNN to be a global average pooling layer, so structural modification and fine-tuning are required for networks that do not meet this condition.

$$\text{Sal}_{\text{CAM}}\left(I; f\right)^c = \sum_k \alpha_k^c \sum_{i,j} A_k\left(i, j\right) \tag{5}$$

α_k^c is the weight of k-th filter connected to class c, A_k is the feature map generated by kth filter.

Due to the inconvenience of modifying network structures in conventional CAM, gradient-based CAMs, represented by GradCAM [20] and GradCAM++ [21], and gradient-free CAMs, represented by ScoreCAM [22] and AblationCAM [23], have emerged.

4   Evaluation Metrics

Quantitative analysis is essential to analyze whether the visualization results are reasonable. This chapter will introduce four ways to evaluate visualization algorithms' performance from causality, anti-disturbance capability, usability, and computational complexity.

Note: In the following descriptions, the input image is denoted as I. The CNN to be explained is denoted as f and the visualization algorithm that generates saliency maps according to the class c will be referred to as Sal^c.

4.1   Causality

Causality mainly measures the correlation between the important area indicated by the saliency map and the network's decision. There are two ways to measure correlation: one is the intersection area between the salient region and the semantic region, and the other is whether there is a positive correlation between the salient region and the network's prediction.

Energy-Based Pointing Game. To measure the causality between salient regions and semantic targets, Zhang [24] proposed Pointing Game(PG) to determine whether the maximum value in the saliency map falls within the boundaries of an object's bounding box. Wang [22] extended PG by considering the sum of energy within the object's bounding box called Energy-based Pointing Game.

$$\text{Proportion} = \frac{\sum_{(i,j)\in box} \left[\text{Sal}^c\left(I\right)\right]}{\sum \text{Sal}^c\left(I\right)} \qquad (6)$$

$(i,j) \in box$ means the pixels within the bounding box of the target.

The Energy-based Pointing Game aims to investigate whether the distribution of saliency values is concentrated on the corresponding semantic targets to verify the causality between the key regions obtained by the visualization algorithm and the semantic targets.

Deletion/Insertion Game. Petsiuk [25] proposed two evaluation metrics: Deletion and Insertion. These metrics evaluate the causality between salient regions and network's predictions. Deletion Game deletes "cause" in order of decreasing importance as indicated in the saliency map while Insertion Game inserts "cause" to a blank image.

$$I_{s+1}^{DI} = DI\left(I_s^{DI}; \text{Sal}^c\left(I\right)\right) \qquad (7)$$

I_s^{DI} means the s iteration of Deletion/Insertion Game. I_0 is the raw input image in deletion game. While in insertion game, I_0 stands for the blurred input image. $DI\left(I; \text{Sal}^c\left(I\right)\right)$ is the method of deleting or inserting pixels according to the saliency map.

During the deletion/insertion process, the curve of the changes in the step-prediction is recorded. The deletion/insertion score is defined as the area under the curve (AUC).

$$\text{Score} = \sum_{j=1}^{k} f^c (I_j) \tag{8}$$

4.2 Anti-disturbance Capability

ADCC. Poppi [8] defined Maximum Coherency, Minimum Complexity, and Minimum Confidence Drop. The Coherency metric examines the ability to maintain consistency in the salient regions when encountering special disturbance. Specifically, it compares the saliency maps of an image before and after the perturbation. The Complexity metric measures the total of the saliency map using the L1-Norm. Confidence Drop measures the drop in CNN's prediction score when applied to the salient region of an image compared to the original image. Based on these metrics, they proposed Average DCC(ADCC), denoted as:

$$\text{ADCC} = 3 \left(\frac{1}{\text{Coh}(I;c)} + \frac{1}{1 - \text{Com}(I;c)} + \frac{1}{1 - \text{AD}(I;c)} \right)^{-1} \tag{9}$$

The Coherency(Coh), Complexity(Com) and Average Confidence Drop(AD) is defined as:

$$\text{Coh}(I;c) = \frac{\text{Cov}\left(\text{Sal}^c\left(I \odot \text{Sal}^c\left(I\right)\right)\text{Sal}^c\left(I\right)\right)}{\sigma_{\text{Sal}^c(I \odot \text{Sal}^c(I))}\sigma_{\text{Sal}^c(I)}} \tag{10}$$

$$\text{Com}(I;c) = \|\text{Sal}^c(I)\|_1 \tag{11}$$

$$\text{AD}(I;c) = \frac{\sum_{I \in X} f^c(I) - f^c(I \odot \text{Sal}^c(I))}{n} \tag{12}$$

Cov indicates the covariance and the σ is the standard deviation. $\odot$ is the element-wise multiplication. X represents all the input images and n is the number of input images.

(In)Fidelity and Sensitivity. Yeh [26] investigated the synchronization ability of visualization algorithms under random perturbations and their sensitivity to noise disturbance. They proposed and analyzed two quantitative metrics, namely the (In)Fidelity and Sensitivity. The definition of (In)Fidelity is the expectation of the difference between the dot product of the input disturbance and the change in prediction scores.

$$\text{InFid} = \mathbb{E}_{\hat{I} \sim \mu_{\hat{I}}} \left[\hat{I}^T \text{Sal}\left(\hat{I}\right) - \left(f(I) - f\left(I - \hat{I}\right)\right)^2 \right] \tag{13}$$

Sensitivity is measured by Monte Carlo multiple sampling to evaluate the maximum change of the visualization algorithm in response to the disturbance added to the input image.

$$\text{Sens}_{\text{Max}} = \max_{\|\hat{I}-I\|\leq r} \left\| \text{Sal}^c \left(f, \hat{I} \right) - \text{Sal}^c \left(f, I \right) \right\| \tag{14}$$

4.3   Usability

A good visualization algorithm requires ease of use and excellent performance in causality and anti-disturbance capability. Visualization algorithms with good usability should be very convenient that can be directly applied, without the need to adjust or retrain.

4.4   Computational Complexity

Suppose a visualization algorithm has high computational complexity and requires hardware with high performance, its applicability will be limited. Therefore computational complexity is an essential factor when choosing a CNN visualization algorithm. Computational complexity indicates the degree of computer resource consumption during the generation of saliency maps. This metric mainly evaluates the dependence of visualization algorithms on computational resources, especially the time consumed during generating saliency maps.

5   Experiments

This experiment mainly evaluates the performance of seven visualization algorithms on ResNet50 and VGG16. First, the networks are trained from scratch on the VOC2007, ImageNet, and Caltech101. The saliency maps obtained from wrong labels are meaningless. Therefore, this experiment uses all correctly classified images as the evaluation dataset. The saliency maps of all images in the evaluation dataset are extracted by the visualization algorithms, and their average reliability on the evaluation dataset is quantitatively evaluated.

In the Deletion and Insertion experiments, the number of deleted/inserted points each time is 224×4. In Deletion, deleting the element replaces the pixel value with 0, and in Insertion, the blur method used is Gaussian blur. In the (In)Fidelity experiment, we randomly select 1000 points in the image and apply random perturbations of magnitude 0.2, and the results are averaged over 10 trials. In the Sensitivity experiment, the input image is also subjected to random perturbations of 0.2, and the results are averaged over 10 trials.

The visualization algorithms used in this experiment include Occlusion(Occ), Deconvolution(DeConv), Gradients(Grad), Integrated Gradients(IG), CAM, GradCAM(GCAM) and ScoreCAM(SCAM). The sliding window step of Occlusion is 9×9 and window size is 60×60. For CAM, the last layer is replaced with a global average pooling layer, and the model is finetuned before testing.

5.1   Causality

Energy-Based Pointing Game. In the Energy-based Pointing Game, all visualization algorithms achieve a high energy level according to our evaluation criteria, as shown in Table 1. CAM-based algorithms outperform other algorithms.

Table 1. Results of Energy-based Pointing Game

Networks	Occ	DeConv	Grad	IG	CAM	GCAM	SCAM
ResNet50	0.711	0.616	0.571	0.607	0.676	**0.745**	0.686
VGG16	0.639	0.503	0.578	0.627	**0.736**	0.680	0.692

Deletion/Insertion Game. The Deletion and Insertion evaluation results are shown in Tables 2 and 3. IG achieves the best results on deletion, while Occlusion, DeConv, Gradients, and CAM-like algorithms obtain relatively close scores. In the Insertion Game, Occlusion achieves the best results, closely followed by CAM-like algorithms, while DeConv, Gradients, and IG perform the worst. The evaluation results obtained on different datasets are consistent.

Table 2. Results of Deletion Game

Datasets	Networks	Occ	DeConv	Grad	IG	CAM	GCAM	SCAM
Caltech101	ResNet50	0.289	0.238	0.272	**0.144**	0.228	0.228	0.251
	VGG16	0.261	0.250	0.226	**0.120**	0.161	0.265	0.246
ImageNet	ResNet50	0.220	0.155	0.149	**0.076**	0.162	0.162	0.187
	VGG16	0.147	0.141	0.097	**0.045**	0.097	0.146	0.130
VOC2007	ResNet50	0.395	0.389	0.397	**0.236**	0.440	0.438	0.470
	VGG16	0.276	0.320	0.280	**0.166**	0.341	0.305	0.295

5.2   Anti-disturbance Capability

ADCC. The ADCC evaluation results are presented in Table 4. Among the CAM-like algorithms, their scores are very close to each other across the three datasets. GradCAM scores highest on all three datasets, whereas DeConv, Gradients, and IG algorithms generally score lower.

Table 3. Results of Insertion Game

Datasets	Networks	Occ	DeConv	Grad	IG	CAM	GCAM	SCAM
Caltech101	ResNet50	**0.887**	0.484	0.571	0.542	0.880	0.880	0.879
	VGG16	**0.889**	0.473	0.590	0.539	0.757	0.876	0.875
ImageNet	ResNet50	**0.764**	0.392	0.530	0.505	0.761	0.761	0.759
	VGG16	**0.731**	0.314	0.446	0.405	0.632	0.717	0.722
VOC2007	ResNet50	**0.836**	0.556	0.586	0.640	0.823	0.822	0.808
	VGG16	0.829	0.466	0.555	0.576	0.825	**0.834**	0.803

Table 4. Results of ADCC

Datasets	Networks	Occ	DeConv	Grad	IG	CAM	GCAM	SCAM
Caltech101	ResNet50	0.747	0.052	0.123	0.057	0.798	**0.801**	0.792
	VGG16	0.771	0.050	0.148	0.061	**0.839**	0.803	0.837
ImageNet	ResNet50	0.673	0.008	0.067	0.011	0.798	**0.799**	0.786
	VGG16	0.766	0.008	0.056	0.014	0.809	0.802	**0.853**
VOC2007	ResNet50	0.798	0.267	0.347	0.164	0.768	**0.822**	0.793
	VGG16	0.809	0.166	0.350	0.193	0.822	0.859	**0.875**

(In)Fidelity and Sensitivity. The evaluation results of (In)Fidelity and Sensitivity are presented in Tables 5 and 6, respectively. In terms of (In)Fidelity evaluation, all algorithms except for IG achieve relatively low levels. IG demonstrates much lower level of infidelity than other algorithms across three datasets. CAM-like algorithms still perform well, while Occlusion, DeConv, and Gradients slightly underperform compared to CAM-like algorithms under the current evaluation criteria. In terms of Sensitivity evaluation, all CAM-like visualization algorithms achieve low levels, while the maximum sensitivity of other methods is higher than that of CAM-like methods. Gradients and IG show the worst performance in terms of maximum sensitivity.

Table 5. Results of (In)Fidelity

Datasets	Networks	Occ	DeConv	Grad	IG	CAM	GCAM	SCAM
Caltech101	ResNet50	0.725	1.474	0.544	3.212	**0.541**	0.554	0.567
	VGG16	1.631	3.614	1.427	10.705	**0.417**	1.443	1.304
ImageNet	ResNet50	0.836	1.257	0.742	4.821	0.746	0.748	**0.731**
	VGG16	1.636	2.562	1.633	10.871	**0.910**	1.542	1.640
VOC2007	ResNet50	0.059	0.070	0.062	0.312	**0.051**	0.054	0.059
	VGG16	0.168	0.239	0.171	0.927	**0.046**	0.163	0.179

Table 6. Results of Max Sensitivity

Datasets	Networks	Occ	DeConv	Grad	IG	CAM	GCAM	SCAM
Caltech101	ResNet50	0.926	0.944	1.107	1.447	**0.362**	0.385	0.401
	VGG16	0.805	1.148	0.938	1.367	**0.492**	0.602	0.631
ImageNet	ResNet50	0.806	0.918	0.996	1.374	**0.300**	0.304	0.380
	VGG16	0.614	1.051	0.964	1.356	**0.400**	0.536	0.438
VOC2007	ResNet50	0.644	0.870	1.022	1.396	0.369	0.469	**0.308**
	VGG16	0.635	1.041	0.977	1.333	**0.393**	0.602	0.481

5.3 Usability

Among all algorithms, CAM requires adjusting the network structure and retraining if the CNN is not ended with a global average pooling layer. So its usability is the worst. Deconvolution only supports the CNN with maxpooling layer. So the usability of Deconvolution is limited. Other algorithms can be directly applied, so their usability is better.

5.4 Computational Complexity

The computational complexity results are presented in Table 7.

Table 7. Results of Computational Complexity (ms)

Networks	Occ	DeConv	Grad	IG	CAM	GCAM	SCAM
ResNet50	1767.13	652.73	11.12	362.31	**6.38**	10.37	2363.45
VGG16	1470.74	12.67	3.82	434.86	**3.37**	4.94	908.15

6 Discussion

6.1 Causality

The Energy-based Pointing Game focuses more on the consistency between salient regions and semantic object regions, that is, the key factor that leads to the current judgment made by CNN should be consistent with human judgment. In the experimental results, the CAM-like visualization algorithms achieve good results due to its weakly localization ability for semantic targets. The feature maps generated by Gradients and DeConv are more dispersed and cannot be concentrated in the semantic target area, so they cannot achieve high scores.

The Deletion/Insertion Game focuses on measuring the consistency between salient regions and network outputs, whether salient regions are the main factor for high scores in the network's output for that class. From the results of

Deletion, IG is in the lead, while the evaluation results of other algorithms are at about the same level. Since IG is derived from the gradient integration from the baseline image to the input image, its ability to capture key regions that affect the network score is stronger, so it scores higher. Analyzing the data of the Insertion Game, due to the presence of Gaussian blurred background, it provides background information, so when inserting salient regions, the performances of Occlusion and CAM-like algorithms are better than other methods.

Therefore, in terms of causality, CAM-like methods and Occlusion are more capable of capturing the regions that affect the critical decisions of the network.

6.2 Anti-disturbance Capability

ADCC measures the anti-disturbance capability of visualization algorithms by disturbing non-target region. Algorithms with weakly localization ability have an advantage on ADCC: the semantic object region is the key factor affecting the network's decision. Therefore, after smoothing the non-salient regions, the semantic target remains intact, resulting in high scores on both the Coherency and AverageDrop metrics for consistency. Other algorithms have low Coherency and AverageDrop scores due to the diffusion of saliency images, resulting in discrete image regions.

The (In)Fidelity focuses on the degree of synchronization between the change in the saliency map and the change in network output when perturbing input images. Occlusion, DeConv, Gradients, and CAM-like algorithms have good anti-disturbance capability, while for IG, the core of IG is to integrate the gradient between the baseline image and the target image to generate a saliency map that satisfies invariance. Therefore, in this metric, the bad performance of (In)fidelity is mainly due to the smoothing of the uncertainty caused by noise during the integration process.

In the Maximum Sensitivity, all CAM-like visualization methods perform well. DeConv, on the other hand, flips the network, causing significant changes in the network feature layer response when perturbations are applied to the input, resulting in a larger maximum sensitivity due to the cumulative effect of layer-by-layer influence.

Overall, in terms of anti-disturbance capability, more focused saliency map will achieve better results. Therefore, CAM-like algorithms are superior to other visualization algorithms.

6.3 Usability

Regarding usability, CAM has unique requirements for the network's structure. Although CAM scores well in other metrics, it cannot be ignored that it performs poorly in usability. DeConv can only record the maxpooling layer, so the usability is limited. Other algorithms can be directly applied and have better performance in usability.

6.4   Computational Complexity

From the computational complexity perspective, CAM only needs to perform corresponding multiplication on the last layer feature map and upsample it to the input layer, so it takes the shortest time. Next are Gradients, GradCAM and DeConv, which require backpropagation of gradients or activation. Visualization algorithms that require iterative solutions need to take the longest time.

7   Conclusion

As the simplest and most intuitive means of uncovering the "black box" secrets of CNN in image recognition, there have been many related studies on visualization algorithms. However, the selection of visualization algorithms is still a difficult problem. This article evaluates seven mainstream visualization algorithms on ResNet50 and VGG from four aspects: causality, anti-disturbance capability, usability, and computational complexity. From the evaluation experiments on three datasets, Caltech101, ImageNet, and VOC2007, weakly localization ability is a basic attribute that visualization algorithms need to possess, so visualization algorithms represented by CAM perform well in causality and anti-disturbance capability metrics. In addition, usability and computational complexity are also important factors to consider when choosing visualization algorithms.

References

1. Ras, G., Xie, N., Van Gerven, M., Doran, D.: Explainable deep learning: a field guide for the uninitiated. J. Artif. Intell. Res. **73**, 329–397 (2022)
2. Fan, F.L., Xiong, J., Li, M., Wang, G.: On interpretability of artificial neural networks: a survey. IEEE Trans. Radiat. Plasma Med. Sci. **5**(6), 741–760 (2021)
3. He, K., Zhang, X., Ren, S., Sun, J.: Deep residual learning for image recognition. In: Proceedings of the IEEE Conference on Computer Vision and Pattern Recognition, pp. 770–778 (2016)
4. Simonyan, K., Zisserman, A.: Very deep convolutional networks for large-scale image recognition. arXiv preprint arXiv:1409.1556 (2014)
5. Yang, F., Du, M., Hu, X.: Evaluating explanation without ground truth in interpretable machine learning. arXiv preprint arXiv:1907.06831 (2019)
6. Yang, M., Kim, B.: Benchmarking attribution methods with relative feature importance. arXiv preprint arXiv:1907.09701 (2019)
7. Brunke, L., Agrawal, P., George, N.: Evaluating input perturbation methods for interpreting CNNs and saliency map comparison. In: Bartoli, A., Fusiello, A. (eds.) ECCV 2020. LNCS, vol. 12535, pp. 120–134. Springer, Cham (2020). https://doi.org/10.1007/978-3-030-66415-2_8
8. Poppi, S., Cornia, M., Baraldi, L., Cucchiara, R.: Revisiting the evaluation of class activation mapping for explainability: a novel metric and experimental analysis. In: Proceedings of the IEEE/CVF Conference on Computer Vision and Pattern Recognition, pp. 2299–2304 (2021)
9. Samuel, S.Z.S., Kamakshi, V., Lodhi, N., Krishnan, N.C.: Evaluation of saliency-based explainability method. arXiv preprint arXiv:2106.12773 (2021)

10. Li, J., Lin, D., Wang, Y., Xu, G., Ding, C.: Towards a reliable evaluation of local interpretation methods. Appl. Sci. **11**(6), 2732 (2021)
11. Brocki, L., Chung, N.C.: Evaluation of interpretability methods and perturbation artifacts in deep neural networks. arXiv preprint arXiv:2203.02928 (2022)
12. Wang, Y., Wang, X.: A unified study of machine learning explanation evaluation metrics. arXiv preprint arXiv:2203.14265 (2022)
13. Kadir, M.A., Mosavi, A., Sonntag, D.: Assessing xai: unveiling evaluation metrics for local explanation, taxonomies, key concepts, and practical applications
14. Li, X.H., et al.: Quantitative evaluations on saliency methods: an experimental study. arXiv preprint arXiv:2012.15616 (2020)
15. Zhou, B., Khosla, A., Lapedriza, A., Oliva, A., Torralba, A.: Object detectors emerge in deep scene CNNs. arXiv preprint arXiv:1412.6856 (2014)
16. Simonyan, K., Vedaldi, A., Zisserman, A.: Deep inside convolutional networks: visualising image classification models and saliency maps. arXiv preprint arXiv:1312.6034 (2013)
17. Sundararajan, M., Taly, A., Yan, Q.: Axiomatic attribution for deep networks. In: International Conference on Machine Learning, pp. 3319–3328. PMLR (2017)
18. Zeiler, M.D., Taylor, G.W., Fergus, R.: Adaptive deconvolutional networks for mid and high level feature learning. In: 2011 International Conference on Computer Vision, pp. 2018–2025. IEEE (2011)
19. Zhou, B., Khosla, A., Lapedriza, A., Oliva, A., Torralba, A.: Learning deep features for discriminative localization. In: Proceedings of the IEEE Conference on Computer Vision and Pattern Recognition, pp. 2921–2929 (2016)
20. Selvaraju, R.R., Cogswell, M., Das, A., Vedantam, R., Parikh, D., Batra, D.: Grad-cam: visual explanations from deep networks via gradient-based localization. In: Proceedings of the IEEE International Conference on Computer Vision, pp. 618–626 (2017)
21. Chattopadhay, A., Sarkar, A., Howlader, P., Balasubramanian, V.N.: Grad-cam++: generalized gradient-based visual explanations for deep convolutional networks. In: 2018 IEEE Winter Conference on Applications of Computer Vision (WACV), pp. 839–847. IEEE (2018)
22. Wang, H., et al.: Score-cam: score-weighted visual explanations for convolutional neural networks. In: Proceedings of the IEEE/CVF Conference on Computer Vision and Pattern Recognition Workshops, pp. 24–25 (2020)
23. Ramaswamy, H.G., et al.: Ablation-cam: visual explanations for deep convolutional network via gradient-free localization. In: Proceedings of the IEEE/CVF Winter Conference on Applications of Computer Vision, pp. 983–991 (2020)
24. Zhang, J., Bargal, S.A., Lin, Z., Brandt, J., Shen, X., Sclaroff, S.: Top-down neural attention by excitation backprop. Int. J. Comput. Vision **126**(10), 1084–1102 (2018)
25. Petsiuk, V., Das, A., Saenko, K.: Rise: randomized input sampling for explanation of black-box models. arXiv preprint arXiv:1806.07421 (2018)
26. Yeh, C.K., Hsieh, C.Y., Suggala, A., Inouye, D.I., Ravikumar, P.K.: On the (in) fidelity and sensitivity of explanations. Adv. Neural Inf. Process. Syst. **32** (2019)

Cross-Domain Few-Shot Sparse-Quantization Aware Learning for Lymphoblast Detection in Blood Smear Images

Dina Aboutahoun[1]([✉]), Rami Zewail[1], Keiji Kimura[2] [ID], and Mostafa I. Soliman[1]

[1] Department of Computer Science and Engineering, Egypt-Japan University for Science and Technology, Alexandria, Egypt
{dina.aboutahoun,rami.zewail,mostafa.soliman}@ejust.edu.eg
[2] Department of Computer Science and Engineering, Waseda University, Tokyo, Japan
kimura@apal.cs.waseda.ac.jp

Abstract. Deep learning for medical image classification has enjoyed increased attention. However, a bottleneck that prevents it from widespread adoption is its dependency on very large, annotated datasets, a condition that cannot always be satisfied. Few-shot learning in the medical domain is still in its infancy but has the potential to overcome these challenges. Compression is a way for models to be deployed on resource-constrained machines. In an attempt to tackle some of the challenges imposed by limited data and high computational resources, we present a few-shot sparse-quantization aware meta-training framework (FS-SQAM). The proposed framework aims to exploit the role of sparsity and quantization for improved adaptability in a low-resource cross-domain setting for the classification of acute lymphocytic leukemia (ALL) in blood cell images. Combining these strategies enables us to approach two of the most common problems that encounter deep learning for medical images: the need for extremely large datasets and high computational resources. Extensive experiments have been conducted to evaluate the performance of the proposed framework on the ALL-IDB2 dataset in a cross-domain few-shot setting. Performance gains in terms of accuracy and compression have been demonstrated, thus serving to realize the suitability of meta-learning on resource-constrained devices. Future advancements in the domain of efficient deep learning computer-aided diagnosis systems will facilitate their adoption in clinical medicine.

Keywords: Few-Shot Learning · Medical Image Analysis · Compression

1 Introduction

The problem of restricted availability of labeled medical data remains a hindrance for conventional deep learning methods as they are dependent on a high volume of data. Conventionally, there are common challenges that plague deep learning for medical applications [1], one is the dataset size, with medical datasets being in the order of hundreds or thousands of samples [2]. Second, is the class imbalance problem of rarer

H. Lu et al. (Eds.): ACPR 2023, LNCS 14408, pp. 213–226, 2023.
https://doi.org/10.1007/978-3-031-47665-5_18

diseases, where some diseases manifest more rarely in a population which is reflected in classes with much fewer samples [3]. Overcoming the data problem in medical applications allows for better diagnostic accuracy and potentially improves pathologists' accuracy [4].

Few-shot learning (FSL) as a concept has been developed to overcome these hurdles by imitating how humans can learn from a few examples. Likewise, when applied to scarce medical datasets, few-shot learning seeks to learn from just a few samples. A more general term, meta-learning, is an approach conventionally described as learning to learn, that aims to generalize to new tasks that are different from the originally trained tasks. Learning to learn from a few examples is a powerful technique that is heavily investigated by the research community. Few-shot meta-learning methods are suited for applications where encountering novel classes with limited samples is a common occurrence as with the case in the field of cancer diagnostics.

Deep learning has been used extensively in various medical image applications such as the detection of abnormalities [5] and segmentation of areas of interest [6], encouraged by the advent of high-quality images and the increase in computational resources. As a result, numerous computer-aided diagnosis (CAD) systems are dependent on deep learning [7].

Encouraged by the efforts in deep learning and few-shot learning healthcare targeted applications, we investigate the role of sparsity and quantization in meta-training in a limited resource medical cross-domain setting. In this work, we exploit sparsity and quantization for the purpose of detecting the presence of blast cells in blood cell images through training on the task of detecting malignant tumors in breast histopathological images.

Our main contributions in this work are as follows:

- We present FS-SQAM, a joint sparse-quantization aware meta-training scheme for the purpose of lymphoblast detection in blood smear images in a cross-domain setting with limited data and computational resources.
- We conduct experiments to assess the influence of sparsity and quantization and the impact of regularization on the performance and efficiency of lymphoblast detection to assist in leukemia diagnosis in a low-resource setting. We observe that the results demonstrate that FS-SQAM allows for strong generalization on the ALL-IDB2 [8] dataset in addition to the gains on the memory footprint reduction front.
- We hope the presented work can encourage more research into approaches that are well-suited for use in challenging clinical environments where both the computational resources and data are limited.

2 Related Works

In this section we start by focusing on previous works that target lymphoblast detection, and then we mention examples in the literature that have utilized FSL for medical applications. We end this section by mentioning some of the influential research directions in efficient few-shot learning and relevant works that examine medical cross-domain FSL.

Acute lymphoblastic leukemia or ALL is a cancer of blood cells and the most common childhood cancer. Early diagnosis is crucial as the disease is characterized by rapid progression. One of the ways to diagnose ALL is through blood testing which requires manual examination by a pathologist. In order to expedite the diagnosis process, many works have proposed approaches for the detection of target cells in microscopic blood smear images that could be incorporated into CAD systems. The literature on ALL detection mainly employs deep learning with transfer learning [9–11] being a dominant approach as training from scratch prerequires the availability of a large dataset. Whilst most studies using deep learning achieve a performance of >95% diagnostic accuracy, efficient resource utilization that targets resource-constrained devices is not taken into account by the majority.

Few-shot learning aims to learn new classes from a few examples, making it a suitable approach for data limited settings, which is the case in most medical applications, making it a method with immense potential benefits for medical classification problems. Metric-learning is a class of FSL approaches where classification is dependent on a learning similarity metric that is capable of discerning similar instances. Among the approaches in this class are Prototypical networks [12], Matching networks [13], and Relation networks [14]. While still a nascent approach, few-shot learning has been gaining interest in the past few years with works applying it to various medical datasets such as histopathological [15], X-rays [16], and cell [17] image datasets among others. A specific subset in few-shot learning problems is cross-domain few-shot learning [18] where the classes used in training and testing are drawn from different domains.

In cross-domain few-shot learning, extreme shifts in the source and target domains are detrimental to performance and provide a challenging problem to overcome. This becomes even more important in medical images, where the data on some diseases are rarer than others, which enables learning for these understudied categories. It has been suggested in [19] that an updatable feature extractor leads to better generalization ability on hard few-shot tasks, as the model can modify its parameters to better suit the task through fine-tuning on the support set. This improves upon using a frozen feature extractor that relies solely on distance calculations to classify.

Compression for neural networks has been studied extensively with the goal of achieving models suitable for devices with limited resources, pruning, and quantization being popular methods. Their combination has been experimented with in general computer vision tasks [20]. For example in [21], the authors devise a quantized sparse training regime that leverages a combined pruning-quantization function that determines the optimal pruning and quantization parameters for each layer.

Further investigation is required to understand how compression techniques can be effectively integrated with few-shot meta-learning, especially in the context of medical applications where models need to generalize quickly and operate within computational constraints. Meta-learning can be memory intensive as reported in [22] due to the requirement of loading the support images to memory in order to obtain a task adapted model. To counteract this effect, the authors devised a training scheme by restricting backpropagation to only a random subset from the support set, making this approach friendly to computationally limited devices. Previous works [23, 24] utilized quantization-aware training (QAT) as a way to quantize the weights of the feature extractor and incorporated both quantization loss and classification loss calculated on the query set. Similarly, incorporating iterative pruning into meta-learning has been attempted in [25] for the purpose of limiting meta-overfitting through pruning the least significant weights and then fine-tuning via a meta algorithm. Another consequence of sparsifying the model is the reduced number of parameters. Thus, if the model allows updates to the feature extractor, this will lead to a task-adapted model with compressed weights.

Since the literature on applying FSL to ALL detection is scarce, we mention a few works that apply cross-domain FSL approaches on histopathological datasets, a related cancer detection task. Examining FSL on histopathological datasets reveals that accuracy ranges from $36.4 \pm 0.51\%$ to $70.0 \pm 0.49\%$ for out-domain CRC-TP (colorectal tissues) [26] $\rightarrow$ BreakHis [27] (breast tissues) classification with an average accuracy of 60% as demonstrated by [28]. The authors stipulate that this is a good starting performance for out-domain settings. Another approach proposed in [29] investigates contrastive learning in various cross-domain scenarios. The approach achieves an accuracy of 67.56% in the out-domain setting (NCT-CRC $\rightarrow$ PAIP) where the source dataset is NCT-CRC-HE-100K (colorectal tissues) [30] and the target dataset is PAIP (liver tissues) [31].

It is well established that deep learning, especially transfer learning, performs well on medical datasets including ALL datasets, however, little work has been done on the topic resource efficient few-shot learning for ALL images and how sparsity and quantization impact meta-learning in general.

3   Methodology

This section describes the methodology adopted in the proposed FS-SQAM framework. The goals of this approach are two-fold: 1) Produce a lightweight model. 2) Equipping the classifier with better generalization ability in a medical cross-domain setting with reasonable performance on a novel dataset with disjoint classes belonging to the medical domain. We test FS-SQAM on the following cross-domain setting BreakHis $\rightarrow$ ALL-IDB2, which belongs to the domain of histopathological images (breast tissue) and blood cell (blood smear) images respectively. Even though the domain gap between the training dataset and the test dataset adds to the problem's difficulty, it presents a realistic scenario where uncommon diseases that manifest less frequently in a population may be encountered by medical practitioners. The described setting can be considered an extreme cross-domain scenario (out-domain) given the great domain shift between these two domains.

The stages underlying the framework are as follows: 1) the pre-trained model undergoes sparse-aware meta-training and then quantization-aware meta-training on the BreakHis dataset. 2) Afterwards, the model is evaluated on test tasks sampled from the ALL-IDB2 dataset to assess the compressed classifier's performance as shown in Fig. 1. To achieve the goal of strong generalization, that is generalization on classes foreign to the training dataset, we used a network capable of fine-tuning on the sampled support sets in order to allow for adaptation for out-domain tasks.

In brief, our framework utilizes an updatable Prototypical based model [12] that undergoes sparse-aware meta-training, and quantization-aware meta-training for blast cell detection we extend the proposal in [19] to achieve an efficient flexible classifier for this task. Although this approach incurs additional training overhead compared to the simpler methods such as one-shot pruning and post-training quantization, it offers

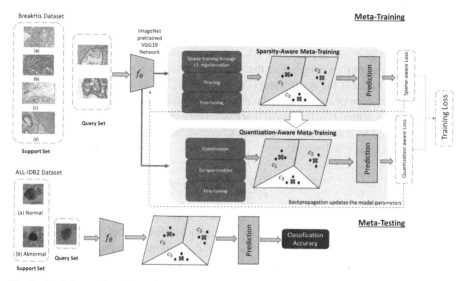

Fig. 1. Training and testing scheme of FS-SQAM, support, and query sets are sampled from BreakHis in the meta-training phase and ALL-IDB2 in the meta-testing phase. In the meta-training stage, the model undergoes 1) sparse training (through L_1 regularization) 2) pruning (part of sparse-aware meta-training 3) quantization-aware meta-training. The support and query samples are projected to the embedded space in order for the query samples be classified.

the significant benefit of preserving accuracy. This is particularly important in medical applications where diagnostic accuracy is crucial.

3.1 Prototypical Networks

Given a situation where there is a training dataset that has a set of classes C_{train} and a set of test classes C_{test}, where C_{train} and C_{test} are disjoint. The goal is to produce a model f_θ capable of adapting to and classifying examples belonging to C_{test} from just a few labeled examples [32]. Episodic learning has been proposed as a way to simulate conditions at test time by sampling examples from the larger training dataset. The episodes are constructed by sampling K-shots from each of the N classes. The K examples are form a support set $S = \{(x_1, y_1), ..., (y_K, y_K)\}_{i=1}^{N}$, alongside a query set Q of different examples from those sampled in the support set, drawn from the same N classes. This setup is referred to as K-shot N-way episode. The model adapts to the support set and the performance is evaluated on the query set with the goal of minimizing loss. Repeating this process on multiple episodes augments the model with the ability to generalize to the examples in the query set. In the literature, the episodic learning setup is termed meta-learning.

Prototypical networks [12] depend on creating a prototype for each class and classifying an instance based on nearness to a class's prototype. The loss function of the training episode of a prototypical network is the cross-entropy loss function but applied to the query set examples, where T is the number of examples in the query set, y is the true class label and x is the query sample to be classified to the closest prototype P_c of class c. The prototype of a class P_c is the mean of the support set embeddings calculated as $\frac{1}{N} \sum_{i=1}^{N} f_\theta(x_i)$ where f_θ is the model that extracts the embeddings of S and Q. A query point is classified by comparing its distance to every class's prototype in the embedding space. The loss can be written as:

$$L_{CE} = -\frac{1}{T} \sum_i log\, p(y_i | x_i, \{p_c\}) \tag{1}$$

Cross-Domain Learning. Violates the assumption that the meta-training and meta-testing tasks T are drawn from the same distribution where it becomes $P_{train}(T) \neq P_{test}(T)$. Hence, in order to account for the novel domain information through transfer learning. The model f_θ is fine-tuned on the classes of interest, specifically, the last k layers are fine-tuned on the target classes. This is in accordance with the idea proposed in [19] that an updatable metric feature extractor is better suited for adapting to unseen classes at test time.

3.2 Sparse-Aware Meta-training

The proposed framework FS-SQAM employs two compression methods, pruning, and quantization where their combination has been utilized in various computer vision tasks to produce an ultra-resource efficient model. In this section, we detail the specific pruning and quantization methods that are incorporated into the framework.

The first compression technique introduced is iterative pruning to enforce sparsity in the network in the sparse-aware meta-training phase through unstructured magnitude-based pruning. Pruning is preceded by sparse training through introducing regularization. Pruning depends on the hypothesis that within overparameterized networks there exists a sparser subnetwork, referred to as a winning ticket [33], that can match the accuracy of the original with the added benefits of fewer parameters and reduced size. We incorporate the L_1 regularization into the training to drive the weights w to zero through the penalization of the absolute sum of weights as indicated by the following loss function of a model f_θ with parameters θ:

$$L(y, \hat{y}) = \frac{1}{N} \sum_{i=1}^{N} L(y_i, f_\theta(x_i)) = L_{CE} + \lambda \sum_{i=1}^{N} |w_i| \qquad (2)$$

where y refers to the ground-truth and $\hat{y}$ is the predicted label. The regularization penalty term consists of the λ hyperparameter and the L_1-norm. We conduct experiments by applying FS-SQAM on a pre-trained VGG19 network with the following values for λ, where $\lambda = \{0.001, 0.005, 0.01\}$. The network is pruned iteratively with the goal of progressively revealing a subnetwork that can achieve comparable accuracy as the unpruned version. Iterative pruning is the preferred approach when accuracy is prioritized as training the network and then subsequently applying one-shot pruning can be harmful to accuracy.

3.3 Quantization-Aware Meta-training

In FS-SQAM, during the quantization-aware meta-training phase, we opt for QAT [34] to reduce the precision from 32-bit floating point to 8-bit integers. QAT relies on compensating for quantization error in the training. Given the input x and the corresponding labels y of a model f_θ and a quantization function q, the quantized value of x in the forward pass becomes $x_q = \min(q_{max}, \max(q_{min}, \frac{x}{s} + z))$ which maps each input weight to an integer. q_{min} And q_{max} stand for the minimum and maximum values for the 8-bit range, s and z represent the scaling factor for the described quantization range and the zero-point respectively. Then dequantization happens through $\hat{x} = (x_q - z)s$ which maps the quantized input x_q back to floating-point. However, this operation $x_q \rightarrow \hat{x}$, yields $\hat{x}$ which is not exactly equal to the original input x, thus inducing quantization noise which is taken into account in the training. Re-training is required to recover accuracy degradation from quantization. The previously mentioned phases are detailed in Fig. 1.

The applied quantization loss, where q is the quantization operation, for the model can be described as:

$$L[y, f_\theta(x, q(\theta))] \qquad (3)$$

Incorporating quantization loss into the training yields the following objective function to be minimized:

$$\min_\theta L(y, \hat{y}) + L[y, f_\theta(x, q(\theta))] \qquad (4)$$

The workflow of FS-SQAM is listed in Algorithm 1, starting with sparsification through L_1 regularization then is proceeded by pruning and applying quantization through QAT.

Algorithm 1. Sparse-QAT Aware Meta-training Algorithm

Input: A pretrained model f_θ with parameters θ, total number of layers L, pruning mask m and pruning percentage p, sampled episodes consisting of support set and query set $S = \{(x_1, y_1), \ldots, (x_{K \times N}, y_{K \times N})\}$ and $Q = \left\{(x_1, y_1), \ldots, \left(x_{K_q \times N}, y_{K_q \times N}\right)\right\}$

Output: Lightweight lymphoblast classifier

   Phase 1: Sparse-Aware Meta-Training

   /*Introduce sparsity to the network*/

1. Set the hyperparameter λ
2. Apply the regularization penalty to trainable layers in f_θ
3. **For** each epoch **do**
4.   **For** each episode **do**
5.   Freeze the first $L - k$ layers of f_θ
6.   Minimize the loss function $\min_\theta L_{CE}$
7. **end**
8. **end**

   /*Iterative pruning*/

9. **For** each epoch **do**
10.   **For** each episode **do**
11.   Prune the smallest p weights (in accordance with the pruning schedule) at every layer by applying a pruning mask m
12.   Fine-tune the masked model, $m \odot \theta$ through minimizing loss in $\min_\theta L_{CE} + \lambda \sum_{i=1}^{N} |w_i|$
13.   Repeat the previous two steps until the desired sparsity is reached
14.   **end**
15. **end**

   Phase 2: Quantization-Aware Meta-Training

   /*Quantization-aware training*/

16. **For** each epoch **do**
17.   **For** each episode **do**
18.   Freeze the first $L - k$ layers of f_θ
19.   Train in simulated quantization
20.   Minimize the objective function $\min_\theta L(y, \hat{y}) + L\left[y, f\left(x, q(\theta)\right)\right]$
21.   **end**
22. **end**
23. Apply quantization to the model

---

4 Experimental Setup

Our initial model is an ImageNet pre-trained VGG19 network. The model undergoes compression as previously detailed. The first 3 convolutional blocks of the network are frozen during the sparse training and quantization-aware meta-training phases.

    The meta-train dataset is the $40\times$ magnification segment from the BreakHis [27] dataset which is where the training tasks are sampled from. The few-shot training tasks are 8-way 10-shots for each episode and the model is trained for 150 epochs where they are divided equally between the sparse training, sparse-aware, and quantization-aware meta-training phases. The model is evaluated on test episodes sampled from the ALL [8] dataset, specifically the ALL-IDB2 segment of the dataset.

4.1 Datasets

The first dataset used is BreakHis [27], which is a dataset of histological images of breast tumors. The dataset has eight classes, where the images of interest are the $40\times$ magnification images which total 1,995 samples. The following table shows the number of images in each of the eight classes (Table 1).

Table 1. The Eight Classes of the BreakHis Dataset.

Classes	Magnification Factor				Total
	$40\times$	$100\times$	$200\times$	$400\times$	
Adenosis (A)	114	113	111	106	444
Fibroadenoma (F)	253	260	264	237	1014
Tubular Adenona (TA)	109	121	108	115	453
Phyllodes Tumor (PT)	149	150	140	130	569
Ductal Carcinoma (DC)	864	903	896	788	3451
Lobular Carcinoma (LC)	156	170	163	137	626
Mucinous Carcinoma (MC)	205	222	196	169	792
Papillary Carcinoma (PC)	145	142	135	138	500
Total	1995	2081	2013	1820	7909

The second dataset included is the ALL-IDB2 [8] dataset, which is a binary dataset consisting of images of blood smears. The image could either be normal or abnormal, reflecting the presence of normal or abnormal blast cells. The dataset is balanced with an equal number of normal and abnormal images, which sums up to a total of 260 images.

5 Results

We present the results of meta-training a prototypical network using FS-SQAM on the BreakHis dataset that is tested on the ALL-IDB2 dataset using a VGG19 backbone. The results of the model's performance are the mean accuracy of three test runs, where each result is the average performance of the classifier across the test tasks. The number of test tasks is set to 600 with the query set size set to four samples for both the training and testing. Experiments were repeated for sparsities of 50%, 70%, and 90% which are shown in Table 2. Results are reported for the use of pruning alone or followed by 8-bit quantization-aware training. The resulting sizes are also reported to provide a view of the accuracy-size tradeoffs for better assessment in Table 3. All of the reported sizes are of.*tflite* [35] files in MBs.

The baseline result without any use of compression is 82.22% accuracy. It is observable that QAT slightly improves the accuracy of the 50% and 70% pruned networks. This leads to an accuracy of 77.95% at 70% sparsity and 8-bit quantized weights. With regards to the obtained compression, the network size is 19.60 MB which is a compression of 3.90× compared to the baseline.

Table 2. Meta-test accuracy for FS-SQAM on ALL-IDB2 dataset using VGG19 network for 2-way 10-shot classification (without regularization).

Sparsity				
	0%	50%	70%	90%
Pruning (Baseline)	0.8222	0.7813	0.7769	0.7485
With QAT	0.8127	0.7888	0.7795	0.7291

Table 3. Model sizes of VGG19 after FS-SQAM in MBs.

Sparsity				
	0%	50%	70%	90%
Sparse-Aware Meta-Training	76.41	55.84	33.60	11.34
FS-SQAM	29.28	32.39	19.60	6.79

Table 4. Meta-test accuracy for FS-SQAM with L_1 regularization applied with varying values of λ on ALL-IDB2 dataset using VGG19 network for 2-way 10-shot classification.

Sparsity			
	50%	70%	90%
$\lambda = 0.001$			
Sparse-Aware Meta-Training	0.7875	0.7743	0.7552
FS-SQAM	0.7864	0.7851	0.7251
$\lambda = 0.005$			
Sparse-Aware Meta-Training	0.7874	0.7867	0.7457
FS-SQAM	0.7898	0.7817	0.7335
$\lambda = 0.01$			
Sparse-Aware Meta-Training	0.7930	0.7826	0.7474
FS-SQAM	**0.7908**	0.7822	0.7338

Table 4 shows the results of using sparse-aware meta-training on its own and FS-SQAM with L_1 regularization applied using $\lambda = \{0.001, 0.005, 0.01\}$ for the sparsity ratios 50%, 70%, and 90%. It is worth noting that applying regularization improves the accuracy at some sparsities compared to not applying regularization. Notably at 50% sparsity, accuracy when $\lambda = 0.005$ and $\lambda = 0.01$ is 78.98% and 79.08% respectively, compared to 78.88% with no regularization applied with a compression ratio of $2.35\times$. Additionally in the FS-SQAM configuration, we find that $\lambda = 0.01$ yields the highest accuracy in this category for 50% and 70% sparsity ratios, which are 79.08% and 78.22%.

While the role of pruning and quantization remains largely unexplored in the context of few-shot learning, pruning has been used to prevent overfitting in meta-learning [36, 37]. The generalization ability of the classifier can be attributed to overcoming the over-parameterization in the network. Over-parameterization has the effect of hurting the generalization ability of the network to unseen examples in normal supervised learning [38]. Thus, expanding this concept to few-shot learning, it is possible to boost generalization to unseen classes through sparsification which also provides the added benefit of compression.

To enhance the compression of the model, QAT has been deemed a method that incurs minimal accuracy loss. Thus, the FS-SQAM framework provides an adaptable classifier that can achieve a fair accuracy-to-size trade-off in a cross-domain setting. Resource-wise, 90% sparsity in FS-SQAM provides an accuracy of 73.38% alongside resulting in the highest compressed model with a compression rate of $11.25\times$.

To provide context for the obtained results, we present some of the results from related works that address few-shot learning for medical datasets, specifically those that involve a significant domain shift in the following table to demonstrate the efficacy of FS-SQAM for lymphoblast detection in an out-domain setting (Table 5).

Table 5. Performance comparison with related works in out-domain setting.

Reference	Accuracy (%)	Out-Domain Setting
[28]	68.1 ± 0.51	CRC-TP $\rightarrow$ BreakHis
[29]	67.56	NCT $\rightarrow$ PAIP
[17]	55.12 ± 0.13	mini-ImageNet $\rightarrow$ HEp-2
50% FS-SQAM	79.08	BreakHis $\rightarrow$ ALL-IDB2

6 Conclusion

Rationing resources is important for real-life clinical scenarios where only restricted computational resources and scarce data are available. We empirically test our framework FS-SQAM which combines sparse-aware training and quantization-aware training in the meta-training process for efficient lymphoblast detection. The obtained results point to the possibility of applying resource-efficient few-shot learning in cross-domain medical settings. The utilization of compression in the meta-training process achieves the goal of minimizing the memory footprint and enabling adaptation to unseen classes which matches the reality of encountering uncommon classes of diseases with very few samples in clinical practice. We empirically investigate the effectiveness of FS-SQAM in BreakHis → ALL-IDB2 cross-domain setting, an extreme case of distribution shift, with a focus on resulting accuracy-size trade-offs. The application of sparse-aware training and quantization-aware training enhances performance and reduces the memory footprint. Additionally, the application of L_1 regularization as a preprocess before pruning yields notable sparse model performance increases at most λ values, especially at 50% sparsity. To further examine the generalizability of the framework, more evaluations need to be undertaken on other medical datasets and domains, we leave this as future work.

References

1. Ellis, R.J., Sander, R.M., Limon, A.: Twelve key challenges in medical machine learning and solutions. Intell. Based Med. **6**, 100068 (2022). https://doi.org/10.1016/j.ibmed.2022.100068
2. Willemink, M.J., et al.: Preparing medical imaging data for machine learning. Radiology **295**, 4–15 (2020). https://doi.org/10.1148/radiol.2020192224
3. Weng, W.-H., Deaton, J., Natarajan, V., Elsayed, G.F., Liu, Y.: Addressing the real-world class imbalance problem in dermatology. In: Proceedings of the Machine Learning for Health NeurIPS Workshop, pp. 415–429. PMLR (2020)
4. Litjens, G., et al.: Deep learning as a tool for increased accuracy and efficiency of histopathological diagnosis. Sci. Rep. **6**, 26286 (2016). https://doi.org/10.1038/srep26286
5. Rajpurkar, P., et al.: CheXaid: deep learning assistance for physician diagnosis of tuberculosis using chest x-rays in patients with HIV. NPJ Digit. Med. **3**, 1–8 (2020). https://doi.org/10.1038/s41746-020-00322-2
6. Altini, N., et al.: Liver, kidney and spleen segmentation from CT scans and MRI with deep learning: a survey. Neurocomputing **490**, 30–53 (2022). https://doi.org/10.1016/j.neucom.2021.08.157
7. Chan, H.-P., Hadjiiski, L.M., Samala, R.K.: Computer-aided diagnosis in the era of deep learning. Med. Phys. **47**, e218–e227 (2020). https://doi.org/10.1002/mp.13764
8. Labati, R.D., Piuri, V., Scotti, F.: All-IDB: The acute lymphoblastic leukemia image database for image processing. In: 2011 18th IEEE International Conference on Image Processing, pp. 2045–2048 (2011). https://doi.org/10.1109/ICIP.2011.6115881
9. Genovese, A.: ALLNet: acute lymphoblastic leukemia detection using lightweight convolutional networks. In: 2022 IEEE 9th International Conference on Computational Intelligence and Virtual Environments for Measurement Systems and Applications (CIVEMSA), pp. 1–6 (2022). https://doi.org/10.1109/CIVEMSA53371.2022.9853691
10. Genovese, A., Hosseini, M.S., Piuri, V., Plataniotis, K.N., Scotti, F.: Histopathological transfer learning for acute lymphoblastic leukemia detection. In: 2021 IEEE International Conference on Computational Intelligence and Virtual Environments for Measurement Systems and Applications (CIVEMSA), pp. 1–6 (2021). https://doi.org/10.1109/CIVEMSA52099.2021.9493677
11. Maaliw, R.R., et al.: A multistage transfer learning approach for acute lymphoblastic leukemia classification. In: 2022 IEEE 13th Annual Ubiquitous Computing, Electronics & Mobile Communication Conference (UEMCON), pp. 0488–0495 (2022). https://doi.org/10.1109/UEMCON54665.2022.9965679
12. Snell, J., Swersky, K., Zemel, R.S.: Prototypical Networks for Few-shot Learning. arXiv preprint http://arxiv.org/abs/1703.05175 (2017). https://doi.org/10.48550/arXiv.1703.05175

13. Vinyals, O., Blundell, C., Lillicrap, T., Kavukcuoglu, K., Wierstra, D.: Matching networks for one shot learning. In: Proceedings of the 30th International Conference on Neural Information Processing Systems, pp. 3637–3645. Curran Associates Inc., Red Hook (2016)

14. Sung, F., Yang, Y., Zhang, L., Xiang, T., Torr, P.H.S., Hospedales, T.M.: Learning to Compare: Relation Network for Few-Shot Learning. arXiv preprint http://arxiv.org/abs/1711.06025 (2018). https://doi.org/10.48550/arXiv.1711.06025

15. Chao, S., Belanger, D.: Generalizing few-shot classification of whole-genome doubling across cancer types. Pac. Symp. Biocomput. **27**, 144–155 (2022)

16. Paul, A., Shen, T.C., Peng, Y., Lu, Z., Summers, R.M.: Learning few-shot chest X-ray diagnosis using images from the published scientific literature. In: 2021 IEEE 18th International Symposium on Biomedical Imaging (ISBI), pp. 344–348 (2021). https://doi.org/10.1109/ISB I48211.2021.9434059

17. Walsh, R., Abdelpakey, M.H., Shehata, M.S., Mohamed, M.M.: Automated human cell classification in sparse datasets using few-shot learning. Sci. Rep. **12**, 2924 (2022). https://doi. org/10.1038/s41598-022-06718-2

18. Guo, Y., et al.: A Broader Study of Cross-Domain Few-Shot Learning. arXiv preprint http:// arxiv.org/abs/1912.07200 (2020)

19. Triantafillou, E., et al.: Meta-Dataset: A Dataset of Datasets for Learning to Learn from Few Examples. arXiv preprint http://arxiv.org/abs/1903.03096 (2020). https://doi.org/10.48550/ arXiv.1903.03096

20. Zhang, X., Colbert, I., Kreutz-Delgado, K., Das, S.: Training Deep Neural Networks with Joint Quantization and Pruning of Weights and Activations. arXiv preprint http://arxiv.org/ abs/2110.08271 (2021). https://doi.org/10.48550/arXiv.2110.08271

21. Park, J.-H., Kim, K.-M., Lee, S.: Quantized sparse training: a unified trainable framework for joint pruning and quantization in DNNs. ACM Trans. Embed. Comput. Syst. **21**, 60:1–60:22 (2022). https://doi.org/10.1145/3524066

22. Bronskill, J., Massiceti, D., Patacchiola, M., Hofmann, K., Nowozin, S., Turner, R.E.: Memory Efficient Meta-Learning with Large Images. arXiv preprint http://arxiv.org/abs/2107.01105 (2021). https://doi.org/10.48550/arXiv.2107.01105

23. Youn, J., Song, J., Kim, H.-S., Bahk, S.: Bitwidth-Adaptive Quantization-Aware Neural Network Training: A Meta-Learning Approach. arXiv preprint http://arxiv.org/abs/2207.10188 (2022). https://doi.org/10.48550/arXiv.2207.10188

24. Chauhan, J., Kwon, Y.D., Mascolo, C.: Exploring On-Device Learning Using Few Shots for Audio Classification **5**

25. Tian, H., Liu, B., Yuan, X.-T., Liu, Q.: Meta-learning with network pruning. In: Vedaldi, A., Bischof, H., Brox, T., Frahm, J.-M. (eds.) ECCV 2020. LNCS, vol. 12364, pp. 675–700. Springer, Cham (2020). https://doi.org/10.1007/978-3-030-58529-7_40

26. Javed, S., Mahmood, A., Werghi, N., Benes, K., Rajpoot, N.: Multiplex cellular communities in multi-gigapixel colorectal cancer histology images for tissue phenotyping. IEEE Trans. Image Process. **29**, 9204–9219 (2020). https://doi.org/10.1109/TIP.2020.3023795

27. Breast Cancer Histopathological Database (BreakHis). Laboratório Visão Robótica e Imagem. https://web.inf.ufpr.br/vri/databases/breast-cancer-histopathological-database-bre akhis/. Accessed 20 Oct 2022

28. Shakeri, F., et al.: FHIST: A Benchmark for Few-shot Classification of Histological Images. http://arxiv.org/abs/2206.00092 (2022). https://doi.org/10.48550/arXiv.2206.00092

29. [2202.09059] Towards better understanding and better generalization of few-shot classification in histology images with contrastive learning. arXiv preprint https://arxiv.org/abs/2202. 09059. Accessed 01 June 2023

30. 100,000 histological images of human colorectal cancer and healthy tissue. Zenodo. https:// zenodo.org/record/1214456. Accessed 02 June 2023

31. Kim, Y.J., et al.: PAIP 2019: liver cancer segmentation challenge. Med. Image Anal. **67**, 101854 (2021). https://doi.org/10.1016/j.media.2020.101854

32. Ren, M., et al.: Meta-Learning for Semi-Supervised Few-Shot Classification. arXiv preprint http://arxiv.org/abs/1803.00676 (2018)

33. Frankle, J., Carbin, M.: The Lottery Ticket Hypothesis: Finding Sparse, Trainable Neural Networks. arXiv preprint http://arxiv.org/abs/1803.03635 (2019). https://doi.org/10.48550/arXiv.1803.03635

34. Jacob, B., et al.: Quantization and Training of Neural Networks for Efficient Integer-Arithmetic-Only Inference. arXiv preprint http://arxiv.org/abs/1712.05877 (2017). https://doi.org/10.48550/arXiv.1712.05877

35. TensorFlow Lite. https://www.tensorflow.org/lite/guide. Accessed 26 Jan 2023

36. Chijiwa, D., Yamaguchi, S., Kumagai, A., Ida, Y.: Meta-ticket: finding optimal subnetworks for few-shot learning within randomly initialized neural networks. Presented at the Advances in Neural Information Processing Systems, 31 October (2022)

37. Liu, Z., et al.: MetaPruning: Meta Learning for Automatic Neural Network Channel Pruning. arXiv preprint http://arxiv.org/abs/1903.10258 (2019). https://doi.org/10.48550/arXiv.1903.10258

38. Hoefler, T., Alistarh, D., Ben-Nun, T., Dryden, N., Peste, A.: Sparsity in Deep Learning: Pruning and Growth for Efficient Inference and Training in Neural Networks. arXiv preprint http://arxiv.org/abs/2102.00554 (2021). https://doi.org/10.48550/arXiv.2102.00554

MAREPVGG: Multi-attention RepPVGG to Facefake Detection

Zhuochao Huang, Rui Yang, Rushi Lan$^{(\boxtimes)}$, Cheng Pang, and Xiaoyan Luo

Guilin University of Electronic Technology, Guilin 541004, China
rslan@guet.edu.cn

Abstract. The threat posed by the increasing means of face forgery and the lowering of the threshold of use is increasing. Although the detection capability of current detection models is improving, most of them need to consume large computational resources and have complex model architectures. Therefore, in this paper, we propose a new deep learning detection framework MARepVGG, which uses RepVGG as the backbone, combines texture enhancement module and multi-attention module to strengthen the network to learn face forgery features through the idea of heavy parameterization to balance training performance and inference speed. We evaluate our method on the kaggle real and fake face detection dataset, which differs from the computer automatically generated images, where the fake faces are high quality images produced by Photoshop experts. Our method improves the accuracy by 14% on this dataset compared to a baseline of forgery detection by repvgg alone, while the number of parameters is only 8.75 M.

Keywords: Facefake Detection · REPVGG · Multi-attention · Texture Enhancement

1 Introduction

With the continuous development of technologies such as computer graphics, deep learning and artificial intelligence, face forgery technology has made great progress. As researchers have developed GAN models that can automatically generate highly realistic face images, face images generated by AI can escape recognition by the naked eye, and it is no longer difficult to accurately forge the victim's face, which poses a huge security risk to society when people can easily forge faces, and face forgery technology will most likely become an accomplice to illegal crimes. Therefore, the research on face forgery detection technology is becoming more and more important. In recent years, deep learning-based detection technology has reached a high level, and many transformer-based deepfake detection models [1] can achieve an accuracy rate of more than 90%.

However, as the accuracy rate increases, the number of parameters of the model tends to increase, because the model needs to learn more complex features or relationships, this detection model becomes very large, and the training process consumes a lot of computational resources and time, which increases the cost of using the model and time cost, and limits their promotion and application in practical applications. Moreover, in mobile or embedded devices, large models often cannot meet the requirements of real-time and low-power consumption. Therefore, we consider how to achieve the detection of face forgery within limited resources, reduce the size and computational complexity of the model and build a more lightweight face forgery detection model at the same time, using some effective feature extraction techniques and classifiers to further improve the detection performance.

To address our proposed scenario above, we propose a hybrid deep learning model called MARepVGG, which uses repvgg-A0 [2] as the backbone of the model to balance training speed and inference speed through parameter reconfiguration, and its entire network consists of standard convolutional layers, which can obtain more hardware optimization support to further accelerate training and inference. At the same time, the attention to different regions is enhanced using the multi-attention module, which captures heterogeneous features by introducing multiple attention mechanisms, thus enabling the model to better learn information from different regions. The texture enhancement module processes the shallow features extracted by the backbone network to make the texture of the image more obvious, which improves the detail representation and compensates for the information loss caused by deep convolution. The generated multi-attention maps and texture features extracted from shallow layers by the texture enhancement block are fused in the bilinear attention pool into a feature representation of the whole image, further enhancing the model's ability to learn forged features. We will evaluate the performance of the model and compare it with other lightweight frameworks in Sect. 4.

The main contributions of our work are the following: We propose a new deep learning model, MARepVGG, which uses multi-attention mechanism and texture enhancement to detect face forgery. Beginning with a lightweight model, we bring a new perspective to face detection. Gains a significant improvement on the baseline approach.

2   Related Work

Most face forgery detection models extract artifact features from images by building various deep convolutions, but with the rapid development of forgery technology, the fineness of forged faces has been greatly improved, so the structure of deepfake detection models [3–5] becomes more complex in order to improve the detection of forged faces. We think whether we can implement the detection of face forgery on a simple model structure, and by reading some literature [6,7] we found that RepVGG can improve the overall network feature representation well and inference speed is similar compared with other mainstream networks. For example, in the YOLOv6 backbone network, Li et al. used RepBlock as a building block for small networks and replaced the CSP module with Rep module in CSP-PAN, which optimized the latency brought by CSP-Net [8] to a certain extent and improved the memory bandwidth utilization.

Meanwhile, mainstream GPUs are highly optimized for 3×3 convolution, and the performance on ImageNet, in terms of RepVGG-A0, for example, is 1.25% and 33% better in terms of accuracy and speed compared to ResNet-18.

The two most common face forgery operations are face swap operation and face attribute operation, in the face swap operation type, the original image is swapped with another person's face, and the representative methods are Sim-Swap [9] and InfoSwap [10]. In face attribute editing operation usually modifies the local part of the original face, which can be achieved by GAN-based methods such as HFGI [11] and StyleCLIP [12]. ordinary deep learning models tend to focus on extracting local features losing other regional features through multi-layer convolution. Facing these problems, we need to improve the complementary fusion for different regional features. Zheng et al. [13] propose a multi-attention method that can learn more regional features by clustering and weighting the spatial channels. A new self-supervised mechanism proposed by Yang et al. [14] can effectively localize the information regions. Using the core ideas of these methods, we propose an adaptation of RepVGG that fuses multi-region features to enhance the discrimination of face authenticity.

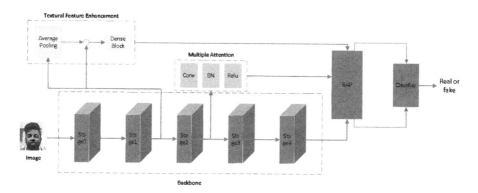

Fig. 1. Shown is the framework of the MARepVGG model proposed in this paper. RepVGG is used as the backbone network to fuse the following main modules: an attention module to generate multiple attention maps, a texture enhancement block to extract and enhance texture information, and a bilinear attention pool to aggregate texture and semantic features.

3   Our Approach

This section provides specific information on the proposed depth detection model (Fig. 1). We will describe our proposed network model in detail in this section. This includes the structure of the backbone network, how the texture enhancement module extracts shallow texture features, the mechanism of the multi-attention module to generate multi-attention graphs and the work of the bilinear pooling layer.

3.1 Backbone

We choose RepVGG-A0 as the backbone network, and we discard its original GAP layer and fully connected layer to keep its RepBlock part. It consists of 5 stages, each containing $[1,2,4,14]$ RepBlocks. the input images are simply edited, including random cropping and left-right flipping, before being fed into the model. The feature maps extracted in stage1 are used as input to the texture enhancement module, and the output of stage2 is passed into the multiple attention module to generate multiple attention maps, and finally the bilinear attention pool is used to fuse the backbone features with local features and perform binary discrimination through the fully connected layer.

3.2 Multiple Attention Maps Generation

The multiple attention module is a lightly weighted model consisting of a 1×1 convolutional layer, a BN layer and a nonlinear activation RELU layer. The difference between real and fake faces may exist in different regions and the degree of difference is subtle. The feature maps extracted from the stage2 stage are passed to the multiple attention module, and the M attention maps obtained by the multiple attention module represent M different regions, and these weights will be applied to the next step of the backbone network to help the model better understand the different features of the input data, which can collect local features more effectively [15].

3.3 Textural Feature Enhancement

In face forgery detection, local texture features are more important than high-level semantic information [16], which is usually present in the shallow layer for identifying artifacts. Therefore, we use the texture feature enhancement module to amplify the artifacts in the shallow features and make it easier for our model to capture these features subsequently. The output feature map F from stage1 is downsampled and averaged in the texture enhancement module to obtain the non-texture feature map D. Then, F is parametrised with D to obtain T. Finally, the densely connected convolution block is used to enhance T [17], and the densely connected convolution block enhances the propagation of features and enhances feature reuse.

3.4 Bilinear Attention Pooling

As shown in Fig. 2, for the shallow texture features output by the texture enhancement block, when the attention map does not match the shallow texture features, the attention map is resized to the same scale as the shallow feature map using linear interpolation, and the fusion of the attention map and the shallow feature map is performed by matrix multiplication and sent to the standard average pooling layer to reduce the influence of the attention map on the pooled feature vector [18] to obtain the texture features P. At the same time, we multi

At the same time, we perform sum operation on the multi-attention map to obtain the single-attention map, and the single-attention map with the features convolved in the last layer is sent to the BAP layer to obtain the global feature G. P and G are sent to the discriminator to obtain the authenticity discrimination result.

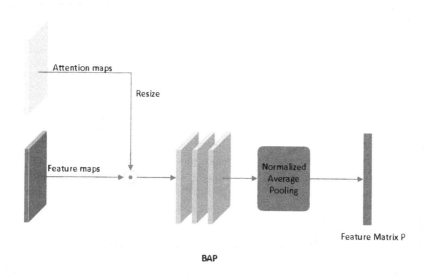

Fig. 2. The process of fusing multi-attention maps generated by the attention module with shallow texture features generated by the texture feature enhancement module.

3.5 Loss

To avoid different attentional maps concentrating on the same region in the image and falling into network degradation, region-independent loss(L_{RIL}) is used to reduce the overlap between attentional feature maps and to reduce the randomness of the information captured by each attentional map [18].

$$
\mathcal{L}_{RIL} = \sum_{i=1}^{B} \sum_{j=1}^{M} \max(\left\|V_j^i - c_j^l\right\|_2^2 - m_{in}(y_i), 0) +
$$
$$
\sum_{i,j \in (M,M), i \neq j} \max\left(m_{out} - \left\|c_i^t - c_j^t\right\|_2^2, 0\right)
\tag{1}
$$

where V is obtained by stacking multiple normalized attention features obtained by BAP from the non-textured feature mapping D. B is the batch volume, M is the number of attentions, and m_{in} represents the margin between the features and the corresponding feature centers, set to different values when y_i is 0 and 1. m_{out} is the margin between each feature center. c is the feature center of V.

Combining the region-independent loss L_{RIL} and the cross-entropy loss L_{CE} is the total loss L function of the model.

$$\mathcal{L} = \lambda_1 * \mathcal{L}_{CE} + \lambda_2 * \mathcal{L}_{RIL} \tag{2}$$

λ_1 and λ_2 are the weights of these two losses in the total loss. In our experiments it is set to $\lambda_1 = \lambda_2 = 1$.

4   Experiment

4.1   Dataset and Implementation Setting

Dataset. The dataset we used contains expertly generated facial images of high quality PS, subjectively classified as easy, medium and difficult, and the number of images is shown in Table 1. These images were synthesized from different faces separated by eyes, nose, mouth or the whole face. Unlike the fake face images generated using the generative model, we hypothesize that the detection model learns some kind of pattern that is easier to recognize in the images generated by the GANs, leading the face forgery detection model to show better accuracy for internally generated and altered face image datasets. This pattern may be futile in the presence of human experts, since the forgery processes of the two are quite different. Using this, we can make the models comparable in a fairer context.

Also, to better understand the performance of our model, we will use a fake face generated based on PGGAN [23] as our dataset. This dataset contains 37566 GAN-generated pseudo-face images, and in order to make this dataset image meet the input requirements of our model, we adjust its resolution to 256×256 and change it to 224×224 by cropping it as we go.

Table 1. Images of real and fake face

sample	train set(count)	test set(count)
real images	1081	1081
fake images	960	960

Implementation Setting. Our proposed model is built using the python module pytorch. pyTorch is a very popular deep learning framework that can quickly build and train neural networks. The Adam optimizer and the loss method proposed in the previous section method method are used to train our proposed model. Our training parameters are set as follows: epoch=100, batch size=64, learning rate=1e-4, betas=(0.9, 0.999), weight_decay=1e-6. These parameters can be adjusted to obtain better training results. The model is executed on 1 NVIDIA Tesla k80 12G GPU.

4.2   Result

Indicator Evaluation. To evaluate our model, we first performed a comparison of several measures of it with the current mainstream lightweight models including RepVGG-A0, ResNet-18 [19], EfficientNet-B4 [20], and inceptionV3 [21]. The comparison results are shown in Table 2. the number of parameters of MARepVGG in the training state is 8.75M, which is 25.08% lower than that of ResNet-18, and the number of floating point operations is 2.3GFLOPs. the speed is tested on 1660ti with a batch size of 16, in instances/second, and the instances are from the true-false face detection dataset [22]. It can be seen that the inference speed is good for batch_size=16, and our model inherits the advantages of RepVGG well. The inference speed on processing images is not much slower.

Table 2. Compare the results of the models on the metrics (Params, FLOPs, Speed)

Model	Params(M)	FLOPs(B)	Speed
RepVGG-A0	8.3	1.4	40.07
ResNet-18	11.7	1.8	39.34
EfficientNet-B4	19	4.2	28.21
InceptionV3	24	5.7	32.25
Ours(MARepVGG)	8.7	2.3	39.70

Comparison with Existing Baseline. We compare the proposed model with RepVGG-A0 as a baseline for face forgery detection accuracy. For the training phase, our training dataset comes from the training_fake class and training_real class in the real and fake face detection dataset, which contains 960 forged face images and 1081 real face images. We first preprocess the images to enhance the generalization ability of the detection model by random rotation flip operation, and resize the images to 224 × 224. For the test set, we use the detection part of the real-fake face detection dataset to evaluate the accuracy of our model. We stored the best training model weights for the detection and the results are shown in Fig. 3. From Fig. 3 we can see that after 100 rounds of training, our proposed model improves the accuracy by 14% over the baseline.

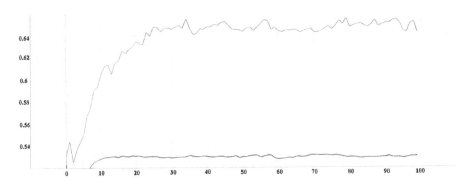

Fig. 3. Comparison of our model and baseline accuracy curves over 100 training rounds, based on NVIDIA k80 GPU. The horizontal axis is the training batch and the vertical axis is the accuracy rate.

Comparison with Other Models. As shown in Table 3, our model is trained uniformly with the compared model on NVIDIA k80 GPU with 100 training rounds, and the dataset used is the real and fake face dataset mentioned in this paper. It can be seen that the detection accuracy of forged faces is higher than that of the comparative model with significantly less number of parameters, which indicates that our model achieves better results in terms of efficient use of limited resources.

Table 3. The accuracy of our model with other lightweight models such as (Resnet-18, EfficientNet-B4, inceptionV3) on the true-false face dataset

Model	ACC(%)
Resnet-18	60.95
EfficientNet-B4	54.04
inceptionV3	65.87
Ours(MARepVGG)	67.07

Experiments on PGGAN. As shown in Fig. 4, our model achieves 94.53% accuracy after 100 rounds of training on the PGGAN dataset. There is a 4% improvement in our proposed method compared to FDFTNet [25], which has training parameters (initial learning rate=0.3, momentum rate =0.9, batch size=128), and an optimal accuracy of 90.29% on the PGGAN dataset after another 300 rounds of training using stochastic gradient descent (SGD). Compared with another model DeepFD [24], which uses contrast loss to enhance the feature retrieval of GAN synthetic images with discriminative feature learning network D1 and classifier D2 with parameters (learning rate=1e-3, maximum epoch=15, batch size=32), the accuracy on the PGGAN dataset after training is 92.6%, and our proposed method still has a 2% improvement.

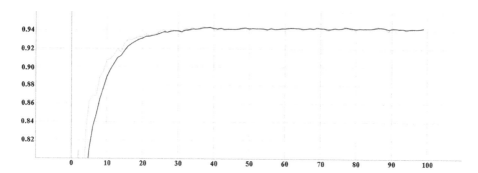

Fig. 4. The performance of our model on the PGGAN dataset with the training batch on the horizontal axis and the accuracy on the vertical axis. The training parameters are recorded in the Implementation Setting section of the text.

Although our proposed method has made some progress relative to the lightweight network model in the comparison experiments, we have to admit that there are still shortcomings in the detection accuracy. Therefore, the next step of our work is to focus on further improving the accuracy of the model. We will further expand and improve the dataset to include more real and fake face samples, so that the model can better learn the features in different scenarios. Second, we will introduce more complex network structures and optimization algorithms to improve the generalization ability and robustness of the model. Finally, we will also combine other technical means, such as multi-task learning, transfer learning, and knowledge distillation, to further improve the accuracy and usefulness of the model.

5   Conclusion

In this paper, after the above experimental comparison, our proposed method makes some progress in inference speed, number of parameters and accuracy relative to the lightweight network model. Our addition of texture enhancement module and multi-attention module to RepVGG improves the model's ability to detect real and fake faces very well. We hope our model can provide a new idea for future applications of face forgery recognition.

Acknowledgements. This research was supported in part by the National Natural Science Foundation of China (Grant Nos. 62172120 and 62002082), Guangxi Natural Science Foundation (Grant Nos. 2019GXNSFFA245014 and ZY20198016), and Guangxi Key Laboratory of Image and Graphic Intelligent Processing Project (Grant No. GIIP2001).

References

1. Wang, J., et al.: M2tr: multi-modal multi-scale transformers for DeepFake detection. In: Proceedings of the 2022 International Conference on Multimedia Retrieval, pp. 615–623 (2022)
2. Ding, X., Zhang, X., Ma, N., Han, J., Ding, G., Sun, J.: RepVGG: making VGG-style convnets great again. In: Proceedings of the IEEE/CVF Conference on Computer Vision and Pattern Recognition, pp. 13733–13742 (2021)
3. Hsu, C.C., Zhuang, Y.X., Lee, C.Y.: Deep fake image detection based on pairwise learning. Appl. Sci. 10(1), 370 (2020)
4. Khalil, S.S., Youssef, S.M., Saleh, S.N.: iCaps-Dfake: an integrated capsule-based model for deepfake image and video detection. Future Internet 13(4), 93 (2021)
5. Dong, X., et al.: Protecting celebrities from deepfake with identity consistency transformer. In: Proceedings of the IEEE/CVF Conference on Computer Vision and Pattern Recognition, pp. 9468–9478 (2022)
6. Li, C., et al.: Yolov6: a single-stage object detection framework for industrial applications. arXiv preprint arXiv:2209.02976 (2022)
7. Weng, K., Chu, X., Xu, X., Huang, J., Wei, X.: EfficientRep: an efficient RepVGG-style convnets with hardware-aware neural network design. arXiv preprint arXiv:2302.00386 (2023)
8. Wang, C.Y., et al.: Cspnet: a new backbone that can enhance learning capability of cnn. In: Proceedings of the IEEE/CVF Conference on Computer Vision and Pattern Recognition Workshops, pp. 390–391 (2020)
9. Chen, R., Chen, X., Ni, B., Ge, Y.: SimSwap: an efficient framework for high fidelity face swapping. In: Proceedings of the 28th ACM International Conference on Multimedia, pp. 2003–2011 (2020)
10. Gao, G., Huang, H., Fu, C., Li, Z., He, R.: Information bottleneck disentanglement for identity swapping. In: Proceedings of the IEEE/CVF Conference on Computer Vision and Pattern Recognition, pp. 3404–3413 (2021)
11. Wang, T., Zhang, Y., Fan, Y., Wang, J., Chen, Q.: High-fidelity GAN inversion for image attribute editing. In: Proceedings of the IEEE/CVF Conference on Computer Vision and Pattern Recognition, pp. 11379–11388 (2022)
12. Patashnik, O., Wu, Z., Shechtman, E., Cohen-Or, D., Lischinski, D.: StyleClip: text-driven manipulation of StyleGan imagery. In: Proceedings of the IEEE/CVF International Conference on Computer Vision, pp. 2085–2094 (2021)
13. Zheng, H., Fu, J., Mei, T., Luo, J.: Learning multi-attention convolutional neural network for fine-grained image recognition. In: Proceedings of the IEEE International Conference on Computer Vision, pp. 5209–5217 (2017)
14. Yang, Z., Luo, T., Wang, D., Hu, Z., Gao, J., Wang, L.: Learning to navigate for fine-grained classification. In: Ferrari, V., Hebert, M., Sminchisescu, C., Weiss, Y. (eds.) Computer Vision – ECCV 2018. LNCS, vol. 11218, pp. 438–454. Springer, Cham (2018). https://doi.org/10.1007/978-3-030-01264-9_26
15. Gan, Y., Chen, J., Yang, Z., Xu, L.: Multiple attention network for facial expression recognition. IEEE Access 8, 7383–7393 (2020)
16. Liu, H., et al.: Spatial-phase shallow learning: rethinking face forgery detection in frequency domain. In: Proceedings of the IEEE/CVF Conference on Computer Vision and Pattern Recognition, pp. 772–781 (2021)
17. Huang, G., Liu, Z., Van Der Maaten, L., Weinberger, K.Q.: Densely connected convolutional networks. In: Proceedings of the IEEE Conference on Computer Vision and Pattern Recognition, pp. 4700–4708 (2017)

18. Zhao, H., Zhou, W., Chen, D., Wei, T., Zhang, W., Yu, N.: Multi-attentional deepfake detection. In: Proceedings of the IEEE/CVF Conference on Computer Vision and Pattern Recognition, pp. 2185–2194 (2021)

19. He, K., Zhang, X., Ren, S., Sun, J.: Deep residual learning for image recognition. In: Proceedings of the IEEE Conference on Computer Vision and Pattern Recognition, pp. 770–778 (2016)

20. Tan, M., Le, Q.: EfficientNet: rethinking model scaling for convolutional neural networks. In: International Conference on Machine Learning, pp. 6105–6114. PMLR (2019)

21. Szegedy, C., Vanhoucke, V., Ioffe, S., Shlens, J., Wojna, Z.: Rethinking the inception architecture for computer vision. In: Proceedings of the IEEE Conference on Computer Vision and Pattern Recognition, pp. 2818–2826 (2016)

22. Real and Fake Face Detection (2019). https://www.kaggle.com/datasets/ciplab/real-and-fake-face-detection

23. Karras, T., Aila, T., Laine, S., Lehtinen, J.: Progressive growing of GANs for improved quality, stability, and variation. arXiv preprint arXiv:1710.10196 (2017)

24. Hsu, C.C., Lee, C.Y., Zhuang, Y.X.: Learning to detect fake face images in the wild. In: 2018 International Symposium on Computer, Consumer and Control (IS3C), pp. 388–391. IEEE (2018)

25. Jeon, H., Bang, Y., Woo, S.S.: FDFtNet: facing off fake images using fake detection fine-tuning network. In: Hölbl, M., Rannenberg, K., Welzer, T. (eds.) SEC 2020. IAICT, vol. 580, pp. 416–430. Springer, Cham (2020). https://doi.org/10.1007/978-3-030-58201-2_28

SGFNeRF: Shape Guided 3D Face Generation in Neural Radiance Fields

Peizhu Zhou, Xuhui Liu, and Baochang Zhang$^{(\boxtimes)}$

School of Automation Science and Electrical Engineering, Beihang University, Beijing 100191, China
{zpz001,1332671326,bczhang}@buaa.edu.cn

Abstract. NeRF (Neural Radiance Fields), as an implicit 3D representation, has demonstrated the capability to generate highly realistic and dynamically consistent images. However, its hierarchical sampling approach introduces a significant amount of redundant computation, leading to erroneous geometric information, particularly in high-frequency facial details. In this paper, we propose SGFNeRF, a novel 3D face generation model by integrating a 2D CNN-based generator and face depth priors optimization method in the same framework. We employ a Gaussian distribution for sampling to extract facial surface information. Additionally, we design a feature decoder to incorporates depth uncertainty into our method, enabling the method to explore regions further away from face surfaces while preserving its ability to capture fine-grained details. We conduct experiments on the FFHQ dataset to evaluate the performance of our proposed method. The results demonstrate a significant improvement compared to previous approaches in terms of various evaluation metrics.

Keywords: 3D scene representation · Face generation · Neural radiance fields · Generative adversarial network

1 Introduction

Portrait synthesis has a wide range of applications in the field of computer graphics, including but not limited to virtual reality (VR), augmented reality (AR), and avatars-based telecommunication. Neural Radiance Fields (NeRF) [1] has attracted significant attention in the realm of three-dimensional object representation. Diverging from conventional explicit visualization approaches such as meshes and point clouds, NeRF implicitly entails the encoding of a model's three-dimensional information within a neural network. One advantage of explicit representation is its ability to model scenes explicitly, thereby synthesizing photorealistic virtual perspectives. However, a disadvantage of this discrete representation is the potential occurrence of artifacts such as overlap-induced pseudo-shadows due to its lack of fine-grained precision. Moreover, and most importantly, the memory constraints imposed by these representations limit their applicability to high-resolution scenes.

H. Lu et al. (Eds.): ACPR 2023, LNCS 14408, pp. 238–249, 2023.
https://doi.org/10.1007/978-3-031-47665-5_20

Many of recent works [2–6] on NeRF have been applied to face generation, with capable of generating high-resolution, photorealistic and dynamic face
images. Generative Adversarial Networks (GANs) [7] have been integrated with
NeRF to produce feature maps, which form the basis for establishing neural
radiance fields. Nevertheless, the computationally intensive nature of volumetric rendering, primarily due to the ray-casting process, significantly slows down
high-resolution generation and incurs high memory requirements. One instance
where volume rendering is employed is by sampling points along individual viewing rays. This process allows for the determination of the ray's color based on the
volume density and radiance of each sampled point. Additionally, oversampling
is utilized during training to account for empty spaces.

In this work. We propose SGFNeRF that optimizes face sampling with depth
priors, which are easy to get from 3DDFA-V2 [8]. Face geometries in NeRF are
guided avoiding of various artifacts. As shown in Fig. 1, many of other relevant
methods without depth priors are prone to generate false images, in which facial
features and the background are generated with equal importance, it results
in the occurrence of facial elements within the background. Moreover, during
extensive facial pose control, there is a tendency for the background to adhere
closely to the face, leading to their fusion or cohesive appearance. In our method,
the application of depth Gaussian sampling is employed. Dense sampling is performed on the surface of the face. Taking into uncertainty of prior depths, we
also develop a feature decoder.

| EG3D | StyleNeRF | IDE-3D | OURS |

Fig. 1. Comparison of visual effects in portrait generation. The images of EG3D,
StyleNeRF and IDE-3D were generated by corresponding official checkpoints. When
facial features and the background are given equal significance in generation, it increases
the likelihood of facial elements appearing in the background. Furthermore, when extensive control is applied to facial poses, there is a tendency to produce artifacts.

To summarize, our contributions are as follows:

- We propose a face depth prior Gaussian sampling and introduce a new loss
  function designed with uncertainty of depth information.
- A feature decoder is designed to generate colors, densities and variances of
  face depths in neural radiance fields from feature maps.
- Through experiments, our model has demonstrated the ability to generate
  face geometry-aware and dynamically consistent portrait images. Especially

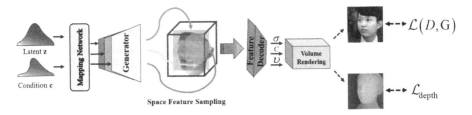

Fig. 2. Overall pipeline of SGFNeRF. A feature generator and mapping network based on pose-conditioned StyleGAN2 are developed, along with a feature decoder and space feature sampling. The Feature Decoder is devised to generate attributes such as colors, densities, and variations in face depths. Additionally, a neural volume renderer is utilized to produce both image and depth maps. The Resolution Upsampler and Discriminator are not depicted in the image.

in scenarios involving large facial angles, it can effectively prevent geometric collapse of the face and reduce the impact between the subject and the background.

2 Related Work

2.1 Neural Radiance Field Representations

Neural implicit representations (i.e. [1,10,12,13]) have shown great potential in 3D reconstruction and novel view synthesis. The three-dimensional scene is stored within the weights of a multi-layer perceptron, enabling the generation of images from arbitrary viewpoints through volume rendering. Explicit representations, such as discrete voxel grids, are efficient in terms of evaluation speed, but they often require a significant amount of memory, making them challenging to scale for high-resolution or complex scenes. On the other hand, implicit representations have the potential to address these memory overheads by representing scenes as continuous functions. This approach provides benefits in terms of efficient memory usage, enabling the handling of complex scenes, and ensuring the generation of dynamically consistent images.

2.2 Generative Face Geometry-Aware Synthesis

Traditionally, image GAN models have relied on convolutional architectures, which have facilitated efficient training and generation for 2D tasks (i.e. [7,14]. In recent times, there has been a growing interest in expanding the capabilities of GANs to enable 3D-aware generation from single-view image datasets. The objective of such advancements is to achieve disentangled control over the content and viewpoint of the generated images. The pcGAN [15] struggle to generate 3D content without 3D priors. Deng et al. [16] adopt a methodology that

incorporates 3D priors to decompose portrait synthesis into distinct and independent factors. However, there is a lack of ability to generate visually dynamic
consistent images [9].

Several studies (i.e. [2,3]) have attempted to integrate NeRF with GAN for
the generation of three-dimensional models. However, these approaches suffer
from significant computational redundancy and errors in the estimation of depth
information.

3 Methods

To address the aforementioned issues, we propose a Gaussian sampling method
based on facial depth priors. Additionally, we introduce a depth loss function that
accounts for depth errors. Moreover, we design a feature decoder that captures
the variance of depth information. Figure 2 illustrates the schematic diagram
of our proposed method. The effectiveness of the proposed method has been
verified through experimental validation.

Feature Generator. In contrast to NeRF, which directly input spatial coordinates into implicit neural fields. Inspired by [17], our approach involves utilizing
a generator to produce space feature maps. The initial step involves feeding the
random latent code and camera parameters into a mapping network, which generates an intermediate latent code. This intermediate latent code is then used to
modulate the convolution kernels of a distinct synthesis network. StyleGAN2 [7]
is selected as the preferred choice for predicting space features due to its well-
established and efficient architecture, which consistently achieves cutting-edge
outcomes in 2D image synthesis. Semantic vectors are sampled in space features
according to coordinates of rays.

Shape Guided Gaussian Sampling. The original NeRF employed a uniform
hierarchical sampling strategy within the neural field. Our strategy is distinct
from evenly dividing the space between near and far bounds. Points along rays
are selected from normal distributions, in which the mean are set by depth priors
and the standard deviations are predicted considering the depth uncertainty
(see in Fig. 3). By employing this approach, the smaller sampling intervals are
implemented on the pertinent section of the ray to accentuate the finer details
on the surface, effectively addressing the broader uncertainty inherent in the
depth estimation, While still preserving the capability to sample in regions that
deviate from the average [11].

To acquire the uncertain values of face depth information, we devised a feature decoder, denoted as F_Θ, which optimizes the parameter Θ to extract features. These features include volume density σ, multi-channel color features c,
and depth uncertainty υ. The whole function of feature decoder can be described
as:

$$F_\Theta : (\mathbf{f}_{xy}, \mathbf{f}_{yz}, \mathbf{f}_{zx}) \mapsto (\sigma, c, \upsilon), \tag{1}$$

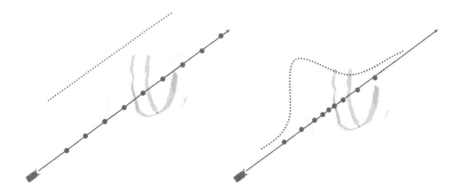

Fig. 3. Comparison of two sampling methods. Left: For spatial uniform sampling, a large number of sampling points require unnecessary computation and do not capture useful information. Right: Gaussian sampling primarily targets surface points and has the potential to sample regions that are distant from the mean.

Volume density σ and multi-channel color features c are used for classical volume rendering [18]. Depth uncertainty v is employed in the calculation of the depth loss function.

Depth Map Optimization. NeRFs have demonstrated remarkable performance in view synthesis tasks. Our method leverages the capabilities of NeRFs to achieve precise depth estimation by directly optimizing implicit volumes. The calculated RGB value, denoted as $C(r)$, can be computed using volume rendering techniques based on finite samples.

$$\hat{Color}(\mathbf{r}) = \sum_{i=1}^{N} T_i \left(1 - \exp\left(-\sigma_i \delta_i\right)\right) \mathbf{c}_i, \tag{2}$$

The function $T(t)$ represents the cumulative transmittance along the ray from t_n to t.

$$T_i = \exp\left(-\sum_{j=1}^{i-1} \sigma_j \delta_j\right), \tag{3}$$

Similar to calculation of RGB values, we compute the depth map values in the neural radiance field, and $D(r)$ can be approximated by evaluating the expectation of the samples along the ray.

$$\hat{Depth}(\mathbf{r}) = \sum_{i=1}^{N} T_i \left(1 - \exp\left(-\sigma_i \delta_i\right)\right) \mathbf{t}_i, \tag{4}$$

The depth values in the depth maps correspond to each pixel in the RGB textures and are utilized for computing the depth loss. Pixels outside the facial region are also generated without the supervision of depth information. Therefore, we devised a region-based depth loss function $\mathcal{L}_{\text{depth}}(\mathbf{r})$.

$$\mathcal{L}_{\text{depth}}(\mathbf{r}) = \begin{cases} \sum_{i=1}^{L} \left(\frac{1}{e^{v_i^2}} + \lambda \|(\hat{D}(\mathbf{r}) - D(\mathbf{r})\|_2 \times e^{v_i^2} \right) & \text{face region} \\ 0 & \text{otherwise}, \end{cases} \tag{5}$$

The depth loss function is not computed in non-depth prior regions, but it is calculated within the facial region. The formula consists of two terms: the first term penalizes the uncertain values, while the second term computes the depth error. The scaling factor, λ, is set to 0.5 in this study.

Resolution Upsampler. Following [7]. We do not directly produce high-resolution images, which cost much more computation to render an image at the exact resolution, but Medium-resolution image maps and depth maps. Additionally, NeRF-based models consume substantial memory for caching intermediate results during gradient back-propagation, posing challenges when working with high-resolution images. These factors together restrict the applicability of NeRF-based models in high-quality image synthesis.

In the resolution upsampler, we utilize the Second Order Attention Network (SAN) [19] for our purposes which upsamples and refines the 32-channel feature image into the final RGB image.

Discriminator. Our model is trained using an adversarial objective, where we leverage the discriminator architecture derived from StyleGAN [4]. To prevent degenerate shape solutions, we incorporate the camera parameters of the incoming image as conditioning information for the discriminator. We utilize the class-conditional discriminator modifications proposed in [20] to incorporate this information.

The loss function of the generative adversarial network is as follows:

$$\mathcal{L}(D, G) = \mathbb{E}_{\mathbf{z} \sim \mathcal{Z}, c \sim \mathcal{C}} \left[f(D(G(\mathbf{z}, \mathbf{p}))) \right] + \mathbb{E}_{I \sim p_{\text{data}}} \left[f\left(-D(I) + \beta \|\nabla D(I)\|^2 \right) \right], \tag{6}$$

where $f(u) = -\log(1 + \exp(-u))$, and p_{data} is the distribution of the data. We set $\beta = 0.5$.

The final objective function is defined as follows:

$$\mathcal{L}_{final} = \mathcal{L}(D, G) + \mathcal{L}_{\text{depth}}, \tag{7}$$

4   Experiments

4.1   Datasets

We conducted extensive experimentation on the FFHQ [7] dataset to validate our approach. The FFHQ dataset is highly valuable for conducting research in domains like face generation, image editing, face recognition, and deep learning.

Table 1. Quantitative comparison of our approach with other relevant methods. Our method does not outperform all of other methods interms of FID and KID on FFHQ dataset, but in terms of visual effects, our method is superior.

Methods	FID↓	KID($\times 10^3$) ↓
Giraffe [21]	31.9	32.7
FENeRF [3]	28.2	17.3
StyleSDF [22]	11.5	2.6
NeRF-GAN [2]	8.3	4.3
StyleNeRF [4]	8	3.7
EG3D [17]	4.7	0.132
IDE-3D [13]	4.6	0.130
Ours	7.2	2.5

It is extensively employed for training Generative Adversarial Network (GAN) models, specifically for the purpose of generating authentic and lifelike face images. These models excel at creating novel face images that possess intricate details and exhibit a remarkable level of realism. We label the face depth maps by 3DDFA-V2 [8].

4.2   Baselines

We compare our method on image generation with relevant methods: NeRF-GAN [2], FENeRF [3], StyleNeRF [4], Giraffe [21], StyleSDF [22], EG3D [17] and IDE-3D [13]. Our model was trained using a batch size of 8. The discriminator was trained with a learning rate of 0.002, while the generator was trained with a learning rate of 0.0025. Our total training time on 2 TITAN V GPUs was about 16 days. Many experiments were conducted to quantitatively and qualitatively evaluate our method. In order to validate the effectiveness of our sampling approach, we also conducted geometric comparisons on the generated three-dimensional models. All experiments were performed under the same platform.

4.3   Quantitative Evaluations

We quantitatively assessed the consistency and quality of the images generated by our approach across FID and KID metrics. The results are showed in Table 1.

Frechet Inception Distance (FID). The FID [23] metric quantitatively measures the similarity between two sets of images: the real images from a dataset and the generated images produced by a GAN or any other generative model.

Fig. 4. Qualitative comparison between StyleNeRF, EG3D and ours in yaw for FFHQ.

Fig. 5. Qualitative comparison between StyleNeRF, EG3D and ours in pitch for FFHQ.

Kernel Inception Distance (KID). KID [23] is based on the Inception Score (IS), which was introduced as a metric for evaluating the quality and diversity of generated images. While IS measures the quality of individual images, KID extends this concept to measure the similarity between the entire distributions of real and generated images.

4.4   Qualitative Results

We have produced multiple images to qualitatively assess our methodology. Our approach demonstrates the ability to generate novel perspectives through direct camera manipulation, effectively generalizing to extreme camera poses that significantly deviate from the distribution of camera poses in the training data. Figures 4 and 5 illustrates the outcomes of our method when applied to challenging camera poses, as well as steep view angles. The results of EG3D and StyleNeRF were produced by corresponding official checkpoints. Figure 4 shows variations in yaw, and Fig. 5 presents variations in pitch. As depicted in the images, our method is capable of generating clear human portraits without generating cluttered backgrounds, and the rendered images exhibit remarkable consistency across various camera positions.

Fig. 6. The comparison of our depth prior Gaussian sampling method in terms of geometric generation. Better differentiation between the face and background.

4.5   Ablation Analysis

To better evaluate the effectiveness of geometry consistency, We conducted a comparative analysis between our method and EG3D, in terms of generating 3D shapes. Iso-surfaces representing shapes are extracted from the density field using the marching cubes algorithm. We present empirical evidence showcasing the successful performance of our approach in this aspect (see Fig. 6). The

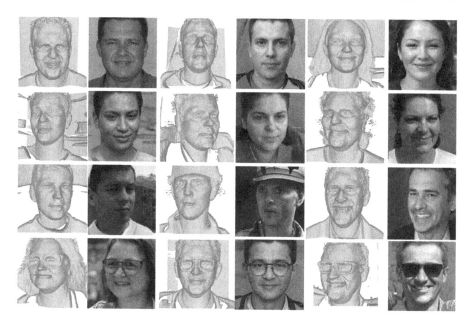

Fig. 7. Numerous experiments have shown that our method can generate relatively independent and complete facial geometric information, which significantly contributes to generating multi-view portraits.

model generated with prior information enables more efficient sampling point placement, thereby avoiding excessive computations and better distinguishing between human subjects and backgrounds. EG3D employs the same sampling method for both human subjects and backgrounds, resulting in a higher density of sampling points. However, this approach often leads to the undesired artifacts, as the background and human subjects tend to become interconnected and visually entangled (see in Fig. 1). More results are shown in Fig. 7. Our experiments demonstrate that the presence of complete and relatively independent geometric information contributes to generating multi-angle portraits.

5   Conclusion

In this paper, we propose SGFNeRF, a deep prior Gaussian sampling approach. Our method utilizes a Gaussian distribution for sampling, focusing on extracting facial surface information and preserving fine-grained details. The incorporation of depth uncertainty in our feature decoder enables exploration of regions further away from face surfaces, expanding the model's capability to capture intricate facial features. We conducted extensive experiments on the FFHQ dataset to evaluate the performance of our proposed method. Our model generates facial images with enhanced visual quality, improved geometric accuracy, and with potential applications in virtual reality and computer vision.

References

1. Mildenhall, B., Srinivasan, P.P., Tancik, M., Barron, J.T., Ramamoorthi, R., Ng, R.: NeRF: representing scenes as neural radiance fields for view synthesis. In: Vedaldi, A., Bischof, H., Brox, T., Frahm, J.-M. (eds.) ECCV 2020. LNCS, vol. 12346, pp. 405–421. Springer, Cham (2020). https://doi.org/10.1007/978-3-030-58452-8_24
2. Shahbazi M, Ntavelis E, Tonioni A, et al.: NeRF-GAN distillation for efficient 3D-aware generation with convolutions. arXiv preprint arXiv:2303.12865 (2023)
3. Sun J, Wang X, Zhang Y, et al.: FENeRF: face editing in neural radiance fields. In: Proceedings of the IEEE/CVF Conference on Computer Vision and Pattern Recognition, pp. 7672–7682 (2022)
4. Gu J, Liu L, Wang P, et al.: StyleNeRF: a style-based 3d-aware generator for high-resolution image synthesis. arXiv preprint arXiv:2110.08985 (2021)
5. Hong Y, Peng B, Xiao H, et al.: HeadNeRF: a real-time nerf-based parametric head model. In: Proceedings of the IEEE/CVF Conference on Computer Vision and Pattern Recognition, pp. 20374–20384(2022)
6. Mihajlovic, M., Bansal, A., Zollhoefer, M., et al.: KeypointNeRF: generalizing image-based volumetric avatars using relative spatial encoding of keypoints. In: Vedaldi, A., Gupta, A., Lempitsky, V., Schiele, B., Fitzgibbon, A. (eds.) ECCV 2022: 17th European Conference, Tel Aviv, Israel, October 23–27, 2022, Proceedings, Part XV, pp. 179–197. Springer Nature Switzerland, Cham (2022). https://doi.org/10.1007/978-3-031-19784-0_11
7. Karras, T., Laine, S., Aila, T.: A style-based generator architecture for generative adversarial networks. In: Proceedings of the IEEE/CVF Conference on Computer Vision and Pattern Recognition, pp. 4401–4410 (2019)
8. Guo, J., Zhu, X., Yang, Y., Yang, F., Lei, Z., Li, S.Z.: Towards fast, accurate and stable 3D dense face alignment. In: Vedaldi, A., Bischof, H., Brox, T., Frahm, J.-M. (eds.) ECCV 2020. LNCS, vol. 12364, pp. 152–168. Springer, Cham (2020). https://doi.org/10.1007/978-3-030-58529-7_10
9. Luo, Y., Lü, J., Jiang, X., Zhang, B.: Learning from architectural redundancy: enhanced deep supervision in deep multipath encoder-decoder networks. In: IEEE Transactions on Neural Networks and Learning Systems (2021). https://doi.org/10.1109/TNNLS.2021.3056384
10. Zhang, K., Riegler, G., Snavely, N., et al.: NeRF++: Analyzing and improving neural radiance fields. arXiv preprint arXiv:2010.07492 (2020)
11. Qu, Q., Liu, K., Wang, W., et al.: Spacecraft proximity maneuvering and rendezvous with collision avoidance based on reinforcement learning. IEEE Trans. Aerosp. Electron. Syst. 58(6), 5823–5834 (2022)
12. Barron, J.T., Mildenhall, B., Tancik, M., et al.: Mip-NeRF: a multiscale representation for anti-aliasing neural radiance fields. In: Proceedings of the IEEE/CVF International Conference on Computer Vision, pp. 5855–5864 (2021)
13. Sun, J., Wang, X., Shi, Y., et al.: IDE-3D: interactive disentangled editing for high-resolution 3D-aware portrait synthesis. ACM Trans. Graph. (TOG) 41(6), 1–10 (2022)
14. Sauer, A., Schwarz, K., Geiger, A.: StyleGAN-XL: scaling StyleGAN to large diverse datasets. In: ACM SIGGRAPH 2022 Conference Proceedings, pp. 1–10 (2022)
15. Liang, D., Wang, R., Tian, X., et al.: PCGAN: partition-controlled human image generation. In: Proceedings of the AAAI Conference on Artificial Intelligence, vol. 33, no. 01, pp. 8698–8705 (2019)

16. Deng, Y., Yang, J., Chen, D., et al.: Disentangled and controllable face image generation via 3D imitative-contrastive learning. In: Proceedings of the IEEE/CVF Conference on Computer Vision and Pattern Recognition, pp. 5154–5163 (2020)
17. Chan, E.R., Lin, C.Z., Chan, M.A., et al.: Efficient geometry-aware 3D generative adversarial networks. In: Proceedings of the IEEE/CVF Conference on Computer Vision and Pattern Recognition, pp. 16123–16133 (2022)
18. Kajiya, J.T., Herzen, B.P.V.: Ray tracing volume densities. In: Computer Graphics (SIGGRAPH) (1984)
19. Dai, T., Cai, J., Zhang, Y., et al.: Second-order attention network for single image super-resolution. In: Proceedings of the IEEE/CVF Conference on Computer Vision and Pattern Recognition, pp. 11065–11074 (2019)
20. Karras, T., Aittala, M., Hellsten, J., et al.: Training generative adversarial networks with limited data. In: Advances in Neural Information Processing Systems, vol. 33, pp. 12104–12114 (2020)
21. Niemeyer, M., Geiger, A.: Giraffe: Representing scenes as compositional generative neural feature fields. In: Proceedings of the IEEE/CVF Conference on Computer Vision and Pattern Recognition, pp. 11453–11464 (2021)
22. Or-El, R., Luo, X., Shan, M., et al.: StylesDF: high-resolution 3D-consistent image and geometry generation. In: Proceedings of the IEEE/CVF Conference on Computer Vision and Pattern Recognition, pp. 13503–13513 (2022)
23. Heusel, M., Ramsauer, H., Unterthiner, T., et al.: GANs trained by a two time-scale update rule converge to a local Nash equilibrium. In: Advances in Neural Information Processing Systems, vol. 30 (2017)

Hybrid Spatio-Temporal Network for Face Forgery Detection

Xuhui Liu[1], Sicheng Gao[1], Peizhu Zhou[1], Jianzhuang Liu[2], Xiaoyan Luo[1],
Luping Zhang[3], and Baochang Zhang[1,4(✉)]

[1] Beihang University, Beijing, China
{1332671326,scgao,luoxy,bczhang}@buaa.edu.cn
[2] Shenzhen Institute of Advanced Technology, Shenzhen, China
jz.liu@siat.ac.cn
[3] National University of Defense Technology, Changsha, China
zhangluping@nudt.edu.cn
[4] Nanchang Institute of Technology, Nanchang, China

Abstract. Facial manipulation techniques have aroused increasing security concerns, leading to various methods to detect forgery videos. However, existing methods suffer from a significant performance gap compared to image manipulation methods, partially because the spatio-temporal information is not well explored. To address the issue, we introduce a Hybrid Spatio-Temporal Network (HSTNet) to integrate spatial and temporal information in the same framework. Specifically, our HSTNet utilizes a hybrid architecture, which consists of a 3D CNN branch and a transformer branch, to jointly learn short- and long-range relations in the spatio-temporal dimension. Due to the feature misalignment between the two branches, we design a Feature Alignment Block (FAB) to recalibrate and efficiently fuse heterogeneous features. Moreover, HSTNet introduces a Vector Selection Block (VSB) to combine the outputs of the two branches and fire important features for classification. Extensive experiments show that HSTNet obtains the best overall performance over state-of-the-art methods.

Keywords: Face Forgery Detection · Hybrid Spatio-Temporal Network · Short- and Long-range Relations · Spatial and Temporal Consistency

1 Introduction

Benefiting from the explosive progress of generative models, especially Generative Adversarial Networks (GANs) [18], current face manipulation techniques [5,28,46,49] are capable of producing ultra-realistic fake videos which are difficult to distinguish by humans. However, it has aroused broad public concerns that these tecniques could be abused for malicious purposes. Therefore, it is crucial to develop more general and practical methods for face forgery detection.

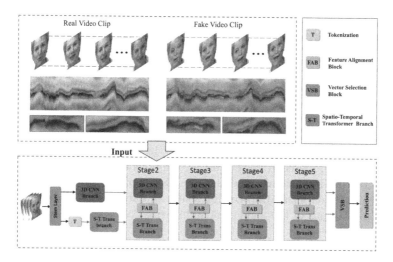

Fig. 1. Top: Visualization of the temporal coherence comparison between real and fake videos. **Bottom:** Overview of the proposed HSTNet. We present the vertical motion at a particular horizontal location. Obviously, the motion of a fake face is sharper than the real one. Considering the above observation, our HSTNet employs a hybrid network to explore the spatio-temporal inconsistency and capture short- and long-range information.

Various frame-based methods which employ 2D deep Convolutional Neural Networks (CNNs) [1,6,27,29,34,42] have been proposed to tackle the problem. They mainly focus on the fine-grained forged spatial details [12,52], or introduce more data domains, such as frequency statistics [27,42], to detect forgery patterns. However, these methods ignore the temporal information and may result in unexpected false predictions. As shown in the upper part of Fig. 1, fake videos often exist visually unnatural image transition or temporal inconsistency, which indicates temporal inconsistency is a vulnerability to be utilized for our face forgery detection. To address this issue, most recent works [2,17,19,30,31,53] pay more attention to video-based methods which extract both the spatial and temporal information. Nonetheless, these methods still have limited ability to comprehensively capture spatial and temporal forgery patterns. Over last two years, the introduction of Vision Transformer (ViT) [15] has brought a boom in the applications of transformer to visual tasks. However, the potential of ViT on fake video forgery is not well explored. The reason might come from its deficiency in local feature extraction.

In this paper, we follow the research line of hybrid networks [8,37,41], and introduce a Hybrid Spatio-Temporal Network (HSTNet) to comprehensively explore the spatial and temporal information for robust face forgery detection. Figure 1 illustrates that our HSTNet adopts a dual-stream architecture, which includes a 3D CNN branch and a spatio-temporal attention based transformer branch to maximize their advantages to extract short- and long-range information, respectively. Therefore, we design Feature Alignment Block (FAB) to align two feature maps at scale and semantic level. It is inserted into every stage of HSTNet to gradually fuse the local and global feature details. Specifically, in order to introduce the local features into the transformer branch, we leverage the attention mechanism to adaptively attach importance weights to each temporal dimension and channel and recalibrate the feature map. After two parallel branches of feature extraction, we introduce the attention mechanism again into the designed Vector Selection Block (VSB) to aggregate local and global features and refine the feature vector for final prediction. In summary, by the dual-stream architecture, the proposed HSTNet entirely employs the advantages of convolution in extracting local details and the advantages of transformer in capturing long-range dependencies and processing sequence data.

The contributions of this paper are summarized as follows:

- We propose a Hybrid Spatio-Temporal Network (HSTNet) to consider both spatial details and temporal consistency for robust face forgery detection. The dual-stream architecture can utilize the full potential of CNN's and transformer's strengths to extract local and global information, respectively.
- We design a Feature Alignment Block (FAB) to perform feature interactions between two heterogeneous features at scale and semantic levels. We also introduce a Vector Selection Block (VSB) to fuse the output vectors of the two branches, fire important features, and suppress redundant features.
- Extensive experiments, including intra-dataset validation and cross-dataset validation, show our HSTNet achieves state-of-the-art (SOTA) performances on four widely used face forgery detection benchmarks.

2   Related Work

Face Forgery Detection. Mainstream face forgery detection can be divided into image-based and video-based methods. At the image level, a significant amount of methods introduce frequency statistics [17,27,42] for capturing artifacts of forgery. Nonetheless, these image-based methods may fail to capture the spatio-temporal inconsistency across continuous frames. More recently, researchers tend to explore the temporal inconsistency and propose several video-based detectors [2,19,30,31,39,44]. Despite achieving a good accuracy on the trained dataset, most of these methods experience a significant performance decline when the manipulation methods are unseen [1,26,43]. To address this issue, many works [16,20,29,32,50,53] are dedicated to improve the generalization capability of detectors. FTCN [53] constraints the extraction of spatial information and concentrates on mining the temporal coherence. It achieves impressive generalization ability, but it is susceptible to common perturbation, such as compression.

Transformers with Convolutions. Compared with vision transformers [15, 25,35], CNNs has unique advantages in extracting local features and translation

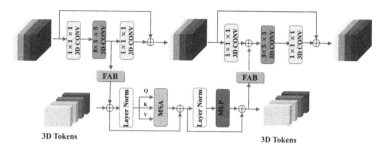

Fig. 2. The feature extraction block, where "⊕" represents point-wise sum. The upper part is 3D CNN blocks, and the lower is a spatio-temporal transformer block. FAB is employed to align heterogeneous features and achieve interactions between the two branches.

invariance. In order to integrate the above merits, many hybrid architectures [37,41,51], including self-attention mechanisms and convolutions, are proposed for enhanced visual representation. Conformer [41] adopts a concurrent structure that comprehensively combines a transformer with a CNN branch via lateral connections to retain the representation capability of local features and global representations. Ds-Net [37] proposes a dual-stream network including convolutions and self-attention layers to extract local and global features simultaneously and efficiently fuse them. Different from existing works, we design a hybrid architecture that consists of a 3D CNN branch and a transformer branch to jointly learn short-long and spatio-temporeal relations in a unified framework. The details of our method are elaborated below.

3   Method

3.1   Overview

Problem Statement. We formulate the face forgery detection task as a binary classification problem and design a video-based network to introduce both spatial and temporal information for more robust and general performance. For a given face video clip $X \in \mathbb{R}^{T \times C \times H \times W}$, where T, C, H, W represent the input frame number, channel dimension, frame spatial height and width, respectively. The goal of our HSTNet is to generate video-level prediction to distinguish the authenticity of the face video.

Two Input Styles. Using [21] as inspiration, the 3D CNN branch takes the video clip X as input directly. The transformer branch takes nonoverlapping 3D patches as input tokens for capturing long-range dependencies. Similar to Timesformer [7], we first partition each frame independently into N nonoverlapping patches, each of size $P \times P$, resulting in a total of $T \times N$ tokens $x_{p,t} \in \mathbb{R}^{TCP^2}$ with C feature channels, where $N = HW/P^2$, $p \in [1, ..., N]$ and $t \in [1, ..., T]$.

Then we employ a linear layer for projection to obtain embedding vectors $\mathbf{Z} \in \mathbb{R}^{T \times (N+1) \times D}$ as follow:

$$\mathbf{Z} = [z_{cls}, \mathbf{E}x_{1,1}, \mathbf{E}x_{1,2}, \ldots, \mathbf{E}x_{1,T}, \mathbf{E}x_{2,1}, \mathbf{E}x_{2,2}, \ldots, \mathbf{E}x_{N,T}], \quad (1)$$

where $\mathbf{E} \in \mathbb{R}^{D \times CP^2}$ denotes the learnable projection matrix. Meanwhile, as in ViT [15], a classification token $z_{cls} \in \mathbb{R}^D$ is added to the first position of the sequence and the classification token at the final transformer layer is used for classification. Considering that the 3D CNN branch ($3 \times 3 \times 3$ convolution) retains positional features and extracts local information [24], spatial and temporal positional embeddings are omitted in our transformer branch [3] .

3.2   Hybrid Architecture for Face Forgery Detection

Our introduced HSTNet is based on a hybrid architecture as shown in Fig. 1, which is composed of a 3D CNN branch and a spatio-temporal transformer branch to jointly capture local and global information. Video-based feature extraction further helps to deeply extract the spatial details and temporal coherence, which play a crucial role in face forgery detection. The whole network consists of a stem layer, four stages of dual-stream feature extraction blocks, FABs to align features, and a VSB to conduct adaptive vectors fusion.

To be specific, the stem layer is instantiated as a $3 \times 7 \times 7$ 3D convolution followed by BatchNorm and a $3 \times 3 \times 3$ max pooling. After initial feature extraction by the stem layer, the feature maps are sent directly to a 3D CNN block and a transformer block after patch embedding. Then these features and tokens go through four stages of HST for deep spatio-temporal learning. Within each stage, dual-stream feature extraction blocks are designed to learn short- and long-range relations. The architecture of the feature extraction blocks is depicted in Fig. 2. FABs are adopted to refine the features adaptively and align two heterogeneous features in resolutions and semantics. Note that the 3D CNN branch is responsible for processing high-resolution feature maps to explore the local forged patterns, while low-resolution features are fed to the transformer branch for mining global inconsistency both in spatial and temporal domains. At the end of HSTNet, VSB combines the two output vectors of the 3D CNN branch and the transformer branch for final prediction.

3D CNN Branch. As stated in [21], 3D convolutional operations are effective to learn spatio-temporal representations. Following ResNet [22], the whole CNN branch is divided into four stages. At each stage $i \in \{2, 3, 4, 5\}$, we stack N_i 3D convolutional blocks sequentially which comprises two $1 \times 1 \times 1$ dimension transformation convolutions, and a $3 \times 3 \times 3$ spatio-temporal convolution. Additionally, we set the downsampling factors to 4, 8, 16, and 32, respectively. Furthermore, since high-resolution inputs preserve more fine-grained spatial details, which are beneficial to detect unnatural inconsistency in forged videos, our 3D CNN branch is effective to extract local spatial details and temporal features across adjacent frames, that is, the short-range relations. With the aid of FABs, these local feature details are gradually integrated into the spatio-temporal transformer branch.

Transformer Branch. Although the receptive field grows consecutively with the increase of convolutional layers, pure CNN network has limited ability in global feature extraction. In contrast to the 3D CNN branch, each transformer block encodes all pairwise relationships among all 3D tokens. Therefore, it can always capture global long-range representations throughout the network. This characteristic enables the transformer to better explore long-range inconsistency for forgery detection. Concretely, we compute attention weights for detecting forgery using multi-head self-attention modules. Firstly, attention operation for each head is defined as:

$$\text{Attention} \left(\mathbf{Q}, \mathbf{K}, \mathbf{V} \right) = \text{Softmax} \left(\frac{\mathbf{Q}\mathbf{K}^{\top}}{\sqrt{d_k}} \right) \mathbf{V}, \tag{2}$$

where d equals $\frac{D}{M}$, M denotes the number of attention heads that we set to 6, queries $\mathbf{Q} = \mathbf{Z}\mathbf{W}_q$, keys $\mathbf{K} = \mathbf{Z}\mathbf{W}_k$ and values $\mathbf{V} = \mathbf{Z}\mathbf{W}_v$ are all linear projections of the input $\mathbf{Z}$ with $\mathbf{Z}, \mathbf{Q}, \mathbf{K}, \mathbf{V} \in \mathbb{R}^{T \times (N+1) \times D}$.

Inspired by the idea of ViT [15], our transformer branch consists of a sequence of transformer layers. Each transformer layer contains three parts: a multi-head self-attention (MSA) module [48] to conduct spatio-temporal dot-product attention, a layer normalization operation (LN) [4] to regularize features and a MLP block for non-linear transformation. Residual connections are deployed in both MSA modules and MLP blocks. With the GELU activation function [23], the calculation of the features at the l-th layer can be defined as:

$$\mathbf{y}^{\ell} = \text{MSA} \left(\text{LN} \left(\mathbf{z}^{\ell} \right) \right) + \mathbf{z}^{\ell}, \tag{3}$$

$$\mathbf{z}^{\ell+1} = \text{MLP} \left(\text{LN} \left(\mathbf{y}^{\ell} \right) \right) + \mathbf{y}^{\ell}, \tag{4}$$

where z^l denotes the summation of the output features of the transformer branch and the CNN branch at layer l, and y^l denotes the output feature of the MSA module. The MLP module has two linear projections separated by the GELU activation function.

3.3   Feature Alignment Block

The interaction between the 3D CNN branch and the spatio-temporal transformer branch plays a critical role on the final prediction. Nevertheless, features of the two branches are misaligned in resolutions and semantics. Hence, we propose FAB to align the heterogeneous features and re-calibrate them adaptively. As illustrated in Fig. 3, given a 3D CNN feature map $x \in \mathbb{R}^{T \times H \times W \times C}$, where T, H, W, C denote the temporal dimension, height, width and channel number respectively, and the 3D tokens $z \in \mathbb{R}^{T \times (N+1) \times D}$, where $T, N+1, D$ denote the temporal dimension, token number and embedding dimensions,

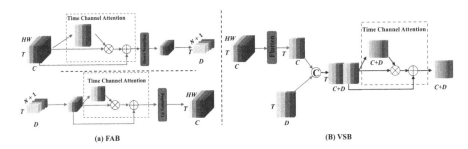

Fig. 3. Illustration of FAB and VSB, where "$\otimes$" indicates matrix multiplication and "$\copyright$" indicates channel-wise concatenation, and T, C, D denote temporal dimension, channel number of 3D CNN vector, and channel number of the 3D class token of the final transformer layer, respectively. The left upper part realizes the mapping from 3D features of the CNN branch to 3D tokens, while the left lower structure achieves the opposite.

respectively, FAB leverages $1 \times 1 \times 1$ 3D convolution to complete channel dimension alignment and down-/up-sampling operations to uniform the spatial resolutions. Meanwhile, layer normalization and batch normalization are introduced to achieve smoother gradients. On the other hand, in order to fill the semantic gap between each local feature and global token pair, instead of simply concatenating the features after spatial alignment, we design a time-channel attention mechanism to refine the features in time and channel dimensions adaptively before down-/up-sampling operations. In details, a global average pooling is first used to flatten the spatial dimension of x_{in} and obtain global representation $u_{in} \in \mathbb{R}^{T \times C}$. Then we utilize a refinement module which comprises two $1 \times 1 \times 1$ 3D convolutions to gradually squeeze u_{in} and generate the time-channel attention map $M_{\alpha} \in \mathbb{R}^{T \times C}$. Finally, we attach the attention map M_{α} to x and obtain refined feature x_{re}. A skip connection is further used to combine x_{in} and x_{re}. The whole process is formulated as follows:

$$M_{\alpha} = \sigma \left(W_{conv,1} * ReLU \left(W_{conv,2} * u_{in} \right) \right), \qquad (5)$$

$$x_{out} = x_{in} + M_{\alpha} x_{in}, \qquad (6)$$

where $W_{conv,1}$ and $W_{conv,2}$ represent the weights of the two 3D convolution layers, and σ and $ReLU$ indicate Sigmoid and ReLU activation functions respectively. The residual structure in Equ. 6 ensures the stability of the training process and accelerates the convergence.

It is worth noting that through continuous information interaction of FAB, the 3D CNN branch introduces sufficient global representations, and the transformer branch also obtains abundant local details. It makes up for the shortcomings of the two branches, and achieves the full integration of short- and long-range information.

3.4   Vector Selection Block

For the final prediction, it is vital to comprehensively consider the outputs of the two branches and select the essential features. Instead of concatenating them simply, we design a VSB to combine them adaptively, in which the time-channel attention mechanism is again employed to comprehensively compare the local and global information in semantics and attach importance weights in the temporal dimension and channels for vector refinement. As shown in Fig. 3 (b), VSB takes the output vector of the 3D CNN branch and the class token of the final transformer layer as input. Different from FAB, we first concatenate two vectors and then leverage the time-channel attention to emphasize the important features and suppress redundant feature maps. Based on this, VSB is applied on the last block of our HSTNet as a joint connection between the backbone and the classification head to achieve better performance.

Table 1. Comparison on the FF++ dataset under the accuracy rate. The best results are highlighted.

Method	FaceForensics++ c23			
	DF	F2F	FS	NT
XN-avg	0.9893	0.9893	0.9964	0.9500
C3D	0.9286	0.8857	0.9179	0.8964
I3D	0.9286	0.9286	0.9643	0.9036
LSTM	0.9964	**0.9929**	0.9821	0.9393
TEI	0.9786	0.9714	0.9750	0.9429
Comotion-70	0.9910	0.9325	0.9830	0.9045
ADDNet-3D	0.9214	0.8393	0.9250	0.7821
STIL	0.9964	**0.9929**	**1.0000**	**0.9536**
Ours	**1.0000**	**0.9929**	0.9929	0.9429

4   Experiments

4.1   Experimental Settings

Datasets. Similar to related works of face forgery detection, our experiments are conducted on the four standardized benchmark dedpfake datasets: FaceForensics++ (FF++) [43], Celeb-DF [33], FaceShifter [28], and DFDC [14].

Evaluation Metrics. In our experiments, we focus on utilizing the Accuracy rate (ACC) and the Area Under Receiver Operating Characteristic Curve (AUC) as our evaluation metrics. As previous related works use a single frame as input, we select video-level AUC and average the prediction for each video clip of the whole video, as in [38]. Consequently, all models utilize the same number of frames to perform predictions.

Implementation Details. In our experiments, we apply a state-of-the-art (SOTA) face extractor RetinaFace [13] to detect and align the faces with a size of 224×224 for both real and fake videos. Each clip used for training and testing comprises 32 frames and random flip is employed during training. All the experiments are conducted on 4 Nvidia TITAN Xp 12 GB GPUs and Intel (R) Core (TM) i7-6850K CPU @ 3.60GHz. Our HSTNet is implemented based on PyTorch v1.7.0, built upon the open source mmaction2 toolbox [11].

We adapt our HSTNet as the backbone of deepfake detector and use I3D class head in the mmaction2 toolbox. All the detectors are trained by using AdamW [36] with the weight decay 0.02 supervised by the binary cross-entropy loss. We apply a warm-up strategy for the training of our model. Specifically, the learning rate first increases from 1e-5 to 1e-4 in the first 2.5 epochs and then decays to 0 for the last 117.5 epochs with the cosine annealing learning rate schedule.

Table 2. Comparison on FF++. Results of some other methods are from [19,52]. The best result are highlighted.

Method	FF++	
	ACC	AUC
XN-avg	95.73	-
MesoNet	83.10	-
Face X-ray	-	87.40
Xception	95.73	96.30
Two Branch	-	98.70
EfficientNet-B4	96.63	99.18
Zhao (Xception)	96.37	98.97
Ours	**97.00**	**99.20**

Table 3. Comparison on Celeb-DF. Results of some other methods are from [19]. The best result are highlighted.

Method	ACC
XN-avg	99.44
I3D	99.23
LSTM	95.73
ADDNet-3D	99.12
S-IML-T	98.84
D-FWA	98.58
STIL	99.78
Ours	**99.99**

4.2 Comparison with SOTA Methods

We conduct a comprehensive comparison with 3D convolution based works I3D [9] and C3D [47]. We mainly compare our method to those with high generalization ability on unknown datasets, such as Xception [10], Face X-ray [29], multi-task learning by Two-branch [38], and LipForensics [20] that captures unnatural mouth motions.

Results on FF++ and Celeb-DF. Firstly, we evaluate our HSTNet on the high-quality FF++ dataset and Celeb-DF dataset. Table 1 illustrates the comparison between our model and SOTA methods. It is evident that our method outperforms the most of opponents especially on Deepfakes setting with 100% accuracy and is slightly lower than the scores of SOTA method STIL on other two settings. The comprehensive evaluation of the results on four manipulated datasets in Table 2 indicates that the accuracy of our method achieves a significant improvement compared with frame-based methods. The reason for this improvement is mainly the local features extracted by the CNN branch and the global spatio-temporal inconsistency captured by the Transformer branch, which provids more coherent and complete information for the whole network. Meanwhile, Fig. 4 also illustrates this point of view.

Table 3 illustrates that our HSTNet outperforms all compared counterparts, e.g., 0.22% higher accuracy than STIL [19] on the Celeb-DF dataset. It indicates that our video-based hybrid model better handles the spatio-temporal inconsistency than frame-based methods. And it strongly demonstrates that the FAB modules between the CNN branch and the Transformer branch extracted better spatio-temporal features than vanilla two-stream neural networks did.

Generalization capability on unseen datasets. In this section, we assess the generalization capability of our HSTNet that is trained on FF++ (HQ) with multiple techniques and tested on unseen manipulation datasets, such as Celeb-DF and FaceShifter. In Table 4, we compare our method with other SOTA models based on frames or videos. HSTNet achieves the best performance on Celeb-DF and DFDC datasets with 4.27% AUC higher than Multi-task [40] and 2.10% AUC than CNN-aug [50], respectively. On the FaceShifter dataset, our method is in second place with only 1.11% AUC lower than Face X-ray [29]. These results in Table 4 verify that our HSTNet has better generalization ability on unseen datasets.

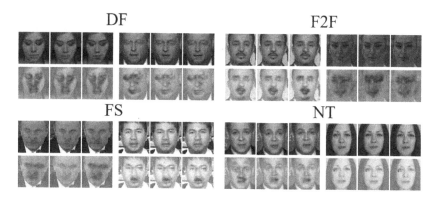

Fig. 4. Visualization of feature analysis for successive frames in videos clips from four different manipulation datasets. The rows beneath original video clips represent corresponding heatmap visualization results. Note that the warmer color indicates a higher detected region and a more suppressed background.

Table 4. Cross-dataset generalization capability evaluation. Video-level AUC (%) on Celeb-DF, FaceShifter (FShifter) and DFDC after training on FaceForensics++ (FF++). Part of the results are from [19]. The best result are highlighted.

Method	Celeb-DF	Fshifter	DFDC
Xception	73.70	72.0	70.90
CNN-aug	75.6	65.70	72.10
Patch-based	69.6	57.80	65.60
Face X-ray	74.76	**92.80**	65.50
CNN-GRU	69.8	80.80	68.90
Multi-task	75.70	66.00	68.10
D-FWA	64.60	65.50	67.30
STIL	75.58	-	-
Ours	**79.97**	91.69	**74.20**

4.3 Ablation Study

We conduct experiments to further demonstrate the effectiveness of FAB and VSB module in our proposed HSTNet. On the one hand, we compare the results of whether FAB introduces time-channel attention or not. Without time-channel attention, FAB will directly perform down-/up-sampling operations and add the two features at pixel level. On the other hand, we explore the effects of different choices on the outputs of two branches, including only convolution vector, only transformer vector, simple concatenated vector, and output of VSB. The results are shown in Table 5. Apparently, both FAB and VSB have significant effectiveness in improving the performance. In particular, FAB with time-channel attention outperforms the other 0.14% in terms of AUC, which states its superiority in integrating short- and long-range information. In addition, selecting the output of VSB for classification achieved the best effect and surpassed the second place by 0.23% demonstrating VSB is the best choice for final prediction.

Table 5. Ablation study results of HSTNet with different model capability. Video-level AUC (%) on FF++ dataset is reported. TC means Time-channel operation in FAB and VSB modules. The best result are highlighted.

	Model	FF++ (AUC)
FAB Structure	FAB (w/o TC)-VSB (w TC)	99.04
	FAB(w TC)-VSB (w TC)	**99.20**
VSB Structure	FAB(w TC)-VSB (conv)	98.82
	FAB(w TC)-VSB (trans)	98.81
	FAB(w TC)-VSB (concat)	98.95
	FAB(w TC)-VSB (w TC)	**99.20**

4.4 Visualization

By using the Grad-CAM method [45], we visualize the heatmaps of the last feature extraction layer of HSTNet to illustrate the locations of spatio-temporal inconsistencies. As depicted in Fig. 4, our HSTNet can locate the unnatural parts of the fake videos not only from the local details, but also from the global consistency. In particular, for those frames that look very real, such as the frames from NeuralTectures at the bottom right of Fig. 4, our method can pay more attention to the positions where there are inconsistencies in the temporal dimension.

5 Conclusions

In this paper, we propose a Hybrid Spatio-Temporal Network (HSTNet) to detect forgery videos. Specifically, our HSTNet utilizes a hybrid architecture consisting of a 3D CNN branch and a spatio-temporal transformer branch to jointly learn short- and long-range relations in space and time. Due to the feature mismatching between the two branches, we design a Feature Alignment Block (FAB) to recalibrate the features and fully integrate them in scales and semantics. We also introduce a Vector Selection Block (VSB) to combine the outputs of the two branches and emphasize essential features for final classification. Extensive experiments illustrate that HSTNet produces state-of-the-art overall results.

Acknowledgments. This work was supported by "One Thousand Plan" projects in Jiangxi Province Jxsg2023102268 and National Key Laboratory on Automatic Target Recognition 220402.

References

1. Afchar, D., Nozick, V., Yamagishi, J., Echizen, I.: Mesonet: a compact facial video forgery detection network. In: 2018 IEEE International Workshop on Information Forensics and Security (WIFS), pp. 1–7. IEEE (2018)
2. Amerini, I., Galteri, L., Caldelli, R., Del Bimbo, A.: Deepfake video detection through optical flow based CNN. In: Proceedings of the IEEE/CVF International Conference on Computer Vision Workshops (2019)
3. Arnab, A., Dehghani, M., Heigold, G., Sun, C., Lučić, M., Schmid, C.: ViViT: a video vision transformer (2021)
4. Ba, J.L., Kiros, J.R., Hinton, G.E.: Layer normalization (2016)
5. Bao, J., Chen, D., Wen, F., Li, H., Hua, G.: Towards open-set identity preserving face synthesis. In: Proceedings of the IEEE conference on Computer Vision and Pattern Recognition, pp. 6713–6722 (2018)
6. Bayar, B., Stamm, M.C.: A deep learning approach to universal image manipulation detection using a new convolutional layer. In: Proceedings of the 4th ACM Workshop on Information Hiding and Multimedia Security, pp. 5–10 (2016)
7. Bertasius, G., Wang, H., Torresani, L.: Is space-time attention all you need for video understanding? (2021)

8. Carion, N., Massa, F., Synnaeve, G., Usunier, N., Kirillov, A., Zagoruyko, S.: End-to-end object detection with transformers. In: Vedaldi, A., Bischof, H., Brox, T., Frahm, J.-M. (eds.) ECCV 2020. LNCS, vol. 12346, pp. 213–229. Springer, Cham (2020). https://doi.org/10.1007/978-3-030-58452-8_13

9. Carreira, J., Zisserman, A.: Quo Vadis, action recognition? A new model and the kinetics dataset. In: proceedings of the IEEE Conference on Computer Vision and Pattern Recognition, pp. 6299–6308 (2017)

10. Chollet, F.: Xception: Deep learning with DepthWise separable convolutions. In: Proceedings of the IEEE conference on Computer Vision and Pattern Recognition, pp. 1251–1258 (2017)

11. Contributors, M.: Openmmlab's next generation video understanding toolbox and benchmark. https://github.com/open-mmlab/mmaction2 (2020)

12. Dang, H., Liu, F., Stehouwer, J., Liu, X., Jain, A.K.: On the detection of digital face manipulation. In: Proceedings of the IEEE/CVF Conference on Computer Vision and Pattern Recognition, pp. 5781–5790 (2020)

13. Deng, J., Guo, J., Ververas, E., Kotsia, I., Zafeiriou, S.: Retinaface: single-shot multi-level face localisation in the wild. In: Proceedings of the IEEE/CVF Conference on Computer Vision and Pattern Recognition, pp. 5203–5212 (2020)

14. Dolhansky, B., et al.: The deepfake detection challenge (DFDC) dataset (2020)

15. Dosovitskiy, A., et al.: An image is worth 16x16 words: Transformers for image recognition at scale (2020)

16. Du, M., Pentyala, S., Li, Y., Hu, X.: Towards generalizable forgery detection with locality-aware autoencoder. pp. arXiv-1909 (2019)

17. Durall, R., Keuper, M., Keuper, J.: Watch your up-convolution: CNN based generative deep neural networks are failing to reproduce spectral distributions. In: Proceedings of the IEEE/CVF Conference on Computer Vision and Pattern Recognition, pp. 7890–7899 (2020)

18. Goodfellow, I., et al.: Generative adversarial nets, vol. 27 (2014)

19. Gu, Z., et al.: Spatiotemporal inconsistency learning for deepfake video detection. In: Proceedings of the 29th ACM International Conference on Multimedia, pp. 3473–3481 (2021)

20. Haliassos, A., Vougioukas, K., Petridis, S., Pantic, M.: Lips don't lie: a generalisable and robust approach to face forgery detection. In: Proceedings of the IEEE/CVF Conference on Computer Vision and Pattern Recognition, pp. 5039–5049 (2021)

21. Hara, K., Kataoka, H., Satoh, Y.: Can spatiotemporal 3d CNNs retrace the history of 2d CNNs and ImageNet? In: Proceedings of the IEEE conference on Computer Vision and Pattern Recognition, pp. 6546–6555 (2018)

22. He, K., Zhang, X., Ren, S., Sun, J.: Deep residual learning for image recognition. In: Proceedings of the IEEE Conference on Computer Vision and Pattern Recognition, pp. 770–778 (2016)

23. Hendrycks, D., Gimpel, K.: Gaussian error linear units (GELUs) (2016)

24. Islam, M.A., Kowal, M., Jia, S., Derpanis, K.G., Bruce, N.D.: Position, padding and predictions: a deeper look at position information in CNNs (2021)

25. Jiang, Z., et al.: Token labeling: Training a 85.5% top-1 accuracy vision transformer with 56m parameters on imagenet (2021)

26. Khodabakhsh, A., Ramachandra, R., Raja, K., Wasnik, P., Busch, C.: Fake face detection methods: can they be generalized? In: 2018 International Conference of the Biometrics Special Interest Group (BIOSIG), pp. 1–6. IEEE (2018)

27. Li, J., Xie, H., Li, J., Wang, Z., Zhang, Y.: Frequency-aware discriminative feature learning supervised by single-center loss for face forgery detection. In: Proceedings

of the IEEE/CVF Conference on Computer Vision and Pattern Recognition, pp. 6458–6467 (2021)

28. Li, L., Bao, J., Yang, H., Chen, D., Wen, F.: Advancing high fidelity identity swapping for forgery detection. In: Proceedings of the IEEE/CVF Conference on Computer Vision and Pattern Recognition, pp. 5074–5083 (2020)

29. Li, L., et al.: Face x-ray for more general face forgery detection. In: Proceedings of the IEEE/CVF Conference on Computer Vision and Pattern Recognition, pp. 5001–5010 (2020)

30. Li, X., et al.: Sharp multiple instance learning for deepfake video detection. In: Proceedings of the 28th ACM International Conference on Multimedia, pp. 1864–1872 (2020)

31. Li, Y., Chang, M.C., Lyu, S.: In ICTU oculi: Exposing AI created fake videos by detecting eye blinking. In: 2018 IEEE International Workshop on Information Forensics and Security (WIFS), pp. 1–7. IEEE (2018)

32. Li, Y., Lyu, S.: Exposing deepfake videos by detecting face warping artifacts (2018)

33. Li, Y., Yang, X., Sun, P., Qi, H., Lyu, S.: Celeb-DF: a large-scale challenging dataset for deepfake forensics. In: Proceedings of the IEEE/CVF Conference on Computer Vision and Pattern Recognition, pp. 3207–3216 (2020)

34. Liu, H., et al.: Spatial-phase shallow learning: rethinking face forgery detection in frequency domain. In: Proceedings of the IEEE/CVF Conference on Computer Vision and Pattern Recognition, pp. 772–781 (2021)

35. Liu, Z., et al.: Swin transformer: hierarchical vision transformer using shifted windows (2021)

36. Loshchilov, I., Hutter, F.: Decoupled weight decay regularization (2017)

37. Mao, M., et al.: Dual-stream network for visual recognition (2021)

38. Masi, I., Killekar, A., Mascarenhas, R.M., Gurudatt, S.P., AbdAlmageed, W.: Two-branch recurrent network for isolating deepfakes in videos. In: Vedaldi, A., Bischof, H., Brox, T., Frahm, J.-M. (eds.) ECCV 2020. LNCS, vol. 12352, pp. 667–684. Springer, Cham (2020). https://doi.org/10.1007/978-3-030-58571-6_39

39. Mittal, T., Bhattacharya, U., Chandra, R., Bera, A., Manocha, D.: Emotions don't lie: An audio-visual deepfake detection method using affective cues. In: Proceedings of the 28th ACM International Conference on Multimedia, pp. 2823–2832 (2020)

40. Nguyen, H.H., Fang, F., Yamagishi, J., Echizen, I.: Multi-task learning for detecting and segmenting manipulated facial images and videos (2019)

41. Peng, Z., et al.: Conformer: local features coupling global representations for visual recognition (2021)

42. Qian, Y., Yin, G., Sheng, L., Chen, Z., Shao, J.: Thinking in frequency: face forgery detection by mining frequency-aware clues. In: Vedaldi, A., Bischof, H., Brox, T., Frahm, J.-M. (eds.) ECCV 2020. LNCS, vol. 12357, pp. 86–103. Springer, Cham (2020). https://doi.org/10.1007/978-3-030-58610-2_6

43. Rossler, A., Cozzolino, D., Verdoliva, L., Riess, C., Thies, J., Nießner, M.: Face-forensics++: learning to detect manipulated facial images. In: Proceedings of the IEEE/CVF International Conference on Computer Vision, pp. 1–11 (2019)

44. Sabir, E., Cheng, J., Jaiswal, A., AbdAlmageed, W., Masi, I., Natarajan, P.: Recurrent convolutional strategies for face manipulation detection in videos. Interfaces 3, 80–87 (2019)

45. Selvaraju, R.R., Cogswell, M., Das, A., Vedantam, R., Parikh, D., Batra, D.: Grad-CAM: visual explanations from deep networks via gradient-based localization. In: Proceedings of the IEEE International Conference on Computer Vision, pp. 618–626 (2017)

46. Thies, J., Elgharib, M., Tewari, A., Theobalt, C., Nießner, M.: Neural voice puppetry: audio-driven facial reenactment. In: Vedaldi, A., Bischof, H., Brox, T., Frahm, J.-M. (eds.) ECCV 2020. LNCS, vol. 12361, pp. 716–731. Springer, Cham (2020). https://doi.org/10.1007/978-3-030-58517-4_42

47. Tran, D., Bourdev, L., Fergus, R., Torresani, L., Paluri, M.: Learning spatiotemporal features with 3d convolutional networks (2015)

48. Vaswani, A., et al.: Attention is all you need. In: Advances in Neural Information Processing Systems, pp. 5998–6008 (2017)

49. Vougioukas, K., Petridis, S., Pantic, M.: End-to-end speech-driven realistic facial animation with temporal GANs. In: IEEE conference on Computer Vision and Pattern Recognition Workshops (CVPRW), pp. 37–40 (2019)

50. Wang, S.Y., Wang, O., Zhang, R., Owens, A., Efros, A.A.: CNN-generated images are surprisingly easy to spot... for now. In: Proceedings of the IEEE/CVF Conference on Computer Vision and Pattern Recognition, pp. 8695–8704 (2020)

51. Wang, W., et al.: Pyramid vision transformer: a versatile backbone for dense prediction without convolutions (2021)

52. Zhao, H., Zhou, W., Chen, D., Wei, T., Zhang, W., Yu, N.: Multi-attentional deepfake detection. In: Proceedings of the IEEE/CVF Conference on Computer Vision and Pattern Recognition, pp. 2185–2194 (2021)

53. Zheng, Y., Bao, J., Chen, D., Zeng, M., Wen, F.: Exploring temporal coherence for more general video face forgery detection. In: Proceedings of the IEEE/CVF International Conference on Computer Vision, pp. 15044–15054 (2021)

Dewarping Document Image in Complex Scene by Geometric Control Points

Run-Xi Li[1($\boxtimes$)], Fei Yin[2], and Lin-Lin Huang[1]

[1] Beijing Jiaotong University, Beijing, China
{21120012,huangll}@bjtu.edu.cn
[2] National Laboratory of Pattern Recognition, Institute of Automation of Chinese,
Academy of Sciences, Beijing, China
fyin@nlpr.ia.ac.cn

Abstract. In the process of document digitization, document images captured by mobile devices suffer from physical distortion, which is detrimental to subsequent document processing. Geometric information of the distorted document images provide global and local constraints that can assist in document dewarping. In this paper, we propose a novel document dewarping method which focus on utilizing the geometric control points such as document boundaries and textlines. Specifically, our method first extracts the boundary source control points and textline source control points and predicts their corresponding forward mapping as target control points. Eventually the sparse mapping between control points is converted into a dense backward mapping by Thin Plate Splines interpolation. Our method can obtain the backward mapping directly and explicitly by interpolation between control points, without solving the time-consuming optimization problem. Quantitative and qualitative evaluation show that our method can dewarp document images with various distortion types, and improve the inference speed by a factor of three over the existing geometric element based rectification methods.

Keywords: Document Dewarping · Geometric Control Points · Deep Learning

1 Introduction

With the advent of the information age, digital document images as an important carrier of information, have been widely used in all aspects of social life because of the advantages of easy storage and intelligent processing. However, in the process of document digitization, the captured document images may be deformed due to the unavoidable physical deformation, the shooting angle of the camera, lighting conditions. These distortions seriously hinder the automated extraction and analysis of document image content. To this end, researchers have proposed many approaches for the rectification of deformed document images.

Early document rectification methods are mainly based on reconstructing the 3D shape of document images. Some methods estimate the 3D shapes by

H. Lu et al. (Eds.): ACPR 2023, LNCS 14408, pp. 265–278, 2023.
https://doi.org/10.1007/978-3-031-47665-5_22

using additional equipment [1, 2, 4] or require multi-view images [5–7], which limits their applicability. Some methods model deformed documents as parametric surfaces and solve for the corresponding parameters by shading [8], text lines [9], and boundaries [10] of the document. However, the parametric model is difficult to handle complex deformation cases.

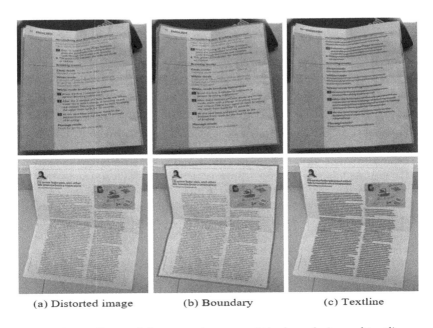

(a) Distorted image   (b) Boundary   (c) Textline

Fig. 1. Input distorted document images and the boundaries and textlines.

Deep learning-based document dewarping methods exhibit greater robustness and generality. To improve the applicability and performance of document dewarping methods. DocUNet [15] predicts the forward mapping by a stacked U-Net. DewarpNet [16] estimates the 3D shape and backward mapping of distorted documents. DocTr [22] is the first method to introduce transformer for document rectification. FDRNet [25] focuses on high-frequency components. Marior [23] follows a progressive strategy to iteratively dewarp the documents. PaperEdge [24] incorporates real-world document images to improve document unwarping. However, most deep learning-based methods directly predict the warping flow, ignoring the geometric information of the documents, such as boundaries and textlines, as shown in Fig. 1). Specifically, document boundaries and textlines should be horizontal or vertical. This provides strong supervision information for document rectification. In order to obtain the warping flow. RDGR [26] solves the optimization problem using the detected document boundaries and text lines as constraints. DocGeoNet [27] learns the geometric elements as auxiliary information and use the feature maps of textline detection branches to predict mapping flow.

On the one hand, solving the optimization problem to obtain the mapping flow is very time-consuming and can be replaced by training a neural network; on the other hand, using the feature maps of geometric elements implicitly ignores part of the explicit spatial mapping information. Motivated by these two aspects, in this paper, we propose a novel approach to rectify distorted document image explicitly uses the geometric information without time-consuming optimization process. More precisely, we first detect the boundaries points and textlines points of the distorted document image. Then we estimate their corresponding forward mapping points in the rectified image through a neural network. Finally, we consider the geometric element points and the corresponding forward mapping points as source control points and target control points, respectively, and take advantage of Thin plate splines interpolation to convert the sparse mapping between control points to the final dense mapping flow, we use bilinear sampling to generate the rectified images through the dense mapping flow.

In summary, the contributions of our paper are as follows:

– We propose a novel document rectification method based on document geo-metric control points, which turns the time-consuming optimization problem required to obtain a mapping flow into the interpolation between pairs of control points.
– We conduct quantitative and qualitative experiments on the DocUNet Bench-mark [15]. Experiment results show that our method based on geometric element control points can rectify various deformed document images and improve the inference efficiency.

2   Related Work

Document dewarping has been studied for many years. In this section, We cate-gorize document dewarping methods into two groups: hand-crafted feature based methods and deep learning based methods.

2.1   Hand Crafted Features Based Methods

Most traditional hand-crafted methods rectify the document images by recon-structing the 3D shape of the distorted document images. Some of these methods used auxiliary device. Brown and Seales [2] employed a structured light projector system and design a mass-spring particle system to flatten the non-planar sur-face. Zhang [1] used a dedicated laser range scanner to capture the 3D shape of the warped document and restored the document by physically-based modeling technique. Yamashita [3] used a stereo vision system to correct and merge two images from two cameras whose directions of optic axes are different from each other. Meng [4] utilized two structured beams to recover the document curves and solved a system of ordinary differential equations to flatten the image. These methods rely on special devices and are limited in practical applications.

Some methods recover the 3D representation multi-view 3D reconstruction. Koo [5] exploited two view images to reconstruct the surface. Tsoi [6] combined multiple images of bound and folded documents and transformed them into a common coordinate frame. You [7] presented a ridge-aware surface reconstruction algorithm and unwrapped the surface by robust conformal mapping. The limitation of this type of method is that is difficult to obtain multi-view images.

To avoid using additional devices and multi view images, another type of method assume that the document can be modeled as a parametric model and estimate the corresponding parameters. Cylindrical surface is the most common model. [12] modeled the curved documents as cylindrical surfaces and compute the shape of the document using Shape from shading. Meng [13] estimated the cylindrical surface parameters through weighted majority voting on the vector fields and solved an ordinary differential equation to obtain the spatial directrix of the surface. Non-Uniform Rational B-Splines (NURBS) are another parametric model. Hironori [14] defined the warping model of a document image as a set of cubic splines and fitted each cubic spline to a text line or a space between text lines. Some early work took advantage of layout elements such as textlines and document boundaries. Among them, Brown [10] compute a corrective mapping to undo common geometric distortions via the 2-D boundary of the imaged material. He [11] extracted page boundary and remove the perspective and geometric distortions of a curled page. Cao [9] locate the textlines and get several projections of direcrixes, then get the mapping from the warping 2D image to the rectified 2D image. However, these low dimensional parametric model are difficult to handle complex deformation.

2.2   Deep Learning Based Methods

Traditional hand-crafted methods depend on assumptions on surface geometry or special devices, which limited the applicability. With the development of deep learning research, researchers began to explore deep networks for document rectification. DocUNet [15] is the first deep learning based method to unwarp distorted documents, it proposed a stacked U-Net to predict the forward mapping. Das [16] contribute the Doc3D dataset, which is the first and largest document image dataset with multiple kinds of annotations, and propose DewarpNet to predict 3D coordinates, backward mapping of distorted documents. Liu [19] propose a Adversarial Gated Unwarping Network (AGUN) to predict the multiple resolutions unwarping grid and generate visually pleasing results based on visual cues. Li [20] learn the distortion flow on small image patches rather than the entire image and then stitch the patch results in the gradient domain. Das [21] design a novel fully-differentiable feature-level stitching module to make piece-wise unwarping networks end-to-end trainable. Xie [17] propose a novel framework for both removing background and estimating pixel-wise displacements using a fully convolutional network (FCN). Moreover, [18] they use a simple Encode structure to effectively estimate control points and reference points and obtain backward mapping by interpolation method. Moreover, Feng [22] introduce Transformer to address geometry and illumination distortion of the document images. Then, Feng [27] introduce geometric representation such as 3D shape and textlines and performs representation learning to promote the performance of network. Xue [25] handles document restoration by focusing on high-frequency components in the Fourier space and dewarps documents by a flexible Thin-Plate Spline transformation. RDGR [26] learns the boundary points and the pixels in the text lines and obtain the final forward mapping by solving an optimization problem with grid regularization term. Ma [24] simultaneously using strong supervision of synthetic data and weak supervision of real data to train the network where only mask annotation of document regions is required for real data.

Although DocGeoNet [27] and RDGR [26] also detect the geometric elements of the distorted documents, DocGeoNet implicitly exploits the features of textlines by means of representation learning to predict the warping flow, RDGR needs to solve a time-consuming optimization problem. Different from the above two methods, we explicitly exploit the geometric elements and their corresponding forward mapping points to interpolate the warping flow.

3   Approach

Similar to many deep learning based methods, the ultimate goal is to obtain a dense mapping flow, such as forward mapping flow $F(x, y)$, which represents a pixel (x, y) in the distorted image should be map to (u, v) in the rectified image:

$$F(x, y) = (u, v) \tag{1}$$

And backward mapping flow $B(u, v)$, values at coordinates (u, v) represents the coordinates of the pixels in the distorted input image:

$$B(u, v) = (x, y) \tag{2}$$

Inspired by Xie [18], instead of directly estimating the dense warping flow, our method predict the sparse control points, i.e. boundaries points and textlines points, and then perform thin plate spline (TPS) interpolation to convert the sparse mapping into a dense backward mapping flow.

More specifically, in order to obtain the two groups of control points, i.e. source control points and target control points, needed for the TPS calculation. We first detect the boundary points and the textline points in the distorted document images as the source control points. Then, we predict the corresponding positions of boundary points and textline points on the rectified image as target control points. After obtaining the dense mapping flow, we sample the corresponding pixel value in the input distorted image to yield the rectified results.

3.1   Network Architecture

As shown in Fig. 2, our network structure is divided into two parts: top and bottom. The top part is the boundary branch and the bottom part is the textline branch. Both branches aim to extract source control points of the distorted document images and predict target control points of geometric elements.

Boundary Source Control Points Extraction. Given an distorted document $I_D \in \mathbb{R}^{H \times W \times 3}$. We use a DocUNet [15] to regress the backward mapping $\hat{B} \in \mathbb{R}^{H \times W \times 2}$ of the distorted image as the source control points. According to the definition of backward mapping $\hat{B}$, the values (x, y) in first row, first column, last row, last column corresponding to the coordinates of the top, left, bottom, right boundary.

Boundary Target Control Points Prediction. The corresponding target control points are the position of the boundaries in the forward mapping which satisfy the following conditions: The value of v equals 0 in the forward mapping value of the top boundary, the value of v equals 1 in the forward mapping of the bottom boundary. Similarity, the value of u equals 0 in the forward mapping of the left boundary and the value of u equals 1 in the forward mapping of the right boundary. And u or v values are equally spaced. Thus based on these properties we can directly obtain the target control points of the document borders without using additional neural networks to predict the target control points.

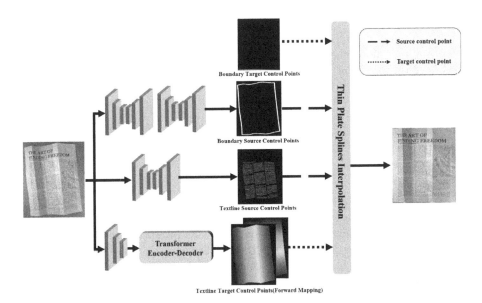

Fig. 2. The network architecture of our method. The input is an distorted document image. Top branch detects the boundary control points of the document and directly obtain the target control points of boundary according to the geometric properties. The bottom branch detects the textline control points and predicts the forward mapping as target control points. Finally, the sparse mapping between source control points target control points will be interpolated by Thin Plate Splines as dense backward mapping.

Textline Source Control Points Extraction. Textlines in distorted documents reflect local deformation information and can provide strong constraint for document unwarping. A curved textline should be rectified to a horizontal or vertical line. We use a UNet to extract textlines in distorted document images in a semantic segmentation way, the network outputs a confidence map $\hat{T} \in \mathbb{R}^{H \times W \times 1}$ in the range of $(0, 1)$ and filtered by a threshold θ. Then morphological operations are performed on the filtered mask to remove burrs from the obtained text line segmentation masks and extract the connected components and sample at equal intervals to get the textline control points.

Textline Target Control Points Prediction. After obtaining the boundary control points and textline source control points, the forward mapping is obtained by solving the optimization problem in RDGR [26], which is time consuming, and the backward mapping is generate by the forward mapping through LinearNDinterpolator. We simplify this process into the prediction of the forward mapping $\hat{F} \in \mathbb{R}^{H \times W \times 2}$ through a Transformer encoder-decoder [22] to capture the long-range deformation information. The forward mapping values at the textline source control points are the textline target control points.

3.2 Post-processing

As mentioned above, textlines should be corrected to horizontal lines or vertical lines, which means that the forward mapping of the points in the same textline should have the same u or v values, we remove the outliers from the forward mapping values by a simple linear segment fitting method. If the forward mapping value of a point deviates far from the fitted straight line, then this point is removed. The remaining points are fitted to the straight line again, and the value on the straight line is used to replace the original forward mapping value.

For example, for horizontal text lines, given the corresponding forward mapping $F_f = \{(u_1, v_1), (u_2, v_2), ..., (u_N, v_N)\}$, we fit a horizontal line $f(v) = a$, $a \in (0, H)$ by least squares method. If the distance of the point (u_i, v_i) from the line is greater than a threshold τ then remove the point.

Finally, we integrate boundary control points and text line control points as source control points, and the corresponding forward mapping as target control points, and employ thin plate splines(TPS) interpolation to interpolate the sparse mapping between control points into a dense backward mapping.

3.3 Loss Functions

We define three loss function to guide the model regress the boundary source control points through backward mapping, extract textline source control points by means of semantic segmentation and predict the corresponding target control points through forward mapping.

The first loss L_{bm} defined as the L_1 distance between predicted backward mapping $\hat{B}$ and the ground truth B_{gt}:

$$L_{bm} = \|B_{gt} - \hat{B}\|_1 \tag{3}$$

The textline segmentation loss L_{text} we use in this work is the binary cross-entropy loss:

$$L_{text} = -\frac{1}{N_T} \sum_{i}^{N} [y_i \log \hat{p}_i + (1 - y_i) \log (1 - \hat{p}_i)] \tag{4}$$

where N_T is the number of elements in textlines, y_i and $\hat{p}_i$ ground-truth and predicted probability.

The forward mapping loss L_f defined as the L_1 distance between predicted forward mapping $\hat{F}$ and the ground truth F:

$$L_f = \frac{1}{N_f} \sum_{i}^{N_f} \|F_i - \hat{F}_i\|_1 \tag{5}$$

where N_f is the number of foreground area. Following [17], we add a local smooth constraint term to expect the predicted forward mapping trend to be as close to the ground-truth flow as possible in a local region:

$$L_{Lsc} = \frac{1}{N_f} \sum_{i}^{N_f} \| \sum_{j=1}^{k} (F_j - \hat{F}_j) - k \times (F_i - \hat{F}_i)\|_1 \tag{6}$$

Total losses of forward mapping prediction branch are defined as a linear combination:

$$L_{fm} = L_f + \alpha L_{Lsc} \tag{7}$$

3.4   Training Details

In our work, the input resolution of boundary module is 128×128. The input resolution of boundary module is 448×448 in order to detect the textlines more precisely. The network is trained with Adam optimizer and the learning rate of 1×10^{-4}. The threshold of confidence map θ is set as 0.3.

4   Experiments

4.1   Datasets

We train our network on the Doc3D dataset and evaluate the quantitative results on the DocUNet benchmark.

Doc3D. Doc3D dataset consists of 100k images with several kinds of annotations, including 3D coordinate map, albedo map, UV map, backward mapping, etc. It is created by using real document data and rendering software according to following steps: captured 3D meshes from deformed real documents and rendered the images in Blender. We randomly split 90k images for training and 10k for validation.

DocUNet Benchmark. This benchmark contains 130 real world warped documents photos captured by mobile cameras with different kinds of distortions and environment. The types of documents are various, including letters, academic papers, magazines, etc.

4.2   Evaluation Metrics

We use two groups of evaluation metrics:(1) Image Similarity and (2) Optical Character Recognition (OCR) accuracy to quantitatively evaluate the performance of our method. For image similarity, we use Multi-Scale Structural Similarity (MS-SSIM) and Local Distortion (LD). For OCR performance, we use Character Error Rate (CER) and Edit Distance (ED).

MS-SSIM. Structural SIMilarity (SSIM) [29] computes the similarity between two images by combining the luminance, contrast and structure comparison measures. Multi-Scale Structural Similarity (MS-SSIM) [28] is the weighted sum of SSIM at different sampling scales, which supplies more flexibility than previous single-scale structural similarity methods in incorporating the variations of viewing conditions. The weights for each scale are set as in the previous work [16].

Local Distortion. Local distortion(LD) is computed by performing dense image registration using SIFTflow [30] between the rectified image and the ground truth image. In the same way as before, all the unwarped results and groundtruth scanned images are resized to a 598400 pixel area.

ED and CER. Edit Distance(ED) is a metric to quantify how similar two strings are to one another, computed by counting the minimum number of operations (i.e. deletions(d), insertions(i) and substitutions(s).) required to transform one string into the other. Character Error Rate (CER) indicates the percentage of characters that were incorrectly predicted, it is calculated based on the Edit Distance:

$$CER = \frac{d + i + s}{N} \tag{8}$$

where N is the number of characters in the reference string obtained from the groundtruth scanned document images. We use Pytesseract (v0.3.8) as the OCR engine to evaluate the text recognition performance of our method. Following DocTr [22], we selected 60 images with rich text information from DocUNet benchmark [15].

4.3   Results

We quantitatively and qualitatively compare our method with recent state-of-the-art deep learning-based methods. For quantitative evaluation, we compare the MS-SSIM, LD, ED, CER with other methods on DocUNet benchmark, we also compare whether the methods use geometric elements. As shown in Table 1. Our method outperforms the DocUNet [15] and DocProj [20] method in all performance aspects, outperforms FCN-based methods in OCR performance.

   We also perform an qualitative evaluation on real world document images by comparing our rectification results with other methods of providing rectification results by visualization. As shown in Fig. 3, our method allows the boundaries to fit around the image and the textlines to be more horizontal.

   In addition to image similarity and OCR performance, We also compare the inference speed (expressed in Frames Per Second or FPS) with RDGR [26]. Our method and RDGR both detect document boundary points and text line points,

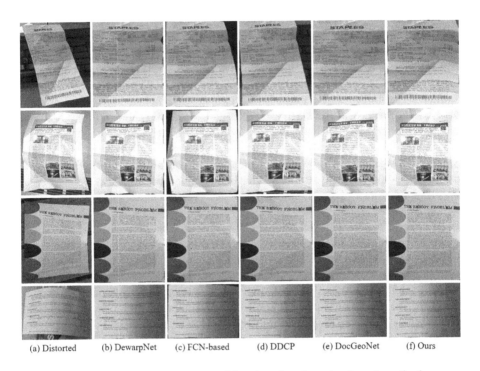

(a) Distorted   (b) DewarpNet   (c) FCN-based   (d) DDCP   (e) DocGeoNet   (f) Ours

Fig. 3. Qualitative comparisons with other deep learning based methods.

Table 1. Comparison of our method with other deep learning-based methods on DocUNet benchmark, "↑" means the higher the better, "↓" means the lower the better. "GeoE" means whether geometric elements are utilized

Methods	GeoE	MS-SSIM↑	LD↓	ED↓	CER↓
DocUNet [15]	×	0.4103	14.19	1552.22	0.5089
DocProj [20]	×	0.2946	18.01	1165.93	0.3818
AGUN [19]	×	-	-	-	-
FCN-based [17]	×	0.4477	7.84	1031.40	0.3156
DewarpNet [16]	×	0.4735	8.39	525.45	0.2626
DDCP [18]	×	0.4729	8.99	745.35	0.2102
Marior [23]	×	0.4780	7.44	593.80	0.2136
PaperEdge [24]	×	0.4724	7.99	375.60	0.1541
RDGR [26]	✓	0.4968	8.51	420.25	0.1559
DocGeoNet [27]	✓	0.5040	7.71	379.00	0.1509
Ours	✓	0.4777	8.68	506.85	0.1968

the difference is that RDGR solves the optimization problem based on these geometric element points to calculate the forward mapping, while we introduce a network to predict forward mapping and Thin plate splines interpolation. We compared the model size and FPS of our method and RDGR, as shown in Table 2. Due to the introduction of the forward mapping prediction branch, the number of parameters of our model is larger than RDGR. Our method has three times the inference speed of RDGR even though it has 35% more parameters. This is because RDGR requires Alternating Direction Method of Multipliers (ADMM) for Quadratic Programming to solve the optimization problem, but the predicted forward mapping and linear fitting can be computed quickly.

Table 2. Comparison of Frames Per Second (FPS) and number of parameters of our method with RDGR, "↑" means the higher the better, "↓" means the lower the better.

Methods	FPS↑	Para/M
RDGR [26]	0.50	49.46
Ours	1.68	66.90

4.4 Ablation Study and Limitation Discussion

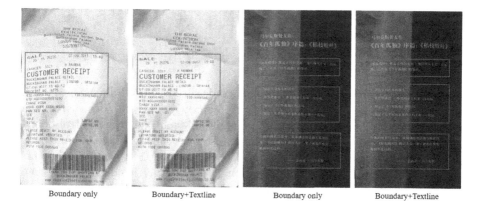

| Boundary only | Boundary+Textline | Boundary only | Boundary+Textline |

Fig. 4. Visualization of the rectification results using different geometric control points. After adding the textline control points, the textlines in the red box is more horizontal (Color figure online)

We conduct ablation study to investigate the influence of geometric elements. As shown in Table 3. The use of geometric elements can provide global and local constraint information for document unwarping, allowing the model to achieve better performance. High image similarity can be achieved using only document boundary points due to the fact that the document's border reflects global deformation information and also serves as a demarcation between foreground and background. And the OCR performance can be further improved by adding textline points, which proves that the addition of textlines makes the rectified document more readable, as can be seen in Fig. 4, the textlines are straighter. Note that we did not do experiments using only textline control points, because all distorted documents have boundaries but not necessarily textlines.

Table 3. The result of using different geometric elements. "↑" means the higher the better, "↓" means the lower the better.

Methods	MS-SSIM↑	LD↓	ED↓	CER↓
Boundary	0.4860	8.62	788.03	0.2800
Boundary+Textline	0.4777	8.68	506.85	0.1968

However, it is worth noting that there is a slight decrease in image similarity when using both boundaries and textlines. This is a limitation of our approach. The reason is that the forward mapping values of textlines are not predicted accurately enough and there are still isolated deviation points even after post-processing filtering. Forward mapping values with large errors can cause local areas of the image to be stretched causing distortion. In the future, We will improve the accuracy of forward mapping prediction by introducing constraint relations.

5   Conclusion

This paper we propose a novel framework to dewarp distorted document image. Different from many existing methods to directly predict the dense mapping flow, we focus on document boundary control points and textline control points and the corresponding forward mapping and then take advantage of thin plate splines(TPS) interpolation to convert the sparse mapping between control points to obtain the final dense backward mapping. The geometric control points can provide global and local structure information for dewarping. Extensive experiment results show our method can achieve better performance. In addition, we analyze the limitations of our approach. In the future, we will focus on improving the accuracy of the forward mapping prediction and introduce some constraints.

Acknowledgments. This work has been supported by the National Key Research and Development Program Grant 2020AAA0109702.

References

1. Zhang, L., Zhang, Y., Tan, C.: An improved physically-based method for geometric restoration of distorted document images. IEEE Trans. Pattern Anal. Mach. Intell. **30**(4), 728–34 (2008)
2. Brown, M.S., Seales, W.B.: Document restoration using 3D shape: a general deskewing algorithm for arbitrarily warped documents. In: Proceedings Eighth IEEE International Conference on Computer Vision, ICCV 2001 2001 Jul 7, vol. 2, pp. 367–374. IEEE (2001)
3. Yamashita, A., Kawarago, A., Kaneko, T., Miura, K.T.: Shape reconstruction and image restoration for non-flat surfaces of documents with a stereo vision system. In: Proceedings of the 17th International Conference on Pattern Recognition, 2004. ICPR 2004. 2004 Aug 26, vol. 1, pp. 482–485. IEEE
4. Meng, G., Wang, Y., Qu, S., Xiang, S., Pan, C.: Active flattening of curved document images via two structured beams. In: Proceedings of the IEEE Conference on Computer Vision and Pattern Recognition, pp. 3890–3897 (2014)
5. Koo, H.I., Kim, J., Cho, N.I.: Composition of a dewarped and enhanced document image from two view images. IEEE Trans. Image Process. **18**(7), 1551–62 (2009)
6. Tsoi, Y.C., Brown, M.S.: Multi-view document rectification using boundary. In: 2007 IEEE Conference on Computer Vision and Pattern Recognition 2007 Jun 17, pp. 1–8. IEEE (2007)
7. You, S., Matsushita, Y., Sinha, S., Bou, Y., Ikeuchi, K.: Multiview rectification of folded documents. IEEE Trans. Pattern Anal. Mach. Intell. **40**(2), 505–11 (2017)
8. Zhang, L., Yip, A.M., Brown, M.S., Tan, C.L.: A unified framework for document restoration using inpainting and shape-from-shading. Pattern Recogn. **42**(11), 2961–78 (2009)
9. Cao, H., Ding, X., Liu, C.: Rectifying the bound document image captured by the camera: A model based approach. In: Seventh International Conference on Document Analysis and Recognition, 2003. Proceedings. 2003 Aug 6, pp. 71–75. IEEE
10. Brown, M.S., Tsoi, Y.C.: Geometric and shading correction for images of printed materials using boundary. IEEE Trans. Image Process. **15**(6), 1544–54 (2006)
11. He, Y., Pan, P., Xie, S., Sun, J., Naoi, S.: A book dewarping system by boundary-based 3D surface reconstruction. In: 2013 12Th international Conference on Document Analysis and Recognition 2013 Aug 25, pp. 403–407. IEEE (2013)
12. Wada, T., Ukida, H., Matsuyama, T.: Shape from shading with interreflections under a proximal light source: distortion-free copying of an unfolded book. Int. J. Comput. Vision **24**, 125–35 (1997)
13. Meng, G., Su, Y., Wu, Y., Xiang, S., Pan, C.: Exploiting vector fields for geometric rectification of distorted document images. In: Proceedings of the European Conference on Computer Vision (ECCV) 2018, pp. 172–187 (2018)
14. Ezaki, H., Uchida, S., Asano, A., Sakoe, H.: Dewarping of document image by global optimization. In: Eighth International Conference on Document Analysis and Recognition (ICDAR'05) 2005 Aug 31, pp. 302–306. IEEE (2005)
15. Ma, K., Shu, Z., Bai, X., Wang, J., Samaras, D.: Docunet: document image unwarping via a stacked u-net. In: Proceedings of the IEEE Conference on Computer Vision and Pattern Recognition 2018, pp. 4700–4709 (2018)
16. Das, S., Ma, K., Shu, Z., Samaras, D., Shilkrot, R.: Dewarpnet: single-image document unwarping with stacked 3d and 2d regression networks. In: Proceedings of the IEEE/CVF International Conference on Computer Vision 2019, pp. 131–140 (2019)

17. Xie, G.-W., Yin, F., Zhang, X.-Y., Liu, C.-L.: Dewarping document image by displacement flow estimation with fully convolutional network. In: Bai, X., Karatzas, D., Lopresti, D. (eds.) DAS 2020. LNCS, vol. 12116, pp. 131–144. Springer, Cham (2020). https://doi.org/10.1007/978-3-030-57058-3_10

18. Xie, G.-W., Yin, F., Zhang, X.-Y., Liu, C.-L.: Document dewarping with control points. In: Lladós, J., Lopresti, D., Uchida, S. (eds.) ICDAR 2021. LNCS, vol. 12821, pp. 466–480. Springer, Cham (2021). https://doi.org/10.1007/978-3-030-86549-8_30

19. Liu, X., Meng, G., Fan, B., Xiang, S., Pan, C.: Geometric rectification of document images using adversarial gated unwarping network. Pattern Recogn. 1(108), 107576 (2020)

20. Li, X., Zhang, B., Liao, J., Sander, P.V.: Document rectification and illumination correction using a patch-based CNN. ACM Trans. Graph. (TOG) 38(6), 1–1 (2019)

21. Das, S., Singh, K.Y., Wu, J., Bas, E., Mahadevan, V., Bhotika, R., Samaras, D.: End-to-end piece-wise unwarping of document images. In: Proceedings of the IEEE/CVF International Conference on Computer Vision 2021, pp. 4268–4277 (2021)

22. Feng, H., Wang, Y., Zhou, W., Deng, J., Li, H.: Doctr: Document image transformer for geometric unwarping and illumination correction. arXiv preprint arXiv:2110.12942. 2021 Oct 25

23. Zhang, J., Luo, C., Jin, L., Guo, F., Ding, K.: Marior: margin removal and iterative content rectification for document dewarping in the wild. arXiv preprint arXiv:2207.11515. 2022 Jul 23

24. Ma, K., Das, S., Shu, Z., Samaras, D.: Learning from documents in the wild to improve document unwarping. In: ACM SIGGRAPH 2022 Conference Proceedings 2022 Jul 27, pp. 1–9

25. Xue, C., Tian, Z., Zhan, F., Lu, S., Bai, S.: Fourier document restoration for robust document dewarping and recognition. In: Proceedings of the IEEE/CVF Conference on Computer Vision and Pattern Recognition 2022, pp. 4573–4582

26. Jiang, X., Long, R., Xue, N., Yang, Z., Yao, C., Xia, G.S.: Revisiting document image dewarping by grid regularization. In: Proceedings of the IEEE/CVF Conference on Computer Vision and Pattern Recognition 2022, pp. 4543–4552 (2022)

27. Feng H, Zhou W, Deng J, Wang Y, Li H. Geometric representation learning for document image rectification. In: European Conference on Computer Vision 2022 Oct 22, pp. 475–492. Springer, Cham (2022). https://doi.org/10.1007/978-3-031-19836-6_27

28. Wang, Z., Simoncelli, E.P., Bovik, A.C.: Multiscale structural similarity for image quality assessment. In: The Thrity-Seventh Asilomar Conference on Signals, Systems & Computers, 2003 2003 Nov 9, vol. 2, pp. 1398–1402. IEEE (2003)

29. Wang, Z., Bovik, A.C., Sheikh, H.R., Simoncelli, E.P.: Image quality assessment: from error visibility to structural similarity. IEEE Trans. Image Process. 13(4), 600–12 (2004)

30. Liu, C., Yuen, J., Torralba, A., Sivic, J., Freeman, W.T.: Sift flow: dense correspondence across different scenes. In: Computer Vision-ECCV 2008: 10th European Conference on Computer Vision, Marseille, France, October 12–18, 2008, Proceedings, Part III 10 2008, pp. 28–42. Springer, Heidelberg

Multi-discriminative Parts Mining for Fine-Grained Visual Classification

Pingping Zhou, Cheng Pang[✉], Rushi Lan, Guanhua Wu, and Yilin Zhang

Guilin University of Electronic Technology, Guilin 541004, China
{pangcheng3,rslan}@guet.edu.cn

Abstract. Fine-Grained Visual Classification (FGVC) aims to differentiate visually similar but subtly different subordinate categories of the same basic category. However, current methods primarily exploit deep-layer features to locate to the strong salient part of the network. This paper finds that some subtle but discernible parts and the rich details in shallow-layer features are also valuable for classification. Consequently, this paper proposes a fine-grained visual classification framework that integrates multiple discriminative parts and multi-layer features. Our framework consists of two modules: 1) The attention map based locate-mine module locates the most discriminate part and masks it, thereby encouraging the network to mine other discriminative parts. 2) The multi-layer feature fusion module combines shallow-layer and deep-layer features to enrich local details in discriminative features. We also introduce an adaptive label loss to distinguish categories with high similarity. Experimental results show that our approach achieves excellent performance on three widely used fine-grained benchmark datasets.

Keywords: Fine-grained visual classification · Multi-discriminative parts · Multi-layer features · Adptive label loss

1 Introduction

In recent times, with the rapid advancements in artificial intelligence, fine-grained vision classification has been widely applied in the fields of autonomous driving [1], biological protection [30] and cancer detection [21]. Unlike coarse-grained vision classification, which only needs to identify the basic class of objects, the objective of FGVC tasks lies to recognize subordinate categories within a given fundamental category, such as bird breeds [29], car types [16] and airplane models [23]. Nevertheless, due to the extremely high visual similarity among subordinate categories and the presence of variations in scale, pose, and illumination, etc., they exhibit small inter-class differences and large intra-class differences, as displayed in Fig. 1. Moreover, a single basic category object can be encompassed hundreds or even thousands of subordinate categories. These factors have brought great challenges for fine-grained visual classification, and

Fig. 1. Partial samples of two subordinate categories of gulls in the CUB-200-2011 dataset. Within gulls of the same subordinate category, there is considerable variations in terms of scale, pose, and illumination (first row), but gulls of different subordinate categories are visually very similar (first column), which making fine-grained visual classification difficult.

it is often difficult to achieve satisfactory results with only the current state-of-the-art coarse-grained convolutional neural networks (CNNs), such as VGG [24], ResNet [12], and Inception [26].

To tackle the above challenges, numerous methods [2,14,17,34] have employed manually annotated bounding boxes and part annotations (e.g., bird head, body) to aid locate target objects or discern parts. However, this reliance on extensive manual intervention introduces drawbacks such as high cost and subjectivity, rendering it less suitable for fine-grained classification tasks. Accordingly, researchers have recently shifted their focus to weakly supervised fine-grained visual classification, where only image labels are used for supervision. These methods can be categorized into two sets.

The first set is based on part locating methods [9,11,31,36]. These methods work by identifying the highly discriminative parts and then taking advantage of specific feature extraction techniques to learn discriminative parts. Yet, the disadvantage of these approaches is their tendency to care about the most prominent parts within the network, eliminating other irrelevant parts to gain the ultimate feature representation. We contend that once the most salient parts are masked or suppressed, the network is compelled to explore other discriminative parts, thus providing greater amount of intricate and supplementary information. Motivated by this intuitive and feasible idea, we introduce the attention map based locate-mine module. This module represents the parts or visual representations of objects through the enhanced map generated by the enhancement mechanism. By randomly selecting a channel from enhanced map as the attention map to assist in localize discriminative parts, and in conjunction with the mining mechanism, further extracting other discriminative parts.

The second set of approaches is based on fine-grained feature learning [15,19,32]. These approaches take into consideration that low-dimensional features may not adequately capture the distinctions for effective classification.

Consequently, they aim to enhance feature representation by learning higher-dimensional features. Lin et al. [19] introduced a bilinear architecture that leverages the product of feature maps obtained from two separate CNNs to acquire higher-order correlations, thus improving visual recognition performance. Yu et al. [32] further explored and proposed a method of applying bilinear pooling on features at different layers of the network, thereby capturing the interactive relationships between multi-layer features. They demonstrated the performance improvement achieved by incorporating shallow-layer features in fine-grained classification tasks. In fact, deep-layer features contain global contextual information and high-level semantic representations in the network. However, due to their coarse spatial resolution, these features often overlook fine-grained details in local regions. Conversely, shallow-layer features possess more abundant local details and finer spatial information, which are crucial for distinguishing local parts in fine-grained datasets. By exploiting the merits of both of deep-layer and shallow-layer features, this paper introduces a fusion approach that combines deep-layer and shallow-layer features to preserve global contextual information in discriminative parts while enhancing the perception of local details.

Furthermore, we observe that existing studies are susceptible to misclassification when dealing with some categories with high similarity. This is because these studies usually use the cross-entropy loss function, which assigns equal weight to all categories and ignores the variations in discrimination difficulty and importance between different categories. To address this limitation, we design adaptive label loss methods that effectively allocate more attention to challenging categories and thus enhance their discrimination.

In summary, the main contributions of this paper are summarized as follows:

- We propose an attention map based locate-mine module, which can precisely locate discriminative parts and mine other discriminable parts;
- We propose a multi-layer feature fusion module, which combine the complementarity of multi-layer features to enrich the detailed information in the discriminate parts;
- We design an adaptive label loss to improves the network's ability to classify similar categories;
- Extensive experiments conducted on three widely used fine-grained classification benchmark datasets (i.e., CUB-200-2011, Stanford-Car and FGVC Aircraft) demonstrate the effectiveness of our method and achieve excellent performance results.

2 Relate Work

In recent studies on fine-grained image recognition, there has been a dedicated effort to locate discriminative parts and learn fine-grained features, resulting in a remarkable advancement in recognition performance.

2.1   Part Locating

The detection of subtle variations in key parts is of utmost importance for recognizing easily confusable categories. Early approaches [8,35] advocated detecting parts by strongly supervised learning using bounding boxes and part annotations. However, this labor-intensive approach is not practical for real-world problems. Recent studies have adopted a weakly supervised approach by providing only class labels, thus alleviating the need for expensive part annotations and localized information regions. Fu et al. [9] designed the Recurrent Attention Convolutional Neural Network (RA-CNN) to localize local regions from coarse to fine by iteratively amplifying local discriminative parts, and enhanced multi-scale feature learning by ranking loss. To simultaneously generate multiple attention locations, Zheng et al. [36] exploited the Multi-Attention Convolutional Neural Network (MA-CNN), which introduced a channel grouping loss to generate multiple rigions by clustering. Yang et al. [31] used a navigator module to gradually learn the ability to select distinctive local regions through self-supervised learning. Zhang et al. [33] proposed the MMAL framework, which is composed of multiple branches that can learn feature information at different scales. Zheng et al. [37] adopted a hierarchical approach, using multiple attention modules to progressively focus on information regions at different levels of granularity. Nevertheless, these methods primarily emphasize the highly discriminative parts and neglect some subtle but distinguishable parts. To overcome this limitation, we propose a module that not only localizes discriminative parts but also explores other discerning parts.

2.2   Fine-Grained Feature Learning

In fine-grained visual classification tasks, it is crucial to fully learn the recognized features. Due to the small differences between subordinate categories, extracting deep semantic features using CNNs only can limit further representation learning. To tackle this issue, Lin et al. [19] devised a bilinear architecture that exploits the outer product of feature maps from two separate CNNs to acquire higher-dimensional feature information for visual recognition tasks. However, the computational capacity is constrained due to the significant computational burden caused by bilinear pooling. They [18] a step further and improved the computational efficiency with learnable dimensionality reduction matrix and grouping operations. To reduce computational complexity while maintaining comparable recognition performance, Gao et al. [10] transformed the traditional bilinear pooling into a more compact form using random mapping and the Hadamard product. Kong et al. [15] further reduced the computational complexity by lowering the rank of the bilinear eigenmatrix. In addition, Cui et al. [4] extract richer feature representations by introducing kernel functions. However, most existing CNN models only use deep-layer semantic features for the final classification, while ignoring the benefit of shallow-layer local features. Therefore, Yu et al. [32] capture the feature interaction information between different levels through hierarchical bilinear pooling operations. Inspired by their utilization of shallow-layer features, we propose an approach to extract diverse various discriminative and complementary visual cues from multiple layers of features instead of a single layer. Moreover, we introduce adaptive label loss to incentivize the network to acquire more generalized features.

3   Method

In this section, we provide a detailed description of the proposed framework. The overall architecture is illustrated in Fig. 2. It is formed by two modules: the Attention Map based Locate-Mine module (AMLM) and the Multi-layer Feature Fusion module (MFF). The AMLM module locates the strong discriminative part and explores other discriminative parts. The MFF module fuses multi-layer features to capture various visual cues that complementary the discriminative parts. Furthermore, we design an adaptive label loss to focus more on highly similar categories.

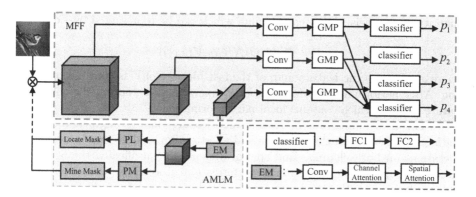

Fig. 2. The overall architecture of our proposed method consists of two modules: the Attention Map-based Locate-Mine module (AMLM) and the Multi-layer Feature Fusion module (MFF). The AMLM module uses the enhanced feature maps generated by the Enhancement Mechanism (EM) to facilitate visual perception of the part. Through the Part Locating component (PL) and the Part Mining component (PM), multiple discriminative parts in the target can be obtained. The MFF module complements the fine-grained details within the discriminative parts by fusing features from multiple layers.

3.1   Attention Map Based Locate-Mine Module (AMLM)

Existing methodologies tend to excessively prioritize parts with elevated response values while disregarding other nuanced but discriminative parts. To mitigate the risk of the network fixating only on the most salient part and to get a larger number of discriminative parts, we introduce the attention map based locate-mine module, as depicted in the orange dashed box within Fig. 2. This module integrates enhancement mechanisms, part locating component, and part mining component.

First the image I^{img} is input into the pre-trained backbone network ResNet. We use $x_n \in R^{H \times W \times C}$ to denote the feature map output by the nth block in the network, where $n \in 1, \ldots, N$, H denotes the height of the feature map, W denotes the width of the feature map, and C represents the size of the feature dimension.

Enhancement Mechanism (EM). In the feature map x_n, each channel has a peak response region that corresponds to a specific part of the target, such as a bird's head, a car's wheel, or an airplane's wing. It is worth noting that certain channels may yield peak responses that correspond to the same part. When employing all channels for localization, the network may inadvertently concentrate on similar parts, thereby getting in a lack of diversity in localization results. To learn more diverse parts, we used a convolutional dimensionality reduction operation, which integrates similar peak responses by reducing the quantity of channels in the feature map, which can be represented by Eq. (1):

$$E = ReLU(BN(ConV(x_n))) \tag{1}$$

where x_n denotes the feature map of the last block, $ConV$ is convolution function. After performing the aforementioned operations, we obtain the enhanced feature map E, which contains local part information.

To effectively integrate the transformed features and strengthen the information associated with the parts, we add an attention module that incorporates operations on both channels and spatial dimension. Specifically, the attention mechanism applied to the channels performs global average pooling on the E and combines it with one-dimensional convolution operations to acquire the importance of parts within the channels. The process of generating the channel-enhanced map E^C, which can be written as Eq. (2):

$$E^C = (\sigma(ConV1D(GAP(E)) \otimes E \tag{2}$$

where GAP is the global average pooling, the $ConV1D$ is the 1D convolution, the σ refers to the sigmoid function, and $\otimes$ denotes element-by-element multiplication.

Next, the E^C will perform spatial operations. Specifically, the E^C is first subjected to global average pooling and global maximum pooling operations along the channel dimension to highlight the information parts. Subsequently, we apply convolution to generate a spatial attention mask, where each element is normalized to a value from 0 to 1 with the help of sigmoid, which reflects the importance of the parts in space. Finally, the spatial importance factor is multiplied with the channel enhanced map E^C to obtain the final spatially enhanced map E^S, as shown in Eq. (3):

$$E^S = (\sigma(ConV[GAP(E^c); GMP(E^C)])) \otimes E^C \tag{3}$$

where σ is the sigmoid activation function. GAP and GMP refer to global average pooling and global maximum pooling respectively, $\otimes$ refer to Hadamard product. To get a specific part and learn its valuable information, we randomly select one channel from the E^S as the attention map to locate the target part, and the attention map is denoted as A.

Part Locating (PL). Using the attention map A, the estimated position of the part can be localized and more detailed local features can be extracted. Specifically, we define locating mask $M^{locate}(u, v)$ based on a threshold valued T^{locate}. The locating mask $M^{locate}(u, v)$ can be obtained from Eq. (4):

$$M^{locate}(u, v) = \begin{cases} 1, if\ A(u, v) > T^{locate} \\ 0, \qquad otherwise \end{cases} \tag{4}$$

where (u, v) denotes a pixel on the attention map A. We choose the smallest bounding box on M^{locate} that encompasses the target part and covers the largest connected region on the locating mask. By multiplying this localization result with $I^i mg$, we acquire the located image I^{locate}. We then feed I^{locate} into the network and obtain the predicted results denoted as p^{locate}.

Part Mining (PM). The mining operation, achieved through masking the highly responsive part, thereby facilitating the exploration of other viable discriminative parts. Similar to the locating operation, we remove response values above a threshold T^{mine} of the region, thus we obtaining the mining mask $M^{mine}(u, v)$, which can be expressed by in Eq. (5):

$$M^{mine}(u, v) = \begin{cases} 0, if\ A(u, v) > T^{mine} \\ 1, \qquad otheiwise \end{cases} \tag{5}$$

the mining mask $M^{mine}(u, v)$ applied to the input image I^{img} yields the image after the mask overlay I^{mine}. The prediction result based on I^{mine} is denoted as p^{mine}. Since the attention map is removed from the image A high response value part, the network will be encouraged to present other discriminative parts, which means that the object can also be seen better.

3.2 Multi-layer Feature Fusion Module (MFF)

Previous works mainly rely on the feature map output from the last block of the network as the feature representation and search for significant information in it. Although it contains powerful semantic information, it has insufficient detail information, which is detrimental to the FGVC task. Therefore, we propose the Multi-layer Feature Fusion module(MFF), indicated by the blue dashed box in Fig. 2. It utilizes features from different layers to improve the classification performance by complementing the detail information within the discriminative features.

When performing feature fusion of different layers, due to the inconsistent feature dimensions among these blocks are, we use convolution layers with batch normalized to align them to a uniform feature dimension. Then, these features are fed into the pooling layer to obtain a compact image representation. Finally, these representations are sent to the classifier for classification, resulting in the predicted results p_n of the image. As shown in Eq. (6):

$$p_n^{img} = GAP(ReLU(ConV_1(ReLU(ConV_2(x_n))))) \tag{6}$$

where $ConV_1$ and $ConV_2$ are the convolution functions, $ReLU$ is the activation function, and GAP is the global average pooling. Finally, an image has a total of $N+1$ predictions, which will be aggregated into the final prediction.

3.3   Adaptive Label Loss

In the context of fine-grained recognition tasks, the selection of the appropriate loss function is crucial for the model to be able to solve the problem effectively. Cross-entropy loss is the most commonly used loss function, where equal weights are assigned to each class. However, in a practical fine-grained visual classification task, there exist variations in discrimination difficulty and importance among different categories. To emphasize the difference between similar categories and motivate the network to learn common features, we devise an adaptive label loss which transforms the labels of individual categories into probability distributions. This method aims to allocate increased attention to challenging categories that exhibit difficulty in discrimination, thus enhancing the network's classification capacity for similar classes. As shown in Eq. (7):

$$\tilde{y}^l = \varepsilon y^l + \frac{1-\varepsilon}{L} \tag{7}$$

where ε refers to the proportion coefficient amongst 0 to 1, it regulates the proportion of real label y^l in the new label $\tilde{y}^l$, l denotes the label vector $y \in R^L$ of indexed elements. Thus, the adaptive label loss can be expressed by Eq. (8):

$$\mathcal{L}_{AL}(I) = -\sum_{n=1}^{N}\sum_{l=0}^{L-1} \tilde{y}_n^l log(p_n^l) \tag{8}$$

Therefore the total loss is calculated by Eq. (9)

$$\mathcal{L}_{total} = \mathcal{L}_{AL}(I^{img}) + \mathcal{L}_{AL}(I^{locate}) + \mathcal{L}_{AL}(I^{mine}) \tag{9}$$

4   Experiment

We validate the proposed method on three publicly available fine-grained visual classification datasets: CUB-200-2011 (CUB) [29], Stanford-Cars (CAR) [16], and FGVC-aircraft (AIR) [23]. In order to ensure the fairness of the comparative experiment, we implement our method using ResNet50 [12] pre-trained on the ImageNet classification dataset as the backbone model. In the experiments, we only use image labels without employing any additional auxiliary annotations. We utilize an SGD optimizer with a momentum of 0.9, a weight decay of 2e-4, and a total training period of 200. To ensure stable training, we adopt a cosine annealing learning rate adaptation strategy. At the beginning of training, the learning rate of the backbone layer is set to 0.0002, and the remaining layers are set to 10 times the learning rate of the backbone layer. For the proportion coefficients ε, we simply set $\{0.7, 0.8, 0.9, 1.0\}$ in ascending order, since larger values indicate higher confidence in class prediction.

4.1 Comparison with the Latest Methods

Table 1. Comparison results of our proposed method with state-of-the-art approaches on three publicly available datasets. All the compared methods employ ResNet50 as the backbone network.

Method	Accuracy (%)		
	CUB	CAR	AIR
NTS [31]	87.5	93.3	91.4
DCL [3]	87.8	94.5	93.0
PA-CNN [37]	87.8	93.3	91.0
FDL [20]	88.6	94.3	93.4
DF-GMM [28]	88.8	94.8	93.8
PMG [7]	89.6	95.1	93.4
MMAL [33]	89.6	95.0	94.7
AP-CNN [6]	88.4	95.4	94.1
SnapMix [13]	87.8	94.3	92.8
FBSD [25]	89.3	94.4	92.7
FRA-MLFF [27]	89.5	94.8	93.0
CHRF [22]	89.4	95.2	93.6
CMN [5]	88.2	-	93.8
Ours	**89.7**	**95.7**	**95.8**

Table 1 presents the evaluation results comparing our proposed method with recent approaches on three publicly available fine-grained visual classification datasets. As shown in the table, utilizing ResNet50 as the backbone network for all comparisons, our method consistently achieves the best performance across all three widely-used datasets.

Specifically, on the CUB dataset, our proposed approach achieves the best performance among the listed methods. Meanwhile, our method gains an accuracy of 95.7% on the CAR dataset, surpassing the previous state-of-the-art accuracy achieved by PMG. On the AIR dataset, our method exhibits a performance improvement of 1.1% over the top accuracy of MMAL, reaching a new state-of-the-art accuracy of 95.8%.

Overall, the method proposed in this paper benefits from two advantages:1) The attention map base locate-mine module learns discriminative features by locating parts, and mines other valuable features by removing the strongly different part, which contributes to the performance improvement;2) By using the learning of multi-layer features on the CNN backbone, our approach effectively captures both high-level semantic information and low-level detailed information. This complementary integration with distinctive features leads to improved classification performance and more accurate localization.

4.2   Ablation Experiments

Table 2. Contribution of the proposed components and their combinations.

Method	Modules(%)					Acc
	EM	PL	PM	MFF	AL-loss	
(a)						85.5
(b)	✓					85.8
(c)	✓	✓				87.5
(d)	✓	✓	✓			88.7
(e)	✓	✓	✓	✓		89.3
(f)	✓	✓	✓	✓	✓	89.7

To assess the impact of each component and the devised adaptive label loss on the performance improvement of the network, we conduct ablation experiments on each module using the CUB-200-2011 dataset. The test results are presented in Table 2. First, by adding the AME component into the ResNet50 backbone network, we achieved an accuracy of 85.8%, indicating that a series of enhancement operations on the feature map contribute to the performance improvement of the network. Subsequently, the addition of the PL component resulted in an accuracy of 87.5%, an improvement of 1.7%, demonstrating that the locating and learning object parts effectively improve accuracy. Moreover, the inclusion of the PM component yielded a further improvement of 1.2%, indicating that the network's performance benefits from capturing multiple discriminative parts. Taking it a step further, by incorporating MFF component, we achieved an accuracy of 89.4%. This result demonstrates the beneficial impact of leveraging detailed information from the rich discriminative parts within the network for fine-grained classification. Finally, when the adaptive label loss was harnessed for supervised training, accuracy increased further to 89.7%, providing evidence that the AL-loss does indeed improve the network's performance.

4.3   Visualization

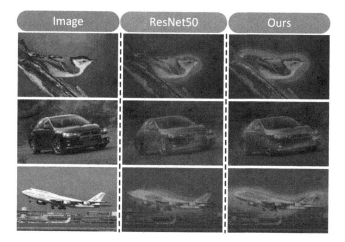

Fig. 3. Heatmaps of test samples from ResNet50 and our proposed method. Comparisons within each row reveal that our method exhibits a greater ability to attend to a larger number of discriminative parts compared to ResNet50.

In order to demonstrate the effectiveness of our proposed method, we have additionally provided visualizations of the heatmaps generated by both the ResNet50 network and our network on a subset of test samples. As illustrated in Fig. 3, the results clearly indicate that our method achieves superior accuracy in locating complete objects and their corresponding parts.

5   Summary

In this paper, we present a novel fine-grained classification network. It introduces the Attention Map-based Locate-Mine (AMLM) module to accurately locate highly discriminative parts and explore other available discriminative regions within the network, thereby facilitating the learning of valuable local part information to achieve favorable classification performance. It introduces the Multi-Layer Feature Fusion (MFF) module, which provides rich and detailed information for the discriminative parts, promoting the network's focus on subtle but crucial local parts. The synergistic collaboration between these two modules enables the network to perceive the holistic view of the target and extract more critical information. Moreover, the adaptive label loss also contributes to improving the discriminability between similar categories. Experimental results demonstrate the remarkable performance of our approach on three widely adopted benchmark datasets.

Acknowledgements. This work is partially supported by the Guangxi Science and Technology Project (AD20159034, ZY20198016), the Open Funds from Guilin University of Electronic Technology, Guangxi Key Laboratory of Image and Graphic Intelligent Processing (GIIP2208) and the National Natural Science Foundation of China (61962014).

References

1. Bojarski, M., et al.: End to end learning for self-driving cars. arXiv preprint arXiv:1604.07316 (2016)
2. Branson, S., Van Horn, G., Belongie, S., Perona, P.: Bird species categorization using pose normalized deep convolutional nets. arXiv preprint arXiv:1406.2952 (2014)
3. Chen, Y., Bai, Y., Zhang, W., Mei, T.: Destruction and construction learning for fine-grained image recognition. In: Proceedings of the IEEE/CVF Conference on Computer Vision and Pattern Recognition, pp. 5157–5166 (2019)
4. Cui, Y., Zhou, F., Wang, J., Liu, X., Lin, Y., Belongie, S.: Kernel pooling for convolutional neural networks. In: Proceedings of the IEEE Conference on Computer Vision and Pattern Recognition, pp. 2921–2930 (2017)
5. Deng, W., Marsh, J., Gould, S., Zheng, L.: Fine-grained classification via categorical memory networks. IEEE Trans. Image Process. **31**, 4186–4196 (2022)
6. Ding, Y.: Ap-cnn: weakly supervised attention pyramid convolutional neural network for fine-grained visual classification. IEEE Trans. Image Process. **30**, 2826–2836 (2021)
7. Du, R., Chang, D., Bhunia, A.K., Xie, J., Ma, Z., Song, Y.-Z., Guo, J.: Fine-grained visual classification via progressive multi-granularity training of jigsaw patches. In: Vedaldi, A., Bischof, H., Brox, T., Frahm, J.-M. (eds.) ECCV 2020. LNCS, vol. 12365, pp. 153–168. Springer, Cham (2020). https://doi.org/10.1007/978-3-030-58565-5_10
8. Fu, J., Wang, J., Rui, Y., Wang, X.J., Mei, T., Lu, H.: Image tag refinement with view-dependent concept representations. IEEE Trans. Circuits Syst. Video Technol. **25**(8), 1409–1422 (2014)
9. Fu, J., Zheng, H., Mei, T.: Look closer to see better: recurrent attention convolutional neural network for fine-grained image recognition. In: Proceedings of the IEEE Conference on Computer Vision and Pattern Recognition, pp. 4438–4446 (2017)
10. Gao, Y., Beijbom, O., Zhang, N., Darrell, T.: Compact bilinear pooling. In: Proceedings of the IEEE Conference on Computer Vision and Pattern Recognition, pp. 317–326 (2016)
11. Ge, W., Lin, X., Yu, Y.: Weakly supervised complementary parts models for fine-grained image classification from the bottom up. In: Proceedings of the IEEE/CVF Conference on Computer Vision and Pattern Recognition, pp. 3034–3043 (2019)
12. He, K., Zhang, X., Ren, S., Sun, J.: Deep residual learning for image recognition. In: Proceedings of the IEEE Conference on Computer Vision and Pattern Recognition, pp. 770–778 (2016)

13. Huang, S., Wang, X., Tao, D.: Snapmix: semantically proportional mixing for augmenting fine-grained data. In: Proceedings of the AAAI Conference on Artificial Intelligence, vol. 35, pp. 1628–1636 (2021)
14. Huang, S., Xu, Z., Tao, D., Zhang, Y.: Part-stacked CNN for fine-grained visual categorization. In: Proceedings of the IEEE Conference on Computer Vision and Pattern Recognition, pp. 1173–1182 (2016)
15. Kong, S., Fowlkes, C.: Low-rank bilinear pooling for fine-grained classification. In: Proceedings of the IEEE Conference on Computer Vision and Pattern Recognition, pp. 365–374 (2017)
16. Krause, J., Stark, M., Deng, J., Fei-Fei, L.: 3d object representations for fine-grained categorization. In: Proceedings of the IEEE International Conference on Computer Vision Workshops, pp. 554–561 (2013)
17. Lin, D., Shen, X., Lu, C., Jia, J.: Deep lac: deep localization, alignment and classification for fine-grained recognition. In: Proceedings of the IEEE Conference on Computer Vision and Pattern Recognition, pp. 1666–1674 (2015)
18. Lin, T.Y., Maji, S.: Improved bilinear pooling with cnns. arXiv preprint arXiv:1707.06772 (2017)
19. Lin, T.Y., RoyChowdhury, A., Maji, S.: Bilinear CNN models for fine-grained visual recognition. In: Proceedings of the IEEE International Conference on Computer Vision, pp. 1449–1457 (2015)
20. Liu, C., Xie, H., Zha, Z.J., Ma, L., Yu, L., Zhang, Y.: Filtration and distillation: enhancing region attention for fine-grained visual categorization. In: Proceedings of the AAAI Conference on Artificial Intelligence, vol. 34, pp. 11555–11562 (2020)
21. Liu, W., Juhas, M., Zhang, Y.: Fine-grained breast cancer classification with bilinear convolutional neural networks (bcnns). Front. Genet. 11, 547327 (2020)
22. Liu, Y., Zhou, L., Zhang, P., Bai, X., Gu, L., Yu, X., Zhou, J., Hancock, E.R.: Where to focus: Investigating hierarchical attention relationship for fine-grained visual classification. In: Computer Vision-ECCV 2022: 17th European Conference, Tel Aviv, Israel, October 23–27, 2022, Proceedings, Part XXIV, pp. 57–73. Springer, Cham (2022). https://doi.org/10.1007/978-3-031-20053-3_4
23. Maji, S., Rahtu, E., Kannala, J., Blaschko, M., Vedaldi, A.: Fine-grained visual classification of aircraft. arXiv preprint arXiv:1306.5151 (2013)
24. Simonyan, K., Zisserman, A.: Very deep convolutional networks for large-scale image recognition. arXiv preprint arXiv:1409.1556 (2014)
25. Song, J., Yang, R.: Feature boosting, suppression, and diversification for fine-grained visual classification. In: 2021 International Joint Conference on Neural Networks (IJCNN), pp. 1–8. IEEE (2021)
26. Szegedy, C., Vanhoucke, V., Ioffe, S., Shlens, J., Wojna, Z.: Rethinking the inception architecture for computer vision. In: Proceedings of the IEEE Conference on Computer Vision and Pattern Recognition, pp. 2818–2826 (2016)
27. Wang, K., Tian, Q., Wang, Y., Liu, B.: Feature re-attention and multi-layer feature fusion for fine-grained visual classification. In: 2022 16th IEEE International Conference on Signal Processing (ICSP), vol. 1, pp. 95–100. IEEE (2022)
28. Wang, Z., Wang, S., Yang, S., Li, H., Li, J., Li, Z.: Weakly supervised fine-grained image classification via Guassian mixture model oriented discriminative learning. In: Proceedings of the IEEE/CVF Conference on Computer Vision and Pattern Recognition, pp. 9749–9758 (2020)
29. Welinder, P., et al.: Caltech-ucsd birds 200 (2010)
30. Xu, X., Yang, C.C., Xiao, Y., Kong, J.L.: A fine-grained recognition neural network with high-order feature maps via graph-based embedding for natural bird diversity conservation. Int. J. Environ. Res. Public Health 20(6), 4924 (2023)

31. Yang, Z., Luo, T., Wang, D., Hu, Z., Gao, J., Wang, L.: Learning to navigate for fine-grained classification. In: Proceedings of the European Conference on Computer Vision (ECCV), pp. 420–435 (2018)
32. Yu, C., Zhao, X., Zheng, Q., Zhang, P., You, X.: Hierarchical bilinear pooling for fine-grained visual recognition. In: Proceedings of the European Conference on Computer Vision (ECCV), pp. 574–589 (2018)
33. Zhang, F., Li, M., Zhai, G., Liu, Y.: Multi-branch and multi-scale attention learning for fine-grained visual categorization. In: MultiMedia Modeling: 27th International Conference, MMM 2021, Prague, Czech Republic, June 22–24, 2021, Proceedings, Part I 27. pp. 136–147. Springer (2021)
34. Zhang, N., Donahue, J., Girshick, R., Darrell, T.: Part-based r-cnns for fine-grained category detection. In: Computer Vision-ECCV 2014: 13th European Conference, Zurich, Switzerland, September 6–12, 2014, Proceedings, Part I 13. pp. 834–849. Springer (2014)
35. Zhao, B., Wu, X., Feng, J., Peng, Q., Yan, S.: Diversified visual attention networks for fine-grained object classification. IEEE Trans. Multimedia **19**(6), 1245–1256 (2017)
36. Zheng, H., Fu, J., Mei, T., Luo, J.: Learning multi-attention convolutional neural network for fine-grained image recognition. In: Proceedings of the IEEE International Conference on Computer Vision, pp. 5209–5217 (2017)
37. Zheng, H., Fu, J., Zha, Z.J., Luo, J., Mei, T.: Learning rich part hierarchies with progressive attention networks for fine-grained image recognition. IEEE Trans. Image Process. **29**, 476–488 (2019)

Geometric Distortion Correction for Extreme Scene Distortion of UAV-Acquired Images

Mark Phil B. Pacot[1,2(✉)] [iD] and Nelson Marcos[2]

[1] Caraga State University, Butuan, Caraga, Philippines
mbpacot@carsu.edu.ph
[2] De La Salle University, Taft Ave., Manila, Philippines
nelson.marcos@dlsu.edu.ph

Abstract. Geometric distortion, especially in extreme cases of scene distortion, is a prevalent issue in images taken by Unmanned Aerial Vehicles (UAVs). This research focuses on tackling this issue using a proposed approach that combines cutting-edge computer vision and photogrammetry techniques. It combines precise feature matching and image-warping algorithms, resulting in a more straightforward approach. By utilizing a Graph Neural Networks-based strategy and fine-tuning hyperparameters to strengthen the algorithm, the feature detection technique is further improved. To rectify spatial deformation within the scene, the homography estimation, which merges the Direct Linear Transform (DLT) approach with Singular Value Decomposition (SVD), is employed. Additionally, at the image registration phase, outliers are rejected using the Random Sample Consensus (RANSAC) technique. The image quality of the rectified images was evaluated using both objective and subjective image quality parameters. Overall, this research produces visually appealing image output in both extreme scene distortion correction and pair-wise image stitching applications, achieving favorable assessment findings based on SSIM, PSNR, and PIQE image quality metrics.

Keywords: Nadir-based Distorted UAV Images · Homography-based Transformation · Graph Neural Networks-based Feature Detection · Image Registration · Rectified Aerial Images

1 Introduction

Unmanned Aerial Vehicles (UAVs) or drones have become increasingly popular in various applications including environmental monitoring, disaster assessment, and agricultural inspections, due to their ability to capture high-resolution images from aerial perspectives [1]. However, the images captured by drones often suffer from distortion, specifically caused by the complex interaction between the camera sensor, lens, and the three-dimensional scene [2]. This interaction is exacerbated by significant spatial transformations and rapid changes in altitude and orientation during image acquisition [3]. Geometric distortion is one of the prevalent issues in images acquired by UAVs [4], particularly in nadir images which are taken from directly above a location, looking straight down towards the Earth's surface. This distortion is termed as Extreme Scene Distortion (ESD), which results in inaccuracies in spatial measurements, hinders the extraction of reliable features, and impedes the subsequent analysis and interpretation of the UAV acquired data.

Efficient correction of this geometric distortion is crucial particularly in UAV applications that require precise measurements and detailed scene reconstruction. In recent years, significant progress has been made, with researchers exploring various approaches, including camera calibration, image rectification, and image-warping techniques, to mitigate the effects of this type of distortion. However, the majority of these methods are limited in their applicability to the extreme scene distortions introduced in this work, as they often assume simplified scene models [5, 6].

By leveraging state-of-the-art techniques from computer vision and photogrammetry, the researchers propose a method that combines robust feature matching and image-warping techniques. This method is less complex and more straightforward compared to non-direct solutions for mitigating the aforementioned problem. The outcomes of this research could potentially enhance the quality and reliability of UAV-based applications, enabling more accurate data analysis, decision-making, and interpretation.

The main contributions of this research work are (1) a simple approach that explores the combination of state-of-the-art robust feature-based matching and image-warping techniques to handle ESD; and (2) a new benchmark dataset representing ESD which is valuable for researchers and practitioners with similar interests in developing new algorithms capable of correcting extreme and challenging distortions in UAV images.

Section 2 of this paper reviews the literature on scene distortion correction in UAV-acquired images. Section 3 presents the proposed method, including the feature-matching algorithm and the image-warping algorithm for extreme scene distortion correction. In Sect. 4, the method is evaluated using objective metrics, including the no-reference image quality metric. Results are analyzed and compared with existing methods, highlighting the performance of rectifying UAV images. The conclusion summarizes the contributions and implications of the research in addressing extreme scene distortion and suggests future research directions in this field of study.

2 Related Work

2.1 Feature-Based Image Recognition

Feature-based image recognition finds applications in computer vision, robotics, medical imaging, and more. By focusing on meaningful features instead of processing the entire image, it mimics the human visual system. This scientific approach combines image processing techniques, pattern recognition algorithms, and machine learning methods to automate visual analysis and understanding. In the realm of image recognition, two broad categories of algorithms have emerged: hand-crafted feature algorithms and deep learning algorithms. Hand-crafted feature algorithms, including Speeded-Up Robust Features (SURF), Scale-Invariant Feature Transform (SIFT), Oriented FAST and Rotated BRIEF (ORB), and Histogram of Oriented Gradients (HOG), have traditionally relied on human-designed features to offer robustness in image analysis tasks. However, their limitations in generalization capabilities have become apparent.

On the other hand, deep learning algorithms, such as Convolutional Neural Networks (CNNs), Recurrent Neural Networks (RNNs), and Generative Adversarial Networks (GANs), have revolutionized the field by automatically learning features from data and showcasing remarkable generalization and adaptability. Nevertheless, they necessitate substantial amounts of labeled training data and computational resources. Their impact is evident in various fields were automated image interpretation and decision-making play crucial roles. For instance, in their pioneering work [7], the researchers significantly advanced by incorporating a hand-crafted feature algorithm into their stitching algorithm for sequentially overlapping UAV images. This innovative approach involved utilizing feature point matching, explicitly leveraging the Oriented FAST and Rotated BRIEF (ORB) feature detection algorithm to characterize the overlapping regions present in the images accurately. Combining the ORB with Grid Motion Statistics achieved remarkable results, effectively clustering UAV images with similar overlaps and enabling real-time image stitching capabilities. In their study, researchers [8] emphasized the significance of analyzing image overlaps for effective image retrieval. They proposed a method that involved down-sampling image resolution and using a simple descriptor or feature-matching technique. The researchers utilized the powerful Scale-Invariant Feature Transform (SIFT) algorithm, which exhibited impressive capabilities in accurately analyzing image overlaps and handling incorrect feature point matches. The inherent characteristics of SIFT, including scale, rotation, and mapping invariance, played a crucial role in the success of overlap analysis. Leveraging the robustness and adaptability of SIFT, the researchers achieved both effectiveness and efficiency in image retrieval, underscoring the algorithm's crucial role in precise image analysis and retrieval tasks.

Additionally, the work of [6] introduces an efficient technique for aerial image stitching, employing a synergistic combination of SURF, PCA, and RANSAC algorithms. Their comparative analysis against SIFT features reveals their proposed algorithm's superior performance in terms of feature extraction and resulting image quality. The computational time required for stitching using SURF is promising, suggesting potential for real-time applications. Recent trends in deep learning-based algorithms for feature-based image recognition have played a significant role in many applications such as medical image retrieval. They include leveraging deep learning for medical decision support systems, utilizing pre-trained models like ResNet-50 and VGG19 with ImageNet weights to identify similar dermatoscopic images and brain tumor MRI scans, employing the deep Siamese CNN architecture to extract fixed-length feature vectors, developing hash code generation methods, and creating systems for retrieving specific lung diseases in CT scans (deep feature-based image recognition approaches) [9]. These methods aim to enhance the efficiency and accuracy of medical image retrieval, catering to various medical domains.

On the other hand, the emergence of 3D Graph Neural Networks (GNNs) has brought remarkable improvements to the field. By leveraging the multi-layer structure of GNNs, it becomes feasible to extract unique features and depth information from RGB images, facilitating robust and accurate segmentation outcomes [10]. These deep learning-based algorithms, with their ability to harness multi-layer networks and exploit contextual information, hold great promise for enhancing the task of image segmentation using RGB images [11]. The remarkable progress made in feature-based image recognition, encompassing both handcrafted and deep learning-based algorithms, has profoundly impacted the applications related to UAV images. By integrating these methods, we can unlock new possibilities in extracting meaningful features and recognizing objects in aerial imagery captured by unmanned aerial vehicles (UAVs). The combination of hand-crafted algorithms, carefully designed feature extraction techniques, and the power of deep learning models capable of learning intricate patterns and representations presents a compelling foundation for advancing UAV image analysis.

2.2   Geometric Distortion Correction

Geometric distortions commonly found in aerial imaging, including radial distortion, tangential distortion, perspective distortion, and keystoning, can impact both the accuracy and visual quality of the images. This study will focus on a specific type of distortion known as perspective distortion or geometric distortion, which has received limited attention in the field of aerial photogrammetry. Figure 1 illustrates the distortions caused by camera rotation in UAV photos, which are categorized as geometric distortion in this study.

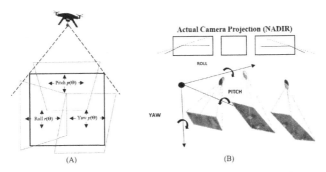

Fig. 1. Extreme Scene Distortion Representation in UAV-Based Imagery.

In Fig. 1A, the box represents the region captured when the aerial camera rotates at various angles, including the pitch angle (p), roll angle (r), and yaw angle (y). Additionally, Fig. 1B displays the corresponding output, showing distortion occurring in one direction parallel to the scanning direction without displacement directly below the image sensor (nadir), and distortion resulting from the rotation of the scanning optics. It is important to note that as the sensor scans across each line, the distance between the sensor and the ground increases, particularly further away from the center of the scanned aerial image. This phenomenon, also known as tangential scale distortion, occurs when picture image features are compressed at positions away from the ground plane's center.

Camera calibration, a technique widely utilized by researchers, involves determining intrinsic and extrinsic parameters to accurately model the behavior of a camera [12]. This process is essential for correcting geometric distortion. However, it should be noted that camera calibration can be a computationally demanding task, often requiring sophisticated algorithms and extensive computational resources [13]. Additionally, achieving accurate calibration results typically requires careful attention to detail, as even small errors in parameter estimation can significantly impact subsequent computer vision algorithms and applications [14]. Previous research has investigated alternative approaches, such as image registration or homography-based correction, which are widely recognized and employed techniques in the field of remotely sensed images.

This technique encompasses crucial steps, including feature detection, feature matching, and homography estimation. For instance, [15] developed a local-adaptive image alignment strategy using triangular facet approximation. This method surpasses the standard homographic technique in aligning both perspective and non-perspective images. Incorporating Gaussian and Student t-weighting parameters enhances alignment and stitching, especially when dealing with diverse camera viewpoints that cause image parallax or ghosting. Their research represents a notable advancement, providing a robust and accurate solution for image alignment and stitching, pushing the boundaries of image processing techniques.

The work of [16] made significant contributions to the field of image alignment and geometric distortion correction. They developed a robust elastic warping-based approach for parallax-tolerant image stitching, resulting in precise alignment and reduced computational overhead. Their work incorporated a Bayesian model for feature refinement, effectively removing inaccurate local matches. Additionally, they introduced a flexible strategy that combined global similarity transformation for the fast reprojection of warped images. These advancements contributed to the correction of geometric distortions, leading to improved alignment accuracy and the creation of seamless panoramic images.

In their research, [17] focused on addressing severe perspective distortions present in a large collection of aerial images. To suppress reprojection errors and image parallax, they developed a reliable technique for achieving precise and globally consistent alignment of ground-scene objects. Their work specifically targeted geometric distortion correction, aiming to create natural-looking panoramas. In a related study, [18] also contributed to the field by creating a natural panorama through adaptive and as-natural-as-possible image stitching. Furthermore, the work of [19] focused on addressing the challenges posed by image parallax and the reliance on post-hoc de-ghosting techniques. To overcome these issues, they introduced a novel approach utilizing a moving direct linear transformation (MLDT) and a unique 2D warp function. Their innovative methodology resulted in an accurate image alignment strategy that effectively eliminated image parallax and reduced the need for post-processing de-ghosting. By incorporating these advancements, they achieved improved alignment consistency and enhanced the overall quality of the aligned images.

The advent of deep learning-based algorithms holds significant promise for addressing geometric distortion correction challenges. These advanced algorithms leverage the power of deep learning techniques to effectively handle and rectify geometric distortions in various types of imagery, including aerial images. By employing neural networks and extensive training on large datasets, these methods demonstrate the potential to achieve accurate and reliable geometric distortion correction results. The ability of deep learning algorithms to learn complex patterns and relationships in data offers new possibilities for enhancing the correction process, potentially leading to improved precision and efficiency in real-world applications [20]. Hence, this research aims to investigate the homography-based technique for geometric distortion correction while integrating deep learning-based feature image recognition to enhance the current approach. Figure 2 shows the block diagram of the proposed study.

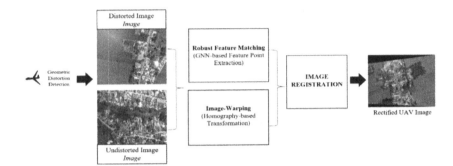

Fig. 2. Block diagram of the Proposed Geometric Distortion Correction Technique.

The block diagram focuses on identifying and correcting geometric distortion in UAV images. First, the researchers employ a human-intervention-free method to recognize acquired UAV images with scene distortion, utilizing PIX4DMapper software. Second, distorted images are manually identified, and they are paired with undistorted images to create distinct image pairs (Image n and Image n + 1) for feature matching. However, if a distorted image lacks an undistorted pair (i.e., a sequence of two distorted images), the proposed solution is to skip it until predetermined criteria are met. Third, a GNN-based feature point extraction technique from [21] was used to extract distinct features, especially in regions where objects are affected by scene distortion. Fourth, a homography-based transformation is integrated, utilizing unique feature points identified by the introduced robust feature matching technique. These points will be fed into the last step. The final step known as image registration, warps the distorted image to align it with its paired undistorted image, thereby correcting the distortion.

3 Proposed Method

Different methods for correcting geometric distortion are available, but they mostly work well with mild distortions and face challenges when dealing with severe distortions. Therefore, there is a pressing need to develop robust and efficient methods specifically tailored to address extreme scene distortion in UAV-acquired images.

3.1 Dataset Description

This research utilizes a carefully selected dataset of images captured by a handheld SONY DSC-RX100M3 camera aboard in a UAV. The camera boasts an impressive 20.1-megapixel Exmor RTM CMOS Sensor, ensuring high-quality images with a spatial resolution of about 2 cm. The dataset consists of carefully captured images obtained during the planned flight, providing valuable visual information for research and analysis purposes. These images are in the standard color format (sRGB) and have been accurately aligned to real-world coordinates using GPS data.

3.2 Geometric Distortion Detection

Pix4Dmapper, a powerful software solution, has demonstrated its potential in this work by automating the identification of images with distortion. By leveraging its advanced features, this software is capable of performing the mentioned task on images acquired by UAVs through its camera calibration functionality. Table 1 presents the detailed specifications of UAV flight instances, including the number of identified images with ESD. It is worth noting that the software serves as a tool used by the researchers to automate the process of identifying distorted images for use in the pairing process, and it does not guarantee superior performance. Instead, it provides valuable insights into the frequency and severity of distortions encountered during image processing.

Table 1. Extreme Scene Distortion Identification Using Pix4Dmapper software.

Flight No	Flight Location	Images with ESD
Observation 1	Site 1 – Candaba, Pampanga (Poblacion), Philippines	$24/338_{images}$
Observation 2	Site 2 – Candaba, Pampanga (Tagalog), Philippines	$4/214_{images}$
Observation 3	Site 1 – Candaba, Pampanga (Poblacion), Philippines	$16/339_{images}$
Observation 4	Site 2 – Candaba, Pampanga (Tagalog), Philippines	$10/212_{images}$

3.3 Extreme Scene Distortion Correction Proposed Solution

Feature Extraction and Detection. The proposed method utilizes deep learning-based feature extraction, detection, and matching using the algorithm made by [21]. This algorithm employs the Graph Neural Network (GNN), which efficiently detects sparse and unique feature points compared to traditional hand-crafted feature descriptor algorithms. By leveraging deep learning and graph-based computations, the GNN identifies and matches sparse and distinctive keypoints, reducing computational complexity and memory requirements.

Hyperparameter tuning is performed by the researchers to optimize the performance of the feature extraction and detection process. The goal is to find the optimal combination of hyperparameter values that yield the best results in terms of extracted features and reliable correspondences between distorted and undistorted images that represent the sets of feature points:

Let:

$$F\Delta = \{(x\delta, y\delta, f\delta)\} and F\Upsilon = \{(x\upsilon, y\upsilon, f\upsilon)\} \tag{1}$$

where $(x\delta, y\delta, f\delta)$ and $(x\upsilon, y\upsilon, f\upsilon)$ are the pixel coordinates, and $F\Delta$ and $F\Upsilon$ are the feature descriptors for the distorted and undistorted images, respectively.

It matches feature points between the distorted and undistorted images, resulting in a set of correspondences:

$$S = \{(x\delta, y\delta, x\upsilon, y\upsilon, \varsigma)\} \tag{2}$$

where $(x\delta, y\delta)$, $(x\upsilon, y\upsilon)$ are the coordinates of matched feature points, ς is the matching score, and S is the resulting set of correspondences.

Figure 3 showcases the representation of the feature points extracted and detected from both the distorted image (on the left) and the undistorted image (on the right), acquired through the utilization of Eq. 1 and Eq. 2. These sets of feature points comprise distinct coordinates, playing a crucial role in facilitating the homography-based transformation process, as explained in Sect. 3.3.

Fig. 3. Sample Output of Feature Points Extraction and Detection.

Homography-Based Transformation. The collected correspondences S are used for homography-based estimation [22]. The homography matrix $\mathcal{H}$ is computed using the Direct Linear Transformation (DLT) method represented as a 3x3 matrix:

$$\mathcal{H} = \begin{pmatrix} h11 & h12 & h13 \\ h21 & h22 & h23 \\ h31 & h32 & h33 \end{pmatrix} \tag{3}$$

Once the homography matrix $\mathcal{H}$ is estimated, it is used to perform a homography-based transformation of the distorted image. The transformation aligns the distorted image with the undistorted image by mapping pixel coordinates from the distorted image to transformed coordinates of the undistorted image, with a scaling factor. In addition to the presented steps, the RANSAC (Random Sample Consensus) algorithm was applied to improve the robustness of the homography estimation. RANSAC helps identify and eliminate outlier correspondences that may negatively affect the accuracy of the estimated homography matrix. By iteratively sampling subsets of correspondences and estimating the homography matrix, RANSAC selects the best-fitting model that maximizes the number of inliers, as shown in Fig. 4.

Figure 4 demonstrates the visual representation of matching distinct and salient feature points within the observed images using RANSAC. This serves as a robust

$$H =$$

$$\begin{matrix} 0.9506 & -0.0138 & 15.3202 \\ -0.0746 & 0.9775 & -101.7876 \\ -0.0000 & -0.0001 & 1.0000 \end{matrix}$$

fx »

(A)   (B)

Fig. 4. Sample Output of Matched Feature Points for Image Registration.

validation mechanism, effectively filtering out erroneous matches among the feature points in an iterative way. This procedure is essential for effective image registration based on homography estimation, deriving a homography matrix. As shown in Fig. 4B, this computed matrix encapsulates the geometric transformation between two images, enabling accurate alignment and possible correction of spatial deformation.

In general, this detailed pipeline could potentially be applied to align and register distorted UAV images with undistorted images. This serves as the proposed geometric distortion correction technique in this work.

3.4 Image Quality Metrics

The researchers employed the Structural Similarity Index (SSIM) and Peak Signal-to-Noise Ratio (PSNR) as evaluation metrics. This was accomplished by comparing the SSIM and PSNR values between the corrected and originally distorted images to measure the enhancement in image quality. Additionally, the researchers utilized a Perceptual Image Quality Evaluator (PIQE) to evaluate the extended application of the proposed solution in pair-wise stitching. This evaluation encompassed visual attributes such as sharpness, contrast, color fidelity, and artifacts.

4   Experimental Results

This section offers insights into the capabilities and limitations of the proposed technique, ultimately validating its potential to address geometric distortion challenges in aerial images captured by Unmanned Aerial Vehicles (UAVs). Figure 5 consists of observed images that require geometric distortion correction due to their minor spatial transformations, resulting in a noticeable erroneous orientation of the Earth's ground scene.

Figure 6 presents the evaluation results of various geometric distortion correction techniques, including the proposed solution, based on the PSNR and SSIM evaluation metrics.

The algorithms compared in this study are from [23–26] with Homography-Based Correction, [27] with Homography-Based Correction, [28] with Homography-Based Correction, [29] with Homography-Based Correction, [30] with Homography-Based

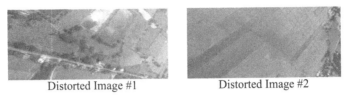

Distorted Image #1   Distorted Image #2

Fig. 5. Sample Input Images with Extreme Scene Distortion.

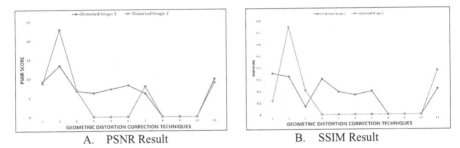

A. PSNR Result   B. SSIM Result

Fig. 6. Quantitative Analysis of the proposed and existing solutions using PSNR and SSIM.

Correction, [31] with Homography-Based Correction, [32] with Homography-Based Correction, and the Proposed solution. Clearly, the introduced algorithm has demonstrated promising results in both the Peak Signal-to-Noise Ratio (PSNR) and Structural Similarity Index (SSIM) image quality metrics by employing Graph Neural Networks (GNN) for feature matching and image-warping techniques. These positive outcomes confirm the algorithm's viability as a method for correcting distortion in Unmanned Aerial Vehicle (UAV) imagery.

Figure 7 showcases the qualitative evaluation of the proposed solution alongside other existing approaches (B) [23] (C) [24] (D) [25] (E) [26], (F) [27], (G) [28], (H) [29], (I) [30], (J) [31], and (K) [32] for correcting distorted UAV images.

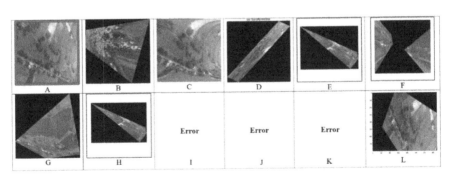

Fig. 7. Qualitative analysis of the proposed and other existing techniques.

In the evaluation, Image A, located in the first row, represents the initial distorted UAV image that requires correction. Subsequently, images B, C, and G display the results obtained from individual existing approaches, each of which produces visually appealing images. However, it is important to note that these approaches were unable to rectify the specific type of distortion mentioned. Conversely, the remaining results in Fig. 7, such as images D to F, exhibit lower-quality outcomes, and images I to K produced errors, with one notable exception. The last image, labeled as L and situated in the second row, showcases the output obtained from the proposed solution. This image stands out as it successfully achieves geometric rectification of the UAV image, thus providing a satisfactory result in terms of a change in scene orientation, which is a valid representation of a nadir-based UAV image.

Figure 8 presents additional experiments conducted to evaluate the effectiveness of the proposed solution in terms of correcting specific types of geometric distortion in UAV images.

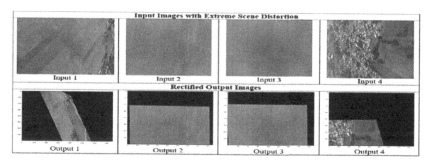

Fig. 8. Qualitative Analysis on additional distorted images using the proposed technique.

These experiments demonstrate successful rectification of the targeted distortions, yielding good-quality output images, as shown in the second row. The results in this figure highlight the capability of the proposed solution to address and correct the specific geometric distortion since it minimizes the insignificant spatial transformation in the ground scene.

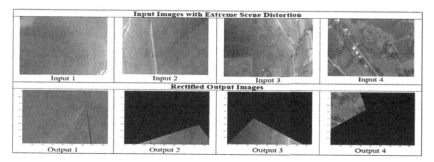

Fig. 9. Qualitative Analysis on additional distorted images using the proposed solution.

However, it is important to note that the proposed solution may have a limitation in terms of the resulting visual quality. While the distortion correction is significant, there may be a slight decrease in overall visual quality compared to the original images. This trade-off between distortion correction and visual quality should be considered when evaluating the effectiveness of this proposed approach. Figure 9 specifically illustrates instances where this work encounters limitations or challenges, emphasizing the need for further improvements to optimize visual quality while effectively correcting the specific geometric distortions.

In Fig. 10, the researchers conducted a comprehensive analysis of the proposed solution in the domain of pairwise image stitching.

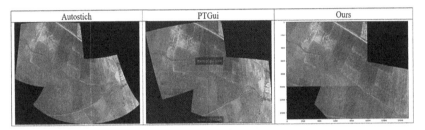

Fig. 10. Extended evaluation of the proposed solution to pair-wise image stitching.

The evaluation, as presented in Table 2 using the PIQE (Perceptual Image Quality Evaluator) evaluation metric, demonstrates that this proposed solution achieves a high-quality outcome in the stitched image, ranking second-best in comparison to other approaches. However, upon subjective assessment through human visual perception, it becomes evident that the proposed solution effectively rectified the minor scene disorientation present in the output image.

Table 2. Quantitative Analysis of Pair-wise Image Stitching using PIQE.

Algorithm Used	PIQE Score ↓
AutoStitch [25]	20.0452
PTGui [26]	35.1569
PROPOSED METHOD	25.0506

5 Conclusion

This study addresses the challenge of correcting geometric distortions in images captured by UAVs, particularly in cases of extreme scene distortion. The proposed approach combines computer vision and photogrammetry techniques to estimate and correct distortions caused by irregular terrains and UAV motion. By utilizing feature matching and image-warping algorithms, the method achieves effective distortion correction. Additionally, a benchmark dataset is introduced to evaluate algorithms specifically designed for extreme distortion in UAV images. This research makes a significant contribution to the field of geometric distortion correction in UAV-acquired images. Furthermore, the proposed method has potential applications beyond distortion correction. It can be used for pair-wise image stitching, enabling the creation of seamless mosaics or panoramas from multiple UAV images. This feature enhances its practicality in various domains such as remote sensing, surveillance, aerial photography, and other fields that rely on accurate visual information.

Overall, this study paves the way for future research in UAV imaging systems, with the potential to improve image quality, enhance analysis capabilities, and expand the applications of UAV-acquired imagery.

References

1. Deliry, S.I., Avdan, U.: Accuracy of unmanned aerial systems photogrammetry and structure from motion in surveying and mapping: a review. J. Indian Soc. Remote Sens. **49**(8), 1997–2017 (2021)
2. Li, A., Guo, J., Guo, Y.: Image stitching based on semantic planar region consensus. IEEE Trans. Image Process. **30**, 5545–5558 (2021)
3. Kim, J.I., Kim, T., Shin, D., Kim, S.: Fast and robust geometric correction for mosaicking UAV images with narrow overlaps. Int. J. Remote Sens. **38**(8–10), 2557–2576 (2017)
4. Wang, Y., Cong, Q., Yao, S., Jia, X., Chen, J., Li, S.: Research on geometric error correction of pushbroom hyperspectral camera carried by UAV. In: Seventh Symposium on Novel Photoelectronic Detection Technology and Applications, vol. 11763, pp. 1214–1220. SPIE (2021)
5. Vinegoni, C., Lee, S., Aguirre, A.D., Weissleder, R.: New techniques for motion-artifact-free in vivo cardiac microscopy. Front. Physiol. **6**, 147 (2015)
6. Rathnayake, R.M.N.B., Seneviratne, L.: An efficient approach towards image stitching in aerial images. In: 2018 3rd International Conference on Information Technology Research (ICITR), pp. 1–6. IEEE (2018)
7. Li, C., Guo, B., Guo, X., Zhi, Y.: Real-time UAV imagery stitching based on grid-based motion statistics. J. Phys. Conf. Ser. **1069**(1), 012163 (2018). IOP Publishing
8. Xing, C., Wang, J., Xu, Y.: Overlap analysis of the images from unmanned aerial vehicles. In: 2010 International Conference on Electrical and Control Engineering, pp. 1459–1462. IEEE (2010)
9. Kose, U., Deperlioglu, O., Alzubi, J., Patrut, B.: Deep Learning for Medical Decision Support Systems. Springer, Berlin (2021)
10. Qi, X., Liao, R., Jia, J., Fidler, S., Urtasun, R.: 3d graph neural networks for RGBD semantic segmentation. In: Proceedings of the IEEE International Conference on Computer Vision, pp. 5199–5208 (2017)
11. Fooladgar, F., Kasaei, S.: A survey on indoor RGB-D semantic segmentation: from hand-crafted features to deep convolutional neural networks. Multim. Tools Appl. **79**, 4499–4524 (2020)
12. Zhang, Z.: Flexible camera calibration by viewing a plane from unknown orientations. In: Proceedings of the Seventh IEEE International Conference on Computer Vision, vol. 1, pp. 666–673. IEEE (1999)
13. Kjaer-Nielsen, A., Jensen, L.B.W., Sørensen, A.S., Krüger, N.: A real-time embedded system for stereo vision preprocessing using an FPGA. In: 2008 International Conference on Reconfigurable Computing and FPGAs, pp. 37–42. IEEE (2008)

14. Liao, K., Lin, C., Zhao, Y.: A deep ordinal distortion estimation approach for distortion rectification. IEEE Trans. Image Process. **30**, 3362–3375 (2021)
15. Li, J., Deng, B., Tang, R., Wang, Z., Yan, Y.: Local-adaptive image alignment based on triangular facet approximation. IEEE Trans. Image Process. **29**, 2356–2369 (2019)
16. Li, J., Wang, Z., Lai, S., Zhai, Y., Zhang, M.: Parallax-tolerant image stitching based on robust elastic warping. IEEE Trans. Multim. **20**(7), 1672–1687 (2017)
17. Xia, M., Yao, M., Li, L., Lu, X.: Globally consistent alignment for mosaicking aerial images. In: 2015 IEEE International Conference on Image Processing (ICIP), pp. 3039–3043. IEEE (2015)
18. Lin, C.C., Pankanti, S.U., Natesan Ramamurthy, K., Aravkin, A.Y.: Adaptive as-natural-as-possible image stitching. In: Proceedings of the IEEE Conference on Computer Vision and Pattern Recognition, pp. 1155–1163 (2015)
19. Zaragoza, J., Chin, T.J., Brown, M.S., Suter, D.: As-projective-as-possible image stitching with moving DLT. In: Proceedings of the IEEE Conference on Computer Vision and Pattern Recognition, pp. 2339–2346 (2013)
20. Qi, X., Chen, G., Li, Y., Cheng, X., Li, C.: Applying neural-network-based machine learning to additive manufacturing: current applications, challenges, and future perspectives. Engineering **5**(4), 721–729 (2019)
21. Sarlin, P.E., DeTone, D., Malisiewicz, T., Rabinovich, A.: Superglue: learning feature matching with graph neural networks. In: Proceedings of the IEEE/CVF Conference on Computer Vision and Pattern Recognition, pp. 4938–4947 (2020)
22. Dubrofsky, E.: Homography Estimation. Diplomová Práce, p. 5. Univerzita Britské Kolumbie, Vancouver (2009)
23. Hartley, R., Zisserman, A.: Multiple View Geometry in Computer Vision. Cambridge University Press (2003)
24. Xu, M.: Comparison and research of fisheye image correction algorithms in coal mine survey. IOP Conf. Ser. Earth Environ. Sci. **300**(2), 022075 (2019). IOP Publishing
25. Guan, B., Zhao, J., Li, Z., Sun, F., Fraunhofer, F.: Minimal solutions for relative pose with a single affine correspondence. In: Proceedings of the IEEE/CVF Conference on Computer Vision and Pattern Recognition, pp. 1929–1938 (2020)
26. Lowe, G.: Sift-the scale invariant feature transform. Int. J. **2**(91–110), 2 (2004)
27. Rublee, E., Rabaud, V., Konolige, K., Bradski, G.: ORB: an efficient alternative to SIFT or SURF. In: 2011 International Conference on Computer Vision, pp. 2564–2571. IEEE (2011)
28. Bay, H., Ess, A., Tuytelaars, T., Van Gool, L.: Speeded-up robust features (SURF). Comput. Vis. Image Underst. **110**(3), 346–359 (2008)
29. Alcantarilla, P.F., Bartoli, A., Davison, A.J.: KAZE features. In: Fitzgibbon, A., Lazebnik, S., Perona, P., Sato, Y., Schmid, C. (eds.) ECCV 2012. LNCS, vol. 7577, pp. 214–227. Springer, Heidelberg (2012). https://doi.org/10.1007/978-3-642-33783-3_16
30. Viswanathan, D.G.: Features from accelerated segment test (FAST). In: Proceedings of the 10th Workshop on Image Analysis for Multimedia Interactive Services, London, pp. 6–8 (2009)
31. Leutenegger, S., Chli, M., Siegwart, R.Y.: BRISK: binary robust invariant scalable keypoints. In: 2011 International Conference on Computer Vision, pp. 2548–2555. IEEE (2011)
32. Derpanis, K.G.: The Harris corner detector. York University **2**, 1–2 (2004)

Q-YOLO: Efficient Inference for Real-Time Object Detection

Mingze Wang[1], Huixin Sun[1], Jun Shi[1], Xuhui Liu[1], Xianbin Cao[1(✉)],
Luping Zhang[2], and Baochang Zhang[1,3]

[1] Beihang University, Beijing, China
xbcao@buaa.edu.cn
[2] National University of Defense Technology, Changsha, China
[3] Nanchang Institute of Technology, Nanchang, China

Abstract. Real-time object detection plays a vital role in various computer vision applications. However, deploying real-time object detectors on resource-constrained platforms poses challenges due to high computational and memory requirements. This paper describes a low-bit quantization method to build a highly efficient one-stage detector, dubbed as Q-YOLO, which can effectively address the performance degradation problem caused by activation distribution imbalance in traditional quantized YOLO models. Q-YOLO introduces a fully end-to-end Post-Training Quantization (PTQ) pipeline with a well-designed Unilateral Histogram-based (UH) activation quantization scheme, which determines the maximum truncation values through histogram analysis by minimizing the Mean Squared Error (MSE) quantization errors. Extensive experiments on the COCO dataset demonstrate the effectiveness of Q-YOLO, outperforming other PTQ methods while achieving a more favorable balance between accuracy and computational cost. This research contributes to advancing the efficient deployment of object detection models on resource-limited edge devices, enabling real-time detection with reduced computational and memory overhead.

Keywords: Real-time Object Detection · Post-training Quantization

1 Introduction

Real-time object detection is a crucial component in various computer vision applications, such as multi-object tracking [42,43], autonomous driving [7,15], and robotics [13,25]. The development of real-time object detectors, particularly YOLO-based detectors, has yielded remarkable performance in terms of accuracy and speed. For example, YOLOv7-E6 [34] object detector achieves 55.9% mAP on COCO 2017, outperforming both transformer-based detector SWINL Cascade-Mask R-CNN [4,22] and convolutional based detector ConvNeXt-XL

M. Wang, H. Sun and J. Shi—Equal contribution.
"One Thousand Plan" projects in Jiangxi Province Jxsg2023102268.

Cascade-Mask R-CNN [4, 36] in both speed and accuracy. Despite their success, the computational cost during inference remains a challenge for real-time object detectors on resource-limited edge devices, such as mobile CPUs or GPUs, limiting their practical usage.

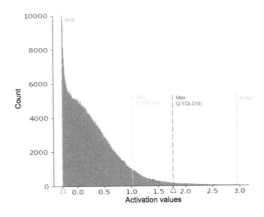

Fig. 1. Activation value distribution histogram (with 2048 bins) of the model.21.conv layer in YOLOv5s. The occurrence of values between 0 and −0.2785 is extremely high, while the frequency of values above zero decreases significantly, reveals an imbalanced pattern. min denotes the fixed minimum truncation value, while max represents the maximum truncation value following the min-max principle. Max Q-YOLO(8) refers to the maximum truncation value when using the Q-YOLO quantization model at 8-bit, and Max Q-YOLO(4) indicates the maximum truncation value when applying the Q-YOLO quantization model at 4-bit. (Color figure online)

Substantial efforts on network compression have been made towards efficient online inference [5, 26, 31, 39]. Methods include enhancing network designs [10, 37, 41], conducting network search [46], network pruning [8, 9], and network quantization [17]. Quantization, in particular, has gained significant popularity for deployment on AI chips by representing a network using low-bit formats. There are two prevailing quantization methods, Quantization-Aware Training (QAT) [17, 38] and Post-Training Quantization (PTQ) [20]. Although QAT generally achieves better results than PTQ, it requires training and optimization of all model parameters during the quantization process. The need for pretraining data and significant GPU resources makes QAT challenging to execute. On the other hand, PTQ is a more efficient approach for quantizing real-time object detectors.

To examine low-bit quantization for real-time object detection, we first establish a PTQ baseline using YOLOv5 [33], a state-of-the-art object detector. Through empirical analysis on the COCO 2017 dataset, we observe notable performance degradation after quantization, as indicated in Table 1. For example, a 4-bit quantized YOLOv5s employing Percentile achieves only 7.0% mAP, resulting in a performance gap of 30.4% compared to the original real-valued model. We find the performance drop of quantized YOLOs can be attributed to the activation distribution imbalance. As shown in Fig. 1, we observe high concentration of values close to the lower bound and the significant decrease in occurrences above zero. When employing fixed truncation values such as Min-Max, representing activation values with extremely low probabilities would consume a considerable number of bits within the limited integer bit width, resulting in further loss of information.

In light of the above issue, we introduce Q-YOLO, a fully end-to-end PTQ quantization architecture for real-time object detection, as depicted in Fig. 2. Q-YOLO quantizes the backbone, neck, and head modules of YOLO models, while employing standard MinMax quantization for weights. To tackle the problem of activation distribution imbalance, we introduce a novel approach called Unilateral Histogram-based (UH) activation quantization. UH iteratively determines the maximum truncation value that minimizes the quantization error through histograms. This technique significantly reduces calibration time and effectively addresses the discrepancy caused by quantization, optimizing the quantization process to maintain stable activation quantization. By mitigating information loss in activation quantization, our method ensures accurate object detection results, thereby enabling precise and reliable low-bit real-time object detection performance. Our contributions can be summarized as follows:

1. We introduce a fully end-to-end PTQ quantization architecture specifically designed for real-time object detection, dubbed as Q-YOLO.
2. A Unilateral Histogram-based (UH) activation quantization method is proposed to leverage histogram analysis to find the maximum truncation values, which can effectively minimize the MSE quantization error.
3. Through extensive experiments on various object detectors, we demonstrate that Q-YOLO outperforms baseline PTQ models by a significant margin. The 8-bit Q-YOLO model applied on YOLOv7 achieves a $3\times$ acceleration while maintaining performance comparable to its full-precision counterpart on COCO, highlighting its potential as a general solution for quantizing real-time object detectors.

2   Related Work

2.1   Quantization

Quantized neural networks are based on low-bit weights and activations to accelerate model inference and save memory. The commonly used model quantization methods include quantization-aware training (QAT) and post-training quantization (PTQ). In QAT, Zhang et al. [40] build a binarized convolutional neural network based on a projection function and a new updated rule during the backpropagation. Li et al. [17] proposed an information rectification module and distribution-guided distillation to push the bit-width in a quantized vision transformer. TTQ [44] uses two real-valued scaling coefficients to quantize the weights to ternary values. Zhuang et al. [45] present a low-bit (2-4 bit) quantization scheme using a two-stage approach to alternately quantize the weights

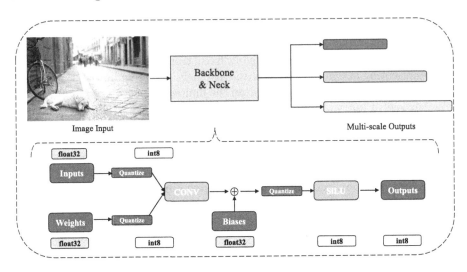

Fig. 2. Architecture of Q-YOLO.

and activations, providing an optimal trade-off among memory, efficiency, and performance. In [12], the quantization intervals are parameterized, and optimal values are obtained by directly minimizing the task loss of the network. ZeroQ [3] supports uniform and mixed-precision quantization by optimizing for a distilled dataset which is engineered to match the statistics of the batch normalization across different network layers. [6] enabled accurate approximation for tensor values that have bell-shaped distributions with long tails and found the entire range by minimizing the quantization error. While QAT often requires high-level expert knowledge and huge GPU resources for training or fine-tuning, especially the large-scale pre-trained model. To reduce the above costs of quantization, PTQ, which is training-free, has received more widespread attention and lots of excellent works arise. MinMax, EMA [11] methods are commonly used to compress or reduce the weights of the PTQ model. MinMax normalizes the weights and bias values in the model to a predefined range, such as [−1, 1], to reduce the storage space and increase the inference speed. MSE quantization involves evaluating and adjusting the quantized activation values to minimize the impact of quantization on model performance.

2.2 Real-Time Object Detection

Deep Learning based object detectors can be generally classified into two categories: two-stage and single-stage object detectors. Two-stage detectors, such as Faster R-CNN [30], RPN [18], and Cascade R-CNN [4], first generate region proposals and then refine them in a second stage. On the other hand, single-stage object detectors have gained significant popularity in real-time object detection due to their efficiency and effectiveness. These detectors aim to predict object bounding boxes and class labels in a single pass of the neural network, eliminating the need for time-consuming region proposal generation. One of the pioneering single-shot detectors is YOLO [27], which divides the input image into a grid and assigns bounding boxes and class probabilities to predefined anchor boxes. The subsequent versions, YOLOv2 [28] and YOLOv3 [29], introduced improvements in terms of network architecture and feature extraction, achieving better accuracy without compromising real-time performance. Another influential single-shot detector is SSD [21], which employs a series of convolutional layers at different scales to detect objects of various sizes. By using feature maps at multiple resolutions, SSD achieves high accuracy while maintaining real-time performance. Variants of SSD, such as MobileNet-SSD [10] and Pelee [35], further optimize the architecture to achieve faster inference on resource-constrained devices.

Efficiency is a critical aspect of real-time object detection, especially for deployment on computationally limited platforms. MobileNet [10] and its subsequent variants, such as MobileNetV2 [32] and MobileNetV3 [14], have received significant attention for their lightweight architectures. These networks utilize depth-wise separable convolutions and other techniques to reduce the number of parameters and operations without significant accuracy degradation. ShuffleNet [41] introduces channel shuffling operations to exploit group convolutions, enabling a trade-off between model size and computational cost. ShuffleNetV2 [23] further improves the efficiency by introducing a more efficient block design and exploring different network scales.

3 Methodology

3.1 Preliminaries

Network Quantization Process. We first review the main steps of the Post-Training Quantization (PTQ) process and supply the details. Firstly, the network is either trained or provided as a pre-trained model using full precision and floating-point arithmetic for weights and activations. Subsequently, numerical representations of weights and activations are suitably transformed for quantization. Finally, the fully-quantized network is deployed either on integer arithmetic hardware or simulated on GPUs, enabling efficient inference with reduced memory storage and computational requirements while maintaining reasonable accuracy levels.

Uniform Quantization. Assuming the quantization bit-width is b, the quantizer $Q(\mathbf{x}|b)$ can be formulated as a function that maps a floating-point number $\mathbf{x} \in \mathbb{R}$ to the nearest quantization bin:

$$Q(\mathbf{x}|b) : \mathbb{R} \to \hat{\mathbf{x}}, \tag{1}$$

$$\hat{\mathbf{x}} = \begin{cases} \{-2^{b-1}, \cdots, 2^{b-1} - 1\} & \text{Signed,} \\ \{0 \cdots, 2^b - 1\} & \text{Unsigned.} \end{cases} \tag{2}$$

There are various quantizer $Q(\mathbf{x}|b)$, where uniform [11] are typically used. Uniform quantization is well supported on most hardware platforms. Its unsigned quantizer $Q(\mathbf{x}|b)$ can be defined as:

$$Q(\mathbf{x}|b) = \text{clip}(\lfloor \frac{\mathbf{x}}{s_{\mathbf{x}}} \rceil + zp_{\mathbf{x}}, 0, 2^b - 1), \qquad (3)$$

where $s_{\mathbf{x}}$ (scale) and $zp_{\mathbf{x}}$ (zero-point) are quantization parameters. In Eq. 4, u (upper) and l (lower) define the quantization grid limits.

$$s_{\mathbf{x}} = \frac{u - l}{2^b - 1}, zp_{\mathbf{x}} = \text{clip}(\lfloor -\frac{l}{s} \rceil, 0, 2^b - 1). \qquad (4)$$

The dequantization process can be formulated as:

$$\tilde{\mathbf{x}} = (\hat{\mathbf{x}} - zp_{\mathbf{x}}) \times s_{\mathbf{x}}. \qquad (5)$$

3.2 Quantization Range Setting

Quantization range setting is the process of establishing the upper and lower clipping thresholds, denoted as u and l respectively, of the quantization grid. The crucial trade-off in range setting lies in the balance between two types of errors: clipping error and rounding error. Clipping error arises when data is truncated to fit within the predefined grid limits, as described in Eq. 4. Such truncation leads to information loss and a decrease in precision in the resulting quantized representation. On the other hand, rounding error occurs due to the imprecision introduced during the rounding operation, as described in Eq. 3. This error can accumulate over time and has an impact on the overall accuracy of the quantized representation. The following methods provide different trade-offs between the two quantities.

MinMax. In the experiments, we use the MinMax method for weight quantization, where clipping thresholds $l_{\mathbf{x}}$ and $u_{\mathbf{x}}$ are formulated as:

$$l_{\mathbf{x}} = \min(\mathbf{x}), u_{\mathbf{x}} = \max(\mathbf{x}). \qquad (6)$$

This leads to no clipping error. However, this approach is sensitive to outliers as strong outliers may cause excessive rounding errors.

Mean Squared Error (MSE). One way to mitigate the problem of large outliers is by employing MSE-based range setting. In this method, we determine $l_{\mathbf{x}}$ and $u_{\mathbf{x}}$ that minimize the mean squared error (MSE) between the original and quantized tensor:

$$\arg \min_{l_{\mathbf{x}}, u_{\mathbf{x}}} \text{MSE}(\mathbf{x}, \mathbf{Q}_{l_{\mathbf{x}}, u_{\mathbf{x}}}), \qquad (7)$$

where $\mathbf{x}$ represents the original tensor and $\mathbf{Q}_{l_{\mathbf{x}}, u_{\mathbf{x}}}$ denotes the quantized tensor produced using the determined clipping thresholds $l_{\mathbf{x}}$ and $u_{\mathbf{x}}$. The optimization problem is commonly solved using grid search, golden section method or analytical approximations with closed-form solution.

3.3   Unilateral Histogram-Based (UH) Activation Quantization

To address the issue of activation value imbalance, we propose a new approach called Unilateral Histogram-based (UH) activation quantization. We first provide an empirical study of the activation values after forward propagation through the calibration dataset. As depicted in Fig. 1, we observe a concentrated distribution of values near the lower bound, accompanied by a noticeable decrease in occurrences above zero. Further analysis of the activation values reveals that the empirical value of -0.2785 serves as the lower bound. This phenomenon can be attributed to the frequent utilization of the Swish (SILU) activation function in the YOLO series.

Algorithm 1. Unilateral Histogram-based (UH) Activation Quantization

---

1: **Input:** FP32 Histogram H with 2048 bins
2: **for** i in range(128, 2048) **do**
3:    Reference distribution $P \leftarrow H[0:i]$
4:    Outliers count $c \leftarrow \sum_{j=i}^{2047} H[j]$
5:    $P[i-1] \leftarrow P[i-1] + c$
6:    $P \leftarrow \frac{P}{\sum_j (P[j])}$
7:    Candidate distribution $C \leftarrow$ Quantize $H[0:i]$ into 128 levels
8:    Expand C to have i bins
9:    $Q \leftarrow \frac{C}{\sum_j (C[j])}$
10:    $MSE[i] \leftarrow$ Mean Squared Error(P, Q)
11: **end for**
12: **Output:** Index m for which $MSE[m]$ is minimal.

Based on the empirical evidence, we introduce an asymmetric quantization approach called Unilateral Histogram-based (UH) activation quantization. In UH, we iteratively determine the maximum truncation value that minimizes the quantization error, while keeping the minimum truncation value fixed at -0.2785, as illustrated in the following:

$$u_{\mathbf{x}} = \arg\min_{l_{\mathbf{x}}, u_{\mathbf{x}}} \text{MSE}(\mathbf{x}, \mathbf{Q}_{l_{\mathbf{x}}, u_{\mathbf{x}}}), l_{\mathbf{x}} = -0.2785. \tag{8}$$

To evaluate the quantization error during the search for the maximum truncation value, we utilize the fp32 floating-point numbers derived from the center values of the gathered 2048 bins, as introduces in Algorithm 1. These numbers are successively quantized, considering the current maximum truncation value under consideration. Through this iterative process, we identify the optimal truncation range. The UH activation quantization method offers two key advantages. Firstly, it significantly reduces calibration time. Secondly, it ensures stable activation quantization by allowing a larger set of integers to represent the frequently occurring activation values between 0 and -0.2785, thereby improving quantization accuracy.

Table 1. A comparison of various quantization methods applied to YOLOv5s [33], YOLOv5m [33], YOLOv7 [34] and YOLOv7x [34], which have an increasing number of parameters, on the COCO `val2017` dataset [19]. The term Bits (W-A) represents the bit-width of weights and activations. The best results are displayed in bold.

Models	Method	Bits	Size$_{(MB)}$	OPs$_{(G)}$	AP	AP$_{50}$	AP$_{75}$	AP$_s$	AP$_m$	AP$_l$
YOLOv5s [33]	Real-valued	32-32	57.6	16.5	37.4	57.1	40.1	21.6	42.3	48.9
	MinMax	8-8	14.4	4.23	37.2	56.9	39.8	21.4	42.2	48.5
	Percentile [16]				36.9	56.4	39.6	21.3	42.4	48.1
	Q-YOLO				**37.4**	**56.9**	**39.8**	**21.4**	**42.4**	**48.8**
	Percentile [16]	4-4	7.7	2.16	7.0	14.2	6.3	4.1	10.7	7.9
	Q-YOLO				**14.0**	**26.2**	**13.5**	**7.9**	**17.6**	**19.0**
YOLOv5m [33]	Real-valued	32-32	169.6	49.0	45.1	64.1	49	28.1	50.6	57.8
	MinMax	8-8	42.4	12.4	44.9	64	48.9	27.8	50.5	57.4
	Percentile [16]				44.6	63.5	48.4	28.4	50.4	57.8
	Q-YOLO				**45.1**	**64.1**	**48.9**	**28**	**50.6**	**57.7**
	Percentile [16]	4-4	21.2	6.33	19.4	35.6	19.1	14.6	28.3	17.2
	Q-YOLO				**28.8**	**46**	**30.5**	**15.4**	**33.8**	**38.7**
YOLOv7 [34]	Real-valued	32-32	295.2	104.7	50.8	69.6	54.9	34.9	55.6	66.3
	MinMax	8-8	73.8	27.2	50.6	69.5	54.8	34.1	55.5	65.9
	Percentile [16]				50.5	69.3	54.6	34.5	55.4	66.2
	Q-YOLO				**50.7**	**69.5**	**54.8**	**34.8**	**55.5**	**66.2**
	Percentile [16]	4-4	36.9	14.1	16.7	26.9	17.8	10.3	20.1	20.2
	Q-YOLO				**37.3**	**55.0**	**40.9**	**21.5**	**41.4**	**53.0**
YOLOv7x [34]	Real-valued	32-32	25.5	189.9	52.5	71.0	56.6	36.6	57.3	68.0
	MinMax	8-8	142.6	49.5	52.3	70.9	56.7	36.6	57.1	67.7
	Percentile [16]				52.0	70.5	56.1	36.0	56.8	67.9
	Q-YOLO				**52.4**	**70.9**	**56.5**	**36.2**	**57.2**	**67.8**
	Percentile [16]	4-4	71.3	25.6	36.8	55.3	40.5	21.2	41.7	49.3
	Q-YOLO				**37.6**	**57.8**	**42.1**	**23.7**	**43.8**	**49.1**

4   Experiments

In order to assess the performance of the proposed Q-YOLO detectors, we conducted a comprehensive series of experiments on the widely recognized COCO 2017 [19] detection benchmark. As one of the most popular object detection datasets, COCO 2017 [19] has become instrumental in benchmarking state-of-the-art object detectors, thanks to its rich annotations and challenging scenarios. Throughout our experimental analysis, we employed standard COCO metrics on the bounding box detection task to evaluate the efficacy of our approach.

4.1   Implementation Details

We randomly selected 1500 training images from the COCO `train2017` dataset [19] as the calibration data, which served as the foundation for optimizing the model parameters. Additionally, the performance evaluation took place on the COCO val2017 dataset [19], comprising 5000 images. The image size is set to 640×640.

In our experiments, unless otherwise noted, we employed symmetric channel-wise quantization for weights and asymmetric layer-wise quantization for activations. To ensure a fair and unbiased comparison, we consistently applied the MinMax approach for quantizing weights. The input and output layers of the model are more sensitive to the loss of accuracy. In order to maintain the overall performance of the model, the original accuracy of these layers is usually retained. We also follow this practice.

4.2   Main Results

We apply our proposed Q-YOLO to quantize YOLOv5s [33], YOLOv5m [33], YOLOv7 [34] and YOLOv7x [34], which have an increasing number of parameters. The results of the full-precision model, as well as the 8-bit and 4-bit quantized models using MinMax, Percentile, and Q-YOLO methods, are all presented in Table. 1.

Table 1 lists the comparison of several quantization approaches and detection methods in computing complexity, storage cost. Our Q-YOLO significantly accelerates computation and reduces storage requirements for various YOLO detectors. Similarly, in terms of detection accuracy, when using Q-YOLO to quantize the YOLOv5 series models to 8 bits, there is virtually no decline in the average precision (AP) value compared to the full-precision model. As the number of model parameters increases dramatically, quantizing the YOLOv7 series models to 8 bits results in an extremely slight decrease in accuracy. When quantizing models to 4 bits, the accuracy experiences a significant loss due to the reduced expressiveness of 4-bit integer representation. Particularly, when using the MinMax quantization method, the model loses all its accuracy; whereas the Percentile method, which roughly truncates 99.99% of the extreme values, fails to bring notable improvement. Differently, Q-YOLO successfully identifies a more appropriate scale for quantization, resulting in a considerable enhancement compared to conventional Post-Training Quantization (PTQ) methods.

4.3   Ablation Study

Symmetry in Activation Quantization. Nowadays, quantization schemes are often subject to hardware limitations; for instance, NVIDIA [24] only supports symmetric quantization, as it is more inference-speed friendly. Therefore, discussing the symmetry in activation value quantization is meaningful. Table 2 presents a comparison of results using Q-YOLO for symmetric and asymmetric quantization, with the latter exhibiting higher accuracy. The range of negative activation values lies between 0 and -0.2785, while the range of positive activation values exceeds that of the negative ones. If we force equal integer expression bit numbers on both positive and negative sides, the accuracy will naturally

Table 2. A comparison of Symmetrical Analysis of Activation Value Quantization. *Asymmetric* indicates the use of an asymmetric activation value quantization scheme, while *Symmetric* refers to the symmetric quantization of activation values.

models	Bits	Symmetry	AP	AP_{50}	AP_{75}	AP_s	AP_m	AP_l
YOLOv5s [33]	Real-valued	-	37.4	57.1	40.1	21.6	42.3	48.9
	6-6	*Asymmetric*	35.9	55.7	38.3	20.4	41.0	47.6
		Symmetric	34.4	53.9	37.0	19.3	39.8	45.0
	4-4	*Asymmetric*	14.0	26.2	13.5	7.9	17.6	19.0
		Symmetric	2.7	5.9	2.2	1.3	4.2	4.6
YOLOv5m [33]	Real-valued	-	45.1	64.1	49.0	28.1	50.6	57.8
	6-6	*Asymmetric*	44.0	63.1	47.7	28	49.9	56.8
		Symmetric	42.4	61.1	46.0	25.3	48.3	55.9
	4-4	*Asymmetric*	28.8	46.0	30.5	15.4	33.8	38.7
		Symmetric	11.3	24.8	8.6	7.5	15.2	14.5

Table 3. A comparison of Quantization type. The term *only weights* signifies that only the weights are quantized, *only activation* indicates that only the activation values are quantized, and *activation+weights* represents the quantization of both activation values and weights.

models	Bits	Quantization type	AP	AP_{50}	AP_{75}	AP_s	AP_m	AP_l
YOLOv5s [33]	Real-valued	-	37.4	57.1	40.1	21.6	42.3	48.9
	6-32	*only weights*	36.7(-0.7)	56.6	39.3	20.9	41.4	48.4
	32-6	*only activation*	36.6(-0.8)	56.2	39.3	21.0	42.0	47.9
	6-6	*weights+activation*	35.9	55.7	38.3	20.4	41.0	47.6
	4-32	*only weights*	19.6(-16.3)	35.6	19.3	11.3	22.5	25.7
	32-4	*only activation*	30.6(-5.3)	49.1	32.6	17.0	36.7	40.7
	4-4	*weights+activation*	14.0	26.2	13.5	7.9	17.6	19
YOLOv5m [33]	Real-valued	-	45.1	64.1	49.0	28.1	50.6	57.8
	6-32	*only weights*	44.7(-0.4)	63.9	48.6	28.0	50.3	57.3
	32-6	*only activation*	44.3(-0.8)	63.4	48.1	28.4	50.3	57.2
	6-6	*weights+activation*	44	63.1	47.7	28.0	49.9	56.8
	4-32	*only weights*	34.6(-9.4)	54.0	37.3	20.0	39.2	45.3
	32-4	*only activation*	37.7(-6.3)	57.3	41 .8	23.7	44.1	51.0
	4-4	*weights+activation*	28.8	46.0	30.5	15.4	33.8	38.7

decrease. Moreover, this decline becomes more pronounced as the quantization bit number decreases.

Quantization Type. In Table 3, we analyze the impact of different quantization types on the performance of the YOLOv5s and YOLOv5m models, considering three cases: quantizing only the weights (*only weights*), quantizing only the activation values (*only activation*), and quantizing both weights and activation values (*weights+activation*). The results demonstrate that, compared to quantizing the activation values, quantizing the weights consistently induces larger performance degradation. Additionally, the lower the number of bits, the greater the loss incurred by quantization. In YOLO, the weights learned by a neural network essentially represent the knowledge acquired by the network, making the precision of the weights crucial for model performance. In contrast, activation values serve as intermediate representations of input data propagating through the network, and can tolerate some degree of quantization error to a certain extent.

4.4   Inference Speed

To practically verify the acceleration benefits brought about by our quantization scheme, we conducted inference speed tests on both GPU and CPU platforms. For the GPU, we selected the commonly used desktop GPU NVIDIA RTX 4090 [24] and the NVIDIA Tesla T4 [24], often used in computing centers for inference tasks. Due to our limited CPU resources, we only tested Intel products, the i7-12700H and i9-10900, both of which have x86 architecture. For deployment tools, we chose TensorRT [1] and OpenVINO [2]. The entire process involved converting the weights from the torch framework into an ONNX model with QDQ nodes and then deploying them onto specific inference frameworks. The inference mode was set to single-image serial inference, with an image size of 640×640. As most current inference frameworks only support symmetric quantization and 8-bit quantization, we had to choose a symmetric 8-bit quantization scheme, which resulted in an extremely small decrease in accuracy compared to asymmetric schemes. As shown in Table. 4, the acceleration is extremely significant, especially for the larger YOLOv7 model, wherein the speedup ratio when using a GPU even exceeded **3×** compared to the full-precision model. This demonstrates that applying quantization in real-time detectors can bring about a remarkable acceleration.

Table 4. The inference speed of the quantized model is essential. The quantization scheme adopts uniform quantization, with single-image inference mode and an image size of 640×640. TensorRT [1]is selected as the GPU inference library, while OpenVINO [2] is chosen for the CPU inference library.

models	Bits	AP	GPU speed/*ms*		Intel CPU speed /*ms*	
			RTX 4090	Tesla T4	i7-12700H(x86)	i9-10900(x86)
YOLOv5s	32-32	37.4	4.9	7.1	48.7	38.7
	8-8	37.3	3.0	4.5	33.6	23.4
YOLOv7	32-32	50.8	16.8	22.4	269.8	307.8
	8-8	50.6	5.4	7.8	120.4	145.2

5   Conclusions

Real-time object detection is crucial in various computer vision applications. However, deploying object detectors on resource-constrained platforms poses challenges due to high computational and memory requirements. This paper introduces Q-YOLO, a highly efficient one-stage detector built using a low-bit quantization method to address the performance degradation caused by activation distribution imbalance in traditional quantized YOLO models. Q-YOLO employs a fully end-to-end Post-Training Quantization (PTQ) pipeline with a well-designed Unilateral Histogram-based (UH) activation quantization scheme. Extensive experiments conducted on the COCO dataset demonstrate the effectiveness of Q-YOLO. It outperforms other PTQ methods while achieving a favorable balance between accuracy and computational cost. This research significantly contributes to advancing the efficient deployment of object detection models on resource-limited edge devices, enabling real-time detection with reduced computational and memory requirements.

Acknowledgement. Supported by the Major Program of the National Nature Science Foundation of China (Grant No.61827901), "One Thousand Plan" projects in Jiangxi Province (Jxsg2023102268) and National Key Laboratory on Automatic Target Recognition 220402.

References

1. NVIDIA TensorRT. https://developer.nvidia.com/tensorrt. Accessed 03 Sep 2022
2. OpenVINO Toolkit. https://docs.openvinotoolkit.org/latest/index.html. Accessed 03 Sept 2022
3. Cai, Y., Yao, Z., Dong, Z., Gholami, A., Mahoney, M.W., Keutzer, K.: Zeroq: a novel zero shot quantization framework. In: Proceedings of the IEEE/CVF Conference on Computer Vision and Pattern Recognition, pp. 13169–13178 (2020)
4. Cai, Z., Vasconcelos, N.: Cascade r-cnn: delving into high quality object detection. In: Proceedings of the IEEE Conference on Computer Vision and Pattern Recognition, pp. 6154–6162 (2018)
5. Denil, M., Shakibi, B., Dinh, L., Ranzato, M., De Freitas, N.: Predicting parameters in deep learning. In: Advances in Neural Information Processing Systems 26 (2013)
6. Fang, J., Shafiee, A., Abdel-Aziz, H., Thorsley, D., Georgiadis, G., Hassoun, J.H.: Post-training piecewise linear quantization for deep neural networks. In: Vedaldi, A., Bischof, H., Brox, T., Frahm, J.-M. (eds.) ECCV 2020. LNCS, vol. 12347, pp. 69–86. Springer, Cham (2020). https://doi.org/10.1007/978-3-030-58536-5_5
7. Feng, D., et al.: Deep multi-modal object detection and semantic segmentation for autonomous driving: datasets, methods, and challenges. IEEE Trans. Intell. Transp. Syst. **22**(3), 1341–1360 (2020)
8. Guo, Y., Yao, A., Chen, Y.: Dynamic network surgery for efficient dnns. In: Advances in neural information processing systems 29 (2016)
9. Han, S., Mao, H., Dally, W.: Compressing deep neural networks with pruning, trained quantization and huffman coding. arxiv 2015. arXiv preprint arXiv:1510.00149 305 (2015)

10. Howard, A.G., etal.: Mobilenets: efficient convolutional neural networks for mobile vision applications. arXiv preprint arXiv:1704.04861 (2017)
11. Jacob, B., et al.: Quantization and training of neural networks for efficient integer-arithmetic-only inference. In: Proceedings of the IEEE Conference on Computer Vision and Pattern Recognition (2018)
12. Jung, S., et al.: Learning to quantize deep networks by optimizing quantization intervals with task loss. In: Proceedings of the IEEE/CVF Conference on Computer Vision and Pattern Recognition, pp. 4350–4359 (2019)
13. Karaoguz, H., Jensfelt, P.: Object detection approach for robot grasp detection. In: 2019 International Conference on Robotics and Automation (ICRA), pp. 4953–4959. IEEE (2019)
14. Koonce, B., Koonce, B.: Mobilenetv3. Convolutional Neural Networks with Swift for Tensorflow: Image Recognition and Dataset Categorization, pp. 125–144 (2021)
15. Li, B., Ouyang, W., Sheng, L., Zeng, X., Wang, X.: Gs3d: an efficient 3d object detection framework for autonomous driving. In: Proceedings of the IEEE/CVF Conference on Computer Vision and Pattern Recognition, pp. 1019–1028 (2019)
16. Li, R., Wang, Y., Liang, F., Qin, H., Yan, J., Fan, R.: Fully quantized network for object detection. In: Proceedings of the IEEE/CVF Conference on Computer Vision and Pattern Recognition, pp. 2810–2819 (2019)
17. Li, Z., Yang, T., Wang, P., Cheng, J.: Q-vit: fully differentiable quantization for vision transformer. arXiv preprint arXiv:2201.07703 (2022)
18. Lin, T.Y., Dollár, P., Girshick, R., He, K., Hariharan, B., Belongie, S.: Feature pyramid networks for object detection. In: Proceedings of the IEEE Conference on Computer Vision and Pattern Recognition, pp. 2117–2125 (2017)
19. Lin, T.-Y., Maire, M., Belongie, S., Hays, J., Perona, P., Ramanan, D., Dollár, P., Zitnick, C.L.: Microsoft COCO: common objects in context. In: Fleet, D., Pajdla, T., Schiele, B., Tuytelaars, T. (eds.) ECCV 2014. LNCS, vol. 8693, pp. 740–755. Springer, Cham (2014). https://doi.org/10.1007/978-3-319-10602-1_48
20. Lin, Y., Zhang, T., Sun, P., Li, Z., Zhou, S.: Fq-vit: fully quantized vision transformer without retraining. arXiv preprint arXiv:2111.13824 (2021)
21. Liu, W., Anguelov, D., Erhan, D., Szegedy, C., Reed, S., Fu, C.-Y., Berg, A.C.: SSD: single shot MultiBox detector. In: Leibe, B., Matas, J., Sebe, N., Welling, M. (eds.) ECCV 2016. LNCS, vol. 9905, pp. 21–37. Springer, Cham (2016). https://doi.org/10.1007/978-3-319-46448-0_2
22. Liu, Z., Lin, Y., Cao, Y., Hu, H., Wei, Y., Zhang, Z., Lin, S., Guo, B.: Swin transformer: hierarchical vision transformer using shifted windows. In: Proceedings of the IEEE/CVF International Conference on Computer Vision, pp. 10012–10022 (2021)
23. Ma, N., Zhang, X., Zheng, H.T., Sun, J.: Shufflenet v2: practical guidelines for efficient cnn architecture design. In: Proceedings of the European Conference on Computer Vision (ECCV), pp. 116–131 (2018)
24. NVIDIA: Nvidia corporation (2022). https://www.nvidia.com/
25. Paul, S.K., Chowdhury, M.T., Nicolescu, M., Nicolescu, M., Feil-Seifer, D.: Object detection and pose estimation from rgb and depth data for real-time, adaptive robotic grasping. In: Advances in Computer Vision and Computational Biology: Proceedings from IPCV'20, HIMS'20, BIOCOMP'20, and BIOENG'20, pp. 121–142. Springer (2021)
26. Qin, H., Gong, R., Liu, X., Shen, M., Wei, Z., Yu, F., Song, J.: Forward and backward information retention for accurate binary neural networks. In: Proceedings of the IEEE/CVF Conference on Computer Vision and Pattern Recognition, pp. 2250–2259 (2020)

27. Redmon, J., Divvala, S., Girshick, R., Farhadi, A.: You only look once: unified, real-time object detection. In: Proceedings of the IEEE Conference on Computer Vision and Pattern Recognition, pp. 779–788 (2016)
28. Redmon, J., Farhadi, A.: Yolo9000: better, faster, stronger. In: Proceedings of the IEEE Conference on Computer Vision and Pattern Recognition, pp. 7263–7271 (2017)
29. Redmon, J., Farhadi, A.: Yolov3: An incremental improvement. arXiv preprint arXiv:1804.02767 (2018)
30. Ren, S., He, K., Girshick, R., Sun, J.: Faster r-cnn: towards real-time object detection with region proposal networks. In: Advances in Neural Information Processing Systems 28 (2015)
31. Romero, A., Ballas, N., Kahou, S.E., Chassang, A., Gatta, C., Bengio, Y.: Fitnets: hints for thin deep nets. arXiv preprint arXiv:1412.6550 (2014)
32. Sandler, M., Howard, A., Zhu, M., Zhmoginov, A., Chen, L.C.: Mobilenetv 2: inverted residuals and linear bottlenecks. In: Proceedings of the IEEE Conference on Computer Vision and Pattern Recognition, pp. 4510–4520 (2018)
33. Ultralytics: YOLOv5: PyTorch implementation of YOLOv5 real-time object detection (2021). https://github.com/ultralytics/yolov5
34. Wang, C.Y., Bochkovskiy, A., Liao, H.Y.M.: Yolov7: trainable bag-of-freebies sets new state-of-the-art for real-time object detectors. In: Proceedings of the IEEE/CVF Conference on Computer Vision and Pattern Recognition, pp. 7464–7475 (2023)
35. Wang, R.J., Li, X., Ling, C.X.: Pelee: a real-time object detection system on mobile devices. In: Advances in Neural Information Processing Systems 31 (2018)
36. Woo, S., Debnath, S., Hu, R., Chen, X., Liu, Z., Kweon, I.S., Xie, S.: Convnext v2: co-designing and scaling convnets with masked autoencoders. arXiv preprint arXiv:2301.00808 (2023)
37. Wu, B., et al.: Shift: a zero flop, zero parameter alternative to spatial convolutions. In: Proceedings of the IEEE Conference on Computer Vision and Pattern Recognition, pp. 9127–9135 (2018)
38. Xu, S., et al.: Q-detr: an efficient low-bit quantized detection transformer. arXiv preprint arXiv:2304.00253 (2023)
39. Xu, S., Li, Y., Wang, T., Ma, T., Zhang, B., Gao, P., Qiao, Y., Lü, J., Guo, G.: Recurrent bilinear optimization for binary neural networks. In: Computer Vision-ECCV 2022: 17th European Conference, Tel Aviv, Israel, October 23–27, 2022, Proceedings, Part XXIV. pp. 19–35. Springer (2022)
40. Zhang, B., Wang, R., Wang, X., Han, J., Ji, R.: Modulated convolutional networks. IEEE Trans. Neural Networks Learn. Syst. (2021)
41. Zhang, X., Zhou, X., Lin, M., Sun, J.: Shufflenet: an extremely efficient convolutional neural network for mobile devices. In: Proceedings of the IEEE Conference on Computer Vision and Pattern Recognition, pp. 6848–6856 (2018)
42. Zhang, Y., Sun, P., Jiang, Y., Yu, D., Weng, F., Yuan, Z., Luo, P., Liu, W., Wang, X.: Bytetrack: Multi-object tracking by associating every detection box. In: Computer Vision-ECCV 2022: 17th European Conference, Tel Aviv, Israel, October 23–27, 2022, Proceedings, Part XXII. pp. 1–21. Springer (2022)
43. Zhang, Y., Wang, C., Wang, X., Zeng, W., Liu, W.: Fairmot: on the fairness of detection and re-identification in multiple object tracking. Int. J. Comput. Vision **129**, 3069–3087 (2021)
44. Zhu, C., Han, S., Mao, H., Dally, W.J.: Trained ternary quantization. ICLR (2016)

45. Zhuang, B., Shen, C., Tan, M., Liu, L., Reid, I.: Towards effective low-bitwidth convolutional neural networks. In: Proceedings of the IEEE Conference on Computer Vision and Pattern Recognition, pp. 7920–7928 (2018)
46. Zoph, B., Vasudevan, V., Shlens, J., Le, Q.V.: Learning transferable architectures for scalable image recognition. In: Proceedings of the IEEE Conference on Computer Vision and Pattern Recognition, pp. 8697–8710 (2018)

VITS, Tacotron or FastSpeech? Challenging Some of the Most Popular Synthesizers

Jindřich Matoušek[1,2] , Daniel Tihelka[1,2](✉) , and Alice Tihelková[1,2]

[1] New Technologies for the Information Society, Faculty of Applied Sciences, University of West Bohemia, Pilsen, Czechia
jmatouse@kky.zcu.cz, dtihelka@ntis.zcu.cz
[2] Department of English Language and Literature, Faculty of Arts, University of West Bohemia, Pilsen, Czechia
atihelko@kaj.zcu.cz

Abstract. The paper presents a comparative study of three neural speech synthesizers, namely VITS, Tacotron2 and FastSpeech2, which belong among the most popular TTS systems nowadays. Due to their varying nature, they have been tested from several points of view, analysing not only the overall quality of the synthesized speech, but also the capability of processing either orthographic or phonetic inputs. The analysis has been carried out on two English and one Czech voices.

Keywords: text-to-speech synthesis · VITS · FastSpeech2 · Tacotron2

1 Introduction

In recent years, a range of *neural speech synthesis* models appeared, often accompanied by open-source implementation. Since various methods are based on different architectures, it is desirable to have a notion of how the individual methods are faring against each other in terms of output speech quality as well as their capabilities of transforming an input into speech.

As indicated by the title, we have tested three well-known neural speech synthesis models, as all the three (or their derivatives) are claimed to be end-to-end systems and are still used for the research [3–5, 15, 23, 26, 36, 37] to name a few. The choice has also been motivated by variations in their architectures; thus, some variations in the synthesized speech can be expected, especially for marginal (or at least not-so-frequent) phenomena in the inputs. Last but not least, since the individual models were originally designed to work with varying input types (phonetic vs. orthographic, see further) to make the comparison fair, all the systems were tested on both of the input types. And finally, in addition to English, we have also used the Czech language in order to prove

This research was supported by the Czech Science Foundation (GA CR), project No. GA22-27800S, and by the grant of the University of West Bohemia, project No. SGS-2022-017. Computational resources were supplied by the project "e-Infrastruktura CZ" (e-INFRA LM2018140) provided within the program Projects of Large Research, Development and Innovations Infrastructures.

H. Lu et al. (Eds.): ACPR 2023, LNCS 14408, pp. 322–335, 2023.
https://doi.org/10.1007/978-3-031-47665-5_26

the language dependency/sensitivity of the systems; this is a significant extension as the LJ Speech dataset is often only used in comparisons.

Contrary to [32], in the present paper the input text is still expected to be passed through a text normalization module, being responsible for the correct expansion of numbers, dates, abbreviations and so on, into text. The only exception, in the case of orthographic input, is the testing of loanwords in Czech and homographs in English, as these are supposed to be handled by a G2P module [6, 14].

2 Systems Description

Let us describe the chosen DNN-based synthesizers in detail. The VITS model [17] can be viewed as a fully end-to-end model in the sense that it directly converts input text into a waveform, avoiding the use of a mel-spectrogram or any other human-understandable inner bridge within the model (still, there is some intermediate representation in between the encoder and the embedded vocoder). Its implementation has been taken from coqui-ai/TTS [8] GitHub repository. In the project, either orthographic text can be used at the input of the model, or G2P conversion is carried out by gruut tokenizer and IPA phonemizer [34] internally. For our experiments, we modified the code to handle both orthographic and phonetic inputs without the use of embedded processors and cleaners in the same way for all the tested systems.

The other two models, namely FastSpeech2 [24] and Tacotron2 [27], follow the two-stage scheme most widely used today: they employ an *acoustic model* (also called *text-to-spectrogram* or *text-to-mel*) which generates intermediate representation of *acoustic* features in the form of mel-spectrograms from an input text, followed by a *vocoder* generating waveform from these acoustic features. Both models are trained independently of each other, usually using features computed from the original speaker's recordings. The main difference between them is that Tacotron2 has been designed not to require phoneme-level alignment, simplifying somewhat the preparation of training data, where only a recording and the corresponding text is required. On the contrary, the FastSpeech2 allows the explicit control of all the prosodic characteristics (duration, F_0, volume), which is still fairly unique feature, provided neither by Tacotron2 nor by VITS nowadays. The drawback of this is the need of duration information prior the training (F_0 and volume are computed from the data), which in turn needs some sort of phonetic alignment. Both the systems were used from TensorFlowTTS GitHub repository [30], as the FastSpeech2 model was not available in the coqui-ai/TTS project at the time the experiments began. Also, the FastSpeech2 model is claimed to be very fast in the inference, which, combined with a very fast Multi-Band MelGAN vocoder, can provide fast responses (low latency output) in commercial applications. Especially when compared to VITS with its embedded HifiGAN vocoder.

For an excellent overview of neural speech synthesis models, please see [29].

As already stated in the present paper, we tried all the TTS models on both orthographic and phonetic inputs. The particular implementations, especially the code of text cleaners, had to be modified in order to handle each of the inputs correctly, e.g., orthographic texts were lowercased while phonetic ones were not (uppercase letters are valid phones). All the numbers, dates, abbreviations, spellings, etc., appearing in the input texts were normalized to their full written forms. To unify the inputs of the models, pause symbols were added to both orthographic and phonetic variants of the inputs into places of audible pauses or breathing, as these are required by FastSpeech2 training data, see Sect. 2.2. Our research in [21] suggests that the use of pause symbols has a positive effect on synthesized speech.

To make it even harder, the number of open implementations of the same method often vary in their quality, which is also a factor to be considered. For example, we experienced that the TensorFlowTTS project provides very stable and easy-to-train two-stage models with very simple switching between acoustic models and vocoders. Also, its Multi-Band MelGAN vocoder is very fast in inference and achieves very natural output quality, much better than the HifiGAN implementation. On the contrary, the coqui-ai provides a promising VITS model (see Sect. 2.3), while the two-stage combination of acoustic models and vocoders is not very robust in that framework, with Multi-Band MelGAN falling behind HifiGAN and even UnivNet vocoders. Overall, we have not yet been able to achieve output of these two-stage models comparable with Tensor-FlowTTS. Therefore, we do not compare the same models between the frameworks in this paper, as the models cannot be transferred between the two frameworks.

Since the performance may depend on a particular implementation, we left the inference speed comparison to future work once the development settles a bit. Moreover, contrary to the inference, the training speed is not a significant factor to consider, especially when a slow-training model provides stable output with a high level of naturalness.

2.1 Tacotron2 + Multi-band MelGAN

The Tacotron2 acoustic model [27] is based on encoder-(attention)-decoder structure, where input text is passed through embeddings, convolution and biLSTM networks, representing the encoder part of the network. The location-sensitive attention network summarizes the full encoded sequence as a fixed-length context vector for each decoder output step. The decoder part is then an auto-regressive recurrent neural network, predicting a mel-spectrogram from the encoded input sequence, one spectrogram frame at a time. The vocoder in the original Tacotron2 was realised by the WaveNet [27] DNN structure (conditioned by mel-spectra instead of linguistic features as in [22]), but the TensorFlowTTS project implements a wide range of alternative vocoders, from which Multi-band MelGAN [35] has been chosen for its highest output quality. The vocoder is based on *generative adversarial networks* (GANs), consisting of an audio data generator and a discriminator to judge the authenticity of the generated audio. MelGAN uses multiple discriminators to judge audios in different scales; thus, in each scale, it can focus on the characteristics in different frequency ranges. Multi-band modeling divides the waveform into multiple sub-bands and enables parallel generation and fast inference.

Let us note that the Multi-band MelGAN vocoder has been chosen deliberately over the HifiGAN vocoder, being internally used by the VITS model (see Sect. 2.3). The reason is that it (or possibly its implementation in the project used, to be more precise) provides a perceptually higher quality of the output speech and is also measurably faster in speech generation.

In our experiments, the Tacotron2 was always trained using the project default parameters, which are AdamW optimizer [20] with $\beta_1 = 0.9$, $\beta_2 = 0.98$, and weight decay $\lambda = 0.001$; the initial and end learning rate were set to 0.001 and 0.00001, respectively, with $4k$ warm-up steps, with no teacher-forcing being used. The batch size was set to 32 and the models were trained up to 200k steps for English, and, due to a much slower training process and time constraints, up to 178k for Czech, both on a single NVIDIA A100 GPU. The Multi-band MelGAN vocoder was trained with Adam [18] optimizer for both generator and discriminator with $\beta_1 = 0.9$, $\beta_2 = 0.999$, using piece-wise learning rate decay starting at 0.0005 going to 0.000001 for generator and 0.00025 to 0.000001 for discriminator, both going down to half after every 100k steps. The batch size was set to 64, and the models were trained up to 4M steps for English and 2.7M for Czech (also due to the time constraints), with a discriminator employed after 200k training steps.

2.2   FastSpeech2 + Multi-band MelGAN

FastSpeech2 [24] is a fast and robust Transformer-based acoustic model proposed to solve issues typical for autoregressive models (such as Tacotron 2) by adopting feed-forward Transformer network to generate mel-spectrograms from an input phone sequence in parallel and replacing the error-prone attention mechanism by an explicit phone duration predictor to match the length of mel-spectrograms. Nowadays, out of the popular DNN models this it the only one accepting the explicit requirement for prosody modifications in the form of phone-related values of duration, F_0 and volume.

On the other hand, the need for phone alignment complicated the use of the Fast-Speech model with orthographic input, as there is no straightforward mapping of graphemes to phoneme signals. In the `TensorFlowTTS` project, the attention mechanism from a trained Tacotron2 model is used to provide this grapheme alignment, but we have found it rather unreliable. Therefore, we used our DNN-based segmentation [10, 11] to obtain the phonetic-level alignment. For the grapheme-level alignment, in the case of orthographic input, we fixated the word boundaries based on phonetic segmentation, and the boundaries of inter-word graphemes were distributed uniformly through the word.

As for the experiments, the FastSpeech2 has also been trained using the project default parameters, which are AdamW optimizer with $\beta_1 = 0.9$, $\beta_2 = 0.98$ and weight decay $\lambda = 0.001$; as in the case of Tacotron2. The initial and end learning rates were set to 0.001 and 0.00005, respectively, also with $4k$ warm-up steps. The batch size was set to 16, and the models were trained up to 200k steps on a single GeForce GTX 1080 Ti GPU.

As the vocoder, the same Multi-band MelGAN model described in Sect. 2.1 was also used. This allows excluding the vocoder effect from the comparison.

2.3   VITS

VITS is a conditional variational autoencoder with adversarial learning [17]. It combines different deep-learning techniques (adversarial learning, normalizing flows, variational autoencoders, transformers) to achieve high-quality natural-sounding output.

VITS is mainly built on the Glow-TTS model but updates the Glow-TTS by introducing the following updates. First, it replaces the duration predictor with a stochastic duration predictor, providing better modeling of the variability in speech. Then, it connects a HifiGAN vocoder [19] to the decoder's output and joins the two with a variational autoencoder (VAE). That allows one-stage training of the model in an end-to-end fashion and finds a better intermediate representation than the traditionally used mel-spectrograms. This results in high fidelity and more precise prosody [2,16]. Unfortunately, we could not replace the HifiGAN vocoder with Multi-band MelGAN, mostly due to the use of a different framework in which the tested VITS is implemented [8].

In our experiments, VITS models were trained using the AdamW optimizer with $\beta_1 = 0.8$, $\beta_2 = 0.99$, and weight decay $\lambda = 0.01$. The learning rate decay was scheduled by a $0.999^{1/8}$ factor in every epoch with an initial learning rate of 2×10^{-4}. The batch size was set to 16, and the models were trained up to 1.3M steps using mixed precision training on a single GeForce GTX 1080 Ti GPU.

3   Test Description

To challenge the capabilities of the given neural speech synthesis models, the test consists of three parts.

First, the question was whether the use of orthographic or phonetic inputs has an impact on speech quality. While [7] showed that phonetic input is better suited for deep convolutional neural sequence-to-sequence TTS models, the use of orthographic input is currently typical for the end-to-end approach, and those models are able to capture speech contexts using the attention mechanism [33]. Therefore, the use of phonetic input, matching the target spectra/sounds fairly closely, may not be essential for neural synthesis models, which is the opposite of the G2P research, where the tendency was always to prefer the finer phonetic alphabet. And it is a fact that both VITS and Tacotron were designed to be indifferent to the use of orthographic or phonetic inputs. This represents a complication for FastSpeech, as described in Sect. 2.2, although it is claimed in [24] to be "end-to-end" system as well. The choice of Czech and English languages has allowed testing this on both the language where the graphemes match phonemes rather closely, as well as on the opposite due to English irregular transcription.

Using the orthographic input brings other problems of their own. Expecting normalized text, as stated in Sect. 1, the neural model must still be able to cope with special pronunciation phenomena such as loanwords or homographs. Similar to [32], the handling of such words has been the second test put on the synthesizers. Indeed, given the limited amount of audio data used to train the model, as opposed to strictly text corpora, which may be an order of magnitude larger, the ability to learn the right pronunciation from a context depends on the number of examples in the data to learn from. For these cases, the phonetic text input has a significant advantage. For Czech, or languages with regular pronunciation, the situation is somewhat simpler, as such words can be rewritten in a "pseudo" orthographic form, such as *designovaný* → *dyzajnovaný* (designed in English). This was not tested in this paper, however.

The last comparison was the quality of the synthetic speech itself. In this research question, we tried to outline which of the models used has the potential to generate speech with the highest perceived quality. Nevertheless, we did not consider the performance of the generation in any way, which may also be important for practical employment.

3.1   Loanwords and Homographs

In the correct Czech pronunciation rendering test, the loanwords not following the regular pronunciation rules were used. There were 21 very short sentences with 32 loanwords (similar to these in [32]) synthesized and analysed:

Stadium agrese.   Exhalace působí *bronchitidu*.
Stage of aggression   Exhalation causes bronchitis
Aktivní frekvence.   *Diskuse* bez pointy.
Active frequency   Pointless discussion
Designovaný premiér.   *Playback* na koncertě místo *etudy*.
Designated Prime Minister   Playback at a concert instead of an etude
. . .

On the contrary, for English we have focused on homographs, which were placed within meaningful phrases designed by the authors. We used 17 words: *record, read, live, minute, tear, wind, conflict, progress, row, import, insult, advocate, research, bow. lead, sow* and *wound*, and put their both pronunciation variants into 17 phrases, the same as these in [32]:

Did you *record*/rɪˈkɔːd/ this *record*/ˈrekərd/?
Have you *read*/red/ that book that all the people *read*/riːd/?
. . .

Both tests, naturally, were carried out for orthographic input only,. as in the case of phonetic input these words are expected to be transcribed into the correct form by a G2P or other NLP module. The evaluation was performed by the authors themselves, simply by listening to the output samples and counting correct/wrong renderings of the evaluated phenomena. There is no need for a multi-listener evaluation, since the use of right or wrong pronunciation variants is clearly recognisable.

3.2   Phonetic vs Orthographic Input

To answer the question of the phonetic vs. orthographic text input, we synthesized 20 ordinary phrases without any words containing phenomena possibly influencing the individual input types. For the orthographic input, the models have to "only" deal with inner- and cross-word assimilation [14] in Czech. In the case of English, the 20 phrases containing common words were synthesized and evaluated. Let us note that we did not examine the correct rendering of OOV words (for English), i.e., these words do not occur in the training recordings. For now, these are considered as a "special" variant of loanwords, and a more detailed survey of this was left to future work.

The same phrases for both languages were phonetically transcribed and synthesized by models trained on phonetic inputs, where a simplified phonetic alphabet was used for both Czech and English [21]. The corresponding orto–phone pairs were then compared in the ABX (CCR) test. Test participants evaluating the Czech voice were native Czech speakers, most of them with a background in speech technology research, while the participants evaluating English voices were undergraduate students of an applied linguistics program with an appropriate level of English skills but without a background in speech technologies. More details about listeners are stated in Sect. 4.

Let us note that the use of an objective acoustic measure, such as PESQ [25], POLQA [1], STOI [28], (perceptual)SNR, and others, was not considered. The reason is that these kinds of tests are unable to distinguish if a stimuli sound correctly from the phonetic point of view.

3.3 Overall System Comparison

The last question was the comparison of the synthetic speech quality generated by the challenged TTS models. To compare that, a "simplified" MUSHRA test [9, 13], was chosen, where the simplification means the absence of reference and anchor test samples. The same set of phrases as described in Sect. 4.2 was used, while in each test stimuli, three samples of the same phrase were presented in randomized order, each rendered by one of the evaluated TTS models for the given input type – i.e., orthographic inputs were evaluated independently on the phonetic inputs. The task for the listeners was to assign scores, ranging from 0 to 100, to the individual samples relative to each other.

Exactly as for the test in Sect. 3.2, test participants for the particular languages were recruited from the same groups. Also, the same reason is for excluding an objective evaluation metric.

3.4 Voices Used in the Experiments

As already stated, Czech and English datasets were used to train the models. For the Czech dataset, we used our own proprietary voice Jan [31], containing $12,241$ phrases giving about 14.7 hours of speech, excluding pauses. Regarding English, we used two voices, the first being our own proprietary voice Jeremy [31] with $10,924$ phrases and 13.6 hours of speech (without pauses), and the second being free LJ Speech Dataset [12], having $13,100$ recordings with a total length of approximately 24 hours.

While Jan and Jeremy were engaged for similar purposes, i.e., unit selection TTS method; they are similar in their properties such as speaking style, unit coverage, and so on. The LJSpeech voice, on the contrary, was obtained from audiobook recordings, and thus, it differs in its properties, especially in the speaking style and no special units balancing, from the former ones.

4   Results

As already noted, the evaluation was carried out by means of listening tests. While there is a large intersection of listeners evaluating the systems in Sect. 4.2 and Sect. 4.3, there were some participating only in one of them. All the listeners were instructed to use headphones and to carry out the tests in a quiet environment. None of them reported any hearing issues or other problems during the evaluation.

Table 1. Results of the synthesis correctness: loanword and homographs.

Model	WER [%]	Wrong
Czech		
FastSpeech2	28.13	serveru, asijsk, Asie, Palestin, kognitivn, playback, etudy, puzzle, melatonin
Tacotron2	**46,88**	
VITS	28.13	
English (Jeremy)		
FastSpeech2	16.67	read, live, minute, progress, research
VITS	**40.00**	
English (LJ Speech)		
FastSpeech2	56.09	live, tear, conflict, progress, research, advocate
Tacotron2	**63.91**	
VITS	**63.04**	

Let us note that the results for Tacotron2, trained on Jeremy voice, are absent. Despite using the same settings as for the other voices, the training of the model started correctly (as checked by analysis of the validation steps), but toward the end of the training, the model was not able to generate intelligible speech. Due to time constraints, we were, unfortunately, unable to analyse the reasons for this behaviour.

4.1 Loanwords and Homographs

The analysis of the synthesized sentences for this part of the evaluation was solely carried out by the authors themselves. Since there is a simple binary decision required, and native speakers or language experts are assumed to be able to recognise correct pronunciation, we do not expect different results in the case of evaluating by means of standard listening tests.

In Table 1, the word error rate (WER) percentages are presented, with the most frequent misses shown. The WER value was computed as the ratio of mispronounced words to the total number of 32 examined loanwords and 34 homographs. In the *wrong* column, we listed the mispronounced loanwords or homographs where all the systems wrongly rendered at least one variant. It can be seen that the Tacotron2 model is rather poor at estimating for both Czech and English, while VITS is rather good for Czech but often misses in English. FastSpeech2, on the other hand, behaves quite robustly, except for the LJ Speech corpus. Overall, the results show quite a large variance, making any clear statement fairly unconvincing. On the other hand, we did not expect any better

Table 2. Results of the preference listening test: orthographic vs phonetic inputs.

Model	Preference [%]		
	ortho	same	phone
Czech			
FastSpeech2	22.50	**42.86**	34.64
Tacotron2	29.29	28.21	**42.50**
VITS	29.29	28.21	**42.50**
English (Jeremy)			
FastSpeech2	**45.44**	15.87	38.70
VITS	**51.74**	9.78	38.48
English (LJ Speech)			
FastSpeech2	**56.09**	17.39	26.52
Tacotron2	**63.91**	13.48	22.69
VITS	**63.04**	9.13	27.86

results, considering that wider text context, and possibly some level of understanding, is required to handle these phenomena correctly. There is a significant advantage of phonetic input, where other DNN models can be used to decide, and they can be trained on much larger (test-only) datasets.

Let us emphasize that this evaluation took into account only the loanword and homograph words. However, we found that there were cases when both evaluated word variants were pronounced correctly, but there was another word either with a wrong accent or pronounced in an otherwise incorrect way. This was left to further analysis, though, and had no influence on the results presented here.

4.2 Phonetic vs Orthographic Input

In Table 2, the results of ABX test comparing speech quality generated by the individual voice models with phonetic vs. orthographic inputs are presented. There were 13 listeners participating in the Czech test, each evaluating 60 test pairs. Similarly, both English voices were evaluated by 23 listeners, each evaluating 100 test pairs in total. The higher number of evaluated pairs for English was caused by joining the evaluated pairs into a single test, purely for practical reasons, while not combining the tested systems in any way.

It can be seen that for English, the orthographic input leads to a higher quality of synthetic speech for all the tested neural models, as clearly preferred by the listeners. For Czech, the opposite is true and phonetic input wins, except for the FastSpeech2 model, where the most listeners evaluated both versions as equal (either good or bad) with a slight preference for phonetic input for the cases where they were able to decide.

This definitely requires further analysis, since we expected the phonetic input would behave better than orthographic for English (as also found in [7], yet for another DNN model), while the results show the clear opposite for all of the systems. On the contrary, with orthographic and phonetic inputs not being so widely different in Czech, there is a surprisingly significant inclination toward the phonetic input.

Table 3. Results of the MUSHRA listening test: overall systems comparison.

Model	MUSHRA score	
	ortho	phone
Czech		
FastSpeech2	72.06 ± 17.49	75.98 ± 15.73
Tacotron2	77.02 ± 14.40	78.80 ± 14.86
VITS	**85.10** ± 12.41	**86.68** ± 11.79
English (Jeremy)		
FastSpeech22	73.91 ± 23.02	71.72 ± 24.56
VITS	**81.83** ± 19.51	**79.97** ± 18.45
English (LJ Speech)		
FastSpeech2	63.74 ± 26.98	57.53 ± 28.58
Tacotron2	**80.66** ± 21.54	69.98 ± 26.09
VITS	**80.55** ± 20.76	**74.01** ± 24.22

4.3   Overall System Comparison

The question of the overall performance of the systems, as evaluated by "simplified" MUSHRA test, is stated in Table 3, and to remind ourselves of the description in Sect. 3.3, the synthesis models using orthographic inputs were evaluated independently of these using phonetic inputs. The test itself contained 40 stimuli and was completed by 13 listeners for the Czech voice, while 80 stimuli were evaluated for English voices, all finished by 23 listeners. And, similar to Sect. 4.2, both English voices were evaluated in a single test.

A more detailed visualization of the results from Table 3 is shown in Fig. 1 and Fig. 2, where it can be seen that the VITS obtained consistently higher scores than the other two synthesizers. Also, the comparison of scores for phonetic and orthographic inputs corresponds with results from Sect. 4.2, although these two inputs were not compared together in any of the stimuli. Analysing the notch intervals, the higher quality of VITS is in the most of the cases statistically significant.

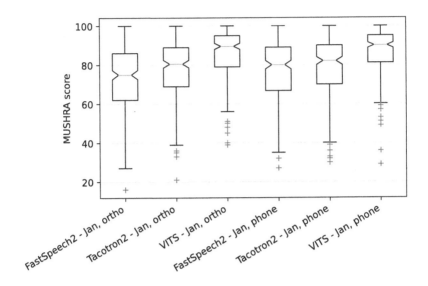

Fig. 1. Results of the MUSHRA listening test: overall systems comparison, Czech.

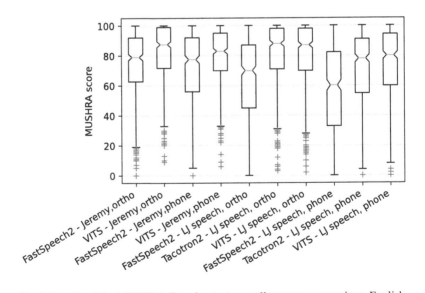

Fig. 2. Results of the MUSHRA listening test: overall systems comparison, English.

5   Conclusions

In the present paper, we have challenged three different modern speech synthesis neural models with various tasks on two different types of input texts (used both for training and inference, naturally).

We have shown by the experiment with loanwords and homographs that the use of raw orthographic input is not reliably capable of providing correct pronunciation for the tested cases, which was more or less expected based on observations in [32]. The FastSpeech2 model is the most successful in this, probably due to the embedding of the transformer model, which is very suitable for the tasks of text conversion [6]. Still, the use of phonetic input is superior to orthographic input. As a byproduct of the evaluation, we have found that even relatively common words may be rendered incorrectly. This is one of our plans for future research in this area.

On the other hand, the use of phonetic input provided, at least for English voices, speech of a lower quality than speech generated from orthographic inputs. This has been a rather surprising finding, and we do not have a full understanding of these results yet. To give a reasoned explanation of such behaviour, a much deeper analysis of the individual outputs will be required, and we would like to continue investigating the issue.

Regarding the overall quality evaluation for the given neural models, the VITS provided synthetic speech ranked by the highest scores more consistently than the other two models. One of the explanations may be the modern structure of its neural model (conditional variational autoencoder), but there may also be an influence on the number of training steps used when training the individual models (although the loss functions no longer significantly decreased at the given training steps). On the other hand, our latest observations of the VITS model from `coqui-ai/TTS` project suggest that it has some problems when synthesizing a Czech phone [r] in some contexts. Also, the VITS model does not allow a full and fine user control of all prosodic characteristics, as opposed to FastSpeech2, which is able to use input character-level relative changes for duration, F_0, and even volume prosodic characteristics. From a practical deployment point of view, this is a significant factor to consider.

Perhaps the most important finding was the influence of the implementation. Nowadays, it is easy to find several open implementations of almost any DNN model published, which is generally the right direction for the research. However, the particular implementations do not provide similar or even comparable results. For example, HifiGAN from `TensorFlowTTS` project provides recognisably worse audio quality than Multi-Band MelGAN from the same project, while it is the opposite in the `coqui` project. Unfortunately, the trained models cannot be transferred easily across the projects. Therefore, let us be prepared that there may be better implementations of the tested models, providing slightly different results than those presented here. We would like to ask anyone to be aware of that fact.

References

1. Beerends, J., et al.: Perceptual objective listening quality assessment (POLQA), the third generation ITU-T standard for end-to-end speech quality measurement part I-temporal alignment. AES: J. Audio Eng. Soc. **61**, 366–384 (2013)
2. Casanova, E., Weber, J., Shulby, C., Junior, A.C., Gölge, E., Ponti, M.A.: YourTTS: towards zero-shot multi-speaker TTS and zero-shot voice conversion for everyone (2021)
3. Cho, H., Jung, W., Lee, J., Woo, S.H.: SANE-TTS: stable and natural end-to-end multilingual text-to-speech. In: Ko, H., Hansen, J.H.L. (eds.) 23rd Annual Conference of the International Speech Communication Association, Interspeech 2022, Incheon, Korea, 18–22 September 2022, pp. 1–5. ISCA (2022). https://doi.org/10.21437/Interspeech.2022-46
4. Delalez, S., Akue, L.: Neural TTS in French: comparing graphemic and phonetic inputs using the SynPaFlex-Corpus and Tacotron2 (2023)
5. Elias, I., et al.: Parallel Tacotron 2: a non-autoregressive neural TTS model with differentiable duration modeling. In: Proceedings of the Interspeech 2021, pp. 141–145 (2021). https://doi.org/10.21437/Interspeech.2021-1461
6. Řezáčková, M., Tihelka, D., Švec, J.: T5G2P: using text-to-text transfer transformer for grapheme-to-phoneme conversion. In: Interspeech 2021, Brno, Czech Republic (2021)
7. Fong, J., Taylor, J., Richmond, K., King, S.: A comparison of letters and phones as input to sequence-to-sequence models for speech synthesis. In: Speech Synthesis Workshop, Vienna, Austria, pp. 223–227 (2019). https://doi.org/10.21437/SSW.2019-40
8. Gölge, E.: Coqui TTS (2021). https://doi.org/10.5281/zenodo.6334862
9. Grůber, M., Chýlek, A., Matoušek, J.: Framework for conducting tasks requiring human assessment. In: Proceedings of the Interspeech 2019, pp. 4626–4627 (2019)
10. Hanzlíček, Z., Vít, J.: LSTM-based speech segmentation trained on different foreign languages. In: Sojka, P., Kopeček, I., Pala, K., Horák, A. (eds.) TSD 2020. LNCS (LNAI), vol. 12284, pp. 456–464. Springer, Cham (2020). https://doi.org/10.1007/978-3-030-58323-1_49
11. Hanzlíček, Z., Vít, J., Tihelka, D.: LSTM-based speech segmentation for TTS synthesis. In: Ekštein, K. (ed.) TSD 2019. LNCS (LNAI), vol. 11697, pp. 361–372. Springer, Cham (2019). https://doi.org/10.1007/978-3-030-27947-9_31
12. Ito, K., Johnson, L.: The LJ speech dataset (2017). https://keithito.com/LJ-Speech-Dataset/
13. ITU Recommendation BS.1534-2: Method for the subjective assessment of intermediate quality level of coding systems. Technical report, International Telecommunication Union (2014)
14. Jůzová, M., Tihelka, D., Vít, J.: Unified language-independent DNN-based G2P converter. In: Kubin, G., Kacic, Z. (eds.) Interspeech 2019, pp. 2085–2089. ISCA (2019). https://doi.org/10.21437/Interspeech.2019-2335
15. Kögel, F., Nguyen, B., Cardinaux, F.: Towards robust FastSpeech 2 by modelling residual multimodality (2023)
16. Kim, J., Kim, S., Kong, J., Yoon, S.: Glow-TTS: a generative flow for text-to-speech via monotonic alignment search. In: Conference on Neural Information Processing Systems, Vancouver, Canada (2020)
17. Kim, J., Kong, J., Son, J.: Conditional variational autoencoder with adversarial learning for end-to-end text-to-speech. In: International Conference on Machine Learning, pp. 5530–5540 (2021)
18. Kingma, D.P., Ba, J.L.: Adam: a method for stochastic optimization. In: International Conference on Learning Representations, San Diego, USA (2015)
19. Kong, J., Kim, J., Bae, J.: HiFi-GAN: generative adversarial networks for efficient and high fidelity speech synthesis. In: Conference on Neural Information Processing Systems (2020)

20. Loshchilov, I., Hutter, F.: Decoupled weight decay regularization. In: International Conference on Learning Representations, New Orleans, USA (2019)

21. Matoušek, J., Tihelka, D.: On comparison of phonetic representations for Czech neural speech synthesis. In: Sojka, P., Horák, A., Kopeček, I., Pala, K. (eds.) Text, Speech, and Dialogue, TSD 2022. LNCS, vol. 13502, pp. 410–422. Springer, Cham. https://doi.org/10.1007/978-3-031-16270-1_34

22. van den Oord, A., et al.: WaveNet: a generative model for raw audio. CoRR abs/1609.03499 (2016)

23. Prasad, A., Zuluaga-Gomez, J., Motlicek, P., Sarfjoo, S., Nigmatulina, I., Vesely, K.: Speech and natural language processing technologies for pseudo-pilot simulator (2022)

24. Ren, Y., et al.: FastSpeech 2: fast and high-quality end-to-end text to speech (2021)

25. Rix, A., Beerends, J., Hollier, M., Hekstra, A.: Perceptual evaluation of speech quality (PESQ) - a new method for speech quality assessment of telephone networks and codecs. In: Proceedings of the 2001 IEEE International Conference on Acoustics, Speech, and Signal Processing, vol. 2, pp. 749–752 (2001). https://doi.org/10.1109/ICASSP.2001.941023

26. Shang, Z., Shi, P., Zhang, P., Wang, L., Zhao, G.: HierTTS: expressive end-to-end text-to-waveform using a multi-scale hierarchical variational auto-encoder. Appl. Sci. 13(2) (2023). https://doi.org/10.3390/app13020868

27. Shen, J., et al.: Natural TTS synthesis by conditioning Wavenet on MEL spectrogram predictions. In: 2018 IEEE International Conference on Acoustics, Speech and Signal Processing (ICASSP), pp. 4779–4783 (2018). https://doi.org/10.1109/ICASSP.2018.8461368

28. Taal, C.H., Hendriks, R.C., Heusdens, R., Jensen, J.: An algorithm for intelligibility prediction of time-frequency weighted noisy speech. IEEE Trans. Audio Speech Lang. Process. 19(7), 2125–2136 (2011). https://doi.org/10.1109/TASL.2011.2114881

29. Tan, X., Qin, T., Soong, F., Liu, T.Y.: A Survey on Neural Speech Synthesis (2021)

30. TensorFlowTTS: Real-time state-of-the-art speech synthesis for TensorFlow 2 (2021). https://github.com/TensorSpeech/TensorFlowTTS

31. Tihelka, D., Hanzlíček, Z., Jůzová, M., Vít, J., Matoušek, J., Grůber, M.: Current state of text-to-speech system ARTIC: a decade of research on the field of speech technologies. In: Sojka, P., Horák, A., Kopeček, I., Pala, K. (eds.) TSD 2018. LNCS (LNAI), vol. 11107, pp. 369–378. Springer, Cham (2018). https://doi.org/10.1007/978-3-030-00794-2_40

32. Tihelka, D., Matoušek, J., Tihelková, A.: How much end-to-end is Tacotron 2 end-to-end TTS system. In: Ekštein, K., Pártl, F., Konopík, M. (eds.) TSD 2021. LNCS (LNAI), vol. 12848, pp. 511–522. Springer, Cham (2021). https://doi.org/10.1007/978-3-030-83527-9_44

33. Vaswani, A., et al.: Attention is all you need (2017)

34. Vervloesem, K., Bachmann, M.: gruut 2.2.0 (2021). https://github.com/rhasspy/gruut

35. Yang, G., Yang, S., Liu, K., Fang, P., Chen, W., Xie, L.: Multi-band MelGAN: faster waveform generation for high-quality text-to-speech. In: 2021 IEEE Spoken Language Technology Workshop (SLT), pp. 492–498 (2021). https://doi.org/10.1109/SLT48900.2021.9383551

36. Zhao, W., Lian, Y., Chai, J., Tu, Z.: Multi-speaker Chinese news broadcasting system based on improved Tacotron2. Multimedia Tools Appl. 4391, 89–100 (2023). https://doi.org/10.1007/s11042-023-15279-z

37. Zhou, Z., Liu, S.: Learning to auto-correct for high-quality spectrograms. In: 2023 IEEE International Conference on Acoustics, Speech and Signal Processing (ICASSP), ICASSP 2023, pp. 1–5 (2023). https://doi.org/10.1109/ICASSP49357.2023.10094762

T5G2P: Multilingual Grapheme-to-Phoneme Conversion with Text-to-Text Transfer Transformer

Markéta Řezáčková[(✉)] [iD], Adam Frémund [iD], Jan Švec [iD],
and Jindřich Matoušek [iD]

New Technologies for the Information Society (NTIS) and Department of Cybernetics
Faculty of applied Sciences, University of West Bohemia, Pilsen, Czech Republic
{juzova,afremun,honzas,jmatouse}@kky.zcu.cz

Abstract. In recent years, the Text-to-Text Transfer Transformer (T5) neural network has proved more powerful for many text-related tasks, including the grapheme-to-phoneme conversion (G2P). The paper describes the training process of T5-base models for several languages. It shows the advantages of training G2P models using that language-specific basis over the G2P models fine-tuned from the multilingual base model. The paper also explains the reasons for training G2P models on whole sentences (not a dictionary) and evaluates the trained G2P models on unseen sentences and words.

Keywords: T5 · transformers · phonetic transcription · grapheme-to-phoneme · TTS system

1 Introduction

For decades, a grapheme-to-phoneme (G2P) module was a crucial part of all text-to-speech (TTS) systems since correct phonetic transcriptions of input sentences were fundamental for high-quality synthetic speech. Nowadays, end-to-end TTS systems, synthesizing from raw texts, appear increasingly often [4,8,11]. Still, the "traditional" composition of TTS systems (i.e., a G2P module and the synthesizer itself) is topical and still used in many approaches (both research and commercial) [9].

The task of phonetic transcription (G2P conversion) is to transcribe the input text into a sequence of phonemes of the given language. Traditional G2P approaches use large dictionaries and (mostly) hand-crafted phonetic rules [9]. Regular languages (regarding the phonetic rules) usually rely on the rule-based approach. However, they still need a dictionary of exceptions (e.g., foreign names, loan words, etc.). That is advantageous, especially for inflected languages, since the pronunciation dictionaries would be enormous when containing all inflected forms. The dictionary-based approaches are often used for languages such as English. However, there is still a need for some post-processing rules, e.g., for out-of-vocabulary words or ambiguities (see below). In both cases, the large dictionaries need to be updated. And despite being supplemented regularly, the

H. Lu et al. (Eds.): ACPR 2023, LNCS 14408, pp. 336–345, 2023.
https://doi.org/10.1007/978-3-031-47665-5_27

dictionaries never contain all words (or all pronunciation exceptions) of the given language.

In recent years, the G2P conversion has relied more often on trained G2P (usually neural network) models [7,10,15,16]. As we know, almost all approaches to G2P work only at the word level – they train models on items of large dictionaries. From our point of view, the main disadvantage of the word-level G2P approach lies in the need to design post-processing rules (which are strongly language-dependent) that would solve the specific phenomena in the particular languages, e.g., cross-word assimilation, homograph disambiguation, etc.

For English, those post-processing rules have to distinguish, for example, between 2 variants in the following phrases[1]:

the [Di:] apple   vs.   **the** [D@] bear
I have not **read** [rEd] the book yet. vs. I **read** [ri:d] every evening.

Some languages, such as Czech, use *assimilation of voice* (sometimes, a voiceless consonant is pronounced voiced, and vice versa – depending on the circumstances):

pod [pot] pokličkou vs. **pod** [pod] dubem vs. **pod** [pot] oknem
under the pot-lid   under the oak   under the window

Četla jsem **text** [tekst]. vs. **Text** [tekzd] byl zajímavý.
I have read a text.   The text was interesting.

The above-mentioned phenomena are the primary motivation for this paper. We applied the G2P on the sentence level without using cross-word rules to catch language-specific inter-sentence word relations. Neural network models trained on whole sentences are presented in recent papers [2,17], and the present paper follows the training process described in [17] and applies that to other languages.

2   T5 Models

As a base model in all our experiments, we used the Text-to-Text Transfer Transformer (T5) model [5]. Generally, the T5 model is trained as the complete encoder-decoder transformer. The training task for the T5 model is defined as a self-supervised task – the model tries to recover missing token spans in the output. The general advantage of the T5 model is the ability to perform many text-to-text tasks like text summarization, topic detection, or sentiment analysis.

For experiments with English data, we used Google's T5-base English model (version from October 21st, 2019)[2] trained from Common Crawl data[3]. We replicated the same pre-processing procedure to obtain the pre-training data in other

---

[1] Note: All examples of pronunciation are in SAMPA alphabet [12].
[2] https://github.com/google-research/text-to-text-transfer-transformer.
[3] https://commoncrawl.org/.

Fig. 1. Example of processing the original text and creating input/output text pairs. Figure taken from [5].

languages considered in this work, and we pre-trained our own T5 models for these languages.

The T5 model is a self-supervised trained variant of the generic textual Transformer architecture [5]. The T5 model is able to construct the internal representation of input on many linguistic layers: starting from phonetic and syntactic through semantic to the pragmatic layer. The T5 model is pre-trained on an artificial self-supervised task – a text restoration task from unlabelled training data. An example of the pre-training input/output text pair is shown in Fig. 1.

The T5 model tries to recover missing tokens in the input sentence masked with sentinel tokens <X> and < Y >. The masked tokens are used as training targets and the output sentence is terminated using another sentinel token < Z >. This way, the T5 learns not only the knowledge required to understand the input sentence but also the knowledge necessary to generate meaningful output sentences.

The original Google's T5-base English model[4] (labeled as *t5-EN* in our paper) was trained from Common Crawl data[5]. We replicated the same pre-processing procedure to obtain the data for other languages tested in the present paper. The pre-processing steps correspond with the steps presented in [6] for building the Colossal Clean Crawled Corpus (C4) on which Google's T5 model was pre-trained. Such rules are generally applied while processing web text:

- Only lines ending in terminal punctuation are retained. Short pages and lines are discarded.
- Pages with dirty and obscene words are removed.
- Lines with the word "JavaScript" and the curly braces { } are removed (remains of incorrect text extraction from the source code of the webpage).
- The pages in the corpus were de-duplicated. The resulting corpus contains each span of three consecutive sentences just once.

For all languages presented in this paper (except for English, for which we use Google's T5-base English model), we have collected the corresponding Common-

---

[4] https://github.com/google-research/text-to-text-transfer-transformer.
[5] https://commoncrawl.org/.

Crawl sub-corpus at the end of October 2021 and pre-trained language-specific T5 models (*t5-XX*) using those data. Textual datasets sizes are presented in Table 1. The T5 training followed the original procedure described in [5].

Table 1. Statistics of textual datasets used for training the language-specific base T5 models.

pre-trained model	dataset size [GB]
t5-CZ	122
t5-DE	649
t5-ES	683
t5-FR	511
t5-IT	274
t5-RU	2.568

We used the `t5-base` architecture consisting of 220M parameters, 2×12 transformer block in the encoder and the decoder. The dimensionality of hidden layers and embeddings was 768. The attention mechanism uses 12 attention heads with inner dimensionality 64.

For comparison with the *t5* model, we also used the "universal" multilingual model `mt5-base` [14] (further denoted as *mt5*), which was pre-trained on CommonCrawl data from 101 languages. Because the *mt5* architecture uses the SentencePiece tokenizer [3] with 250k pieces, the overall number of trainable parameters is 580M. The increased number of parameters lies in the extra embedding vectors required to represent additional sentence pieces from the tokenizer. The remaining architecture of the encoder and the decoder is the same for both the *t5* and *mt5* models. Because all 101 languages share the same tokenizer, the input/output texts are tokenized into the higher count of shorter pieces than the language-specific `t5` models. To recap, the language-specific SentencePiece tokenizers consistently use 32k pieces.

3   G2P Data and Models

As explained in Sect. 1, this paper focuses on training sentence-level G2P models. The recently published study [17] showed that the T5G2P model (i.e., a T5 trained for G2P task) was able to outperform the baseline *rules+dictionary* approaches (or at least almost beat them) for English and Czech languages. Following the mentioned paper, we trained T5-based G2P models for seven languages.

We have collected sentences with their phonetic transcriptions for Czech (CZ), German (DE), English (EN), Spanish (ES), Italian (IT), French (FR), and Russian (RU) languages[6]. The transcriptions were generated automatically and checked by our phonetic experts. The statistics are summarized in Table 2. The sizes of data available are different (and the average sentence lengths as well), and also, the total numbers of unique phonemes in particular language data vary significantly – which would probably affect the accuracy values calculated on the generated transcriptions (see Sect. 4). The Spanish language has the smallest phoneme set (according to data we had at our disposal) since there is no distinguishing between short and long variants of vowels. On the other hand, the largest set for the Italian language is related to the phonetic phenomenon "gemination", a consonant lengthening (a consonant articulation for a longer period of time compared to a singleton consonant), which is typical (besides other languages) for Italian [1].

For each language, a subset of 10% randomly selected sentences was used for testing. Note that the testing data contain "just" sentences unseen during the training phase. Still, many single words were seen during the training process – which is evident since common words (prepositions, basic verb forms, pronouns, and others) appear very often. That is also a reason why our *word accuracy* values in Table 3 can not be compared to the word accuracy values in studies working with dictionary items. Therefore, we also focused on unseen words in the testing sentences (see Sect. 4.1).

Table 2. G2P data statistics.

language	No. of sentence	avg. sentence length (in words)	avg. sentence length (in phones)	No. of phones
CZ	442,027	11.5	65.9	53
DE	275,572	16.3	80.8	52
EN	160,668	11.8	45.4	49
ES	605,470	22.0	107.5	34
FR	635,605	17.1	62.9	46
IT	450,766	10.7	54.7	85
RU	405,844	10.5	61.4	54

We used the Tensorflow implementation of Hugging-Face Transformers library [13] together with the T5s[7] library. We fine-tuned the base (both language-dependent and language-independent) T5G2P models (described in Sect. 2) to generate the corresponding phonetic transcription. As the T5 model is an encoder-decoder model that converts all NLP problems into a text-to-text format, we easily used the whole sentences of a particular language at the input. The desired output is also defined as a sequence. The examples of input and output sequences (for Czech) are shown below:

---

[6] Note: We do not explicitly work with word stress position because we believe that this information (if necessary) is hidden implicitly in the phonetic transcription for all languages in use.

[7] https://github.com/honzas83/t5s

Input sequence: *Dodnes tak ale neučinil.*
Output sequence: *dodnes tak !ale ne!uCiJil.*

Input sequence: *Že papež skutečně nosí místní církve ve svém srdci.*
Output sequence: *Ze papeS skuteCJe nosI mIstJI cIrkve ve svEm sPci.*

Input sequence: *Nedávno skončily Vánoce a opět se slaví.*
Output sequence: *nedAvno skonℂili vAnoce !a !opjet se slavI.*

The training lasted 100 epochs with 1000 update steps per each epoch. As the learning rate scheduler we used Inverse Square Root Scheduler with starting learning rate equals to $1 \cdot 10^{-4}$. All parameters are set as trainable.

4   T5G2P Results

The output sentences generated by our trained T5G2P models fine-tuned from language-specific (*t5-XX*) and multilingual (*mt5*) models were compared to the reference and evaluated using the following measures: *sentence accuracy*, *word accuracy* and *phoneme accuracy*. The results are shown in Table 3.

Table 3. Sentence, word, and phoneme accuracies in % for different languages. Comparison of *t5-XX* and *mt5* models.

language	base T5 model	sentence accuracy	word accuracy	phone accuracy
CZ	mt5	98.32	99.85	99.95
	t5-CZ	98.90	99.90	99.97
DE	mt5	97.02	99.81	99.93
	t5-DE	98.02	99.88	99.95
EN	mt5	91.96	99.01	99.55
	t5-EN	93.77	99.04	99.68
ES	mt5	98.70	99.94	99.97
	t5-ES	99.40	99.97	99.98
FR	mt5	96.95	99.80	99.96
	t5-FR	98.18	99.88	99.98
IT	mt5	95.41	99.32	99.87
	t5-IT	95.74	99.38	99.88
RU	mt5	96.29	99.73	99.90
	t5-RU	97.86	99.83	99.92

The results clearly show the advantage of language-specific base T5 models (compared to the multilingual *mt5* model) – the G2P models using the *t5-XX* base models outperformed the models trained from a multilingual base in all three observed measures for all tested languages. More specifically, the *sentence error rate* (i.e., sentence accuracy complement to 100%) decreases, for example, from approx. 3% to less than 2% for German and French, and (surprisingly) it also decreases noticeably for English.

For greater clarity, the values of sentence accuracy are drawn in Fig. 2. Regarding the dependence of sentence accuracy values on the size of the dataset available for the particular language, we can confirm that the sentence accuracy tends to increase with the increasing dataset size. Nevertheless, there are some "anomalies". For example, the results on Italian are significantly worse compared to languages with a similar number of sentences available (see Table 2) – but that "drop" might be explained by the most extensive set of phonemes (and maybe, the 2nd smallest dataset used for training the pre-trained *t5-IT* model (see also Table 1). The worst results regarding the accuracy evaluated on our G2P task were recorded for English. However, let us emphasize that (besides complex English phonetic transcription) we had the smallest G2P dataset for this language. The two Slavic languages (Czech and Russian) do not differ much in the G2P data size. However, the results are a bit better for Czech – in our opinion, the Czech phonetic transcription is more straightforward than Russian since there is a fixed word stress position. The graph in Fig. 2 also shows a significant difference between results for Spanish and French (despite similar numbers of G2P sentences available), but, again, those languages vary in phoneme set size (French has third more phonemes than Spanish).

4.1 Unseen Words in Testing Data

In Sect. 3, we mentioned that words in testing data are not entirely unseen – a certain number of those words is also included in the training data and the T5, therefore, saw them during the training phase (and probably, it also learned how to transcribe them correctly). Therefore, the word accuracy values for all languages are very high. Considering English (which is used frequently in many G2P studies, e.g. [10,16]), our word error rate (WER) is approximately 1%, while the state-of-the-art values on publicly available dictionaries are about (or less) than 20%.

The numbers of unseen words in the subset of sentences used for testing are shown in Table 4 – the second column contains numbers of all unique words in the testing set, and the third column shows how many of those do not occur in the training set (only several percent or less than 1%, depending on a language). The *word error rate* values for those unseen words (*uWER*) are shown in the last column. The uWER values mostly range from 14% to 20% (with 2 exceptions analyzed below), meaning approx. every sixth word not seen in the training data is transcribed incorrectly by the trained G2P models.

The numbers in the first row (CZ) might be surprising. The testing data for Czech consist of many words (compared to the other languages) despite not having the largest set of sentences at disposal. However, that only confirms that the Czech language has a rich vocabulary. But because the Czech phonetic transcription is very regular (excluding foreign and loan words), the uWER

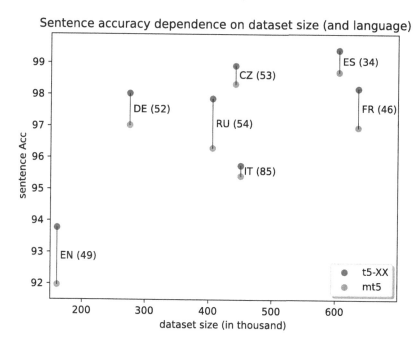

Fig. 2. Sentence accuracy and dataset size (the phoneme set sizes in brackets).

Table 4. Word error rates of unseen words (uWER) in the test set for different languages. Evaluated using the *t5-XX* models.

language	No. of unique words	No. of unseen words	uWER (%)
CZ	202.923	7.807	2.66
DE	111.811	1.496	14.84
EN	30.182	625	27.76
ES	93.160	412	15.29
FR	76.597	498	17.67
IT	71.442	1.039	19.92
RU	68.731	1.229	17.49

value is the smallest one in our study. The highest uWER value for English (27%) means that approximately one-quarter of unknown word transcriptions generated by our trained G2P model contains an error. This is, of course, higher compared to state-of-the-art WER. Still, those WER values were calculated on a testing subset of all words – in our case, the uWER was evaluated on words that did not appear in any of more than 140 thousand training sentences so those words are mostly names (often of foreign origin and, therefore, with a less predictable pronunciation) or other rare English words – which was also confirmed by the analysis of incorrect transcriptions.

5   Conclusion

In the present paper, we used T5 neural network for training grapheme-to-phoneme models for 7 different languages. We followed the process of training T5G2P models described in [17]. First of all, we collected a huge amount of data for particular languages and pre-trained language-specific base models (in the same way as Google's T5-base model was trained). Afterward, those models were fine-tuned for the G2P task, having whole sentences at the input and their phonetic transcriptions at the output.

The results presented in Sect. 4 clearly showed the benefits of language-specific base models, compared to the multilingual *mt5* model. The other advantage, already described in Sect. 2, lies in a number of training parameters which is significantly higher for the *mt5* model. We also focused on words in testing data that were unknown to the T5G2P models ("unseen words") and compared the word error rate for different languages.

For future work, we want to analyze the incorrect transcriptions for particular languages in depth. And we also deal with the number of phonemes in each language and the possibility of reducing the phoneme set (especially for some applications of G2P and some languages like Italian). And finally, we aim to apply the same process of pre-training *t5-XX* models and fine-tuning the T5G2P models for other languages.

Acknowledgement. This research was supported by the Czech Science Foundation (GA CR), project No. GA21-14758S, and by the grant of the University of West Bohemia, project No. SGS-2022-017.

References

1. Di Benedetto, M.G., et al.: Lexical and syntactic gemination in Italian consonants - does a geminate Italian consonant consist of a repeated or a strengthened consonant? J. Acoust. Soc. Am. **149**(5), 3375–3386 (2021). https://doi.org/10.1121/10.0004987
2. Jůzová, M., Tihelka, D., Vít, J.: Unified language-independent DNN-based G2P converter. In: Kubin, G., Kacic, Z. (eds.) 20th Annual Conference of the International Speech Communication Association, Interspeech 2019, Graz, Austria, 15–19 September 2019, pp. 2085–2089. ISCA (2019). https://doi.org/10.21437/Interspeech.2019-2335
3. Kudo, T., Richardson, J.: SentencePiece: a simple and language independent subword tokenizer and detokenizer for neural text processing. In: Proceedings of the 2018 Conference on Empirical Methods in Natural Language Processing: System Demonstrations, Brussels, Belgium, November 2018, pp. 66–71. Association for Computational Linguistics (2018). https://doi.org/10.18653/v1/D18-2012. https://aclanthology.org/D18-2012
4. Matoušek, J., Tihelka, D.: VITS: quality vs. speed analysis. In: Ekštein, K., Pártl, F., Konopík, M. (eds.) Text, Speech, and Dialogue, TSD 2023. LNCS, vol. 14102. Springer, Cham (2023). https://doi.org/10.1007/978-3-031-40498-6_19

5. Raffel, C., et al.: Exploring the limits of transfer learning with a unified text-to-text transformer. J. Mach. Learn. Res. **21**(140), 1–67 (2020)
6. Raffel, C., et al.: Exploring the limits of transfer learning with a unified text-to-text transformer. arXiv arXiv:1910.10683 (2020)
7. Rao, K., Peng, F., Sak, H., Beaufays, F.: Grapheme-to-phoneme conversion using long short-term memory recurrent neural networks. In: 2015 IEEE International Conference on Acoustics, Speech and Signal Processing (ICASSP), pp. 4225–4229 (2015)
8. Sotelo, J., et al.: Char2Wav: end-to-end speech synthesis. In: ICLR (2017)
9. Tihelka, D., Hanzlíček, Z., Jůzová, M., Vít, J., Matoušek, J., Grůber, M.: Current state of text-to-speech system ARTIC: a decade of research on the field of speech technologies. In: Sojka, P., Horák, A., Kopeček, I., Pala, K. (eds.) TSD 2018. LNCS (LNAI), vol. 11107, pp. 369–378. Springer, Cham (2018). https://doi.org/10.1007/978-3-030-00794-2_40
10. Vaswani, A., et al.: Attention is all you need. arXiv arXiv:1706.03762 (2017)
11. Wang, Y., et al.: Tacotron: towards end-to-end speech synthesis (2017). https://arxiv.org/abs/1703.10135
12. Wells, J.C.: SAMPA computer readable phonetic alphabet. In: Gibbon, D., Moore, R., Winski, R. (eds.) Handbook of Standards and Resources for Spoken Language Systems. Mouton de Gruyter, Berlin and New York (1997)
13. Wolf, T., et al.: Transformers: state-of-the-art natural language processing. In: Proceedings of the 2020 Conference on Empirical Methods in Natural Language Processing: System Demonstrations, October 2020, pp. 38–45. Association for Computational Linguistics (2020)
14. Xue, L., et al.: mT5: a massively multilingual pre-trained text-to-text transformer. CoRR abs/2010.11934 (2020). https://arxiv.org/abs/2010.11934
15. Yao, K., Zweig, G.: Sequence-to-sequence neural net models for grapheme-to-phoneme conversion. CoRR abs/1506.00196 (2015)
16. Yolchuyeva, S., Németh, G., Gyires-Tóth, B.: Transformer based grapheme-to-phoneme conversion. In: Interspeech 2019, September 2019. https://doi.org/10.21437/interspeech.2019-1954
17. Řezáčková, M., Švec, J., Tihelka, D.: T5G2P: using text-to-text transfer transformer for grapheme-to-phoneme conversion. In: Hermansky, H., Cernocký, H., Burget, L., Lamel, L., Scharenborg, O., Motlícek, P. (eds.) 22nd Annual Conference of the International Speech Communication Association, Interspeech 2021, Brno, Czechia, 30 August–3 September 2021, pp. 6–10. ISCA (2021). https://doi.org/10.21437/Interspeech.2021-546

Transformer-Based Encoder-Encoder Architecture for Spoken Term Detection

Jan Švec[✉] , Luboš Šmídl , and Jan Lehečka

Department of Cybernetics, University of West Bohemia, Pilsen, Czech Republic
{honzas,smidl,jlehecka}@kky.zcu.cz

Abstract. The paper presents a method for spoken term detection based on the Transformer architecture. We propose the encoder-encoder architecture employing two BERT-like encoders with additional modifications, including attention masking, convolutional and upsampling layers. The encoders project a recognized hypothesis and a searched term into a shared embedding space, where the score of the putative hit is computed using the calibrated dot product. In the experiments, we used the Wav2Vec 2.0 speech recognizer. The proposed system outperformed a baseline method based on deep LSTMs on the English and Czech STD datasets based on USC Shoah Foundation Visual History Archive (MALACH).

Keywords: Neural networks · Transformer architecture · Spoken term detection

1 Introduction

Searching through large amounts of audio data is a common feature of several tasks in speech processing, namely keyword spotting (KWS), wake word detection (WWD), query-by-example (QbE), or spoken term detection (STD). These tasks differ both with the requirements imposed on the form of the query: for example, audio snippet (QbE) or sequence of graphemes (STD) and computational resources required: low resource (WWD), real-time processing (KWS), or off-line processing (STD). In recent works, the architecture of such systems is often based on acoustic embeddings extracted using deep neural networks [16]. Such embeddings are further used to classify or detect keywords, terms, or examples. The embeddings could be extracted using convolution networks, recurrent networks, or – more recently – Transformer networks.

Many recent papers have used Transformer architecture for the mentioned tasks. The Keyword Transformer [2] is designed for the Google Speech Command (GSC) task, which directly uses the Transformer architecture to project the input

This research was supported by the Ministry of the Interior of the Czech Republic, project No. VJ01010108 and by the Czech Science Foundation (GA CR), project No. GA22-27800S.

audio data into a single vector used for keyword classification. A similar approach is the architecture called LETR [4]. Unfortunately, the GSC-related works often present a solution for keyword classification instead of KWS or STD in long, streamed audio data.

The multi-headed self-attention mechanism is also used in the QbE scenario. For example, [21] proposes a combination of recursive neural networks, self-attention layers, and a hashing layer for learning binary embeddings for fast QbE speech search.

The works related to WWD also study the use of the Transformer architecture. The streaming variant of Transformer was proposed in [18]. The Transformer was modified for real-time usage and outperformed the system based on the convolution network. Another architecture called Catt-KWS [20] uses a cascaded Transformer in the encoder-decoder setup for real-time keyword spotting.

In this work, we do not focus on the direct processing of the input speech signal. Instead, we use the speech recognizer to convert an audio signal into a graphemic recognition hypothesis. The representation of speech at the grapheme level allows preprocessing of the input audio into a compact confusion network and further to a sequence of embedding vectors. A Deep LSTM architecture proposed in [24] uses the projection of both the input speech and searched term into a shared embedding space. The hybrid DNN-HMM speech recognizer produces phoneme confusion networks representing the input speech. The DNN-HMM speech recognizer can be replaced with the Wav2Vec 2.0 recognizer [1] with CTC loss – an algorithm for converting the CTC grapheme posteriors into grapheme confusion network was proposed in [22]. The grapheme confusion networks were subsequently used in the Deep LSTM STD. Moving from DNN-HMM to the Wav2Vec speech recognizer significantly improves the STD performance.

This work describes a modification of the STD neural network (Sect. 2) by replacing the Deep LSTMs with the Transformer encoder (Sect. 3). The core of the Transformer encoder has the same architecture as BERT-like (Bidirectional Transformers for Language Understanding) models [3, 10] (Sect. 3.4), but a simple drop-in replacement of LSTMs with vanilla Transformer encoder brings a significant degradation in STD performance which contradicts the common understanding of Transformers as the more superior class of models. This observation motivated the research presented in this paper. To overcome the LSTM baseline, we propose a set of well-motivated modifications (Sect. 3.2). The proposed method is experimentally evaluated in the domain of oral history archives (Holocaust testimonies from the USC Shoah Foundation Visual History Archive) in two languages (Sect. 4). The experimental results (Sect. 5) show that the proposed Transformer architecture outperforms the baseline Deep LSTM.

2 Neural Spoken Term Detection Framework

The design of the encoder-encoder STD based on neural networks consists of two independent processing pipelines: (1) the recognition output projection by a *hypothesis encoder* and (2) the searched term projection and minimum length estimation by a *query encoder*. Suppose the input audio is represented by the recognized hypothesis, which is a sequence of time-aligned segments c_i, $i = 1, \ldots N$. Each segment c_i is projected into a vector $\mathbf{C}_i$. The query g is expressed as the sequence of graphemes g_j, $j = 1, \ldots M$ mapped using an input embedding layer to vectors $\mathbf{G}_j$.

The hypothesis encoder is used to map the sequence of vectors $\mathbf{C}_{i=1}^N$ to a sequence of embedding vectors $\mathbf{R}_{i=1}^N$. The query encoder maps the vectors $\mathbf{G}_{j=1}^M$ to a sequence of query embeddings $\mathbf{Q}_{k=1}^K$. Here we assume that the length of sequences $\mathbf{C}_i$ and $\mathbf{R}_i$ is the same to keep the time correspondence of $\mathbf{R}_i$ to the input audio. The number of query embeddings K is independent of the length of the query M. For example, the query can be represented by a single vector ($K = 1$) or, like in [24], by three vectors ($K = 3$, then $\mathbf{Q}_1$ represents the first half of the query, $\mathbf{Q}_2$ the middle of the query, and $\mathbf{Q}_3$ the second half).

The embedding vectors $\mathbf{R}_i$ and $\mathbf{Q}_k$ are then used to compute per-segment probabilities of segment c_i being the part of the putative hit of the query g. To compute the calibrated probabilities $r_i, i = 1, \ldots N$, we use the dot-product of the embedding vectors:

$$r_i = \sigma \left(\alpha \cdot \max_{k=1}^K (\mathbf{R}_i \cdot \mathbf{Q}_k) + \beta \right) \tag{1}$$

where $\sigma(x)$ denotes the sigmoid function and α and β are trainable calibration parameters. The maximum is used to select the most similar (in terms of dot-product) query embedding $\mathbf{Q}_k$ of all K embeddings (see Fig. 1).

To determine the putative hits of the query g, the minimum number of segments $L(g)$ is estimated in the query encoder and used to find all spans (I, J) satisfying the conditions $r_i > t$ $\forall i : I \leq i \leq J$ and $J - I + 1 \geq L(g)$ where t is the decision threshold. In other words, we search for peaks in r_i threshold t which span at least $L(g)$ time-aligned segments c_i. The overall score for the putative hit is determined as an average probability:

$$\text{score}(g, I, J) = \frac{1}{J - I + 1} \sum_{i=I}^J r_i \tag{2}$$

If there are multiple overlapping spans for a given query, only the span with the highest score is kept as a putative hit.

The NN-based model is trained using a binary cross-entropy loss function. The training data can be generated on the fly by randomly selecting a word from a time-aligned transcript as a query. Because we target oral history archives, we can exploit a huge amount of speech data they contain by blindly recognizing the speech data and using the correctly recognized in-vocabulary words (in terms of confidence scores) to generate the queries. The main focus of STD in oral history archives is on out-of-vocabulary words; a data augmentation technique can be used. For example, two or more consecutive in-vocabulary words can be randomly merged to simulate OOVs [24].

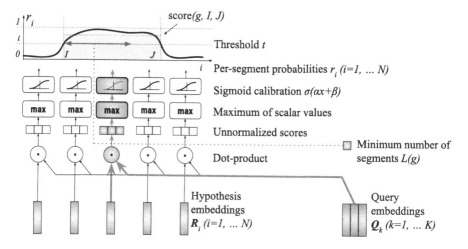

Fig. 1. Neural STD framework. Per-segment probabilities are intentionally displayed as a continuous function for clarity, although they are represented as discrete values r_i.

3 Transformer-Based Architecture

In this section, we will describe an application of the Transformer neural network architecture in the STD framework described in Sect. 2. The basic idea of our proposed architecture is to use just the encoder part of the Transformer to extract context-dependent vector representations of the input. This approach is similar to using a Transformer in the BERT family of models [3]. The novelty of our approach is to convert both the input audio and the searched query into a shared embedding space and then score each segment of the input audio using a simple similarity measure consisting of a sigmoid-calibrated dot-product between two vectors in this embedding space. In an analogy to the encoder-decoder approach, we can call this architecture the *encoder-encoder*.

3.1 Preliminary Experiments

Since the Transformer architecture is believed to achieve better performance than the LSTMs in many NLP and speech processing tasks [5,8], we first experimented with the Deep LSTM architecture where the LSTMs were simply replaced with Transformer blocks and positional embeddings added to the input. Surprisingly, those experiments showed that the STD performance dropped below the LSTMs. The results of this vanilla Transformer evaluated under the experimental setup described in Sects. 4 and 5 are reported in Tables 2 and 3. To improve the performance of the Transformer-based STD model, we suggest some extensions of the vanilla BERT-like architecture.

3.2 Proposed Architecture

First, we hypothesize that the worse performance of the vanilla Transformer architecture is caused by the format of the input – the sequence of single graphemes. Therefore, we used the trainable *1D convolutional filter* with a stride larger than 1 to reduce the temporal dimensionality of the input and to find latent projections of larger subsequences of graphemes corresponding with larger subword units. The Transformer is applied on top of such projections (output of the convolutional layer). To restore the input-output relation with the time-alignment of the segments c_i, we also applied the upsampling layer (also called transposed convolution or deconvolution) on the output of the Transformer (Fig. 2). BERT-like architectures [3] use the GELU functions [7] as activations and therefore we used it not only in the encoder but also as activations in the convolutional layer. The upsampling layer contained linear activation. The standard positional embeddings are added after applying convolution before feeding input into the Transformer.

To estimate the minimum number of segments $L(g)$, we add an extra token called *[CLS]* to the input of the query encoder. A similar approach can be found in BERT pre-training where the *[CLS]* token is used for the next-sentence-prediction task [3]. The corresponding encoder output is transformed using a linear fully-connected layer to a scalar value $L(g)$. The training loss function of this network output is standard MSE (Fig. 4).

While the ability to condition the outputs on very distant parts of the input is one of the strongest features of the Transformer model, in STD, the occurrence of the putative hit depends only on local input features and distant dependencies are very rare. Therefore, we used *attention masking* to limit the multi-headed attentions to attend only to a few neighboring input segments. Although attention masking is a common mechanism to introduce causality into Transformer models [11], we use it to introduce locality. The masking is implemented using the masking matrix containing ones on the diagonal and on a fixed number of super- and sub-diagonals.

3.3 Simplifications over Deep LSTM

The proposed Transformer-based encoder-encoder architecture brings some advantages over the baseline Deep LSTM. The Transformer can compensate for inaccurate time alignment of the CTC output and therefore we did not use the output masking as used in [22]. In addition, the estimation of the minimum number of segments $L(g)$ for a given query is performed as a part of query embedding computation without requiring a separate model.

3.4 Transformer Block

We used a classical Transformer block as presented in [17] with GELU activation functions in feed-forward layers. The hyperparameter setting was similar to the BERT models, particularly the BERT-Mini architecture [6]. BERT-Mini has a

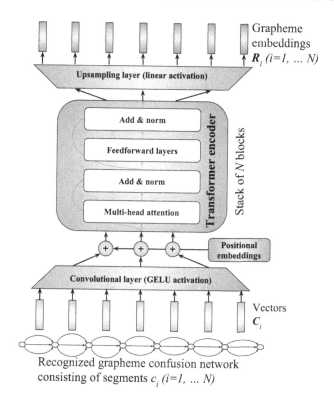

Fig. 2. Architecture of the hypothesis encoder.

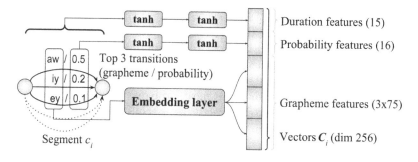

Fig. 3. Mapping of confusion segments c_i to vectors $\mathbf{C}_i$.

stack of four Transformer blocks with four self-attention heads, the dimensionality of embedding vectors is 256, and the dimensionality of feed-forward layers is 1024. The dropout probability used was 0.15.

3.5 Input Transformation

The proposed STD system does not process the input audio directly. Instead, it uses the fine-tuned Wav2Vec 2.0 model to recognize the grapheme-based

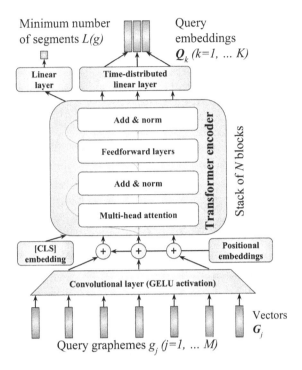

Fig. 4. Architecture of the query encoder.

representation of the input converted into the grapheme confusion network using the deterministic procedure [22]. For each segment of the confusion network, the 3-top most probable transitions are taken into account. Each segment is encoded to a 256-dimensional vector consisting of 15 duration features generated from a scalar duration of the segment using two $tanh()$ fully connected layers, 16 transition probability features generated by another set of fully connected layers, and 3×75 grapheme embeddings for three most probable symbols of the segment (Fig. 3). The query is represented directly as a sequence of query graphemes projected into a 256-dimensional embedding space.

4   Dataset and Model Description

The presented method was evaluated on the data from a USC-SFI MALACH archive in two languages – English [15] and Czech [14]. The training data for NN-based STD were extracted by blindly recognizing the archive using the DNN-HMM hybrid ASR with acoustic and language models trained from the manually transcribed part of the archives. Basic statistics are summarized in Table 1 (more details are provided in [23]).

We used the Wav2Vec model fine-tuned on the MALACH data to generate the grapheme confusion networks. For English, we started with publicly available pre-trained Wav2Vec 2.0 Base model [12]. For Czech, we used the ClTRUS model [9] pre-trained from more than 80 thousand hours of Czech speech data following the same pretraining steps as for the base Wav2Vec 2.0 model [1].

The Fairseq tool [13] was used for fine-tuning. We sliced long training audio signals on speech pauses not to exceed the length of 30 s. We removed non-speech events and punctuation from the transcripts and mapped all graphemes into lowercase. The pre-trained models were fine-tuned for 80k updates with a peak learning rate of 8×10^{-5} for English and 2×10^{-5} for Czech, respectively. The CTC classification layer predicts probabilities of 53 symbols for English and 51 for Czech, and the output frame length is 0.02 s for both models.

It is important to note, that the CTC loss does not guarantee the precise time alignment of the generated sequence of symbols. However, the timing produced by the fine-tuned models is sufficient to perform STD over the generated hypothesis as was shown for in-vocabulary terms in [22].

The in-vocabulary (IV) and out-of-vocabulary (OOV) terms were selected automatically from the development and test data based on the DNN-HMM recognition vocabulary. We filtered all possible terms so that the terms are not substrings of other terms in the dataset nor the words in the vocabulary. The numbers reported in this paper are directly comparable to results presented in [22–24].

5   Experimental Results

For training the Transformer-based encoder-encoder architecture, we used ADAM optimizer with a learning rate warm-up. The warm-up raised the learning rate from 0 to 10^{-4} in the initial 80k training steps and then the learning rate decayed linearly to 0 in the next 720k training steps. The batch size was 32. We used lower learning rates and longer training than Deep LSTM because the training of Transformers tends to collapse if higher rates are used. The models were trained using $N = 256$ (number of confusion network segments in the

Table 1. Statistics of development and test sets [23]. ASR means DNN-HMM hybrid ASR.

	English		Czech	
	Dev	Test	Dev	Test
ASR vocabulary size	243,699		252,082	
#speakers	10	10	10	10
OOV rate	0.5%	3.2%	0.3%	2.6%
ASR word error rate	24.10	19.66	23.98	19.11
#IV terms	597	601	1680	1673
#OOV terms	31	6	1145	948
dataset length [hours]	11.1	11.3	20.4	19.4

input) and $M = 16$ (maximum length of the query). The thresholding parameter $t = 0.5$ was used to determine the putative hit spans.

In the experiments, we first optimized the MTWV metric [19] on the development dataset (Table 2). Then, using a given architecture, the optimal decision threshold was determined and applied to the test dataset and the ATWV metric was computed (Table 3). In the experiments, we used both the in- and out-of-vocabulary terms. The presented method is designed to generalize from seen IV terms to detect the OOV terms.

Table 2 follows the changes proposed in Sect. 3. The drop-in replacement of Deep LSTM with the vanilla Transformer degraded the performance. The addition of convolutional and upsampling layers led to a minor improvement. We searched for an optimum 1D convolution width and stride in the experiments with a grid search (widths 1 to 5, strides 2 to 4). We found that width 3 and stride 2 maximized the MTWV, which leads to $K = 8$ query embeddings per each query.

In the next step, we added attention masking. Again, we swept across an interval of different widths of the attention mask: diagonal matrices of ones with 1 to 5 super- and sub-diagonals of ones. Finally, we used the diagonal matrix with two super- and two sub-diagonals. In other words, each Transformer block attends to the current, two preceding, and two following time steps. We have to mention that this does not imply the context is just five segments because several Transformer blocks are stacked; therefore, the context of the last layer is wider than these five segments. Overall, the proposed network architecture has a slightly larger number of trainable parameters (7.3M) in comparison with the Deep LSTMs (6.9M)

Table 2. Results on the development dataset (MTWV↑).

	English	Czech
Deep LSTM (baseline [22])	0.8308	0.8987
Vanilla Transformer	0.8163	0.8808
Transformer (proposed method)		
+ Convolution layers	0.8395	0.8905
+ Attention masking	**0.8588**	**0.9261**
In-vocabulary terms	0.8613	0.9355
Out-of-vocabulary terms	0.8156	0.9112

As the final step, the presented architectures were evaluated on the test dataset (Table 3). The ATWV on test data follows the improvement in MTWV on the development dataset. For illustration, the differences between MTWV evaluated on IV and OOV terms are shown on the last two lines of Table 2. The optimal ATWV decision threshold for IV and OOV terms was almost the same for English (0.83 vs 0.81) and exactly the same for Czech (both 0.77). As expected, the MTWV for IV terms is slightly higher than for the OOV terms.

Table 3. Results on the test dataset (ATWV↑).

	English	Czech
Deep LSTM (baseline [22])	0.7616	0.9100
Vanilla Transformer	0.7319	0.8745
Transformer (proposed method)	**0.7919**	**0.9138**

6   Conclusion

We proposed an NN-based STD method employing two BERT-like encoders. We modify the vanilla Transformer by adding convolutional and upsampling layers. For the hypothesis encoder, we also used the attention masking mechanism. The presented modifications of the NN-based STD employing the Transformer encoder-encoder architecture achieved more than 0.04 improvement in MTWV/ATWV on development and test datasets over the baseline vanilla Transformer. The achieved results also outperform the baseline Deep LSTM architecture on all datasets.

The proposed modifications are usable not only in Transformer-based STD task employing graphemic queries and recognized hypotheses but also in related tasks such as QbE, KWS, or WWD. The architecture of the Transformer encoder-encoder model opens further research questions, such as the possibility of combining STD (graphemic query) and QbE (spoken query) in a single, multi-task trained model.

Acknowledgement. Computational resources were supplied by the project "e-Infrastruktura CZ" (e-INFRA CZ LM2018140) supported by the Ministry of Education, Youth, and Sports of the Czech Republic.

References

1. Baevski, A., Zhou, H., Mohamed, A., Auli, M.: Wav2Vec 2.0: a framework for self-supervised learning of speech representations. In: Proceedings of the 34th International Conference on Neural Information Processing Systems, NIPS 2020. Curran Associates Inc., Red Hook, NY, USA (2020)
2. Berg, A., O'Connor, M., Cruz, M.T.: Keyword transformer: a self-attention model for keyword spotting. In: Proceedings of Interspeech 2021, pp. 4249–4253 (2021). https://doi.org/10.21437/Interspeech.2021-1286
3. Devlin, J., Chang, M.W., Lee, K., Toutanova, K.: BERT: pre-training of deep bidirectional transformers for language understanding. arXiv preprint arXiv:1810.04805 (2018)
4. Ding, K., Zong, M., Li, J., Li, B.: LETR: a lightweight and efficient transformer for keyword spotting. In: ICASSP 2022–2022 IEEE International Conference on Acoustics, Speech and Signal Processing (ICASSP), pp. 7987–7991 (2022). https://doi.org/10.1109/ICASSP43922.2022.9747295

5. Gillioz, A., Casas, J., Mugellini, E., Khaled, O.A.: Overview of the transformer-based models for NLP tasks. In: 2020 15th Conference on Computer Science and Information Systems (FedCSIS), pp. 179–183 (2020). https://doi.org/10.15439/2020F20

6. Google Research: TensorFlow code and pre-trained models for BERT, March 2020. https://github.com/google-research/bert

7. Hendrycks, D., Gimpel, K.: Gaussian Error Linear Units (GELUs). arXiv preprint arXiv:1606.08415 (2016)

8. Karita, S., et al.: A comparative study on transformer vs RNN in speech applications. In: 2019 IEEE Automatic Speech Recognition and Understanding Workshop (ASRU), pp. 449–456 (2019). https://doi.org/10.1109/ASRU46091.2019.9003750

9. Lehečka, J., Švec, J., Prazak, A., Psutka, J.: Exploring capabilities of monolingual audio transformers using large datasets in automatic speech recognition of Czech. In: Proceedings of Interspeech 2022, pp. 1831–1835 (2022). https://doi.org/10.21437/Interspeech.2022-10439

10. Liu, Y., et al.: RoBERTa: a robustly optimized BERT pretraining approach. arXiv (1), July 2019. http://arxiv.org/abs/1907.11692

11. Luo, Z., et al.: DecBERT: enhancing the language understanding of BERT with causal attention masks. In: Findings of the Association for Computational Linguistics: NAACL 2022, pp. 1185–1197. Association for Computational Linguistics, Seattle, United States, July 2022. https://doi.org/10.18653/v1/2022.findings-naacl.89, https://aclanthology.org/2022.findings-naacl.89

12. Meta Research: Wav2Vec 2.0, April 2022. https://github.com/facebookresearch/fairseq/blob/main/examples/wav2vec/README.md

13. Ott, M., et al.: fairseq: a fast, extensible toolkit for sequence modeling. In: Proceedings of the 2019 Conference of the North American Chapter of the Association for Computational Linguistics (Demonstrations), pp. 48–53. Association for Computational Linguistics, Minneapolis, Minnesota, June 2019. https://doi.org/10.18653/v1/N19-4009, https://aclanthology.org/N19-4009

14. Psutka, J., Radová, V., Ircing, P., Matoušek, J., Müller, L.: USC-SFI MALACH Interviews and Transcripts Czech LDC2014S04. Linguistic Data Consortium, Philadelphia (2014). https://catalog.ldc.upenn.edu/LDC2014S04

15. Ramabhadran, B., et al.: USC-SFI MALACH Interviews and Transcripts English LDC2012S05. Linguistic Data Consortium, Philadelphia (2012). https://catalog.ldc.upenn.edu/LDC2012s05 (2012)

16. Settle, S., Livescu, K.: Discriminative acoustic word embeddings: recurrent neural network-based approaches. In: 2016 IEEE Spoken Language Technology Workshop (SLT), pp. 503–510 (2016). https://doi.org/10.1109/SLT.2016.7846310

17. Vaswani, A., et al.: Attention is all you need. In: Advances in Neural Information Processing Systems, pp. 5999–6009 (2017)

18. Wang, Y., Lv, H., Povey, D., Xie, L., Khudanpur, S.: Wake word detection with streaming transformers. In: ICASSP 2021–2021 IEEE International Conference on Acoustics, Speech and Signal Processing (ICASSP), pp. 5864–5868 (2021). https://doi.org/10.1109/ICASSP39728.2021.9414777

19. Wegmann, S., Faria, A., Janin, A., Riedhammer, K., Morgan, N.: The TAO of ATWV: probing the mysteries of keyword search performance. In: 2013 IEEE Workshop on Automatic Speech Recognition and Understanding, ASRU 2013 - Proceedings, pp. 192–197 (2013). https://doi.org/10.1109/ASRU.2013.6707728

20. Yang, D., et al.: CaTT-KWS: a multi-stage customized keyword spotting framework based on cascaded transducer-transformer. In: Proceedings of Interspeech 2022, pp. 1681–1685 (2022). https://doi.org/10.21437/Interspeech.2022-10258

21. Yuan, Y., Xie, L., Leung, C.C., Chen, H., Ma, B.: Fast query-by-example speech search using attention-based deep binary embeddings. IEEE/ACM Trans. Audio Speech Lang. Process. **28**, 1988–2000 (2020). https://doi.org/10.1109/TASLP.2020.2998277

22. Švec, J., Lehečka, J., Šmídl, L.: Deep LSTM spoken term detection using Wav2Vec 2.0 recognizer. In: Proceedings of Interspeech 2022, pp. 1886–1890 (2022). https://doi.org/10.21437/Interspeech.2022-10409

23. Švec, J., Psutka, J.V., Šmídl, L., Trmal, J.: A relevance score estimation for spoken term detection based on RNN-generated pronunciation embeddings. In: Proceedings of Interspeech 2017, pp. 2934–2938 (2017). https://doi.org/10.21437/Interspeech.2017-1087

24. Švec, J., Šmídl, L., Psutka, J.V., Pražák, A.: Spoken term detection and relevance score estimation using dot-product of pronunciation embeddings. In: Proceedings of Interspeech 2021, pp. 4398–4402 (2021). https://doi.org/10.21437/Interspeech.2021-1704

Will XAI Provide Real Explanation
or Just a Plausible Rationalization?

Pavel Ircing[(⊠)] and Jan Švec

Department of Cybernetics, Faculty of Applied Sciences, University of West Bohemia,
Univerzitní 8, 301 00 Plzeň, Czech Republic
{ircing,honzas}@kky.zcu.cz

Abstract. This paper discusses the analogies between the mainstream
theory of human mind and the two broad paradigms that are employed
when building artificial intelligence systems. Then it ponders the idea
how those analogies could be utilized in building a truly explainable
artificial intelligence (AI) applications. The core part is devoted to the
problem of unwanted rationalization that could disguise the true reasons
lying behind the decisions of the explainable AI systems.

Keywords: explainable AI · dual process theory · rationalization

1   Introduction

The idea of Explainable Artificial Intelligence (XAI) has become very prominent
recently, both in the AI research community [7] and in the society in general.
This trend is only natural, given the increasing number of areas where important decisions are entrusted to various machine learning algorithms. Such areas
include (but are not limited to) health, employment, financial and even law
enforcement and justice sectors, so it is of no surprise that the concerned stake-
holders demand the explanation and/or justification of those decisions (more
about this terminology is given in Sect. 3). The "right to explanation" is even
enshrined in the EU's General Data Protection Regulation (GDPR) (see [13] for
a commentary)

This paper, however, is not meant as an overview of the existing XAI
approaches (this could be found for example in [26]) nor to discuss any particular method that could be used to explain the AI decisions. Instead, it would
like to elaborate on one of the pitfalls of AI explanations that stems from the
very nature of both the human mind and the AI that was – at least to some
extent – designed to imitate it.

The work has been supported by the grant of the University of West Bohemia, project
No. SGS-2022-017.

2   The Relation of the AI Paradigms to the Working of the Human Mind

2.1   Two Major AI Paradigms

Let us first recap here a couple of the well-known facts. In principle, there are two broad major approaches to building AI systems. The older one is usually called *symbolic AI* or, somehow pejoratively, "Good Old Fashioned AI" (GOFAI) [10]. The systems employing symbolic AI – be it the problem-solving and game-playing algorithms or the more practical expert systems – were based on mostly human-designed rules that were readable by both humans and the computers. As such, those systems had a naturally built-in ability to explain its decisions, often simply by presenting the rules that were used during the inference of a particular outcome.

On the other hand, there were three major drawbacks of the symbolic AI systems that have prevented them to be used on a larger scale. First, it turned out to be close to impossible to manually design a set of rules that would be able to accurately capture even a relatively small real-world task with all of the possible inconsistencies and/or exceptions. For the few cases where a comprehensive set of rules was successfully designed, the rule system was so complex that the resulting system suffered from the combinatorial explosion that even contemporary computational resources would not be able to deal with. And finally, the GOFAI systems had significant problems with connecting to the physical world – a lot of "cognitive work" had to be done by the users that needed convert the "signals" from the physical world into an appropriate symbolic representation.

Due to the reasons given above, essentially all successful AI systems that are used today are based on the other paradigm – the one that is sometimes referred to as *subsymbolic AI* but most commonly known as *machine learning*. In the recent years, when the neural networks are most frequently used as the underlying machine learning model, the term *deep learning* is gaining popularity. Yet another term for employing neural networks in AI – *connectionist AI* – is in fact rather old [23] but being used much more often by the cognitive scientists than the AI researchers themselves. Regardless of the name, the machine learning (we will prefer this term throughout the paper) methods are – in comparison with the symbolic AI systems – much more efficient in terms of performance and usage of computational resources, require very little (target) domain expert knowledge and "manual" expert work. They are also able to deal better with the inconsistencies present in the majority of real-life tasks and connect relatively well to the physical world as they can seamlessly process signals from various sensors. And of course possibly the biggest advantage over the GOFAI systems is their explicitly declared ability to learn – in other words, to improve their performance over time as more data from the task are observed. The downside of the machine learning approach – again in comparison with the symbolic AI – is the somehow inherent "opacity" of the system; it yields a result that is correct most of the time but it's hard for a human to understand why such an outcome has been produced.

2.2   Human Mind - The Dual Process Theory

The previous section essentially presents the summary of the facts that are being taught in almost all introductory AI courses. What is however much less frequently discussed is the remarkable similarity of the two aforementioned AI paradigms to the *dual process theory* of human mind. This theory – which was most probably formalized for the first time in [27] and widely popularized by Daniel Kahneman a couple of decades later [12] – posits that the human mind works in two rather distinct operational modes. Or, as Kahneman puts it, that our mind is composed of two different systems [12]:

- *System 1* is fast, unconscious and virtually effortless, automatic and intuitive. It is based on experience. memories and emotions. It constantly "monitors" the environment and evaluates the situation. It generates impressions, feelings and inclinations – those could become beliefs, attitudes when endorsed by System 2.
- *System 2* is slow, conscious and effortful and requires full attention (and thus uses a lot of "mental resources"). It is analytical, logical and performs reasoning in its true sense. It is in a "stand-by mode" most of the time and is called into action when needed.

It's important to stress out that the concept of those two systems is of course only a model and therefore partially a metaphor and certainly a simplification. It does not suggest that we can actually locate those two systems in distinct areas of the brain. Also, it is not true that the working of those two systems is hierarchical as it's often implicitly understood – more accurately, they work in a somehow parallel fashion. And finally, the common simplification that the System 1 is the only one prone to errors and cognitive biases whereas System 2 is strictly rational is also a misconception that has been frequently refuted by Kahneman himself.

2.3   The Relation Between the AI and the Mind

However, if we really look at the two systems described in the previous section as separate entities for a moment, there is a striking resemblance to the properties of the AI systems based on the two paradigms described in Sect. 2.1.

First, let us consider a couple of most widespread AI application employing machine learning paradigm – various image processing engines including those performing face recognition and OCR but also the visual components of the autonomous vehicles' sensing systems; speech recognition and machine translation applications etc. Those are clear examples of the systems that monitor the environment (almost) constantly and provide quick and most of the time rather accurate results. It certainly does remind the workings of System 1 as described in Sect. 2.2.

Moreover, one of the rules of thumbs shared by the AI practitioners says that if one instance of the task at hand can be solved by a human in approximately 1 s (or faster), then there is a good chance that it will be possible to train a machine learning system for this task (assuming, of course, that we are able to obtain sufficient amount of training data) [19]. Let us think about it for a moment – how long does it take for a human to recognize a familiar face? Or evaluate the situation at the crossroad? Or even translate a sentence from one language to another, given that he/she is fluent in both languages? At the same time, those humans – who have just used their System 1 to perform the mentioned tasks – are not able to immediately explain how exactly they have reached a given outcome – it was actually found out that they need to activate System 2 for this (see for example [3]). So even in this sense is the System 1 similar to a standard machine learning AI system.

On the other hand, the tasks solved by the original, symbolic AI systems were actually those requiring long, systematic and concentrated human mental effort – such as proving of the mathematical theorems [18] or playing chess [14]. Those are the tasks which humans can solve only using System 2 (however, see the brief note about chess playing below). In fact, this type of cognitive work was sometimes considered to be the *only* true expression of human intelligence – in all fields ranging from psychology through cognitive science to artificial intelligence. As roboticist Rodney Brooks states in [5]:

> Judging by projects chosen in the early days of AI, intelligence was thought to be best characterized as the things that highly educated male scientists found challenging.

As was already mentioned above, both the human System 2 and the symbolic AI systems are (relatively) slow and use up a lot of "computational resources"; but they are also both able to provide at least some explanation of their conclusions.

Let us now make a brief sidenote. One might argue that chess is actually a counterexample for this AI-mind analogy since the best chess algorithms are nowadays based on the machine learning paradigm (and thus also humans should be playing them with their System 1). However, we can refer to Kahneman [12] once more to refute this objection:

> When confronted with a problem-choosing a chess move or deciding whether to invest in a stock-the machinery of intuitive thought (*i.e., System 1 – author's remark*) does the best it can. If the individual has relevant expertise, she will recognize the situation, and the intuitive solution that comes to her mind is likely to be correct. This is what happens when a chess master looks at a complex position: the few moves that immediately occur to him are all strong.
> . . .
> Studies of chess masters have shown that at least 10,000 hours of dedicated practice (about 6 years of playing chess 5 h a day) are required to attain the highest levels of performance. During those hours of intense concentration, a serious chess player becomes familiar with thousands of configurations, each consisting of an arrangement of related pieces that can threaten or defend each other.

The quote above – although of course not meant as such – looks like a (popular) textbook description of a machine learning algorithm. So we see a very good mind-AI analogy once again.

Now let's go back to the main topic of this paper. Since we have just argued that there is a strong resemblance between the two systems of human mind and the two paradigms of AI, we could use the human mind "setup" – where, roughly speaking, the System 1 often provides fast and accurate result and System 2 adds an explanation, if necessary – as an inspiration for explainable AI systems. But before elaborating on such a concept, let us first review what exactly is understood by the "explainability" within the context of AI.

3   More Detailed Specification of Explainability

Although the "explainable AI" is currently a hot research topic, upon closer inspection it turns out that the term itself is often poorly defined [15] and/or understood differently by different research communities or even individual researchers. A concise and well-thought-out conceptualization of different possible views of the general notion of "explainability" is given in [6].

Let us briefly summarize their view here. The authors of [6] specify 4 broad classes of AI systems - see below - with regard to the user's chances to understand the inner workings of the system. Unfortunately, they sometimes use a terminology that contradicts the one used in other influential XAI papers (e.g. [21]) and thus we will need to adjust the terms slightly and put them into context of other related work.

The classes are the following:

Opaque systems are the standard machine learning systems where the user can only see the input and the corresponding output of the system (the proverbial"black-box" situation).

Transparent systems [1] are the ones that allow user to see the mathematical model used with the AI system [20] (the "glass-box" scenario). So, at least in theory, a user can interpret how the system works inside – of course only if he/she has a very good understanding of the given model formalism. And even in such a case, the direct interpretability of the state-of-the-art models based on deep neural networks is very limited. That it the reason why some other authors classify both *opaque* and *transparent* systems to one class of the *black-box* systems. For example, Rudin distinguishes *black box of the first type* – "a

---

[1] The authors of the original paper [6] actually use the term **interpretable systems** for this class. However, this term is standardly used to describe a rather different class of the AI systems (see [21] and the following sections). The term *transparent* is also sometimes being used in a slightly different meaning within XAI community but the deviation from our usage is not so striking and the term was chosen here to express the opposite of *opaque*.

function that is too complicated for any human to comprehend" [21], which is basically a case of the vast majority of the current machine learning models even in the "glass-box" setting – and the *black-box of the second type* – "a function that is proprietary" [21], i.e. hidden from the user mostly in an attempt to protect trade secret.

While the distinction could between the two classes above is interesting and also in many contexts important, we can leave it aside for our purposes as we are interested in the AI systems that actually *do* provide some kind of explanation. Such systems are in [6] divided into two further classes:

Comprehensible systems are the AI engines that provide not only the standard output (e.g. the classification decision) but also a set o auxiliary symbols that should help user to understand why the system produced such output. Those symbols are most often words[2] but can also take other forms, such as visualisations highlighting a specific segments of the image etc.

It is important to point out that in this case the system still does not really explain its decisions. It provides just cues for humans where to start their own deliberation about the reasons that led to the specific outcome. It is only natural that different people can arrive at – sometimes substantially – different conclusions. Those conclusions will be affected not only by the person's knowledge of domain from which the input data are sampled, cultural and education background but also by his/her beliefs and attitudes (see Sect. 4 for details).

Explainable systems worthy of this name are, according to the authors, only the systems that can actually explicitly formulate the line of reasoning that explains the systems output using full sentences in natural language understandable even for non-experts in AI.[3]

Although it is not explicitly stated, the authors of [6] silently assume that all the (successful) machine learning models are *inherently* black boxes that require a post-hoc explanation. Rudin in [21] offers a contrasting approach, advocating the usage of so-called **interpretable** models, i.e. models that are designed in a way that naturally allows human interpretation/understanding, without a need for additional "explaining" machinery. She gives an example of such a model – CORELS, a rule-based system where the rules are not handcrafted but learned automatically [2].

---

[2] Authors of [6] give an example where the image recognition system is presented with a photo of a factory and the system outputs the classification results *factory* together with the "explanatory" words *halogen lights, machines, concrete floor*.

[3] In an example analogous to the one given above, the system would output something like *The image has halogen lights, a concrete floor and many machines. These objects are often present in and related to the factory operations. The system thus believes the image is of a factory scene* [6].

However, if we look at the state-of-the-art in the AI field, it seems that we will in fact really have to build a system that would be able to explain the decision of some neural network. When doing so, it seems only natural to once again take an inspiration from the human mind as suggested in Sect. 2.3 and construct the hybrid model where the neural networks and symbolic AI approaches would be intertwined and able to provide fast and correct results together with an explicit explanation. However, the current attempts to design such a system are still in the stage of a theoretical concepts [4] or they are designed for studying the cognitive processes themselves, not for solving difficult real-world tasks [24] (i.e., they belong rather to the field of cognitive science, not artificial intelligence).

But even if there were such hybrid AI system available – and they probably sooner or later will be – they will still face the possible bias inherent to the human mind and described in the following section.

4   The Danger of Rationalization

The fact that the specifics of human cognitive processes need to be taken into account when designing comprehensible/explainable AI systems has already attracted the attention of many researchers. However, not even the extremely well-structured and unusually thorough paper [17] that presents many ways in which the XAI researchers should explore and exploit the findings of social scientists mentions the danger of rationalization.

The concept of rationalization was introduced to psychology more than a century ago [11]. Although the name suggests that it is something directly connected with the rational reasoning/behavior and as such a highly desirable trait, both in humans and machines (modern AI often uses the overarching notion of designing *rational agents* [22]), the opposite is actually true.

The term *rationalization* is used for in fact irrational or logically faulted explanation of the decisions or actions that a person makes instinctively or on the basis of his/her beliefs, attitudes, desires or social pressure. When a person is rationalizing, he/she is creating a seemingly logical construct that explains the decision/action in a manner that would justify it for themselves or – maybe even more often – for their social group.

Using the terminology of the dual process theory from Sect. 2.2, the System 2 is trying to come up with a line of reasoning that would explain the decision of the System 1. In this process, the System 2 is trying to reduce the *cognitive dissonance* [9] – the perceived inconsistency between the performed decision, action or observed facts and the inner beliefs, attitudes and values of the person. So once again, there is a close analogy with AI systems – we can think of cognitive dissonance as the objective function that we are striving to minimize.

A truly **rational** agent should take the observation (info about the performed decision, action – state of the environment in general) and the inner logic of reasoning for granted and if there is a cognitive dissonance, it is the inner beliefs/attitudes/values that should be adjusted.

However, the **rationalizing** agent would do something rather different. In fact, we find it useful to actually distinguish two types of rationalizing agents here. The first type would be *rationalizing for themselves*, just as the humans do. Such agents would strongly prefers to keep their inner settings intact – instead, they will try to achieve consistency by either ignoring (part of) the observation or bending the logic of reasoning. But designing the agents that would be able to "deceive" themselves in such a way would not make much sense, at least not from the "practical AI" point of view (although it might be interesting e.g. for cognitive scientists).

What is more interesting to study for the "engineering" branch of AI are the rationalizing agents of the second type – that ones that would produce the *rationalized explanation*[4] *for the human users*. The designers of such systems often – either consciously or just intuitively – exploit the findings from the field of cognitive sciences, especially the one regarding coherence. Thagard in his influential work [25] argues that the coherence is the most important criterion defining a good explanation – that is, not only coherence within the explanation itself but also the coherence with the prior beliefs of the *explainee* (the person for whom the explanation is intended), with the prevailing societal narratives (e.g. concerning climate changes or human rights) and possibly other contexts. It has been experimentally proven (see e.g. again [25] or [17]) that (at least apparent) coherence of the explanation is valued more than its completeness.

So, the designers of the AI systems often use explaining mechanisms that intentionally produce *rationalized* output – i.e., the output (often in natural language) that is plausible and seemingly logical but cares more about the plausibility than about the true correspondence with the real grounds for the AI system's decisions.

There may be several motivations for using the rationalization as described in the previous paragraph. First of them could be to actually conceal the true inner mechanism of the used algorithms – in such cases, the rationalization is designed to intentionally mislead the "social group" of system's users.[5]

Second possible motivation is actually well-intended – the developers just want to produce the explanation that would be perceived positively by human users. A natural way of producing such an explanation is to "mimic" the sentences that the actual humans usually use in similar context. Given the recent progress in NLP, such a thing could be rather easily achieved either by taking the machine translation approach that "translates" the states of the AI agent into natural language [8] or, even more generally, by using the state-of-the-art natural language generation models such as GPT-3 [28]. At the time when the first version of this paper was drafted (June 2021), the idea of producing the "most plausible text output/explanation" was mostly a theoretical concept that

---

[4] It is probably clear from the context that the following paragraphs deal with the class of **explainable** systems as defined in Sect. 3. However, the rationalization – in this case on the human side – plays an important role in the **comprehensible** systems as well, since it is the human user who constructs the actual full-scale explanation from the "hints" provided by the system.

[5] There could be several motivations for creating such a misleading systems – one of the frequent ones would be to make a false impression that the system respect some desirable ethical standards [1].

was being tested in OpenAI labs [29]. However, the deployment of ChatGPT in late November 2022 has made this approach widely known even for the general public under the term Reinforcement Learning from Human Feedback (RLHF).

The "pre-ChatGPT" versions of GPT large language models were in fact known to reinforce rather then mitigate the inherent human biases [16]. The OpenAI developers apparently make a continuous effort to suppress the bias in ChatGPT but it's most probably performed by (a rather ad-hoc) filtering and post-processing the output of the foundation GPT models which still remain biased as they were trained using human-produced text data that are, of course, human-biased by definition.

Possibly a way to construct a good XAI system would be to indeed take the known human biases into account but not to *abuse* them – either malevolently (see motivation one above) or just to make the developer's job easier (motivation two). One possible direction could be to provide *customized explanation*, tailored to the beliefs of a particular user, in order to increase his/her acceptance of a particular AI systems. In such a case, however, the developer must never sacrifice the truthfulness of the explanation to its plausibility. Our experience with ChatGPT so far suggests the opposite - we have a feeling that plausibility is weighted most in the RLHF, despite the claims that people involved in RLHF scoring should reward mainly actualness and truthfulness.

5   Conclusion

There is no doubt that the issues discussed above will gain significantly more attention once the truly explainable systems start to be deployed in real-life applications. The aim of this position paper is to keep those questions in the debate. It is also interesting to note that the conceptual XAI papers published before (roughly) 2021 usually illustrate their ideas using examples from image recognition domains, demanding the XAI systems to be able to explain things like: *"How did you arrive at the decision that there is a golden retriever in the picture?"* or *"Why the autonomous car failed to register the stop sign?"*. Nowadays, on the other hand, the focus has - quite naturally - shifted to the generative AI systems like ChatGPT for text or Midjourney for images.

In the case of the text chatbots, one should bear in mind a trivial but very important distinction in the meaning of the term "explanation" – if you, for example, ask ChatGPT a question (e.g. *"What is the meaning of life?"*), it will provide you with a lengthy answer, addressing the question from various viewpoints. Consequently, you can of course ask for an "explanation" (e.g. by typing *"Why did you produce exactly this answer?"*). What you get is however definitely not the explanation in the sense that was used thorough this paper - instead, it is another elaborate list of *general* principles that guide the ChatGPT functioning.

References

1. Aivodji, U., Arai, H., Fortineau, O., Gambs, S., Hara, S., Tapp, A.: Fairwashing: the risk of rationalization. In: Chaudhuri, K., Salakhutdinov, R. (eds.) Proceedings of the 36th International Conference on Machine Learning. Proceedings of Machine Learning Research, vol. 97, pp. 161–170. PMLR, 9–15 June 2019
2. Angelino, E., Larus-Stone, N., Alabi, D., Seltzer, M., Rudin, C.: Learning certifiably optimal rule lists for categorical data. arXiv preprint arXiv:1704.01701 (2017)
3. Bago, B., Neys, W.D.: The smart system 1: evidence for the intuitive nature of correct responding on the bat-and-ball problem. Thinking Reasoning **25**(3), 257–299 (2019). https://doi.org/10.1080/13546783.2018.1507949
4. Besold, T.R., et al.: Neural-symbolic learning and reasoning: a survey and interpretation. arXiv preprint arXiv:1711.03902 (2017)
5. Brooks, R.: Flesh and Machines: How Robots Will Change Us. Pantheon (2002)
6. Doran, D., Schulz, S., Besold, T.R.: What does explainable AI really mean? A new conceptualization of perspectives. arXiv preprint arXiv:1710.00794 (2017)
7. Doshi-Velez, F., Kim, B.: Towards a rigorous science of interpretable machine learning. arXiv preprint arXiv:1702.08608 (2017)
8. Ehsan, U., Harrison, B., Chan, L., Riedl, M.O.: Rationalization: a neural machine translation approach to generating natural language explanations. In: Proceedings of the 2018 AAAI/ACM Conference on AI, Ethics, and Society, pp. 81–87 (2018). https://doi.org/10.1145/3278721.3278736
9. Festinger, L.: A Theory of Cognitive Dissonance. Stanford University Press, Stanford (1957)
10. Haugeland, J.: Artificial Intelligence: The Very Idea. Bradford Books, Bradford (1989)
11. Jones, E.: Rationalization in every-day life. J. Abnorm. Psychol. **3**(3), 161–169 (1908). https://doi.org/10.1037/h0070692
12. Kahneman, D.: Thinking, Fast and Slow. Farrar, Straus and Giroux, New York (2011)
13. Kaminski, M.E.: The right to explanation, explained. Berkeley Technol. Law J. **34**(1), 189–218 (2019). https://doi.org/10.15779/Z38TD9N83H
14. Kotok, A.: A chess playing program for the IBM 7090 computer. In: Levy, D. (ed.) Computer Chess Compendium, pp. 48–55 (1988). https://doi.org/10.1007/978-1-4757-1968-0_6
15. Lipton, Z.C.: The mythos of model interpretability. arXiv preprint arXiv:1606.03490 (2016)
16. McGuffie, K., Newhouse, A.: The radicalization risks of GPT-3 and advanced neural language models. arXiv preprint arXiv:2009.06807 (2021)
17. Miller, T.: Explanation in artificial intelligence: insights from the social sciences. Artif. Intell. **267**, 1–38 (2019). https://doi.org/10.1016/j.artint.2018.07.007, https://www.sciencedirect.com/science/article/pii/S0004370218305988
18. Newell, A., Simon, H.: The logic theory machine - a complex information processing system. IRE Trans. Inf. Theory **2**(3), 61–79 (1956). https://doi.org/10.1109/TIT.1956.1056797
19. Ng, A.: AI For Everyone (MOOC) (2022). https://www.coursera.org/learn/ai-for-everyone. Accessed 26 May 2018
20. Ribeiro, M.T., Singh, S., Guestrin, C.: Model-agnostic interpretability of machine learning. arXiv preprint arXiv:1606.05386 (2016)

21. Rudin, C.: Stop explaining black box machine learning models for high stakes decisions and use interpretable models instead. Nat. Mach. Intell. **1**(5), 206–215 (2019)
22. Russell, S., Norvig, P.: Artificial Intelligence: A Modern Approach (4th edn.). Pearson, Boston (2020)
23. Smolensky, P.: Connectionist AI, symbolic AI, and the brain. Artif. Intell. Rev. **1**(2), 95–109 (1987). https://doi.org/10.1007/BF00130011
24. Sun, R.: The CLARION cognitive architecture: toward a comprehensive theory of the mind. In: Chipman, S.E.F. (ed.) The Oxford Handbook of Cognitive Science, pp. 117–133 (2017)
25. Thagard, P.: Explanatory coherence (plus commentary). Behav. Brain Sci. **12**(3), 435–467 (1989). https://doi.org/10.1017/s0140525x00057046
26. Vilone, G., Longo, L.: Explainable artificial intelligence: a systematic review. arXiv preprint arXiv:2006.00093 (2020)
27. Wason, P., Evans, J.: Dual processes in reasoning? Cognition **3**(2), 141–154 (1974). https://doi.org/10.1016/0010-0277(74)90017-1
28. Wiegreffe, S., Hessel, J., Swayamdipta, S., Riedl, M., Choi, Y.: Reframing human-AI collaboration for generating free-text explanations. arXiv preprint arXiv:2112.08674 (2021)
29. Ziegler, D.M., et al.: Fine-tuning language models from human preferences. arXiv preprint arXiv:1909.08593 (2019)

Voice-Interactive Learning Dialogue on a Low-Cost Device

Martin Bulín$^{(\boxtimes)}$, Martin Adamec , Petr Neduchal , Marek Hrúz ,
and Jan Švec

University of West Bohemia, Univerzitní 8, 301 00 Pilsen, Czech Republic
{bulinm,neduchal,hruz,honzas}@kky.zcu.cz, adamecm@students.zcu.cz

Abstract. Traditional offline learning approaches are reaching their limits in meeting the dynamic demands of specialized applications, such
as real-time human-robot interaction. While high benchmark scores
attained through offline fine-tuning large models on extensive data, offer
a glimpse of their potential, the true functionality is validated when these
models are deployed on target devices and utilized in real-life scenarios.
This paper presents a method incorporating humans in an interactive
learning loop, using their real-time feedback for online neural network
retraining. By leveraging the power of transfer learning, we can profi-
ciently adapt the model to suit the specific requirements of the target
application through natural voice-based dialogue. The approach is evaluated on the image classification task utilizing a unique low-cost device
and a practical example of the real-time dialogue is presented to demonstrate the functionality.

Keywords: Human in the Loop · Interactive Learning · Low-Cost
Device Deployment · Audio-Visual Dialogue · Image Classification

1 Introduction

Conventional machine learning methods heavily rely on extensive datasets, and
the performance of a model is typically measured under controlled lab conditions
using a benchmark evaluation. Despite these models being fine-tuned offline and
training processes can span hours or even days, it is rare for models to achieve
absolute perfection. The abundance of training samples and model parameters
makes it often challenging for developers to pinpoint specific instances where
and why the models may fail. This paper addresses two key challenges: (1)
deploying a model on a physical entity and ensuring its effective operation in
real-life conditions, and (2) enabling interactive adaptation and refinement of
the model's behaviour based on user requirements and feedback.

We introduce a newly developed custom 3D-printed robotic entity based on
Raspberry Pi 4B[1] and complemented by multiple interfaces that enable audio,

---

[1] https://www.raspberrypi.com/products/raspberry-pi-4-model-b/.

© The Author(s), under exclusive license to Springer Nature Switzerland AG 2023
H. Lu et al. (Eds.): ACPR 2023, LNCS 14408, pp. 369–382, 2023.
https://doi.org/10.1007/978-3-031-47665-5_30

visual, and even tactile interactions. This device is used to deploy the proposed learning method integrating a human into a voice-interactive dialogue loop. By utilising transfer learning and human feedback in the learning loop, we can effectively customize the model to meet the precise user's demands. The method is experimentally evaluated on the task of image classification. The robot can learn and recognize new objects through natural dialogue by integrating computer vision techniques with advanced speech technologies. Furthermore, the learning loop is augmented with face recognition, enhancing the overall learning process and facilitating user engagement.

Section 2 presents a comprehensive review of relevant methodologies. The target physical device is introduced in Sect. 3, while Sect. 4 provides an in-depth description of the utilized datasets. Section 5 provides a detailed exposition of the interactive loop and its constituent elements. The experimental evaluation is documented in Sect. 6, while Sect. 7 summarises this work's key findings and contributions.

2   Related Work

In this section, related work to this paper is introduced. In particular, the section is divided into two parts. The first part is focused on interactive learning - i.e., human-in-the-loop - research, and the second part deals with its applications for various modalities, in particular, images, audio, video, and multimodal systems.

2.1   Interactive Learning

Interactive learning or Interactive Machine Learning (IML) is the subfield of Human-in-the-loop research that focuses on a learning process where a human is interactively supplying training target information. In other words, the human is used to build classifiers - whether he is an expert or non-expert - online by using the system instead of traditional offline machine learning. This principle is based on the idea presented in the paper [30]. A similar technique was proposed in the paper [7], where it is mentioned that the learning process is repeated until desired results are met.

A more current definition of interactive learning is mentioned in the paper [10]. The authors said that IMLs are algorithms that can interact with agents and can optimize their learning behaviour through these interactions, where the agents can also be human. IML is redefined in multiple papers such as [6] or [23], but all of them have similar properties, such as interactivity and incremental learning process, and should be fast enough.

The other question is the role of the human in the IML. The role, in this case, has two meanings. The first one is the expertise of the human. The human can be an expert in machine learning, a domain-specific expert, or a non-expert user of the IML system. Moreover, the role can be seen as a position of the human in the machine learning process. He can be placed at the beginning of the process to provide annotations or preprocess of the data in real-time. The second option is to place humans at the end to check and correct the results of the IML system. Moreover, a third option belongs to another part of the Human-in-the-loop research field [20]. In particular, it is Active Learning (AL), where the mutual position between machine and human differs from the one in IML. In IML, they are equal, or the human is in the lead, but in AL, the machine is the lead, and it uses a human only in cases in which it is not sure about the correct result (i.e., the confidence of the result is poor).

This paper presents the IML system running on a low-cost device capable of interacting with humans through multiple modalities – in our case, through video and audio channels.

The use of images in IML is offered because it is a natural and very under-standable modality for humans. One of the first systems based on images was CueFlik [8]. It was a web search system that users could use to learn their own classification rules by providing examples and counterexamples of individual classes. Another similar and more current example is an open-source image anno-tation framework for ecological surveys called AIDE [15]. Other use cases [13] of image-based IML are for example interactive information retrieval [3], visual topic analysis [28], or interactive anomaly detection [31].

As an example of video-based IML (i.e., a stream of images), the paper by Kabra et al. [14] can be mentioned. The authors proposed a system for biologists designed as an annotation tool for certain animals' behaviour. An audio modality also has several examples of applications that are similar to this paper. It is, for example, Spoken Language Understanding presented in the paper [2] or the work of Ishibashi et al [12] where an interactive sound recognition using visualization - e.g. stereograms or deep learning audio-to-image retrieval - is performed. In other words, audio files are visualized to provide the user with more information to classify the sound. An example of an audiovisual IML system is the research of Visi and Tanaka [29]. The authors proposed a system for recognizing musical gestures consisting of motion and gesture tracking of a human and then synthesis of the appropriate sound. Finally, the paper of Qureshi et al. [22] proposed a system for multimodal deep reinforcement learning of a humanoid robot. In this case, multimodal means that the robot used its RGB-D camera and a hand touch sensor for its operations.

3   Target Device

One of the key foundations of this project is to implement the developed method for interactive learning on an actual robotic entity and assess its performance in real-world conditions. For this purpose, we employed a unique physical device known as *Robot.v1*, which was developed at the Department of Cybernetics of the University of West Bohemia in 2023 [4]. It is a multimodal low-cost 3D-printed entity of a rotund shape (see Fig. 1) equipped with the following interfaces:

- *Touch screen (7")* facilitates visual interaction from the robot's side and offers tactile-based human feedback.

- *RPi Camera module V2* enables the robot's visual perception.
- High-performance *microphone array* [24] is employed for sound perception and sound source localization, complemented by a *speaker* for audio output.

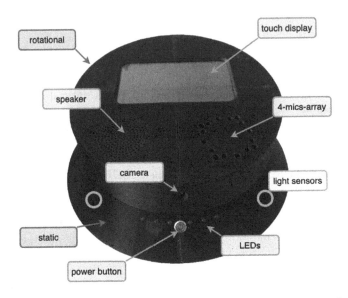

Fig. 1. Picture of the target device for deploying the proposed method, known as *Robot.v1*.

The robot structure comprises a static part, a rotational element, and several components. These include a solar panel for efficient charging, light sensors to determine the optimal orientation towards the incoming sun source, a stepper motor facilitating the rotation of the upper part, or LEDs for arbitrary robot status indication. The computational tasks are executed on a Raspberry Pi 4B, the core processing unit. The software implementation relies on the Robot Operating System [21], serving as the central framework for integrating and coordinating various individual tasks, ensuring stable main processing.

The speech-related tasks - Automatic Speech Recognition (ASR) and Text-To-Speech Synthesis (TTS) are addressed by the in-house technology called SpeechCloud [26]. The platform is also connected to a remote server with GPU capabilities through an HTTP API. This connection enables using powerful computational resources for intensive tasks such as neural network retraining. As depicted in Fig. 2, among the extensive selection of pre-programmed ROS nodes and services available on *Robot.v1*, we utilized the *speech* package, specifically the *ASR* and *TTS* services, and the *gui* package using the touch screen for capturing human feedbacks. Additionally, through this project, we enhanced the *camera* package by incorporating face recognition and object detection capabilities.

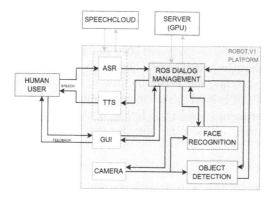

Fig. 2. A component diagram of the target device employed in project [1].

4 Datasets

This section aims to introduce datasets used either for pre-training neural networks or directly during experiments in the interactive learning loop.

The Intel Image Classification dataset[2] is composed of approximately 25 000 natural scene images divided into 6 classes labelled as buildings, forest, glacier, mountain, sea, and street.

Fig. 3. Example images of each class of Intel Image Classification dataset.

---

[2] https://www.kaggle.com/datasets/puneet6060/intel-image-classification.

Most of the images have a resolution of 150 by 150 pixels, with some of the images being smaller. The dataset is distributed in three parts. 14000 images are in the train set, 3000 in the test set, and 7000 in a prediction set, which was used in the Image Classification Challenge[3]. Originally, the dataset was used in the task of scene understanding but it can be used in the task of object recognition as well. In this paper, it is used to test image embeddings – see Sect. 5.2, as well as for the final experiment – see Fig. 7. In Fig. 3, there is an example of 6 images from the dataset, each representing one class in the same order as mentioned before.

The COCO dataset [19] is a popular large-scale dataset composed of 123287 images of various resolutions. Each image contains one or multiple classes of the overall number of 80 classes. Initially, it is widely used in object detection, object segmentation, and object captioning tasks. Moreover, it is commonly used to benchmark models in computer vision tasks. This dataset was also used to pre-train the *Mobilenet V3 Large* network architecture [17] used in this research. An example of images from the dataset is shown in Fig. 4.

Fig. 4. Examples from the COCO dataset. Left: An image of an airport containing multiple classes. Right: Same image with visible annotations of aeroplane class.

5   Interactive Learning Loop

The central concept presented in this paper is to incorporate a human into a voice-interactive learning loop of an artificial system. In addition to conventional machine learning approaches, this allows for direct interaction with a deployed model, enabling iterative customization based on specific requirements. The method is showcased using a toy example of the image classification task and assessed on a physical robotic platform. Additionally, a face recognition tool is added to simulate a realistic human-robot interaction scenario, acting as

---

[3] https://datahack.analyticsvidhya.com.

a wake-up gate that initiates the main loop for learning objects when a known face is detected (depicted in Fig. 5).

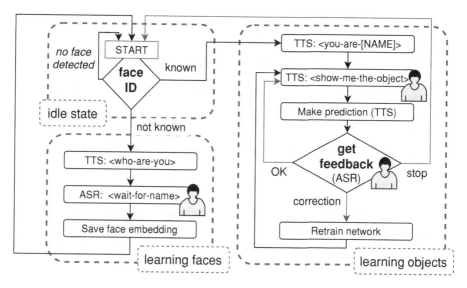

Fig. 5. A scheme of the dialogue for evaluating the developed voice-interactive learning method. The red icon highlights the specific parts, where human interaction is utilized within the loop.eps (Color figure online)

Several design choices needed to be considered, with two primary constraints to be addressed. Since the robotic entity's objective is to maintain a dialogue loop with *a minimal time delay* between user input and the response (ideally in real-time), computational speed emerges as the paramount parameter alongside *algorithmic accuracy*.

5.1   FaceID and Learning New Faces

The inclusion of the *faceID* tool in the application, as illustrated in Fig. 5, acts as the entry point to the main loop of interactive learning. The system initially operates in an idle state, and upon detecting a familiar face through the camera, it transitions into the loop for learning objects. In the event of detecting a new and unfamiliar face, the user is prompted to provide their name, and the captured facial sample is subsequently incorporated into the database for future reference.

It was decided to utilize the open-source *face-recognition* Python library[4], primarily due to its user-friendly API. This library, built on top of the *dlib*[5] [16] library written in C++, enhances the efficiency of computationally intensive tasks, thereby accelerating their execution. The process of face recognition from the image comprises two parts: *face localization* and *face classification*.

---

[4] https://github.com/ageitgey/face_recognition.
[5] https://github.com/davisking/dlib.

Face Localization. The objective is to detect the presence of a face in the camera image. To achieve this, two library-provided methods were thoroughly evaluated, with a particular focus on computational efficiency. The first method, based on convolutional neural networks and considered more robust to face angle and rotation changes, was found unsuitable for the target device due to an average inference time of 3.64 s across 100 trials.

In contrast, the second method available in the library, known as *Histogram of Oriented Gradients* (HOG) [5], demonstrated slightly lower accuracy; however, its inference time of 0.58 s was more suitable for our real-time application. Consequently, the HOG method was chosen for the project.

Face Classification. After detecting a face in the image, it is encoded into a vector representing its distinctive features, i.e. its identity. Firstly, facial landmarks representing corners of the mouth, eyes, nose tip, etc. are detected. These landmarks provide a geometric pose of the face which is then "frontalized" into a mean camera-facing face shape using a geometric transform. There are two systems for face landmarks detection, one that detects 5 landmarks and one that detects 68 landmarks. We found no significant difference in the inference times between the two models through experimentation. Consequently, we opted to implement the 68-feature model. The face is then cropped and the image is passed through a pre-trained custom ResNet [9] model to produce a 128-dimensional embedding.

In the real-life application, the newly detected face is encoded into its vector representation and compared to the embeddings of already-known faces using the library's internal metrics and thresholding techniques. This enables real-time face detection in the application while efficiently storing new embeddings. If multiple faces are detected in the image, only the first face on the list is used, as the default application assumes that only one user interacts with the device.

5.2 Network Architecture for Image Classification

When the camera detects a familiar face, the system seamlessly transitions into the main loop of learning objects, as depicted in Fig. 5. The model depicted in Fig. 6 is responsible for predicting the object presented to the camera by the user. Its design is focused on two primary aspects that distinguish our task from traditional offline image classification:

1. the presence of *timing constraints*, where the real-time settings heavily rely on both inference time and network retraining time;
2. the network must demonstrate exceptional and rapid *generalization*, as we often encounter a limited number of training examples per desired class, aiming to alter the model's behaviour.

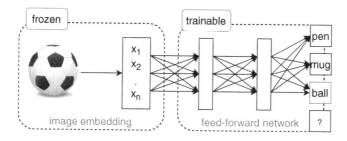

Fig. 6. Network architecture for interactive image classification.

To fulfil these specifications, we employ transfer learning, specifically utilizing a network that has been pre-trained on a large-scale computer vision task. This pre-trained network serves as an embedding model for our task, enabling us to leverage its learned representations for newly added examples. By employing this approach, we are able to train a relatively small number of parameters in a subsequent feed-forward neural network, which consists of two hidden layers and a softmax output layer. Leveraging the current computing power and hardware capabilities, this setup enables real-time processing, making it feasible to integrate even the re-training part seamlessly into the dialogue loop.

The selection of the embedding model is a critical aspect of the design choice. We conducted an experiment using the *Intel Classification Dataset* with nine different methods to address this.

Table 1. Performance comparison of different image embedding extractors.

Embedding model	Mean embedding time	Train time	Accuracy
Resnet-18 [9]	0.0365 ± 0.0033 s	0.42 s	0.882
Alexnet [18]	0.0246 ± 0.0039 s	0.37 s	0.874
Vgg-11 [25]	0.1258 ± 0.0143 s	1.09 s	0.896
Densenet [11]	0.1194 ± 0.0216 s	4.98 s	0.884
Efficientnet B0 [27]	0.0460 ± 0.0090 s	3.61 s	0.895
Efficientnet B1 [27]	0.0591 ± 0.0063 s	6.63 s	0.889
Efficientnet B2 [27]	0.0605 ± 0.0105 s	7.84 s	0.898
Efficientnet B3 [27]	0.0846 ± 0.0112 s	9.56 s	0.883
Mobilenet V3 Large [17]	**0.0358 ± 0.0092 s**	**0.80 s**	**0.915**

In order to maintain fair conditions, we utilized the same subsequent feed-forward network, consisting of a single hidden layer with 50 neurons, for all methods, and during the evaluation, we considered three metrics:

- *embedding time* of a single image;
- *train time* - refers to the duration of training the network until the stopping condition was reached;

– maximal *classification accuracy* reached.

In order to simulate real-world conditions relevant to the target application for which we were selecting the embedding model, we conducted the classification task with six distinct classes and limited the dataset to 50 training samples, and 20 validation samples per class. This closely aligns with the desired capabilities of our final model, where it should be able to generalize and acquire knowledge effectively even with a minimal number of training examples. Then we used 300 testing samples per class, which served as a representation of the knowledge that the model was expected to acquire.

After conducting the experiment summarized in Table 1, we determined that the *Mobilenet V3 Large* architecture [17] is the optimal choice as the embedder for our pipeline. To extract feature embedding vectors with a dimensionality of 1280 from this model, we utilized the *timm* library[6].

5.3   Human Feedback and Network Retraining

At this stage, we are approaching the crucial component of the interactive dialogue, which involves human feedback on the model's predictions. Since the dialogue uses audio and visual modality, the feedback can be provided through two channels: automatic speech recognition (ASR) or the touch screen and graphical user interface (GUI). As illustrated in Fig. 5, the feedback can fall into one of three possibilities:

– *Stop* - The dialogue finishes.
– *Ok* - The model's prediction was correct. In this case, the last shown example is added to the training set with the correctly predicted label.
– *Correction* - The model's prediction was incorrect. In that case, the feedback is parsed using rule-based operators. For instance, in the case of ASR, if the recognized text is *No, it is not a mug. It is a pen*, the feedback type *correction* and the correct class *pen* would be extracted from the parsed information.

The network is re-trained, as described below, with every new training sample. To enhance the fluidity of the dialogue, the system automatically proceeds along the *ok* path if no additional feedback is provided within 3 s after each prediction.

Network On-the-Fly Retraining. As depicted in Fig. 2, the model undergoes retraining on a remote server, specifically on a machine equipped with an NVIDIA GeForce GTX 1080 GPU. The newly collected samples and trained model parameters are transferred in binary format using the HTTP protocol between the remote server and the target device. By leveraging the frozen embedding model (which is not retrained) and employing a small training set, the retraining process is sufficiently fast (less than a second), even when factoring in the time required for the HTTP transfer.

---

[6] https://timm.fast.ai.

A unique scenario arises when the user attempts to introduce a new object that the network has not encountered before. In such cases, the final network layer must be restructured, and a new output class (and its corresponding neuron) must be added. Through experimentation, we discovered that maintaining the trained weights associated with the existing known classes while initializing only the weights connected to the new class greatly facilitates overall convergence. This approach outperforms the alternative method of completely reinitializing the output layer from scratch.

6   Experimental Setup and Evaluation

This section presents the experimental evaluation of the interactive learning dialogue framework. Based on the results in Table 1, we employed the Mobilenet V3 Large architecture [17] for our task, which was originally pre-trained on the COCO dataset for object detection and recognition purposes (see Sect. 4). As shown in Fig. 6, this pre-trained model was utilized to obtain image embeddings, which were then combined with a feed-forward neural network consisting of two hidden layers (512 and 256 hidden neurons) and an output softmax layer.

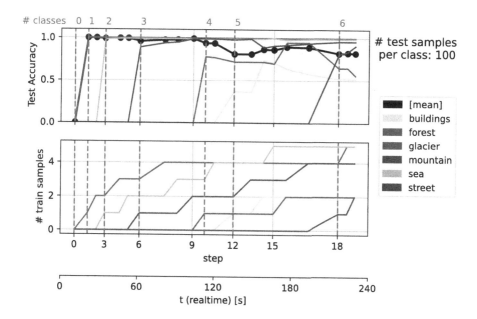

Fig. 7. An exemplary instance of the human-robot learning dialogue. The real-time axis is depicted at the bottom. The training samples were incrementally introduced one by one, and the system was regularly evaluated using 600 testing samples (100 per class) that represented the desired "knowledge". The vertical red lines indicate the progressive increase in the number of learned classes. (Color figure online)

Regarding retraining, we used the cross-entropy loss function, the ADAM optimizer with a learning rate of 0.001, and a maximum of 50 training epochs. We implemented an early stopping condition, where training would halt if the training loss did not show improvement for ten consecutive epochs.

Interactive Learning Loop Evaluation. The experiment is performed on six classes' Intel Image Classification dataset. The dataset samples were loaded directly into the algorithm without relying on the physical display through the robot's camera. However, all other settings and conditions of the real-time scenario remained unchanged. The experimental setup for this study differs from conventional supervised learning. Firstly, we establish a concept called *knowledge*, which refers to the desired behaviour we aim to train our system to achieve. This knowledge is represented by the classical testing data partition, where in this specific case, we utilize 100 samples per class, resulting in a total of 600 samples.

Figure 7 illustrates a selected example of the human-robot learning dialogue. At the beginning of the process, there are no training samples available. Instead, they are progressively introduced to the system as the real-time application runs. Each sample is accompanied by a label that is derived from human feedback, and these pairs are one by one added into the training data partition. The experiment yields the following observations: (1) The chosen model effectively meets the timing constraints for both inference and retraining; (2) The utilization of a pre-trained model as the embedder enhances the generalization capabilities, allowing solid accuracy to be achieved on 100 testing samples with only 2–4 training samples per class; (3) The introduction of a new class to the system does not significantly impact the accuracy of previously learned classes.

7   Conclusion

This work addresses the limitations of traditional offline learning methods and explores their potential for deployment in real-life applications. Initially, we introduced a novel, cost-effective device that features multiple interfaces, making it suitable for testing machine learning systems. Subsequently, we proposed a learning method incorporating a human within the learning loop, leveraging their feedback to adapt and refine the system's behaviour. The concept was tested on the image classification task and enveloped into a working framework. The experimental evaluation of the workflow yielded several promising findings, establishing a robust foundation for future endeavours. Notably, we successfully demonstrated a use case involving sorting images into categories. Building upon this achievement, the next logical progression would be to explore the potential of learning a scene description using natural language. Importantly, the method is versatile and has the potential to be applied across multiple domains.

Acknowledgements. This research was supported by the Czech Science Foundation (GA CR), project No. GA22-27800S, and by the grant of the University of West Bohemia, project No. SGS-2022-017.

References

1. Adamec, M.: Voice-Interactive Computer Vision on Raspberry Pi. Bachelor thesis, University of West Bohemia (2023)
2. Begeja, L., Renger, B., Gibbon, D., Liu, Z., Shahraray, B.: Interactive machine learning techniques for improving SLU models. In: Proceedings of the HLT-NAACL 2004 Workshop on Spoken Language Understanding for Conversational Systems and Higher Level Linguistic Information for Speech Processing, pp. 10–16 (2004)
3. Behrisch, M., et al.: Magnostics: image-based search of interesting matrix views for guided network exploration. IEEE Trans. Visual Comput. Graph. **23**(1), 31–40 (2016)
4. Bulín, M.: Multimodal low-cost robotic entity based on raspberry pi. In: Rendl, J. (ed.) SVK FAV 2023 - Magisterské a Doktorské Studijní Programy, pp. 38–39. University of West Bohemia, Pilsen, University of West Bohemia, Pilsen (2023)
5. Dalal, N., Triggs, B.: Histograms of oriented gradients for human detection. In: 2005 IEEE Computer Society Conference on Computer Vision and Pattern Recognition (CVPR'05), vol. 1, pp. 886–893 (2005). https://doi.org/10.1109/CVPR.2005.177
6. Dudley, J.J., Kristensson, P.O.: A review of user interface design for interactive machine learning. ACM Trans. Interact. Intell. Syst. (TiiS) **8**(2), 1–37 (2018)
7. Fails, J.A., Olsen Jr, D.R.: Interactive machine learning. In: Proceedings of the 8th International Conference on Intelligent User Interfaces, pp. 39–45 (2003)
8. Fogarty, J., Tan, D., Kapoor, A., Winder, S.: Cueflik: interactive concept learning in image search. In: Proceedings of the Sigchi Conference on Human Factors in Computing Systems, pp. 29–38 (2008)
9. He, K., Zhang, X., Ren, S., Sun, J.: Deep residual learning for image recognition. arXiv preprint arXiv:1512.03385 (2015)
10. Holzinger, A.: Interactive machine learning for health informatics: when do we need the human-in-the-loop? Brain Informatics **3**(2), 119–131 (2016)
11. Huang, G., Liu, Z., Van Der Maaten, L., Weinberger, K.Q.: Densely connected convolutional networks. In: Proceedings of the IEEE Conference on Computer Vision and Pattern Recognition, pp. 4700–4708 (2017)
12. Ishibashi, T., Nakao, Y., Sugano, Y.: Investigating audio data visualization for interactive sound recognition. In: Proceedings of the 25th International Conference on Intelligent User Interfaces, pp. 67–77 (2020)
13. Jiang, L., Liu, S., Chen, C.: Recent research advances on interactive machine learning. J. Visualization **22**, 401–417 (2019)
14. Kabra, M., Robie, A.A., Rivera-Alba, M., Branson, S., Branson, K.: Jaaba: interactive machine learning for automatic annotation of animal behavior. Nat. Methods **10**(1), 64–67 (2013)
15. Kellenberger, B., Tuia, D., Morris, D.: Aide: accelerating image-based ecological surveys with interactive machine learning. Methods Ecol. Evol. **11**(12), 1716–1727 (2020)
16. King, D.E.: Dlib-ml: a machine learning toolkit. J. Mach. Learn. Res. **10**, 1755–1758 (2009)
17. Koonce, B., Koonce, B.: Mobilenetv3. In: Convolutional Neural Networks with Swift for Tensorflow: Image Recognition and Dataset Categorization, pp. 125–144 (2021)
18. Krizhevsky, A., Sutskever, I., Hinton, G.E.: Imagenet classification with deep convolutional neural networks. Commun. ACM **60**(6), 84–90 (2017)

19. Lin, T.-Y., et al.: Microsoft COCO: common objects in context. In: Fleet, D., Pajdla, T., Schiele, B., Tuytelaars, T. (eds.) ECCV 2014. LNCS, vol. 8693, pp. 740–755. Springer, Cham (2014). https://doi.org/10.1007/978-3-319-10602-1_48

20. Mosqueira-Rey, E., Hernández-Pereira, E., Alonso-Ríos, D., Bobes-Bascarán, J., Fernández-Leal, Á.: Human-in-the-loop machine learning: a state of the art. Artif. Intell. Rev. **56**(4), 3005–3054 (2023)

21. Quigley, M., et al.: Ros: an open-source robot operating system. In: Proceedings of the IEEE International Conference on Robotics and Automation (ICRA) Workshop on Open Source Robotics, Kobe (2009)

22. Qureshi, A.H., Nakamura, Y., Yoshikawa, Y., Ishiguro, H.: Robot gains social intelligence through multimodal deep reinforcement learning. In: 2016 IEEE-RAS 16th International Conference on Humanoid Robots (Humanoids), pp. 745–751. IEEE (2016)

23. Ramos, G., Meek, C., Simard, P., Suh, J., Ghorashi, S.: Interactive machine teaching: a human-centered approach to building machine-learned models. Hum. Comput. Interact. **35**(5-6), 413–451 (2020)

24. SeeedStudio: Respeaker mic array v2.0 (2023). https://wiki.seeedstudio.com/ReSpeaker_Mic_Array_v2.0/

25. Simonyan, K., Zisserman, A.: Very deep convolutional networks for large-scale image recognition. In: International Conference on Learning Representations (2015)

26. Švec, J., Neduchal, P., Hrúz, M.: Multi-modal communication system for mobile robot. IFAC-PapersOnLine **55**(4), 133–138 (2022)

27. Tan, M., Le, Q.: Efficientnet: rethinking model scaling for convolutional neural networks. In: International Conference on Machine Learning, pp. 6105–6114. PMLR (2019)

28. Thom, D., et al.: Can twitter really save your life? a case study of visual social media analytics for situation awareness. In: 2015 IEEE Pacific Visualization Symposium (PacificVis), pp. 183–190. IEEE (2015)

29. Visi, F.G., Tanaka, A.: Interactive machine learning of musical gesture. In: Handbook of Artificial Intelligence for Music: Foundations, Advanced Approaches, and Developments for Creativity, pp. 771–798 (2021)

30. Ware, M., Frank, E., Holmes, G., Hall, M., Witten, I.H.: Interactive machine learning: letting users build classifiers. Int. J. Hum Comput Stud. **55**(3), 281–292 (2001)

31. Xu, P., Mei, H., Ren, L., Chen, W.: Vidx: visual diagnostics of assembly line performance in smart factories. IEEE Trans. Visual Comput. Graph. **23**(1), 291–300 (2016)

Composite Restoration of Infrared Image Based on Adaptive Threshold Multi-parameter Wavelet

Shuai Liu[1] ⓘ, Peng Chen[1], Zhengxiang Shen[1], and Zhanshan Wang[1,2](✉)

[1] School of Physical Science and Engineering, Tongji University, Shanghai 200092, China
wangzs@tongji.edu.cn
[2] Institute of Precision Optical Engineering, Tongji University, Shanghai 200092, China

Abstract. The multiplicative speckle noise and additive background noise of an infrared image are significant elements impacting image quality. To address the issue of image degradation caused by noise superposition and enhance the infrared image quality in terms of noise suppression, a composite restoration method based on adaptive threshold multi-parameter wavelet is proposed. First, based on the noise distribution characteristics of the infrared image, the multiplicative noise in the infrared image is transformed into additive noise, and the image is restored using the wavelet transform coefficient of the converted infrared image. Then, the benefits and drawbacks of soft and hard threshold functions are analysed in depth, and an adaptive double threshold function with adjustable parameters is developed. Finally, a fast non-local means method is used to suppress the effect of background noise on image quality. The experimental results show that the proposed method reduces 111.03 dB on average over the MSE index, 6.67 dB on the PSNR index and 6.92 dB on the SNR index.

Keywords: frared image · image denoising · adaptive threshold wavelet

1 Introduction

As a passive detection technology, infrared imaging has been widely used in the military, industry, agriculture, and other fields [1, 2]. Simultaneously, the imaging quality requirements of infrared systems are constantly improving, and certain technical problems are becoming increasingly prominent. One of the problems that need to be solved is infrared image restoration [3]. In comparison with visible images, infrared images are easily affected by the additive noise caused by the detector, detection environment, and hardware conditions of photoelectric conversion circuits. Additionally, the multiplicative noise generated by the channel is not ideal for acquisition and transmission leading to poor imaging quality of infrared systems [4]. Figure 1 shows the comparison of an infrared image that is affected by additive noise, multiplicative noise, and their combination.

This work was supported by National Natural Science Foundation of China (No. 12373100), and the Fundamental Research Funds for the Central Universities.

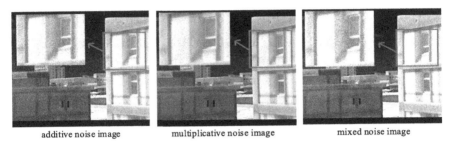

additive noise image   multiplicative noise image   mixed noise image

Fig. 1. Composition of noisy images

The discrete wavelet transform (DWT) [5] has many excellent characteristics, such as fast decomposition, decorrelation, and low entropy, so that the wavelet transform can realize well the separation of desired signal and noise. Therefore, many scholars have conducted research on this problem in recent years [6]. Donoho et al. [7] proposed the wavelet threshold denoising method, which has a simple principle and remarkable denoising effect. However, the discontinuity of the hard threshold function at the threshold point results in visual distortion, such as the pseudo-Gibbs phenomenon and ringing in the denoised image [8, 9]. The constant deviation caused by the soft threshold function leads to blurred image edge details after denoising [10–12]. Therefore, many researchers have proposed a variety of adaptive threshold denoising methods. Guo et al. [13] proposed an improved wavelet threshold calculation method and a new threshold function to denoise ultraviolet signals in view of the existing problems of the soft and hard threshold functions. Chen [14] improved the classical wavelet threshold denoising algorithm, and innovatively adopted a combination of soft and hard thresholds. Zhang et al. [15] proposed an adaptive threshold function for underwater signal noise under complex ocean conditions. Kumar et al. [16] proposed an signal denoising method based on the stationary wavelet transform. Binbin [17] proposed an infrared image processing method based on adaptive threshold denoising. These methods not only open up broader prospects for the full advantages of wavelet threshold denoising methods but also provide a basis for further exploration of adaptive denoising methods.

According to the specific imaging mechanism and characteristics of infrared imaging, an infrared imaging system has both multiplicative and additive background noise. The existing single wavelet denoising algorithms for multiplicative speckle and additive noise cannot simultaneously remove two different types of noise; thus, there are problems such as residual noise, blurred details, and limited image quality improvement effects in denoised images [18]. Therefore, a composite restoration method based on adaptive threshold multi-parameter wavelet (ATMW) is proposed in this paper, which can remove at once background light, additive detector, and multiplicative speckle noise, and effectively improve the image quality of infrared systems. First, a method based on ATMW is proposed to remove multiplicative speckle noise in infrared images. This method converts speckle noise into additive noise through logarithmic transformation, and then, the wavelet coefficients of the transformed infrared images are processed by threshold denoising. Based on the wavelet coefficient threshold processing method for infrared image denoising, the advantages and disadvantages of soft and hard threshold functions are analysed, an adaptive threshold function with adjustable parameters is constructed, and double threshold mapping is adopted. Then, the additive noise (such as background light) is removed by a fast non-local means algorithm (FNLM), which can effectively remove the noise and retain the image details.

2 Mixed Noise Model

The composition of the infrared imaging system is shown in Fig. 2. According to Fig. 2, noise sources mainly include the background, amplifier, and detector in the field of view. Background noise includes scene radiation noise and noise caused by atmospheric dithering. Amplifier noise is mainly transistor noise. The detector noise mainly includes 1/f noise, noise caused by the complex fluctuation of the carrier, thermal noise, and so on.

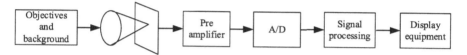

Fig. 2. Composition of infrared imaging system

From the essence of noise analysis, infrared image noise signals can be divided into additive noise and multiplicative noise [19–23]. The inherent noise of circuit components in the shooting equipment and transmission process, as well as the Gaussian, salt and pepper, and Poisson noises generated by their mutual influence are associated with additive noise. Additive noise is inherent in the presence or absence of image signals. The multiplicative noise is generally caused by the unsatisfactory channel, which is multiplied by the image signal. It is just the opposite of additive noise and depends on the image signal. When the image signal disappears, the multiplicative noise disappears as well [24–26].

Generally, the noise model of infrared images can be expressed as:

$$Y_{ij} = X_{ij} * \delta + N \tag{1}$$

where X is the original signal of the image, Y is the image containing noise, δ represents multiplicative noise, N represents additive noise, and i and j are the position coordinates of a pixel in a two-dimensional space.

3 Compound Restoration Method Based on ATMW

The existing infrared image denoising methods are mainly divided into two categories. The first case involves ignoring the additive noise in the image and then converting the multiplicative noise into additive noise through transformation for denoising. The second one involves ignoring the multiplicative noise in the image and only denoising the additive noise. Neither of them can effectively suppress the two different types of noise in infrared images simultaneously, and the improvement in image quality after denoising is limited. Therefore, aiming at the characteristics of background, other additive and multiplicative speckle noise in the imaging system, this study proposes an ATMW combined with FNLM to suppress noise. It cannot only remove background, detector, and other additive noise but also suppress multiplicative speckle noise. This method can effectively improve the image quality of an infrared image.

The process of infrared image restoration is shown in Fig. 3. First, the multiplicative noise component in the image is processed by the wavelet threshold method; then, the additive background noise is denoised in the image.

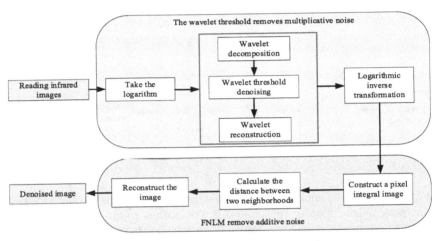

Fig. 3. Flowchart of infrared image restoration

3.1   ATMW for Multiplicative Noise Removal

The wavelet transform is an ideal mathematical model for human visual information processing. The image with noise is decomposed by the wavelet transform in multiple layers, and the wavelet high and low-frequency coefficients are obtained. Wavelet threshold image denoising retains the wavelet low-frequency coefficients, sets an appropriate threshold to separate the noise signal in the wavelet high-frequency coefficients, setting it to zero, and then reconstructs the wavelet high frequency coefficients using the wavelet threshold function. Finally, the wavelet coefficients are reconstructed to obtain the denoised image. The design of the threshold value and function required will greatly affect wavelet denoising. If the threshold is too large, the effective signal will be set to zero, and the image will be damaged and blurred. Meanwhile, if the threshold is too low, a portion of the noise signal is retained, and the image denoising is incomplete, failing to achieve the desired denoising effect. The threshold function determines the approximation between the reconstructed and original wavelet coefficients. If the threshold function is discontinuous at the threshold point, it will cause visual distortion such as ringing and pseudo-Gibbs phenomenon in the reconstructed denoised image. If there is a constant deviation between the reconstructed and actual wavelet signals, the accuracy of the reconstruction will be reduced and the edge of the image will be blurred. Therefore, the design of an appropriate threshold value and function is the key to the wavelet image denoising method.

In wavelet threshold technology, the choice of the threshold is the key factor determining the algorithm's performance. On the one hand, it needs to be large enough to remove as much noise as possible. On the other hand, it should be small enough to retain as much signal energy as possible. The VisuShrink threshold [27] is currently a widely used threshold. The same threshold is selected for each wavelet decomposition level, which can be described using formula (2):

$$\lambda = \sigma \sqrt{2 \ln(M * N)} \tag{2}$$

M and N are the rows and columns of image pixels, and σ is the noise standard deviation. As the wavelet transform is a multi-resolution analysis, the threshold value can be selected at each layer. Therefore, a variable adaptive wavelet threshold is proposed in this paper, which can decrease with the increase of the number of wavelet decomposition layers and corresponds to the actual wavelet decomposition. The variable wavelet threshold is presented in formula (3):

$$\lambda = \frac{\sigma \sqrt{2 \ln(M * N)}}{\ln(i^2 + 1)} \tag{3}$$

where i is the number of decomposition layers of the wavelet transform, and σ is the standard deviation of noise; $\ln(i^2 + 1)$ is the contraction factor, which can automatically adjust the size of the wavelet threshold according to the number of layers of wavelet decomposition and has the characteristics of self-adaptation. The proposed variable wavelet threshold can better solve the problem of the VisuShrink threshold, and effectively improve the recognition of the noise signal and the accuracy of image reconstruction.

This study presents a multi-parameter double mapping threshold function, which has more advantages and flexibility compared with hard and soft threshold functions, i.e., it can perform wavelet coefficient processing and complete adaptive denoising of images. Thresholds are introduced to adjust the translation of the function. According to parameter m, the difference between the estimated and actual wavelet coefficients can be adjusted. The expression is presented in formula (4):

$$\hat{w}_{j,k}^i = \begin{cases} sign(w_{j,k}^i) * \left(\left| w_{j,k}^i \right| - \dfrac{m\lambda_i}{1 + e^{-(|w_{j,k}^i| - \lambda_i)}} \right), & \left| w_{j,k}^i \right| \geq \lambda_i \\ w_{j,k}^i, & \dfrac{\lambda_i}{2} \leq \left| w_{j,k}^i \right| \leq \lambda_i \\ 0, & \left| w_{j,k}^i \right| < \dfrac{\lambda_i}{2} \end{cases} \tag{4}$$

where $\hat{w}_{j,k}^i$ is the estimated coefficient of the image, $w_{j,k}^i$ is the original coefficient of the image after wavelet decomposition, λ_i is the ith wavelet threshold, and m is the adjustment parameter. The value of m will affect the trend of the threshold function, thus adjusting its steady-state error and continuity.

As can be seen from the above adaptive double threshold function, when the parameter m = 0, the function becomes a hard threshold function. When m = 1 and $w^i_{j,k} \to \infty$, the function becomes a soft threshold function. When $\left| w^i_{j,k} \right| \to \infty, \left| \hat{w}^i_{j,k} - w^i_{j,k} \right| \to m\lambda_i$, i.e., with the increase of $\left| w^i_{j,k} \right|$, the absolute value of deviation between the estimated wavelet coefficient $\hat{w}^i_{j,k}$ and wavelet coefficients $w^i_{j,k}$ tends to $m\lambda_i$. As m is a parameter, the absolute value of the deviation can be controlled by adjusting its size, which effectively improves the constant deviation between the estimated wavelet coefficients and the wavelet coefficients generated in the soft threshold function.

In comparison with the soft and hard threshold functions, the multi−parameter wavelet threshold function proposed in this paper is a better and more flexible choice. The proposed threshold function can correctly determine the size of m according to different images, realize the different processing of wavelet coefficients, and complete the image adaptive denoising. The improved wavelet denoising process is shown in Fig. 4.

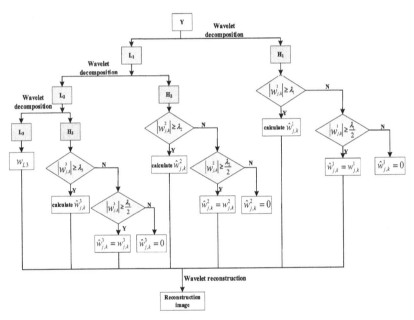

Fig. 4. Flowchart of adaptive threshold multi-parameter wavelet denoising

In summary, the algorithm is described in the following steps:

1. The infrared image containing multiplicative noise is expressed with formula (5); with 4 as the base, the logarithm of formula (5) is taken, and the multiplicative noise is changed into additive noise, and expressed with formula (6)

$$Y_{ij} = X_{ij} * \delta \tag{5}$$

$$\log 4Y_{ij} = \log 4X_{ij} + \log 4\delta \tag{6}$$

To avoid taking the logarithm of 0 as the base when implementing the algorithm, special order $Y_{ij} = Y_{ij} + \zeta, \zeta \in (0.0000001, 0.0000002)$.

2. A three-layer wavelet decomposition is performed for the infrared image $\log 4Y_{ij}$, and the db4 wavelet base is selected. First, the noisy image is decomposed into a low-frequency part L1 and a high-frequency part H1 in the first layer. Then, the low-frequency part of the first layer L1 is decomposed into the second low-frequency part L2 and second high-frequency part H2 by wavelet decomposition. Finally, the low-frequency part of the second layer L2 is decomposed into the third low-frequency part L3 and third high-frequency part H3.

3. Threshold quantization is performed for high-frequency coefficients; $w_{j,k}^i$ represents the high-frequency coefficient in Hi ($i = 1,2,3$ and indicates the number of layers currently decomposed).

   (1) The threshold of each layer is calculated according to the threshold formula (3).

   (2) If $\left| w_{j,k}^i \right| < \lambda_i$, $w_{j,k}^i$ is the noise coefficient, set it to zero. If $\left| w_{j,k}^i \right| \geq \lambda_i$, $w_{j,k}^i$ is a useful signal, and its corresponding new coefficient can be calculated using the threshold function proposed in formula (4). If $\lambda_i / 2 \leq \left| w_{j,k}^i \right| \leq \lambda_i$, $\hat{w}_{j,k}^i = w_{j,k}^i$.

4. The infrared image $\log 4Y_{ij}$ is reconstructed. The new coefficient $\hat{w}_{j,k}^i$ and third layer low-frequency coefficients are reconstructed to obtain the denoised image.

5. The image obtained in the previous step is subjected to a power of 4 to acquire a denoised image.

3.2 Fast Non-local Means (FNLM) Algorithm for Additive Noise Removal

FNLM not only effectively removes speckle noise and maintains structural similarity but also minimizes the operation time and greatly improves the denoising performance. Therefore, the FNLM method is used to remove background, detector, and other additive noise from the image signal after wavelet reconstruction.

FNLM uses integral image technology to accelerate the non-local means (NLM) algorithm. The pixels in the image are N; the size of the search window is D*D (D = 2Ds + 1), and the size of the neighboring window is d*d (d = 2ds + 1). Therefore, the integral image of the pixel difference is constructed, as shown in formula (7):

$$S_t(x) = \sum_{\{z=(z1,z2)\in N^2 : 0 \leq z1 \leq x1, 0 \leq z2 \leq x2\}} S_t(z), x = (x_1, x_2) \in \Omega \qquad (7)$$

where x is the pixel point in the noisy image. $S_t(z) = \|V(z) - V(z+t)\|^2$ represents the gray value distance between pixels z and $z+t$ in the noisy image.

Then, the Euclidean distance between $V(x)$ and $V(y)(y = x + z)$ can be calculated, as shown in formula (8). $V(x)$ is the size of $d * d$ neighbourhood centred on x in the noisy image; $V(y)$ is the size of $d * d$ neighbourhood centred on y in the noisy image.

$$\|V(x) - V(y)\|^2 = \frac{1}{d^2}(S_t(x_1 + ds, x_2 + ds) + S_t(x_1 - ds - 1, x_2 - ds - 1) - S_t(x_1 + ds, x_2 - ds - 1)$$
$$-S_t(x_1 - ds - 1, x_2 + ds))$$

$$(8)$$

In summary, when the FNLM algorithm is used to calculate the similarity of two neighbouring windows, we only need to calculate the difference, which greatly reduces the time complexity.

4   Results and Discussion

The simulated images comprised 2000 480 p infrared images captured by a REPT-O-330 15–330 mm F/4.0 infrared camera from the REPT company. The proposed algorithm was compared to the soft threshold function, hard threshold function, and FNLM algorithm. The simulation was performed using Windows 10 and Matlab R2020a. This study uses subjective and objective evaluation criteria to analyse the results. The subjective evaluation is the subjective visual effect; the objective evaluation indices are mean square error (MSE), peak signal-to-noise ratio (PSNR), and signal-to-noise ratio (SNR).

4.1   Analysis of Experimental Results

Five infrared images were added with multiplicative noise with a mean of zero and a standard deviation of 10 and Gaussian noise with a mean of zero and a standard deviation of 15. Using this algorithm, the wavelet was decomposed three times and db4 was selected as the wavelet base. The results are shown in Fig. 5; Fig. 5a is the original image, Fig. 5b is the noisy image, Fig. 5c is the result of the hard threshold function denoising algorithm, Fig. 5d is the result of the soft threshold function denoising algorithm, Fig. 5e is the result of the FNLM denoising algorithm, and Fig. 5f is the result of the compound restoration algorithm proposed herein. In Fig. 5, we can see that the images denoised by the soft and hard threshold function denoising algorithms still have a large amount of noise compared with the original infrared image, and the visual effect is not greatly improved. Although the FNLM algorithm has some denoising effect, it still has more residual noise. The overall effect of the denoising image obtained by the adaptive threshold multi-parameter wavelet compound restoration algorithm proposed herein is relatively smooth and clear. The image denoised by this algorithm retains its edge features and effectively improves the Gibbs phenomenon near the edge. The image details are clearer, and the visual effect is better than the traditional wavelet denoising method and FNLM algorithm.

To better compare the performance of the adaptive threshold multi-parameter wavelet compound restoration algorithm and assess its effectiveness, the denoising effects of different methods were compared using objective data of the images. The MSE, PSNR, and SNR were used as measurement indicators, and the comparison results are shown in Tables 1, 2, and 3.

It can be seen from Table 1 that the MSE of the proposed ATWM composite algorithm is 172.223 lower than that of the noisy image on average, 164.309 lower than that of the hard threshold denoising algorithm, 54.180 lower than that of the soft threshold denoising algorithm, and 6.213 lower than that of the FNLM algorithm. From Table 2, the average value of the proposed adaptive double threshold composite algorithm for the PSNR is 8.228 higher than that of the noisy image, 8.055 higher than that of the hard threshold denoising algorithm, 4.653 higher than that of the soft threshold denoising algorithm, and 0.820 higher than that of the FNLM algorithm. As shown in Table 3, the mean value of the proposed ATWM composite algorithm for the SNR is 8.551 higher than that of the noisy image, 8.375 higher than that of the hard threshold denoising algorithm, 5.001 higher than that of the soft threshold denoising algorithm, and 0.650 higher than that of the FNLM algorithm.

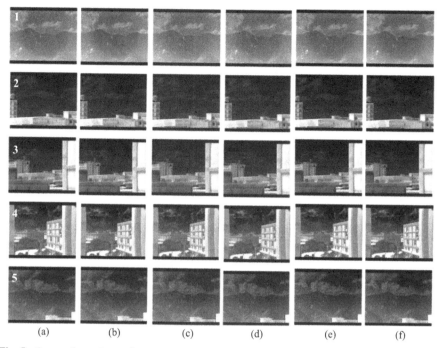

Fig. 5. Comparison of experimental results on infrared images of different algorithms. a. Original images; b. Noisy images; c. Hard threshold denoising; d. Soft threshold denoising; e. FNLM; f. Proposed

Table 1. Comparison of MSE among different algorithms

	Noisy images	Hard threshold denoising	Soft threshold denoising	FNLM	Proposed
1	208.6455	200.5881	89.8706	35.8593	30.8885
2	206.7074	198.3135	92.2750	41.2801	33.1628
3	192.1573	183.9526	83.9982	34.1382	27.5156
4	192.3205	184.3500	80.9782	28.0985	21.9653
5	217.9521	211.0079	100.4487	48.3590	43.1370
average	203.55656	195.64242	89.51414	37.54702	31.33384

The average values of MSE, PSNR, and SNR of the 20 randomly sampled denoised images were used to draw histograms, as shown in Fig. 6. For the MSE, the denoised image of the hard threshold algorithm is 7.68 dB lower than the noisy image; the denoised image of the soft threshold algorithm is 113.10 dB lower than the noisy image, and the FNLM is 165.13 dB lower than the noisy image. However, the proposed algorithm can reduce the MSE by 171.47 dB, which is higher than the other algorithms. In terms of

Table 2. Comparison of PSNR among different algorithms

	Noisy images	Hard threshold denoising	Soft threshold denoising	FNLM	Proposed
1	24.9367	25.1078	28.5946	32.5848	33.2328
2	24.9772	25.1573	28.4800	31.9734	32.9243
3	25.2942	25.4837	28.8881	32.7984	33.7350
4	25.2905	25.4744	29.0471	33.6440	34.7134
5	24.7472	24.8878	28.1114	31.2860	31.7823
average	25.04916	25.2222	28.62424	32.45732	33.27756

Table 3. Comparison of SNR among different algorithms

	Noisy images	Hard threshold denoising	Soft threshold denoising	FNLM	Proposed
1	9.5272	9.6931	13.1382	17.4558	17.9458
2	14.3052	14.4909	17.7858	21.8503	22.6102
3	15.1510	15.3467	18.7180	23.2975	24.0918
4	13.4047	13.5928	17.1253	22.3003	23.1891
5	9.6874	9.8322	13.0220	16.6772	16.9919
average	12.4151	12.59114	15.95786	20.31622	20.96576

the PSNR, the image denoised by the hard threshold is improved by 0.22 dB, the image denoised by the soft threshold is improved by 3.59 dB, and the FNLM is improved by 6.52 dB. Still, the algorithm proposed in this paper can improve by 8.50 dB and has a high PSNR. In terms of SNR, the denoised image by hard threshold is improved by 0.23 dB; the denoised image by soft threshold is improved by 3.56 dB, and the denoised image by the FNLM is improved by 7.05 dB. The SNR of the proposed algorithm can be improved by 8.80 dB.

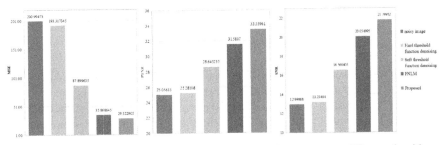

Fig. 6. Average MSE, PSNR, and SNR comparison of 20 images among different algorithms

In addition, the superiority of the algorithm was verified by changing the standard deviation of the initial Gaussian noise. We assume $\sigma = 15$, $\sigma = 25$, and $\sigma = 35$. As shown in Fig. 7, the five rows represent the infrared image reconstructed according to the following algorithms: the first row is the noisy image, the second row is the hard threshold denoising, the third row is the soft threshold denoising, the fourth row is the FNLM, and the fifth row is the ATMW composite restoration algorithm proposed in this paper. The level of initial Gaussian noise varies according to each column: (a) $\sigma = 15$, (b) $\sigma = 25$, and (c) $\sigma = 35$.

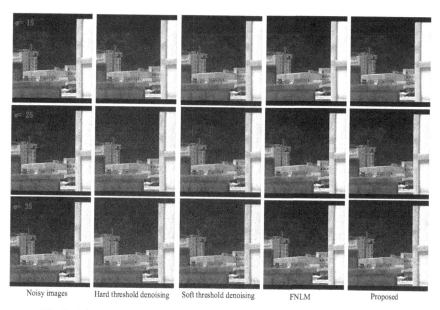

Noisy images   Hard threshold denoising   Soft threshold denoising   FNLM   Proposed

Fig. 7. Visual comparison of reconstruction quality for different noise levels

Figure 7 presents the visual results processed by different algorithms under various noise levels. The images in Fig. 7 are relatively complex, with rich texture and geometric structure. Thus, the algorithm proposed in this paper has a strong ability to remove noise at various noise intensities, while retaining image details and texture. The composite restoration method based on ATMW has the best image quality when compared to other methods.

Next, these algorithms are quantitatively compared to evaluate image quality after denoising. The calculation results of MSE, PSNR, and SNR values for different algorithms are presented in Table 4. The lower the MSE value, the smaller the difference between the denoised and original images and the better the image quality will be. The higher the PSNR and SNR values, the better the algorithm's performance and image quality after denoising will be. From Table 4, the proposed algorithm generates higher PSNR and SNR values and a lower MSE value than other methods. Table 4 verifies the superiority of the compound restoration method in image reconstruction compared with the other methods.

Table 4. Denoising results of different algorithms under various noise levels

		Noisy images	Hard threshold denoising	Soft threshold denoising	FNLM	Proposed
σ = 15	MSE	192.1573	183.9526	83.9982	34.1382	27.5156
	PSNR	25.2942	25.4837	28.8881	32.7984	33.735
	SNR	15.151	15.3467	18.718	23.2975	24.0918
σ = 25	MSE	492.7197	480.0999	252.2641	147.7367	90.9133
	PSNR	21.2048	21.3175	24.1122	26.4359	28.5445
	SNR	11.0359	11.1524	13.9283	16.3297	18.6178
σ = 35	MSE	910.673	896.091	511.4623	401.3401	261.3104
	PSNR	18.5372	18.6073	21.0427	22.0957	23.9592
	SNR	8.3684	8.4429	10.8631	12.0227	13.8954

In summary, the experiments indicate that the proposed infrared image denoising method has better performance than the traditional wavelet threshold denoising and FNLM algorithms and can effectively suppress the Gibbs phenomenon.

5   Conclusions

Infrared imaging has the potential for several significant applications. Because infrared images are affected by not only the detector and the additive background noise but also multiplicative speckle noise, there are problems such as blurred image details and information loss, which cannot be cannot simultaneously and effectively be suppressed by the current denoising techniques. In this paper, we propose a composite restoration approach based on ATMW and FNLM that can suppress both multiplicative speckle and additive background noise on image quality. According to the experimental findings, this method is superior to FNLM and conventional wavelet threshold infrared image denoising techniques. Additionally, after performing experiments on 20 images, it was proven that there are benefits in retaining image details and target specifics, with average increases in PSNR and SNR of 8.51 and 8.90, respectively, and a decrease in MSE of 171.47.

References

1. Johnson, J.E., et al.: Comparison of long-wave infrared imaging and visible/near-infrared imaging of vegetation for detecting leaking CO2 gas. IEEE J-STARS **7**(5), 1651–1657 (2014)
2. Panigrahy, C., Seal, A., Mahato, N.K.: Parameter adaptive unit-linking dual-channel PCNN based infrared and visible image fusion. Neurocomputing **514**, 21–38 (2022)
3. Zhang, Z., Chen, X., Liu, L., Li, Y.F., Deng, Y.B.: A sparse representation denoising algorithm for visible and infrared image based on orthogonal matching pursuit. Signal Image Video Process. **14**(4), 737–745 (2020)

4. Shen, Y., et al.: Improved Anscombe transformation and total variation for denoising of lowlight infrared images. Infrared Phys. Technol. **93**, 192–198 (2018)
5. He, Z.C., Wei, B.L., Zhou, L.F., Zhou, E.L., Li, E., Xing, Z.Y.: The crack detection of acoustic metamaterials using a weighted mode shape-wavelet-based strategy. Eng. Anal. Bound. Elements **145**, 286–298 (2022)
6. Agah, G.R., Rahideh, A., Khodadadzadeh, H., Khoshnazar, S.M., Kia, S.H.: Broken rotor bar and rotor eccentricity fault detection in induction motors using a combination of discrete wavelet transform and Teager-Kaiser energy operator. IEEE Trans. Energy Convers. **37**(3), 2199–2206 (2022)
7. Donoho, D.L.: De-noising by soft-thresholding. IEEE Trans. Inf. Theory **41**(3), 613–627 (1995)
8. Chen, G.Y., Bui, T.D., Krzyzak, A.: Image denoising with neighbour dependency and customized wavelet and threshold. Pattern Recognit. **38**(1), 115–124 (2005)
9. Lu, R.L., Wu, T.J., Yu, L.: Performance analysis of threshold denoising via different kinds of mother wavelets. Spectroscopy and Spectral Analysis **24**(7), 826–829 (2004)
10. Guo, X.L., Yang, K.L., Guo, Y.X.: Hydraulic pressure signal denoising using threshold self-learning wavelet algorithm. J. Hydrodyn. **20**(4), 433–439 (2008)
11. Smith, C.B., Agaian, S., Akopian, D.: A wavelet-denoising approach using polynomial threshold operators. IEEE Signal Process. Lett. **15**, 906–909 (2008)
12. Poornachandra, S.: Wavelet-based denoising using subband dependent threshold for ECG signals. Digital Signal Process. **18**(1), 49–55 (2008)
13. Guo, H., Yue, L.H., Song, P., Tan, Y.M., Zhang, L.J.: Denoising of an ultraviolet light received signal based on improved wavelet transform threshold and threshold function. Appl. Opt. **60**(28), 8983–8990 (2021)
14. Chen, Z.: Signal recognition for English speech translation based on improved wavelet denoising method. Adv. Math. Phys. **9**, 6811192 (2021)
15. Zhang, N., Lin, P., Xu, L.: Application of weak signal denoising based on improved wavelet threshold. IOP Conf. Ser.: Mater. Sci. Eng. **751**(1), 12073 (2020)
16. Kumar, A., Tomar, H., Mehla, V.K., Komaragiri, R., Kumar, M.: Stationary wavelet transform based ECG signal denoising method. ISA Trans. **114**, 251–262 (2021)
17. Binbin, Y.: An improved infrared image processing method based on adaptive threshold denoising. EURASIP J. Image Video Process. **1**, 5 (2019)
18. Kim, D.C., Kim, M., Yoon, I., Momjian, E., Kim, J.H., Letai, J., Evans, A.S.: Adaptive optics and VLBA imaging observations of recoiling supermassive black hole candidates. Monthly Notices Roy. Astron. Soc. **517**(3), 4081–4091 (2022)
19. Shao, Y.Y., et al.: Infrared image stripe noise removing using least squares and gradient domain guided filtering. Infrared Phys. Technol. **119**, 103968 (2021)
20. Guan, J.T., Lai, R., Xiong, A., Liu, Z.S., Gu, L.: Fixed pattern noise reduction for infrared images based on cascade residual attention CNN. Neurocomputing **377**, 301–313 (2020)
21. Jiang, H.X., et al.: A resource-efficient parallel architecture for infrared image stripe noise removal based on the most stable window. Infrared Phys. Technol. **97**, 258–269 (2019)
22. Jiang, M.: Edge enhancement and noise suppression for infrared image based on feature analysis. Infrared Phys. Technol. **91**, 142–152 (2018)
23. Wang, W.J., Wei, X.G., Li, J., Wang, G.Y.: Noise suppression algorithm of short-wave infrared star image for daytime star sensor. Infrared Phys. Technol. **85**, 382–394 (2017)
24. Zhang, J., Zhou, X., Li, L., Hu, T., Fansheng, C.: A combined stripe noise removal and deblurring recovering method for thermal infrared remote sensing images. IEEE Trans. Geosci. Remote Sens. **60**, 5003214 (2022)
25. Xiao, P., Guo, Y., Zhuang, P.: Removing stripe noise from infrared cloud images via deep convolutional networks. IEEE Photon. J. **10**(4), 7801114 (2018)

26. Kuang, X., Sui, X., Liu, Y., Chen, Q., Gu, G.: Single infrared image optical noise removal using a deep convolutional neural network. IEEE Photon. J. **10**(2), 78006154 (2018)
27. Bal, A., Banerjee, M., Sharma, P., Maitra, M.: An efficient wavelet and curvelet-based PET image denoising technique. Med. Biol. Eng. Comput. **57**(12), 2567–2598 (2019)

Author Index

© The Editor(s) (if applicable) and The Author(s), under exclusive license
to Springer Nature Switzerland AG 2023
H. Lu et al. (Eds.): ACPR 2023, LNCS 14408, pp. 397–401, 2023.
https://doi.org/10.1007/978-3-031-47665-5

Printed in the United States
by Baker & Taylor Publisher Services